Accounting
Theory and Practice

Visit the *Accounting Theory and Practice* ... ...tion Companion Website at **www.pearsoned.co.uk/glautie...** ...able **student** learning material including:

- Multiple choice questions to ...st your understanding
- Additional notes on selected multiple questions give insight into problem solving

PEARSON

We work with leading authors to develop the
strongest educational materials in accounting
bringing cutting-edge thinking and best learning
practice to a global market.

Under a range of well-known imprints, including
Financial Times Prentice Hall, we craft high-quality
print and electronic publications which help readers
to understand and apply their content, whether
studying or at work.

To find out more about the complete range of our
publishing, please visit us on the World Wide Web at:
www.pearsoned.co.uk

Accounting
Theory and Practice

EIGHTH EDITION

M. W. E. Glautier

B. Underdown

D. Morris

Financial Times
Prentice Hall
is an imprint of

Harlow, England • London • New York • Boston • San Francisco • Toronto • Sydney • Singapore • Hong Kong
Tokyo • Seoul • Taipei • New Delhi • Cape Town • Madrid • Mexico City • Amsterdam • Munich • Paris • Milan

Pearson Education Limited

Edinburgh Gate
Harlow
Essex CM20 2JE
England

and Associated Companies throughout the world

Visit us on the World Wide Web at:
www.pearsoned.co.uk

First published in Great Britain in 1976
Seventh edition 2001
Eighth edition published 2011

ISBN: 978-0-273-69385-7

British Library Cataloguing-in-Publication Data
A catalogue record for this book is available from the British Library

Library of Congress Cataloging-in-Publication Data
Glautier, M.W. E.
   Accouting theory and practice / M.W.E. Glautier, D. Morris, B.
Underdown. -- 8th ed.
      p. cm.
   ISBN 978-0-273-69385-7 (pbk.)
   1. Accounting. I. Morris, D. (Deigan) II. Underdown, Brian. III.
Title. IV. Title: Accounting.
   HF5636.G57 2011
   657--dc22
                                                   2010033774

10 9 8 7 6 5 4 3 2
14 13 12

Typeset in 10/12pt Sabon by 30
Printed and bound by Ashford Colour Press Ltd, Gosport

Dedication

For Barbara Morris and the late Jean Shepherd who gave us so much encouragement and support in writing this eighth edition

Contents

Preface to the eighth edition

The tradition in accounting education has been to focus the teaching of accounting mainly on procedures for processing financial data. The treatment of accounting as a skill, rather than as a body of knowledge, is based on the belief that 'accounting is what accountants do'. While this assertion undoubtedly holds good as a statement of what accountants do, such a view of accounting has serious shortcomings as regards the educational qualities of accounting courses and the education of accountants. First, by restricting the nature and scope of accounting to an exposure of its procedures, it fails to provide an adequate understanding of these procedures in relation to the problems facing accountants. Second, it impedes the recognition of economic and social changes which bear directly on these problems. Third, it supports a conviction widespread among students and practitioners that what they have been taught is in the nature of everlasting truth.

This textbook is committed to a different view of accounting education in a number of important respects. First, as its title *Accounting: Theory and Practice* implies, it attempts to provide a theoretical framework for the understanding of the nature of accounting and an appreciation of the purpose of various accounting practices. This approach permits accounting practices to be exposed to critical analysis by means of which their usefulness and relevance may be assessed and their shortcomings exposed. Second, the nature and the scope of accounting is extended beyond accounting procedures by conceiving the essential function of accounting as facilitating socio-economic activities and decisions. Accordingly, we give a global and rounded view of accounting in which the emphasis is appropriately placed on the role of accounting as being the provision of information for decision making.

We have interpreted the broad objectives of accounting as being to provide information for the following purposes:

1 decision making regarding the use of limited resources, including the identification of crucial decision areas, and the determination of objectives and goals;
2 effectively directing and controlling human and material resources;
3 maintaining and reporting on the custodianship of resources;
4 facilitating social functions and controls.

This new edition has been updated to take account of new international financial accounting standards, of advances in the areas of costing and management control, corporate governance, company taxation, social accounting, as well as a concern with ethical values arising from the recent and on-going credit and banking crisis.

It is our intention in this eighth edition to maintain the original objective that gave this text its specific character in its attempt to relate the theory of accounting with its expression in accounting practices over both financial and cost accounting. We maintain also the original structure through which the discussion of the problems of financial accounting was extended to financial reporting and cost accounting and led into the problems of management control and decision making.

Adjusting to the way the market has progressively shifted away from social concerns, as they were treated in their different aspects in the seventh edition and in the light of the public debate on social accounting at the time, it is now clear that the market is giving much greater emphasis to corporate financial performance and the shareholder value criterion in that regard. Accordingly, we have removed chapters of the seventh edition which we consider redundant in the present context, while maintaining material that remains relevant to the debate about business and society as it relates to accounting.

The most significant changes that distinguish the seventh from the eighth edition are intended to address those related to our perceived impact of the global market economy on the teaching of accounting. For this reason, this eighth edition is proposed as an international edition. English remains the ultimate lingua franca and the natural vehicle for an international accounting text that will have worldwide market relevance and acceptance. To ensure the degree of market relevance that is our ambition, we have substituted the international accounting standards issued by the International Accounting Standards Board (IASB) for the UK standards on which the seventh edition relied. This change is in line with the intention that national accounting standards boards shall seek convergence with the IASB standards and giving explanation in each case where there is divergence. In this international edition, the IASB standards are referred in each case to the relevant standard of the Accounting Standard Board of the United Kingdom, so that UK readers can follow the convergence towards the IASB standards that are the operative standards for the global economy. It may be noted that even the USA is in the process of subscribing to these standards for their own national purposes, thereby acknowledging the universality of accounting rules and methods for regulatory purposes.

We have gone further than the seventh edition in another important respect through the structure that we have chosen for the elaboration of the teaching through successive course levels, thereby giving the book sufficient flexibility to accompany teachers and students as they progress to more rigorous and higher learning levels and more difficult material. Parts 1, 2 and 3 are horizontally and vertically integrated as packages relevant to first- and second-level courses respectively. They represent basic knowledge that is taught on MBA and executive programmes in business schools, even though they are also found on university and professional accounting training courses. The audiences are different, but their knowledge and teaching requirements share similarities.

Part 1 provides an overview of accounting theory and the nature and the importance of theory for developing accounting knowledge and incorporating that knowledge into a unified whole, the purpose of which is the provision of information for decision making. It is common to the entire book and its importance lies in the statement of the moral values that are implicit in accountability in all social relationships and particularly in those where, in the nature of things, accounting methods have to do with truth, trust, care and transparency. Several notorious financial scandals of recent years have revealed the extent to which moral hazard has infected the accounting process and how inadequate has been the regulatory framework in sufficiently upholding moral values in a climate of deregulation. Accounting has as much to do today with the social conscience as when Pacioli during the Renaissance made explicit the moral rules that were fundamental to the Italian method of double-entry bookkeeping.

Part 2 examines the nature of financial and cost information based on the historical cost approach. It explains the thinking underlying financial and cost accounting practices in the context of accounting conventions and standards.

Part 3 considers the role of accounting information for decision making by shareholders and investors, as well as by management. Shareholders and investors have to rely on accounting information released in the form of periodic financial reports for decisions on their investment.

Part 4 is a new and unique feature, distinct from the seventh edition in its ambition to meet the teaching needs of courses at business schools that reach higher levels on advanced sections of MBA programmes and on senior management programmes. As an integrated package, it recognizes that most participants on advanced MBA and senior executive programmes are themselves employees of large multinational groups. Earlier editions had two chapters dealing with the accounting rules for preparing consolidated accounts. A new logic is found in refocusing the chapters on group accounts on the basis of international accounting standards relevant to multinational groups and associated with the concept of group performance management. It is intended that participants on such programmes will gain in knowledge and learning experience through a structured awareness of the link between financial reporting for groups of companies, through which financial performance is evaluated and management control systems necessary to the effective functioning of complex organizations.

We would emphasize that although this textbook is divided into four parts, each addressed to a special aspect of accounting, they are nevertheless linked through a theoretical framework which brings them together and establishes their purposes in the provision of information for decision making. The topics examined through this structure are as follows:

Part 1   Accounting theory: an overview (relevant to all readership levels)

Part 2   Accounting information (relevant to first-level courses)
Section 1. Financial accounting
Section 2. Cost accounting

Part 3   Accounting information for decision making (relevant to second-level courses)
Section 1. Financial reporting
Section 2. Management control

Part 4   Accounting for multinational corporations (relevant to advanced level courses)
Section 1. Financial reporting for groups of companies
Section 2. Management control systems for multinational corporations

Acknowledgements

We wish to place on record our gratitude to colleagues and friends for the advice and help which they have given us in the course of first writing this text. We owe a particular debt to Professor W. Rotch and Charles Clark, who were both closely associated with every aspect of the book and who helped us unstintingly, as well as Professor T.A. Lee, Professor R.H. Parker, Professor A. Hopwood, C.P. Rickwood, G.J. Harris, Dr H.C. Dekker, E.C. Johnson, C. Burke, O.A. Bello and P.J. Taylor.

For help with the subsequent editions, thanks are due to: R.W. Wallis, M.H.C. Lunt, A.J. Naughton, M. Sherer, A. Southworth and A. Chandiok; to F.S. Hall, M.A. Nardone, R.A. Coates, M. Skenfield, R.W. Wallis, Dr A. Goodacre and P. Hughes; to C.J. Jones and J. Maltby of the University of Sheffield, and Professor J.C. Scheid of the Conservatoire Nationale des Arts et Métiers, Paris; and to G.L. Axelby, M. Rimmington, Leslie Chadwick, David Citron, Judy Day, Paul Gordon, Robert Greenhalgh, Gillian Holmes, Peter Miller, Lydia Thompson, Alan Witts and David Welch. For help with the seventh edition, thanks are due to Debbie and Nick Reed, G.L. Axelby and Anne Underdown. For the eighth edition, thanks are due to Alison Mclintock and Jean Shepherd.

We have been privileged as authors to have had so much support from our publishers, and this book is indeed the outcome of a close partnership between authors and publishers. We wish to thank all those members of the Pearson staff who have worked with us. We are deeply indebted to Simon Lake, Pat Bond and Elizabeth Tarrant for their assistance in planning previous editions. We thank Catherine Newman and Lyn Roberts for their assistance in planning the seventh edition. We are indebted to Matthew Smith, Robin Lupton and Louise Andrew for their help with this new and international edition. We remember the late Dr K.W. Watkins of Sheffield University, who was one of the original instigators of this book. We owe much to his friendship.

We thank Professor Dr Han van Dissel, Director General of the European Centre for Executive Development (CEDEP), Fontainebleau for allowing us access to CEDEP resources.

Publisher's acknowledgements

We are grateful to the following for permission to reproduce copyright material:

Figures

Figure 38.1 adapted from *Competitive Advantage: Creating and Sustaining Superior Performance*, The Free Press (Porter, M.E. 1985), Adapted with the permission of The Free Press, a Division of Simon & Schuster, Inc., from Competitive Advantage: Creating and Sustaining Superior Performance by Michael E. Porter, Copyright © 1985, 1988 by Michael E. Porter. All rights reserved.; Figure 38.3 adapted from Using the balanced Scorecard as a Strategic Management System, *Harvard Business Review*, January/February (Kaplan, Robert S. and Norton, David P. 1996); Figure 41.2 adapted from Mastering the Management System, *Harvard Business Review*, January (Kaplan, R.S and Norton, D.P. 2008)

Text

Epigraphs on page 56, 9, page 165, 26 from Americal Institute of Certified Public Accountants, Improving Business Reporting – A Customer Focus (The Jenkins Report), 1994; General Displayed Text on page 81 from www.iasb.org

In some instances we have been unable to trace the owners of copyright material, and we would appreciate any information that would enable us to do so.

PART 1

Accounting theory: an overview

Introduction to Part 1

As a field of knowledge, accounting falls within the social sciences. It is defined in terms of a set of problems and a methodology for dealing with these problems through principles and practices that have their validity in consensus. Generally, this consensus is formalized into accounting law that authorizes specific accounting practices. The practice of accounting is subject to regulatory control through the standardization of accounting practices. It has now provided the global economy with a set of rules that ensure uniformity and comparability in accounting information used for financial reporting purposes. Over the last 150 years, accounting progressively has achieved professional status in the most countries. As a result, professional accounting bodies have obtained a measure of delegated authority for regulating admission into the profession and enforcing rules applicable to accounting practice.

An important consequence of professional status has been the increasing concern in recent years with deontology that looks beyond clearly defined rules of law to the moral principles that are the foundation of jurisprudence. The recognition that decisions often imply moral choice broadens the perspective on the nature of choice and the limits to choice in accounting. Moral hazard has become a major consideration in dealing with the failure of the regulatory framework in preventing corruption and fraud that have led to massive financial corporate scandal. The reputation of financial institutions at all levels and of governmental agencies, has been tarnished by the debacle that has accompanied the credit and banking crisis that began in the USA in 2007 and rapidly affected the entire world.

Ethical values, such as truth, sincerity, fairness, care and transparency, are considered fundamental for creating trust in both the accounting profession and in the information provided to users of accounting information. Their importance goes much beyond the confines of the market economy to question the sustainability of a social order based on free markets and capitalistic organization able to deal with the frightening array of problems now facing humanity. The argument in favour of free trade through competitive markets assumes that markets are self-regulating. The credit and banking crisis showed this assumption to be false in the case of recession and confirmed the experience of the Great Depression for the need for government intervention in such a situation. It has revealed also the urgency for the re-enforcement of regulatory controls with regards to the responsibility and accountability of business corporations to society.

The very success of the market economy has ensured economic growth and raised living standards. It has increased the disparity between the rich and developed economies that have profited from exploitation of the earth's resources and the poor, whose numbers are rapidly increasing in the less-developed countries. Even within the developed and industrialized nations, social cohesion is threatened by conflicting interests that a competitive market economy creates.

In its concern with business capital, accounting has focused on money values and has justified choice by reference to shareholder value. Accounting principles and practices refer to money values and use money measurements in interpreting business performance in terms of profitability and improvements in shareholder value. Different approaches to accounting theory, whether these approaches be descriptive or empirical about accounting knowledge; positive or normative as regards the direction of accounting research, reflect a continuing interest in business success as resulting ultimately from financial efficiency.

Part 1 provides an overview of the various influences that are at play in the evolution of accounting theory, as seen in their historical, social, economic, ethical and political aspects.

CHAPTER 1

Accountability and accounting

Setting the scene

Social relationships involve duties, responsibilities and accountability. The nature of these duties and responsibilities determine the extent of accountability and the manner and content of accounting. It follows that the subject matter of accounting may be referred to social theory for an understanding of the issues with which it is concerned.

The social context that leads to the existence of duties and responsibilities is a complex network of personal, social and public relationships that define the nature of society. The social conscience ensures social cohesion through moral values that are universally accepted in individual conscience and expressed in law. Accountability through transparency is a major bulwark of truth and promotes trust necessary to social cohesion.

The context, content of accountability and manner of accounting may be discussed in as many different perspectives as there are formal and informal social structures within society.

Learning objectives

After studying this chapter you should have:

1 acquired an understanding that social relationships of every kind involve responsibility and accountability;
2 understood that the subject matter of accounting resides in social theory;
3 become aware of the fundamental importance of truth, trust, care and transparency in accounting;
4 realized the significance of accountability and the role of accounting to social cohesion.

Responsibility and accountability

The pre-condition to accounting is the presence of responsibility towards others which imposes an obligation to account for one's actions. Responsibility and accountability have their roots in social relationship and are joined together in all personal and business relationships, as well as in the wider field of public and government responsibility that is the very nature of democracy.

Responsibility and accountability cement social relationships, ensuring their stability and permanence. They are key elements in all social structures and, in a broader sense, are essential to social order and are defined in rules of conduct recognised, accepted and enforced in law.

In a very broad sense, accounting is the process that defines the form, content and procedures required to meet the nature and standard of accountability implicit in a given situation.

Accountability and the social conscience

The social conscience is a shared conscience which, embodied in each one of us, is the collective of all individuals seeking to do 'what is right' (Glautier, 2007). It is the consensus that individual and group behaviour should conform to rules of conduct that are universally applicable and accepted. It is the basis of the social contract on which the social order is founded. It may be understood as the unity of consciousness that guides social action towards 'what is right'. In a general sense, the social conscience considers 'what is right' by reference to moral values that are conducive to the common good.

As expressed at an individual level, the term 'conscience' is a personal experience that describes the way in which individuals take stock of their action by referring them to conscience as their awareness and acceptance of 'what is right'. As with the social conscience, individual conscience admits responsibility by referring actions to a standard that seeks 'what is right'. This standard or benchmark is found in moral values, which are instrumental to social order.

The social conscience is the basis of jurisprudence and the rule of law. Given that no individual is an island, but rather a social being that experiences life through relationships with others, moral values determine behaviour in a caring society. In its universal meaning, the social conscience, which is derived from an awareness of 'what is right', may also be assumed as an awareness of 'what is truth'.

From the viewpoint of science, truth is the sole criterion that defines the quintessence of knowledge. As regards the natural sciences, knowledge results from a process of discovery in which the laws of nature are accepted as representing the ultimate truth. The scientific method of enquiry uncovers knowledge initially through observations of the material world, which may be defined as material facts. Using the logic of reason, observations are transformed into scientific knowledge through testing hypotheses for reliability. This approach to formulating knowledge is known as empiricism. Hence, scientific knowledge is empirical knowledge and scientific truth is factual truth.

The acquisition of knowledge in the social sciences concerned with social, as distinct from physical behaviour, has been strongly influenced by beliefs about truth that are conditioned by moral value judgements. Although social scientists begin with observations of social facts in the form of 'what is', these observations are judged by reference to 'what should be' for the purpose of developing social theories. Such theories are described as normative theories, as distinct from the empirical theories found in the natural sciences.

In effect, the natural sciences accept the laws of nature as representing the truth concerning the material world and all material life forms and rely on the logic of reason for developing scientific theories. Moral value judgements have no relevance in formulating scientific theories as regards material forms. By contrast, moral value judgements are central to developing theories in the social conscience concerned with social relationships. It is faith in the validity of such judgements that leads social scientists to formulate social theories. The significance of moral values to the development of accounting theory is shown in the considerable interest shown in ethics in accounting literature of recent years and in the insistence within the accounting profession of the observance of rules of deontology in accounting practices.

Accountability, truth and transparency

Responsibility and accountability under law requires that truth be established. Equally, the nature and level of personal, social, business, or governmental accountability involved in making decisions can be made only in the light of truth. Transparency is needed for truth to be seen. Concealment allows falsehood, dishonesty and deceit to thrive.

Truth as an absolute condition is an extremely difficult requirement. Not only does it insist on complete knowledge, but it requires also the ability to comprehend that knowledge. Insisting on the absolute truth is a too strict condition for practical purposes. For this reason, the intention to be truthful is a sufficient condition, even though there may be innocent error with respect to the truth. It explains why the standard of truth in accountability is modified to the less demanding requirement of sincerity, defined as an honest belief in the truth of statements.

Accountability, trust and care

Trust may be defined as the confidence needed to ensure successful and permanent social relationships. Trust depends upon truth. Without truth, there is no trust. Without trust, there can be no relationship. Both truth and trust are necessary conditions without which relationships cannot endure. They are general expectations that are present in the social conscience. Falsehood, deceit and dishonesty destroy the initial trust and confidence that exist when relationships are first formed. It is said that trust is easily given, but cannot be recovered once lost. Trust contains an additional expectation, which is the duty of care, manifested in the implicit intention that parties will seek to do 'what is right'. The duty of care is formally defined as due diligence in the performance of accounting tasks.

Accountability and responsibility: the duty of care

Accountability is determined by the responsibility deemed to exist towards others. Under law, the duty of care may be general or specific. It exists as a general prohibition not to harm another in his or her person, property or reputation. The absence of care seen in deliberate negligence is a breach of law. Generally, the law does not impose a duty of care, rather it forbids harm or criminal negligence.

Specific responsibility arises by reason of the nature of a relationship, such as parental responsibility or contractual responsibility. Specific responsibility is stated in law or in formal agreements. Thus, the responsibility of corporate directors is the duty of care to act in the interest of shareholders. Under accounting law, there is legal obligation to prepare and submit to shareholders annual accounts in the form of financial reports showing the financial results for the year and the year-end financial position of the business.

Business law imposes strict and extensive duties and obligations as contractual terms. These determine the nature and the extent of the duty of care that is implicit in all business relationships. The failure to observe these conditions may lead to breaches of contract and to the recovery of financial damages. Accountability is a function of the responsibility determined under contract.

Truth and fairness

Truth is said to be 'indivisible'. This means that it must be the truth, the whole truth and nothing but the truth. A partial or half truth is not the truth and cannot be accepted as valid. 'Spinning' is the manipulation of truth that fosters the pretence that falsehood may be transformed into truth.

Likewise, trust is indivisible. Unqualified truth results in complete trust, that is, unqualified trust. Business relationships depend upon truth to maintain trust. Truth is a demanding standard that is satisfied by sincerity.

Trust implicitly relates to the duty of care. In the same way as truth is met by sincerity, so the duty of care is met by the notion of 'fairness'. It relates to justice as seen in fairness in treating legal rights and duties.

As a standard of care, fairness brings reasonableness as a criterion for determining what constitutes a reasonable expectation. It does not modify the insistence for truth or sincerity. However, inevitably it suffers from an inherent lack of precision by becoming a matter of opinion leading to debate as to what is fair.

The true and fair criterion is used worldwide for the purpose of certifying financial accounting reports to shareholders. Countries that belong to the Anglo-Saxon accounting tradition were able to persuade other countries to follow suit in using the true and fair criterion for audit purposes, instead of the criterion that referred to sincerity and conformity with accounting law.

Summary

In terms of social theory, society may be construed as functioning through a complex network of personal, social, business, political and public relationships. Social cohesion is established through the various responsibilities which these relationships create. They impose also a duty of accountability on which social order is founded. Accounting is the process that defines the form, content and procedures used for accountability.

The social conscience provides the basis of the social contract on which the social order is founded. It may be understood as the unity of consciousness that guides social action towards 'what is right' by reference to moral values, which are also reflected in jurisprudence and formal law. The moral values that are fundamental to accountability and accounting are truth, trust, transparency, care and fairness.

Social theories are normative in nature and concerned with 'what should be'. They differ from theory construction in the natural sciences that are concerned with 'what is'. They reflect beliefs that have much to do with social progress within civil society and the market economy. Such diversity leads to many different forms of accounting having different objectives. Business accounting is concerned with accountability in the market economy. Government accounting has to do with accountability for governmental institutions. In all cases, truth, trust, transparency, care and fairness are fundamental and instrumental to social cohesion in a caring society that justifies itself in terms of a social conscience.

Self-assessment questions

1 In what sense do social relationships create duties, responsibility and accountability?

2 What do you understand by the social conscience?

3 What moral values are implied in social relationships and for social cohesion?

4 What is the nature of social theory?

5 Discuss the importance of truth in accounting?

6 Discuss accountability and accounting by reference to truth, trust, transparency and care.

References

Cottell, P.G. and Perlin, T.M. (1990) *Accounting Ethics: A Practical Guide for Professionals*, Connecticut: Quorum Books.

Glautier, M.W.E. (2007)*The Social Conscience*, London: Shepheard-Walwyn (Publishers) Ltd.

Habermas, J. (1990) *Moral Consciousness and Communication*, Cambridge MIT Press, translated by Lenhardt, C. and Nicholson, S.

Hoffman, W.M., Brown Kamman, J., Frederick, R.E. and Petry, E.S. (1996) *The Ethics of Accounting & Finance: Trust, Responsibility & Control*, Connecticut: Quorum Books.

Reynolds, M.A. and Yuthas, K. (2007) Moral Discourse and Corporate Social Reporting, *Journal of Business Ethics*, Spring, pp. 47–62.

Riahi-Belkaoui, A. (1992) *Morality in Accounting*, Connecticut: Quorum Books.

Stolowy, H. (2005) Nothing Like the Enron Affair Could Happen in France!, *European Accounting Review*, Vol. 14, No. 2, pp. 405–415.

CHAPTER 2

The scope of business accounting

Setting the scene

Accountants may seem unlikely revolutionaries, but we shall see profound transformations in the ways in which they assess and report corporate performance. And the accounting challenge becomes even more urgent now that the sustainability agenda is opening up to embrace not only environmental and economic dimensions, but also social and ethical dimensions. This is why we increasingly talk of the 'triple bottom line' of sustainable development. Simply stated, this means that business people must increasingly recognise that the challenge now is to help to deliver simultaneously economic prosperity, environmental quality and social equity. Accounting practice must recognise the new challenge.

(Elkington, 1998)

Learning objectives

After studying this chapter you should be able to:

1 explain how the changing environment has extended definitions of accounting;
2 describe how accounting has developed through time;
3 identify the factors which have caused accounting to be criticized in recent years;
4 show how accountants have responded to these concerns.

The definition of accounting

Accounting is in an age of rapid transition; its environment has undergone vast changes in the last two decades and an accelerating rate of change is in prospect for the future. Changing social attitudes combined with developments in information and manufacturing technology, the adoption of new management philosophies and the growing intensity of competition, both local and global affect radically the environment in which accounting operates today. It creates the need to re-evaluate the objectives of accounting in a wide perspective. Accounting is moving away from its traditional procedural base, encompassing record-keeping and such related work as the preparation of budgets and final accounts, towards a role which emphasizes its social importance.

The changing environment has not only extended the boundaries of business accounting, but has created a problem in defining the scope of the subject. There is a need for a definition which is broad enough to delineate its boundaries, while at the same time being sufficiently precise as a statement of its essential nature. It is interesting to contrast definitions which were accepted a little time ago with more recent statements. According to a definition made in 1953, 'The central purpose of accounting is to make possible the periodic matching of costs (efforts) and revenues (accomplishments) in the calculation of result. This concept is the nucleus of accounting theory, and a benchmark that affords a fixed point of reference for accounting discussions' (Littleton, 1953).

The Committee on Terminology of the American Institute of Certified Public Accountants formulated the following definition in 1961: 'Accounting is the art of recording, classifying and summarizing in a significant manner and in terms of money, transactions and events which are, in part at least, of a financial character, and interpreting the result thereof' (AICPA, 1961).

A more recent definition is less restrictive and interprets accounting as the provision of 'information about the reporting entity's financial performance and financial position that is useful to a wide range of users for assessing the stewardship of management and for making economic decisions' (ASB, 1999).

An earlier definition which additionally acknowledges social welfare objectives is closer to our own interpretation of the scope of accounting and the manner in which we should like to treat the subject. We would add the rider that accounting is moving towards a consideration of social welfare objectives. Accordingly the purpose of accounting is to provide information which is potentially useful for making economic decisions and 'aims to assess the impact of an organisation or company on people both inside and outside' (Gonella *et al.*, 1998).

According to this latter viewpoint, the scope of accounting should not be restricted to the private use of information, which has the limited perspective of being concerned with the impact of information on the welfare of individuals as such. The social welfare viewpoint is concerned with improving the allocation of scarce resources. Another aspect of this viewpoint is reflected in the development of social accounting. In the past, the interests of shareholders, investors, creditors and managers have exerted a dominating influence on the development of accounting practices. The social welfare theory of accounting requires that the interests of employees, trade unions and consumers be taken into account, and that the traditional imbalance existing in the supply of information should be corrected. Social accounting draws attention to the gulf existing between the sectarian interests represented in conventional business accounting and its focus on profit, and the need to see the entire social role of business organization in the context of all those affected by its activities.

This debate has progressed to the notion of 'triple bottom line' (TBL) reporting that focuses on sustainable development. According to Group 100, 'in its purest sense, the concept of TBL reporting refers to the publication of economic, environmental and social information that reflects activities and outcomes across these three dimensions of a company's performance' (Group 100 Incorporated, 2003). This guide provides a clear and concise explanation of this important subject prepared under the auspices of the Business Council of Australia.

The emerging role of accounting

The history of accounting illustrates how accounting is a product of its social and economic environment and at the same time a force for changing it. From today's perspective, we may distinguish four phases which may be said to correspond with its developing role.

1 Stewardship accounting has its origins in the function which accounting served from the earliest times in the history of our society of providing the owners of wealth with a means of safeguarding it from embezzlement. Wealthy men employed 'stewards' to manage their property. These stewards rendered periodical accounts of their stewardship, and this notion still lies at the root of financial reporting today. Essentially, stewardship accounting involves the orderly recording of business transactions, and accounting records of this type date back to as early as 4500 BC. Stewardship accounting is associated, therefore, with the need of those in business to keep records of their transactions, the manner in which they invested their wealth and the debts owed to them and by them.

2 Financial reporting has a more recent origin, and dates from the development of large-scale businesses which were made possible by the Industrial Revolution. Indeed, the new technology not only destroyed the existing social framework, but altered completely the method by which business was financed. The industrial expansion in the early part of the nineteenth century necessitated access to large amounts of capital. This led to the advent of the joint stock company, which enables the public to provide capital in return for 'shares' in the assets and the income of the company. In the United Kingdom, the Joint Stock Companies Act 1844 permitted the incorporation of such companies by registration without the need to obtain a Royal Charter or a special Act of Parliament. In 1855, however, the Limited Liability Act permitted such companies to limit the liability of their members to the nominal value of their shares. This meant that the liability of shareholders for the debts incurred by the company was limited to the amount which they had agreed to subscribe. In effect, by applying for a £1 share, a shareholder agreed to subscribe £1, and, once he had paid that £1, he was not liable to make any further contribution in the event of the company's insolvency. Parliament eventually restated the doctrine of stewardship in a legal form. It made the disclosure of information to shareholders a condition attached to the privilege of joint-stock status and of limited liability. This information was required to be in the form of annual income statements and balance sheets. We may say briefly that the former is a statement of the income or loss made during the year of the report, and the balance sheet indicates the assets held by the firm and how those assets were financed.

The reluctance of company directors to disclose more than the minimum information required by law, along with growing public disquiet as to the usefulness of the information contained in financial accounts culminated in the extension of disclosure requirements in the United Kingdom by means of the Companies Acts 1948 to 2006.

The demand for improvements in corporate governance, i.e. the system by which companies are directed and controlled, has continued this process. For example, the Turnbull Committee's report (ICAEW, 1999) provides guidance to assist companies to implement disclosure requirements in respect of internal controls. This report requires directors to disclose in their annual report that there is an on-going process for identifying, evaluating and managing the significant risks faced by a company.

The legal importance attached to financial accounting statements stems directly from the need of a capitalist society to mobilize savings and direct them into profitable investments. Investors, be they large or small, must be provided with reliable and relevant information in order to be able to make efficient investment decisions.

3 Management accounting is also associated with the advent of industrial capitalism, for the Industrial Revolution of the eighteenth century presented a challenge to the development of accounting as a tool of industrial management. In isolated cases there were some, notably Josiah Wedgwood, who developed costing techniques as guides to management decisions. But the practice of using accounting information as a direct aid to management was not one of the achievements of the Industrial Revolution: this new role for accounting really belongs to the twentieth century.

Certainly, the genesis of modern management with its emphasis on detailed information for decision making provided a tremendous impetus to the development of management accounting in the early decades of this century, and in so doing considerably extended the boundaries of accounting. Management accounting shifted the focus of accounting from recording and analysing financial transactions to using information for decisions affecting the future.

The advent of management accounting demonstrated once more the ability and capacity of accounting to develop and meet changing socio-economic needs. Management accounting has contributed in a most significant way to the success with which modern capitalism has succeeded in expanding the scale of production and raising standards of living.

4 The credit and banking crisis that began in 2007 marked a watershed in the deregulation accorded to the market economy and the recognition of the need for stronger and more effective regulatory controls. The first signs appeared in the enactment of the Sarbanes–Oxley Act 2002 (Public Company Accounting Reform and Protection of Investor Act, 2002) as a governmental response to the corrupt accounting practices and deviant managerial behaviour that resulted in several high profile corporate scandals in the USA. Other governments, notably the United Kingdom, failed to follow the American lead, but were caught up with the subsequent collapse of their own financial markets that necessitated extensive governmental intervention and financial support and the nationalization of major banks and credit institutions. The extent of this crisis is yet to be fully manifested in needed reforms and in the discussion among nations for the creation of an effective international regulatory framework under international authority.

Accounting in a changing environment

The process of change has had a dramatic impact on accounting theory and practice in recent years. Rapid changes in the environment have caused much concern and necessitated changes in accounting. The following factors may be identified:

1 The status of the accounting profession has depended to some extent on its monopoly of the auditing and external financial reporting function. However, an important discussion document has attacked the concepts upon which external

financial statements are based on the grounds that they are 'neither consistent nor logical and do not lead to a portrayal of economic reality' (ICAS, 1988). Much criticism has been directed at the lack of uniformity in the manner in which periodic income is measured and the financial position of the enterprise represented. Also severe criticism has been directed at an external financial reporting system that allows management to provide cosmetic improvements to the firm's accounting performance, by the phenomenon of 'creative accounting' (Whelan and McBarnet, 1999). Furthermore, historic cost accounting produces misleadingly high profits in times of inflation.

2 Accounting is shaped by the environment in which it operates. Since this differs from country to country (due to legal, economic, political, cultural, etc. differences) very diverse national financial accounting systems have developed. For example, in some countries financial accounting developed to ensure that the proper amount of income tax is collected by the national government. In an expanding global economy where management and investors are increasingly making cross-border decisions through international markets, the comparability of financial information is essential. The internationalization of accounting standards under the auspices of the International Accounting Standards Committee has revealed the need of an international agency having effective regulatory control over financial reporting practices. The credit and banking crisis has served to magnify the need for international cooperation in this area.

3 Since the mid-1980s, following changes in the social and economic environment in which many organizations operate, traditional management accounting practices have attracted criticism for lagging behind the times, especially in view of technological developments. The argument has largely centred on the view that managers faced with having to make decisions in fully technology-driven situations are supplied with information by their firm's internal management systems which is inadequate. Johnson and Kaplan (1987) came to the conclusion that, in general, management accounting systems 'are not providing useful, timely information for process control, product costing and performance evaluation of managers'.

4 Increasingly, management is being held responsible not only for the efficient conduct of business as expressed in profitability, but also for what it does about an endless number of social problems. Hence, with changing attitudes, the time-honoured standards by which performance is measured have fallen into disrepute. There is a growing consensus that the concepts of growth and income as measured in traditional balance sheets and income statements are too narrow to reflect what many companies are trying, or are supposed to be trying, to achieve.

5 Effective control over large public corporations, whose shares are quoted on stock exchanges, has shifted significantly over the years from shareholders to their directors, who have been granted extensive and exclusive rights over a wide range of decisions that do not require shareholders' approval. The context of deregulation that has existed over many years, together with a weakened regulatory framework, has fostered a climate of corporate corruption. As a result, managers have been able to increasingly appropriate to themselves an unwarranted proportion of the income attributable to investors in excessive remuneration in the form of bonuses, share options and other prerequisites. The pendulum is now shifting to give increasing importance to ethical values and to dealing with the problem of moral hazard through government intervention, tightening of regulatory controls and corporate governance.

Responses to these concerns have been as follows:

1 In the United Kingdom, the need to improve accounting practice was recognized formally by the creation of the Accounting Standards Committee in 1970. More recently, the Dearing Report's (1988) proposals have led to a new administrative structure for accounting standard setting that is designed to improve the quality of accounting standards and to strengthen the enforcement process.

  Much effort has been directed towards developing a theoretical framework for validating external financial reporting practices in terms of their perceived objectives, and to enable future development to take place in accordance with those objectives. In the United States the Financial Accounting Standards Board, since its inception in 1972, has been engaged in developing a series of statements which have established a conceptual framework for financial reporting. More recently, conceptual frameworks have been issued by the Institute of Chartered Accountants of Scotland (*Making Corporate Reports Valuable*, ICAS, 1988), the International Accounting Standards Committee (*Framework for the Preparation and Presentation of Financial Statements*, IASC, 1989), the Institute of Chartered Accountants in England and Wales (*Guidelines for Financial Reporting Standards, the Solomons Report*, ICAEW, (Solomons, 1989)) and the Accounting Standards Board (*Statement of Principles for Financial Reporting*, ASB, 1999).

2 In 1973 the International Accounting Standards Committee (IASC) was founded by the accountancy bodies of nine countries with the fundamental aim of increasing comparability of financial information worldwide – or, more formally, 'to formulate and publish, in the public interest, accounting standards to be observed in the presentation of financial statements and to promote their worldwide acceptance and observance'. The IASC has expanded rapidly and now has 128 member bodies in 91 countries.

3 New management accounting systems have emerged in recent years. These systems have prompted the following comments:

  Management accounting techniques have moved with the times and new techniques and approaches have grown in response to an increasingly competitive market environment for almost all businesses. As a consequence the breadth of activity and the rigour with which it is being monitored and measured within most companies has grown rapidly in the last ten years.

  (Eccles and Kahn, 1999)

4 Awareness of corporate social responsibility has imposed new information objectives for accountants, which will require a new accounting methodology. In recent years, the concept of social accounting has been enlarged to include a concern for ecology in the form of what has become known as 'green accounting'.

Summary

In this chapter, we have examined the development of accounting from its earliest form as a recording activity to its present importance which stems from the objective of providing socio-economic information for decision making. The history of accounting development reflects the ability to respond to changing social needs.

Self-assessment questions

1 In what ways have the definitions of accounting changed over time?

2 Consider the concepts of stewardship accounting, financial and management accounting.

3 Consider the reasons why accounting has attracted criticism in recent years.

4 Describe how accountants have responded to those criticisms.

References

Accounting Standards Board (ASB) (1999) *Statement of Principles for Financial Reporting.*

AICPA (1961) *Committee on Terminology*, American Institute Publishing Co. p. 9.

Dearing Report (1988) *The Making of Accounting Standards*, Report of the Review Committee.

Eccles, R.G. and Kahn, H.D. (1999) *Value Reporting Forecast: 2000*, Price Waterhouse Coopers.

Elkington, J. (1998) The Sustainability Agenda: Not For The Short Sighted, *Accounting and Business*, September.

Gonella, C., Pilling, A. and Zadek, S. (1998) *Making Values Count*, ACCA Research Report No. 57.

Group 100 Incorporated (2003) *Sustainability: A guide to triple bottom line reporting*, Melbourne.

Institute of Chartered Accountants of Scotland (1988) *Making Corporate Reports Valuable.*

International Accounting Standards Committee (1989) *Framework for the Preparation and Presentation of Financial Statements.*

Johnson, H.T. and Kaplan, R. (1987) *Relevance Lost*, Harvard Business School.

Littleton A.C. (1953) *The Structure of Accounting Theory*, AAA Monograph, No. 5, p. 30.

Solomons, D. (1989) *Guidelines for Financial Reporting Standards*, Research Board of the ICAEW.

Van Cauwenberge, P. and De Beelde, I. (2007) On the IASB Comprehensive Income Project: An Analysis of the Case for Dual Income Display, *ABACUS*, Vol. 43, No. 1, pp. 1–26.

Whelan, C. and McBarnet, D. (1999) *Creative Accounting and the Cross-Eyed Javelin Thrower*, John Wiley and Sons.

Whittington, G. (2008) Fair Value and the IASB/FASB Conceptual Framework Project: An Alternative View, *ABACUS*, Vol. 44, No. 2, pp. 139–168.

CHAPTER 3

Accounting as an information system

Setting the scene

The accountants' basic role as 'informative people' will become increasingly important. To prosper, an information-era company must have even more information and knowledge and use it even more quickly than ever before. The positioning of the accountancy profession is ideal to capitalise on these opportunities.

(R. K. Elliot, quoted in Fleming, 1999)

Learning objectives

After studying this chapter you should be able to:

1 identify the boundaries between the accounting system and its environment;

2 analyse the information needs of the groups of people who have vested interests in a business organization;

3 explain how accounting assists the allocation of resources.

Accountants select raw data relevant to their purposes. The filtering process by which they select accounting data is provided by the conventions of accounting, which play a deterministic role in defining accounting information. This filtering process may be taken as one boundary between the accounting system and its environment: that point at which raw data becomes input data. The data selected forms the input into the processing system which provides accounting information. This information output is used by groups of decision makers, which are identifiable, and it is evident that a decision-oriented information system should produce information which meets the needs of its users. Clearly, these should be specified in accordance with a theory of users' requirements. Hence, the other boundary to an accounting information system is established by the specific information needs of its users. We may model these boundaries as in Figure 3.1.

This analysis of accounting as an information system leads to some important deductions. First, the goal of the system is to provide information which meets the needs of its users. The nature and character of the output of the system can be specified, if these needs can be sufficiently and accurately identified. Second, the output requirements should determine the type of data selected as the input for processing into information output. Third, welfare considerations may be taken into account in the selection of data, in accordance with the objectives of accounting stated in Chapter 2.

Figure 3.1

The concept of *control* indicated (in Figure 3.1) shows that users' needs should define not only the nature of data input, but also the extent of the data input which should be determined by a cost–benefit analysis related to these needs and the impact of their decisions on society.

The output of an information system

The foregoing discussion serves to indicate the importance of the needs of users of accounting information, for such needs determine the objectives of an accounting information system.

There are several groups of people who have vested interests in a business organization – managers, shareholders, employees, customers and creditors. Additionally, the community at large has economic and social interests in the activities of business organizations. This interest is expressed at national level by the concern of government in various aspects of corporate activities, such as the economic well-being of business firms, their contribution to welfare, their part in the growth of the national product, to mention but a few obvious examples; and at local level by the concern of local authorities and bodies in the direct socio-economic impact of the activities of local businesses. These concerns are addressed in the notion of 'triple bottom line' reporting discussed in the previous chapter.

According to the decision-usefulness approach to accounting theory, users of accounting information should be regarded as decision makers interested in determining the sacrifices which must be made to obtain the benefits that are expected to flow from the decisions. Since all the sacrifices and the benefits necessarily materialize in the future, uncertainty plays a critical role in assessing the sacrifices and benefits associated with particular decisions.

The information needs of shareholders and investors

Long before the Industrial Revolution that began in the United Kingdom in the late eighteenth century and spread to continental Europe, business accounting served the sole purpose of supplying information for control purposes to those who had invested their wealth in business ventures. The Industrial Revolution saw the emergence of industrial capitalism and the mobilization of wealth for capital investment. This was facilitated through the creation of the joint-stock company structure, pioneered in English law, which led to the separation of ownership and management of incorporated businesses. Although retaining ownership rights under the law to the assets and income, the English Joint Stock Companies Acts of 1844–1856 recognized the need to protect the rights of investors in joint stock companies under the control of separate Boards of Directors. The legal rules that defined the ownership rights of shareholders and investors included a strict requirement for the disclosure to shareholders of annual financial information in the form of published balance sheets and income statements. Similar developments took place in other industrial nations. Part 2 Section 1 examines the nature of the financial accounting information disclosed to shareholders and investors. Part 3 Section 1 discusses the problems of financial reporting in terms of a critical analysis of the objectives of financial reporting to investors.

The information needs of management

Organizations fall into two broad classes: those having profit objectives, and those having welfare objectives. This text is concerned mainly with business organizations, but it should be remembered that many accounting methods employed in business organizations are also employed by other forms of organizations, including governmental agencies and non-profit organizations. As regards the management of organizations, little difference may exist between the information needs of managers of businesses and other forms of organization.

The management process may be seen as consisting of three main functions – planning, organizing and controlling activities. These various management functions have the common purpose of making decisions that have their own specific information requirements. Planning decisions, for example, are directed towards realizing broad goals which, in addition to the organization's survival and its profitability, usually include growth targets as well as growth in market share. Other goals include product leadership, increased productivity and improved industrial relations. It is the function of management to reconcile the conflict that may arise between these various goals through the planning process. Cost management is a key success factor requiring cost information for product and service costing as well as cost control. Part 2 Section 2 examines the nature of cost accounting. Part 3 Section 3 discusses the nature of management control.

The information needs of employees

The theory of finance assumes that the objective of business corporations is to optimize shareholder value. Under this assumption, there is a conflict of interests between corporate objectives as management objectives and those of employees, whose salaries and other entitlements are treated as costs in the calculation of accounting income.

Unless employees are able to share in the income of business organizations, they are effectively dissociated from their activities, if we suppose that the objective of business organizations is to maximize accounting income and maximize returns to shareholders. This classical concept of the objective of business enterprises is being replaced as a result of the social changes taking place in our society, and there is a broadening view of the social and economic responsibilities of management. It is recognized that employees have a vested interest in the outcome of management decisions of every kind. Improvements in industrial democracy through employee participation in management decisions have important implications for the supply of information to employees. Many firms are already investigating this question.

As regards the settlement of wage disputes, the question of profit-sharing between employees, shareholders and management can only be settled properly on the basis of a full disclosure of the relevant facts. The expansion of the global market economy and the creation of supra-national bodies, such as the European Union, have extended the cultural background in which the importance of human rights generally as well as social rights, is given full recognition.

The information needs of governments

Government agencies, such as the taxation services, central statistical services, ministries of commerce, industry, employment, etc., collect information about the various aspects of the activities of business organizations. Much of this information is a direct output of the accounting system, for example, levels of sales activity, income, investments, inventory, liquidity, dividend levels, taxation, etc. This information is very important in evolving policies for managing the economy.

Governments, in addition, can compel the disclosure of information which is not otherwise made available to the public, such as future investment plans, expected future financial performance and so on.

By and large, however, governments expect accounting information to be presented in a uniform manner, so that the rules applying to accounting methods and the preparation of accounting reports for government use are the same as those which govern the nature of accounting information disclosed to investors and shareholders. If governments base policy decisions on accounting information which distorts the true position, it is evident that the ill effects of such decisions will be widely felt.

The information needs of creditors

Creditors consist of all those who have provided goods, money or services to business organizations and have accepted a delay in payment or repayment. Creditors may be short-term or long-term lenders. Short-term creditors include suppliers of materials and goods, normally described as trade creditors, credit institutions such as banks and hire-purchase firms which lend money at interest on a relatively short-term basis, and those who have provided services and are awaiting payment, for example, employees, outside contractors who have made repairs or electricity and gas undertakings which have rendered invoices and have not yet been paid. Long-term creditors are those who have lent money for a long period, often in the form of secured loans.

The main concern of creditors is whether or not the enterprise is creditworthy, that is, will it be able to meet its financial obligations? Creditors are interested in the enterprise's profitability only insofar as it affects its ability to pay its debts. On the other hand, creditors are very concerned with the firm's liquidity, that is, those cash or near-cash resources which may be mobilized to pay them, as well as the willingness of banks and other creditors to await payment. Creditors react quickly to changes of opinion about a firm's creditworthiness, and if there is any doubt about a firm's ability to pay, they will press for immediate settlement of debts and probably drive into liquidation a firm whose prospects in the medium and longer term are not necessarily bad. Creditors are interested, therefore, mainly in financial accounting information which affects solvency, liquidity and profitability, that is, with obtaining reports which will describe a firm's financial standing.

The information needs of other groups

There are two other groups in society interested in the activities of business organizations, and which are pretty well excluded from receiving information: the local community and customers.

The information needs of the local community

Local communities are very dependent on local industries, not only because they provide employment, but also because they directly affect the entire socio-economic structure of the environment. Firms provide employment, create a demand for local services and an expansion in commercial activities, as well as extensions in the provision of welfare services as the economic well-being of the community improves. Large firms, in particular, are able to exert a dominating influence on the local social framework which often is reflected in the corporate personality of the inhabitants. Local industries have both positive and negative influences on the locality. Pollution, despoliation and congestion are all negative aspects of their activities that constitute external direct and indirect social and economic costs, which are borne by the community.

The local community has an interest in the activities of local industries, and requires much more information on social benefits and costs than the public-relations-type information which is presently disclosed. The social audit points to a possible remedy for the lack of objectivity in the information presently disclosed.

The information needs of customers

In recent years, consumer councils and other bodies have restored in some measure the disproportionate balance of power which has appeared in our society between the large and powerful producers of consumer goods and the voiceless masses of our population who have been at the former's mercy. In a few instances, the Monopolies Commission has acted to protect consumers, but its power to intervene is based upon law.

Customers may well have little influence in markets increasingly dominated by large business organizations, and it is difficult to see how, even if more information were made available, the balance might be redressed. Certainly, customers are interested in information indicating the fairness of pricing policies, such as the relative proportion of unit price which consists of costs, profits and taxes, and in the differential costs between one product and another produced by the same firm at a different price. For example, why should one electric shaver cost £10 more than another, and in what ways is this difference value for money? Clearly, there will be many more social changes in our society before questions of this sort will be recognized and adequately answered.

Accounting information and the allocation of resources

The various groups of information users just discussed share a common concern, which is to make decisions about the allocation of scarce resources between competing ends. Students of economics will find that such a statement echoes a popular definition of the subject matter of economics. The importance of accounting information is that it makes such an allocation possible in a market economy, where individuals and organizations are largely free to allocate the resources which they control between competing ends. Hence, one objective of an accounting information system is to enable information users to make decisions which improve the allocation of available resources within their control. Such decision making may be understood only in relation to the objectives of decision makers, so that the various groups of information users whose needs may be said to have very different and occasionally competing decision objectives. Accordingly, the objective of accounting information systems is to enable decision makers to improve the allocation of the resources which they control and to assess the actual results of their decisions against the forecast results.

Behavioural aspects of decision making

The purpose of accounting is to produce information which will influence behaviour. Unless accounting reports have the potential to influence decisions and actions, it is difficult to justify the cost of preparing such reports. Traditionally, accounting reports have been addressed to shareholders and investors. In Part 3 Section 1, the behavioural aspects of investor decision making are discussed and the role of accounting information in that context will be examined. In particular, the response of the Stock Exchange to the disclosure of accounting information through the reaction of share prices will be seen to be one way in which the influence of accounting reports of investors may be judged. In Part 3 Section 2, the behavioural aspects of decision making within organizations are examined and the role of management accounting information as an influence in this respect will be discussed.

From a management point of view, the purpose of accounting information is to enable the organization to attain its goals. Hence, the effectiveness of accounting information is evidenced in the manner in which it affects behaviour. Unless accounting information produces the desired action, it has served no purpose at all. Research has shown, for example, that even when managers have all the information which they need, they do not always make good decisions. The human process which leads managers to recognize or fail to recognize the significance of accounting information requires better understanding and accountants need to be aware of the role of accounting information to enable managers to identify and to learn from their mistakes. Feedback information plays an important part in this process.

Summary

Accounting may be examined from the viewpoint of information system theory as a system consisting of three activities – input, processing and output. Its relevance and usefulness extends beyond purely operational consideration to an evaluation of the degree to which the needs of the users of accounting information are satisfied. Defining the basic goal of an accounting information system as being the provision of information for decision making provides the means of judging its effectiveness.

There are many approaches to the study of decision making – economic, behavioural and quantitative – and the interdisciplinary nature of decision theory has the inevitable consequence that accounting has also become an interdisciplinary subject. The systems approach facilitates an interdisciplinary study of accounting because it requires that it be viewed, not in isolation, but as one element in a broad informational context.

Self-assessment questions

1 State the groups of persons having vested interests in a business organization and examine the nature of their information needs.

2 Evaluate the role of accounting information in the allocation of resources.

Reference   Fleming, P. D. (1999) Steering a Course for the Future, *Journal of Accountancy*, November.

CHAPTER 4

The universality of business accounting method

Setting the scene

The context in which business accounting has its universal significance resides in the community of nations that has been brought together through the emergence of a global economy. It is also a context that has been uniquely influenced by the universal adoption of the double-entry method of bookkeeping, which had its origins in new business methods inspired during the Italian Renaissance, then known as the Italian method of bookkeeping. The first formal text on double-entry bookkeeping was written by Pacioli, in 1494, as part of a treatise on mathematics (Pacioli, 1494). Each chapter on the double-entry method of bookkeeping began with a statement of the moral principle implied in the method. It is a tradition that has been maintained and is illustrated in the explanatory note to each international accounting standard, setting out the principle prior to stipulating the method.

Learning objectives

After studying this chapter you should be able to:

1 understand the nature of accounting responsibility as a specific social responsibility;

2 understand the implications of the transaction principle in defining business accounting method;

3 understand the principles on which double-entry bookkeeping is based;

4 know the meaning of debit and credit;

5 appreciate the importance of objectivity in accounting doctrine;

6 perceive the different ways in which business accounting method has universal usefulness;

7 realize that business accounting method has social implications that flow from the structure of modern capitalist society.

Historically, accounting responsibility was rooted in the idea of stewardship accounting. Estate owners appointed stewards with the responsibility for managing their property. They were required to keep proper records of all transactions and to submit year-end accounts. Subject to the approval of these accounts, they were 'discharged' from the responsibility for good management with which they had been 'charged' at the beginning of the year. This system, known as 'charge and discharge accounting', continues to be reflected in current practice that requires proper records to be maintained and audited prior to submission for approval by shareholders.

The concept of stewardship accounting remains enshrined in accounting theory, which has retained the double-entry method principle as its methodology. Although the keeping of manual records in ledgers and cash books now has been superseded by computerized accounting systems, computerized accounting systems function exclusively on the basis of the double-entry principle. With the computer age, old-fashioned terminology that referred to bookkeeping and bookkeepers has been replaced by the terms accounting and accountants.

The transaction principle and double-entry bookkeeping

The transaction principle is the key to understanding the very nature of accounting information. The only business activity that is recognized and recorded in accounting systems is the transaction that occurs whenever a business enters into contractual relationships of whatever nature with external parties. Generally, transactions are evidenced in invoices that state the date, the nature of the transaction, the price and the amount involved. No transaction may be recorded without an invoice and no data other than that shown on the invoice may be used for recording purposes.

The transaction principle strictly limits the nature of accounting data that is recorded to that which appears in invoices. Consequently, all other information that cannot be evidenced by invoice is not recognized as accounting data and will not appear as financial information prepared from accounting records. This rule excludes a great deal of information that would be relevant knowledge about a business.

According to the double-entry principle, the transaction is replicated in its legal nature and the invoice acting both as legal and accounting proof. In legal terms, a transaction involves an exchange in which something is given in exchange for something else which is received. For example, a cash sale for £10 is a sale valued at £10 that has resulted in the receipt of £10. The double-entry principle requires that both these aspects of the transaction be shown in the accounting record through interlocking accounts. Accordingly, two accounts are used for recording the transaction, namely, the sales account in which is shown the £10 sales and the cash account in which the receipt of £10 from the sale is recorded, as follows:

Sales account: £10 given in cash

Cash account: £10 received from sales

These two accounts are interlocked through showing the transaction as a flow of a constant money value, namely, £10, from the Sales account to the Cash account. The starting point is the account from which the flow begins and is signalled by the term 'credit'. It terminates in the account in which the flow is received. The term 'credit' is derived from the Latin expression 'creditum', which means 'I give'; the term 'debit' is derived from 'debitum', meaning 'I receive'. These terms are historical relics from the Italian origins of double-entry bookkeeping, 'creditum' being simply reduced to 'credit' and 'debitum' reduced to 'debit'. They are common to all languages today for all accounting or financial purposes being further shortened to 'Cr' and 'Dr' respectively on accounting and financial statements, such as invoices, bank statements, bills of exchange etc.

Accordingly, these two accounts will be fully detailed in the accounting system as a flow of £10 cash from the Sales account to the Cash account as follows:

Sales a/c   Cash £10   Cash a/c   Sales £10

25

Reference to the Sales a/c only will indicate that the Cash a/c has received £10. Correspondingly, reference to the Cash a/c only will indicate that £10 has originated from the Sales a/c.

The accounting data recorded from invoices bears the date of the transaction. Hence, accounting information drawn from accounting systems is historical in nature and refers to past and current transactions only. It records the legal rights and obligations created through transactions as stated on invoices and may be verified from invoices. The process of auditing year-end financial statements involves using sampling procedures to check that invoices have been properly recorded and are available, if needed.

The doctrinal purity of double-entry bookkeeping

Accounting purports to record the truth with respect to transactions that have been completed during an accounting period. Truth that is founded on facts is known as objective truth and is validated by facts. Absolute truth is beyond human knowledge and sincere belief, as truth, is subjective and has only the value of opinion.

Objectivity ensures the purity of accounting data by preventing mere opinion from polluting the quality of truth that exists in unadulterated invoices. Objectivity as the test of truth in accounting is ensured through the sole use of invoices for obtaining data inputs into accounting systems. Malpractice and fraudulent accounting is often attributable to the manipulation of invoices in a variety of ways that include fictitious or falsified invoices.

The preparation of financial reports using data drawn from accounting records introduces subjectivity whenever it is necessary to alter recorded historical values to meet the specific information needs. For example, when preparing year-end results, it may be necessary to anticipate future losses. The value of such losses inevitably are subjective, being unknown with certainty at the date of valuation. This is typically the case with unrealized losses in year-end inventories that have to be estimated in order not to overstate reported earnings and mislead investors as a result.

Doctrinal purity founded on the objectivity of historical values is threatened whenever such values are modified in the preparation of accounting information through alternative valuations that abandon the objectivity of historic values. Consequent upon the credit and banking crisis starting in 2007, political pressure was exerted on regulatory authorities in the United States and elsewhere for easing the mark-to-market rule[1] in favour of fair values in financial reporting. This had particular significance for financial institutions that were adversely affected by the credit and banking crisis and appeared to deny the unambiguous truth that resides in the objectivity of accounting values. An Exposure Draft issued in 2009, *Fair Value Measurements*' (IASB, 2009), defined fair value as 'the price that would be received to sell an asset or paid to transfer a liability in an orderly transaction between market participants at the measurement date (an exit price)'. Some critics have suggested that this departure from historical values in favour of fair values impairs truth in accounting and undermines trust in accounting information.

---

[1] Conservative accounting practice based on the principle of prudence is to value current assets on balance sheets at their current market value and, in the case of inventories, at the lower of cost and market value.

Stewardship accounting defines ownership control as the objective for accounting records of transactions kept at their historical value. Periodic financial reports prepared in that context are addressed to the ex-post evaluation of financial results, asset and risk management. Interpretations of the social context of business that look beyond capitalism to admit that there are other stakeholders in the enterprise are fallacious, since they do not have any proprietary interest. Equally, the claim that the social role of business extends beyond financial considerations imposes normative concepts that would require validation through the reform of the structure of modern society.

Finally, the role of the accounting profession is defined in terms of the stewardship accounting model. Its mission is to elaborate rules and standards that relate to this mission and that ensure that financial reports based on historical accounts are as objective as possible for ownership control purposes. It has long been argued that accountants are not valuers. They are concerned with the analysis and allocation of historical costs that are not useful for making valid projections of future values that are relevant to the decision needs of investors.

Universal double-entry bookkeeping

The double-entry principle is used in all forms of accounting activity, whether in public or in private sector business firms, in financial companies, such as insurance and banking, for government and local authority accounting purposes, in non-profit organisations and global institutions, such as the World Bank and the IMF.

In all the foregoing organizations, double-entry bookkeeping is the vital core of an information system that collects, analyses and transforms data into meaningful information and provides a permanent record of all activities in their financial expression. The management of economic resources in the production of goods and services would be impossible without the information that is made continuously and permanently available through an accounting control system based on the logic and principle of the double-entry bookkeeping system.

The importance of universal double-entry bookkeeping reaches much beyond the management of economic resources in providing that level of cohesion necessary to the functioning of a modern market society. The reliance and trust invested in the accounting information allows all parties to realize their own interest by committing their efforts in collaborative activities. Thus, investors that commit their own capital to business firms in the expectation that their investment will be both secure and profitable, rely on the veracity of accounting information. Investor confidence in business firms disappears when that sense of cohesion, which is a function of trust in accounting information, is shattered by fraud and corruption. Likewise, governments that finance the budgets of public bodies and agencies that provide social services have to justify, verify and account to taxpayers with regard to the social purposes to which public funds are committed. In this sense, social cohesion within democratic societies is ensured through political action that is validated through the sound management of public funds. The high level of social cohesion necessary to business success implies that the interests of stakeholders, such as shareholders, employees, creditors and customers, are reconciled through management action that is rationalized in a consensus founded on common understanding. Accounting information provides that essential reference.

A further contribution to social cohesion provided by the logic and language of double-entry bookkeeping is the provision of a common meaning in the communication of information throughout society. By describing actions and communicating their consequences using such terms as 'debit' and 'credit', their meaning is made immediately transparent. The recipient of correspondence from a bank or business firm informing them that their account has been debited with a stated sum immediately realizes, without any education in accounting, that the sender is stating that, according to information recorded in the accounting system, the recipient is indebted in the amount stated for goods or services that they have received. The logic and language of double-entry bookkeeping has acquired universal use for communicating information and decisions in terms of commonly shared meanings.

The transaction principle that determines the nature of the data input recorded on the basis of the double-entry principle also provides the calculus for periodic income measurement, based exclusively on the concept of realization. Sales recorded either on the basis of cash receipt or sales invoices are compared with invoices that relate to the cost of goods or services sold, the resulting difference appearing either as a surplus or deficit, as the case may be. That surplus or deficit is the income or loss that has been realized.

The universal acceptance of accounting income as income realized and quantified through double-entry bookkeeping data is reflected also in universal agreement that accounting income should have its ultimate meaning as an unconditional number. For this reason, accountants have been traditionally wary of references to values that are not attested through invoices at their recorded value. In accounting logic, income concepts based on value-added that economists consider as more appropriate, are rejected since they may include unrealized gains that are future expectations having their validity only in conjecture.

The understanding of accounting income provides social cohesion in the global market economy through agreement as to the calculus of periodic income. It has acted as a point of resistance to the manipulation of recorded accounting data that are justified as adjustments considered necessary to eliminate the uncertainty attaching to future events, for example, provisions for future losses.

All business organizations, whether structured on capitalistic lines or mutual and cooperative lines are united in agreeing that the accounting income concept is the only practical basis for evaluating business efficiency. This logic is universally accepted in the determination of accounting income as a transaction-based surplus based on historical values.

The integration of financial and cost management

Corporate management may be seen as presenting two distinct problems, namely, dealing with relations with external parties and managing the internal processes involved in producing goods and services. The double-entry principle is employed in collecting and processing data for recording transactions with external parties, which include suppliers, employees and services, through invoices that are exchanged in the normal course of business.

In the case of manufacturing companies, the purpose of cost accounting is to calculate the cost of production of finished goods. This information is necessary for product pricing in order to ensure profitability. At the same time, it provides a knowledge base for determining the financing requirement implied in the level of production. Cost accounting relates only to the processes involved in transforming raw materials into finished goods. Its objective is to record the build-up of production costs as raw materials are transformed through several processes and production departments into finished goods at the factory warehouse.

Double-entry bookkeeping at factory level treats the transfer of costs to products, as they are processed through different stages of production, through a cost accounting system defined in terms of different departments. Production costs accumulated in one department are transferred to the next department in line by crediting the account of the originating department with the product costs transferred to the next department and recorded by debiting that department with the cost of production transferred. Cost accounting through double-entry bookkeeping allows the ultimate integration of product costs transferred to sales as the cost of goods sold.

The same principle is adopted for other forms of activities, such as services of various kinds. It is through precise knowledge of the costs of goods and services that businesses are able to formulate pricing policies that allow costs to be covered and competitive prices to be assessed as to their impact on incomes.

Social aspects of double-entry bookkeeping

Double-entry bookkeeping assumes that a business is an independent entity operating in an open market through which it is related to other parties by a series of on-going transactions, which are evidenced in invoices. The peculiarity of double-entry bookkeeping is the distinction drawn between shareholders as owners and other parties that have no ownership interests. This distinction is formalized in business law that grants the legal right to the assets and the incomes to shareholders, leaving employees as merely servants paid for their services at market rate.

Summary

Accounting responsibility remains defined in terms of stewardship accounting, imposing upon corporate management the duty of preparing annual financial reports to shareholders. Business activity is viewed as manifested through realized transactions, conferring unique importance of the transaction principle in accounting method. Double-entry bookkeeping that developed during the Italian Renaissance is universally used throughout the global economy. It is a relatively simple method of recording transactions as financial flows through integrated accounts using a system of notation in which such flows appear as debits and credits. This method is used for all accounting purposes, whether in public or private enterprises and including financial and cost accounting. Double-entry bookkeeping has social connotations that stem from the distinctive treatment accorded to ownership interests.

Self-assessment questions

1 Why is accounting responsibility defined in terms of stewardship accounting?

2 Explain the significance of the transaction principle for accounting method.

3 Briefly explain the principles underlying double-entry bookkeeping.

4 Explain the meaning of the terms 'debit' and 'credit'.

5 What is meant by doctrinal purity in double-entry bookkeeping?

6 Explain why double-entry bookkeeping has universal applicability.

References   IASB (2009) Exposure Draft ED/2009/5, *Fair Value Measurement*, IASB Publications, May.

Pacioli, Luca (1494) *Summa di arithmetica, geometria, proportioni et proportinalita*, Venice.

CHAPTER 5

International rules for business accounting

Setting the scene

The development of international accounting rules began in 1973, with the creation of the International Accounting Standards Committee (IASC), now the International Accounting Standards Board (IASB). As regards member countries of the European Union, the European Commission published two important directives for financial reporting by companies within the European Union. There now exists an international framework of rules of business accounting, which have been incorporated in the accounting law of nations that are members of these various international bodies.

The globalization of the market economy is creating new and different social and economic problems, extending the social responsibilities of business and thereby enlarging the dimensions of accounting responsibility.

Learning objectives

After studying this chapter you should know that:

1 the nature of business accounting is concerned with profitability, asset values and financial risk;

2 business activity is financed by capital supplied by investors and the annual net income as the financial return due to shareholders for financing business risk;

3 accounting income is calculated as the net difference between annual revenues and the cost of earning those revenues. When the cost of earning revenues exceeds annual revenues, the difference is shown as a net loss;

4 business accounting is based on three fundamental concepts, the entity, the transaction and the money measurement concepts;

5 accounting is a social science that refers to business as a specific area of social behaviour;

6 the globalization of the market economy has changed the accounting environment through the influence of international accounting bodies and the creation of a regulatory framework of international accounting standards.

The global expansion of the market economy of recent years has been conducted largely in a significantly deregulated business environment, making it easier for business to move across national frontiers in the search for profit. Such rules as apply to the conduct of international business are found in both country and international laws and regulations. They define the nature and extent of accountability for business activities in terms of those laws and regulations. They cover the panoply of political concerns that ranges from fiscal and tariff considerations to social and environmental issues and may be seen as constraints on an absolute freedom of trade. However, such is the importance of economic growth and business expansion that governments and the international community have been very concerned with means of encouraging business expansion rather than imposing restrictions.

The context of business accounting

Capitalism provides the theory, logic and structure of business organization in Western society. Based on capitalism, classical economic theory defines the sole aim of business as concerned with the production of goods and services with the intention of realizing profit through trading in open markets. This definition commonly supposes the existence of free trade though which business enjoys the undisputed right to seek its own interests without interference from government.

As a political philosophy, free trade is associated with classical economic theory expounded by Adam Smith in *An Inquiry into the Nature and Causes of the Wealth of Nations*. It is founded on the belief that man, led by an invisible hand and pursuing his own interests, frequently promoted that of society, an end that was not part of his intention. In arguing for free trade, Jeremy Bentham, in *An Introduction to the Principles of Morals and Legislation*, pleaded that every man was the best judge of his own advantage and should be allowed to pursue it without hindrance.

Business organizations are owned by shareholders collectively committing personal wealth to finance business ventures under conditions of risk with the expectation of profit. As a body, they are the owners of the business and are empowered to nominate Boards of Directors, who are responsible and accountable to them for the management of business activities. Employees have no ownership rights and receive wages and salaries for their services. These are treated as business expenses in the calculation of income.

Profit is the reward for financing business risk. It is also expressed as the annual return on invested capital. Accounting income is based on a simple arithmetic formula based on matching annual revenues with the expenses of earning those revenues. The difference that arises from this process is the net periodic income or net loss, as the case may be.

Accounting responsibility covers two major areas of accountability. First, maintaining proper records of business transactions on an on-going basis and ensuring that they are correctly recorded in accordance with generally accepted accounting principles, as stipulated in accounting law. Second, preparing periodic financial reports for shareholders showing the periodic financial result and the financial situation at the end of the period, in accordance with accounting law and certified as to truth and fairness by professional auditors. Financial reports normally refer to accounting years, defined as covering twelve months.

Financial reports focus on three particular areas of management responsibility and accountability, namely profitability, asset values and financial risk. These concerns are addressed in the financial reports published to shareholders. These are interpreted using tools of financial analysis into information relevant to their own decision needs, as well as information essential to the functioning of financial markets concerned ultimately with the efficient allocation of resources throughout the economy.

The development of international rules for business accounting

The evolution of business accounting rules may be seen as an organic process showing a pattern of adaptation to the needs of a market economy under constant progress and a market society under social change. Three distinct stages may be identified:

1 The early development of markets and of nascent capitalism prior to the Industrial Revolution of the seventeenth and eighteenth centuries.
2 The Industrial Revolution in Western Europe and rapid economic progress driven by commercial and industrial capitalism, flowing from manufacturing activities.
3 The recent global expansion of Western capitalism fuelled by financial capitalism, in the form of international financial capital flows, provoking revolutionary changes in world social order.

The origin of accounting may be traced to antiquity and the need to keep records for administrative and business purposes. These records were maintained in literary and descriptive form. The so-called golden period of accounting in Roman times occurred in the last two centuries BC, when heads of families were expected at law to maintain proper records of their stewardship of family property and transactions. The concept of responsibility that defines accountability has its earliest formal statement in the Roman *Jus Civilis* (Roman Civil Law).

Modern business structures and methods, as well as accounting rules have their roots in the emergence of Western society during the Italian Renaissance and through the expansion of business across Western Europe under the aegis of Italian firms. It led to the creation of international branches, new types of financial documents and, especially the Italian method of double-entry bookkeeping that eventually became the international standard for business accounting. Accounting rules during this period took the form of a consensus about the practice of accounting resulting in a series of accounting concepts, variously referred to as accounting convention or accounting principles. They provided the basic framework of modern accounting theory and acquired professional authority with the appearance of accounting bodies in the latter part of the nineteenth century. In the aftermath of the Second World War, they were given legal authority under accounting law in several European countries that had adopted a national accounting plan.

Until the beginning of the Industrial Revolution, double-entry bookkeeping coexisted with single-entry bookkeeping, known in England as the English Method of Bookkeeping. Neither system was subject to formal law and recognized simply as business practices. The Industrial Revolution marked the decisive point in the evolution of modern capitalism and business accounting, as it changed completely the business environment. Notably the factory system of industrial production led to an enormous increase in the output of goods and a corresponding increase in the volume of trade. The need to mobilize private wealth in providing the necessary financial support marked a decisive stage in the evolution of accounting rules, as the result of government intervention through legislation that authorized joint-stock companies to issue shares in return for capital subscribed by investors. This development altered the dimension of accounting responsibility by conferring on business managers the legal responsibility for corporate management and the duty of accountability to shareholders. It marked the formalization under law of the basic rules for financial reporting to shareholders. This development eventually led to an audit requirement, which was later to become a core accounting responsibility for an accounting profession that was eventually to consolidate itself under statute. Accounting conventions remained unregulated until quite recent times. The freedom which accountants enjoyed led to the development of practices that lacked uniformity and comparability as between different companies. The Industrial Revolution occurred in the aftermath of the English Enlightenment and in the spirit of free trade. There were no specific accounting laws and, interestingly methods of cost accounting were primitive and made it impossible to produce accurate product costs.

Until well after the Second World War, nation states acted independently in developing their own economies in their own interests and under their own laws. The evolution of accounting practices differed according to legal and cultural traditions in different countries. Although double-entry bookkeeping was the accepted methodology, accounting responsibility was defined differently as between nation states. The Anglo-Saxon tradition based on individual freedom and freedom of trade left the regulation of accounting practices to the accounting profession. Elsewhere in Western Europe, the regulation of accounting practices was subject to state authority and under bureaucratic control. Accounting law was formalized in terms of governmental regulation and government accounting plans. This gave rise to two different accounting cultures that were to come into conflict within the European Union.

Unregulated accounting practices within the Anglo-Saxon community of nations began to create problems in financial reporting in the 1970s, when financial markets and investors began to criticize the inadequacy of conventional accounting reports in terms of their relevance and usefulness for investor decision making. Massive inflation accentuated this problem and there began a new trend within the accounting profession, which focused on defining an objective framework for accounting rules for ensuring greater uniformity and comparability in financial reporting.

The next stage in the development of international accounting rules began in 1973, when the accounting bodies from nine countries founded the International Accounting Standards Committee (IASC), which changed its name to the International Accounting Standards Board in 2001. Its purpose is to promote worldwide acceptance of accounting standards that would improve comparability of financial information. As regards accounting rules within the European Union, the European Commission published two important directives concerning the annual accounts of companies within the European Union. These were the Directive on the Annual Accounts of Companies with limited liability, issued 25 July 1978, and the Directive on the Consolidated Accounts of Companies with limited liability, issued on 13 June 1983. Finally, the OECD itself had a considerable influence on these movements through an on-going concern with the development of accounting rules in an international context.

The IASB took its inspiration from the work of the accounting bodies in the USA and the UK, which were emphatically concerned with the substance of accounting information. By contrast, the EEC was more concerned with harmonizing the form in which accounting information should be presented. This divergence was reconciled when the EEC decided on 3 November 2008 to adopt the consolidated International Financial Reporting Standards (IFRS) of the IASB, after having adopted several individual IFRS since 2003. By 2008, the USA had also decided to follow suit with respect to its own financial reporting standards. As a result, under the auspices of the IASB, there now is a set of international accounting standards that has effective universal applicability throughout the global market economy.

Concepts that determine the nature of business accounting

Three basic concepts define the nature of business accounting, namely the entity, the transaction and the money measurement concepts. The nature of business accounting and accounting responsibility remain determined by the foregoing three concepts and their crucial importance in these respects has been maintained in the series of international accounting standards issued to date.

The entity concept establishes the business as separate from its owner. In the case of unincorporated businesses such as sole traders and partnerships, the separate identity of the owner(s) is established through a capital account on the balance sheet, recording invested capital as a source of funds. In the case of incorporated businesses, the share capital account represents the separate identity of shareholders established under law. The business is a separate legal person. The responsibility for management is vested in a Board of Directors having executive authority.

The transaction concept defines business activity as consisting of transactions in a market context with clients and suppliers of goods and services, assets and finance. The transaction concept limits the recognition of business to those activities that may be identified as legally enforceable contracts. As a result, whatever else may be associated with its actions, such as sustainability, environmental and other social effects is ignored.

Finally, the money measurement concept means that money is the sole valuation base for business activity, which is viewed as concerned strictly with money values. Public concern with moral and ethical values has been heightened in recent years as a result of such financial scandals as Enron, Parmalat and Madoff. Truth, trust and transparency have now become serious issues for regulators.

The emergence of the global market economy

The emergence of the global market economy under the auspices, direction and in the interests of financial capitalism is creating a new world order in which the incompatibility of free trade and regulatory intervention will need resolving. This incompatibility was made evident through the credit and banking crisis that began in the USA in 2007 and rapidly affected Europe and Asia by 2008.

It showed how rapidly countries could be affected by shared problems originating elsewhere in the global market economy and had to seek together common solutions. In particular, it indicated the shortcomings in the regulatory framework applying to the business sector and the urgent need to develop new accounting rules enabling the closer supervision of business enterprises. It led to massive injections of public funds into the corporate business sector, as governments took majority ownership stakes in publicly quoted companies. It revealed a flawed financial capital system that was unable to regulate itself and acted with disregard to the economic and social consequences caused by greed and socially irresponsible corporate management behaviour.

A permanent solution to the problems that this crisis revealed called for international agreement on an appropriate structure for developing an effective international regulatory framework. It remains to be seen whether high levels of international regulation will interfere unduly with the efficient functioning of financial markets.

Summary

International rules for business accounting rely on the procedures that professional accountants evolved through time to deal with the responsibility of providing financial information about business entities to their owners. The evolution of the global market economy has made necessary the rationalization of practices in different countries into uniform international accounting standards for accounting as well as financial reporting purposes.

Considerable progress has been made in recent decades under the aegis of the International Accounting Standards Board (IASB) in providing the global economy with a set of accounting standards aimed at securing greater uniformity and comparability in financial reporting. However, weaknesses in the regulatory framework have persisted.

Self-assessment questions

1 How does capitalism define the context of business accounting?

2 What does the concept of free trade imply for international accounting rules?

3 What is accounting income and how is it calculated?

4 What are the two major areas of accounting responsibility?

5 What are the three areas of management responsibility and accountability?

6 Briefly review the three stages in the evolution of international accounting rules?

7 What is the role of the International Accounting Standards Board?

8 What are the defining concepts underlying international accounting rules?

9 Discuss the implications of the emergence of the global market economy for the development of international accounting rules?

CHAPTER 6

The scope and role of accounting theory

Setting the scene

The construction of an accounting theory requires the justification or refutation of exist-ing accounting practices. Under the traditional approach, construction and verification of a theory were considered virtually synonymous. In the past ten years, however, a new approach that employs a distinct verification process has emerged. The underlying objective of both approaches is the same: to develop a conceptual framework for what accountants do or are expected to be doing.

(Belkaoui, 1992)

Learning objectives

After studying this chapter you should be able to:

1 appreciate the nature of theories;
2 explain how theory in accounting differs from that in the natural sciences;
3 understand the reasons why there has been no progress towards a general theory of accounting;
4 explain the nature of different approaches to accounting theory;
5 appreciate the importance of concepts and standards in accounting theory construction;
6 understand the relevance of a conceptual framework for developing financial reporting standards;
7 perceive the significance of ethics for policy makers and regulators.

Knowledge is uncovered by the mind. It provides understanding of the various phe-nomena that constitute the experience of life. The idea of progress through the acquisition of knowledge is closely associated with the Enlightenment, the period that signalled the Age of Science. The logic of reason relying on the scientific method of enquiry continues to promote progress and better understanding of matter and material life forms, which is the domain of the natural sciences. It has revealed that all material life forms are subject to immutable laws of nature. Scientific knowledge is concerned solely with the discovery of the laws of nature through observations that yield data that is rationalized into theories. The essential usefulness of scientific theories lies in their reliability in making predictions, namely that the repetition of the same facts and circumstances will produce the same results in the future.

The social sciences are concerned with gaining understanding of social behaviour and also rely on the logic of reason and the scientific method of enquiry in the treatment of data that is rationalized into theories that explain social behaviour. As Darwin (1859) explained, the laws of nature have an important part to play in providing an understanding of aspects of social behaviour, such as the self instinct and the survival of the fittest (Dawkins, 1976). However, social behaviour is also subject to man-made laws that are not immutable but are conditioned by value judgements.

The definition of good theory

The word 'theory' itself gives rise to misunderstanding, and may mean different things to different people. This arises because explanations are made at different levels. At one extreme, explanations are purely speculative, resulting in speculative theories, for example that 'outer-space probes are affecting the weather'. To the natural scientist, speculative theories are not really theories at all and explanations have to be conclusive before they are given the status of theories. To this end, their assumptions require verification by the test of experience. At another extreme are to be found explanations which are accepted only when they have been verified. Empirical theories are constructed by the process of verifying assumptions, or hypotheses, through the test of experience. This process is known as the 'scientific method', and is illustrated in Figure 6.1.

Essentially, theories are generalizations which serve to organize masses of data in order to establish significant relationships from that data. Data constitute the facts and significant relationships are developed through reasoning. The close association of theory and facts is fundamental to the notion of good theory, for the reliability of a theory depends not only upon the facts to which it refers, but also upon the reasoning applied to the interpretation of those facts, which requires validation.

A misunderstanding of the relationship that exists between facts and theories gives rise to a great deal of misconception about the role of theories. Thus, the complaint that 'it's all right in theory but not in practice' implies that the person making the complaint must hold the belief that an alternative theory provides a different explanation of the facts in question.

Theories are concerned with explanation. Explanation relates a set of observations to a theoretical construction of reality which fits those observations. If no theoretical scheme that does this reasonably well is available, the desire for explanation leads to the creation of a scheme of ideas which provides a definition of the problem observed, as well as an understanding of it, in the form of explanation. In both cases, relating observations to existing theory and constructing theory to fit observations, have the objective of providing an explanation of those observations.

According to Hawking (1995), 'a theory is a good theory if it satisfies two requirements. It must accurately describe a large class of observations on the basis of a model that contains only a few arbitrary elements. And it must make definite predictions about the results of future observations'.

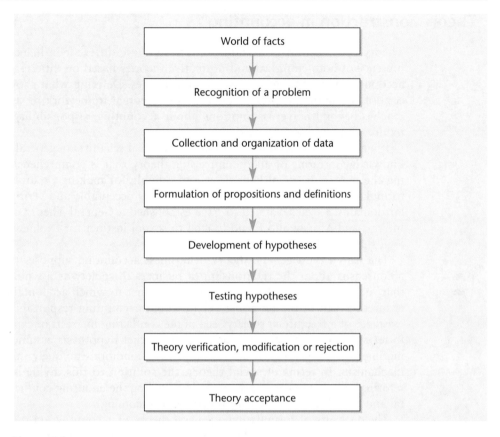

Figure 6.1

Theory construction

The construction of theories requires a process of reasoning about the problems implicit in the data under observation, in order to distinguish basic relationships. It is a process of simplification, which requires assumptions that permit the representation of reality by a generalization that is easily understood.

Theory construction in the natural sciences begins with observations that lead to hypotheses about 'what is', which are then tested and verified prior to being formalized as theory. This process is known as 'empiricism' and scientific theories are empirical theories. Theory construction in the social sciences may be empirical and resulting from observations and also may begin by developing hypotheses or postulates on the basis of value judgements about 'what should be' and not 'what is'. Such theories are referred to as normative theories. They seek to develop rules for social behaviour that rely on man-made laws for their implementation.

Empirical theories assist in making 'predictions', for while they consist of generalizations which explain the present, future occurrences also replicate the same conditions. It is in providing both explanations and predictions that empirical theories have acquired such importance in making decisions about the future which are based on assumptions derived from experience.

Theory construction in accounting

Theory construction in accounting reflects these different influences through the presence of both empirical and normative theories based on differing perceptions of accounting facts and accounting responsibilities. Defining what should be the concern of accounting, expressed through a conceptual framework of stated objectives, reaches beyond naïve assumptions about accounting responsibility to that of the nature of modern society itself.

It may be suggested that the ambition of social scientists in general is to formulate knowledge in terms of all-encompassing theory that is comprehensive for explaining the nature of social behaviour and reliable for making predictions. It implies formulating generalizations that are reasonably acceptable and verifiable in particular domains. Keynes claimed to have established a General Theory of Employment, Interest and Money and Freud looked to sexual instinct for explanation of psychological behaviour.

The search for a general theory of business accounting supposes that there exists a consensus about the relationship of business to society as a whole and, equally, that such a consensus also applies to the manner in which accountability should be ensured. Much of the on-going debate about accounting responsibility accepts the existence of a fracture in society seen in the conflicting interests of capital and labour. In terms of economic theory, the efficient market hypothesis assumes that conflicting interests are reconciled under competitive conditions uniquely through a pricing mechanism. In terms of social theory, the solution to this divide is seen in social reforms and promoting structures for reconciling the enduring conflict between capital and labour at the workplace (Glautier, forthcoming).

The difficulty of formulating a general theory of accounting on the basis of 'what accountants do' lies in establishing a view of 'what accountants should do' in the context of a philosophy or system of ideas that transcends descriptions of practice and reaches out to an ideal in which a wider social purpose may be found.

As long ago as 1955, Chambers argued that it is possible to build up a theory of (business) accounting without reference to the practice of accounting. At the time, this view met with intense hostility, but the subsequent debate about accounting has looked beyond the confines of accounting to the role of business in society and its implications for business accountability and business accounting. This debate has inspired two distinct trends. Under the aegis of the accounting profession and regulatory authorities, the concern has been establishing a conceptual framework for financial reporting based on conventional accounting practice and financial accounting standards. Watts and Zimmerman (1978, 1986) attempted to construct a positive theory of accounting on the basis of accounting practices for determining accounting standards. Financial markets, the accounting profession and regulatory authorities found common purpose in promoting the interests of financial capitalism and its influence over the global market economy. Not surprisingly, the theory of finance acted as an intellectual beacon for questioning traditional accounting theory that had its central concern with legal rights with respect to assets and liabilities.

On a broader social level, the relationship between business and society has led to a fierce public and political debate. The accounting profession, as well as academics, social scientists and social reformers joined together in an on-going debate that has focused on business accountability defined as corporate social responsibility for the social and environmental aspects of business activities. Although both financial and corporate social responsibility reports are published in combined annual reports to shareholders, financial reports using exclusively financial measurements are audited for truth and fairness, whereas corporate social reports are formulated generally in terms of non-financial measurements. These are not subject to formal audit and are prepared by public relations rather than accounting personnel. As such, they are an evaluation of corporate social performance that is partly influenced by the desire to create a favourable public image.

Different approaches to accounting theory construction

The term 'theory' is also used at different levels in the literature of accounting. References to 'accounting theory' may mean purely speculative interpretations or empirical explanations. These references usually do not indicate the level of theory which is implied.

According to Hendriksen,

Accounting theory may be defined as logical reasoning in the form of a set of broad principles that (1) provide a general frame of reference by which accounting practice can be evaluated, and (2) guide the development of new practices and procedures. Accounting theory may also be used to explain existing practices to obtain a better understanding of them. But the most important goal of accounting theory should be to provide a coherent set of logical principles that form the general frame of reference for the evaluation and development of sound accounting practices.

(Hendriksen, 1992)

The relationship between accounting theory and accounting practice is indicated in Figure 6.2, as is the influence of policy makers in relating accounting theory to accounting practice.

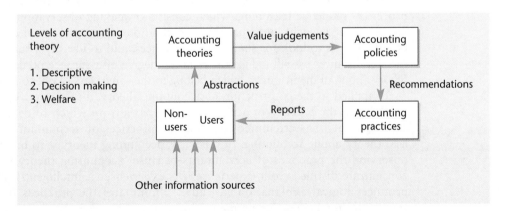

Figure 6.2

Figure 6.2 shows that the role played by theory in accounting is very different from that played in the natural sciences, where theories are developed from empirical observations. The converse is the case in accounting, since practice may be changed to accommodate theory.

According to Ijiri,

Contrary to the fields of linguistics, meteorology or chemistry, accountants can change their practices relatively easily. Therefore, it becomes an essential problem for accountants to know how accounting practices should be developed in the future. The sanctions by which accounting policies have become implemented are quite essential in understanding the field of accounting, since it is possible to change practices to fit theories!! This is unthinkable for scientists in other fields for whom phenomena are almighty. No matter how beautiful and elegant the theory may be, if it does not fit the empirical phenomena, it is replaced by one which fits better.

(Ijiri, 1971)

Figure 6.2 also illustrates how the form of accounting information reported to decision makers depends on the practices adopted. These practices are imposed by accounting policy makers who, having knowledge of accounting theories, have the responsibility of responding to the needs of users of accounting information.

Several approaches to the development of accounting theory have emerged in recent decades, as follows:

1 descriptive;
2 decision usefulness:
   (i) empirical;
   (ii) normative;
3 welfare.

1 The descriptive approach

Theories developed using the descriptive approach are essentially concerned with what accountants do. In developing such explanations, descriptive theories rely on a process of inductive reasoning, which consists of making observations and of drawing generalized conclusions from those observations. In effect, the objective of making observations is to look for similarity of instances, and to identify a sufficient number of such instances as will induce the required degree of assurance needed to develop a theory about all the instances which belong to the same class of phenomena.

As applied to the construction of accounting theory, the descriptive approach has emphasized the *practice* of accounting as a basis from which to develop theories. This approach has attempted to relate the practices of accountants to a generalized theory about accounting. In this view, accounting theory is to be discovered by observing the practices of accountants because 'accounting theory is primarily a concentrate distilled from experience it is experience … intelligently analysed that produces logical explanation … and … illuminates the practices from which it springs' (Littleton and Zimmerman, 1962).

The descriptive approach results in descriptive or positive theories of accounting, which explain what accountants do and enable predictions to be made about behaviour, for example, how a particular matter will be treated. Thus, it is possible to predict that the receipt of cash will be entered in the debit side of the cash book.

In effect, the descriptive approach is concerned with observing the functional tasks which accountants have traditionally performed. In 1952, the Institute of Chartered Accountants in England and Wales stated that 'the primary purpose of the annual accounts of a business is to present information to proprietors showing how their funds have been utilized, and the profits derived from such use' (ICAEW, 1952).

Underlying the descriptive approach is the belief that the objective of financial statements is associated with the stewardship concept of the management role, and the need to provide the owners of businesses with information relating to the manner in which their assets have been managed. In this view, company directors occupy a position of trust with responsibility and accountability to shareholders and the discharge of these obligations requires the publication of annual reports to shareholders. With the growth of large corporate enterprises, the weakening of the links between ownership and management created a need for a more focused notion of stewardship, in which the disclosure of financial information was aimed at protecting shareholders from fraudulent management practices.

As regards the development of international accounting standards, it is evident that the descriptive approach to theory construction in accounting plays an influential role in shaping perceptions of the problems of accounting and the manner in which they should be solved. The IASB has been concerned with discussing the varied practices used by accountants and reaching a consensus on the most feasible basis on which to reduce the diversity of these practices through the process of standardization.

Figure 6.3 illustrates the framework within which descriptive accounting theory has developed.

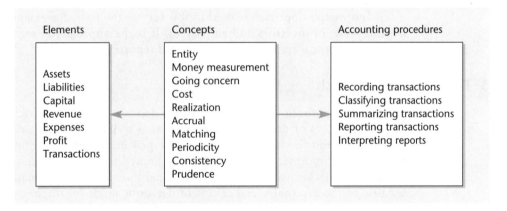

Elements	Concepts	Accounting procedures
Assets Liabilities Capital Revenue Expenses Profit Transactions	Entity Money measurement Going concern Cost Realization Accrual Matching Periodicity Consistency Prudence	Recording transactions Classifying transactions Summarizing transactions Reporting transactions Interpreting reports

Figure 6.3

2 Decision usefulness approaches

The expansion of behavioural research into accounting during the 1970s resulted in an interest in decision usefulness theories of accounting. This mood was well captured in the following statement by the American Accounting Association in 1971:

> To state the matter concisely, the principal purpose of accounting reports is to influence action, that is, behavior. Additionally, it can be hypothesized that the very process of accumulating information, as well as the behavior of those who do the accounting, will affect the behaviour of others. In short, by its very nature, accounting is a behavioral process.

(AAA, 1971)

Two types of decision usefulness theories of accounting have resulted from this approach, namely, empirical and normative theories.

The empirical approach

The early 1970s witnessed a substantial increase in empirical research which was designed to make accounting research more rigorous and to improve the reliability of results. Sophisticated statistical techniques became increasingly used for this purpose. Furthermore, the expansion of university courses in accounting increased the number of students with a mathematical background, who could conduct research in this way. The implications of the empirical approach to research in accounting were significant in the development of accounting theory.

The normative approach

Unlike the empirical research, which concentrates on how users of accounting information apply this information in decision making, the normative approach to theory construction is concerned with specifying the decisions that ought to be made as a precondition to considering the information requirement.

The normative approach focuses on the decision models which should be used by decision makers seeking to make rational decisions. This focus is seen as providing insights on the information needs of decision makers, as a basis for developing accounting theory.

The normative approach is used in this text as the basis for examining the information needs of investors and employees. It is the approach in recent attempts to develop conceptual frameworks for financial reporting.

3 The welfare approach

The welfare approach is an extension of the decision-making approaches, which considers the effects of decision making on social welfare. Basically, decision-making approaches limit the field of interest to the private use of accounting information. If accounting information had a relevance limited to private interests, the decision-making approaches would provide a sufficient analysis of information needs. It is because of the external social effects of decisions made on the basis of accounting information that there is imputed a social-welfare dimension to accounting theory. The effects of financial information on welfare may be viewed from the standpoint of the vested interests of groups within an organization. The alteration of accounting policies in favour of one group and away from another will affect the distribution of income and wealth within society.

The ethics of accounting standards

The responsibility and authority for the development of international accounting standards now rests with the IASB. It consists of 14 board members representing more than 100 different countries. Its influence over the financial information flowing through the global market economy is likely to grow in importance by virtue of the confidence placed in its authority and ability for maintaining trust in financial reporting throughout the global market economy.

The development of the global market economy is seen as resulting from the expansion of Western capitalism. In a societal context, the global market economy is also a melting pot in which different cultures find their expression, often conflicting with Western traditional values. Through the breakdown of international barriers to trade and the harmonization of the regulatory framework for the conduct of business, it is also creating a universal business culture. Reconciling different cultures and different traditions in the making of rules applicable to so many countries is an extremely complicated task for so few board members. Achieving acceptable levels of technical competence and, at the same time, acting as an effective regulatory body supposes that its moral authority will be unquestioned. The recent worldwide credit crisis has undermined faith in the ability of the global market economy to deal with the causal factors that had their roots in the nature of financial capitalism and the influence of corruptive greed within Western financial institutions.

Accounting policies cannot only address purely technical problems through accounting standards. Ethical problems are now in the forefront of universal criticisms of the ineffectiveness of regulatory bodies that have their membership drawn from a business community concerned with its own interests.

Accounting practices have remained firmly anchored in the age-old tradition of stewardship accounting aimed at controlling of assets, liabilities and profitability through the maintenance of proper records of transactions having their validity in law as legal rights and obligations, expressed in monetary terms having reference to contract date. The unimpeachable truth that resides in the objectivity of accounting data recorded in such manner is threatened whenever modifications are made to that data, under whatever pretext, for managing information supplied to shareholders and other parties. This suggests that accounting standards that modify established accounting practices should be exposed to moral value judgements, rather than criteria of expediency in submitting to the demands of influential interests. For example, the recognition of the loss of value of non-current assets through their use in current operations provides the moral justification for charging depreciation as a cost in the calculation of current income, thereby financing non-current asset replacements out of incomes and at refunding the cost of original investments in fixed assets through the tax savings realized over time. By contrast, as mentioned earlier, the recent modification of the mark-to-market rule for valuing current assets held by banks in favour of the fair-value rule may be criticized as a manipulation that distorts balance sheets as regards toxic assets that had led to many banks being technically bankrupt. Showing the value of toxic financial assets at their market value would have implied their complete write-off to zero value on the asset side of balance sheets and, on the liabilities side, massive debt in respect of government aid that would have revealed the accounting truth, namely total bankruptcy through the destruction of the capital base. This situation was unacceptable to the banking industry as well as governments concerned with the financial stability of economies under crisis and had to be fudged by spinning the truth.

It is evident that deficiencies in four significant areas, namely accounting theory, policy making (by the profession and the government), accounting practice and the use of accounting information, impair the usefulness of an accounting information service. The failure of policy makers to incorporate research findings in the policies they devise may reduce the potential usefulness of accounting information.

Summary

This chapter has been concerned with an examination of the scope and the role of accounting theory in developing knowledge through the construction of theories. The importance of such theory construction for the improvement of accounting practice has also been discussed. The nature of theory was examined in detail in order to establish precisely the significance of theory to knowledge in general, and to accounting in particular. There has been little effective agreement or progress towards a comprehensive or general theory of accounting, beyond the acceptance and rationalization of accounting practices into formal accounting standards.

Several approaches to the development of accounting theory were reviewed. Attention was drawn to successive stages beginning with descriptive theories, leading to normative and decision-making theories of accounting. The fundamental principles applying to double-entry bookkeeping, in particular the transaction principle, the money measurement and the historic cost principle that provide accounting data with a high level of objectivity, would be impaired if they were to be modified or abandoned in the course of defining alternative postulates than those used heretofore for stewardship reporting.

The chapter concluded with a discussion of the responsibility of accounting policy makers and of regulators, as guarantors of truth and trust in accounting information, not only to ensure the relevance and usefulness of such information, but in so doing to resist the pressure from political and professional lobbies for objectivity to cede to opinion, thereby increasing the scope for creative accounting allowing moral hazard to infect accounting information disclosed to investors and decision makers.

Self-assessment questions

1 Examine the nature of theories.

2 Analyse the relationship between accounting theory, accounting policy and accounting practice. To what extent does the quality of accounting policy and accounting practice depend on accounting theory?

3 Distinguish between 'principles', 'concepts' and 'accounting procedures'.

4 Contrast the descriptive and normative approaches to theory construction.

5 Explain how the welfare approach to accounting theory differs from other approaches.

References AAA (1971) *Report of the Committee on the Behavioural Science Content of the Accounting Curriculum*, Accounting Review Supplement, 46.

Belkaoui, A.R. (1992) *Accounting Theory*, 3rd edn, Academic Press.

Chambers, R.J. (1955) Blueprint for a Theory of Accounting, *Accounting Research*, Vol 6, No. 1, January.

Darwin, C. (1859) *The Origin of Species by Means of Natural Selection*, John Murray.

Dawkins, R. (1976) *The Selfish Gene*, Oxford University Press.

Glautier, M.W.E. (forthcoming) *The Caring Society*.

Hawking, S. (1995) *A Brief History of Time: From the Big Bang to Black Holes*, Bantam Press.

Hendriksen, E.S. (1992) *Accounting Theory*, 5th edn, Richard D. Irwin.

ICAEW (1952) *Accounting in Relation to Changes in the Purchasing Power of Money*, Recommendation No. 15, paragraph 1, May.

Ijiri, Y. (1971) Logic and sanctions in accounting, in Sterling R.R. and Bentz W.F. (eds) *Accounting in Perspective*, South Western Publishing Co.

King T.A. (2006) *More than a Numbers Game: A Brief History of Accounting*, John Wiley & Sons Inc.

Littleton A.C. and Zimmerman, V.K. (1962) *Accounting Theory: Continuity and Change*, Prentice Hall.

Watts, R.L. and Zimmerman, J.L. (1978) Towards a positive theory of the determination of accounting standards, *The Accounting Review*, Vol. 53, No. 1, 112–34.

Watts R.L. and Zimmerman J.L. (1986) *Positive Accounting Theory*, Prentice Hall.

PART 2

Accounting information

Introduction to Part 2

A distinction is made in business accounting between *financial accounting*, which is the activity of recording and analysing the financial results of transactions as a means of arriving at a measure of the firm's success and financial soundness and *cost accounting* that aims to produce product and service costs information to enable management to make efficient pricing decisions, as well as other decisions. The source of the data used in financial and cost accounting is the same and is obtained from recorded transactions. Financial accounting and cost accounting concepts differ depending upon the purpose for which they are intended.

Section 1a examines the traditional practices of financial accounting based on historical cost. The approach used is based on a descriptive analysis of the practices of accountants and leads to a descriptive theory of financial accounting reflecting *what* accountants do and the conventions and standards by which their activities are regulated.

As pointed out in Chapter 6, financial reports produced on the basis of financial records may be analysed in terms of the relevance of the information provided to users for the purposes of decision making. We suggest that such analysis should be conducted in terms of normative theory. Users' needs are addressed using normative theories for that purpose.

Financial accounting practices are concerned with the following activities:

1 recording financial transactions;
2 summarizing and presenting financial information in reports.

The nature and methods of financial accounting are determined to a considerable extent by the concepts listed in Chapter 8 used by accountants for identifying, evaluating and communicating financial information. This is particularly true of the information provided to external users such as shareholders and investors. It is evident that unless accountants obey the same rules as regards selecting, measuring and communicating information to external users, the latter will be at a disadvantage in respect of the reliance which may be attached to the information they receive. The usefulness of accounting concepts lies in the uniformity and comparability of information that depend on accountants following the same rules for selecting, measuring and communicating information to external users. They ensure a greater degree of comparability in the information provided by the same firm over a period of years. Accountants do not in general attempt to meet the specific information needs of external users. The information that they provide is dictated by the concepts which they have followed for a very long time, rather than by the information needs of external users.

The users of external reports have no direct control over their contents. We may contrast Figure P2.1, which illustrates the boundaries of the financial accounting system for external users, with the user-orientated model shown in Figure 3.1. In this case, there is no direct control by the user over the final output. Hence, it may be suggested that the information system for external decision makers is not user-orientated. The output, and therefore also the input, into this system is determined by concepts embodied in accounting tradition and in law.

Figure P2.1

A basic assumption underlying communication is that there is a clear separation between the transmitter and the receiver of information. This is acknowledged in financial reporting by the distinction drawn between the function of the accountant as the transmitter of information and the external user as the receiver of information. External users rely upon accountants to provide them with a significant supply of information for making economic decisions. It is for each user to evaluate and interpret this information when formulating decisions which only he or she may make. It is not the objective of the accountant as the preparer of financial reports to make such evaluations and draw conclusions for the external user. Consequently, it is not the function of the internal accountant to value a firm for the external user: on the contrary, it is for the investor to establish the value of the firm as an investment and to bear the risk involved in acting on such a valuation. The function of the internal accountant is to comply with the legal and other regulations that apply.

In line with this reasoning, Section 1 discusses the problems associated with the production of financial accounting information. We examine how data is selected from the environment, and the manner in which it becomes an input into the financial accounting system. We discuss also the manner in which the output of the financial accounting system is formulated as financial reports. We examine in Part 3 the relevance of these reports to the decisions which shareholders and investors wish to make.

Our analysis of financial accounting information is limited to those aspects that are considered important and relevant to the textbook as a whole. Section 1 examines financial accounting method to gain an understanding of its nature and of the principles underlying its procedures and analyses the process of periodic measurement, which is one of its main applications.

One important application of financial accounting method relates to the use of accounting records for the day-to-day control of assets and liabilities. These technical aspects of control are treated as a 'background subject' in this text, so as not to detract from the important theoretical and practical aspects of the accountant's role in providing information for decision-making purposes.

Section 2 examines the nature and purpose of cost accounting for management purposes. Managers are defined as internal users of information that is prepared specifically for their needs for decision making regarding, for example, the cost of product and services and the implications for costs of changes in activity level. The data recorded in the financial accounting system that is transferred routinely to the cost accounting department is reconfigured to meet different decision needs. Recorded as historical costs directly from invoices, they reflect the actual costs incurred in producing goods and services, such as raw material, labour costs and overhead costs.

Different decisions require different cost accounting concepts. One of the principal objectives of cost information is to enable management to making pricing decisions, that enable the recovery of costs and obtaining the desired income margin on sales. To this end, product and service costs are analysed as between direct and indirect cost for the purpose of associating costs with product or services. Another main objective of cost information is to perceive how changes in activity volume impact on unit costs and on overall incomes. For this purpose, the same basic cost data is analysed as between fixed costs and variable costs. This classification examines costs in accordance with their behaviour at different output levels.

The provision of cost information to management is less constrained by those conventions that affect the information supplied to shareholders and investor. It is confidential information that is not released to external users and is developed at the request of management.

Product and service costs are systematically collected and processed in formalized cost accounting systems in the same way as financial accounting information is recorded in the financial accounting system. They are under the responsibility of separate departments under the overall authority of the Financial Director. In the case of a manufacturing company, the cost accounting system is operated at the factory level and falls under the authority of the Factory Director.

The variety and complexity of management decisions consistently demand clarification of the purpose for which information is needed. What are the special circumstances for which information is needed and what are the costs that are relevant to a particular decision? These questions open a vista of interesting areas of management concerns that have at the origin the search for improved profitability. They are the subject matter of Section 2.

The concern with the management of costs as a means of improving profitability and the freedom accorded to innovative concepts and methods has inspired many new and exciting ideas in the area of cost accounting for management control. These are discussed in Part 3.

Financial accounting

CHAPTER 7

Financial accounting statements

Setting the scene

Without adequate information, users of business reporting cannot judge properly the opportunities and risks of investment opportunities. To make informed decisions, they need a variety of information, including data about the economy, industries, companies and securities. Complete information provided by the best sources enhances the probability that the best decisions will be made. And for company-specific information – which is key because companies are the sources of cash flows that ultimately result in the return on securities or the repayment of loans – management often is the best source. In particular, . . . financial statements are viewed as an excellent framework for capturing and organizing financial information.

(AICPA, 1994)

Learning objectives

After studying this chapter you should be able to:

1 **identify the main elements of an income statement;**

2 **explain the structure of a balance sheet, differentiating between non-current and current assets;**

3 **appreciate the accrual basis of accounting;**

4 **classify the sources and uses of cash flow from business activities.**

The descriptive approach as used in financial accounting was explained in Chapter 6 as a framework based on transactions, revenues, expenses, income, assets, liabilities and capital. This chapter examines these elements and illustrates how they are incorporated in financial statements that summarize all the individual transactions recorded during an accounting period. These transactions are financial in nature and are expressed in money terms. Financial statements are the end products of the accounting function. They provide readers with neat summaries of what has occurred during an accounting period and comprise three basic statements that are linked together:

1 the income account;
2 the balance sheet;
3 the statement of cash flows.

The income statement

The measurement of income is probably one most important functions of financial accounting. Investors, managers, bankers and others are interested in knowing how well a business is doing. The income statement shows the results of the 'flow' of activity and transactions and is designed to report the income performance of a business for a specific period of time, such as a year, quarter or month. Income represents the difference between revenues and expenses. The income statement reports for a specific period of time the items that comprise the total revenue and total expense and the resulting net income.

The income statement of Albert Trader is shown below. Note how the heading of the statement specifically identifies the name of the business, the title of the report and the period of time over which the reported net income was earned.

Albert Trader
Income statement for the year ended 31 December 20X1

	£000	£000
Sales revenue		220
Cost of sales		103
Gross trading income		117
Less: Other expenses		
Rent and rates	6	
Lighting and heating	4	
Wages	40	
Depreciation of shop equipment	8	
		58
Income before interest and tax		59
Less: Interest expense		1
Income before taxation		58
Taxation		20
Net income		38

Sales revenue

A business earns revenue by selling goods and services. Whereas a trading business such as Albert Trader will derive revenue mainly from sale of merchandise, a business which renders services, such as an accounting firm, will derive revenue by charging clients for its services. It is not necessary for a business to receive cash before recognizing that revenue has been earned. As discussed later in this chapter, and more fully in Chapter 8, the accruals concept recognizes revenue that arises from the sale of goods or services on credit.

Cost of sales

This shows the cost of goods sold to produce the revenue. For a trading business like Albert Trader, the cost of sales equals opening inventory, plus purchases, minus closing inventory. When calculating business income for a period, the sales revenue for that period and the costs of earning that revenue must be matched with one another in the income statement.

Other expenses

In addition to the cost of goods sold, other expenses such as rent and rates, lighting and heating and wages, as shown in Albert Trader's income statement, are incurred in earning revenue. Such expenses may require the immediate payment of cash, or, in the case of credit, the payment of cash some time after the expense is incurred. In some cases, cash is paid before the expense is incurred, for example, the payment of office rent in advance. For accounting purposes, an expense is recognized in the period in which it is incurred, which is not necessarily the same as the period in which the cash is paid. The period in which an expense is deemed to be incurred is the period in which the goods are used or the services are received.

An expense may represent the cost of using equipment or buildings acquired and held for use in operating the business rather than for sale. Such items often have a high initial cost at the date of acquisition and are utilized over an extended period of time, known as their useful life. As they are used in operating the business, a portion of their initial cost becomes an expense, known as depreciation. In Albert Trader's income statement £8,000 depreciation of shop equipment is recorded.

Net income

Net income is the excess of total revenues over total expenses, which include net interest and taxation. If the total expenses exceed the total revenues, a net loss is reported. Where revenues and expenses are equal for the period, the business is said to break-even.

The balance sheet

The balance sheet, sometimes called the statement of financial position, lists the assets owned by a business, the liabilities owed to others and the accumulated investment of its owners. The balance sheet shows these balances at a specific date. Even though the business is trading over time, the balance sheet is only a 'snapshot' of what the business's resources and obligations are at a stated time. This differs from the income statement which reports inflows and outflows of resources over a period of time.

The balance sheet may provide helpful information in determining the degree of financial risk. For example, a bank considering a short-term loan to a business would want to know the financial position of the business at the time of the loan.

Albert Trader's balance sheet is shown below. Note how the heading of the balance sheet specifically identifies the name of the business, the title of the report and the specific date of the statement. To assist the preparation of the cash flow statement later in the chapter, the balance sheet figures are shown for two years.

Albert Trader
Balance sheet at 31 December 20X1 and 20X0

	31.12.20X1		31.12.20X0	
Non-current assets	£000	£000	£000	£000
Store equipment at cost		90		60
Accumulated depreciation		20		12
Net book value		70		48
Current assets				
Inventories	80		60	
Debtors	21		10	
Cash	1		2	
	102		72	
Current liabilities				
Trade creditors	26		32	
Working capital		76		40
		146		88
Capital account				
Opening balance	88		56	
Net income for year	38	126	32	88
Long-term liability				
Loan		20		0
		146		88

Assets

Assets are things of value which are possessed by a business. In order to be classified as an asset the money measurement concept, which will be discussed in Chapter 8, demands that a thing must be susceptible of being measurable in terms of money. The assets of a business are classified into non-current and current assets, as shown in Albert Trader's balance sheet.

Non-current assets

Non-current assets are used for the purpose of business and are not intended for resale. They include assets having a long life in use such as buildings, equipment and vehicles. Non-current assets, with the exception of land, are depreciated over time as they are used. Since their productive life is limited, their initial cost is apportioned to expense over their estimated useful life. As noted earlier, the amount of depreciation for the year is recorded in the income statement as an expense. The cumulative amount of depreciation expense for all past periods since acquisition is deducted on the balance sheet from the cost of the asset to derive the net book value of the asset. This does not represent the current value of the asset. In the case of Albert Trader the net book value of non-current assets is shown as £70,000 at 31.12.20X1.

A non-current asset for one business may be a current asset for another. For example, a car is a non-current asset if it is to be used by a salesman, but a current asset if it is held as inventory for sale by a car sales company.

Current assets

Current assets are those which are expected to be transformed into cash in the near future, usually within one year. They include inventories such as materials, supplies, work-in-progress and finished goods as well as debtors. Debtors represent amounts due from customers in respect of past sales on credit. Cash is the amount of cash on the premises, or at the bank, on balance sheet date.

The practice of reporting assets on balance sheets varies according to countries. In the United Kingdom and in other European countries, they are shown in order of increasing liquidity, that is the list starts with the items least likely to be turned into cash in the near future. In the United States, the reverse is the case.

Current liabilities

Current liabilities are the amounts owing by the business which will fall due for payment within one year. Most firms find it convenient to buy merchandise and services on credit terms rather than to pay cash. This gives rise to liabilities known as trade creditors – £26,000 at 31.12.20X1 in the case of Albert Trader. The reason why sums of money owed to the creditors of a business are known as liabilities is that the business is liable to creditors for the amounts owed.

Working capital

A business must have sufficient working capital to be able to pay its way and settle its immediate obligations. This implies that there must be funds available for the purchase of inventories, for the payment of trade creditors and the general running expenses of the business. Working capital (also known as 'net current assets') is the difference between current assets and current liabilities. The working capital of Albert Trader at 31.12.20X1 is:

Current assets – Current liabilities = Working capital
£102,000   £26,000   £76,000

The business has an excess of £76,000 to use in operations after the current assets are converted into cash and the current liabilities are paid. From a banker's viewpoint, a trader with a large amount of working capital may be considered a good credit risk because the business can cover its debt obligations. However, it may also show that the trader is mismanaging his inventories by holding too many goods or too much cash. The appropriate level of working capital depends on the industry concerned.

The capital account

The capital account represents the ownership interest in the business. Albert Trader's balance sheet shows that the net income for the year is added to the owner's opening capital.

Loan

The loan shown in Albert Trader's balance sheet is classified as a long-term liability. Long-term liabilities are deemed as due after a period exceeding one year and arise when money is borrowed as a means of supplementing the funds invested by the owner. In the case of Albert Trader, the income statement shows that £1,000 was paid in interest on the loan during the year.

The accrual basis of accounting

The income statement and balance sheet are based on accrual accounting. As noted earlier, income or loss is measured by matching a period's sales revenue with the expenses incurred in earning those revenues. Under the accrual method of accounting, it is the revenues earned and the expenses incurred that are recorded, rather than cash receipts and payments in cheque or cash form. The unpaid amounts at year end in the form of outstanding amounts receivable and payable are recorded as debtors or creditors (as the case may be) in the balance sheet at the end of the period. It is generally agreed that income measured in this way is a better indicator of a business's economic performance in a period than income determined on a cash in/out basis.

The statement of cash flows

Cash is the lifeblood of a business. A healthy cash flow (measured as cash inflows minus cash outflows) is fundamental to a business's ability to survive and prosper. Users of financial statements who look merely at the income statement for a measure of financial health can be deceived. Indeed, many businesses with apparently strong profitability have foundered through poor control over their cash flow. The statement of cash flows can be used by management to avoid liquidity problems. Its purpose is to show what cash has been generated by a business's operations and where the cash has gone. The importance of cash flow was recognized by the Accounting Standards Board's first standard which came into effect in 1992, and replaced by FRS 1 'Cash Flow Statements' in 1996. The International Accounting Standards Board issued its IAS 7 'Statement of Cash Flows' in 1992, revised in 1977, 2007 and 2009. Both standards are examined in detail in Chapter 25, page 391.

Under the United Kingdom's Accounting Standard Board FRS 1, a statement of cash flows classifies the sources and uses of cash flow from several types of business activities.

- *Operating activities.* Cash flows from operating activities are the cash effects of transactions relating to operating or trading activities. They are the cash effects of transactions that enter into the determination of operating income, that is income before interest and tax.
- *Returns on investments and servicing of finance.* These are receipts resulting from the ownership of an investment and payments to providers of finance. They include interest received and interest paid.
- *Taxation.* These are cash flows to and from taxation authorities.
- *Capital expenditure.* These are cash flows associated with the acquisition and disposal of non-current assets.
- *Financing activities.* These comprise receipts from, or repayments to, external providers of finances.

Preparation of the statement of cash flows

The preparation of the statement of cash flows requires the following information:

1 the income statement for the current period;
2 the balance sheet for the current period;
3 the balance sheet for the prior period.

Operating activities

In the operating activities section of the statement of cash flows accountants calculate the cash generated from the day-to-day operations of a business. The accrual basis net income is converted to a cash basis by two adjustments:

1 Add back non-cash expenses. For example, depreciation is a 'book item' only and does not represent an outflow of cash. Such an outflow occurs when non-current assets are purchased or disposed of, an occurrence which is included later in the 'Investing activities' section.
2 Adjust net income for changes in working capital. A comparison of the inventory figure in Albert Trader's balance sheet shows that this item increased by £20,000 during the current period (from £60,000 to £80,000). This indicates an increase in cash requirements. Similarly, both Albert Trader's debtors and creditors require an increase in cash. In total, changes in working capital over the years required the use of £37,000 additional cash.

Interest paid

Albert Trader paid £1,000 in interest on the loan he took out during the year.

Tax paid

Albert Trader paid £20,000 in tax.

Capital expenditure

When a business buys or sells a long-term asset like a building or item of equipment, the cash relating to the transaction is reflected in the capital expenditure section of the statement of cash flows. In the case of Albert Trader, £30,000 was invested in shop equipment between the two balance sheet dates and this is shown on the cash flow statement.

Financing activities

The two balance sheets show that Albert Trader borrowed £20,000 during the year in order to finance the increase in working capital and the purchase of shop equipment.

Decrease in cash balance

The reader will note that Albert Trader's statement of cash flows explains why the cash balance has decreased by £1,000 despite borrowing £20,000 in the form of a loan and generating £67,000 from operating income plus depreciation. A total of £37,000 was required to adjust for changes in working capital and £30,000 was required to finance the purchase of non-current assets.

These activities are disclosed clearly in the statement of cash flows as illustrated in the case of Albert Trader below. It conforms with Financial Reporting Standard 1 (FRS 1).

Albert Trader
Statement of cash flows for the year ended 31 December 20X1

Operating activities	£000	£000
Operating income		59
Add back non-cash expenses		
Depreciation charges		8
		67
Adjust for changes in working capital		
Inventories (increase)	(20)	
Debtors (increase)	(11)	
Creditors (decrease)	(6)	
		(37)
Net cash inflow from operating activities		30
Returns on investment and servicing of finance:		
Interest paid		(1)
Tax paid		(20)
Capital expenditure		(30)
Financing activities:		
Proceeds from loan		20
Decrease in cash		(1)

The International Accounting Standards Board IAS 7 'Statement of Cash Flows' adopts a presentation that differs from FRS 1 in the manner in which cash-flow data are organized to show four separate components of a firm's cash flow, namely, cash flow from operations, cash flow from investing, cash flow from financing and net change in cash flow over the period, as shown below:

Albert Trader
Statement of cash flows for the year ended 31 December 20X1

Operations	£000
Net income	38
Depreciation	8
Increase in inventories	(20)
Increase in debtors	(11)
Increase in trade creditors	(6)
Cash from operations	9
Investing	
Non-current assets acquired	(30)
Cash from investing	(30)
Financing	
Increase in long term borrowing	20
Cash flow from financing	20
Change in cash	(1)
Cash – Beginning year	2
Cash – End of Year	1

Summary

This chapter has introduced the three basic statements – the income statement, the balance sheet and the statement of cash flows. The income statement reflects only operating activities, the matching of revenues and expenses in earning income. The balance sheet describes a business's financial position at a point in time. The statement of cash flows, unlike the other two statements, is not based on accrual accounting. It reports on cash received and cash payments.

Self-assessment questions

1 What is the purpose of an income statement?

2 What is the purpose of a balance sheet?

3 What is the relationship between the income statement and the balance sheet?

4 Briefly define (a) non-current assets; (b) current assets; (c) current liabilities; (d) working capital.

5 In respect of non-current assets as reported on the balance sheet explain (a) cost; (b) accummulated depreciation; (c) net book value.

6 Explain the difference between an income statement and a statement of cash flows.

7 What are the main sections of a statement of cash flows?

Reference   *AICPA (1994) Improving Business Reporting – A Customer Focus* (The Jenkins Report), American Institute of Certified Public Accountants.

CHAPTER 8

Financial accounting concepts

Setting the scene

Certain kinds of accounting conventions seem puzzling, even arbitrary, to laymen. Some expenses are accrued as they are incurred, but others are accrued as they are likely to be; some revenue is recognized all at once, other revenue is recognized as time passes. It should be one objective of accounting theory to furnish explanations of seeming inconsistencies in practice, explanations which could be given to laymen if necessary. Perhaps further examination would show that these practices are not, as they might seem, conventional customs that have become coloured with a tinge of arbitrariness. Good and sufficient reasons still control all so-called conventional accounting actions.

(Littleton, 1953)

Learning objectives

After studying this chapter you should be able to:

1 explain how the entity, the money measurement and the going concern concepts affect the basic financial accounting statements;
2 discuss the assumptions inherent in the cost and realization concepts;
3 describe the role of the accruals and matching concepts in financial statement preparation;
4 discuss the periodicity, consistency and prudence concepts.

The concepts of accounting discussed in this chapter may be seen as related to the general problem of developing viable theories of financial accounting. As we shall see, their origin lies in a historical process of development. The on-going nature of this process is discussed in Chapter 9, where the review of the concepts of financial accounting by the accounting profession is seen to focus on the formulation of standard accounting practices.

We mentioned in the Introduction to this part that the nature of financial accounting information is not dictated by the needs of external users, but rather is determined to a considerable extent by the concepts which exist among accountants for identifying, evaluating and communicating financial information. In this chapter, we analyse the nature and the effects of accounting concepts on the manner in which accountants generate financial information. The need for these concepts is discussed, as well as the problems which they pose.

The nature of financial accounting concepts

Accounting concepts define the assumptions on which the financial accounts of a business are prepared. Financial transactions are interpreted in the light of the concepts which govern accounting methods. In effect, financial accounting concepts largely determine the interpretations given in financial reports of the events and results which they portray. For example, the concept relating to the recognition of revenue determines the dimension of the income reported to shareholders and the value of the enterprise as judged from the balance sheet.

Figure 8.1 illustrates the manner in which financial accounting concepts act as filters in selecting data as input into the processing system and as output of information for users.

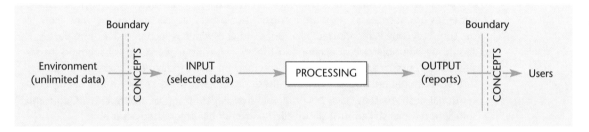

Figure 8.1

Financial accounting concepts

Financial accounting is founded on the following concepts:

1 entity
2 money measurement
3 going concern
4 cost
5 realization
6 accruals
7 matching
8 periodicity
9 consistency
10 prudence/conservatism.

The entity concept

The practice of distinguishing the affairs of the business from the personal affairs of its owners originated in the early days of double-entry bookkeeping some 500 years ago. Accounting has a history which reaches back to the beginning of civilization, and archaeologists have found accounting records that date as far back as 4000 BC, well before the invention of money. Nevertheless, it was not until the fifteenth century that the separation of the owner's wealth from the wealth invested in a business venture was recognized as necessary. This arose from using paid managers or stewards to run a business and requiring them to render accounts of their stewardship. Consequently, the 'capital' invested in the business represented not only the initial assets of the business but a measure of its indebtedness to the owner. The notion of stewardship accounting remains enshrined in modern financial accounting, the owner being entitled to both the 'capital' invested in the business and the incomes made during the year. The accounting and legal relationship between the business and its owner is shown on the balance sheet, which states the firm's assets and liabilities and hence indicates its financial position and well-being.

Example 8.1

J Soap recently inherited £30,000 and decides that the moment is opportune for him to realize his lifetime ambition and open a hairdressing salon. Accordingly, he makes all the necessary arrangements to begin on 1 April 20X0, under the name 'J Soap – Ladies' Hairdresser', and commits £10,000 of his money to that business. He therefore opens an account at his bank under the business name 'J Soap – Ladies' Hairdresser'.

The financial position of the firm on 1 April 20X0, from an accounting point of view, will appear as follows:

J Soap – Ladies' Hairdresser
Balance sheet at 1 April 20X0

Capital	£10,000	Bank balance	£10,000

The business is shown as having £10,000 as its asset at that date, and that this has been financed by the £10,000 from J. Soap, which in the normal course of things will not be repaid. The Capital account recognizing the indebtedness of the business to J. Soap in respect of the capital of £10 000 that he has invested.

The accounting effect of the entity concept is to make a clear distinction between J Soap's private affairs and his business affairs: what he does with his remaining £20,000 is of no concern to the accountant, but what happens to the £10,000 invested in the business becomes the subject matter of accounting.

The interesting aspect of the entity concept is that it establishes a fictional distinction between J Soap and the business which is not recognized in law: he remains legally liable for the debts of the business, and should the business fail, he will have to pay the creditors out of his private funds.

In the case of corporations, however, there is a legal distinction between the owners, that is the shareholders, and the business, so that the shareholders are not liable for the corporation's debts beyond the capital which they have agreed to invest. The accounting treatment of the relationship between the shareholders and the corporation is no different from that accorded to the sole trader and his business, except of course that the capital of the corporation is divided into a number of shares.

Example 8.2

Multiform Toys plc Iwas registered on 1 April 20X0 as a public limited company, the objective being to manufacture a wide range of children's toys. The promoters need £100,000 to launch the company. They offer for sale 100,000 £1 ordinary shares to the public, and agree themselves to subscribe for 25,000 shares.

If we assume that all the shares have been issued and paid for on 1 May 20X0, the balance sheet will be as follows:

Multiform Toys plc
Balance sheet at 1 May 20X0

Share capital	£100,000	Bank balance	£100,000

The promoters are now shareholders, together with those members of the public who have subscribed for the shares. The liability of the company to the shareholders amounts to £100,000, and the company has £100,000 cash to pursue its objectives.

The effect of the entity concept in the case of an incorporated business is to recognize the separate identity of the company from that of its shareholders. The shareholders themselves are not liable for the debts of the company, and their liability is limited to the £100,000 which they have subscribed. We shall discuss the full implications of incorporation from an accounting point of view in Chapter 23.

The money measurement concept

Trade and accounting existed before the invention of money, which we know began to circulate in the sixth century BC. Its role as a common denominator, by which the value of assets of different kinds could be compared, encouraged the expansion of trade. By Roman times, money had become the language of commerce, and accounts were kept in money terms. Hence, there is an accounting tradition which dates back some 2,000 years of keeping the records of valuable assets and of transactions in monetary terms. It is not surprising, therefore, that accounting information today reflects the time-hallowed practice of dealing only with matters capable of expression in money.

The money measurement concept sets an absolute limit to the type of information which may be selected and measured by accountants, and hence limits the type of information which accountants may communicate about a business enterprise.

Example 8.3 The Solidex Engineering Co Ltd is a long-established company which specializes in the production of a single component used in the manufacture of mining gear. The balance sheet at 31 December 20X0 reveals the following position:

The Solidex Engineering Co Ltd
Balance sheet at 31 December 20X0

	£	£
Non-current assets		
Land and buildings	30,000	
Equipment	25,000	
		55,000
Current assets		
Inventories	30,000	
Bank balance	15,000	
		45,000
Total assets		100,000
Share capital		100,000
Total liabilities and equity		100,000

For some time, it has been known that a competitor has developed a better product, and that the company is likely to lose its market. The managing director is ill, the production manager and the accountant are not on speaking terms and the labour force is resentful about the deterioration in working conditions in the factory. The buildings are dilapidated, but the land itself is valuable. The equipment is old and needs a great deal of maintenance, and as a result, there is a considerable wastage of labour hours because of machinery breakdowns.

It is clear from the foregoing example that the most significant information of interest to shareholders is not what is contained in the balance sheet but the information which is left out of it, which is much more relevant to an understanding of the firm's position. Yet, the accountant is unable to measure and communicate that information to shareholders directly in money terms, although all these facts may explain poor income figures. The reader of a financial accounting report should not expect, therefore, that all or perhaps even the most important facts about the business will be disclosed. This explains why there is such a premium on 'insider' information to make correct assessments of a firm's true position. One of the major problems of accounting today is to find means of solving the measurement problem: how to extend the quality and the coverage of information in a meaningful way. The advantage of money values is that the layman is able to grasp the meaning of facts that are stated in money, and it remains the obvious standard of measurement.

There are further problems associated with the practice of using money as a standard of measurement in accounting. Money does not have a constant value through time, nor does the value of specific assets remain the same in relation to money. Until recently, accountants turned a blind eye to this problem by assuming that the money standard did have a constant value. The rising rates of inflation in the 1960s and 1970s destroyed this fiction.

Financial accounting records serve two distinct and important purposes. First, they provide evidence of the financial rights and obligations resulting from legal contracts. For this purpose these records must be kept in the form of unadjusted money measurements. Second, they are used as a basis for providing financial information for shareholders, investors and a variety of users who need such information for decision-making. In this part, we discuss the first purpose of financial accounting records, and in Part 3 we discuss the second.

The going concern concept

The valuation of assets used in a business is based on the assumption that the business is a continuing one, not on the verge of cessation. This concept is important as many assets derive their value from their employment in the firm, and should the firm cease to operate the value which could be obtained for these assets on a closing-down sale would probably be much less than their book value.

Example 8.4   The Zimbabwe Gold Mining Company Ltd has been mining gold for many years. Its assets consist of a mineshaft half a mile deep which enables the company to reach the gold reef, small-gauge railway tracks and trucks within the mine, lifting gear, conveyor belts, crushing plant and sundry equipment. The balance sheet at 1 April 20X0 shows the following position:

The Zimbabwe Gold Mining Company Ltd
Balance sheet at 1 April 20X0

Non-current assets	£	£
Mineshaft	500,000	
Land and buildings	25,000	
Plant and equipment	200,000	
		725,000
Current assets		
Tools	15,000	
Gold in transit	50,000	
Bank balance	10,000	
Total assets		75,000
		800,000
Owners' capital		
Share capital		500,000
Retained income		300,000
Total liabilities and equity		800,000

The mineshaft was sunk originally with the money raised by the issue of shares, and the other assets were financed out of loans which were repaid out of income, which was not distributed to shareholders. In terms of the entity convention the total debt of the company to shareholders is, therefore, £800,000 – which is the amount they might expect to receive if the company ceased to operate. For the time being, apart from £60,000 in gold or cash, their interest is substantially the mineshaft and the plant and equipment amounting to £700,000. If the gold reef ceased to be economically workable and the mine had to be abandoned, the mineshaft, being purely a hole in the ground, would become valueless, as would much of the plant. Hence, it is unlikely that shareholders would get back even a fraction of their investment.

The going concern concept underpins the historical cost values shown in the balance sheet. To abandon this concept would imply that assets should be valued on a realizable value basis. In recent years, as we will see in Chapter 9, the concept has been extended to include the survival of the enterprise for the 'foreseeable future'.

The cost concept

Accountants calculate the value of an asset by reference to the cost of acquisition, and not by reference to the value of the returns which are expected to be realized. Hence, the 'value in use' of assets which the going concern concept maintains is the cost of acquisition. To the accountant, the difference between the value in use and the cost of acquisition of an asset is the income it generates:

$$\text{Value in use} - \text{Cost of acquisition} = \text{Income}$$

Example 8.5 W. E. Audent & Son is a firm of chartered accountants with a large audit practice. Its major asset is the staff of audit clerks. The value in use of the staff may be calculated by reference to the hourly rate at which their services are charged out to clients; the cost of securing their services to the firm is represented by their salaries; and the annual income of the firm is the difference, less, of course, the administrative expenses of running the firm.

In accounting, cost is used as a measure of the financial 'effort' exerted in gaining access to the resources which will be deployed in earning revenues. Since these resources are secured through financial transactions, the financial effort is measured at the time of acquisition, which coincides, of course, with the legal obligation to pay for those resources in money. The cost concept raises the following problems:

1 The historical cost of acquisition of assets is not a dependable guide to their current value because it fails to reflect:
   (a) changes in the general purchasing power of money;
   (b) changes in the specific value of individual assets in relation to money.
2 The historical cost of acquisition of assets used up in the activity of earning income does not form a dependable basis for calculating income.

Example 8.6 | John Smith is a dealer in hides. He obtains his yearly supplies from Canada in the autumn, and sells them in the United Kingdom during the ensuing 12 months. In October 20X0 he bought 2,000 hides at an average cost of £20 Canadian, equivalent to, let us say, £10, and by September 20X1 had sold them all at an average price of £20, making an income of £20,000. Meanwhile, the price of Canadian hides has increased by 50 per cent so that to replace inventory he has sold during the year he will now have to pay an average of £15 a hide. Hence, while the income of £20,000 is correct for last year's trading, it overstates what can be expected next year by £10,000 because the hides sold have been valued at £10 instead of £15 each – which is their current value in Canada.

3 The accounting practice of writing off the cost of certain assets as depreciation against revenue means that it is possible to remove the cost of these assets from the accounts altogether. For a long time, for example, it was the practice of banks to reduce the value of land and buildings to £1 and so create secret reserves by understating the value of these assets and the amount of owners' equity.
4 Since incurring a cost depends upon a financial transaction, there are assets which create income for the firm which can never appear as such in the accounts. Often the major asset of a highly successful firm is the knowledge and the skill created as a result of teamwork and good organization. This asset will not appear in the accounts, since the firm has paid nothing for it, except in terms of salaries that have been charged against yearly income. Allied to this problem is the failure to make any mention in the balance sheet of the value of the human assets of the firm. Long ago, the economist Alfred Marshall stated that 'the most valuable of all capital is that invested in human beings'. It is universally recognized that the firm's human assets are its chief source of wealth. Accountants have not yet been able to agree on how information on the value of human assets may be most appropriately presented. Other important assets of which no mention is made in financial accounting statements are, for example, the value to the firm of its market position, which may be a very valuable asset if the firm enjoys a monopoly and the value of the firm's own information system, which will affect the quality of its decisions.

Many of the most controversial issues in financial accounting theory and practice revolve around the cost concept. External users of financial statements basically wish to have information on the current worth of the firm on the basis of which they may make investment decisions. In order to make their balance sheets more realistic many companies carry some non-current assets, especially properties, in their accounts at revalued amounts.

The realization concept

The realization concept is also closely related to the cost concept, for as the recorded value of an asset to the firm is determined by the transaction which was necessary to acquire it, so any change in its value may only be recognized at the moment the firm realizes or disposes of that asset. The realization concept reflects totally the historical origin of accounting as a method for recording the results of transactions. To an accountant there is no certainty of income until a sale has been realized. Hence, increases in value which have not been realized are not recorded as income.

The realization concept is strongly criticized by economists. They argue that if an asset has increased in value, it is irrelevant that it has not been sold. For economists, it is sufficient that the gain in value could be realized for that gain to be recognized. The realization concept, it is true, may lead to absurd conclusions.

Example 8.7 William James and George Lloyd have bought a pair of dilapidated cottages in Gwynedd for £50,000. They spend £20,000 on restoring the cottages, so that their total cost amounts to £70,000. Both cottages are identical and form part of one unit, that is, they are semi-detached. The cottages were bought as part of a speculative venture to earn income out of the popularity of Welsh cottages as holiday homes. A businessman from Manchester offers to buy both cottages for £100,000 each, but the partners decide to sell only one of the cottages and to retain the other for sale at a higher price in the future.

From an accounting point of view, the cottage which is sold is recognized as being worth £100,000, and the difference of £65,000 between the accounting cost and the sale price is the realized income. The second cottage, which could also have been sold for £100,000 to the same man, is recorded as being worth only £35,000 – being the costs associated with acquiring and restoring it.

Unrealized gains in value are widely recognized by non-accountants. Banks are prepared to lend money on unrealized values: business people reckon as gains increases in the value of assets even though they are unsold – yet accountants will not do so unless and until a contract of sale has been signed.

As a result of the realization concept, two classes of gains may be distinguished 'holding gains', which are increases in value resulting from holding an asset; and 'operating gains', which are gains realized as a result of selling assets. 'Holding gains' are not recorded, but 'operating gains' are reported. The realization concept means, in effect, that the reported income of a business is only a part of the total increases in value which accrue to a firm during an accounting period.

The realization concept does not require the accountant to await the receipt of cash before recording a transaction. Indeed, in many cases the delivery of goods and the receipt of cash occur after the legal agreement which determines the timing of the transaction.

Example 8.8 On 1 January 20X0, Midlands Motor Engineers receive an order from one of their accredited dealers for five tractor engines each costing £400. The engines are despatched on 10 January, and on 5 February a cheque for £2,000 is received in payment.

From a legal point of view, the acceptance of the order on 1 January marks the timing of the sale, and the creation of the contractual obligation to deliver the engines as well as the contractual right to receive payment. Accounting follows the law in this respect, and it is common practice to write to confirm the receipt of an order and its acceptance, so as to leave no doubt as to the legal and accounting position.

On occasions, however, when a contract is for work which cannot be completed for a long period of time, the contract may stipulate when rights to payment arise. This is particularly the case as regards large civil-engineering contracts, shipbuilding contracts and large government contracts. In these situations, accounting practices once more follow the law, and the timing of the right to receive cash is determined by the contract.

Example 8.9   Westlands Civil Engineering Co. is awarded a government contract for the building of a fifty-mile section of a motorway. The work is required to be completed in three years. Payments are to be made by the government on the basis of work completed in each three-monthly period. It is agreed that an independent firm of quantity surveyors will certify the cost of work completed in each period, and that these certificates will form the basis for calculating the period payments to the company on the 'percentage-of-completion' method.

In accordance with this contract, the timing of the realizations will depend upon the issue of the certificates by the quantity surveyors.

The accruals concept

The realization concept asserts that gains in value may not be recognized until the occurrence of a transaction is reinforced by the accruals concept, which applies equally to revenues and expenses.

The accruals concept makes the distinction between the receipt of cash and the right to receive cash, and the payment of cash and the legal obligation to pay cash, because in practice there is usually no coincidence in time between cash movements and the legal obligations to which they relate.

Let us examine first the manner in which the accruals concept applies to revenue recognition. Revenue may be defined as the right to receive cash, and accountants are concerned with recording these rights. Cash receipts may occur as follows:

1 concurrently with the sale;
2 before a right to receive arises;
3 after the right to receive has been created;
4 in error.

The accruals concept provides a guideline as to how to treat these cash receipts and the rights related thereto.

Example 8.10   Mrs Smith is an old lady who occupies a flat owned by Mereworth Properties Ltd. The rent is payable monthly in advance on the first day of each month, and amounts to £250 a month. She is very forgetful, and rarely does a month pass without some complication in the payment of her rent.

On 1 January she sends her cheque for £250 for the rent due for January. This rent is due and payable to the company, and must be included as revenue for that month. On 10 January Mrs Smith sends another cheque for £250, thinking that she had not paid her rent for January. This is a cash receipt to which the company is not presently entitled, and it must either be returned to Mrs Smith, or kept on her behalf as a payment in advance of her

February rent. The company returns her cheque saying that she has already paid her rent for January, and she receives this letter on 20 January. She forgets to pay her rent on 1 February. The accountant is obliged to include the rent due in February in the revenue for that month, even though it is only ultimately paid on 15 March. Until Mrs Smith has paid her rent for February, she will be a debtor of the company for the rent owing.

Similar rules apply to the treatment of expenses incurred by the firm. Expenses may be defined as legal obligations incurred by the firm to pay in money or money's worth for goods or services which it has received. Cash payments may occur as follows:

1 at the time of purchase;
2 before they are due for payment;
3 after due date for payment;
4 in error.

The accruals concept requires the company to treat as expenses only those sums which are due and payable. If a payment is made in advance, it must not be treated as an expense, and the recipient is a debtor until his/her right to receive the cash matures. Cash paid in error is never an expense, and until it is recovered the person to whom it was paid is also a debtor. Where an expense had been incurred, however, and no payment has been made, the expense must be recorded, and the person to whom the payment should have been made is shown as a creditor.

We will see in Chapter 12 the importance of the accruals concept as regards record-keeping and the presentation of financial accounting statements.

The matching concept

One of the important purposes of financial accounting is to calculate income resulting from transactions. This means identifying the gains resulting from transactions and setting off against those gains the expenses which are related to those transactions. The realization concept identifies the timing of gains, and the accruals concept enables the accountant properly to record revenues and expenses; neither, however, helps the accountant to calculate income. The matching concept links revenues with their relevant expenses.

Example 8.11 On 1 April Cash and Carry Ltd purchase for resale 2,000 tins of beans at a cost of 5p a tin. The selling price is 8p a tin. During the month of April 1,000 tins are sold. What is the income for the month which is attributable to this line of goods?

We know that the expenses are 2,000 × 5p = £100, and that the revenues are 1,000 × 8p = £80. On the face of it, therefore, Cash and Carry Ltd have made a loss of £100 less £80, that is, £20. This conclusion is nonsense, because we are setting off against the sale proceeds of 1,000 tins the cost of acquiring 2,000 tins.

In accordance with the matching concept, the accountant establishes the income for the month of April by calculating the cost of purchasing 1,000 tins of beans and setting this expense against the revenue realized from the sale of these tins:

Sales revenue	1,000 tins @ 8p = £80
Cost of sales	1,000 tins @ 5p = £50
Income	£30

The 1,000 tins remaining unsold remain in the accounting records as assets, and when they are eventually sold, income from sales will be calculated by deducting the cost of acquisition from the sales revenue realized.

The matching of revenues and expenses is sometimes a most difficult problem in accounting, because many types of expense are not easily identifiable with revenues.

Example 8.12 Bloxwich Pharmaceutical Co Ltd manufactures and sells pharmaceutical products. Its major activity is the manufacture of antibiotics, which accounts for 80 per cent of its sales revenue. The remaining 20 per cent of its sales is derived from beauty creams. Its expenses for the year 20X0 are as follows:

Manufacturing costs of antibiotics	£500,000
Manufacturing costs of beauty creams	20,000
Administrative costs	100,000
Selling and financial costs	50,000
Research and development costs	150,000
Total expenses for the year	£820,000

In the same year, the total revenue from sales of both antibiotics and beauty creams amounts to £1,000,000. Calculate the income on the antibiotics side of the business.

We can begin to answer this problem as follows:

Sales revenue from antibiotics (80% of total)	£800,000
Manufacturing costs of antibiotics	500,000
	300,000
Other expenses	?
Income on antibiotics	?

Clearly, we need more information in order to allocate the administrative, selling and financial costs between antibiotics and beauty creams. It is unlikely that an exact allocation could be made, and in the end, an estimate would be made.

The research and development costs of new antibiotics and beauty creams are a more difficult problem. Strictly speaking, we should not set these costs against the revenues of the year, since the benefit will not occur in this year. Much of it, however, may not lead to new products. Therefore, if we ignore this expenditure, the company's reported income will be inflated and unrealistic.

From the foregoing example, it is seen that the exact matching of revenues and expenses is often impossible. Nevertheless, the computation of periodic income requires that expenses be allocated, where necessary, in order that the financial results may be stated in a consistent manner.

The concept of periodicity

The custom of making periodic reports to the owner of a business dates from the time when wealthy persons employed servants to manage and oversee their affairs. Periodic accounting has its origin in the idea of control. Company law sees the role of financial reports as being essentially the communication of information from the managers of the business, that is the directors, to the owners, that is the shareholders. There is an element of shareholder control over directors which stems from the legal duty laid on the latter to issue reports on their stewardship of the firm's assets.

The concept of periodicity is now established by law as regards certain types of reports such as balance sheets and income statements. Company legislation in all countries generally requires the publication of annual reports to shareholders, and tax laws require accounts for all businesses to be submitted annually. However, there is nothing to prevent companies from providing information at more frequent intervals to investors, if they so wish.

The fact that reports are annual has grown out of custom, and many would question the wisdom of selecting an arbitrary period of twelve months as a basis for reporting upon the activities of a business. The idea of annual reports is deeply entrenched, and even governments runs their business on a yearly basis preparing annual budgets for taxation revenues and government expenditure, although many activities are on-going and cannot be seen correctly in the perspective of twelve months. This is also true for all large companies, and many smaller businesses.

Example 8.13   Universal Chemicals Ltd manufactures a wide range of chemical products and has factories throughout the country. Owing to unusually difficult labour relations, rising raw material costs and stiffening competition, its reported income for the year ended 31 December 20X0 has decreased by 10 per cent from that of the previous year. Its borrowings, however, have increased by 20 per cent owing to an enlarged capital investment programme which is designed to add substantially to income in about five years' time.

Clearly, in this case the reader of the report for the year 20X0 should consider the report in context, and look to the long-term trend of income and to the better financial position which is expected in the future.

The concept of periodicity as expressed in yearly accounting fails to make the important distinction between the long-term trend and the short-term position. Hence, it limits the usefulness of the information communicated to shareholders and investors.

The matching and periodicity concepts seek to relate the transactions of one particular year with the expenses attributable to those transactions. From a practical point of view, accountants carry forward expenses until they can be identified with the revenues of a particular year, and carry forward receipts until they can be regarded as the revenue of a particular year in accordance with the realization convention. Since all assets become 'costs' in accounting, the convention of periodicity creates difficulties with regard to the allocation of non-current assets as expenses of particular years. We examine this matter when we discuss depreciation in Chapter 13.

So far we have mentioned the effect of the concept of periodicity on the usefulness of information communicated to external users; we now comment on its effect on income measurement. The majority of economists treat accounting income as the 'income' of a business, and hence as a measure of the income which investors and shareholders derive from their investment in the firm. As a result, they impose the economic criteria appropriate to the measurement of economic income to accounting and disapprove of the shortcomings of accounting which they see as stemming from accounting concepts for calculating periodic income. Ideally, an accurate measurement of the income of a business can be made only after the business has ceased operating, sold off all its assets and paid off all its liabilities. The net income accruing to investors would then be the difference between the sum total of all their receipts, either as dividends or capital repayments, and their initial investment. It is clear, however, that accounting income is merely the result of completed transactions during a stated period: the concept of periodicity is a statement of this view.

The concept of consistency

The usefulness of financial information lies to a considerable extent in the conclusions which may be drawn from the comparison of the financial statements of one year with those of a preceding year, and the financial reports of one company with those of another. It is in this way that we may deduce some of the most important information for decision making, such as an indication that there has been an improvement in income since last year and that therefore it is worth buying more shares, or the income of Company A is better than that of Company B and given current share prices one should switch from holding shares in Company B and buy those of Company A.

The comparability of financial statements depends largely upon the choice of accounting methods and the consistency with which they are applied. A change in the basis on which a firm values inventories, for example, may produce in a different result from that which would have been computed had the accountant adhered to a consistent basis of valuation. If firms wish to change their method for treating a particular problem, such as the valuation of inventories or the value attached to a particular asset, they may do so, but they should mention the effect of the change in accounting methods.

Comparing the accounts of different companies is much more difficult. The accounting methods of individual firms are not always the same. There is no uniformity of accounting methods which would provide consistency of treatment necessary for the comparison of the accounts of different companies. Whereas the accounting concept of consistency is generally followed by individual firms, there is no agreement that different firms should use the same accounting methods. Hence, the needs of investors for greater comparability of information between companies is frustrated by accounting concepts which insist on consistency, but allow different methods of measurement and treatment which cannot yield comparable results. The International Accounting Standards Board (IASB) is charged with the task of trying to secure international agreement on appropriate accounting methods which will ensure a higher degree of international comparability of accounting information. Progress made in this regard will be discussed in Chapter 9.

The concept of prudence/conservatism

Prudence reflects the view of accountants of their social role and of their responsibilities towards those to whom they provide information. It is seen in some of the concepts that have examined in this chapter, for example the realization concept which requires the realization of a gain before it may be recognized, and the cost convention which holds that the value of an asset is the cost of acquisition.

There are two principal rules which stem directly from the concept of prudence:

1 the accountant should not anticipate income and should recognize immediately all possible losses;
2 faced with two or more methods of valuing an asset, the accountant should choose the more conservative value.

These two rules contravene some accounting concepts, for example the cost concept, for if the market value of inventories and marketable securities has fallen below the cost of acquisition they must be valued at the market value. Equally, the logic which underlies the realization concept as regards gains, that there is no certainty of a gain until there is a sale, does not extend to the treatment of anticipated losses. Thus, accountants provide for losses in value which are sufficiently foreseeable to make them a present reality, on the basis that to ignore such losses might mislead the user of accounting information. One of the clearest explanations of the policy of prudence was made by G.O. May as long ago as 1946, as follows:

> *The great majority of ventures fail, and the fact that enterprises nevertheless continue is attributable to the incurable optimism (often dissociated from experience) as well as to the courage of mankind. In my experience, also, losses from unsound accounting have most commonly resulted from the hopes rather than the achievements of management being allowed to influence accounting dispositions. To me, conservatism is still the first virtue of accounting, and I am wholly unable to agree with those who would bar it from the books of accounts and statements prepared therefrom and would relegate it to footnotes.*

(May, 1946)

The caution of the accountant may well be a foil for the optimism of business people but, although it may be desirable for the accountant to be prudent in the estimates which are made, the selection of accounting methods for recording and presenting information on the basis that they deliberately understate assets or earnings should not be an overriding principle. Investors and shareholders need reliable and useful information: to understate is as bad as to overstate – investment in a business may be discouraged if it appears to be less valuable than it really is. The credit and banking crisis that began in 2007 has raised the entire problem of the valuation of 'toxic assets' on the balance sheets of financial institutions with respect to the concept of prudence.

Users of accounting information, like others who are faced with making decisions, look for guidance to the lowest value, the highest value and the probable value. In restricting accounting information to the statement of the lowest value, the accountant is not fulfilling the social role expected of a supplier of comprehensive financial information.

Summary

Accounting concepts serve as guideposts, but tend to emphasize the reliability of information rather than its usefulness. The conflict between reliability and usefulness is controversial. At one extreme, some accountants contend that if a measurement is useful, further justification is unnecessary. At the other extreme, others hold that the reliability of accounting information is the most important criterion, and will ultimately determine the extent to which external users accept accounting statements for making investment decisions.

1 Examine the role of so-called concepts in the analysis of accounting transactions and the preparation of financial statements.

1 Consultat Inc. is a firm of consulting engineers, newly established to advise on a large project taking three years to complete. Their fee for this work is a percentage of the total project costs, payable on completion of the project. In the interim, advances on the final fee are made at six-monthly intervals. The total project costs will not be known until the project is completed. The following advances were received by Consultat Inc. during the three-year period:

year ended 31 December 20X0	£25,000
year ended 31 December 20X1	£30,000
year ended 31 December 20X2	£30,000

When the total costs were computed during the year ended 31 December 20X0, it was found that a further sum of £50,000 was due to Consultat Inc.

Required:

(a) Explain how Consultat Inc. would show the payments made during the periods covered by the project. Justify your explanation in terms of the concepts of accounting which you consider apply to this situation.

(b) Would you change your reasoning at all in the light of the following information?

(i) the advance payments are not contractual but discretionary on the part of the paying company;

(ii) a clause in the consulting agreement requires Consultat Inc. to undertake – free of charge – extra work to remedy defects appearing within three years of the completion of the project.

Suggest how you would treat these problems by reference to accounting concepts.

2 Bloxwich Engineers Ltd borrows £100,000 at a fixed interest rate of 10 per cent for a period of five years for the purpose of acquiring a stamping press of advanced design. Suggest how you would treat the accounting aspects of the transactions associated with the acquisition and the financing of the stamping press in the following circumstances:

(a) by the end of the third year of use, the stamping press has been depreciated to £70,000, but due to a new design having appeared, its market value is only £30,000. The stamping press, nevertheless, continues to generate the same level of revenue as it did in the first year of use;

(b) during the fourth year, the stamping press generates only £8,000 of revenues, and the Managing Director of Bloxwich Engineers Ltd has written an instruction to the effect that 'since the press is now making a loss of £2,000 when interest is taken into account', it should be sold forthwith. The market value has now fallen to £15,000. The monies realized are to be applied to the acquisition of further plant, and the interest charge remains to be paid during the following and final year of the loan.

Support your discussion of the accounting problems you have identified by reference to the conventions which justify your reasoning.

3* Lewis, Jones and Peers, newly qualified as architects, decide to form a partnership on 1 January 20X0. During their first year of business, a substantial operating loss is realized, amounting to £20,000. They had anticipated such a loss and had provided sufficient funds to cover it when they first formed the partnership. 'After all', said Peers, 'it is well known that the first year of practice for architects always produces a loss, since they are really establishing the business. They do, in fact, earn little money as they build up contacts which will earn future revenues'. 'That's right', continued Lewis, as he was explaining to the accountant, who has prepared the income statement showing the loss of £20,000, 'you can't show the £20,000 as a loss, when it is the cost of setting up the business. To be consistent with the facts, you have to show the £20,000 as an asset on the balance sheet.' 'Yes, I agree,' concluded Jones, 'that is the most conservative way of looking at the situation. Then, we recognize the creation of an asset we can write off over several years and match against the future revenues which are really the result of this year's efforts.'

How would you deal with the arguments of your clients if you were the accountant in this situation? Refer the problems you see to such accounting concepts as are applicable to them, and in particular, explain how you would deal with the terms 'consistent' and 'prudence' used by the partners in their discussion with you.

References Littleton, A.C. (1953) *Structure of Accounting Theory*, American Accounting Association.

Marshall, A. (1964) *Principles of Economics*, 8th edn, London: Macmillan.

May, G.O. (1946) *Financial Accounting: A Distillation of Experience*, New York: Macmillan.

CHAPTER 9

Financial accounting standards

Setting the scene

People in every walk of life are affected by business reporting, the cornerstone on which our process of capital allocation is built. An effective allocation process is critical to a healthy economy that promotes productivity, encourages innovation, and provides an efficient and liquid market for buying and selling securities and obtaining and granting credit. Conversely, a flawed allocation process supports unproductive practices, denies cost-effective capital to companies that may offer innovative products and services that add value, and undermines the securities market ... Reporting standards play an important role in helping the market mechanism work effectively for the benefit of companies, users, and the public.

(AICPA, 1994)

Learning objectives

After studying this chapter you should be able to:

1   discuss the purpose underlying the issue of financial accounting standards;

2   identify four 'fundamental concepts' originally stated in SSAP 2 and replaced by FRS 18, and the EU's Fourth Directive on Company Accounts and compare them with the corresponding concepts discussed in Chapter 8;

3   explain the meaning and role of 'accounting bases'.

The financial accounting concepts discussed in Chapter 8 were seen as core elements in the development of a descriptive theory of financial accounting. The review of the concepts of financial accounting which was conducted by the accounting profession in the United Kingdom in the 1970s resulted in the publication of a series of financial accounting standards, is part of the on-going process of developing international accounting standards through seeking consensus.

Accounting concepts allow a variety of alternative practices to coexist. As a result, the financial results of different companies cannot be compared and evaluated unless full information is available about the accounting methods which have been used. Not only have the variety of accounting practices permitted by the conventions of financial accounting made it difficult to compare the financial results of different companies, but the application of alternative accounting methods to the preparation of the financial reports of the same company have enabled entirely different results to be reported to shareholders.

The need for the imposition of standards arose because of the lack of uniformity existing as to the manner in which periodic income was measured and the financial position of the enterprise represented. The purpose of this chapter is to examine the significance of the development of accounting standards for a descriptive theory of financial accounting based on concepts and consensus.

The importance of comparability

The information contained in published financial statements is especially important to external users, such as shareholders and investors, for without such information they would have to take decisions about their investments under a considerable degree of uncertainty. A major problem is that there are no formal channels for communicating to companies the type and nature of the financial information which external users believe they require, and the manner in which such information ought to be presented. Traditionally, Government has assumed the responsibility for legislation specifying the type and the minimum level of information which companies should disclose. In some countries, Government has prescribed a legal format for financial accounting and financial reporting purposes along the lines of a comprehensive Accounting Chart or Plan specifying in detail accounts by name and number. In Anglo-Saxon countries, such as the UK, the USA, Canada, Australia, India etc., the accounting profession has assumed the responsibility for ensuring the proper presentation of such information. In time, it became accepted that the concepts applied to the presentation of financial information should not permit too much discretion, and that the manner in which financial information is treated in financial statements should conform to carefully considered standards.

The function of accounting standards may best be examined by reference to the basic purpose of financial statements, namely the communication of information affecting the allocation of resources. Ideally, such information should make it possible for investors to evaluate the investment opportunities offered by different firms and to allocate scarce resources to the most efficient. In theory, this process should result in the optimal distribution of resources within the economy, and should maximize their potential benefit to society.

One of the most important criteria for the presentation of financial information is ensuring an appropriate basis of comparison between different firms. The accounting methods used by different firms for presenting information should allow appropriate comparisons to be made. For example, they should not enable a company to report income which results simply from a change in accounting methods, rather than from increased efficiency. If companies were free to choose their accounting methods in this way, the consequence might well be that deliberate distortions would be introduced in the pricing of shares on the Stock Exchange, leading eventually to a misallocation of resources. This would occur if relatively less efficient companies were able to report fictitious income, and as a result divert capital to themselves from more efficient companies having more rigorous accounting methods.

Reasons for concern about standards

In the United Kingdom, the Institute of Chartered Accountants in England and Wales began to make recommendations about accounting practices as early as 1942. Ultimately, a series of 29 recommendations on accounting practices were issued with the objective of codifying the best practices to be used in particular circumstances. However, there were several disadvantages to this procedure:

1 The recommendations were not mandatory, and were issued for the guidance of members of the Institute.
2 The recommendations did not result from fundamental research into the objectives of accounting, but merely codified existing practices.
3 The recommendations did not reduce the diversity of accounting methods. For example, Recommendation No. 22, 1960, concerned with inventory valuation, advocated five different methods of computing the cost of inventory. Furthermore, four of these methods could be computed differently for partly and fully finished inventory. To complicate matters further, Recommendation 22 stated that cost could be defined in three different ways!

In the late 1960s, there was a spate of public criticism of financial reporting methods, which arose from the publicity accorded to aspects of the financial statements of a number of companies. These included Pergamon Press and the General Electric Company. The manner in which these cases jolted the accounting profession may be judged from the example of the General Electric Company.

In 1967, the General Electric Company (GEC) made a takeover bid for Associated Electric Industries (AEI). AEI produced an income forecast for that year of £10 million, which was based on ten months' actual income and two months' budgeted income. The GEC takeover bid was successful, and afterwards GEC reported that, in fact, AEI had made a loss of £4.5 million for the year. According to GEC auditors, £9.5 million of the £14.5 million difference between the two calculations of income for 1967 was due to a difference in judgement about amounts written off inventories and the provision for estimated losses.

The angry reaction of the press to the disclosure of the amended figures for 1967 centred on the fact that two accounting firms could justifiably produce such widely differing results for the same year. One observer commented that it appeared that accounting was really an art form, and two firms of accountants looking at the same figures were capable of producing income numbers as far apart as a painting by Rubens is from a Rembrandt.

The accounting standards movement that developed in the 1970s in the USA and in the UK had its origin in the perception that financial reports drawn up on the basis of generally accepted accounting principles were failing to meet the needs of users for information relevant to decision making. Moreover, accounting measurements based on historic cost under conditions of high inflation levels prevalent during this period singularly distorted the meaning of accounting income and the underlying reality of balance sheet values. In effect, the information produced under generally accepted accounting principles appeared unrelated to the realities facing shareholders and investors.

The accounting standards movement marked the beginning of a long-lasting debate that revisited the very foundations of accounting concepts, questioned the relevance of accounting methods and saw the essential problem as residing in the need for an objective framework that would establish the relevance of accounting information for the decision needs of users. The creation in 1970 of the Accounting Standards Committee, replaced in 1990 by the Accounting Standards Board, marked the beginning of the task of improving accounting practice. It was quickly followed by the setting up of the International Accounting Standards Committee in 1973, both bodies being based in London and composed of personalities sharing similar concerns.

The Accounting Standards Board (ASB) and the International Accounting Standards Board (IASB)

The prime objective of the Accounting Standards Committee in the United Kingdom was to narrow the areas of difference and variety in accounting practice. The procedure began with the issue of an 'Exposure Draft' on a specific topic for discussion by accountants and the public at large. Comments made on an Exposure Draft were taken into consideration when drawing up a formal statement of the accounting method to be applied in the form of a Statement of Standard Accounting Practice (SSAP). Once formally adopted, any material departure from the standard had to be disclosed. The topics on which Statements of Standard Accounting Practice (SSAPs) were issued show that the work of the Accounting Standards Committee profoundly affected the development of accounting theory and methods.

The experience in the United Kingdom closely paralleled that of the United States and a close association between these two countries was to result in the creation of the International Accounting Standards Committee in 1973. Thereafter, the International Accounting Standards Board was established to develop high quality, global accounting standards and to cooperate with national accounting standard setters in seeking convergence between standards throughout the world. The Anglo-Saxon tradition in setting accounting standards was very influential on the approach adopted by the IASB. The conflict with the more bureaucratic approach of accounting regulators within the European Union was ultimately resolved through the acceptance of the IASB's standards. The way was clear for the development of worldwide accounting standards that would meet the needs for uniformity in accounting and financial reporting practices in an expanding global market economy.

Accounting concepts, accounting methods and policy

The relationship between accounting concepts and methods involves matters of accounting policy. The disclosure of accounting policies is highly significant to the central issue of identifying the objectives for formulating accounting standards and a theoretical framework for developing accounting policies.

The Accounting Standards Committee released its first authoritative statement SSAP 2 'Disclosure of Accounting Policies' in 1971. It dealt with the relationship between accounting concepts, methods and policies. The relationship is illustrated in Figure 9.1, where it is seen that accounting concepts provide the foundations to both accounting methods and policies. These are defined by SSAP 2 as follows:

- *Fundamental accounting concepts* are broad general assumptions which underlie the financial statements of business enterprises.
- *Accounting bases* are the methods for expressing or applying fundamental accounting concepts to financial transactions and items. Accounting bases are more diverse and numerous than fundamental concepts, since they have evolved in response to the variety and complexity of types of business and business transactions. For this reason, there may exist more than one recognized accounting base for dealing with particular items.
- *Accounting policies* are the specific accounting bases judged by business enterprises to be most appropriate to their circumstances and adopted by them for the purpose of preparing financial statements.

Figure 9.1

SSAP 2 stated that four accounting concepts should be regarded as fundamental. These were replicated in the European Union's Fourth Directive on Company Accounts, together with the entity concept as the fifth as follows:

- The *going-concern concept* implies that the enterprise will continue in existence for the foreseeable future. It is on this assumption that the income statement and balance sheet are formulated.
- The *accruals concept* requires that revenues and costs be accounted for in the period to which they relate and not when cash is received or paid.
- The *consistency concept* requires that the treatment of like items within each accounting period and from one period to the next should be the same.
- The *concept of prudence* requires that revenue and income should not be anticipated, but accounted for only when realized. However, losses should be anticipated and provided for as soon as they become known with reasonable certainty.

In 2000 the Accounting Standards Board replaced SSAP 2 by Financial Reporting Standard 18 (FRS 18) 'Accounting Policies'. Consistency and prudence ceased to be fundamental concepts and comparability, relevance, reliability and understandability became the four fundamental accounting concepts. It emphasized comparability rather than consistency and linked prudence to reliability rather than realization.

SSAP 2 was concerned with ensuring that accounting bases are disclosed in financial statements whenever items are shown which have their significance in value judgements, estimated outcomes of future events or uncompleted transactions, rather than ascertained amounts. In the words of SSAP 2:

In circumstances where more than one accounting base is acceptable in principle, the accounting policy followed can significantly affect a company's reported results and financial position, and the view presented can be properly appreciated only if the principal policies followed are also described. For this reason, adequate disclosure of the accounting policies should be regarded as essential to the fair presentation of financial accounts.

In 1992, concern that the public should receive information about the risks of business failure led the Cadbury Committee to recommend additional disclosures relating to the going concern concept. In 1994 the Auditing Practices Board issued a statement of Auditing Standards (SAS 130) which provided guidance for auditors on the application of the going concern base. According to this standard, auditors should look for evidence that the going concern concept was not valid. They should obtain confirmation from the directors that the company is a going concern. In forming such a confirmation, the auditors should look one year ahead from the date of the directors' approval of the accounts.

The International Accounting Standards Board (IASB) followed the initiative of the Accounting Standards Committee in IFRS 1 'First-time adoption of International Financial Reporting Standards'. It required an undertaking from an entity adopting IFRS standards would select its accounting policies based on the IFRSs in force. It was followed by IAS 8 'Accounting Policies, Changes in Accounting Estimates and Errors'.

The Accounting Standards Board (ASB) responded to the increasing demand for uniform international standards in the following terms:

The ASB has accepted the argument that there should really be only one way of accounting for similar transactions throughout the world ... Unless we disagree with the international trend we try to align our standards closely to those of the International Accounting Standards Committee.

(Tweedie, 1999)

By 1 January 2009, the IASB had released the following IFRSs and IASs (reproduced by kind permission of the IASB):

- **IFRSs**
  IFRS 1 First-time Adoption of International Financial Reporting Standards
  IFRS 2 Share-based Payment
  IFRS 3 Business Combinations
  IFRS 4 Insurance Contracts
  IFRS 5 Non-current Assets Held for Sale and Discontinued Operations
  IFRS 6 Exploration for and evaluation of Mineral Resources
  IFRS 7 Financial Instruments: Disclosures
  IFRS 8 Operating Segments
- **IASs**
  IAS 1   Presentation of Financial Statements
  IAS 2   Inventories
  IAS 7   Statement of Cash Flows
  IAS 8   Accounting Policies, Changes in Accounting Estimates and Errors
  IAS 10 Events After the Balance Sheet Date
  IAS 11 Construction Contracts
  IAS 12 Income Taxes
  IAS 16 Property, Plant and Equipment

IAS 17 Leases
IAS 18 Revenue
IAS 19 Employee Benefits
IAS 20 Accounting for Government Grants and Disclosure of Government Assistance
IAS 21 The Effects of Changes in Foreign Exchange Rates
IAS 23 Borrowing Costs
IAS 24 Related Party Disclosures
IAS 26 Accounting and Reporting by Retirement Benefit Plans
IAS 27 Consolidated and Separate Financial Statements
IAS 28 Investments in Associates
IAS 29 Financial Reporting in Hyperinflationary Economies
IAS 31 Interests in Joint Ventures
IAS 32 Financial Instruments: Presentation
IAS 33 Earnings per Share
IAS 34 Interim Financial Reporting
IAS 36 Impairment of Assets
IAS 37 Provisions, Contingent Liabilities and Contingent Assets
IAS 38 Intangible Assets
IAS 39 Financial Instruments: Recognition and Measurement
IAS 40 Investment Property
IAS 41 Agriculture

Company legislation and International Accounting Standards

In Chapter 13 we examine the legal requirements applying to the financial statements of companies and the manner in which financial accounting information must be disclosed in the income statements and balance sheets. Two aspects of these requirements are directly related to the accounting concepts and standards considered in this chapter.

First, the four fundamental accounting concepts of SSAP 2 have become enshrined in the accounting law of member countries of the IASB (formerly IASC) pursuing a policy of convergence between their own national accounting regulation and international accounting standards. Final accounts prepared in accordance with accounting laws must follow the four concepts outlined earlier and replicated in the 4th Directive on Company Law of the European Union. Second, all final accounts prepared for the purpose of compliance with the IAS must now give a 'true and fair view'; an obligation described as 'overriding'. This implies that if the final accounts are to contain information which is sufficient in quantity and quality to satisfy the reasonable expectations of users then they should be prepared in accordance with the concepts and standards formulated by the regulatory authorities. Third, in the United Kingdom, the Companies Act 1989 introduced a requirement to state whether the accounts have been prepared in accordance with applicable accounting standards and give details of, and reason for, any material departures.

Summary

Financial accounting concepts and standards constitute a descriptive theory which has evolved from accounting practices.

Accounting concepts allowed a variety of practices to evolve. The lack of uniformity made it difficult for users of financial reports to compare the results of different companies. The need for comparability is one of the most important criteria for the presentation of financial reports. The reasons for concern about the quality of accounting information were seen to relate to the different results which could be drawn from the same set of data. The work of the standard setting boards has resulted in the reduction of variety of accounting practices.

Self-assessment questions

1 Discuss the purpose underlying UK accounting standards.

2 Identify the four 'fundamental accounting concepts' mentioned in FRS 18 and compare them with the ten concepts discussed in Chapter 8.

3 Explain the meaning of an 'accounting base'. State why accounting bases are more diverse than fundamental concepts.

References   AICPA (1994) *Improving Business Reporting – A Customer Focus*, (The Jenkins Report) American Institute of Certified Public Accountants.

Dearing, Sir Ron (Chairman) (1988) *The Making of Accounting Standards*, Report of the Review Committee, ICAEW.

Tweedie, D. (1999) *The 1998 Annual Review of the Financial Reporting Council*. Financial Reporting Council.

CHAPTER 10

The generation of financial accounting data

Setting the scene

We have a duty to present timely and accurate information to decision makers from the information systems we direct. Over the past ten years, our ability to extract information from raw data has undergone something of a transformation. One of the fundamental skills required of an accountant is to excel at defining what information is and placing it in context. So it follows that we must have a good understanding of the different ways to extract data and be familiar with the tools available for such an exercise. It also follows that we must have a really good understanding of what constitutes data – how data are gathered, stored and used.

(Williams, 1999)

Learning objectives

After studying this chapter you should be able to:

1 explain the meaning and importance of 'source documents' in the financial accounting process;

2 discuss the role of the journal, day books and cash book in the recording of financial accounting data;

3 describe the development of data-processing systems.

Earlier we examined the nature and the boundaries of the financial accounting system. We noted that the concepts of financial accounting constituted one of the boundaries in the filtering process for the data which are fed into the financial accounting system. We concluded that these concepts played a crucial role in determining the nature of financial accounting information.

This chapter examines the processes involved in the generation of financial accounting data prior to their transformation into accounting information.

An outline of the information generation process

Financial accounting information results from a process involving the following stages:

1 the preparation of source documents;
2 the entry of basic data into source records;
3 the posting of data from the source records into the ledger, which is a permanent record.

The production of financial accounting information in the form of reports is illustrated in Figure 10.1.

Figure 10.1

Although the concepts underlying the financial accounting system have remained unchanged, its processes have undergone and are continually undergoing modification and improvement. In particular, technological change has dramatically affected these processes. The advent of the computer has considerably speeded up and streamlined data recording, and has permitted the integration of several stages of this process into a single operation.

This chapter is concerned with an analysis of traditional data recording practices relating to source documents and source books, and examines the impact of the computer on these practices. The process of preparing financial reports will be examined in subsequent chapters.

Source documents

As explained in Chapter 8, financial accounting data originates in transactions. Source documents capture the details of these accounting events. They also have a very important functional purpose as regards the activities of an enterprise.

Data flows are generated and classified according to their sources:

1 Financial accounting data flows are generated from activities conducted between the firm and external groups such as customers and suppliers of materials, goods, services and finance.
2 Data flows generated internally constitute a substantial volume of the total information flows.

These flows are generated and channelled through a management information system (MIS), the function of which is to meet the needs of management for planning and control. The relationship between external and internal data flows and the documentation involved are illustrated in Figure 10.2. This shows the focal role played by accounting data in relation to the firm's basic operations as well as the nature of the source documents involved in the generation of financial accounting data.

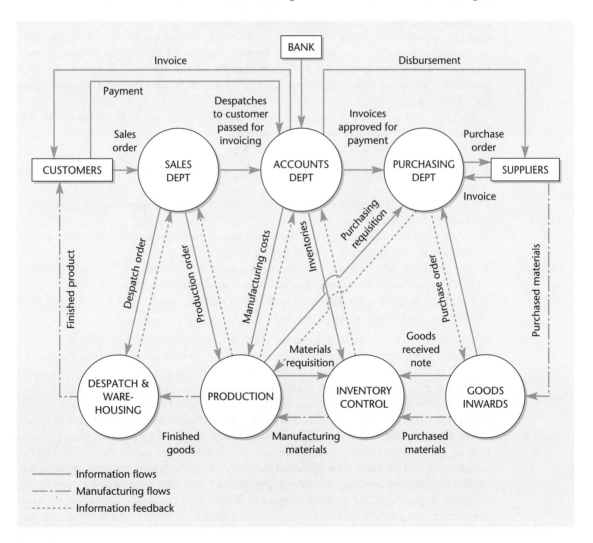

Figure 10.2

Source documents related to sales

A sales order form is completed on conclusion of a sale. The original is sent to the customer as acknowledgement of the order, and in the case of a credit sale, one copy goes to the credit control department for approval. If the goods are in inventory, the credit control department will pass the authenticated sales order form to the inventory control department for the release and dispatch of the goods. An advice note is sent to the customer advising of the date of despatch and mode of delivery. The goods are normally accompanied by a delivery note stating the description of the goods and the quantity involved though not the price. The customer acknowledges receipt of the goods by signing the delivery note.

When the goods have been released by the inventory control department for despatch, a further copy of the sales order stating the date of despatch is sent to the sales invoice section of the accounts department, so that the sales invoice may be prepared. The sales invoice states the nature, quantity and price of the goods ordered and the amount due from the customer. The sales invoice will also state the payment terms, including the delay of payment. This would typically be one month. Customers may be required to pay on receipt of the invoice. Some firms issue monthly statements showing the number of statements sent during the month and the total sum due.

The copy sales invoice is the source document which provides the data which will be recorded in the financial accounting system.

The sales order form is used for the following purposes:

1 As a record and confirmation of a sale. One copy will be kept by the sales department.
2 For checking the creditworthiness of a customer prior to proceeding with the completion of the order.
3 As a document authorizing the release of goods from inventory. One copy will be retained by the inventory control department.
4 For checking and despatching the right goods to the right customer by the despatch department. One copy is kept by this department for this purpose.
5 For preparing the sales invoice which will state the amount due. One copy will be retained by the accounts department.

Where goods are not kept in inventory but are manufactured to order, the receipt of an order puts the production process in motion. We examine the cost accounting process in a subsequent section. We may note that a copy of the production order will be sent to the production manager and one copy to the accounts department, which is responsible for collecting all the costs associated with the manufacture of the goods ordered. Figure 10.2 shows that the materials required may be obtained either from existing inventories or by purchase. Where the required materials are held in inventory, the issue of a materials requisition form to the inventory control department will procure their release. One copy of the materials requisition form will be retained by the inventory control department and one copy will be sent to the accounts department for costing purposes. Where the required materials have to be purchased, the production department issues a purchase requisition form to the purchasing department.

Source documents related to purchases

The purchasing department obtains the raw materials, equipment and supplies needed. Each request is made on a requisition form stating the nature and the quantity required, which is signed by an authorized person. The purchasing department selects a supplier and sends a purchase order form setting out the description, quantity and required delivery date of the goods, together with instructions for despatch and invoicing. The purchase order refers to the quoted price according to the supplier's catalogue or quoted price. The purchase order form is an offer to purchase and when accepted by the supplier creates a legal contract between buyer and seller. Copies of the purchase order are distributed to the departments concerned: namely receiving, inventory control, accounts and ordering.

Source documents related to the receipt of goods

Upon delivery of the goods, the receiving department verifies that the goods delivered compare in every detail with the purchase order. Then, a goods received note is prepared detailing the description of the goods received, their quantity, quality and condition. A copy of the goods received note is sent to the department concerned with the audit of the receipt of goods, which is usually the purchasing department. A copy is also sent to the accounts department and the department responsible for the order. The inventory control department is also notified because it is responsible for the storage, distribution and control of inventories. It keeps records of inventories, and ensures that adequate inventory levels are maintained.

In due course, the supplier sends an invoice stating the description, quantity and price of the goods ordered, the date of acceptance of the order, which is usually shown as the date of despatch of the goods, and the amount now owing. The invoice is checked by the accounts department against the goods received note, and cleared for payment in due course. Normally, invoices are paid monthly allowing the workflow in the accounting department to be efficiently organized and the payment procedures to be properly supervised.

The entry of basic data in the source books

The recording process begins with the issue or receipt of invoices. Although a legal contract is created by the acceptance of an order, nothing is recorded until formally stated. The appropriate source document provides evidence of the existence of an order.

The practice of keeping daily records of accounting events in a diary or roughbook dates from the early history of accounting. It was recommended by Pacioli in 1494 to enable the owner of a business to check daily the records kept by his clerks. Once agreed, they were entered into the ledger. It became a golden rule in accounting that no entry should appear in the ledger which has not first been entered in the journal.

At first, the journal was used to record all commercial transactions. They were entered chronologically and showed the details of these transactions as well as the ledger account to which the entry was ultimately posted, as shown below.

The data entered in the journal consisted of:

1 the date of the transaction;
2 the name of the purchaser or the asset purchased;
3 the name of the seller or the asset sold;
4 the sum involved;
5 a short narrative describing the transaction.

Date	Journal description	Folio	Dr £	Cr £
5 Jan	Goods Dr	L5	100	
	To A Smith	L7		100
	Being 100 shirts bought for resale			
5 Jan	B Jones Dr	L10	5	
	To Cash			5
	Being wages due to the week ending 5 January			

Periodically, the entries in the journal were transferred to the main record, described as the ledger, by a procedure known as posting. The folio references in the journal indicated the pages in the ledger to which the postings were made.

As trade expanded and the number of transactions increased, it became the practice to group the entries made in the journal into the following classes:

1 purchases of trading goods on credit;
2 sales of trading goods on credit;
3 cash receipts and payments;
4 all other transactions.

This classification enabled entries of like nature to be kept together, and facilitated the operation of entering data into the source books. It led to the division of the journal into four parts, which were renamed as follows:

1 the purchases day book, in which were entered credit purchases;
2 the sales day book, in which were recorded credit sales;
3 the cash book, in which were recorded all cash transactions;
4 the journal proper, in which were recorded transactions which could not be recorded in the other source books. The journal proper has been retained as a book of original entry for such transactions.

The day books

Since the bulk of source documents relate to the purchase or sale of goods, the function of the purchases and sales day books is to allow such data to be collected and posted to the ledger. An example of a purchases day book is given below.

Purchases day book

Date	Name	Invoice no.	Folio	£
1 June	S Smith	101	L15	50
2	W Wright and Co	113	L20	35
2	J James	148	L10	140
3	T Tennant	184	L16	20
3	Transferred to purchases account		L50	245

The posting of the purchases day book to the ledger is made by crediting the account of each supplier with the value of the goods supplied and transferring the total value of all purchases in the period to the purchases account. The details entered in the day books are obtained from the invoices which are filed and kept.

The sales day book is written up in the same manner, except that the source document is a copy of the invoice sent to the customer.

The cash book

Only cash transactions are entered in the cash book, which records all receipts and payments of cash. The cash book has a dual role, being a journal and a ledger account.

As the practice grew of using cheques, so the cash book came to reflect this practice, and record all payments in and out of the bank account.

Unlike the day books, the cash book records receipts and payments side by side, so that flows in and out are seen together and their impact on the balance may be readily seen. At the end of the accounting period, the cash book is reconciled with the bank statement through a bank reconciliation statement which explains any difference between the balance recorded in the cash book and that recorded by the bank. This difference is due to the time-lag between the posting of a cheque to a creditor and its clearing through the bank, delays in clearing cheques paid in, bank charges and direct payments into and out of the bank.

Where transactions take place in cash as well as by cheques, and cash discounts are given and allowed, the cash book is given extra columns, and becomes known as a 'three-column cash book'. The transfer of cash in and out of the bank account is recorded as well as the receipts and payments by cheques, as follows:

Cash book

Date	Details	Folio	Discounts allowed £	Cash £	Bank £	Date	Details	Folio	Discounts received £	Cash £	Bank £
1 Jan	Balance	J1		50	800	1 Jan	B Brown	L3	7		103
1	Sales	L15		60		1	Purchases	L14		20	
1	W White	L9	5		95	1	Cash				20
1	Bank			20							

The explanation of some of these entries is as follows:

1 Jan   B Brown – this represents the payment of an account owing to Brown amounting to £110 which was settled by the payment of £103, the balance being in the form of a discount which was received.

1 Jan   W White – this represents the receipt of a cheque for £95 in settlement of an amount owing of £100, a discount of £5 being allowed.

1 Jan   Bank – this represents a cash cheque drawn on the bank for £20. The corresponding payment of cash by the bank is shown on the other side of the cash book.

For security reasons, firms do not keep large sums in cash about their premises. Cash takings are banked daily. It is the practice to use cheques for the payments of debts, so that there is no need to keep cash on hand beyond relatively small sums. A petty cash box is used to meet immediate need for cash, for example enabling a secretary or porter to take a taxi to deliver a document, or to buy a small article which is urgently required.

The cashier is usually entrusted with the petty cash box and any payments must be claimed by means of a petty cash voucher signed by an authorized person. The cashier is given a petty cash float and pays out petty cash only against vouchers, which are retained. As the petty cash float decreases, petty cash vouchers of an equivalent value accumulate in the petty cash box. In due course, they are checked and the petty cash paid out is refunded to the cashier, thereby restoring the petty cash float to its original sum.

The ledger

The ledger is divided into sales, purchases and nominal ledgers. The sales ledger (or debtors ledger) contains all the customers' accounts; the purchases ledger (or creditors ledger) those of suppliers and the nominal ledger (also general ledger or private ledger) contains the rest of the firm's accounts. The main reason for dividing the ledger is to permit specialization in the recording process.

Computerized accounting systems

Developments in hardware and software have revolutionized the entire accounting function. Standard packages by companies such as SAP and Oracle handle everything from the capturing and processing of data, the production of reports as well as such tasks as resource planning and control, supply chain management, product life-cycle management, customer and supplier relationship management, etc.

Example 10.1   Figure 10.3 illustrates the facilities available in an integrated computer system for processing a sales order. The sales order is fed into the computer, which then accesses information from the debtor's ledger and up-to-date information from inventory records.

First, the computer provides information on the outstanding customer's balance and shows whether the customer is creditworthy. Credit limits are established in advance for each customer. The computer adds the value of the order to the balance outstanding on the customer's account in the sales ledger, and compares the total with the credit limit. If the credit limit has not been reached, the order is cleared for further processing. If the credit limit has been reached, the operative will need to confirm that the order will or will not be processed. This procedure allows the company to exercise a meaningful credit control check and to avoid processing any orders for customers with an excessive debt.

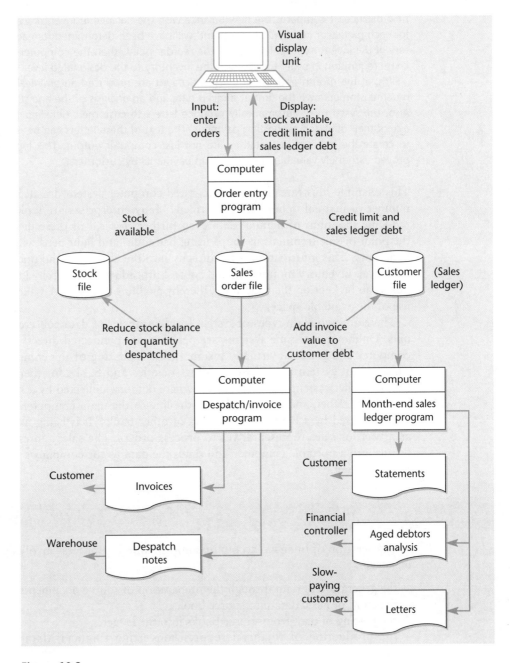

Figure 10.3

Second, the computer provides details of the inventory available and allows the firm to identify immediately which items can be despatched. For these items, the computer's despatch/invoice program would automatically produce a despatch note (to send to the warehouse) and an invoice (to send to the customer).

Third, the invoice is automatically posted to the customer's account in the sales ledger and, via the sales day book, to the sales account in the nominal ledger.

Fourth, the computer adjusts the inventory records in respect of the order and calculates a new balance. It compares the new balance with the balance in inventory which is required for each particular item. A 'reorder point' will have been determined for each item of inventory. If the inventory level falls below the reorder point, then the computer produces a purchase requisition in order to replenish the inventory to the designated level.

Fifth, at the month end, statements of account are produced automatically showing how much customers owe the firm at a given date and an analysis of the age structure of debts. Also, the system will automatically produce letters to customers detailing the amount and age of their debt and requesting payment. The text of these letters can be modified in order to create the impression that they are not just computer output. This type of facility has proved extremely valuable in speeding up payments by customers.

This example illustrates how an integrated computer system drastically reduces the number of manual operations performed. Many enterprises are looking at ways of reducing the input of manual data even further. Typical of these developments are the point-of-sale terminals in shops using bar codes and light pens which identify the items sold. This information is fed directly into the computer and updates the inventory level. Inventory monitoring and control procedures are thereby improved. Fewer items can be kept on the shop floor, thereby enabling retailers to make more effective use of the available space.

There are two main types of system for the transfer of data collected by the terminals. Online or real-time systems are permanently connected directly to the central computer and produce virtually instantaneous updating of the computer's records. This type of system is used by building societies and banks for their own customers. The other system is batch transfer where data are collected by a small computer, grouped together, and then sent down the line to the main computer. Such a system might be used by a bank for customers of other banks. It is being used increasingly as a way for sales representatives to process orders. The sales representative enters details into a portable computer and sends the data to the company's main computer for processing.

Summary

The generation of financial accounting information is a process involving the following stages:

1 the generation of data through the preparation of source documents;
2 the entry of basic data into source books;
3 the posting of data from source books into the ledger;
4 the production of financial reports converting financial data into financial information.

By making data processing more cost-effective, developments in computers have enabled smaller firms to take advantage of computer techniques. User-friendly systems can be operated by people who have no previous computer experience. Integrated computer systems reduce overall clerical requirements and improve the accuracy and speed of processing data.

Self-assessment question

1 What do you understand by a 'source document'? Give three examples of source documents, and explain their importance to the accounting process.

Problems *(* indicates that a solution is to be found in the Lecturer's Guide)*

1 Name the books of original entry to be used for recording the following transactions and state the accounts to be debited and credited:

Transaction (a)   Purchase of equipment on credit.

Transaction (b)   Payment of cash to a creditor.

Transaction (c)   Bank charges paid.

Transaction (d)   Receipt of cash from a customer.

Transaction (e)   Sale to a customer on credit.

Transaction (f)   Goods returned by a customer.

2 Prepare journal entries for the following transactions and indicate the journal in which they would normally appear:

1 April   Received invoice for £400 being equipment purchased from Equipment Supplies Ltd.

2 April   Received invoice for £700 for goods supplied by Jones Ltd.

4 April   Received cheque for £50 from J Brown for goods supplied. Sent cheque to S Supplier for £250 in payment of purchases effected in March.

5 April   Received an invoice from Standfast Supplies Ltd for goods supplied £800.

6 April   Invoiced J Shepherd for goods sold £98.

7 April   Received a cheque for £70 from W Smith in settlement of his account for goods sold.

8 April   Received rates statement showing rates due £500.

9 April   Banked weekly cash takings of £700.

3* Show the following entries as they would appear in a three-column cash book:

1 May   Credit balance (on bank statement) at bank £700, cash in hand £5. Cash drawn from bank for the till £30. Cheque sent to Brown for £67 in settlement of amount due of £70, discount being received for prompt payment.

2 May   Received cheque from Jones for £45 in payment of invoiced amount of £47, less cash discount.

3 May   Cash sales for the day £190.

4 May   Banked cash sales of previous day £190.

5 May   Sent cheque to Blewett £100 being instalment due on loan repayment.

6 May   Took £10 out of till for taxi fares.

Reference   Williams (1999) 'Reporting with a Purpose', *Ca (Canada) Magazine*, March.

CHAPTER 11

Data processing and double-entry bookkeeping

Setting the scene

The resources that come into the company are equal to the resources that are recognized as going out, whether at the present time or at some future date. This equality between the resources that come into a company and those that go out forms a vital part of the accountant's view of the company. It reflects the fact that a company only owns assets on behalf of third parties. These third parties are shareholders and others who are financing the company's operations. The company never really owns assets on its own behalf, but only holds them prior to passing the benefit of ownership on to another party. This means that, whenever the company acquires assets, it must also acquire the finance to hold those assets. This gives rise to the double-entry system which records this twofold aspect of each transaction.

(Chopping and Skerratt, 1995)

Learning objectives

After studying this chapter you should be able to:

1 show the effects of transactions on the accounting equation;

2 describe the nature of double-entry bookkeeping;

3 enter transactions in accounting records and take out a trial balance;

4 identify errors which are not revealed by the trial balance.

There are two very important aspects of data generation. First, when reporting to external users, accounting information is presented in a form showing the monetary aspects of a firm's activities. Second, financial accounting concepts determine the nature and the quality of the data which are processed.

The purpose of this chapter is to examine the structure which has evolved for handling financial accounting data.

The accounting equation

The accounting equation depicts the equality which exists between the resources owned by the enterprise and the claims against it. One side of the accounting equation expresses, in monetary terms, the resources held by the enterprise. These are known as 'assets'. The other side of the accounting equation describes how their acquisition has been financed and the claims which exist against the business as a result. The acquisition of assets by the enterprise will have been financed by funds provided either by shareholders as owner(s) or by borrowings. The funds provided by shareholders constitute the 'capital' of the enterprise. The funds borrowed exist as liabilities.

The accounting equation may be stated as follows:

$$\text{Capital} + \text{Liabilities} = \text{Assets}$$

The accounting equation assumes that the enterprise is a vehicle through which assets are held and utilized, and that claims exist against those assets to their full monetary value. Given that liabilities arising from borrowings are stated as legal debts of determined monetary amounts, the owners of the enterprise are entitled to the balance of the assets after liabilities have been settled. Accordingly, the accounting equation may be expressed as follows:

$$\text{Capital} = \text{Assets} - \text{Liabilities}$$

The balance sheet is founded on the accounting equation, for it is a list of the assets held by the enterprise against which is set a list of the claims existing against the enterprise. Both lists are equal in total.

Transactions and the accounting equation

The balance sheet shows the financial position of an enterprise at a stated point in time. Successive transactions maintain the accounting equation on which the balance sheet rests. It is possible to record the effects of successive transactions on the balance sheet equation.

Transaction 1

J Soap invested £10,000 on 1 April 20X0 in a ladies' hairdressing business, on 1 April 20X0 the opening transaction would be shown as follows:

Balance sheet 1

	£		£
Capital	10,000	Assets: Bank balance	10,000

Subsequent transactions affect the balance sheet through the accounting equation.

Transaction 2

J Soap paid the monthly rent for the business amounting to £500. This is an expense which will have to be taken into account in determining the income or loss for the period. Since the income made, or loss suffered, augments or diminishes the funds contributed to the business by the proprietor, the expense may be shown as a temporary reduction in proprietorship equity. From the point of view of the accounting equation, therefore, the effect of the transaction on the balance sheet is to reduce cash by £500, and at the same time reduce the capital by the same amount. The balance sheet after this transaction would appear as:

Balance sheet 2

	£		£
Capital	9,500	Assets: Bank balance	9,500

Transaction 3

J Soap purchased equipment for £2,000 from Hairdressers' Supplies Ltd on credit. As a result, a new asset appears on the balance sheet as the equipment, and a liability of £2,000 appears in respect of the amount owing. The balance sheet now appears as follows:

Balance sheet 3

	£		£
Capital	9,500	Assets: Equipment	2,000
Liability:			
Creditor	2,000	Bank balance	9,500
	11,500		11,500

Although the balance sheet totals increase by £2,000, there is no change in the capital of the business. Instead, the balance sheet shows that the equipment purchased has been financed by a liability of exactly that amount.

Transaction 4

J Soap paid wages of £200 in cash for part-time assistance. This is an expense of the month, and its effect on the balance sheet is to reduce cash by £200 and the capital by the same amount. The balance sheet now appears as follows:

Balance sheet 4

	£		£
Capital	9,300	Assets: Equipment	2,000
Liability:			
Creditor	2,000	Bank balance	9,300
	11,300		11,300

Transaction 5

J Soap's revenue from clients for April amounted to £1,500, of which £1,400 was received in cash. The effect of these transactions is to increase the capital by £1,500 and to increase cash at bank by £1,400. The difference of £100 requires a new asset account to be opened – Debtors – in the sum of £100. The balance sheet now appears as follows:

Balance sheet 5

	£			£
Capital	10,800	Assets:	Equipment	2,000
Liability:			Debtor	100
Creditor	2,000		Bank balance	10,700
	12,800			12,800

Transaction 6

J Soap withdraws the sum of £400 in cash for his own use. This withdrawal reduces capital by £400 and cash by the same amount. The withdrawal of cash from the business is the reverse of the first transaction in which J Soap invested in the business. Consequently, the capital account is reduced by the amount of the withdrawal. The balance sheet now stands as follows:

Balance sheet 6

	£			£
Capital	10,400	Assets:	Equipment	2,000
Liability:			Debtor	100
Creditor	2,000		Bank balance	10,300
	12,400			12,400

Simplifying the recording of transactions

The process of drawing up a new balance sheet after each transaction would be extremely cumbersome in practice, given the large number of daily transactions. The problems are threefold. First, how to calculate the impact of successive transactions in terms of the income they generate? Such a calculation would have to explain why there occurred an increase in the capital from an original amount of £10,000 to £10,800, prior to the withdrawal made by J Soap. Second, how to reflect J. Soap's investment as owner in a convenient manner? It would involve summarizing the effects of transactions on the capital account at the end of the accounting period. Third, how to devise a method of recording transactions that avoids drawing up successive balance sheets?

The first problem is resolved by summarizing all transactions associated with income-earning during the period in a statement known as the income statement. Unlike the balance sheet, which states the financial position at different points in time, the income statement seeks to establish the gains or losses of the enterprise as the result of transactions over a period of time. The preparation of the income statement involves identifying the revenues of the period, and the expenses which may properly be charged against those revenues. In the example of J Soap above, the successive balance sheets for the month of April, which resulted in the increase in the capital account from £10,000 to £10,800 by balance sheet 5, may be summarized by an income statement for April 20X0 as follows:

J Soap – Ladies' Hairdresser
Income statement for April 20X0

	£	£
Revenue		1,500
Expenses:		
Rent	500	
Salaries	200	700
Net income for April		800

The second problem, namely portraying the investment of the owner of the business at the close of the accounting period, involves using both the income statement of the period and the balance sheet at the close of the period. In this respect, the income statement and the balance sheet complement each other. The income statement summarizes the operating results between successive balance sheets, and these results are reflected in the capital shown on the closing balance sheet. The factors which have affected the amount of the owner's capital at the date of the closing balance sheet may be summarized in a detailed statement of the capital account. As regards the example of J Soap given above, the analysis of the capital account would be shown on the closing balance sheet as follows:

J Soap – Ladies' Hairdresser
Capital account as at 30 April 20X0

	£	£
Balance, 1 April 20X0		10,000
Net income for April	800	
Less: Drawings	400	400
Balance, 30 April 20X0		10,400

The third problem, that of devising a system of recording transactions which avoids drawing up successive balance sheets, was resolved several centuries ago by the invention of the system of double-entry bookkeeping.

The nature of double-entry bookkeeping

The collection and recording of data is known as bookkeeping. The practice of recording financial data in 'books' dates from a very long time ago. These books were usually 'bound books' – bound so as to prevent the possibility of fraud by either the insertion or the removal of pages. Nowadays, mechanical and electronic data processing have frequently removed the bookkeeper as a person concerned with entering the results of financial transactions into the books.

The double-entry system of bookkeeping, however, remains the basis for record keeping regardless of whether or not a firm employs advanced data-processing techniques, mechanical or manual methods. It is the logical method for recording financial information, and as such the basis of financial accounting practice. The universality of double-entry bookkeeping was discussed briefly in Chapter 4 in terms of its importance in accounting theory.

The term 'double-entry' adds a special meaning to the process of bookkeeping. It is a method of recording financial data as transactions involving flows of money or money value between different accounts. It involves a network of integrated accounts, in which an account is designated for each accounting item. The entries recorded on the successive balance sheets of J Soap for April 20X0 would appear in a double-entry bookkeeping system.

Transaction 1

The initial investment of £10,000 cash by J Soap in the ladies' hairdressing business is shown as a flow of money from the capital account to the cash book, as follows:

Capital account	Cash book
—————— £10,000 ———→	

Business transactions are represented in double-entry bookkeeping as flows of money or money value between the various accounts concerned, but clearly any one transaction involves only one flow, as shown above. In order to identify the direction of any one flow, all accounts are divided into two parts. A flow out of the account is recorded on the right-hand side, and a flow into an account is recorded on the left-hand side. Hence, the transaction shown above would appear as follows:

Capital account	Cash book
—————— £10,000 ———→	

Flows out could conveniently be described by a minus sign, but the accounting convention which dates from the Italian origins of bookkeeping utilizes the term *Credit* (Cr), which means 'to give'. Likewise, flows in could be described by a positive sign, but the accounting appellation is *Debit* (Dr), which means 'to owe'. Hence, this additional information may be inserted in the accounts to identify the direction of the flow, and replacing the arrow which we have used up to now.

Capital account		Cash book	
Cr		Dr	
£10,000		£10,000	

There are now only two additional items of information which are required to identify the transaction flow, namely the point of origin and the point of destination.

These, too, are made easy in bookkeeping by the simple expedient of describing in the credited account where the flow has gone, and by inserting in the debited account the source of the flow.

Capital account		Cash book	
	Cr	Dr	
	Cash £10,000	Capital £10,000	

In practice, accountants know very well that the left-hand side of an account is the debit side, and vice versa for the right-hand side, so that they do not head up the accounts with Dr or Cr. In the old days, they used to add the word *By* on the narration of credit entries, and *To* on the narration of debit entries – but this too is unnecessary, and most accountants have abandoned the practice. The reader will occasionally find entries recorded as follows:

Capital account	
	By cash £10,000

Cash book	
To capital £10,000	

These terms are now superfluous

Lastly, the date of the transaction must be recorded, and it is done as follows:

Capital account	
	20X0
	1 April Cash £10,000

Cash book	
20X0	
1 April Capital £10,000	

To simplify the exposition of the double-entry bookkeeping system in the examples which follow, the dates will be omitted.

In the manner in which transactions are recorded under this method, the reader will have been quick to notice an important feature – the flow has remained constant in value as it has moved from the credited account to the debited account. As a result, double-entry bookkeeping possesses a mathematical foundation which has its logic in the simple proposition that as regards any one transaction the credit must be equal to the debit. At any time, therefore, the arithmetical precision of the bookkeeping process may be checked by adding up all the debit entries and all the credit entries. If the total debit entries do not equal, that is balance with, the credit entries, there has been an error in the recording process. As we see on page 114, the trial balance is the means whereby accountants check for arithmetical errors in recording transactions. If the trial balance shows a difference as little as 1p between the total debits and the total credits, the error must be found. This is because accountants know that the result of a great many cumulative errors may boil down to a difference of only 1p.

Double-entry bookkeeping is a logical and precise system for recording financial transactions as flows of money or money value. It is easy to operate, and simple to adapt to modern computer methods by using positive and negative electric charges to signal whether an account should be debited or credited.

Transaction 2

The payment of £500 rent by J Soap is interpreted as a flow of money from the cash book to the rent account. It reduces cash by £500 and appears as an increase in the balance shown in the rent account by £500. The rent account is an 'expense' account which will be transferred later for the purposes of calculating the net income for April. The entries will appear as follows:

Cash book			Rent account		
		£			£
	Rent	500	Cash	500	

Transaction 3

The purchase of equipment on credit for £2,000 by J Soap from Hairdressers' Supplies Ltd does not yet involve the payment of cash, but requires the debt owing to Hairdressers' Supplies Ltd to be shown. This is effected by crediting the account of Hairdressers' Supplies Ltd with £2,000. Therefore the firm acquires a liability in order to acquire an asset. The entries would be as follows:

Hairdressers' Supplies Ltd account			
			£
		Equipment	2,000

Equipment account		
	£	
Hairdressers' Supplies Ltd	2,000	

Transaction 4

The payment of £200 as wages is another example of an expense account. Note that in the case of such accounts, the persons receiving payment are not named on the accounts themselves. Separate records would be kept in the form of a wages book, rent book, etc. This transaction decreases cash by £200 and increases wages by the same amount. The entries would be as follows:

Cash book			Wages account		
		£			£
	Wages	200	Cash		200

Transaction 5

The treatment of the revenue generated from the sale of hairdressing services involves two problems. First, the cash sales involving the receipt of cash amounting to £1,400 are entered directly as follows:

Sales book			Cash book		
		£			£
	Cash	1,400	Sales		1,400

The treatment of credit customers is rather more complex. First, the individuals concerned are shown in the debtors' ledger. The total amount of credit sales during the month of £100 appears in a summary account known as the debtors account. The entries are as follows:

Sales account			Debtors account		
		£			£
	Debtors	100	Sales		100

The payments made by debtors during the month totalled £1,400, leaving an amount outstanding of £100 at the end of April and shown as follows:

Debtors account				
		£		£
Sales		1,500	Cash	1,400
			Balance	100
		1,500		1,500

Transaction 6

J Soap withdrew £400 for his personal use. This transaction, which reduces his capital account by £400, could be entered directly as follows:

Capital account					Cash book		
		£		£			£
Cash		400	Cash	10,000		Capital	400

The effect of this transaction would be to reduce the capital account by £400 to £9,600. This reduction could be shown as follows:

Capital account

	£		£
Cash	400		
Balance c/d	9,600	Cash	10,000
	10,000		10,000
		Balance b/d	10,000

In order to minimize entries in the capital account in respect of regular withdrawals by the owner of a business, the normal practice is to show them in a separate drawings account. At the end of the accounting period, the drawings account is transferred to the capital account, so that only one entry is made in respect of drawings. Using the drawings account, the withdrawal of £400 would be shown as follows:

Drawings account		Cash book	
	£		£
Cash	400	Drawings	400

The capital account illustrates a technical operation known as balancing an account. Where there is more than one entry in an account the net effect of transactions affecting that account may be determined by calculating the balance of the account. This is the difference between the sum of the credit entries and the sum of the debit entries. In the case of the capital account the sum of the credit entries exceeds the sum of the debit entries. The balance is described as a credit balance. A debit entry is made in the account for the balance, which is said to be carried down (c/d); a credit entry is made on the next line to record the amount of the balance brought down (b/d) and to preserve the principle of double entry.

Double-entry bookkeeping as a 'closed' system

The term 'system' is commonly used to mean any unit which may be identified as an independent whole, having its own objectives and its own internal functions. An 'open' system is one whose behaviour is affected by external factors. The economy of any country is an 'open system' because it is affected by its trading relationships with the rest of the world. A 'closed' system is one in which all the functions are internalized in the system, and are not affected by outside factors. Double-entry bookkeeping has the characteristics of a closed system in that all the transactions recorded take place within the accounts system. This means that all flows resulting from transactions are depicted as having their origin in an account which is found in the system, and they have their destination in another account in the system. It is impossible for a flow to originate from an account outside the accounts system. Likewise, it is impossible for a flow of money or of money value to go to an account outside the accounts system.

Example 11.1 Let us go back to the example given above. J Soap opens up a business under the name of 'J Soap – Ladies' Hairdresser'. He invests £10,000 in cash into the business. The effect of the entity convention is that J Soap opens and keeps separate books for the business of J Soap – Ladies' Hairdresser, which is regarded as a separate entity from J Soap himself. Double-entry bookkeeping gives expression to the entity convention since all the accounts of J Soap – Ladies' Hairdresser relate only to the financial transactions of that business. J Soap himself is an external party as far as the business is concerned.

The question is – how can the flow of £10,000 from J Soap into the business be depicted, given that no flow may originate from outside the accounts system. The answer is the existence of an account within the accounts system whence it has originated. That account is the account of J Soap himself in his capacity as owner of the business, which is described above as the capital account. The source of the flow of £10,000 is therefore found in the capital account, and its destination is the cash account.

Capital account

			£
	20X0		
	1 April		10,000

Cash book

	£	
20X0		
1 April	10,000	

Suppose for a moment that on 2 April J Soap decides that he has put too much money in the business and wishes to take out £3,000. In the accounts system, the transaction could be shown as follows:

Capital account

		£			£
20X0			20X0		
2 April	Cash	3,000	1 April	Cash	10,000

Cash book

		£			£
20X0			20X0		
1 April	Capital	10,000	2 April	Capital	3,000

The significance of these entries reflects the fact that accounting is not concerned with the ultimate destination of the actual sums of money, but simply with portraying the full transaction as a *record* of the flow of money. Successive entries are made in accounts which have been opened, and where a transaction involves a new account then that account is opened. Likewise, if an account is no longer needed, it is closed.

The implications of these statements as far as bookkeeping being a closed system of accounts are:

1 The bookkeeping system of any firm is infinitely elastic in size. As many accounts are opened as are necessary to record in full the transactions which have taken place. It is not surprising, therefore, that large businesses have many thousands of accounts.

2 All the accounting flows of money or of money value take place between the various accounts found in the system. The accounts system, therefore, consists of a set of 'interlocking accounts'.

3 The accounts themselves represent 'realities' – whether they are persons or assets involved in transactions.

4 Firms are continually involved in transactions: this activity is mirrored in the constant flow of money and of money value in the accounts system.

5 Since all the flows have both their source and their destination in the accounts to be found in the system, the total debits and the total credits remain equal at all times. If this is not so, there are one or more errors.

Accounts as descriptions of transactions

We have already noted that the accounts system is used to describe the direction of a flow of money or of money value, as well as the timing of the flow. Business transactions affect a firm in different ways: some are concerned with the acquisition of assets to be used in earning incomes, others concern the supply of finance to the firm, either by the owner or by lenders, others relate to goods purchased or sold to persons so that the exchange of goods expressed as money value creates rights or liabilities in money terms, and others yet relate to revenues and costs.

If a firm is to make any sense of the large number of accounts kept, some grouping is necessary, so that accounts of the same business nature are kept together. The integration of accounts into groupings enables the accountant to extract information with much greater ease. For example, to find out how much is owed to persons by the business, the accountant has merely to go to the accounts of the creditors. This term means that such persons have been the source of a flow of money, or of money value to the firm, and have not been repaid. Likewise, the debtors accounts are consulted to find out how much is owing to the business by those people who have received money or money value and have not settled their accounts.

Transactions frequently involve two or more different classes of accounts.

Example 11.2 J Soap supplies hairdressing services to Mrs B Brown to the value of £20 on 1 April 20X0. In the accounts of J Soap, the transaction will be shown as a flow of money value (services) from the sales account, which is a nominal account, to Mrs B Brown's account, which is a personal account. Nominal accounts contain all of the items that are transferred to the income statement and so include items such as sales, purchases, wages and expenses.

Sales account

		£
	20X0	
	1 April Mrs B Brown	20

Mrs B Brown account

	£	
20X0		
1 April Sales	20	

Since Mrs Brown has received services from J Soap she is a debtor to the amount of £20. At the end of the month, J Soap will send her a statement showing that £20 is due for payment. Mrs B Brown sends her cheque for £20, which will be banked on 1 May. This is shown as another transaction, the settlement of a debt, as follows:

Mrs B Brown account

	£			£
20X0			20X0	
1 April Sales	20		1 May Cash	20

Cash book

	£	
20X0		
1 May Mrs B Brown	20	

This transaction is between a personal account and a real account. At this point, two interesting observations may be made:

1 A 'credit' transaction is a flow of money value to or from a personal account, and involves the creation of a debt towards the business, or a liability against the business. Hence, the use of the terms debtor and creditor respectively to denote the nature of such legal rights and obligations.
2 The payment of any liability involves another accounting transaction which records the flow of money from or to the appropriate personal account to or from the cash book. In this connection, the cash book records all the money flows through the firm's bank account.

The mathematical implications of double-entry bookkeeping

The arithmetical accuracy of the entries made in the accounts may be verified by means of a trial balance which involves comparing the total debits with the total credits.

During any accounting period, there may have been several entries in an account, so that several debits and several credits may be shown. A simple calculation may be made to calculate the net balance, for the purpose of the trial balance itself, and to ascertain the net state of the account.

Example 11.3 In the foregoing example several cash transactions took place during the month of April, as follows:

Cash book

	£		£
Capital	10,000	Rent	500
Sales	400	Wages	200
Debtors	1,000	Drawings	400

If we wish to ascertain the balance on the cash book, the procedure for so doing is simply to add up both sides of the account and to calculate the difference. This difference is the balance.

Cash book

	£		£
Capital	10,000	Rent	500
Sales	400	Wages	200
Debtors	1,000	Drawings	400
		Balance	10,300
	11,400		11,400

This balance represents the excess of the debits over the credits and it indicates that the bank balance is £10,300 in hand. In order to show this fact in the account after it has been balanced, the balance is brought down as a debit balance.

Cash book

	£		£
Capital	10,000	Rent	500
Sales	400	Wages	200
Debtors	1,000	Drawings	400
		Balance c/d	10,300
	11,400		11,400
Balance b/d	10,300		

Balancing the accounts is the first stage in preparing the trial balance. Some accounts will have debit balances and others will have credit balances. When we compare the total balances, they should be equal.

The trial balance

The trial balance is a list of balances extracted from all the accounts arranged so that the debit balances are listed on one side and the credit balances on the other side.

Example 11.4 The following trial balance was extracted on 30 April 20X0 from the books of J Soap – Ladies Hairdresser:

Trial balance as on 30 April 20X0

	Debit balances	Credit balances
	£	£
Capital account on 1 April 20X0		10,000
Drawings	400	
Cash	10,300	
Rent	500	
Wages	200	
Equipment	2,000	
Sales		1,500
Debtors	100	
Creditors		2,000
	13,500	13,500

The trial balance not only serves as a check on the arithmetical accuracy of the book-keeping process, but is a summary of the balances of all the accounts, which, as we shall see in the next chapter, serves as a working paper in the course of preparing financial statements. We note that in the process of summarizing information for the purpose of the trial balance, the personal accounts of the debtors and the creditors have been totalled.

The trial balance will not reveal the following types of errors:

1 errors of omission, where a transaction has been completely overlooked;
2 errors of principle, where an amount is correctly recorded but is placed in the wrong class of account – for example, where the purchase of equipment is shown under purchases rather than under equipment;
3 errors of commission, where an amount is correctly recorded in the correct class of account, but is entered in the wrong account – for example, where a sale of £50 to Mr B Brown is entered in Mrs B Brown's account;
4 errors of original entry, where the transaction is recorded in the wrong amount – for example, where a sale to Mrs B Brown of goods to the value of £20 is recorded as £2 in the sales journal;
5 errors in recording the direction of the flow, although the correct account is recorded – for example, instead of being shown as a debit to the cash book and a credit to Mrs B Brown's account it is shown the other way round;
6 compensating errors which cancel each other out will not be revealed. Thus, an error in adding up the trade debtors which is cancelled out by a similar error in adding up the trade creditors will not be revealed.

Example 11.5 Fairburn is a retailer and on 1 January 20X0 his assets were:

	£
Cash in bank	686
Inventories	916
Furniture and fittings	396
Sundry debtors – Grime	36
Spear	78
Murta	52

His only liabilities were to the following suppliers:

	£
Windle	24
Naik	42

The following transactions took place during January:

Event	January		£
1	1	Sold goods to Spear on credit	248
2	5	Paid wages	24
3	6	Bought goods on credit from Windle	300
4	8	Grime settled his account	
5	9	Paid the amount owing Naik	
6	10	Cash sales	128
7	13	Paid wages	28
8	17	Bought goods for cash	150
9	18	Paid Windle the balance on his account	
10	19	Bought a new office desk for cash	64
11	20	Paid wages	34
12	23	Cash sales	220
13	24	Paid office expenses	6
14	25	Spear paid on account	50
15	26	Cash sales	168
16	27	Paid wages	30
17	30	Cash sales	60

Required:
Enter these transactions in Fairburn's accounting records and test the arithmetical accuracy of your work by preparing a trial balance at 31 January 20X0.

Bank account

		£			£
	Balance b/d	686	(2)	Wages	24
(4)	Grime	36	(5)	Naik	42
(6)	Sales	128	(7)	Wages	28
(12)	Sales	220	(8)	Purchases	150
(14)	Spear	50	(9)	Windle	324
(15)	Sales	168	(10)	Fixtures and fittings	64
(17)	Sales	60	(11)	Wages	34
			(13)	Office expenses	6
			(16)	Wages	30
				Balance c/d	646
		1,348			1,348
	Balance b/d	646			

Capital account

	£		£
Balance c/d	2,098	Balance b/d	2,098
		Balance b/d	2,098

Fixtures and fittings account

	£		£
Balance b/d	396		
(10) Bank	64	Balance c/d	460
	460		460
Balance b/d	460		

Sales account

	£			£
		(1)	Spear	248
		(6)	Bank	128
		(12)	Bank	220
		(15)	Bank	168
Balance c/d	824	(17)	Bank	60
	824			824
			Balance b/d	824

Wages account

		£		£
(2)	Bank	24		
(7)	Bank	28		
(11)	Bank	34		
(16)	Bank	30	Balance c/d	116
		116		116
	Balance b/d	116		

Purchases account

		£		£
(3)	Windle	300		
(8)	Bank	150	Balance c/d	450
		450		450
	Balance b/d	450		

Office expenses account

		£		£
(13)	Bank	6	Balance c/d	6
		6		6
	Balance b/d	6		

Grime's account

	£			£
Balance b/d	36	(4)	Bank	36

Spear's account

		£			£
	Balance b/d	78	(14)	Bank	50
(1)	Sales	248		Balance c/d	276
		326			326
	Balance c/d	276			

Murta's account

	£		£
Balance b/d	52	Balance c/d	52
Balance b/d	52		

Windle's account

(9)	Bank	£ 324		Balance b/d	£ 24
			(3)	Purchases	300
		324			324

Naik's account

(5)	Bank	£ 42	Balance b/d	£ 42

Fairburn trial balance 31.1.20X0

	£ Dr	£ Cr
Bank	646	
Capital		2,098
Inventory	916	
Fixtures and fittings	460	
Sales		824
Wages	116	
Purchases	450	
Office expenses	6	
Debtors – Spear	276	
Murta	52	
	2,922	2,922

Summary

The evolution of double-entry bookkeeping has provided accountants with a method of processing data in a systematic manner, and with a means of checking the accuracy of accounting records which was built into its processes by virtue of the interlocking nature of the accounts system. At the end of an accounting period, it is axiomatic that the total debit entries must be equal to the total credit entries and vice versa.

With the advent of the computer, the usefulness of the double-entry method as a check on the accuracy of record keeping has largely disappeared. Nevertheless, double-entry bookkeeping remains the basis for recording financial transactions as flows of money, or of money value from one account to another, whether or not the accounts system is computerized.

Far more significant, however, as regards the usefulness of the data recorded in the double-entry system are the effects of accounting conventions, which require in particular that the values recorded should be determined by transactions.

1 Show the effects of the following transactions on the accounting equation. For this purpose, enter these transactions in columns as under:

Col 1	+	Col 2	=	Col 3
Capital		Liabilities		Assets
....		....		....
....		....		....

Transaction (a)   J Johnson opens a garage by investing £20,000 in cash in the business.

Transaction (b)   He borrows £5,000 from the bank.

Transaction (c)   He purchases petrol for £1,000 and pays in cash.

Transaction (d)   He buys equipment to the value of £10,000 and agrees to pay that amount within four weeks.

Transaction (e)   He purchases second-hand cars from Middleton Motors and pays £15,000, being the agreed amount.

Transaction (f)   Customers pay £2,000 for services rendered.

Transaction (g)   Wages paid amount to £1,000.

2 Show the accounting effects of the following transactions by reference to the balance sheet and the income statement. (Example: cash sale £200 would add £200 to revenue on the income statement and £200 to the asset cash on the balance sheet.)

	Accounting effects	
Transaction	*Balance sheet*	*Income statement*
Cash sales £400	....	....
Cash purchases £75	....	....
Received from trade debtor £35	....	....
Equipment purchased on credit terms £345	....	....
Invoice received for repairs to machinery £67	....	....
Wages paid £78	....	....
Payment of rent due last month £90	....	....
Equipment sold as scrap £20 (book value £10)	....	....
Loan received £600	....	....
Bank interest charged £49	....	....

3 Bill Cashing sets up practice as an architect, investing £10,000 of his own money into the business and effecting a transfer of that sum from his personal account to his business account at Barclays Bank Ltd. The transfer is effected on 1 January 20X0, the date on which he formally commences business. The following transactions take place in the following month:

Event

1	1 January	Paid office rent for January £200.
2	1 January	Purchased office equipment on account from Equipit Ltd £1,000.
3	1 January	Purchased office supplies on account from W Brown for £150.
4	3 January	Hired a junior out of school.
5	4 January	Surveyed a property for A Bond and sent out an invoice of £50.
6	7 January	Decided to transfer his own car to the business at a value of £2,000.
7	10 January	Bought petrol for £10, paid by cheque.
8	11 January	Took a client to lunch at a cost of £20, and was asked to prepare plans for a new factory for which work he estimated he would earn £1,200.
9	17 January	Conducted another property survey for A Bond and invoiced him for £60.
10	20 January	Took another prospective client to lunch at a cost of £30, and found that he would not be able to undertake work for that client.
11	30 January	Paid the office junior his monthly wage of £70.
12	30 January	Sent a cheque to Equipit Ltd for £1,000.
13	30 January	Sent a cheque to W Brown for office supplies £150.
14	30 January	Banked a cheque received from A Bond for £50.

Required:

Enter these transactions in Bill Cashing's accounting records, and test the arithmetical accuracy of your work by preparing a trial balance when you have completed the entries needed to be made.

4 As at 31 December 20X0, the accountant of AB Ltd extracted a trial balance from the firm's accounting records and, there being a difference, inserted a balancing figure in a suspense account.

Later, it was found that:

(a) a payment of £150 for stationery in the cash book had been posted in the ledger as £50;

(b) a total of £637 in the sales day book had been carried forward as £673;

(c) an amount of £60 paid to S Jones on 2 January 20X1 had been included in the purchase ledger balances shown in the trial balance;

(d) goods which cost £75 had been returned to R Brown and, while a correct entry had been made in the purchases returns book, £175 had been posted to the credit of R Brown's account in the sales ledger;

(e) at the beginning and end of the accounting period inventores were valued at £1,250 and £2,250 respectively. In error, the latter figure had been shown in the trial balance;

(f) discounts allowed amounting to £325 had been credited to the appropriate nominal ledger account;

(g) £256, being the amount of discounts received, had been debited to the nominal ledger as £265;

(h) cash at bank was shown in the trial balance as £350. In fact this was the balance shown by the bank statement which on 31 December 20X0 was £20 in excess of the bank balance correctly recorded in the cash book.

After rectification of the above discrepancies the books balanced.

Required:

Show journal entries necessary to correct the above errors and set out the suspense account as it would finally appear in the books.

5* (a) Harold Davies is the proprietor of a small building firm. He does not understand the term 'balance sheet' and asks you to explain to him whether the following items should be on his balance sheet. Indicate the nature of the items (e.g. current asset, long-term liability, not applicable, etc.) and give the reason for your answer.

    (i)   inventories of sand and cement;

    (ii)   air compressor purchased for cash;

    (iii) air compressor hired for three weeks;

    (iv) wages paid to labourer;

    (v)   lorry used for transporting materials;

    (vi) diesel fuel in lorry fuel tank;

    (vii) washing machine bought for Mrs Davies;

    (viii) bank overdraft;

    (ix) petty cash in hand;

    (x)   £2,000 owing to an uncle who says Harold need not pay until five years have elapsed.

  (b) Explain what effect the following transactions will have on a balance sheet to which they relate:

    (i)   Shareholders invest a further £20,000 in the company.

    (ii)   The company buys raw material for cash £1,200.

    (iii) The company buys raw material on credit £4,000.

    (iv) The company pays £5,000 to its creditors.

    (v)   The wages payable are paid £2,000.

6 Oliver commenced business on 1 June 20X0. The following transactions took place during the month of June.

Event	June	
1	1	Introduced cash of £4,000 and car valued at £1,750.
2	2	Bought goods for cash at a cost of £1,130.
3	8	Paid wages of £13 and sundry expenses of £2.
4	9	Sold goods on credit to Victor for £190.
5	14	Sold goods on credit to Susan for £240.
6	18	Bought goods on credit from William for £85.
7	22	Bought fixtures and fittings at a cost of £350.
8	25	Paid wages of £38.
9	26	Paid drawings to himself of £80.
10	30	Victor paid the full amount owing.
11	30	Paid rent of £500.

Required:

Enter these transactions in Oliver's accounting records and take out a trial balance at 30 June 20X0.

7 Richard started up a business as a butcher on 1 March 20X0. His transactions during March were:

1 Borrowed £10,000 from his father and paid the money into a business bank account.
2 Made cash purchases totalling £6,000.
3 Made cash sales totalling £8,000.
4 Bought a delivery bicycle for £140 cash.
5 Paid rent for one month £240.
6 Made credit purchases totalling £4,000 and by the end of the month had paid all but £1,000 of this amount.
7 Made credit sales totalling £7,600 and at the end of the month debtors still owed £3,400 of this amount.
8 Received a legacy of £2,000 and paid this into the business.
9 Paid for electricity for one month £180.
10 Drew £240 for his personal expenses.

Required:

Enter the transactions in Richard's accounting records and take out a trial balance at 31 March 20X0.

8* Simon is a retailer and on 1 June 20X0 his balance sheet was as follows:

	£	£		£	£
Capital		14,000	**Non-current assets**		
			Premises	10,000	
			Fixtures	2,000	12,000
Current liabilities			**Current assets**		
William	2,000		Inventories	5,000	
Paul	3,000	5,000	Debtor – Sam	600	
			Bank	1,400	7,000
		19,000			19,000

His transactions during June were:

June

1	Purchased goods on credit from William for £1,000.
2	Cash sales £2,000.
3	Sold items £600 on credit to Clare.
4	Paid William £600 on account.
5	Sam paid £560 in full settlement, which allowed him a discount of £40.
8	Cash sales £1,800.
9	Purchased fixtures £700 cash.

10	Sold goods on credit to Sam for £800.
11	Sold goods to Ann for £300.
16	Purchased goods on credit from Paul for £4,000.
17	Purchased items from William on credit for £2,000.
19	Paid Paul £6,600 in full settlement.
21	Returned goods cost £200 to William.
23	Returns received from Ann selling price £200.
26	Ann paid £90 in full settlement.
28	Cash sales £4,600.
30	Paid William £1,800 on account.

Required:

Enter these transactions in Simon's accounting records and take out a trial balance at 30 June 20X0.

Reference   Chopping, D. and Skerratt, L. (1995) *Applying GAAP 1995/96*, Accountancy Books.

Periodic measurement

CHAPTER 12

Double-entry bookkeeping and periodic measurement

Setting the scene

The accounts system is merely a repository of financial data about transactions. To be meaningful, this data must be extracted from the accounts system and organized in such a way that it is useful to those who need information for decision making. The two accounting statements employed for this purpose are the income statement for the year and the balance sheet as at the end of the year. This chapter examines the preliminary stages in the preparation of these statements.

Learning objectives

After studying this chapter you should be able to:

1   distinguish between revenue and capital expenses;

2   explain how revenue and expenses are attributed to the accounting period;

3   calculate accruals and prepayments and enter them in the accounting records.

Chapter 11 examined the double-entry method as a means of recording financial transactions as flows of money or of money value. Firms are continually involved in transactions, and this activity is mirrored in the double-entry bookkeeping process by the constant flow through the accounts system of the money or money values involved in those transactions.

The concept of periodicity, which was mentioned in Chapter 8, represents the view that, although the activities of a firm continue through time, and the decisions taken at one point in time cannot be separated from their effects whenever they materialize, nevertheless those activities should be regularly reported on. In other words, the financial health of a business should be tested at periodic intervals. The concept of periodicity poses problems in adapting the data recorded in the accounts system so that it will correctly reflect the result of the transactions concluded in the selected period, and the financial health of the firm at the end of that period.

Problems in periodic measurement

We noted when discussing the concept of periodicity in Chapter 8, not only that the transactions of a period should be identified, but also that the expenses attributable to those transactions should be matched with the revenues derived from them in accordance with the matching concept.

The first major problem, therefore, in adapting the information recorded in the accounts system has a twofold aspect, i.e. to identify:

1 the revenues attributable to transactions during the year;
2 the expenses related to those revenues.

The second major problem concerns adjustments which must be made in order to arrive at a measure of the surplus or deficit of revenues over expenses. These adjustments involve an element of judgement, for example, how much to provide for depreciation and bad debts, and what adjustments to make in respect of expected losses. Such adjustments are made because the end product is a statement of the income or loss made in the accounting period. We consider these problems in the next chapter.

Identifying the revenues and expenses of the period

The data recorded in the accounts system provides the basis for identifying the revenues and expenses of an accounting period. First, there must be extracted from the accounts system the data recorded in respect of all the transactions concluded in the period. As seen in Chapter 11 the summary of all the transactions is obtainable by means of a trial balance drawn up on the last day of the accounting period.

Example 12.1 The following trial balance was extracted from the books of John Smith on 31 December 20X0, being the end of the first year of trading.

	£ Dr	£ Cr
Capital		25,000
Motor vehicles	10,000	
Furniture and fittings	2,500	
Purchases	31,000	
Bank balance	6,000	
Sales		70,000
Debtors	18,000	
Creditors		3,500
Rent	4,500	
Salaries	22,800	
Insurances	400	
Motor expenses	2,000	
Light and heat	1,000	
General expenses	300	
	98,500	98,500

The meaning of revenue and expense

The trial balance does not distinguish between flows of income and flows of capital, neither does it make a distinction between expenditure incurred to earn revenue and expenditure on the acquisition of assets. The first problem is to identify the revenues of the year, and this is a matter of definition. By revenue we mean the flows of funds, that is money or rights to money, which have resulted from the trading activities of the business, as distinct from funds (capital) invested by the owner or loans made by creditors and others. In this case, the only revenue item shown on the trial balance is from sales amounting to £70,000. The second problem is to identify the expenses. We define revenue expenses as the costs of running the business during the accounting period. In contrast, capital expenses are the costs incurred in acquiring non-current assets or adding to the income-earning structure of the firm. The calculation of periodic income is by means of a formula which deducts expenses from revenues:

periodic income = revenues – expenses

Looking at the trial balance, the expenses of the year, as defined, are as follows:

	£
Purchases	31,000
Rent	4,500
Salaries	22,800
Insurances	400
Motor expenses	2,000
Light and heat	1,000
General expenses	300

An alternative definition of expenses is that adopted by accountants, who treat as expenses all those costs the benefit of which has been used up during the year. Looking at the expenses which we have identified in the trial balance, it is clear that the benefit derived by the firm from expenditure on these items is limited to the accounting period. The only exception is the goods purchased which have not been sold by the end of the year, and we discuss this problem in Chapter 14.

We have completed the first stage in periodic measurement by identifying the revenue and expenses attributable to the 'income-earning' transactions of the firm during the year, which we may list as follows:

	£		£
Purchases	31,000	Sales	70,000
Rent	4,500		
Salaries	22,800		
Insurance	400		
Motor expenses	2,000		
Light and heat	1,000		
General expenses	300		

Periodic measurement and the accruals concept

The next task of the accountant is to ensure that the revenues and expenses are attributable to the accounting period. It is the normal practice to record in the expense accounts only those amounts actually paid during the period. As a result, at the end of the period, these accounts may be understated or overstated. Likewise, it is possible that there may be some outstanding revenue due to the business, other than sales revenue, which must be brought into the year's income.

The governing principle which affects these adjustments is the accruals concept discussed in Chapter 8. The accruals concept, it will be recalled, makes a distinction between the receipt of cash and the right to receive cash, and the payment of cash and the legal obligation to pay cash. As there is often no coincidence in time between the creation of legal rights and obligations and the transfer of cash, it follows that the accountant must scrutinize the revenue and expenses accounts to make sure that amounts due and payable are accrued. Similarly, payments made in advance must be excluded and carried forward to the next accounting period. The adjustments are effected in the accounts themselves.

An accrued expense is a cost that has expired during the accounting period but has not been recognized in the accounts. Accrued expenses often include salaries, interest, business rent, taxes and other expenses. In the case of an accrued expense, both an expense and a liability exist at the end of the accounting period without having been recorded in the books. The nature of the problem becomes clear when we look at some examples.

The accrual of income

At the end of an accounting period, the total sales revenue will have been recorded in the accounts system, and the amounts unpaid by customers in respect of these sales will have been included under sundry debtors. The outstanding income which may not already have been recorded is limited, therefore, to income other than sales, such as rent receivable, commissions receivable, etc. The accountant must adjust his end-of-year figures so as to include all the income to which the business is legally entitled, even though it has not been received.

Example 12.2 On 1 December 20X0, John Smith had sublet a portion of his premises which had never been utilized for a monthly rent of £60 payable in advance on the first of each month. By 31 December 20X0, the date on which the trial balance was extracted, the rent receivable had not yet been received. To accrue the rent receivable, the accountant must enter the amount accrued in the rent receivable account as follows:

Rent receivable account

	20X0	£
	31 Dec Accrued	60

This amount is taken to the income statement as income for the year 20X0:

Rent receivable account

20X0	£	20X0	£
13 Dec Income statement	60	31 Dec Accrued c/d	60
	60		60
20X1			
1 Jan Accrued b/d	60		

Students are often puzzled that rent receivable should be a credit. The reason is that the rent receivable account is used to denote the source of a flow of funds so that there is a flow out from the rent receivable account into the cash account. Let us assume that on 1 January 20X1, the rent outstanding is paid. The entries would be as follows:

Rent receivable account

20X1	£	20X1	£
1 Jan Accrued b/d	60	1 Jan Cash	60

Cash book

20X1	£		
1 Jan Rent receivable	60		

In adjusting the receipts for the year so that they will correctly show the income of the year, the accountant accrues income not yet received, as we have seen above, but also carries forward to the following year any receipts of the current year which are the income of the following year.

If, however, there had been an omission of income from the accounts of the preceding year, and this income is received in the current year, it would not be practical to go back and adjust the accounts of the previous year. Those accounts will have been closed at the end of that accounting period. The accountant will include last year's income in the current year's account, and indicate that it was an omission from last year, or explain how this income arose. Adjustments of this nature often arise out of the settlement of legal disputes or compensation claims.

The accrual of expenses

The accrual of expenses occurs much more frequently than the accrual of income, for it is the nature of things that firms delay the payment of expenses. As a result, nominal accounts such as rent, insurance, wages, light and heat, etc. have to be adjusted to show the total payments due and payable in respect of the accounting year. Occasionally, however, firms are obliged to pay in advance for services, so that there is a possibility that a portion of the payment relates to the next accounting period. Accordingly, the accrual of expenses involves two types of adjustments:

1 an accrual in respect of expenses of the year which have not yet been paid;
2 an exclusion from the recorded expenses of that part which relates to the next year.

Example 12.3 Let us return to the trial balance extracted from John Smith's books. We are informed that:

1 The yearly rent is £6,000 payable quarterly. The rent of £1,500 payable on 1 December had not been paid.
2 Insurance premiums paid amounting to £400 included a payment of £50 in respect of a new policy taken out on 31 December 20X0.

It is clear, therefore, that the legal obligation in respect of the rent is understated in the rent account by £1,500. Equally, the insurance premiums applicable to the year ended 31 December 20X0 amount to £350 and not £400. It is necessary to adjust these accounts as follows:

1 to increase the rent chargeable as an expense by £1,500;
2 to decrease the insurance chargeable as an expense by £50.

Underpayment of rent

Let us assume that the rent payments were made on due date as follows:

Rent account

20X0		£	
1 Feb	Cash	1,500	
1 May	Cash	1,500	
1 Aug	Cash	1,500	

The amount which should be charged against the income for the year ended 31 December 20X0 is £6,000. The rent unpaid at 31 December 20X0 may be accrued as follows:

Rent account

20X0		£	
1 Feb	Cash	1,500	
1 May	Cash	1,500	
1 Aug	Cash	1,500	
31 Dec	Accrued	1,500	

Having made this adjustment, the rent account for the year ended 31 December 20X0 may be closed by transferring the rent of £6,000 to the income statement for the year ended 31 December 20X0. The rent unpaid is, of course, a liability of the firm on 31 December 20X0, and is shown by bringing down the amount accrued as a credit balance on the rent account. The adjusted rent account will appear as follows:

Rent account

20X0		£	20X0		£
1 Feb	Cash	1,500	31 Dec	Income statement	6,000
1 May	Cash	1,500			
1 Aug	Cash	1,500			
31 Dec	Accrued c/d	1,500			
		6,000			6,000
			20X1		
			1 Jan	Accrued b/d	1,500

We note the rent outstanding at 31 December 20X0 is £1,500, and we have brought this amount down to show:

1 that there is a credit balance outstanding at 31 December 20X0;
2 that on 1 January 20X1 there is an outstanding liability in respect of the previous year, so that the firm will have to pay £7,500 during the year ended 31 December 20X1.

The trial balance on 31 December 20X0 may now be adjusted as follows:

	£	£
Rent	6,000	
Rent accrued		1,500

If the firm pays the rent outstanding on 2 January 20X1, and thereafter pays the rent on due date, the rent account for the year 20X1 will appear as follows:

Rent account

20X1		£	20X1		£
2 Jan	Cash	1,500	1 Jan	Accrued b/d	1,500
1 Feb	Cash	1,500	31 Dec	Income statement	6,000
1 May	Cash	1,500			
1 Aug	Cash	1,500			
1 Dec	Cash	1,500			
		7,500			7,500

Prepayment of insurance

For certain services, payments are made before the associated benefits are received, i.e. the payment is made in advance. In these cases an arithmetic apportionment of the amount paid must be made between the two consecutive accounting periods.

Let us assume that the insurance premiums were paid in advance as follows:

1 January 20X0	£350
31 December 20X0	50
	£400

These transactions will be shown in the insurance account as follows:

Insurance account

20X0		£	
1 Jan	Cash	350	
31 Dec	Cash	50	

The premium paid on 31 December 20X0 is the prepayment of an expense for the year ending 31 December 20X1. Hence, it cannot be shown as an expense for the year ended 31 December 20X0. Thus the purpose of the adjustment is:

1 to measure the expense applicable to the year ended 31 December 20X0, and to transfer this amount to the income statement for that year;
2 to carry forward the premium paid in advance to the following year.

The adjusted account will appear as follows:

Insurance account

20X0		£	20X0		£
1 Jan	Cash	350	31 Dec	Income statement	350
31 Dec	Cash	50	31 Dec	Prepaid c/d	50
		400			400
20X1					
1 Jan	Prepaid b/d	50			

We may note that the insurance prepaid at 31 December 20X0 is brought down as a debit balance on 1 January 20X1, and as a result:

1 there is a debit balance in favour of the firm on 31 December 20X0;
2 the firm will not have to pay the premium of £50 in the subsequent year, if the yearly premium is only due and payable on 1 January each year.

The trial balance on 31 December 20X0 may now be adjusted to read as follows:

	£	£
Insurance	350	
Insurance prepaid	50	

Assuming that the firm pays the insurance premium in the following year on the due date, the insurance account for that year will be as follows:

Insurance account

20X1		£	20X1		£
1 Jan	Prepaid b/d	50	31 Dec	Income statement	400
1 Jan	Cash	350			
		400			400

The reader will observe how easily the accounts system permits the adjustments made in respect of the accruals of revenue and expenses to be reconciled with the subsequent receipts and payment of cash. Although we have interfered with the recording process in order to adjust the accounts so as to reflect the true picture at the end of the accounting period, the double-entry system continues to record the accounting flows and is not itself affected by the adjustments which have been made.

The results of the accrual adjustments

The reader will recall that the trial balance is merely a working paper which the accountant uses to extract the information which he requires from the accounts system, and to check its accuracy. We may alter the original details shown on the first trial balance to reflect the adjustments which we have so far made.

Example 12.4 The adjusted trial balance for John Smith's business as at 31 December 20X0 may be set out as follows:

	£ Dr	£ Cr
Capital		25,000
Motor vehicles	10,000	
Furniture and fittings	2,500	
Purchases	31,000	
Bank balance	6,000	
Sales		70,000
Debtors	18,060	
Creditors		3,500
Rent	6,000	
Rent accrued		1,500
Insurance	350	
Insurance prepaid	50	
Salaries	22,800	
Motor expenses	2,000	
Light and heat	1,000	
General expenses	300	
Rent receivable		60
	100,060	100,060

The effect of these adjustments on the revenues and expenses for the year ended 31 December 20X0 may be summarized as follows:

	£		£
Purchases	31,000	Sales	70,000
Rent	6,000	Rent receivable	60
Salaries	22,800		
Insurance	350		
Motor expenses	2,000		
Light and heat	1,000		
General expenses	300		

It will be noted also that the adjustments have given rise to the following balances on the accounts:

	£ Dr	£ Cr
Rent accrued		1,500
Insurance prepaid	50	
Rent receivable	60	

As these balances represent sums owing by the business and debts due to the business, they will be shown, as we shall see in Chapter 14, as liabilities and assets respectively at the end of the accounting period.

The matching of revenues and expenses

The purpose underlying the accountant's efforts to identify and correctly measure the revenues and expenses of an accounting period is to attempt to match them so as to obtain a measure of the 'financial effort' of earning the revenues of that period. The matching of expenses and revenues is far more complicated than appears at first sight. So far, we have assumed that by correctly measuring the revenues and expenses attributable to the accounting year they have been correctly matched. In other words, we have made the assumption that the expenses of the accounting period are the expenses related to the revenues of that period. The realization concept permits the accountant to recognize only financial results in the form of sales revenues. It is well known that there is a time-lag between buying or manufacturing goods for sale and selling them. At the end of an accounting period, therefore, there will always be goods awaiting sale and raw materials unused. The expenses attributable to unsold goods and unused materials, usually described as inventories, must be excluded from the expenses of the period and carried forward to the next accounting period, when the goods will have been sold and the materials used. The importance of inventory adjustments to the correct measurement of periodic income is crucial.

Example 12.5 Mr Hancock's trial balance at 31 December 20X0 included the following debits:

	£
Rent	1,800
Business rates	760
Light and heating	1,180
Insurance	520

Rent of £600 for the last three months of 20X0 had not been paid and no entry had been made in the books. Of the rates, £560 was for the year ended 31 March 20X1. The remaining £200 was for the three months ended 31 March 20X0. In accordance with the matching concept the rates included in the income statement would be £200 + (£560 × $^3/_4$) = £620.

Fuel had been delivered on 10 December 20X0 at a cost of £30 and had been consumed before the end of 20X0. The invoice had been received for this fuel in 20X0; however, no entry had been made in the records of the business. £70 of the insurance paid was in respect of insurance cover for the year 20X1.

135

The above information would be recorded in the following accounts which show transfers to the income statement for the year ended 31 December 20X0.

Rent account

		£			£
31 Dec	Balance b/d	1,800	31 Dec	Income statement	2,400
31 Dec	Balance c/d	600			
		2,400			2,400
			1 Jan	Balance b/d	600

Rates account

		£			£
31 Dec	Balance b/d	760	31 Dec	Income statement	620
			31 Dec	Balance c/d	140
		760			760
1 Jan	Balance b/d	140			

Light and heating account

		£			£
31 Dec	Balance b/d	1,180	31 Dec	Income statement	1,210
31 Dec	Balance c/d	30			
		1,210			1,210
				Balance b/d	30

Insurance account

		£			£
31 Dec	Balance b/d	520	31 Dec	Income statement	450
			31 Dec	Balance c/d	70
		520			520
1 Jan	Balance b/d	70			

Inventory adjustments

By definition, the closing inventory at the end of an accounting period is the residue of the purchases of that period which remains unsold or unused.

Example 12.6 John Smith's purchases account includes all goods purchased during the year ended 31 December 20X0. At the end of the year, the inventory of materials unused is quantified, and its cost price is valued at £3,000. The accounting problems relating to this inventory are as follows:

1 Since the business has to pay for all goods purchased, it would be imprudent to reduce the purchases account by the amount of inventory at the end of the year. Hence, the purchases account must not be adjusted and the total purchases must be charged as expenses.

2 By charging all purchases against sales, however, the income for the year would be understated by £3,000. Means must be found, therefore, to take the closing inventory out of the income calculation. This is effected by opening an inventory account on 31 December 20X0 and posting the inventory to it.

Inventory account

20X0	£	
31 Dec	3,000	

As soon as an account is opened for the purpose of recording a flow of value it is necessary to describe the source of the flow and its destination. We know that the purchases account is not the source of the flow of inventory to the inventory account, because we have deliberately refused to adjust the purchases account. We need to value inventories in order to calculate the income or loss for the period. The accountant states that the inventory adjustment comes from the income statement which is employed to measure income. The full accounting entries are, therefore, as follows:

Income statement for the year ended 31 December 20X0

		20X0	£
		31 Dec Inventory	3,000

Inventory account

20X0	£	
31 Dec Income statement	3,000	

The effect of these entries is to solve the problem of income measurement, because the *credit* flow from the income statement is taken into the calculation of income, as follows:

	£		£
Purchases	31,000	Sales	70,000
		Closing inventory	3,000

The inventory account is an interesting account because it exists to measure income and since that is done on the last day of the accounting year, the inventory account only exists for one day. In fact, the closing inventoy on the last day of the year is the opening inventory on the first day of the next accounting year. Hence, on the first day of the next accounting period, the inventory must be posted to the income statement of the next period, as follows:

Income statement for the year ended 31 December 20X1

20X1	£	
1 Jan Inventory	3,000	

Inventory account

20X0	£	20X1	£
31 Dec Income statement	3,000	1 Jan Income statement	3,000

The reader will now observe that the inventory account has served its purpose and may be closed. This is done by drawing a double line beneath the entries.

Inventory account

20X0	£	20X1	£
31 Dec Income statement	3,000	1 Jan Income statement	3,000

In practice, the accountant will not reverse the inventory into the income statement of the year 20X1 until 31 December 20X1 when s/he prepares that account. As a result, the trial balance for the year ended 31 December 20X1 will include a debit balance in respect of the inventory account in the amount of £3,000. As the trial balance is always extracted before the inventory adjustment is made, the opening inventory always appears on the trial balance but the closing inventory is never shown.

Summary

In this section of Part 2, we consider the procedural problems involved in periodic measurement. This chapter deals with the problems of adapting the financial accounting data lodged in the data-processing system to the objective of measuring periodic income.

The first stages in the measurement of periodic income are:

1 the identification of the revenues attributable to transactions concluded in the accounting period;
2 the identification of the expenses related to those revenues.

The accruals concept requires the inclusion of amounts receivable and payable, as well as amounts received and paid, in the measurement of revenues and expenses. We examined the accounting procedures involved in accruing revenue and expenses.

The objective of periodic measurement is the matching of revenues and expenses to establish accounting income. The exclusion of inventory unsold at the end of the accounting period is a further problem in periodic measurement considered in this chapter.

Self-assessment question

1 State the concepts which apply to the manner in which periodic revenues and expenses are identified and related. Illustrate your answer.

Problems *(* indicates that a solution is to be found in the Lecturer's Guide)*

1 If goods which cost £10,000 were in inventory on 1 January, goods purchased during the year amounted to £40,000 and goods costing £15,000 were in inventory at 31 December, state the cost of the goods which were sold during the year.

2 From the following information construct the combined Rent and Rates Account for the year ended 30 June 20X1 showing the figures that would appear for rent and rates in the income statement and the figures that would appear in the balance sheet as at 30 June 20X1.

The property of the business was rented at £1,600 per annum payable quarterly in arrears on the usual quarter days. The rates were £600 per annum payable half yearly in advance on 1 October and 1 April in each year. The rent was one quarter in arrears on 30 June 20X0 and the rates for the half year to 30 September 20X0 had not been paid.

The following transactions took place during the year to 30 June 20X1:

20X0

July 2 Cash – One quarter's rent to 24 June 20X0
July 2 Cash – Half year's rates to 30 September 20X0
Oct 10 Cash – Half year's rates to 31 March 20X1
Oct 10 Cash – One quarter's rent to 29 September 20X0

20X1

Jan 4 Cash – One quarter's rent to 25 December 20X0
April 6 Cash – Half year's rates to 30 September 20X1
April 6 Cash – One quarter's rent to 25 March 20X1

3* Star Enterprises Ltd is a company formed to manage the affairs of a successful pop group. All the group's revenue and expenses are recorded in the company's books. The group's recording contract with IME Records stipulates a payment of advance royalties of £50,000 on the recording of a record. Actual royalties are 50p per record. Any sales in excess of 100,000 copies will result in additional royalties being paid. If sales are less than 100,000, then any excess advance is recouped from future payments.

During the year ended 31 March 20X1 the company received the following royalties:

	£	£
Advance Record 1		50,000
Advance Record 2	50,000	
Less: Shortfall on Record 1	17,000	33,000
Additional royalties Record 2		44,000
Advance Record 3		50,000

Record 3 was recorded and released shortly before the year end. No sales figures are yet available.

The company has also incurred advance expenditure of £35,000 on promoting a tour the group will undertake during April 20X1.

Required:

(a) State the accounting principles which are used in revenue and expense recognition.

(b) Write a report to the management of the company advising on the treatment of royalties and advance expenditure, and showing how these items will be treated in the accounts to 31 March 20X1.   (Problem supplied by A J Naughton)

4 Norman is preparing a statement of income for the year ended 31 December 20X0. The following payments and income appear as balances on their individual ledger accounts:

	£	
Rent	300	Rent is payable £100 per quarter in arrears.
Telephone	60	The last quarter's bill is outstanding.
Rates	400	Rates of £200 were paid for a half-year from 1 October 20X0.
Insurance	100	Premium paid for year from 31 March 20X0.
Electricity	80	Last bill paid on 31 October 20X0.
Rent receivable	500	Rent receivable £100 per quarter in advance.
Commission receivable	300	Commission of £200 due from September to 31 December 20X0 not yet received.

Required:

Prepare ledger accounts and balance off all relevant debtors and creditors. Assume no opening debtors and creditors; all adjustments to be calculated on a time basis. The rateable year runs from 6 April to 5 April (i.e. for accounts purposes April to March).

5* Alistair rents three shops and maintains one account for rent and rates for all three premises. The rents are fixed for each year and increases take effect as from 1 January.

At 1 January 20X0, he had paid all of the rent up to date, but there was a prepayment in relation to rates of £1,100.

During the year ended 31 December 20X0 he made the following payments:

Date	Shop	£	
10 January	A	540	Rent for January 20X0–June 20X0
10 April	A	800	Rates for April 20X0–March 20X1
3 July	A	540	Rent for July 20X0–December 20X0
29 December	A	600	Rent for January 20X1–June 20X1
3 February	B	1,200	Rent for January 20X0–December 20X0
28 March	B	1,060	Rates for April 20X0–March 20X1
6 January	C	350	Rent for January 20X0–March 20X0
24 March	C	1,600	Rates for April 20X0–March 20X1
15 May	C	350	Rent for April 20X0–June 20X0
10 September	C	350	Rent for July 20X0–September 20X0

Required:

Write up the rent and rates account for 20X0 showing the total income statement charge.

CHAPTER 13

Losses in asset values and periodic measurement

Setting the scene

High-tech hearing aid supplier Hidden Hearing has suffered a sharp setback, with news that an accounting 'error' will drag its interim results into the red. Directors expect to report a loss up to £100,000 for the half year, after providing for auditor's costs and also a £200,000 termination payment for its finance director. The accounting 'error', which was the use of a lower depreciation rate than required on computer equipment, also saw the restatement of 1999 annual pre-tax income from £2.03m to £1.43m.

The company sells advanced and unobtrusive hearing aids which are designed and fitted for customers at between £700 and £2,400 a pair.

(*The Daily Telegraph*, 27 December 1999)

Learning objectives

After studying this chapter you should be able to:

1 explain the nature of depreciation;

2 calculate depreciation and incorporate the figures in the accounting records;

3 account for the disposal of non-current assets;

4 make adjustments for bad and doubtful debts.

In the previous chapter, various adjustments to the data in the double-entry book-keeping system were discussed in order that these data might correctly reflect the income and expenses appropriate to the activities conducted during the accounting period in question. The accrual of revenues and expenses involved the exclusion of payments and receipts for other periods.

This chapter discusses the accounting adjustments made in respect of losses in asset values. The first adjustment concerns the depreciation of non-current assets. The second is the loss in the value of debtors resulting from the recognition that some debtor balances will not be paid and must be treated as bad debts, and that a further portion may ultimately prove to be bad, requiring making a provision for doubtful debts.

The treatment of losses in asset values

The concept of prudence requires that losses should be recognized as soon as they become evident to ensure that income and capital values are not overstated in financial reports. Losses in asset values appear under a variety of guises. Losses of cash and of inventory by theft, embezzlement or accidental damage are written off immediately against income, insurance recoveries being treated as a separate matter. Losses to non-current assets due to accidental damage, theft or other causes are also written off against income, as are losses arising on the sale of non-current assets which result from a difference between the sale price and the book value of the assets sold. (The book value means the value according to the accounting records.) Most non-current assets also diminish in value as their usefulness is exhausted over a period of years. Finally, losses in asset values also result from the exercise of judgement, as in the case of bad debts when accountants have to decide whether a recorded value does exist at all.

Losses in the value of non-current assets

Losses in the value of non-current assets arising through sale, accidental loss or theft present no difficulties from an accounting viewpoint, for such losses are written off immediately against income. By contrast, the diminution in value described as depreciation has been the subject of much controversy. Depreciation is of a complex nature and now occupies an important role in three different areas of the subject. First, it is related to the problem of cost allocation, both as regards the matching of revenues and expenses in the process of income measurement, and as regards product costing in management accounting. Second, it is related to the concept of capital maintenance in income theory. Third, it is central to decision making as regards the life and the replacement of non-current assets. The notion of depreciation has varied and multiplied in such a way that its analysis is not an easy matter. In this chapter, we take a limited view of depreciation, and concern ourselves solely with its financial accounting implications.

The nature of depreciation

The term 'depreciation' is susceptible to four different meanings:

1 a fall in price;
2 physical deterioration;
3 a fall in value;
4 an allocation of non-current asset costs.

Depreciation as a fall in price

A fall in the price of an asset is one aspect of depreciation, but it is not a reliable guide to a valid accounting concept of depreciation. A fall in price may occur independently of any decrease in the usefulness of an asset, for example the immediate fall in price occurring on the purchase of a new asset.

Depreciation as physical deterioration

Depreciation in this sense means impaired utility arising directly through deterioration or indirectly through obsolescence. It is implied in much of the discussion of this concept of depreciation that an asset is 'used up', so that the 'use' of an asset is the extent to which it has been used up. It is evident that these ideas are represented in the rates of depreciation which are attached to depreciable assets. It should be noted, however, that an asset is not necessarily 'used up' through use, because adequate maintenance may prevent deterioration in some cases. Thus, for example, if irrigation ditches are well maintained, they will not deteriorate through use.

The concept of depreciation as deferred maintenance has not been properly investigated, although it is a concept of depreciation which may be more relevant than conventional concepts as regards certain types of assets.

Depreciation as a fall in value

There are problems associated with the use of the term 'value' and the relationship of depreciation to the concept of value. Value may mean 'cost value', 'exchange value', 'use value' (utility) or 'esteem value'. Clearly, 'cost value' is not affected by events occurring after acquisition, so that it is not meaningful to relate depreciation in this sense to a fall in cost value. 'Exchange value' changes only twice in the experience of the owner of an asset – at the point of purchase and at the point of sale. In this sense, depreciation may mean only a fall in price between two points, and we have already discussed this concept of depreciation. Depreciation as a decrease in utility is also already covered by the concept of physical deterioration, while the notion of the esteem value of an asset is entirely subjective and not amenable to an objective concept of measurement.

If one attempts to relate the notion of depreciation to economic income, however, one would have the basis of an accounting concept of particular usefulness for decision making. The economic value of an asset is regarded as the discounted value of expected future cash flows associated with that asset in a particular use (Irving Fisher, 1906). Hence, depreciation may be conceptualized and measured as the progressive decrease in the net cash flows yielded by the asset as its economic utility declines through time, for whatever reason. Normally its income-earning capacity falls due to increasing inefficiency arising from physical deterioration. As regards certain classes of assets, for example computers, falls in economic value have occurred more rapidly from obsolescence.

Depreciation as cost allocation

The orthodox view of accountants is that depreciation represents that part of the cost of a non-current asset which is not recoverable when the asset is finally retired from use. Provision for this loss of capital is an integral cost of conducting the business during the effective commercial life of the asset and is not dependent upon the amount of income earned.

The practice of treating depreciation as an allocation of historical cost is based on the assumptions that:

1 the expected benefit to be derived from an asset is proportional to an estimated usage rate;
2 it is possible to measure that benefit.

The current practice is part of the procedure of matching periodic revenues with the cost of earning those revenues. The essential difference between non-current assets and current operating expenses is that the former are regarded as costs which yield benefits over a period of years, and hence must be allocated as expenses against the revenues of those years, whereas the latter yield all their benefits in the current year and may be treated as the expenses of that year and matched against the revenues which they have helped create.

The practice of treating depreciation as an allocation of costs presents a number of difficult theoretical problems. The known objective facts about an asset are few, and adequate records are not usually kept of the various incidents during the useful life of an asset apart from its purchase price. Repair and maintenance costs, for example, are charged separately, as are running costs. Other unresolved problems concern the selection of appropriate bases for allocating the cost of depreciable assets; for example should depreciation be calculated by reference to units of actual use rather than the passage of time? Finally, should the residual value of an asset be regarded as a windfall gain at the end of its useful life, should it be set off against the replacement cost of the asset, or should it be used as a point of reference for calculating the proportion of the cost of non-current assets allocated as depreciation?

The accounting concept of depreciation

According to the AICPA, depreciation accounting is 'a system of accounting which aims to distribute the cost . . . of tangible capital assets, less salvage (if any), over the estimated useful life of the unit . . . in a systematic and rational manner. It is a process of allocation, not of valuation' (AICPA, 1953).

From the foregoing definition, two important points may be made:

1 Depreciation accounting is not concerned with any attempt to measure the value of an asset at any point of time. One is trying to measure the value of the benefit the asset has provided during a given accounting period, and that benefit is valued as a portion of the cost of the asset. Hence, the balance sheet value of depreciable assets is that portion of the original cost which has not yet been allocated as a periodic expense in the process of income measurement. It does not purport to represent the current value of those assets.

2 Depreciation accounting does not itself provide funds for the replacement of depreciable assets, but the charging of depreciation ensures the maintenance intact of the original money capital of the entity. Thus, if £100 is paid out of capital to acquire an asset and at the end of year 1 depreciation is charged at 20 per cent, it follows that £20 is retained out of net income and not distributed. The original money capital of £100 is maintained at the end of year 1, consisting of £80 remaining of the original money value of the asset plus £20 retained out of income. Note, however, that a provision for depreciation is not identified with cash or any specific asset or assets.

Factors in the measurement of depreciation

Four factors are important in the process of measuring depreciation from an accounting viewpoint, as follows:

1 identifying the cost of the asset;
2 ascertaining its useful life;
3 determining the expected residual value;
4 selecting an appropriate method of depreciation which must be systematic and rational.

Identifying the cost of the asset

Depreciation is calculated on historical cost values, which include acquisition costs and all incidental costs involved in bringing an asset into use. In the case of buildings, for example, cost includes any commissions, survey, legal and other charges involved in the purchase, together with the costs incurred in preparing and modifying buildings for a particular use. In the case of plant and machinery, all freight, insurance and installation costs should be capitalized.

Problems occur where a firm manufactures assets, for example, if an engineering firm constructs a foundry. In such cases, the cost of labour, materials, etc. associated with the activity of construction should be segregated from those associated with the normal trading activities, and capitalized. Ascertaining such costs is not a trivial matter. Moreover, improvements to existing assets should also be capitalized. The distinction between a repair and an improvement is not always easy to establish. In some circumstances, the intention may be to repair but the cheaper solution is a replacement. An old boiler, for example, may be replaced more cheaply than repaired. The cost of repairs is chargeable as a current expense: the cost of replacement is an investment and should be capitalized.

Ascertaining the useful life of an asset

The useful life of an asset is defined as that period during which it is expected to be useful in the income-earning operations of the firm. In most cases, the useful life is determined by two factors:

1 the rate of deterioration;
2 obsolescence.

The rate of deterioration is a function of the type of use to which the asset is put, and the extent of that use. A lorry used by civil engineering contractors may have a shorter life expectancy than a lorry employed by cartage contractors, for the former may operate in rough terrain, whereas the latter is used on roads. It is not unusual to find that the estimated useful life of a lorry in the first case may be two years or less, whereas the estimated life in the second may well be four years. Moreover, an asset used intensively will have a shorter life than one used less frequently. In this respect, assets are built to certain specifications which determine to some extent their durability in use. The useful life is determined on the basis of past experience, which is a good indicator of the probable life of a particular asset.

It should be pointed out, however, that the estimated useful life of an asset is also a question of policy and may be determined accordingly. Thus, a car-hire firm may decide to renew its fleet each year, and in this case the useful life of its fleet of cars is one year for the purpose of calculating depreciation.

The problem of taking obsolescence into account in assessing the useful life of an asset is altogether more complex, for obsolescence occurs with the appearance of an asset incorporating the result of technological developments. In respect of certain assets, such as cars, each year may see the introduction of an improved model, so that owners of fleets of cars may decide that obsolescence, or assumed obsolescence, is a more important factor in the useful life of cars than depreciation. Relying on new models or improved versions each year, a firm may decide to renew its fleet each year. However, it is hard to distinguish the extent to which such decisions are influenced by the need to have the latest product or to avoid excessive repair bills stemming from large mileages. It would seem, therefore, that obsolescence is one factor which affects the useful life of non-current assets and accelerates their progress towards the scrapheap. Accordingly, the estimated useful life of an asset is determined by that length of time for which, as a matter of policy, it is wished to employ an asset. That length of time will be a function of a number of factors, but the most important will be the increasing cost of employing that asset due to higher yearly maintenance cost and possible declining revenues.

From a theoretical point of view, there is a point at which the net cash inflows associated with an asset are equal to the costs of operating that asset. Those costs may be expressed as the opportunity costs represented by revenues forgone as a result of using that asset rather than replacing it, or the opportunity costs represented by alternative returns which may be derived from cash outlays committed to repairs and maintenance. These two measures of opportunity cost are not necessarily equivalent. In terms of this analysis, the length of useful life of an asset would be determined as in Figure 13.1.

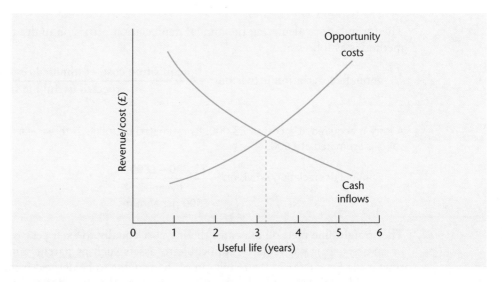

Figure 13.1

Determining the expected residual value

The residual value of an asset is estimated at the time of acquisition so that the net cost may be allocated to the accounting periods during which the asset is usefully employed. The residual value is the expected realizable value of the asset at the end of its useful life. Hence, the residual value will depend on the manner and on the length of time that the asset is to be used. Where, for example, it is intended to use an asset until it is completely worn out or obsolete, its residual value will be negligible. Where, as in the case of the replacement of fleets of cars, the length of useful life is shortened to one year, the residual value will be higher.

Where it is intended to extract the maximum use from an asset, the residual value should be nominal: where it is intended to replace the asset when it still has some useful life, its residual value should be estimated on a conservative basis so as to minimize the effect of variations in the price of second-hand assets. The cost allocated against the revenues of the accounting periods involved are calculated as follows:

	£
Cost of acquisition (say)	£2,000
Residual value (say)	200
Cost to be allocated as depreciation	1,800

Selecting the method of depreciation

There are several methods of depreciation but the most common are the straight-line method and the decreasing-balance method.

The matching concept requires that 'the choice of the method of allocating the cost of a long-term asset over its effective working life should depend upon the pattern of expected benefits obtainable in each period from its use' (Barton, 1984).

(a) The straight-line method

The formula for calculating the annual depreciation provision under the straight-line method is as follows:

$$\text{annual depreciation provision} = \frac{\text{acquisition cost} - \text{estimated residual value}}{\text{expected useful life in years}}$$

Example 13.1 A lorry is acquired at a cost of £3,000. Its estimated useful life is three years, and its residual value is estimated at £600.

$$\text{annual depreciation provision} = \frac{£3,000 - £600}{3 \text{ years}}$$
$$= £800 \text{ per annum}$$

The straight-line method allocates the net cost equally to each year of the useful life of an asset. It is particularly applicable to assets such as patents and leases where time is the key factor in the reduction of the benefits to be derived from the use of an asset. Although the method is in general use for other non-current assets, it suffers from the following disadvantages:

1 it does not reflect the fact that the greatest loss in the market value occurs in the first year of use;
2 it does not reflect the unevenness of the loss in the market value over several years;
3 it does not reflect the diminishing losses in value which occur in later years, as the asset approaches the end of its useful life.

For these reasons, the straight-line method of depreciation does not provide an accurate measure of the cost of the service potential allocated to the respective accounting periods during which an asset is employed.

(b) The decreasing-balance method

To calculate the annual depreciation provision under this method, a fixed percentage is applied to the balance of the net costs not yet allocated as an expense at the end of the previous accounting period. The balance of unallocated costs decreases each year, and, theoretically, the balance of the unallocated costs at the end of the estimated useful life should equal the estimated residual value. The formula used to calculate the fixed percentage to be applied to the allocation of net costs as depreciation is:

$$r = 1 - n\sqrt{\frac{s}{c}}$$

where n = the expected useful life in years
s = the residual value (this value must be significant or the depreciation rate will be nearly one)
c = the acquisition cost
r = the rate of depreciation to be applied.

Example 13.2   Calculate the rate of depreciation to be applied to a lorry acquired at a cost of £3,000, having an expected useful life of three years and an estimated residual value of £600.

$$r = 1 - 3\sqrt{\frac{£600}{£3,000}}$$

$$= 0.4152 \text{ or } 41.52\%$$

The depreciation calculation for each of the three years would be as follows:

		£
	Cost	3,000
Year 1	Depreciation at 41.52% of £3,000	1,246
	Unallocated costs end of year 1	1,754
Year 2	Depreciation at 41.52% of £1,754	728
	Unallocated costs end of year 2	1,026
Year 3	Depreciation at 41.52% of £1,026	426
	Residual value at end of year 3	600

In practice, the annual percentage rate of depreciation is not calculated so precisely. A rate is selected which approximates to the estimated useful life, for example an estimated useful life of three years would imply a $33\frac{1}{3}$ per cent rate of depreciation. The advantage of the decreasing-balance method is that it approximates reality in respect of certain assets, for example motor vehicles, where the depreciation calculated in the first year is greatest, thereby reflecting the greater loss in market value at this stage of a vehicle's life.

Depreciation and total asset costs

The total costs associated with the benefits derived from non-current assets consist of depreciation and the costs of repairs and maintenance. It follows that the proper application of the matching concept to the allocation of total asset costs requires that depreciation and repairs and maintenance be considered jointly as regards the selection of an appropriate method for allocating total asset costs to the accounting periods benefiting from their use. The depreciation calculated under the two methods which have been examined may be compared in Figures 13.2 and 13.3.

Figure 13.2

Figure 13.3

The cost of repairs and maintenance may be assumed to increase through time, as the asset deteriorates through use. This is reflected in real life by the expectation that the first year in use should be relatively trouble free. The pattern of repair and maintenance cost is illustrated in Figure 13.4. The total annual assets costs under the straight-line and decreasing-balance methods of depreciation may be compared as in Figures 13.5 and 13.6.

Figure 13.4

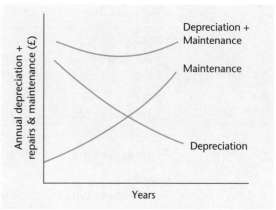

Figure 13.5   **Figure 13.6**

From the foregoing illustrations, it may be seen that the decreasing-balance method provides a better allocation of total asset costs over the useful life of an asset than the straight-line method.

Accounting for depreciation

There are several methods for providing for depreciation. Legislation requires that the following information in respect of non-current assets be shown on the balance sheet:

1 the cost or valuation, as the case may be;
2 the aggregate amount provided or written off since the date of acquisition or valuation, as the case may be, for depreciation or diminution in value.

The net book value of non-current assets is the difference between 1 and 2 above.

Example 13.3 The historical cost of plant and machinery is £100,000. Accumulated depreciation to date is £60,000 and the net book value is, therefore, £40,000. This information is disclosed as follows:

Non-current assets	Cost	Accumulated depreciation	Net book value
	£	£	£
Plant and machinery	100,000	60,000	40,000

The accounting procedure required to generate this information is to debit the acquisition cost, or valuation as the case may be, in the asset account, and to accumulate depreciation yearly in a provision for depreciation account. The annual provision for depreciation is charged to the income statement.

Example 13.4 Assume that the plant and machinery shown in the previous example was acquired on 1 January 20X0 for £100,000, that its estimated useful life is five years, the expected residual value is nil, and that depreciation is calculated on a straight-line basis at the rate of £20,000 a year. The appropriate accounts would record the following data by the end of the year 20X2.

151

Plant and machinery account

20X0		£	20X0		£
1 Jan Cash		100,000	31 Dec Balance c/d		100,000
		100,000			100,000
20X1			20X1		
1 Jan Balance b/d		100,000	31 Dec Balance c/d		100,000
20X2			20X2		
1 Jan Balance b/d		100,000	31 Dec Balance c/d		100,000
20X3					
1 Jan Balance b/d		100,000			

Provision for depreciation account

20X0		£	20X0		£
31 Dec Balance c/d		20,000	31 Dec Income statement		20,000
		20,000			20,000
20X1			20X1		
			1 Jan Balance b/d		20,000
31 Dec Balance c/d		40,000	31 Dec Income statement		20,000
		40,000			40,000
20X2			20X2		
			1 Jan Balance b/d		40,000
31 Dec Balance c/d		60,000	31 Dec Income statement		20,000
		60,000			60,000
			20X3		
			1 Jan Balance b/d		60,000

Income statement for the year ended 31 December 20X0

	£	
Provision for depreciation	20,000	

Income statement for the year ended 31 December 20X1

	£	
Provision for depreciation	20,000	

Income statement for the year ended 31 December 20X2

	£	
Provision for depreciation	20,000	

Accounting for the disposal of assets

The cost of the benefits derived from the use of assets cannot be ascertained until the assets have completed their useful life and have been sold or otherwise disposed of. In the meantime, the annual provision for depreciation is merely an estimate of that actual cost. The practice is to make an adjustment to the income for the year of sale in respect of any difference between the book value and the realized value of the asset. It is not the practice, therefore, to attempt to reopen previous years to make a correction for the actual depreciation suffered.

The method is to open an asset realization account, often called a 'disposal account', and to reverse the existing entries in the asset realization account and the provision for depreciation account in respect of the asset sold or disposed of, recording directly in the asset realization account the sale price, if any, obtained.

Example 13.5 On 31 December 20X0, plant and machinery acquired at a cost of £100,000 three years ago was sold for £30,000. The accumulated depreciation to date was £60,000. The accounting procedure for dealing with this event is as follows:

Plant and machinery account

20X0		£	20X0		£
1 Jan	Balance b/d	100,000	31 Dec	Asset realization	100,000
		100,000			100,000

Provision for depreciation account

20X0		£	20X0		£
31 Dec	Asset realization	60,000	1 Jan	Balance b/d	60,000
		60,000			60,000

Cash book

20X0		£		
31 Dec	Asset realization	30,000		

Asset realization account

20X0		£	20X0		£
31 Dec	Plant & machinery	100,000	31 Dec	Cash	30,000
			31 Dec	Provision for depreciation	60,000
			31 Dec	Income statement	10,000
		100,000			100,000

Income statement for the year ended 31 December 20X0

	£	
Loss on sale of plant and machinery	10,000	

Therefore the gain or loss on disposal of non-current assets would be reported on the income statement, and the machinery would no longer be reported on the balance sheet.

Narrowing accounting differences: the role of standards

In Chapter 9 we discussed the problems created in the financial reporting process by the existence of a variety of practices permitted by the concepts of accounting. These problems appear in the lack of comparability between the financial reports of different companies, and in the consequent inability of users of financial reports to make informed judgements about different enterprises. The purpose for which the International Accounting Standards Board was established is to narrow the areas of difference and variety present in accounting and financial reporting practices on an international level.

Depreciation is one area where substantial differences exist between accounting methods permitted by the concepts of accounting. In common with other controversial topics in accounting, many of the differences have their origins in the means adopted for allocating costs. As it is impossible to devise cost allocation methods which are entirely objective, accountants resort to methods which are more or less arbitrary. For example, the straight-line method of depreciation assumes that asset costs should be allocated to successive periods in uniform amounts, whereas the decreasing-balance method of depreciation assumes that rate of allocation should be constant through time. The assumptions underlying these alternative methods are defensible in the context of the circumstances which they also assume. In effect, 'for each situation in which allocation is contemplated, there is a variety of possible allocation methods, each of which could be defended. The allocation problem arises because there is no conclusive way to choose one method in preference to all others, except arbitrarily' (Thomas, 1974, p. 2).

Although there is no solution to the problems posed by the existence of competing methods of allocating non-current asset costs through depreciation to successive accounting periods, users of financial reports may be assisted in evaluating the financial results reported, and making the adjustments necessary when comparing different companies. It was for this reason that, in the United Kingdom, the Accounting Standards Committee issued SSAP 12 'Accounting for Depreciation', which was later superseded by FRS 15 'Tangible Non-current assets'. These reinforced the requirement in the Companies Act 1985 (now replaced by the Companies Act 2006) that tangible non-current assets must be depreciated.

Depreciation is defined in FRS 15 as the 'measure of the cost of the economic benefits of the fixed asset that have been consumed during the period. Consumption includes the wearing out, using up or other reduction in the useful economic life of a fixed asset whether arising from use, effluxion of time or obsolescence through either changes in technology or demand for the goods and services produced by the asset.' Freehold land need not normally be depreciated but all other tangible non-current assets should be.

However, the FRS acknowledges that there may be exceptional circumstances where a long useful economic life or high residual value can be justified, giving rise to immaterial depreciation. But annual impairment reviews must be performed on such assets in accordance with FRS 11, 'Impairment of Non-current assets and Goodwill', a complicated procedure, and for all assets with lives greater than fifty years.

Depreciation should represent a fair allocation of the asset's value over the useful life of the asset. To determine a fair allocation requires consideration of the cost or valuation of the asset, its nature and expected useful life and its estimated residual value. Cost less residual value should then be allocated over the periods which benefit from the asset's use throughout its expected useful life.

The standard requires that provision for depreciation of non-current assets having a finite useful life be made by allocating the cost or revalued amount less estimated residual values of the assets as fairly as possible to the periods expected to benefit from their use. On a revision of the estimated useful life of an asset, the undepreciated cost should be charged over the revised remaining useful life. Where the method of depreciation is changed, which is permissible only where the new method will give a fairer presentation of the results and financial position, the undepreciated cost should be written off over the remaining useful life on the new basis, commencing with the period in which the change is made, and the effect, if material, disclosed in the year of change. Where assets are revalued, depreciation should be based on the revalued amount and current estimate of remaining useful life with the effect, if material, disclosed in the year of change.

The following should be disclosed in the financial statements for each major class of depreciable asset:

1 the depreciation methods used;
2 the useful lives or the depreciation rates used;
3 total depreciation allocated for the period;
4 the gross amount of depreciable assets and the related accumulated depreciation.

No specific method of depreciation is laid down in the standard, this being the responsibility of the management of the business, i.e. to select a method most appropriate to the asset in question. Freehold land need not normally be depreciated but buildings with a limited life should be. This latter requirement was a major innovation. Prior to SSAP 12, it was common practice for depreciation not to be provided for buildings on the ground that market values tended to exceed net book values shown on the balance sheet. SSAP 12 took the view, reiterated by FRS 15, that because buildings have a limited life, they should be depreciated using the same criteria applied to other non-current assets. This requirement provoked strong objection from property investment companies. SSAP 19 'Accounting for Investment Properties' (1981) allowed companies not to provide for depreciation in respect of investment properties. An investment property is defined as an interest in land and/or buildings, where construction work and development are completed and which is held for its investment potential.

International Accounting Standards Board IAS 16 'Property, Plant and Equipment' (1982) (and successively revised and amended) prescribes the accounting treatment for property, plant and equipment, setting out the rules applicable to the timing of recognition of assets, the carrying amounts and the depreciation methods. Assets may be carried at cost less accumulated depreciation and impairment (Cost Model) or may be carried at a revalued amount, being the fair value at the date of revaluation less subsequent depreciation, provided that fair value can be measured reliably (Valuation

Model). IAS 36 'Impairment of Assets' (1998) (revised 2009) prescribes the procedures to ensure that assets are carried at no more than their recoverable value.

IASB 17 'Leases' 1982 (revised 2003 and 2010) prescribes the procedures to be applied to non-current assets in the form of finance and operating leases, other than those relating to natural resources and licensing agreements for patents, copyrights, films, manuscripts etc. Finance leases are defined as those that transfer risk and rewards to ownership and all other leases are classified as operating leases.

Losses arising from the default of debtors

The necessity to give credit to customers results in the investment of substantial funds in what are in effect short-term loans. There are three important financial aspects as regards debtors which are of interest to both management and investors. First, there is the problem of working capital management in respect of the balance of claims in favour of and against the firm, and its implications in respect of liquidity and solvency. Second, there is the problem of the overall level of debtors in relation to other assets, and the need for the firm to have sufficient funds to invest in the maintenance and expansion of its income-earning structure. This has implications for present and future profitability. Third, there is the risk associated with the recovery of amounts due from debtors. This is a problem of credit control and the prevention of losses due to default by debtors.

The valuation of amounts due from debtors at the end of an accounting period presents no difficulty as regards determining debtor balances in an objective manner. Provided that accounting records have been kept properly, the objectivity of the valuation of debtors is founded in the law of contract and is a claim enforceable at law against debtors. The recoverability of debts, however, is a question to which the accountant must address himself, since the concept of prudence requires that losses be recognized when they arise. The recoverability of debts for financial reporting purposes is a question of law in some cases and of judgement in others. Thus, where a debtor has been declared bankrupt the recoverability of the debt is subject to the law of bankruptcy, and where no dividend is likely, the loss must be recognized and the amount written off as bad. When, however, a debtor cannot be traced or is unable to pay owing to personal circumstances and the sum involved does not warrant legal action, then the decision to recognize the loss is a matter of judgement. By and large, accountants examine the debtors' ledger at the end of the financial year and identify those debts likely to be bad debts by reference to the delay in payment and the attempts made to secure payment. Debts considered irrecoverable are written off by debiting the income statement account and crediting debtors, and if they should be recovered subsequently, then the debt is restored in the debtors' ledger.

Failure to deal adequately with the problem of defaulting debtors will distort the measurement of income and asset values in the following respects:

1 The measurement of income for an accounting period will be overstated to the extent that any credit sales taken into income have created debts which are not recoverable.

2 The measurement of income for the subsequent accounting period will be understated to the extent that debts created in the previous accounting period are recognized belatedly as bad and written off against the income of the subsequent accounting year.

3 The balance sheet statement of the value of debtors includes debts which, though legally enforceable, are irrecoverable. It is not possible, for example, to recover debts from bankrupt persons, or persons who cannot be traced.

Accordingly:

1 bad debts should be recognized as soon as they arise;
2 the risk of further possible losses should be anticipated in accordance with the concept of prudence.

Accounting practice is to deal separately with the problem of debts which are recognized as bad, and to anticipate further losses in the future. In effect, three types of debts are distinguished:

1 good debts;
2 bad debts;
3 doubtful debts.

The treatment of bad debts

Careful supervision of debtors' accounts will minimize bad debts. The enforcement of time limits for settlement of accounts helps in the prevention of a build-up of arrears and in identifying doubtful debts. Once a debt is recognized as bad, it should be written off immediately, so that the list of debtor accounts represents only good debts, that is, those expected to be paid in full.

Example 13.6 H Smith Ltd, a firm of building contractors, had been regular customers of Hervey Building Supplies Ltd and enjoyed a credit limit of £1,000. On 1 January 20X0 the balance on its account in the books of Hervey was £900, and purchases in January 20X0 totalled £150. H Smith informed Hervey on 5 February of its inability to pay its account. Hervey stopped further credit to H Smith until the position was clarified. Shortly thereafter, it was discovered that H Smith was insolvent, and that it was unlikely that any of the debt of £1,050 would be paid. On 1 March, it was decided to treat the debt as a bad debt.

The accounting entries in the books of Hervey would be as follows:

H Smith Ltd account

20X0	£	20X0	£
1 Jan Balance	900	1 Mar Bad debt	1,050
31 Jan Sales	150		
	1,050		1,050

Bad debts account

20X0	£		
1 Mar H Smith Ltd	1,050		

At the end of the accounting period, the total on the bad debts account is debited to the income statement.

Example 13.7 Assume that the only bad debt suffered by Hervey Building Supplies Ltd was in respect of H Smith Ltd in the sum of £1,050, as above. The bad debts account for the year ended 31 December 20X0 would be closed as follows:

Bad debts account

20X0	£	20X0	£
1 Mar H Smith Ltd	1,050	31 Dec Income statement	1,050
	1,050		1,050

Income statement for the year ended 31 December 20X0

20X0	£	
Bad debts	1,050	

The treatment of doubtful debts

The question of doubtful debts, as distinct from bad debts, is examined only at the end of each accounting period. A final scrutiny of the debtors account will elimi-nate all those accounts considered to be bad and the necessary transfers will be made to the bad debts account. Of the remaining debtors, some may ultimately prove to be bad but there may be reasonable grounds for hoping that all remaining debtors will settle their accounts. The concept of prudence requires that the risk should be discounted of further debts proving to be bad. The normal practice is to create a provision for doubtful debts out of the current year's income, without seeking to identify particular debts as being doubtful of recovery. There are several methods of estimating doubtful debts. The most common method is to allow past experience to establish the percentage of debtors which has proved to be bad, and to calculate the provision for doubtful debts by applying this percentage to the debtors outstanding at the end of the accounting period. A more accurate method is to classify debtor balances in terms of their age, and to apply to the several groups of debts the loss rates established by experience.

Example 13.8 The sales ledger balances existing in the books of the Bumpa Trading Company at the end of the financial year are as follows:

Duration of debts	Amount	Loss rate %	Provision
	£		£
Less than 1 month	10,000	1	100
1–2 months	3,000	3	90
2–3 months	1,000	5	50
3–4 months	500	10	50
Over 4 months	100	20	20
	14,600		310

One of the advantages of this method of creating a provision for doubtful debts is that it enables management to understand the relationship between the slow collection of debts and the financial losses caused by defaulting debtors.

The accounting entries would be as follows:

Income statement for the year ended 31 December 20X0

	£	
Provision for doubtful debts	310	

Provision for doubtful debts account

		20X0	£
		Income statement y/e 31 Dec	310

The provision for doubtful debts is not identified with any individual debtors. It is carried forward as an estimated liability, and may be shown on the balance sheet as follows:

Balance sheet as at 31 December 20X0

		£	£
	Debtors	14,600	
	less Provision for doubtful debts	310	
			14,290

In this manner, the objective of presenting a realistic valuation of trade debts is achieved.

Example 13.9 During 20X0 J Snow had to write off the debts of C Wild and J Hope who owed £80 and £260 respectively. At 31 December 20X0 the total of sundry debtors was £2,880. Snow made a provision for doubtful debts of 5 per cent.

On 3 March 20X1 J Hope unexpectedly paid his debt. At 31 December 20X1 the total of sundry debtors, other than Wild and Hope, was £2,520 and the provision was maintained at 5 per cent.

J Snow's accounting entries would be as follows:

Bad debts account

20X0		£	20X0	£
31 Dec	C Wild	80	31 Dec Income statement	484
	J Hope	260		
	Provision for doubtful debts	144		
		484		484

Income statement for the year ended 31 December 20X0

	£
Bad debts	340
Provision for bad debts	144

Balance sheet as at 31 December 20X0

	£	£
Debtors	2,880	
less Provision	144	2,736

C Wild

20X0		£	20X0		£
1 Jan	Balance b/d	80	31 Dec	Bad debts	80

J Hope

20X0		£	20X0		£
1 Jan	Balance b/d	260	31 Dec	Bad debts	260

Provision for doubtful debts account

20X1		£	20X0		£
31 Dec	Bad debts (excess provision)	18	31 Dec	Bad debts	144
	Balance c/d	126			
		144			144
			20X1		
			1 Jan	Balance b/d	126

Bad debts recovered

20X1		£	20X1		£
31 Dec	Income statement	260	3 Mar	J Hope	260

Income statement for the year ended 31 December 20X1

	£
Bad debts recovered	260
Excess provision for doubtful debts	18

Balance sheet as at 31 December 20X1

	£	£
Debtors	2,520	
Less Provision	126	2,394

The decrease in sundry debtors from £2,880 to £2,520 reduces the provision for doubtful debts by £18 (5 per cent of £360) at 31 December 20X1.

Summary

This chapter examined two important items in the measurement of periodic income, namely, depreciation and financial losses resulting from bad debts. Both are concerned with the manner in which losses in asset values should be recognized. Depreciation is a difficult problem from a theoretical viewpoint, and its treatment in accounting as an allocation of historical costs is a limited view of this problem. Nevertheless, such treatment is compatible with the matching concept for the allocation of asset costs to the revenues derived from their use. Not all assets are depreciable, and depreciation should take into account all the relevant costs of acquisition as well as the useful life of assets.

Two methods of depreciation were examined, and their implications discussed. The adjustments required on the sale or disposal of assets were also examined.

Losses caused by defaulting debtors were analysed and their impact on the measurement of periodic income was discussed. Accounting adopts a two-stage approach to this problem, namely the recognition of losses actually incurred by declaring certain debts as *bad*, and the provision against the risk of loss through creating provisions for doubtful debts.

Self-assessment questions

1 Analyse the main factors which should be considered when selecting a policy for depreciating non-current assets.

2 Explain the main provisions of FRS 15.

Problems (* *indicates that a solution is to be found in the Lecturer's Guide*)

1 Lodgemoor Company acquired a machine on 1 July 20X0 for £48,000 and immediately spent a further £2,000 on its installation. The machine was estimated to have a useful life of eight years and a scrap value of £4,000 at the end of this time.

Required:

Compute the depreciation provision for the year ended 30 June 20X1 and 20X2 if the company chooses to use:

   (a) the straight-line method;

   (b) the reducing-balance method.

2 Beale Company purchased a machine on 1 January 19X9, at an invoice price of £142,600. Transportation charges amounted to £2,000, and £3,400 was spent to install the machine. Costs of removing an old machine to make room for the new one amounted to £1,200, and £200 was received for the scrap value of the old machine.

Required:

   (a) State the amounts of depreciation which would be provided on the machine for the first year on a straight-line basis and on a decreasing-balance basis, assuming an estimated life of eight years and no salvage value expected at the end of that time.

   (b) Compute the depreciation provision for the year ended 31 December 20X1, assuming a revised total life expectancy for the machine of 12 years; assume that depreciation has been recorded through 31 December 20X0 on a straight-line basis.

3 From the following information relating to the non-current assets of a business prepare the following accounts as they should appear in the ledger:

   (a) plant and machinery;

   (b) motor vehicles;

   (c) plant and machinery provision for depreciation;

   (d) motor vehicles provision for depreciation;

   (e) asset realization.

The plant and machinery was acquired on 1 January 19X6, at a cost of £7,500, and the motor vehicles were acquired on 1 July 19X8, at a cost of £3,500.

It has been the practice of the business to depreciate assets using the straight-line method and they estimate the life of the plant to be ten years and that of the motor vehicles to be five years.

The accounts of the business are made up to 31 December in each year and it is usual to calculate depreciation for a full year on the assets in the possession of the business at balance sheet date.

During the year to 31 December 20X0, a new machine costing £1,000 was acquired and a machine bought on 1 January 19X6 for £500 was sold for £325; and a car costing £750 on 1 July 19X8 was sold for £400.

4* The year-end balance on the debtors account amounted to £100,000. Net sales for the year totalled £1,200,000. Explain how you would deal with the following information.

   (a) An analysis of the sales ledger indicates that irrecoverable debts amount to £11,400.

   (b) Past trends suggest that 5 per cent of debts eventually should be provided as doubtful.

   (c) The existing provision for doubtful debts is £3,000.

5 A business maintains in its ledger a combined bad debts and provision for doubtful debts account. The provision was created in the accounts for the year ended 31 March 19X9 by calculating an amount equal to 5 per cent of the £10,000 outstanding debts at that date. During the year ended 31 March 20X0 bad debts of £250 were incurred and at the bal-

ance sheet date the outstanding debts amounted to £12,500. It was decided to maintain the provision for doubtful debts at 5 per cent of the outstanding debts. During the year to 31 March 20X1, bad debts of £270 were incurred and the debts outstanding at balance sheet date amounted to £10,000. It was decided to adjust the doubtful debts provision to an amount equal to 4 per cent of the debts outstanding at 31 March 20X1.

Required:

(a) Record the above in the ledger of the business.
(b) Show the entries that would appear in the income and loss account for each of the years to 31 March 19X9, 20X0 and 20X1 and on each of the three balance sheets made up to those dates.

6 An airline company purchased and put into operation a jet aircraft on 1 February 19X7 for £7,000,000. The expectation then was that the aircraft would be flown for a total of 10,000 hours over a period of 4 years and then traded in for a new model. The trade-in value was expected to be £1,500,000 at the end of January 20X1. The number of flying hours actually logged by the aircraft was as follows:

1 February 19X1–31 January 19X8	3,000
1 February 19X2–31 January 19X9	2,800
1 February 19X3–31 January 20X0	2,300
1 February 19X4–31 January 20X1	500

The aircraft had a serious accident in June 20X0 and was a total write-off – although an insurance company agreed to pay £1,200,000 in settlement.

Required:

(a) Calculate the depreciation charges for each of the four financial years to 31 January 20X1
    (i) using the straight-line method (applied on a full-year basis), and
    (ii) on a basis of flying hours logged.
(b) Show the appropriate ledger accounts for the year ended 31 January 20X1 for the two methods.

7 A Mayberry Ltd, a company with a turnover of £30,000 per year, acquired a machine on 1 January 20X0 for £8,000. It was company policy to depreciate machinery on a straight-line basis at 20 per cent per year. During 20X0, a modification was made to the machine to improve its technical reliability at a cost of £800 which it was considered would extend the useful life of the machine by two years. At the same time, an important component of the machine was replaced at a cost of £500, because of excessive wear and tear. Routine maintenance during the year cost £250.

Required:

Show the asset account, the provision for depreciation account, and the charge to the income statement in respect of the machine for the year ended 31 December 20X0.

8* Brannan own plant and equipment which is used on their construction sites. The depreciation policy of the company is to charge a full year's depreciation in the year of acquisition but none in the year of disposal.

During the year ended 31 March 20X1 the following changes took place:

Purchases 20X0/1

Date	Cost
	£
1 July	8,200
31 August	6,800
1 December	12,600
28 February	7,500

Sales 20X0/1

Date	Cost	Date of purchase	Receipts
	£		£
15 August	4,200	15 May 19X6	250
30 September	5,800	1 December 19X4	100
29 December	9,000	1 February 19X8	510
1 March	11,000	31 March 19X9	3,000

All the remaining assets had been owned for less than four years. Depreciation is charged on a straight-line basis using a rate of 25 per cent per annum. The balance on the plant and equipment account at 1 April 20X0 was £187,600 and on the provision for depreciation account £62,100.

Required:

Prepare the following accounts:

(a) A plant and equipment account.
(b) A plant and equipment provision for depreciation account.
(c) A disposal account.

References   AICPA (1953) Accounting Research Bulletin No. 43.

Barton, A.D. (1984) *The Anatomy of Accounting*, University of Queensland Press.

Fisher, I. (1906) *The Nature of Capital and Income*, New York: Macmillan.

Thomas, A.L. (1974) *The allocation problem: Part 2*, Studies in Accounting Research, AAA.

CHAPTER 14

Preparing an income statement and a balance sheet

Setting the scene

Financial statements are at the centre of business reporting. They represent the financial picture of a company, both at a point in time and over a period of time, translating into financial terms many, but not all, of the events and activities that affect it . . . Many investment decisions – such as whether to lend money, whether to buy, hold or sell securities – are based, in large part, on the information in financial statements.

(AICPA, 1994)

Learning objectives

After studying this chapter you should be able to:

1 prepare an income statement after making adjustments for accruals, inventories and depreciation;

2 prepare a balance sheet;

3 reconcile the balance on the bank account in the ledger with the balance shown on the bank statement.

In Chapter 11, we examined the role of the trial balance as a working paper which enables the accountant not only to check the arithmetical accuracy of the entries recorded during an accounting period, but which also serves as a basis for considering adjustments to be made for the purpose of measuring periodic income. The extraction of a trial balance at the close of the accounting period is the first step, therefore, in the preparation of an income statement and a balance sheet.

We noted in Chapter 12 how the trial balance is adjusted in respect of the accrual into the accounting period of revenues and expenses, and we analysed in Chapter 13 the nature of the losses in asset values which have to be taken into consideration in the measurement of periodic income.

The purpose of this chapter is to summarize the various adjustments which must be made to the trial balance, and the manner in which these adjustments are incorporated into the process of preparing an income statement and a balance sheet.

Preparing an income statement

The preparation of a income statement is a two-stage exercise. The first stage is an informal one and consists of using the trial balance as a worksheet for accumulating all the data which incorporate the various adjustments we referred to earlier. The adjustments are then entered in the appropriate accounts, and the income statement is formally included in the accounts system. It is important to remember that the income statement is an account to which the revenue and expense accounts for the accounting period are transferred as summarized totals, and which exists solely for the purpose of measuring the accounting income for that period.

The following example illustrates the nature of the income statement.

Example 14.1 Let us return to the trial balance given on page 127, which listed the balances extracted from the books of John Smith on 31 December 20X0 at the end of the first year of trading:

	£ Dr	£ Cr
Capital		25,000
Motor vehicles	10,000	
Furniture and fittings	2,500	
Purchases	31,000	
Bank balance	6,000	
Sales		70,000
Debtors	18,000	
Creditors		3,500
Rent	4,500	
Salaries	22,800	
Insurances	400	
Motor expenses	2,000	
Light and heat	1,000	
General expenses	300	
	98,500	98,500

We noted in Chapter 9 that the following adjustments were required:

1 Rent unpaid at the end of the year was £1,500.
2 Insurance paid in advance amounted to £50.
3 Rent receivable, but not recorded in the account, amounted to £60.
4 Closing inventory at 31 December 20X0 was valued at £3,000.

We are now given the following additional information:

1 Depreciation is to be provided on the undermentioned assets and calculated on the reducing-balance method. Their estimated residual values are shown in brackets.

Motor vehicles	20%	(£1,000)
Furniture and fittings	10%	(£250)

2 Bad debts to be written off amount to £180, and a provision for doubtful debts is to be made of £178.

Adjusting for accruals

We saw also that the adjustments for accruals and prepayments resulted in the following revisions of balances in the trial balance:

	Original balance	Adjustment	New balance
	£	£	£
1 Rent	4,500	1,500	6,000
2 Insurance	400	50	350
3 Insurance prepaid	–	50	50
4 Rent receivable	–	60	60

We explained in Chapter 12 that items 1, 2 and 3 represented adjustments to the revenues and expenses of the year and affected the income statement. The following resulting balances of the accounts affect the balance sheet and we shall see later in this chapter how they are incorporated in that statement:

	£ Dr	£ Cr
Rent accrued		1,500
Insurance prepaid	50	
Rent receivable	60	

The corrected total revenues and expenses may now be listed on a worksheet used in the preparation of the income statement:

Draft income statement for the year ended 31 December 20X0

	£		£
Purchases	31,000	Sales	70,000
Rent	6,000	Rent receivable	60
Salaries	22,800		
Insurance	350		
Motor expenses	2,000		
Light and heat	1,000		
General expenses	300		

Adjusting for inventory

We noted in Chapter 12 that periodic measurement involved valuing inventories of goods unsold at the end of the accounting period. The closing inventory is valued in accordance with the cost concept, and represents the residue of the purchases of the year which have not been sold at the year end, though they may be sold in the next accounting period. Opening inventories are shown, therefore, as a *debit balance* in the trial balance, whereas closing inventories do not appear, since they are valued after the close of the accounting period. It is for this reason that the appropriate entries must be made in the inventory account to make possible the measurement of periodic income. In the example in question, there is no opening inventory because it is the first year of trading.

We also saw in Chapter 12 that the adjustment for closing inventories had a two-fold effect. First, it is carried out by means of a credit to the income statement and a debit to the inventory account. Second, it results in a debit balance in the inventory account which must be incorporated in the balance sheet.

The closing inventory is entered on the draft income statement as follows:

Draft income statement for the year ended 31 December 20X0

	£		£
Purchases	31,000	Sales	70,000
Rent	6,000	Rent receivable	60
Salaries	22,800	Closing inventory	
Insurance	350	31 December 20X0	3,000
Motor expenses	2,000		
Light and heat	1,000		
General expenses	300		

Adjusting for loss in asset values

We mentioned in Chapter 13 the most important losses in asset values that the accountant has to recognize in the measurement of periodic income. It is not proposed to deal here with the variety of gains and losses in asset values that may occur, since we are concerned only with the process of periodic measurement and with the most significant losses in asset values which enter into that process.

In the example, we are required to deal with depreciation, bad and doubtful debts.

Calculation of depreciation

It is the usual practice to detail in the income statement the component elements of the provision for depreciation, and as will be seen later non-current assets are also described in their categories on the balance sheet. The provision for depreciation in respect of the different non-current assets may be reconciled, therefore, with the yearly provision for depreciation shown on the balance sheet.

1 Motor vehicles	£	£
Cost	10,000	
Estimated residual value	1,000	
Net cost for depreciation purposes	9,000	
Depreciation for the year 20X0 at 20%	1,800	1,800
Residual balance for depreciation in following years	7,200	

2 Furniture and fittings	£	£
Cost	2,500	
Estimated residual value	250	
Net cost for depreciation purposes	2,250	
Depreciation for the year 20X0 at 10%	225	225
Residual balance for depreciation in following years	2,025	
Total depreciation for the year		2,025

Calculation of the provision for doubtful debts

Duration of debt	Balance £	Loss rate, %	Provision £
Less than 1 month	15,960	$\frac{1}{2}$	80
1–2 months	1,800	5	90
2–3 months	40	10	4
over 3 months	20	20	4
	17,820		178

These adjustments may be included in the draft income statement as shown below:

	£		£
Purchases	31,000	Sales	70,000
Rent	6,000	Rent receivable	60
Salaries	22,800	Closing inventory at	
Insurance	350	31 December 20X0	3,000
Motor expenses	2,000		
Light and heat	1,000		
General expenses	300		
Depreciation			
Motor vehicles	1,800		
Furniture and fittings	225		
	2,025		
Bad debts	180		
Provision for doubtful debts	178		

Calculating the periodic income

The details shown on the draft income statement above are sufficient to permit the calculation of the income for the year ended 31 December 20X0. The income statement is set out to enable significant information to be immediately apparent. In this respect, a distinction is made between *gross* income and *net* income, the former being the income resulting after the deduction from the gross sales revenue of expenses directly connected with the product or purchase cost of goods sold, while the latter

169

reflects the deduction of overhead expenses from gross income. Although the net income is the most important result, dividing the income statement into two parts highlights the burden of overhead expenses, as well as focusing attention on important aspects of business activity.

Calculating gross income

In the case of a trading business – as is the case in the example quoted – the gross income from trading may be shown as follows:

	£		£
Purchases	31,000	Sales	70,000
Less: Closing inventory at			
31 December 20X0	3,000		
Cost of sales	28,000		
Gross trading income	42,000		
	70,000		70,000

This arrangement shows the following points:

1 Although purchases amounted to £31,000, the cost of goods actually sold amounted to only £28,000. Hence, the gross trading income expressed as a percentage of sales is:

$$\frac{42,000}{70,000} \times 100 = 60\%$$

This percentage is often referred to as the gross income ratio. Expressed as a percentage of cost of sales, the gross trading income is:

$$\frac{42,000}{28,000} \times 100 = 150\%$$

2 The level of trading activity may also be judged from the average length of time inventory is held. The rate of inventory turnover may be calculated as follows:

$$\frac{\text{cost of sales}}{\text{average inventory}}$$

The average inventory is obtained by the arithmetic mean of the opening and closing inventory. In the example under consideration, the rate of inventory turnover for the year was as follows:

$$\frac{28,000}{3,000} = 9.3 \text{ times}$$

so that inventory was held for approximately 39 days (365 days ÷ 9.3), or replaced approximately 9.3 times in the year.

The segregation of the gross trading income in the process of calculating periodic income provides useful ratios for the analysis of trading performance, and for indicating areas of trading where efficiency might be improved.

It is the practice for firms to identify the nature of gross income, for example manufacturing firms show manufacturing gross income and contracting firms show contracting gross income.

The problem of deciding which expenses to include in the calculation of gross income lies in defining direct as distinct from indirect operating expenses. Direct expenses, such as purchases, freight and other expenses associated with the acquisition of goods for resale are included in the calculation of gross income.

Calculating the net income

The calculation of the net income is effected by charging against the gross income the indirect expenses accumulated in the trial balance, and other expenses such as depreciation, bad debts and provisions for the year ended 31 December 20X0 may be calculated as shown:

Net income for year ended 31 December 20X0

	£		£
Rent	6,000	Gross trading income	42,000
Salaries	22,800	Rent receivable	60
Insurance	350		
Motor expenses	2,000		
Light and heat	1,000		
General expenses	300		
Depreciation			
Motor vehicles	1,800		
Furniture and fittings	225		
	2,025		
Bad debts	180		
Provision for doubtful debts	178		
	34,833		
Net income	7,227		
	42,060		42,060

Miscellaneous income, such as interest, rents and dividends, which forms a minor element in the business income, is usually shown in the calculation of the net income rather than in the calculation of the gross income.

The segregation of the net income calculation also affords a clearer view of significant ratios. The net income is itself the most significant performance result, and its dimensions may be assessed not only in relation to the gross trading income, but also to gross revenue. The net income as a percentage of sales indicates the level of activity required to produce £1 of net income, and may be calculated as follows:

$$\frac{\text{Net income before interest and tax}}{\text{sales}}$$

Thus, whereas the percentage of gross income to sales was 60 per cent, the percentage of net income to sales was only 13 per cent, indicating thereby not only the relative burden of direct and indirect expenses but also the relative efficiency of the business.

The formal presentation of the income statement

Although the income statement is part of the accounts system, and may be shown in an account form, its formal presentation has been influenced by its use as a financial reporting statement. This influence has encouraged the further classification of indirect expenses into selling, administration and financial expenses, and the presentation of the income statement in a vertical form as follows:

John Smith trading as general dealer
Income statement for the year ended 31 December 20X0

	£	£	£
Sales			70,000
Cost of sales			
Purchases		31,000	
Less: Closing inventory		3,000	
			28,000
Gross trading income			42,000
Other income			
Rent			60
Total income			42,060
Selling and distribution expenses			
Sales representatives' salaries	12,000		
Motor expenses	2,000		
Depreciation – motor vehicles	1,800	15,800	
Administrative expenses			
Rent	6,000		
Office salaries	10,800		
Insurance	350		
Light and heat	1,000		
General expenses	300		
Depreciation – furniture and fittings	225		
		18,675	
Financial expenses			
Bad debts	180		
Provision for doubtful debts	178	358	
Total overhead expenses			34,833
Net income			7,227

Preparing a balance sheet

The preparation of the balance sheet is a two-stage process. It follows the same pattern as the preparation of the income statement, that is, an informal stage based on a worksheet, and a formal stage represented by the balance sheet presented as a financial report. There are, however, a number of important differences between an income statement and a balance sheet. First, from a procedural point of view, the income statement is part of the accounts system and, as explained earlier, it is itself an account. By contrast, the balance sheet is not an account, but a list showing the balances of the accounts which remain following the preparation of the income statement. Second, the income statement is the effective instrument for periodic measurement in accounting, whereas the balance sheet only states residual balances. Third, residual debit balances are shown on the balance sheet as assets, but there are problems stemming from this description which are discussed in Chapter 15. Fourth, by attaching accounting measurements to debit and credit balances described as assets and liabilities respectively, the balance sheet is often interpreted as indicating the net worth of the business. This is a misconception, and in the case of corporations has led to much controversy. We explore these problems further in Part 3.

Collecting and classifying balances

The preparation of the balance sheet need not await the entry of all the adjustments into the individual accounts following the preparation of the income statement. It may be prepared in draft form from the trial balance and the finalized draft of the income statement.

Debit balances are either assets, losses or expenses. The preparation of the income statement involves the removal from the trial balance of all expenses in respect of the year, so that any debit balances remaining are treated as assets. These assets, as defined, are classified as follows:

1 Long-term assets representing an enduring benefit to the enterprise. Long-term assets, described as non-current assets, for example plant and machinery, are subject to depreciation. Other long-term assets, such as land and intangible assets, may or may not be subject to depreciation or other changes in their book value. We examine these problems in Chapter 15.
2 Short-term assets, described as current assets, include the following:
   (a) closing inventories at the end of the accounting period;
   (b) trade debtors;
   (c) prepayments on expense accounts, for example, insurance paid in advance;
   (d) bank balances and cash.

The measurement of closing inventories presents particular problems, which are discussed in Chapter 15. The accounting problems relating to trade debtors which arise from the writing-off of bad debts and the making of provisions for doubtful debts have already been discussed. We shall deal presently with the verification of bank balances and overdrafts.

By contrast, credit balances are either liabilities, revenues or investments in the firm in the form of capital and long-term loans. The removal of periodic revenues from the trial balance means that the remaining credit balances are either liabilities or investments. The provision for depreciation is one of a number of exceptions to this rule. These exceptions, as in the case of prepayments shown as debit balances, arise from accounting procedures. Credit balances are collected and classified as follows:

1 capital account, representing the owner's original investment in the firm and accumulated incomes less drawings;
2 long-term borrowings;
3 short-term liabilities, described as current liabilities, which include such credit balances as sundry creditors, accrued expenses, payments received in advance, provisions for taxation and bank overdrafts.

Verifying balances

Accounts are usually subjected to yearly audits, that is, they are checked by a firm of professional accountants. The purpose of the audit is not only to check the accuracy of the records, but also to ensure that the statements contained in those records are correct. Thus, the physical existence of the assets in the assets accounts is verified, as is the existence of liabilities in various creditors' accounts. In the case of large corporations, audits are obligatory and auditors are appointed by shareholders. In this connection, they are required to report that both the income statement and the balance sheet reflect a true and fair view of the information they are legally required to convey.

The bank reconciliation statement

It is unlikely that on any specific day the bank balance shown in the cash book will correspond with the statement of the balance in the bank account issued by the bank. This is due not only to the normal delays occurring in the process of clearing cheques, but also to delays in lodging and presenting cheques for payment. Moreover, payments and receipts may be effected directly through the bank. For example, dividends and interest receivable may be paid directly into the bank account, and routine payments may be effected by standing orders and direct debit procedures. The bank routinely charges commission, fees and interest directly to bank accounts, and the bank statement is used to convey these details to the client.

The bank reconciliation statement reconciles the balance at the bank as per the bank statement with the bank balance as per the cash book, whenever a bank statement is received.

When preparing a balance sheet, the bank balance as shown in the cash book must be supported by a bank statement showing the balance on the last day of the accounting period, and the bank reconciliation statement explains any differences which have not been already adjusted in the cash book. Any charges such as bank commission and interest will be entered in the cash book and will be shown as expenses in the income statement. In effect, the bank reconciliation statement explains the nature of the unadjusted differences between the cash book and the bank statement.

Example 14.2 The bank balance according to the cash book was £6,000 on 31 December 20X0. The bank statement balance was £6,500. The difference is explained as follows:

1 cheques received from debtors on 31 December 20X0 which were not banked until after 1st January 20X1 amounted to £250;
2 cheques sent to creditors on 31 December 20X0 and not presented for payment until after 1 January 20X1 amounted to £750.

Bank reconciliation statement as on 31 December 20X0

	£
Balance at bank as per bank statement	6,500
Add: Cheques received but not credited	250
	6,750
Less: Cheques issued but not presented	750
Balance at bank per cash book	6,000

The formal presentation of the balance sheet

In the case of corporations, legislation provides rules for the presentation of both the income statement and the balance sheet. As we shall see in Chapter 16, these rules apply to published financial reports. The rules reflect the practices of the accounting profession, and are designed not only to secure sufficient disclosure but also to permit salient features to be quickly recognized.

It is usual to classify assets and liabilities in groupings and to rank them in order of liquidity. Thus, asset groupings are shown from the most fixed to the most liquid, and liabilities from the long-term to the most current.

The importance of the balance sheet, together with the income statement financial reporting and investment decision-making, has focused attention on the arrangement of particular groupings to assist the interpretation and the analysis of results. This will be discussed in Chapter 19, but it may be mentioned at this stage that the relationship between long-term finance and long-term investment needs of the firm (long-term capital as defined in finance) and short-term finance and short-term financial needs (working capital) is important to financial analysts. Other areas of interest are the return on capital employed which is the ratio of net income to equity capital (owner's investment in the firm), liquidity and solvency.

The vertical form of presentation of the balance sheet is illustrated below.

John Smith Incorporated Balance sheet at 31 December 20X0

Non-current assets	Cost	Depreciation to date	Net		
	£	£	£	£	£
Motor vehicles	10,000	1,800	8,200		
Furniture and fittings	2,500	225	2,275		
	12,500	2,025	10,475	10,475	
Current assets					
Inventory at cost			3,000		
Debtors		17,820			
Less: Provision for doubtful debts		178	17,642		
Accruals and prepayments			110		
Bank balance			6,000		
			26,752		
Current liabilities					
Creditors		3,500			
Accruals		1,500	5,000		
Net current assets				21,752	
Capital employed					32,227
Shareholders' equity				25,000	
Net income for the year				7,227	
					32,227

Example 14.3 The following trial balance was extracted from the books of Peter Ardron Incorporated as at 31 December 20X0:

	£	£
Purchases	54,520	
Sales		79,060
Salaries	8,760	
Rates	1,170	
Office expenses	3,950	
Motor expenses	3,790	
Shareholders' equity 1 January 20X0		13,640
Freehold properties at cost	7,500	
Furniture and fittings at cost	2,000	
Motor cars at cost	6,300	
Accumulated depreciation		
Freehold properties		450
Furniture and fittings		800
Motor cars		2,370
Inventory 1 January 20X0	6,740	
Drawings	4,800	
Provision for doubtful debts 1 January 20X0		600
Loan		4,000
Debtors	9,240	
Creditors		10,040
Bank balance	2,190	
	110,960	110,960

The following matters are to be taken into account:

1 Inventory at 31 December £7,330.
2 Rates paid in advance 31 December £250.
3 Provision for doubtful debts to be made equal to 5 per cent of debtors at 31 December.
4 Provide depreciation for the year at the following annual rates calculated on cost, assuming no scrap value:

freehold properties	1%
furniture and fittings	10%
motor cars	20%

5 Provide for interest on the loan at 5 per cent per annum.

Peter Ardron Incorporated income statement for the year ended 31 December 20X0 and a balance sheet at that date appear as follows:

Peter Ardron Incorporated
Income statement for the year ended 31 December 20X0

	£	£	£
Sales			79,060
Cost of sales			
Opening inventory		6,740	
Purchases		54,520	
		61,260	
Less Closing inventory		7,330	53,930
Gross income			25,130
Expenses			
Salaries		8,760	
Rates £(1,170 – 250)		920	
Office expenses		3,950	
Motor expenses		3,790	
Doubtful debts provision not required		(138)	
Loan interest		200	
Depreciation: Freehold properties	75		
Fixtures and fittings	200		
Motor cars	1,260	1,535	19,017
Net income			6,113

Balance sheet at 31 December 20X0

	£ (Cost)	£ (Dep'n)	£ (NBV)
Non-current assets			
Freehold properties	7,500	525	6,975
Furniture and fittings	2,000	1,000	1,000
Motor cars	6,300	3,630	2,670
	15,800	5,155	10,645
Current assets			
Inventory		7,330	
Debtors	9,240		
Less Provision for doubtful debts	462		
		8,778	
Prepayments		250	
Bank balance		2,190	
		18,548	
Current liabilities			
Creditors	10,040		
Accruals	200	10,240	8,308
Net current assets			18,953

Shareholders' equity

Balance b/d	13,640	
Income for year	6,113	
	19,753	
Drawings	4,800	14,953
Loan		4,000
		18,953

Workings
Provision for doubtful debts account

	£		£
Balance c/d (5% × £9,240)	462	Balance b/d	600
Income statement			
(provision no longer	138		
required)			
	600		600

Summary

This chapter has been concerned with the accounting procedures for preparing and presenting the two main financial reports, namely the income statement and the balance sheet.

The extraction of the trial balance at the close of the accounting period marks the first stage in the preparation of these reports. Earlier chapters have examined the adjustments required for the purposes of periodic measurement. These include accruals, depreciation and adjustments in respect of bad and doubtful debts. All these adjustments are effected informally on working sheets, and once they have been verified and confirmed, the final accounts are drawn up.

The importance of the income statement lies not only in the fact that it is the main vehicle of periodic measurement and provides the measurement of periodic income, but also in that it is part of the accounts system. The objective purpose underlying the preparation of the income statement is the measurement of net income, which is used as a basis for measuring business efficiency. The distinction between gross income and net income facilitates the analysis of the financial results, as does the classification of expenses under various categories.

By contrast, the balance sheet is a list of residual balances following the preparation of the income statement. It forms no part of the accounts system. The balance sheet is used in conjunction with the income statement in the analysis of the financial performance of the business, and the treatment and classification of assets and liabilities are important to this analysis. Consequently, particular attention is paid to the manner in which important financial aspects of the business are highlighted in the presentation of the balance sheet.

1 Jack Daw Incorporated have prepared the following balance sheet as at 30 June 20X1:

	£		£	£
Shareholders' equity		Plant at cost	8,000	
Balance, 1 July 20X0	10,000	*Less*: Depreciation	2,000	6,000
Income for the year	2,050	Vehicles at cost	3,000	
	12,050	*Less*: Depreciation	1,000	
				2,000
Creditors and provisions	5,000	Inventory		7,000
Bank overdraft	1,000	Debtors	3,200	
		Less: Provision for	200	3,000
		doubtful debts		
		Cash	–	50
	18,050			18,050

You are asked to audit his accounts and in the course of your examination you find the following:

(a) A dividend of £100 has been paid direct to the bank and no entry has been made in the books.

(b) A debt of £100 is irrecoverable and you agree with the company that the provision for doubtful debts should be fixed at 10 per cent of the remaining debtors.

(c) A purchase of plant, costing £500, has been charged to repairs. It was agreed that this should be depreciated by 10 per cent on cost.

(d) The inventory on 30 June 20X1 was overvalued by £250.

(e) On counting the petty cash you find there is only £10 in the box. It seems likely that the balance has been stolen by an employee.

Required:

(a) A statement showing the necessary adjustments to the income statement for the year to 30 June 20X1.

(b) The amended balance sheet as at 30 June 20X1.

2 The balances in the books of account for John Reeve at 31 March 20X1 are given below:

	£
Sales	50,000
Purchases	30,000
Inventory, 1 April 20X0	35,000
Administration expenses	5,000
Selling expenses	5,000
Trade creditors	27,000
Bank overdraft	32,000
Trade debtors	55,000
Debentures	50,000
Plant and machinery, at cost	80,000
Plant and machinery, depreciation provision, 1 April 20X0	30,000

	£
Fixtures and equipment, at cost	40,000
Fixtures and equipment, depreciation provision, 1 April 20X0	10,000
Shareholders' equity account, 1 April 20X0	51,000

You are also given the following information:

(a) On 31 March 20X1, the inventory was valued at £40,000.

(b) Depreciation of plant and machinery and fixtures and fittings is to be calculated at the rate of 20 per cent of cost.

Required:

Using the vertical form of presentation, prepare the income statement for the year ended 31 March 20X1 and a balance sheet as at that date.

3* The following trial balance was extracted from the books of T Bone Incorporated as at 31 December 20X0:

	£	£
Shareholders' equity		20,500
Purchases	46,500	
Sales		60,900
Repairs	848	
Motor car (cost)	950	
Car expenses	318	
Freehold land and buildings	10,000	
Bank balance	540	
Furniture and fittings (cost)	1,460	
Wages and salaries	8,606	
Discounts allowed	1,061	
Discounts received		814
Drawings	2,400	
Rates and insurances	248	
Bad debts	359	
Provision for bad debts, 1 Jan 20X0		140
Trade debtors	5,213	
Trade creditors		4,035
General expenses	1,586	
Inventory, 1 Jan 20X0	6,300	
	86,389	86,389

The following matters are to be taken into account:

(a) Inventory at 31 December 20X0 was £8,800.

(b) Wages and salaries outstanding at 31 December 20X0 were £318.

(c) Rates and insurances paid in advance at 31 December 20X0 amounted to £45.

(d) During the year, goods ex-inventory valued at £200 were taken for personal use of the C.E.O. No entry has been made in the books in this respect.

(e) Depreciation is to be provided at the rate of 20 per cent on the motor and at 10 per cent on furniture and fittings.

(f) The provision for bad debts is to be reduced to £100.

Required:

Prepare an income statement for the year ended 31 December 20X0, and a balance sheet as at that date.

4 Matt Spode Incorporated is a china wholesaler. A trial balance extracted from his books on 31 December 20X0 revealed the following balances:

	£	£
Shareholders' equity		112,000
Purchases	92,400	
Sales		157,240
Premises at cost	64,000	
Motor vehicles at cost	30,000	
Accumulated depreciation of motors		8,200
Fixtures and fittings at cost	6,500	
Accumulated depreciation – fixtures and fittings		1,100
Motor expenses	7,300	
Rates	2,300	
Balance at bank	4,200	
Wages and salaries	42,000	
Drawings	9,600	
Insurance	2,000	
Trade debtors	18,000	
Provision for doubtful debts		560
Trade creditors		15,000
Sundry expenses	16,200	
Long-term loan		20,000
Inventory at 1 Jan 20X0	19,250	
Cash in hand	350	
	314,100	314,100

The following information was available at 31 December 20X0:

(a) Inventory at 31 December was £22,400.
(b) There were wages and salaries of £1,200 owing.
(c) There was a payment of £1,200 on 30 September to cover 12 months' insurance.
(d) On reviewing debtors, it was discovered that a debt of £800 would not be recovered and that a further £1,200 was doubtful.
(e) Depreciation is 25 per cent reducing-balance on motors and 10 per cent straight-line on fixtures and fittings.
(f) Loan interest at 10 per cent has not been allowed for.

Required:

Prepare an income statement and balance sheet for Matt Spode Incorpated to cover the period in question.

5 The following trial balance was drawn up from the books of A Merchant Incorporated at 31 December 20X0:

	£	£
Shareholders' equity		
As at 1 January 20X0:		90,000
Additionl funds raised during the year		1,500
Dividends paid during the year	8,000	
Gross income for the year		27,000
Inventory, 31 December 20X0	23,600	
Selling and distribution expenses	4,500	
Motor vehicles at cost	20,000	
Freehold premises at cost	30,000	
Provision for depreciation of motor vehicles at 1 January 20X0		4,000
Debtors and creditors	52,000	31,100
Bank balance	8,750	
Rates and insurances	6,000	
Office salaries	3,000	
Office expenses	1,250	
Doubtful debts provision		2,500
Bad debts written off	500	
Discounts	1,500	3,000
	159,100	159,100

Required:

Prepare an income statement for the year ending 31 December 20X0, and a balance sheet as at that date, taking into account the following:

(a) Provision is to be made for depreciation of motor vehicles for the year at the rate of 20 per cent per annum on the cost of the vehicles.
(b) The doubtful debts provision is to be adjusted to an amount equal to 5 per cent of the outstanding debtors.
(c) The rates are £4,000 per annum and have been paid to 31 March 20X1.

6 Jackson owns a retail shop The following information is available from the few records kept for the beginning and end of 20X0:

	1 January	31 December
	£	£
Cash in shop till	350	250
Bank overdraft	800	300
Inventory	2,600	3,300
Owed by customers	4,500	5,100
Owed to suppliers	1,450	1,900
Loan from wife	4,000	2,500

Notes:

(a) Jackson tells you that during 20X0 he took from the till, before making the weekly bankings:
  (i) £200 a week for his personal expenses, and
  (ii) £80 a week for his assistant's wages.
(b) Returned cheques show that all payments out of the bank account were to suppliers except:
  (i) a payment of £250 to an insurance company, being £150 for the insurance of the shop's contents and £100 for the insurance of Jackson's own house, and
  (ii) a payment of £600 for furniture for Jackson's own house.
(c) During the year Jackson had paid business expenses of £3,100 through his private bank account.
(d) Although no record of it is kept, Jackson owned the shop purchased on 1 January 19X6 for £40,000 and shop fittings and fixtures purchased on the same date for £6,000. It is agreed that fair rates of depreciation are 5 per cent per annum on cost for the shop and 10 per cent per annum on cost for the fittings and fixtures.

Required:

(a) Calculate Jackson's income for 20X0.
(b) Compile a statement of the financial position of this business on 31 December 20X0.

7* A businessman has no double-entry records of his transactions but has a cash book from which the following summary for the year ended 31 December 20X1 has been prepared:

	£
Bank overdraft, 31 December 20X0	7,500
Receipts from trade debtors	90,000
Further capital introduced	30,000
Loan from X on 31 March on which interest is payable at the rate of 5 per cent a year	20,000
Payments to trade creditors	35,000
General expenses	9,000
Wages	12,000
Drawings	22,000
On 3 December 20X0, the business had	
trade debtors for	70,000
trade creditors for	50,000
inventory valued at	30,000
sundry non-current assets which had cost	60,000
provision for depreciation	10,000
On 31 December 20X1 there were	
trade debtors for	85,000
trade creditors for	65,000
inventory valued at	27,000
sundry fixed assets which had cost	68,000

Draft an income statement for the year ended 31 December 20X1, and a balance sheet as at that date, providing for 5 per cent depreciation of the fixed assets on a straight-line basis.

8 From the following information relating to Snailsby, a village shopkeeper who keeps no proper books of account, prepare accounts for the year ended 30 June 20X1.

Summary of banking account

	£		£
Opening balance	2,600	Payments for goods bought	
Shop takings paid in	98,740	for inventory	57,180
Sale of motor van, 1 Jan 20X1	3,600	Payments of business expenses	6,720
		Private items	5,400
		Purchase of new motor van,	
		1 Jan 20X1	8,500
		Closing balance	27,140
	104,940		104,940

	30 June 20X0 £	30 June 20X1 £
Inventory	24,000	29,000
Amount owing for goods sold	800	1,250
Amount owing for goods bought	7,640	18,400
Amount owing for business expenses	1,320	730
Furniture, fixtures and fittings	6,000	6,000
Motor van	4,500	8,500
Cash in hand	800	350

Of shop takings of £6,000 which were not banked, £1,500 were used to pay various business expenses.

Estimated annual depreciation on written-down values: furniture, fixtures and fittings, 5 per cent; motor van, 20 per cent.

The cost of the van sold during the year was £5,625.

9 On 30 June 20X1 the bank column of John Smith's cash book showed a debit balance of £12,600. On examination of the cash book and bank statement the following was revealed:

(a) Cheques amounting to £935 which were issued to creditors and entered in the cash book before 30 June were not presented for payment until after that date.

(b) Cheques amounting to £230 had been recorded in the cash book as having been paid into the bank on 30 June, but were entered on the bank statement on 1 July.

(c) A cheque for £70 had been dishonoured prior to 30 June, but no record of this fact appeared in the cash book.

(d) A dividend of £340 paid direct to the bank had not been recorded in the cash book.

(e) Bank interest and charges of £60 had been charged in the bank statement but not entered in the cash book.

(f) No entry had been made in the cash book for a trade subscription of £15 paid by banker's order in January 20X1.

Required:

(a) To make appropriate adjustments in the cash book bringing down the correct balance.

(b) To prepare a statement reconciling the adjusted balance in the cash book with the balance shown in the bank statement for 30 June 20X1 which was a credit balance of £13,500.

10* The following balances were extracted from the books of D Stowe at 31 December 20X0:

	£
Sales	15,620
Purchases	10,400
Inventory at 1 January 20X0	4,140
Motor vehicles	16,400
Provision for depreciation at 1 January 20X0	7,900
Debtors	12,300
Creditors	15,600
Cash at bank	3,215
Motor expenses	620
Rent and rates	1,160
Insurance	185
Electricity	120
Postage and telephone	250
Drawings	4,100
Sundry expenses	270
Capital at 1 January 20X0	14,040

The following matters are to be taken into account:

1 Inventory at 31 December 20X0 were £7,350.
2 Depreciation of £1,200 is to be charged.
3 Expenses accrued at 31 December 20X0 were electricity £45, telephone £65 and sundry expenses £24.
4 Expenses prepaid at 31 December 20X0 were rent and rates £240, insurance £40.

Required:

Prepare an income statement for the year ended 31 December 20X0, and a balance sheet at that date.

11 The following trial balance was extracted from the books of Tim Russell at 31 December 20X0.

	£	£
Sales		105,560
Purchases	71,224	
Discounts allowed and received	1,206	684
Carriage	2,588	
Drawings	431	
Rent, rates and insurance	5,973	
Postage and stationery	1,213	
Advertising	1,852	
Salaries and wages	13,076	
Bad debts	1,234	
Debtors	13,170	
Creditors		11,640
Cash in hand	312	
Cash at bank	3,054	
Inventory as at 1 January	7,154	
Equipment –		
at cost	48,700	
accumulated depreciation		21,650
Capital		31,653
	171,187	171,187

The following additional information as at 31 December 20X0 is available:

1 £588 of the carriage represents carriage inwards on purchases.
2 Equipment is to be depreciated at 10 per cent per annum using the straight-line method.
3 Rates have been prepaid by £213.
4 Advertising is accrued by £177.
5 Salaries and wages includes £5,500 which was paid on a weekly basis to Tim.
6 Inventory at the close of business was valued at £8,221.

Required:

Prepare a trading and income statement for the year ended 31 December 20X0 and a balance sheet as at that date.

Reference   AICPA (1994) *Improving Business Reporting – A Customer Focus* (The Jenkins Report), American Institute of Certified Public Accountants.

CHAPTER 15

Reporting recorded assets and liabilities

Setting the scene

This chapter further examines the logic and methodology which underlie the traditional manner in which assets and liabilities are recorded and depicted on the balance sheet. First, we discuss the conventional historical cost valuation of assets and the implications of this method of valuation for balance sheet purposes. Second, we discuss the adjustments to historical cost values which are made at the stage of preparing the balance sheet. Third, we review the implications of the variety of different results obtained from traditional accounting practices. In this chapter, therefore, the concern is with historical cost valuation. The discussion of alternative valuation bases is deferred to Part 3.

Learning objectives

After studying this chapter you should be able to:

1 identify the general rules for valuing non-current assets;

2 demonstrate how the various methods used for valuing inventory affect income measurement;

3 explain the problem of recognizing income or loss on long-term contracts;

4 discuss the problems inherent in valuing intangible assets;

5 explain how liabilities are valued in the financial statements.

The financial accounting concepts examined in Chapter 8 may be said to have their origin in the concept of stewardship accounting. A number of these concepts have a determining influence on valuation for financial reporting purposes, and reflect the stewardship concept of financial reporting as regards the manner in which boards of directors should communicate information to shareholders concerning the manner in which their funds have been handled. For example, when a transaction occurs, it is said that both parties to the transaction are agreed as to the exchange value of the asset involved. That value may be verified at that point. It is an objective measure of value for accounting purposes. It follows that the cost of acquiring assets has traditionally been thought to provide the best method of valuing assets for financial reporting purposes on the assumption that the objective of financial reporting is to explain to shareholders how their funds have been utilized.

Since the stewardship concept of financial reporting has its roots also in the prevention of frauds, it is interesting to note that one of the major arguments in favour of historical cost valuation is the prevention of fraud. Accountants feel that to depart from this basis of valuation would open the way to fraudulent practices since other measures of value are essentially in the nature of opinions and judgements.

Note that the concept of prudence leads to a modification of the cost concept in certain cases, and to reporting to shareholders the lowest likely value. For example, if the net realizable value of inventory is lower than its historical cost value, the concept of prudence requires that the net realizable value be adopted.

The concept of consistency requires that once a basis of valuation has been adopted, it should not be changed except for valid reasons.

Finally, it should be noted that company law stipulates the manner in which values should be reported. Generally, in most countries, the law reflects the concepts of accounting, and in this respect we may say that in developing legal rules for financial reporting, the law has followed its tradition of codifying concepts existing among practitioners. This has certainly been the case in countries in the Anglo-Saxon tradition, such as the United Kingdom and the USA.

The valuation of assets

The key to an understanding of the manner in which the accountant approaches the problem of valuation is to be found in the classification of assets. Non-current assets are long-term assets whose usefulness in the operations of the firm is likely to extend beyond one accounting period. They are not intended for resale, so that their economic value depends upon the expected future cash flows they are intended to generate. By contrast, current assets are those intended to be exhausted in the income-earning operations of the next accounting period, and this includes their availability for meeting current liabilities.

The valuation of non-current assets

There are three general rules for valuing non-current assets:

1 The enterprise should be considered as a going concern, unless the facts indicate the contrary. Thus the valuation of non-current assets should reflect the continued expectation of their usefulness to the enterprise. For this reason, their realizable value is inappropriate, and their historical cost is regarded as the most objective measure of value. Historical cost includes the original purchase price and, in addition, all other costs incurred in rendering the asset ready for use.
2 Changes in the market value of non-current assets have traditionally been ignored in the valuation process, although, as we shall see, this position has changed in recent years.
3 Losses in value attributable to wear and tear should always be recognized.

The main requirements for the recognition, measurement and depreciation of tangible non-current assets are included in International Accounting Standard (IAS) 16 'Property, Plant and Equipment'. Some other relevant requirements are included in IAS 23 'Borrowing Costs'. As regards the United Kingdom, for example, these requirements broadly correspond with the Accounting Standards Board FRS 15 'Tangible Fixed Assets'. Compliance with FRS 15 leads to compliance with IAS 16 in stipulating that fixed assets should initially be recorded at cost. 'Cost' here includes those costs that are directly attributable to bringing the asset into working condition for its intended use.

The valuation of land

Land has traditionally been valued at cost despite rises or falls in market value. Cost includes broker's commission, surveying and legal fees and insurance charges. In addition, draining, levelling and landscaping costs and other improvements such as fencing, sewerage and water mains should be included, though it is quite common in the case of farm accounts for these improvements to be shown separately because of the different tax allowances which they occasionally enjoy. Land is not generally regarded as susceptible to depreciation.

The valuation of buildings

Buildings have traditionally been valued on a historical cost basis – whether they have been acquired or constructed. Construction costs include such incidental expenses as architects' fees, inspection fees and insurance costs applicable to a construction project. Where an existing building is purchased, the costs of rendering the building suitable for its intended purpose should be added to the purchase price in arriving at its historical cost value.

The valuation process for buildings differs from that of land in two ways:

1 A cost of maintenance is involved in the repairs which have to be made from time to time in the upkeep of the building. Such maintenance expenses are charged as they are incurred to the income statement. Additions and improvements to the building, which are distinguished from repairs, must be capitalized and added to the value of the building.
2 Buildings depreciate with age. The accounts value should be shown at cost less the accumulated depreciation to date.

The valuation of plant and machinery and other non-current assets

Plant and machinery, furniture and fittings, motor vehicles, tools and sundry equipment are usually valued at historical cost with proper allowance for depreciation. Cost includes purchase price, freight charges, insurance in transit and all installation costs. As we saw in Chapter 13, the purpose of depreciation in accounting is to allocate the cost of non-current assets to the several years of their useful life to the firm.

The revaluation of non-current assets

There are interesting differences between IAS 16 and the relevant requirement of IAS 23 and the practice allowed in the United Kingdom under FRS 15, which illustrate how these differences are resolved with respect to the applicability of international accounting standards and national standards. They relate to 'fair value' as distinct to 'current value' as an appropriate valuation base for revaluation purposes and to the treatment of revaluation gains and losses.

The practice of revaluing assets was recognized by legislation in the United Kingdom in 1948, when the Companies Act of that year stipulated that non-current assets should be shown at cost, or, if they stand in the company's books at a valuation, the amount of the valuation. However, no guidance was given by the Act as to when a valuation should be made, except in the case of property where a 'substantial difference' between cost and market value should be indicated in the balance sheet.

Before FRS 15 was issued, companies could freely pick and choose which of their assets they wished to revalue and when, enabling them to manipulate their published results. FRS 15 does not require companies to revalue assets but it does stipulate that, where a revaluation policy is adopted, it should be applied consistently to individual classes of assets and the revaluations must be kept up-to-date.

Both IAS 16 'Property, Plant and Equipment' and FRS 15 'Tangible Fixed Assets' require that, where a policy of revaluation is adopted, the revalued tangible non-current assets should be carried forward at current value. IAS 16 uses the term 'fair value', which in the case of land and buildings, plant and equipment is usually their market value, whereas FRS 15 defines current value as the lower of replacement cost and recoverable amount, believing that this is a more precise and clearer indication of the amount at which the asset should be revalued. FRS 15 ensures some internal consistency in a company's accounting, but it does not directly provide for comparability between companies. Analysts of financial statements will still need to make allowances for different accounting policies on tangible fixed asset valuation.

Revaluation gains and losses should be reported in the income statement. IAS 16 permits only those losses that reverse revaluation gains previously recognized to be recognized, whereas FRS 15 requires other losses to be recognized in the statement of total recognized gains and losses to the extent that an asset's recoverable amount is greater than the recoverable amount arguing that such losses that do not result from impairement are caused by a general fall in prices.

The valuation of current assets

Current assets consist of cash and other assets, such as debtors and inventories that are expected to be converted into cash or to be used in the operations of the enterprise within one year. The most complex problems lie in the valuation of the three different types of inventory – raw materials, work-in-progress and finished goods. The production process may be viewed as adding value to successive categories of inventories, that is, from raw material to finished goods. Furthermore, inventory values affect the income statement as well as the balance sheet. Since they are an important constituent of the expenses chargeable against sales revenue, they occupy a key position in the determination of periodic income.

Inventories

Inventories are valued at the lower of cost and net realizable value. International Accounting Standard 2 Inventories (IAS 2) states that inventories shall be measured at the lower of cost and net realizable value, net realizable value being the estimated selling price in the ordinary course of business less the estimated cost of completion and the estimated costs necessary to make the sale. The corresponding regulation in the United Kingdom, SSAP 9 'Stocks and Long-Term Contracts' dates from 1975 and required that the cost of inventory 'should comprise that expenditure which has been incurred in the normal course of business in bringing the product or service to its present location and condition'. Acquisition costs reflected in inventory values should be added to the costs of purchasing, of packaging and of transport. Where applicable, trade discounts should be deducted from the purchase price. There are, however, many different methods for determining the cost value of inventories, and these methods produce valuations which differ markedly from each other. A simple example serves to illustrate how three different valuation methods lead to divergent values.

Example 15.1 A firm has an opening inventory of 100 items valued at £1.00 each. During the accounting period, 100 units were purchased for £1.20 each and a further 100 units were purchased for £1.30 each. There remained 100 units in inventory at the end of the accounting period, that is, after 200 units had been sold for £300.

The firm is considering the effects of the undermentioned three methods of inventory valuation:

1 first in, first out (FIFO);
2 last in, first out (LIFO);
3 weighted average cost.

The effects of these alternative methods may be seen from the tabulation of inventory data below:

	Unit	Unit cost (£)	Value (£)
Opening inventory	100	1.00	100
First purchase	100	1.20	120
Second purchase	100	1.30	130

1 The FIFO method assumes that the oldest items in inventory are used first, so that the items in inventory are assumed to be the remnants of more recent purchases. The result of the application of FIFO to the given data is that the cost of goods sold during the year is taken to be £220, and the value of the closing inventory is £130.

Advocates of the FIFO method argue that its underlying assumption is in accordance with conventional practice that goods purchased first are sold first, and that this method eliminates the opportunities for management to manipulate income and inventory values by selecting out of the existing inventory the values which serve their purposes best. Under conditions of rising prices, FIFO requires that the inventory of the earliest date and prices be deemed sold first, with the effect that the income statement reflects a higher level of income than would have been the case if current replacement costs had been used. Closing inventory values are shown at the more recent acquisition prices and thus approximate current replacement costs.

2 The LIFO method assumes that the most recently purchased inventories are used first, so that the items remaining in inventory at the end of the year are assumed to be the remnants of earlier purchases. Under this method, the cost of goods sold during the year is taken to be £250, and the value of the closing ionventory is £100. The LIFO method has the opposite effect, therefore, to that of FIFO on the measurement of income and the valuation of closing inventory.

Though LIFO approximates the replacement cost basis of valuation as regards the input of resources to the income-earning process, it does not necessarily correspond with replacement cost valuation. LIFO reflects the latest cost price of the specific commodity, which may or may not be the actual replacement cost. In the case of seasonal buying, for example, the cost of the last purchase may not be equivalent to the current replacement cost. As a result, LIFO eliminates only an indeterminate part of the effects of specific price changes. Indeed, when sales exceed purchases, that is, when inventories are being depleted, the gap between replacement cost and LIFO may become very great. A classic example of this situation arose in the United States during the Korean War, which resulted in inventory reduction on such a scale that Congressional approval was given for next-in-first-out inventory valuation as a relief for taxpayers who were on the LIFO basis! A further disadvantage of the LIFO method of inventory valuation is that it leads to distortions in balance sheet valuations. If the quantity in inventory remains stable or increases LIFO can result in an asset balance that is substantially out of line with current costs.

3 The weighted average cost method requires the calculation of the unit cost of closing inventory by means of a formula which divides the total cost of all inventories available for sale during the accounting period by the physical units of inventory available for sale

The weighted average cost of the 300 units available for sale may be calculated as follows:

$$\frac{\text{Total cost of annual inventory}}{\text{Total annual units in inventory}} = \frac{£350}{300} = £1.167 \text{ per unit}$$

Hence, the cost of goods sold during the year is £233, while the value of the closing inventory is £117. The weighted average cost method is a compromise, therefore, between the extreme points established by FIFO and LIFO respectively.

Example 15.2 The effects of different methods of inventory valuation on the calculation of income may be seen in the example given below. For simplicity, it is assumed that the business is considering a change in the method of valuation which gave an opening inventory value of £100.

	FIFO	LIFO	Weighted average
	£	£	£
Purchases	250	250	250
Add: Opening inventory	100	100	100
	350	350	350
Less: Closing inventory	130	100	117
Cost of goods sold	220	250	233
Sales	300	300	300
Net income	80	50	67

This simple example shows that the closing inventory may be valued at £130, £100 or £117, depending on the assumptions made about the flow of costs. Three different income figures result from using different inventory valuation methods, namely £80, £50 and £67. It should be remembered that the closing inventory for one year becomes the opening inventory of the following year. Therefore, in the long term, there will be no difference in the calculation of the net income of the business. It is in the short term that different inventory valuation methods give different results. This fact emphasizes the significance of any changes in the inventory valuation method used.

IAS 2 'Inventories' prescribes that the cost of inventories shall be assigned using the FIFO or weighted average method. It precludes the use of the LIFO method. In the United Kingdom, although the Companies Act 1985 allowed the use of LIFO, SSAP 9 stated that the LIFO method does not usually bear a reasonable relationship to actual cost where balance sheet values are concerned, and so at present LIFO is not usually appropriate as a method of inventory valuation. In May 2002, the Accounting Standards Board in the United Kingdom issued FRED 28 (Financial Reporting Exposure Draft) 'Inventories, Construction and Service Contracts' with the purpose of bringing convergence between IAS 2 'Inventories' and IAS 11 'Construction Contracts' by breaking up SSAP 9 into two new accounting standards. It proposed also to abolish LIFO as a legitimate method of inventory valuation.

Long-term contracts

Construction contracts, such as those for dams, roads, ships and industrial plants, may take years to complete. At the end of a given accounting period, a contracting company has to determine the extent to which income or loss should be recognized as arising only on the completion of the contract. Income realization rests on a factual basis. On completion date, all revenues and costs are known, and the income earned on the contract may be determined readily. If the contract covers several accounting periods, this method of reporting income will result in wide income fluctuations over these periods.

IAS 11 'Construction Contracts' provides that if the outcome of a construction contract can be estimated reliably, revenues and costs should be recognized in proportion to the stage of completion of contract activity, in accordance with the percentage of completion method of accounting. To be able to estimate the outcome reliably, the enterprise must be able to make reliable estimates of total contract revenue, the stage of completion and the costs to complete the contract. If the outcome cannot be estimated reliably, no income should be recognized. Instead, contract revenue should be recognized only to the extent that contract costs are expected to be recoverable and contract costs should be expenses as incurred.

In line with the policy of establishing convergence with international accounting standards in the United Kingdom, FRED 28 re-affirmed the Accounting Standards Board's position on long-term contracts stated in SSAP 9 'Stocks and Long-Term Contracts', namely, that 'where the business carries out long-term contracts and it is considered that their outcomes can be assessed with reasonable certainty before their conclusion, the attributable income should be calculated on a prudent basis and included in the accounts for the period under review'. Attributable income may be calculated as follows:

$$\text{accrued profits} = [\text{total contact price} - (\text{costs to date} + \text{estimated costs of completion})]$$
$$\times \frac{\text{work certified to date}}{\text{total contract price}}$$

It is the normal practice in long-term contracts to have stages certified as completed for the purpose of determining progress payments. The issue of a work-completed certificate justifies the calculation of the income or loss to be taken at that point. No income should be recognized until it may be predicted with reasonable certainty. As soon as it becomes evident that a loss on completion is likely, the entire loss and not merely the accrued proportion must be recognized immediately.

Example 15.3 J Nicholl, contractor, had undertaken to extend a factory building for I McClure at a contract price of £100,000, estimating the work would take 18 months to complete. At the financial year end he estimated that costs to date were £30,000 and that a further £50,000 would be involved in completing the project. The value of work certified was £25,000. J Nicholl would estimate attributable income as follows:

	£	£
Contract price		100,000
Costs to financial year end	30,000	
Estimated costs to complete	50,000	
		80,000
Estimated total income		20,000

$$\text{attributable profit} = \frac{\text{work certified to date}}{\text{total contract price}} \times \text{estimated total profit}$$

$$= \frac{£25,000}{£100,000} \times £20,000 = £5,000$$

Debtors

The problems associated with the valuation of debtors were discussed in Chapter 13.

The valuation of other assets

Investments

In financial accounting, investments are defined as shares and other legal rights acquired by a firm through the investment of its funds. Investments may be long term or short term, depending upon the intention of the firm at the time of acquisition. Where investments are intended to be held for a period of more than one year, they are in the nature of non-current assets: where they are held for a shorter period, they are in the nature of current assets. Shares in subsidiary and associated companies are usually not held for resale, and hence would be classified as being of the nature of non-current assets. Short-dated government inventories, for example, may provide a convenient vehicle for the investment of excess funds not immediately needed. Such short-term holdings would be classified as current assets in the balance sheet.

Investments, therefore can be found in two places on the balance sheet – non-current assets or current assets. Like any other non-current assets, long-term investments must be shown at cost less any necessary provisions. If the net realizable value falls below the cost valuation, a provision will have to be made to cover impairment in value'. As an alternative to showing non-current asset investments at their cost, a market valuation may be used.

Current asset investments are normally stated at the lower of their purchase price and net realizable value. Where a current asset investment has been written down to its net realizable value, but the provision which has been made proves not to have been required, then the provision must be eliminated or reduced, as appropriate. Current asset investments may also be stated at their current cost.

Two special categories of investments that have considerable economic importance require separate treatment. They are investments made in subsidiary and associated companies consequent upon the growth of large groups of companies through the process of mergers and acquisitions and the extensive trading in financial instruments taking place in financial markets. Financial reporting for groups of companies will be discussed in Part 4.

International Accounting Standard Board IAS 39 'Financial Instruments: Recognition and Measurement', corresponding to the UK Accounting Standards Board FRS 26 'Financial Instruments: Recognition and Measurement', defines a financial instrument as 'a contract that gives rise to a financial asset of one entity and a financial liability or equity instrument of another entity'. Common examples of financial instruments within the scope of IAS 39 are cash, demand and time deposits, commercial paper, notes and loans receivable and payable, debt and equity securities, asset backed securities such as collaterized mortgage obligations, repurchase agreements and securitized packages of receivables. Specifically, the definition includes financial derivates that constitute major market trading in options, rights, warrants, futures contracts, forward contracts and swaps.

The credit and banking crisis that threatened the collapse of the international financial system was rooted in the expansion of sub-prime mortgages which fuelled an explosive growth in complex financial instruments such as financial derivatives secured on packaged mortgages. Widely used by financial institutions, these derivatives that collaterized debt obligations and were treated as asset-backed securities resulted in an uncontrolled credit expansion and as securities in interbank lending. They were accepted at face values that escaped verification by reason of their structured complexity that few really understood. The total volume of these instruments that became toxic assets ran into several trillion dollars in the USA. Shown as assets on balance sheets of financial institutions that ranged from investment banks and mortage companies to savings and loans institutions, they proved ultimately to be effectively worthless and had no evident current recoverable value. Governments committed huge sums in preventing the collapse of the international financial system and in the rescue of major banks. Even in the USA, the authorities feared the demise of the capitalist system and, unheard in a world committed to free markets, both the USA and the UK effectively nationalized major financial institutions by taking over financial responsibility for financial institutions that were technically bankrupt. This action resulted in toxic assets held in accordance with normal accounting valuation rules stated above and with corresponding huge debts to government. Maintaining conventional accounting valuation rules in this situation was unacceptable to both Government and the regulatory authorities and led to a proposal for replacing the mark-to-market rule, namely the lower of cost or market value as a 'fair value' rule based on a hypothetical value of what such assets might be expected to have in normal circumstances.

Intangible assets

Intangible assets do not have any physical features, rather they represent legal rights and relationships beneficial to their owner. The most important single characteristic of intangible assets is the high degree of uncertainty regarding the value and existence of the future benefits to be received. The most common examples are:

1 patents, copyrights, and trademarks;
2 research and development costs;
3 goodwill.

IAS 38 'Intangible Assets' provides rules for the recognition and measurement of intangible assets and provides that, initially intangible assets shall be measured at cost. A distinction is made between intangible assets that have been acquired through purchase or in the course of a business combination. If acquired separately, the cost value applies and if acquired in a business combination, it is the fair value that applies. The corresponding UK Accounting Standard FRS 10 'Goodwill and Intangible Assets' provides recognition and measurement rules.

An important distinction is made between purchased intangible assets and internally generated intangible assets, such as internally generated goodwill and research on new product development. IAS 38 provides that internally generated goodwill shall not be recognized as an asset and expenditure on research and intangible items shall be recognized as an expense as it is incurred.

Patents

A patent is a legal right to exploit a new invention, and is obtained following the registration of its specification with the Designs Registry of the Patent Office. Patents are recorded at cost and are amortized (written off) over their effective life, usually on a straight-line basis. A similar treatment is applied to other such exclusive rights which are granted by government authority, for example copyrights and trademarks.

Research and development costs

Research and development costs fall under three main headings:

1 *pure research:* experimental or theoretical work undertaken primarily to acquire new scientific knowledge or technical knowledge for its own sake;
2 *applied research:* original or critical investigation undertaken in order to gain new scientific or technical knowledge and directed towards a specific practical aim or objective;
3 *development:* use of scientific or technical knowledge in order to produce new or substantially improved materials, devices, products or services, to install new processes or systems prior to the commencement of commercial production or commercial applications, or to improving substantially those already produced or installed.

As regards expenditure falling within the first two categories, which may be regarded as part of a continuing operation required to maintain a company's business and its competitive position, this should be written off against revenue in the year in which expenditure is incurred. This excludes the cost of non-current assets acquired or constructed for research and development activities over a period of time which should be capitalized and written off over the useful life of the assets. IAS 38 'Intangible Assets' and in the UK FRS 'Goodwill and Intangible Assets' provide similarly that expenditure on development should be written off in the year of expenditure except in the following circumstances, where it may be deferred to future periods:

1 there is a clearly defined project;
2 the related expenditure is separately identifiable;
3 the outcome of such a project has been assessed with reasonable certainty as to its technical feasibility, and its ultimate commercial viability;

4 if further development costs are to be incurred on the same project, the aggregate of such costs, together with related production, selling and administration costs are reasonably expected to be more than covered by related future revenues; and

5 adequate resources exist, or are reasonably expected to be available, to enable the project to be completed and to provide any consequential increases in working capital.

In the circumstances defined above, development expenditure may be deferred to subsequent years, and shown on the balance sheet as an asset to the extent that its recovery can be regarded as reasonably assured. Such expenditure will be subsequently amortized against revenue. Deferred development expenditure should be reviewed at the end of each accounting period, and when the circumstances which have justified the deferral of the expenditure no longer apply then the expenditure to the extent considered irrecoverable should be written off immediately.

Goodwill

Goodwill may be described as the sum of those intangible attributes of a business which contribute to its success, such as a favourable location, a good reputation, the ability and skill of its employees and management, and its long-standing relationships with creditors, suppliers and customers. The valuation of goodwill is a controversial topic in accounting because of its vague nature and the difficulty of arriving at a valuation which is verifiable. Hence, in view of its lack of accounting objectivity, it is generally excluded from the balance sheet. Goodwill only enters the accounting system in connection with a valuation ascribed to it in the acquisition price of a business. In such a case, that portion of the purchase price which exceeds the total value of the assets, less the liabilities taken over, represents the amount paid for goodwill. At this point, therefore, there is no objective measure of the value of goodwill.

The treatment of acquired goodwill arises in connection with its carrying value as an asset shown on the balance sheet. ISA 36 Impairment of Assets seeks to ensure that assets are carried at no more than their recoverable value. An asset is deemed to be impaired when its carrying value exceeds the amount that could be recovered through use or sale of the asset, in which case an impairment loss must be recognized. Accordingly, IAS 36 requires an annual impairment test to be carried out. An impairment loss must be written off immediately to the income statement.

FRS 10 'Goodwill and Intangible Assets' issued by the Accounting Stantard Board in the UK deal at length with the treatment of purchased good to ensure that purchased goodwill and intangible assets are charged to the income statement in the period in which they are depleted'. FRS 10 is based on the matching concept which links revenues with their relevant expenses. The option of writing off goodwill immediately against reserves, which was available and almost exclusively adopted by UK companies prior to FRS 10 was ruled out completely and FRS 10 provided that purchased goodwill be capitalized and amortized (i.e. depreciated) over its expected useful economic life, which in general will not exceed twenty years.

However, FRS 10 allows a company to amortize more slowly, or indeed not at all, if it can demonstrate that such a policy is justifiable. But if a company either amortizes goodwill over more than twenty years, or does not amortize it at all, it has to carry out an impairment test in accordance with FRS 11 'Impairment of Fixed Assets and Goodwill', which is a complex exercise. Since the requirements of FRS 10 impact adversely on company income statements, it is not surprising that most companies choose to amortize goodwill over the maximum useful economic life generally acceptable to standard setters. Twenty years is likely to be regarded as a norm to be departed from comparatively rarely by most companies.

Brands

Brands play a major influence on corporate valuations and profitability in today's highly competitive environment. From an accounting viewpoint, they are regarded as a form of goodwill and are treated in the same way. The value of acquired brands are capitalized and reported on balance sheets, whereas the enormous financial outlays expended on the creation of brand names are treated as current expenses. The decision of two major companies in the United Kingdom to give recognition of the cost of significant brands acquired began a heated controversy regarding accounting for brands. Grand Metropolitan plc decided to recognize brands acquired since 1985 in their 1988 balance sheet, but specifically excluded created brands. However, Rank Hovis McDougall plc in their 1988 balance sheet showed the value of all brands currently used by the group and appeared to have treated acquired and created brands on the same footing.

The objectives of these companies were to add strength to their balance sheets, improve their share prices, diminish their vulnerability to takeover and increase their borrowing power. Certainly, the balance sheets of these companies were transformed by their decision on brands. Two major issues relate to these decisions. First, there is no generally accepted method of objectively valuing brands. The uncertainties surrounding the calculations of brand values cast doubts on their usefulness to users. Second, as stated in the Introduction to this part, it is not the objective of the balance sheet to place a value on a company.

IAS 38 'Intangible Assets' specifically prohibits the recognition of internally generated brands. In their report to the ICAEW's Research Board, Barwise *et al.* (1989) concluded that the issue of brand accounting is 'inseparable from the accounting treatment of goodwill'. The Accounting Standards Committee adopted the same view in a technical release (TR 780) which was published in 1990:

> *The ASC's analysis leads it to conclude that whatever definition is adopted the term 'brand' describes what is generally regarded for accounting purposes as goodwill. It is concluded that for such purposes brands are subsumed within goodwill and this should be accounted for in accordance with the requirements for accounting for goodwill.*

Leases

A lease is a contract which grants the right to operate or use property for a specified period of time. The lessor retains the ownership of the asset, but conveys to the lessee the right of use in consideration of the payment of a specified rent.

The traditional approach to accounting for leases has been to record the transactions in their legal form. The lessee merely debits the rent due and payable to the income statement. Since the lessee has no ownership right, no asset is shown on the balance sheet. The lessor, on the other hand, remains the owner of the asset leased, which is recorded as an asset on the lessor's balance sheet. At the same time, the rent receivable is recorded as revenue in the lessor's income statement. Seen from a business viewpoint, the lessee acquires the use of an asset without needing to buy it, therefore avoiding the necessity of raising finance for its acquisition. Had the lessee acquired the asset, and borrowed money to that end, both the assets and the debt would have been recorded on the balance sheet. For this reason, leasing is frequently referred to as 'off-balance-sheet financing'. The leasing of assets is a practice which is increasing. The traditional treatment of leases in accounting may be misleading to users of financial statements wishing to assess a company's state of affairs.

International Accounting Standard (IAS 17) 'Leases' applies to all leases other than lease agreements for minerals, oil, natural gas and similar resources and licensing agreements for films, videos, plays, manuscripts, patents, copyrights and similar items. It provides that finance leases should be recorded as an asset and a liability at the lower of its fair value and the present value of the minimum lease payments. The lease payments should be apportioned between the finance charge and the reduction of the outstanding liability. Assets held under financial leases should be depreciated in line with owned assets, while operating lease payments should be recognized as expenses over the lease term.

Similarly, in the United Kingdom, SSAP 21 'Accounting for Leases and Hire Purchase Contracts' seeks to reflect the economic nature of a leasing transaction by bringing leases on to balance sheets. The principal requirement of SSAP 21 is for lessees to capitalize finance leases, i.e. those which transfer substantially all the risks and rewards of ownership of a leased asset to the lessee. A capitalized asset is then depreciated over its useful life. A corresponding liability for future lease payments is recorded at the net present value of the future payments. The interest rate applied to find net present value is the rate 'implicit in the lease'. Part of each lease payment is treated as being payment of interest on the outstanding liability: the balance is debited against the liability. Therefore, instead of charging the full amount of lease payments against income, the lessee charges depreciation and interest. In any one year, the sum of these two charges may exceed or fall short of the lease payment but over the period of the life of the asset the total of depreciation and interest will equal total lease payments.

In the lessor's accounts, the lease transaction is treated as though it were an outright sale. A deferred receivable is recorded which is the counterpart of the lessee's liability.

| Example 15.4 | A lessee enters into a lease for an item of plant. The following details apply: |

Fair value of asset	£100,000
Residual value of asset	nil after 5 years
Lease terms	£25,000 for 5 years commencing 1 Jan 20X0

The implicit rate of return which equates five payments of £25,000 annually in advance to the purchase price of £100,000 is approximately 12.5 per cent. The lessee's income statement will reflect both the finance charge and depreciation on the asset as follows:

Income statements

Year	Average amount outstanding	Charge to interest at 12.5%	Depreciation, 20% straight line	Total
	£	£	£	£
20X0	75,000	9,375	20,000	29,375
20X1	59,375	7,422	20,000	27,422
20X2	41,797	5,225	20,000	25,225
20X3	22,022	2,978	20,000	22,978
20X4			20,000	20,000
		25,000	100,000	125,000

The balance sheets would record the net book value of the asset and the obligations show the outstanding principal of the loan together with the accrued interest for the year. The amount of principal outstanding is apportioned to show the amount falling due within one year and that which falls due after more than one year of the balance sheet date.

Balance sheets

Year	20X0	20X1	20X2	20X3	20X4
Cost	100,000	100,000	100,000	100,000	100,000
Depreciation	20,000	40,000	60,000	80,000	100,000
	80,000	60,000	40,000	20,000	–
Current liabilities					
Obligations under finance lease	15,625	17,578	19,775	22,022	–
Accrued interest	9,375	7,422	5,225	2,978	–
	25,000	25,000	25,000	25,000	–
Deferred liabilities					
Obligations under finance lease	59,375	41,797	22,022	–	–
	84,375	66,797	47,022	25,000	–

In this example we have used the actuarial approach for capitalizing the finance lease. SSAP 21 states that the rule-of-78/sum-of-digits method may normally be regarded as an acceptable method. The calculations using the rule of 78 are shown below.

Year	Rental (£)	Interest charge (£)
20X0	25,000 × 4/10	10,000
20X1	25,000 × 3/10	7,500
20X2	25,000 × 2/10	5,000
20X3	25,000 × 1/10	2,500
20X4	–	–
		25,000

Provisions, contingent liabilities and contingent assets

International Accounting Standard 37 'Provisions, Contingent Liabilities and Contingent Assets' and, its equivalent in the United Kingdom FRS 12 which was promulgated in 1999, seek to ensure that provisions, contingent liabilities and contingent assets are recognized and measured on a consistent basis by providing appropriate recognition criteria and measurement bases to enable users of financial statements to understand their nature, timing and amount. IAS 37 provides the following definitions:

1 A provision is a liability of uncertain timing or amount.
2 A liability is a present obligation as a result of past events, settlement expected to result in payment.
3 A contingent liability is a possible obligation depending on whether some uncertain future event occurs, or a present obligation, but payment is not probable or the amount cannot be measured reliably.
4 A contingent asset is a possible asset that arises from past events and whose existence will be confirmed only by the occurrence or non-occurrence of one or more uncertain future events not wholly within the control of the enterprise.

Provisions

Prior to IAS 37 and FRS 12, provisions were often used to smooth the trend of reported income. For example, a company could establish a general provision for future reorganization expenses in a year of very good profitability without having any actual obligation to carry out the reorganization. The decision to reorganize could then be subsequently reversed, with the effect that the provision would then be released to a future income statement to improve otherwise poor results.

The changes which were introduced by IAS 37 and FRS 12 stem from the new definition of a liability as an 'obligation of an entity to transfer economic benefits as a result of past transactions or events'. For there to be a liability there has to be a past event that has given rise to present obligations. A provision, which is in fact a liability, requires two further conditions relating to outflow of benefits and reliable measurement. Provisions should only be made when:

1 there is a present obligation arising from a past event;
2 there will be a probable outflow of economic benefits;
3 the amount can be reliably measured.

The reference to 'past event' means that there must be a condition at the balance sheet date. A decision or intention to do things in the future is not enough.

Contingent liabilities

Both IAS 37 and FRS 12 define a contingent liability as 'a possible obligation that arises from past events and whose existence will be confirmed only by the occurrence of one or more uncertain future events not wholly within the entity's control'. A contingent liability must never be recognized but instead should be disclosed in the notes to the accounts unless it is unlikely to be incurred.

Contingent assets

Contingent assets usually arise from unplanned or other unexpected events that give rise to the possibility of an inflow of economic benefits to the entity. Contingent assets are not recognized in financial statements because to do so could result in the recognition of income that may never be realized. However, when the realization of the income is virtually certain, the related asset is not a contingent asset and its recognition is appropriate.

Summary

It is necessary to understand the logic and methodology which underlie the recorded values of assets and liabilities in order to appreciate the nature of financial accounting information. A number of concepts surround the problem of valuation of assets and liabilities shown on income statements and balance sheets.

This chapter examines the accounting approach to the valuation of non-current and current assets, and considers the effects of inflation in modifying the historical cost concept for non-current asset valuation. The chapter also illustrates the effects of traditional accounting practices in creating variety in the accounting treatment of different items. We also saw how FRS 12 aims to ensure that provisions, contingent liabilities and contingent assets are recognized and measured on a consistent basis.

Self-assessment question

1 Examine the problems of accounting for research and development expenditure, and explain the requirements of IAS 38 Intangible Assets.

Problems (* indicates that a solution is to be found in the Lecturer's Guide)

1* You are the Chief Accountant of a retailing company which operates from a number of department stores throughout the country. You are approached early in 20X1 by a member of your staff who is preparing the annual accounts for the Barnsley store for the year ended 31 December 20X0. He seeks your advice on the following matters:

(a) how to treat the goodwill arising on the acquisition of a local bakery during 20X0. The Barnsley store acquired the bakery for the purpose of securing its own supply of bread. The cost was £85,000 including goodwill of £20,000;

(b) whether to depreciate the cost of the freehold of the furniture department's warehouse which was purchased during the year. The cost was £44,000 split between land £10,000 and buildings £34,000. Legal fees of £800 were incurred;

(c) how to value two items of inventory about which he is unsure. These are:
   (i) a large inventory of over-ordered Christmas cards costing £780;
   (ii) an inventory of skateboards purchased in 19X9 for £1,000;

(d) whether to treat an advertising campaign as an expense in 20X0 or to carry it forward to 20X1. The campaign costing involved a series of advertisements in the *Barnsley Sun* newspaper in December 20X0 informing readers of the January sale. The sale was not as popular as it has been in recent years.

Required:

Draft a memorandum to your staff setting out the accounting principles to be followed in each of the above cases and give advice on the most appropriate treatment in the circumstances given.

(Problem supplied by A J Naughton)

2 The summarized balance sheet of Demiwood Ltd for 31 December 20X0 is shown below.

	£	£
Share capital		250,000
Revenue reserves		95,000
		345,000
10% debentures		86,000
		431,000
Non-current assets (all tangible)		295,000
Current assets	221,000	
Current liabilities	(85,000)	
Net current assets		136,000
		431,000

On 1 January 20X1 Demiwood Ltd bought out the McMaltby Company which was a private company with a summarized balance sheet at 31 December 20X0 as follows:

	£	£
Capital		62,000
Represented by:		
Tangible non-current assets		
Freehold premises		25,000
Plant		20,000
		45,000
Current assets	32,000	
Current liabilities	(15,000)	
Net current assets		17,000
		62,000

An independent valuer estimated that McMaltby's premises were worth £60,000 and its plant was worth £25,000 at replacement cost. It was also estimated that inventory was undervalued by £5,000 but that debtors were overvalued by £3,000.

The agreed price for McMaltby was £120,000 which was made up of cash from a new loan of £100,000 and £20,000 in liquid assets that Demiwood already owned. The McMaltby Company ceased to exist on 1 January 20X1 and all its assets and business activities became part of Demiwood Ltd.

Required:

(a)   Calculate the goodwill arising on the takeover of the McMaltby Company.
(b)   Explain how goodwill should be treated in Demiwood's books.
(c)   Prepare a summarized balance sheet for Demiwood immediately following the takeover.

3   A fire completely destroyed Arthur's timber yard and all his accounting records, during the night of 31 December 20X0.

From duplicate bank statements and circularization of his debtors and creditors, Arthur was able to ascertain the following figures.

	£
Debtors, 1 January 20X0	5,130
Creditors, 1 January 20X0	1,790
Cash paid to creditors during the year	22,220
Cash received from debtors during the year	30,080
Creditors, 31 December 20X0	1,870
Debtors, 31 December 20X0	6,050

Arthur's trading accounts for the two years ended 31 December 19X9 were as follows:

	Year ended Dec 19X8	Year ended Dec 19X9	Year ended Dec 19X8	Year ended Dec 19X9
	£	£	£	£
Opening inventory	1,235	1,700	Sales 18,850	25,740
Purchases	13,660	17,718		
	14,895	19,418		
Less: Closing inventory	1,700	1,400		
	13,195	18,018		
Gross income	5,655	7,722		
	18,850	25,740	18,850	25,740

Assuming that the ratio of gross income to sales was the same in 20X0 as in previous years, calculate the value of the inventory destroyed by fire. Submit your workings.

4* Viva Ltd does not keep records of inventory movements. A physical inventory is made at the end of each quarter and priced at cost. This figure is used for compiling quarterly accounts. Draft accounts have been prepared for the year ended 31 March 20X0, but have not been completed as the details of the inventory account on 31 March 20X0 have been mislaid and cannot be found. The company operates on a gross-income markup of 33 per cent of cost.

You have ascertained the following facts:

(a)   the total of sales invoiced to customers during January, February and March 20X1 was £53,764. This figure includes £4,028 relating to goods despatched on or before 31 December 20X0. The total of the goods despatched to customers before 31 March 20X1 but invoiced in the following month was £5,512;

(b) the total of purchase invoices entered in the purchase day book during January, February and March 20X1 was £40,580 and this figure includes £2,940 in respect of goods received on or before 31 December 20X0. Invoices relating to goods received in March 20X1 but which were not entered in the purchase day book until April 20X1 totalled £3,880;

(c) the value of the inventory at cost on 31 December 20X0 was £42,640;

(d) in the inventory sheets at that date;

  (i) the total of one page was over-cast by £85;

  (ii) 120 items, the cost of which was £2 each, had been priced at 40p each;

  (iii) the total of the inventory in one section, which was £5,260, had been included in the summary as £5,620.

Required:

Show how you would arrive at the figure for the inventory at cost as on 31 March 20X1.

(Problem supplied by A J Naughton)

5 Purchases and sales data for the first three years of a firm's operation were as follows (purchases are listed in order of acquisition):

	19X8	19X9	20X0
	£	£	£
Sales	12,000 units @ 50	15,000 units @ 60	18,000 units @ 65
Purchases	4,000 units @ 22	5,500 units @ 32	7,000 units @ 40
	6,000 units @ 25	6,000 units @ 34	4,500 units @ 43
	5,000 units @ 30	4,000 units @ 37	5,000 units @ 45

Required:

(a) Prepare a schedule showing the number of units on hand at the end of each year.

(b) Compute the year-end inventories for each of the three years using (i) FIFO, (ii) LIFO, (iii) average cost.

(c) Calculate the gross income for each of the three years based on (i) FIFO, (ii) LIFO and (iii) weighted average.

(d) Which method of inventory valuation do you consider the most appropriate? Why?

6 Z Ltd is engaged upon a contract the price of which is £250,000. At 31 December 20X0 the expenditure on the contract is as follows:

	£
Materials issued from store	42,000
Wages	39,820
Expenses directly chargeable to the contract	12,130
Materials purchased and delivered direct to the site	4,910
Plant in use on site valued at	6,840
Proportion of overhead charges	790

The amount of work completed to date as certified by the architect after 20 per cent retention money was £100,000. Materials in inventory at the site were valued at £970 and depreciation is to be charged at 5 per cent. Prepare the contract account showing the proportion of income you would advise should be taken to the income statement.

7 Builders Ltd commenced work on 1 July 20X0 on a contract the agreed price of which was £250,000. Expenditure incurred during the year to 30 June 20X1 was as follows:

Wages £60,000; plant £17,500; materials £42,500; sundry expenses £4,000; and head office charges allocated to the contract amounted to £5,500. Part of the plant which had cost £1,300 was sold for £1,500.

Of the contract price £100,000 representing 80 per cent of the work certified had been received by 30 June 20X1 and on that date the value of the plant on the site was deemed to be £4,500 and that of the unused materials £1,250. Work costing £12,500 had been completed but not certified at 30 June 20X1.

It was decided to estimate what further expenditure would be incurred in completing the contract for the purpose of computing the estimated total income that would be made on the contract and to take to the credit of the income statement for the year a proper proportion thereof.

The estimate of additional expenditure that would be required, based on the assumption that the contract would be finished in six months' time, was as follows:

(a) Wages to complete £52,800.
(b) Materials in addition to those in inventory on 30 June 20X1 would cost £35,000.
(c) Sundry expenses would amount to £1,800.
(d) Plant in addition to plant in hand at 30 June 20X1 would cost £6,500 and the residual value of plant at 31 December 20X1 would be £3,750.
(e) Contingencies would require a further £3,500.

Prepare a contract account at 30 June 20X1.

8* Rover Company leases certain heavy equipment from the London Leasing Company under an eight-year lease. The economic life of the equipment is ten years. No residual value will remain at the end of that period. The lease agreement calls for eight annual payments of £150,000 beginning at the inception of the lease. The first payment is to be made on 1 January 20X1. Each payment thereafter falls to be made on the first day of the year. The fair value of the equipment is £1 million. Rover Company depreciates similar assets by the straight-line method.

Required:

Show how the transaction would be recorded in Rover Company's final accounts.

Reference　　Barwise, P., Higson, C., Likierman, A. and Marsh, P. (1989) *Accounting for Brands*, ICAEW and London Business School.

SECTION 2

Cost accounting

Introduction to Section 2

Whereas financial accounting information plays a major role in financial reporting to shareholders and investors, cost accounting provides vital information for the management of business enterprises, both private and public and for all forms of organization that manage economic resources in achieving their objectives. Cost management is widely regarded as one of the key success factors for profit improvement and is at the basis of sound budget management and control. This applies in all types of organizations: manufacturing, merchandising (wholesaling and retailing) and service. Although manufacturing firms require a greater quantity and variety of accounting information, most of the management accounting practices discussed in this part are applicable to all organizational settings.

Being identified with management theory, the nature and the objectives of cost accounting information is a central aspect of management control. No single management accounting system is suitable for all enterprises, management accounting requirements being contingent upon the particular characteristics of each individual business. However, every system has the following objectives:

1 It must provide reasonably accurate costs of products and services. As a subset of management accounting, cost accounting focuses on the determination of product or service cost. Cost accounting is also essentially a link between financial and management accounting for two reasons:
   (a) It provides managers with a means to follow the flow of costs through the company's accounts as the inputs they represent are converted to outputs. Such information is needed for company accounts – the balance sheet inventory values and profit and loss statement of cost of goods sold.
   (b) It provides managers with information that is useful for them in carrying out the functions considered below – decision making, planning, and controlling and evaluating performance.
2 It must provide information for making decisions. It is helpful to distinguish between recurring and non-recurring decisions. Examples of the former are the pricing of products and services, the launching of new products (in e.g. cosmetics and clothes) and changes in volumes produced and sold. Examples of the latter are restructuring, outsourcing and building new facilities.
3 It must provide sufficient useful information to help managers adequately perform their functions of planning, controlling and evaluating performance. Planning is the process of choosing objectives for a business and developing a strategy for achieving them in a systematic manner. Control is the exertion of managerial influence on operations so that they conform to plans. Essentially, the control process first involves setting performance standards or norms against which actual results are measured. The management accountant helps in determining standards for various quantities, times and costs in all operating areas. Performance is then measured and compared with the standards on a regular basis; the management

accountant's role is to provide managers with timely, relevant and reliable reports. The processes involved in management control are discussed in Part 3.

Management accountants have been criticized for placing an overemphasis on 1(a) above to the detriment of the other objectives (Johnson and Kaplan, 1987). Where this occurs, financial reporting becomes the driving force for the design of management accounting systems. These organizations may need to review the data they capture as well as the systems for processing them, in order to satisfy more fully the needs of internal users. This situation has become more serious since the mid-1980s, following changes in the environment in which many organizations operate. These changes have intensified the criticisms of traditional management accounting practices. In particular:

1 the performance measurements adopted by traditional management accounting may be of limited usefulness in certain circumstances (e.g. not capturing the costs of variety and complexity);
2 the internal orientation of management accounting restricts the usefulness of the information provided (e.g. failure to capture information on relative market shares or quality versus competitors or even the reasons non-customers do not buy the product or service);
3 the product and service costs which are produced by traditional costing methods could be incorrect and, therefore, misleading for managerial decision making (the reasons for this are legion; for example wrong cost drivers, wrong overhead rates, the failure to capture the costs of complexity, etc.).

As we stressed in Part 1 of this book, the accounting function should reflect the environment at a particular time. It is, therefore, essential to understand how the business environment has changed in recent years.

World-class manufacturing

As far as manufacturing industry is concerned the most important recent change in the environment has been the development of 'world-class manufacturing', a phrase first used by Schonberger (1986) as the title of his book. He suggests that the term 'nicely captures the breadth and the essence of the fundamental changes taking place in industrial enterprises'. The term encapsulates the dynamic changes to manufacturing processes brought on by:

1 global competition;
2 advanced manufacturing technology;
3 the adoption of new management philosophies, often developed by the Japanese, e.g. just-in-time, total quality management, six sigma and lean manufacturing.

These changes are intended to make radical improvements to the company's competitiveness and to enhance profitability. They involve improving quality, reducing lead times (the time a service or product takes to get through the process), simplifying work flows and production processes, reducing costs and enhancing product flexibility. The aim is to provide significant increases in consumer satisfaction and significant reductions in cost. Although these changes have developed under the heading of 'world-class manufacturing' (WCM), it must be stressed that these improvements are not the sole domain of manufacturing industry. While they started in manufacturing other industries have adopted the ideas and adapted them to their circumstances: this is particularly true of the service sector.

WCM introduces a new approach to product quality. This is quite different from the traditional approach because the primary emphasis is placed on resolving problems that cause poor quality, rather than merely detecting it. The purpose is systematically to expose and resolve the root causes of quality problems so that the company can eventually achieve zero defects – or 100 per cent quality. The purpose is not to increase the number of people involved with inspecting and tracing defects but to develop an awareness of quality issues within shop floor operators so that the entire workforce is harnessed to the quest for product perfection. This requires changes to both the design and manufacturing processes so that high quality can be built into the product instead of poor quality being inspected out. The introduction of advanced manufacturing technology with increased use of new machine tools with strict tolerances in manufacturing, and automated inspection not only of the finished product but also of component parts at every stage in the manufacturing cycle, result in substantial improvements in quality. A style of management aimed at producing high-quality products and services and eliminating waste is called total quality management (TQM).

WCM enhances product flexibility, the capability to adapt to new, different and changing requirements. The ability to set up and change production lines quickly increases production flexibility and enables firms to be more responsive to customers' needs. Consumers today are more sophisticated and demand greater variety and customized products and services. Therefore, products need to be more varied, display increasing complexity and have shorter life cycles in virtually all markets. Investment in advanced manufacturing technology (AMT) provides a new flexibility which is of strategic importance. Such systems enable a rapid shift with minimal disruption from one product to another and thus reduce significantly the cost penalty of product diversity. AMT also enables new products and modifications to be introduced more quickly.

Lower costs will result from the changes discussed above. For example, as a result of reduced human involvement with simplified tooling and setting up, and thus the reduction of potential human error, and with the ability to produce tight tolerances, fewer material rejects could be expected. Furthermore, total costs will be reduced by the reduction in labour costs. One of the main motivations for companies investing in robotics is to improve labour productivity and thus save on labour costs. Costs can also be reduced by the introduction of just-in-time (JIT) manufacturing which aims to change the production processes so that stocks which are not immediately required for production are eliminated. JIT will be considered in Chapter 18.

A conspicuous example of the cumulative effects of these initiatives is the Toyota Motor Company, which pioneered many of these ideas and over the years has perfected them into what has become known as the Toyota System. They have enabled the company to become the largest and most profitable car manufacturer in the world.

Growth of the service industry

Developed economies used to be dominated by manufacturing and their associated industries (extractive industries, heavy industries, heavy and light manufacturing). This is no longer the case. Manufacturing has moved increasingly to low-cost countries: China, Korea, Taiwan; while the high-cost developed economies focus on the service sectors: education, health, financial services, retail, telecommunications, transport. The transformation is striking and still has further to go. In 1945 manufacturing accounted for 75 per cent of the output of the British economy; today the figure is nearer 15 per cent. Due partly to the deregulation of many services such as insurance, banking and airlines, increased competition in the service industry has made many managers much more conscious of the need to use accounting information for planning, control and decision making. For example the attention to costs in budget airlines, such as Ryanair and the pioneering Southwest Airlines, is legendary. Both are significantly more profitable than the traditional mixed route, high cost, high price 'competitors' such as BA, American Airlines and Air Lingus. The increased competition has forced airlines to invest heavily in yield management software and route profitability systems. An example of how the unique characteristics of service firms have necessitated the extension of cost accounting to their particular circumstances.

Implications for management accounting

With changes in business in recent years managements' information needs have significantly expanded in scope and variety. Criticism of management accounting made by some commentators has largely centred on the view that managers, faced with having to make decisions in complex technology-driven situations, are supplied with information by their firm's internal management systems which is inadequate (Bromwich and Bhimani, 1994). The changes in management accounting practices which have been called for by these commentators are briefly considered below.

New measures of performance needed

Since companies now compete on quality of design, on the performance of the resulting product and on the ability to bring new products to the market quickly, as well as the provision of fast reliable delivery, measures to track performance in these areas are now essential. Over time, the pre-eminence of financial measures will diminish as non-financial measures to account for such factors are developed.

Strategic management accounting

The internal orientation of traditional accounting information is too narrow for strategic decision making. However, the competitive positioning of business in national and world markets requires that accountants, as part of top management teams, adopt a strategic perspective. Similarly, technology cost in highly automated companies is becoming very large and managers in high-tech firms need to take a longer-run perspective in making decisions (for example a new wafer fab plant costs several billion dollars). Strategic management accounting has developed to assist senior management in taking a genuinely long-term view of their business by providing information which (a) enables them to monitor and control the organization's activities in a manner measurable against the strategy and objectives, and (b) contributes to the strategic decision-making process. Strategic management accounting is considered in Part 3.

Activity-based costing

Traditional systems of product costing were designed for relatively simple, routine manufacturing processes, usually with high labour content. These systems appeared to provide satisfactory information for managers in traditional industries. However, today none of these conditions prevail: manufacturing processes are neither simple nor routine, products are not standard, product variety is high and involves considerable complexity. These have called into question traditional methods of cost accounting. Activity-based costing (ABC), which has developed to address this problem, is considered in Chapter 18.

This section examines the processes of management, describes traditional cost accounting, some recent developments, together with activity-based costing. It also examines how cost accounting information facilitates decision making, which is the process of choosing among competing alternative courses of action.

References   Bromwich, M. and Bhimani, A. (1994) *Management Accounting: Pathway to Progress*, Chartered Institute of Management Accountants.

Johnson, H.T. and Kaplan, R.S. (1987) *Relevance Lost: The Rise and Fall of Management Accounting*, Harvard Business School Press.

Schonberger, R.I. (1986) *World Class Manufacturing*, New York: Free Press.

CHAPTER 16

The processes of management

Setting the scene

Myths come and go in accounting as in other endeavours of mankind. Accountants, however, should be careful to consider the focus of their efforts to make sure that they are not just following the latest fad that may turn out to be just another myth.

Management accountants should do what their operations colleagues are doing: Go back to the basics and understand your operation. If a management accountant spends time studying the operations of his or her company to understand thoroughly what makes the organization function, then that accountant probably will create a system that helps the managers of that company regardless of whether it includes the latest gimmicks. Solid, relevant information is what managers need, and the accountant who can help managers solve their problems is the accountant who is valuable to the organization. Forget the myths, and concentrate on the fundamentals.

(Böer, 1994)

Learning objectives

After studying this chapter you should be able to:

1 identify the five stages of planning;

2 demonstrate how management coordinates the tasks necessary to achieve strategic goals;

3 analyse the relationship between control and planning;

4 discuss the role of communication in achieving organizational goals;

5 explain the importance of motivation;

6 discuss the role of information in decision making at three levels – strategic planning, management control and operational control.

There are two conflicting schools of thought regarding the extent to which the firm is in charge of its own destiny. One school postulates that firm profitability is explained almost entirely by the economics of the industry in which it competes. The other maintains that firm profitability is explained by the choices and skills of management. Paradoxically the position of both schools can be illustrated by reference to the airline industry. It is claimed that the world airline industry, since its inception, has made cumulative losses not profits. That is to say the industry is profoundly and perhaps inherently unprofitable. However, it is also true that Southwest Airlines has made a profit every single year except one. Clearly Southwest is doing something right and is used to prove the point that good management can earn good profits in a 'bad' industry. This is what planning and control theory asserts: management has control over the firm's future and believes that the firm's destiny may be manipulated and hence planned and controlled. In this view, the quality of managerial planning and control decisions is the key factor for success.

In reality, business organizations normally operate somewhere in between these two extreme views: many elements, such as raw material prices, are completely outside their control; on the other hand some elements, such as the selling price of its product, are determined by the organization itself. One may make a distinction, therefore, between controllable and non-controllable items. It is the function of management to manipulate the controllable items to the firm's best advantage, and to ensure that it is prepared to meet changes in the non-controllable ones, so as to take full advantage of favourable changes and minimize the impact of unfavourable ones. Planning is essential for all the factors which affect the organization, irrespective of whether they are controllable or non-controllable. We may infer from this fact that the greater the degree to which a firm's management reflects the views of control theorists the greater are its chances of success.

Although there are different schools of thought as to what may be understood by the term 'management' and how it should be practised, it is generally accepted that management has five main functions: planning, organizing, controlling, communicating and motivating.

Planning

Planning is the most basic of all management functions, and the skill with which this function is performed determines the success of all operations. Planning is a rational process for helping management choose between alternative courses of action. Choice is inescapable as management seeks the best uses for scarce resources. Theoretically, the function of planning is to improve the quality of decision making by careful consideration of all the relevant factors before a decision is made, thus ensuring that they conform with a strategy by which the firm's future is to be shaped. Planning may be seen as consisting of five stages:

1 Setting organizational objectives.
2 Assessing the environment in which the organization will be operating, by reference to the external factors which are likely to affect its operations. For this purpose, forecasts have to be made which attempt to predict what will happen in the future, with and without policy changes on the part of the organization.
3 Assessing existing resources, for management is concerned with making the most efficient use of those scarce resources, often called the four Ms: men, machines, materials and money. This aspect of the planning function involves making an estimate both of external resources which are accessible, and resources already held which are either idle or which might be more efficiently utilized.
4 Determining the strategy for achieving stated objectives by means of an overall plan which specifies strategic goals. Strategic decisions are concerned with establishing the relationship between the firm and its environment.

5 Designing a programme of action to achieve selected strategic goals by means of both long-range programmes and short-range programmes, the latter covering a period of a year or less and containing sets of instructions of the type found in annual budgets.

Organizing

Organizing involves setting up the administrative structure for implementing strategic decisions. The administrative design area is concerned with establishing the structure and the shape of the firm or organization, and defining responsibilities and lines of authority. It involves a definition of the tasks necessary to achieve strategic goals, determining who is to perform these tasks and assigning responsibility for their performance. The formal representation of these arrangements is summarized in the organization chart, to be found in all organizations. The function of organizing is to coordinate these tasks in such a way that the organization is able to work efficiently in fulfilling its objectives. The process of organizing is achieved through departmentalization, by which different specialisms are hived off into separate departments. These departments are linked in a hierarchy, a formal communication structure that enables instructions to be passed downwards and information to be passed upwards to senior management as well as horizontally to other departments [i.e. the sales department has to pass information to production]. Figure 16.1 shows a partial organization structure or chart for a firm which is concerned with two main activities – furniture and floor covering.

Each box and its associated activities will be the responsibility of a manager; the lines represent the formal channels of communication between them. The top five boxes represent the five major functions of this firm – marketing, manufacturing, finance, personnel and research and development. For administrative purposes, the firm is organized according to its product categories; therefore, two divisions – furniture and floor covering – are established.

At the bottom of the pyramid in the figure are the basic organizational units, known as departments; the figure illustrates the six departments belonging to the furniture division. Departments form an occupational classification – in this case they are divided into production and service departments.

A major purpose of any organizational structure is to facilitate the flow of information to and from decision makers. Since management may be said to be the process of converting information into action, organizations should be designed around information flows. Each decision point in this process is a sub-information system having its own elements at input, processor and output. Hence, information networks shape the structure of the organization. The structure of the organization is also used as the basis for data gathering through the use of responsibility centres [cost, revenue, profit or investment], with a manager being responsible for each responsibility centre.

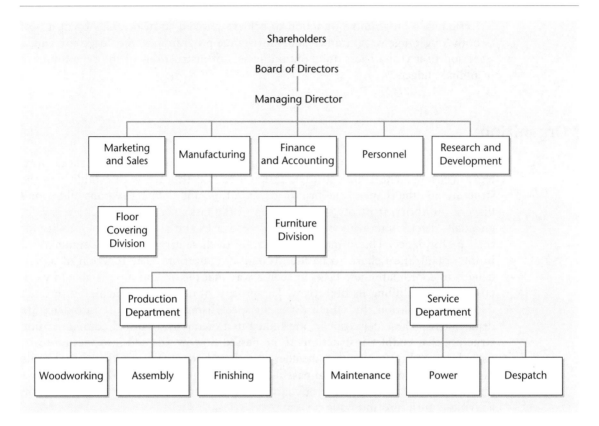

Figure 16.1

Control

The decisions involved in this area stem from two main activities: first, comparing actual performance against that stipulated in the plan [it could also be a budget], and second, determining whether the plan itself should be modified in the light of this comparison (Figure 16.2).

Control is closely linked to the planning function in that its purpose is to ensure that the firm's activities conform to its plans. It is effected by means of an information feedback system which enables performance to be compared with planned targets. Control is essential to the realization of long-range and short-term plans (often called annual budgets).

Figure 16.2

In long-range planning, information feedback enables management to assess what progress has been made towards the realization of the long-range objectives specified in the long-range plan. Additionally, it allows management to review long-range objectives in the light of new circumstances which may have rendered those objectives unrealistic.

In practice, by far the greatest emphasis is attached to the control of operations so as to meet the objectives contained in the annual budget which, as we noted earlier, should be seen as part of the long-range plan. Information feedback is an integral part of budgetary control procedures which are intended to be highly sensitive to operational variations on a day-to-day basis. Their aim is to highlight deviations from the budget as soon as possible so that remedial action may be taken immediately.

A prerequisite of the successful performance of the control function is an efficient information system which will reveal the need for corrective action at an appropriate time, enabling managers to judge whether their targets are still appropriate as the environment changes month by month and year by year. The control function is closely linked to the planning function by means of a feedback system which provides information on the results of past decisions. Such a system is necessary to the assessment of the quality of the decision-making process and to its improvement, and is illustrated in Figure 16.3.

The feedback system provides the great bulk of analytical information used in the planning process. It provides a means also of evaluating planned objectives. Should, for example, the economic climate change, the efficiency of the organization's operations will depend on the swiftness of its reaction to this change by way of alterations to the planned objectives. The feedback system is also instrumental to the making of control decisions, for it provides a means of continuously assessing current performance against the strategic plan. Decision making in this sense thus involves making day-to-day adjustments to changing conditions in order to map out the most appropriate course of action needed to implement strategic decisions. Thus, information is the lifeblood of any system, and the responsibility for the design of adequate information systems is of paramount concern to management.

Figure 16.3

Communication

Communication is an exchange of facts, ideas and opinions by two or more persons. The exchange is successful only when actual understanding results. Merely saying is not enough; a receiver of information must understand the message which the sender is trying to communicate. Communication occurs when the former understands what the latter means to convey.

Communication involves linking all the management functions by transmitting information and instructions within the organization. Additionally, the communication process relates the organization to its environment by linking it to suppliers of resources, and to the consumers for whom its products are intended.

In any organization, the specialization of tasks and the consequent division of labour creates a situation in which an unrestricted flow of ideas and facts is necessary if it is to function efficiently. A high degree of communication binds the various members of the organization together, uniting them in the pursuit of organizational goals. Hence, an organization may be viewed not only as a decision-making system, but also as a communication system.

The way in which information is communicated and related to planning and control may be illustrated as in Figure 16.4, which shows how environmental and analytical information is combined in the plans which are designed to meet the organization's objectives. These plans are implemented as resources become inputs which are converted into products and services. The feedback and control systems should function so as to ensure the effectiveness of the plans.

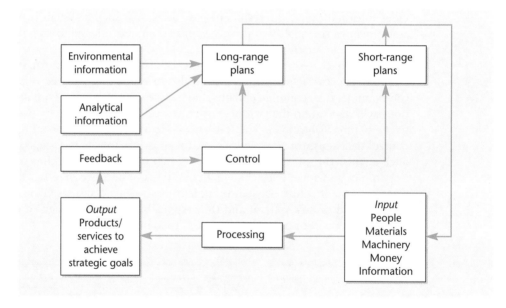

Figure 16.4

Motivation

This involves getting all the members of the organization to pull their weight, making sure that they are pulling in the same direction, and finding ways in which individual performance may be improved. When we study motivation, we are studying the influences on human beings and what affects their behaviour. For example, when we ask someone to perform a certain task which we know to be within their capability and experience and it is not done satisfactorily, this failure may well be the result of poor motivation rather than lack of ability.

Some motivating factors are related to social needs, and these are influenced by the organization of the work situation. Many studies have examined the effects of these needs, and they illustrate how the size, cohesiveness and motives of the group act as controls on the members' own motives. Hence, the organization should create a situation in which group and individual goals coincide to as great a degree as possible.

Information and decision making

Decision making has received increasing attention in recent years, and some authorities have argued that management and decision making are synonymous terms. Indeed, there is very little managerial activity which does not involve decision making in some form. Since the quality of information available is crucial to the quality of decision making, an efficient and adequate information system is a pre-requisite of managerial success. The hallmark of efficient management may thus be seen in the ability to specify accurately the information needed, and this ability is in itself a function of clear definition of objectives, sound planning and control capability and satisfactory organizational arrangements.

Information is an integrating force which combines organizational resources into a cohesive whole directed towards the realization of organizational objectives. Since information affects the fortunes of an organization in such a fundamental way, it is important that information should be effectively organized and efficiently handled, and this is achieved through what has become known as a management information system. A management information system provides individual managers with the information required for making decisions within their own particular areas of responsibility. It may be likened to the central nervous system of an organism in that it consists of a network of information flows to which each decision may be related. The management accounting information system and the financial accounting information system are two systems within the management information system which tend to be concentrated on financial information. Other information systems are used within a company and these may be of equal importance in management decision making.

Within this information network, decision points may be identified at three levels – strategic planning, management control and operational control (Anthony, 1965, p. 24).

Strategic planning involves the determination of corporate objectives and goals, as well as the development of broad policies and strategies by which they may be achieved. This activity relies heavily on information about the environment, and has an irregular pattern. Management control is a lower-level activity which is concerned with the implementation of the strategic plan; it assures that the necessary resources have been obtained, also that they are being used effectively and efficiently. This activity is rhythmic, and follows a weekly, monthly or quarterly pattern. Operational control is the process of ensuring that specific tasks are being carried out effectively and efficiently. It is an activity which focuses on individuals' jobs and transactions, and its tempo is 'real time' (that is, data reported as events occur). Operational control is thus exercised over operating systems, and these include inventory records, personnel records, data handling and maintenance records. Examples of the relationship between these levels of activity are illustrated as follows:

Strategic planning	Management control	Operation control
Setting marketing policies	Formulating advertising programmes	Controlling the placement of advertisements
Setting personnel policies	Planning staff levels	Hiring and controlling staff

The relationship between these three levels of activities and the information flows is shown in Figure 16.5.

Figure 16.5

Strategic planning decisions are based upon data derived both from outside and within the system in the form of environmental and analytical information; the latter identifies the organization's strengths and weaknesses, and the former enables it to formulate its strategy.

The constraints imposed upon management control decisions emanate from the strategic decisions incorporated in the strategic plan, and for the purposes of management control decisions these constraints are contained in long- and short-term plans. These plans themselves are broken down into detailed programmes for the various operational subsystems, and into specified information for the purposes of operational control. Hence, management control decisions are based on summarized information which compares the actual performance of cost and profit centres against their planned performance. In order that management should not be inundated with irrelevant information, reports to management should be in the form of statements of variances from the budget, and the reasons why these variances have occurred. Management control exercised in this way is known as management by exception. Management control decisions are thus concerned with investigating variances, and issuing instructions to operating managers on how to deal with them. Alternatively, management may recognize that the variances are inevitable and uncontrollable, and therefore recommend that the strategic plan should be altered to take account of this fact. In such a case, the decision will take the form of a recommendation of an adjustment to the strategic plan.

Operational control decisions are made at the meeting point between specified and operating information associated with the various subsystems. Specified information sets up standards of performance in terms of volume and costs of production and allocated time. Operating information discloses the results in the form of items produced, and production performance in terms of time actually taken. Operational control decisions, unlike management control decisions, are concerned with day-to-day variances occurring in detailed operations, such as the time taken to perform individual tasks.

Summary

Planning occurs at all management levels, and the success of other management functions depends upon the quality of planning.

Management is also concerned with such activities (functions has been used earlier to describe the top five boxes in Figure 16.1 and therefore probably should not now be used in the sense of tasks or activities) as organization, control, communication and motivation. Since decision making is a key characteristic of all management activities, decision making has become synonymous with management.

Information is necessary for decision making, and the quality of information will affect the quality of decisions. Hence, an adequate and efficient information system is a prerequisite of managerial success.

Decision making may be classified according to the following areas:

1 strategic planning – which involves the determination of corporate objectives and goals as well as the broad policies and strategies by which they may be achieved;
2 management control – which is concerned with implementing the strategic plans;
3 operational control – which is the process of ensuring that specific tasks are carried out effectively and efficiently.

In Part 2 we shall consider the role of accounting as the most important element of a management information system, and we shall also examine the manner in which accounting information assists management in its various activities.

Self-assessment questions

1 Explain what is meant by 'organizing' as a management activity.

2 What is the significance of an 'organizational structure'?

3 What is meant by 'control'?

4 Why is communication of critical importance in the management process?

5 Discuss motivation in a management context.

6 Discuss the role played by information in management decision making.

7 Explain the different levels of management activity, and comment on their relative importance.

1* The Daniels Corporation is a medium-sized company specializing in the leisure industry. The company comprises a hotel, a restaurant, a chauffeur-driven taxi service, a health studio and pool, a coffee shop, a bar and a conference centre. The hotel can accommodate 100 guests and the restaurant 80 places; the taxi service has 10 vehicles; the health studio has 400 members, who use the facilities of the swimming pool, jacuzzi, sauna and multigym; the bar holds 150 people.

Required:

(a) What kind of organization structure should be used for the leisure complex?

(b) What type of decision would be taken at the strategic level? Give examples and explain what information would be useful in making the decision and where the information would be obtained.

(c) Specify the management control system which would be needed to run the business. What information would be needed by the managers, and why?

(d) Choose a task at the operational level and write the operational manual for this task.

References Anthony, R.N. (1965) *Planning and Control Systems: A Framework for Analysis*, Harvard Business School.

Böer, G. (1994) Five modern management accounting myths, *Management Accounting* (USA), January.

CHAPTER 17

Traditional cost accounting

Setting the scene

Manufacturing cost accounting (cost accounting's rarely used full name) is the third leg of the stool – the other legs being scientific management and the assembly line – on which modern manufacturing industry rests. Without cost accounting, these two could never have become fully effective. It too is American in origin. Developed in the 1920s by General Motors, General Electric, and Western Electric, the new cost accounting, not technology, gave GM and GE the competitive edge that made them worldwide industry leaders. Following World War II, cost accounting became a major US export....

Henry Ford's epigram, 'The customer can have any colour as long as it is black,' has entered American folklore. But few people realize what Ford meant: flexibility costs time and money, and the customer won't pay for it. Even fewer people realize that in the mid-1920s the 'new' cost accounting made it possible for GM to beat Ford by giving customers both colours and annual model changes at no additional cost.

(Drucker, 1990)

Learning objectives

After studying this chapter you should be able to:

1 identify the objectives of cost analysis;

2 describe the elements of cost;

3 explain the stages involved in the ascertainment of overhead costs applicable to a unit of product (or service);

4 contrast the accuracy of department and plant-wide overhead rates;

5 consider the case for a level of activity based on normal capacity;

6 discuss the limitations of full-cost calculations;

7 describe five major types of product-costing systems.

Costs represent money measurements of the efforts that an organization has to make to achieve its objectives. Consequently, costs play a very important role in management decision making.

It is important to know the meaning of the cost terminology commonly in use and the purpose for which cost information is needed. The question that must always be asked is 'costs for what purpose?' The following different cost classifications relate to different questions.

1 Relationship classification: how are costs related to a given cost object?
   Direct costs are those that are caused by, traced to and measured for the cost
   object in question. Indirect costs are not caused by, traced to and measured
   for the cost object. Consequently they can only be associated with the cost object
   through an allocation mechanism. Failure to identify the cost object renders the
   direct/indirect classification meaningless.

2 Behavioural classification: how do costs behave with respect to changes in
   volume?
   Variable costs change directly and proportionately with changes in volume (i.e.
   are a linear function of volume). Fixed costs are all other costs. Note that contrary to popular usage, fixed costs are not costs that do not change with volume,
   but are costs that are not variable. Also, variable costs are not simply costs that
   vary, but are costs that vary in a very special manner – linearly – with respect to
   volume. The division of costs into these two categories depends on a number of
   assumptions that will be discussed later.

3 Responsibility classification: who is responsible for costs?
   A cost centre is a responsibility centre for which costs are accumulated by nature.
   This definition has several important characteristics: a responsibility centre is a
   physical location – you can go to it (there is a 'where'); there is someone who is
   responsible for the performance of the tasks which have been assigned to it (there
   is a 'who'); different types of costs are accumulated (there is more than one type
   of cost associated with the centre); costs by nature are a list of what the money is
   being spent on (salaries, supplies, utilities, etc. – there is a 'what').

4 Decision making classification: what costs are relevant to a stated decision?
   Relevant costs are those that vary according to alternatives being considered.
   Relevant costs are future costs that will be incurred as a result of the decision.
   Irrelevant costs are all the other costs that remain unchanged irrespective of the
   decision taken.

5 Costs that change with very small changes in volume.
   Marginal costs are those additional costs of producing one more unit, for example
   the costs of producing one more light bulb, in a factory already producing mil-
   lions. Marginal costs often are incorrectly taken to mean costs that change with a
   decision, irrespective of the size of the change or the definition of the base case.

6 Costs which are not relevant for a given decision because they have already been
   incurred.
   Sunk costs are costs that have already been incurred and have been expended on
   a good or a service that has no present or future use (and therefore no value).
   Note that a sunk cost is not a past cost, it is a past cost that has no further use or
   value, for example expenditure on special purpose tooling to make a specific car is
   a sunk cost.

The foregoing classifications apply to the most commonly used cost terminology.
They also happen to be the most commonly misused. Different cost classification defined the relevant information for different types of decision. For example,
costs required for the purpose of product costing are analysed, in the first instance,
as direct and indirect costs of the product. Costs that reflect the impact of different
activity levels and are relevant to decisions relating to activity volume are expressed
in the form of fixed and variable costs. Accordingly, the various cost terms that are
used in accounting, such as direct and indirect costs, fixed and variable costs, sunk

costs, differential costs, discretionary and engineered costs, controllable and non-controllable, all have a specific meaning and a specific decision use. These terms will be examined in this and subsequent chapters.

Objectives of cost analysis

Costs are collected for three major purposes:

1 to assist in the measurement of reported income;
2 to assist in decision making such as the pricing of products or services;
3 to assist in planning, controlling and evaluating performance.

Product or service costs are accumulated according to two classifications. First, according to responsibility in order to control costs by associating them with individual managers. This form of accounting plays a central role in the management control of operations, discussed in Part 3.

Second, according to products or services and to determine their full costs. Full costs include total manufacturing costs incurred in bringing a product to a marketable state or the full costs of providing a service. One application of full product costs is calculating inventory values, which in the case of manufactured products include all manufacturing costs and only manufacturing costs. Sometimes, non-manufacturing costs such as administrative and marketing costs are added to the full product costs for the purpose of determining the profitability of products and for establishing pricing policies. Product costs are also used in government contracts which seek to establish a 'fair price' on the basis of total costs.

The elements of cost

In manufacturing industry, costs are classified into two major categories, namely, manufacturing and non-manufacturing costs, the former being the costs incurred in transforming raw materials into finished products. For companies providing services, the terms 'direct' and 'indirect' costs are more useful.

Manufacturing costs

Product costs comprise three elements:

1 direct material costs;
2 direct labour costs;
3 indirect costs (for factory overhead).

The term 'direct' cost applies only to those costs that can be readily identified with a product. Direct material costs include only those costs which can be directly associated with the product. Direct labour costs include only the wages of employees directly engaged in making a product. Direct material and direct labour costs are referred to collectively as prime costs.

In deciding which costs to treat as direct costs, the accountant takes into consideration the materiality of the item. The expense of recording such small items as washers, nuts and bolts as direct costs, rather than as part of factory overhead costs, far outweighs any benefit attached to this information. Factory overhead costs include all the remaining production costs, after direct product costs have been determined. Some obvious examples are:

1 indirect material costs such as lubricants, and supplies of materials for repairs and maintenance;
2 indirect labour costs such as the salaries and wages of inspectors, timekeepers and workers who do not work on specific products;
3 factory overhead costs also include other indirect product costs such as heat, light, power and the depreciation of factory buildings, plant and equipment.

Manufacturing costs comprise the total of all direct and indirect product costs, which is recorded as the inventory value of finished products awaiting sale. Upon sale, manufacturing costs are included in the cost of sale for calculating the gross margin.

Non-manufacturing costs

Non-manufacturing costs are 'period' rather than 'product' costs, and are associated with accounting periods rather than with output. They include administrative and marketing costs. Administrative costs are defined as the costs incurred on executive salaries, head office staff expenses including all clerical and secretarial staff, legal expenses and depreciation on office equipment, furniture, etc. Marketing costs include the activities associated with obtaining orders, such as advertising and selling costs, and activities concerned with fulfilling orders, such as warehousing, packing and delivery. These costs are not included in the cost of manufacturing products, and are not included in the cost of sales for income measurement purposes.

Full product costs

The elements of cost involved in the calculation of full product costs for a unit of a product may be summarized by the following ascertained unit costs:

	£
Direct material costs	4
Direct labour costs	6
Direct cost per unit	10
Indirect – factory overhead costs	8
Manufacturing cost per unit	18
Full product cost	18

In calculating full product costs, the accounting problem is to find means of associating with units of products their appropriate costs for the various decisions which management has to make. The task of calculating the direct material and direct labour costs assigned to individual products is relatively easy. The direct material costs are calculated by ascertaining the quantities of materials used in the product, making due allowance for normal waste, and multiplying the quantity by the raw material purchase price. Similarly, the direct labour costs are obtained by specifying the operations involved in production and the time taken, and multiplying the time by the appropriate labour rates. It is in the calculation of total overhead costs per unit that the major accounting problem of cost determination lies.

Full service costs in service firms

Many accountants now work for service organizations in areas such as hotels and leisure, transport, health services, farming, training, retailing, banking and insurance and so on. The relative importance of different types of costs is significantly different from that in manufacturing organizations. In particular, labour costs are a much greater proportion of costs in service organizations than in manufacturing companies and material costs are much greater in manufacturing than in service organizations. Other differences also exist that make it more difficult to identify costs with the service delivered. For example, in retailing firms, most counter staff will be assigned to an area and not a product, whereas in manufacturing companies, the production staff on a food production line will be assigned to a product. Fewer costs can be directly identified with a service than a product and so more will be classified as indirect (i.e. overheads).

As regards non-manufacturing costs – administration, selling and distribution costs – these also apply to service organizations but will be labelled as administration or selling instead of non-manufacturing.

The problem of overhead costs

The problem of ascertaining the overhead costs to apply to a unit of product is first and foremost a function of the number of different products which the firm manufactures or the different types of service which an organization provides. When the firm manufactures only one product, or provides only one service, the problem is relatively simple. For example, if the firm produces 1,000 units of the product, and the overhead costs total £2,000, the total overhead cost per unit is £2. This example could also be applied to some service organizations, e.g. the number of X-rays divided into the cost of the X-ray department of a hospital would result in a cost per X-ray.

Where the firm manufactures more than one product or provides more than one service, however, problems arise in computing unit product or service overhead costs. The process of calculating indirect product costs in manufacturing firms involves three stages:

1 associating factory overhead costs with production cost centres;
2 allocating the costs of production cost centres to individual products;
3 selecting an appropriate level of activity for calculating unit product costs, since unit costs vary with activity levels and make it necessary to select the activity level applicable to future output.

The above stages also apply to a certain extent to service organizations for service costing, except that the unit of product is usually tangible in manufacturing and intangible in service organizations.

The association of factory overhead costs with production cost centres

Cost centres are locations with which costs may conveniently be associated for the purpose of product (or service) costing. Basically, there are two types of cost centres for which costs are accumulated – production and service or support cost centres.

Production cost centres are those involved in production, such as machining and assembling departments. 'Production' is used fairly loosely here to represent the area where a product is manufactured. Service cost centres are those which exist to facilitate production, for example, maintenance, stores and canteen. The same basic distinction can be made in service industries: part of the organization delivers the service and other parts provide support. For example in the public transport industry, there are direct costs of each route (salaries of drivers, fuel for buses, wear and tear of tyres, etc.), and then the indirect route costs comprising all the costs of the depot which have to be allocated to routes (maintenance of buses, supervisors, rostering of drivers, etc.).

The first step in associating factory overhead costs with cost centres is to collect and classify factory overhead costs into identifiable cost categories (e.g. material and labour that are not direct to products, utilities, depreciation, rent rates). Some of these will be direct costs to different cost centres, where it is known exactly where they belong and to which cost centre they should go, such as depreciation and maintenance of equipment in a particular cost centre. Others will be indirect costs to cost centres and will be allocated to cost centres on the basis of an allocation key, for example square footage of space occupied, horsepower of machines, and so forth. At the conclusion of this first stage, direct and indirect costs throughout the factory will have been identified with each production and service cost centre, direct costs having been traced to cost centres and indirect allocated to cost centres.

The second step is to allocate the costs of the service/support cost centres to production cost centres. Asume that a firm has three service cost centres (maintenance, stores, canteen) and two production cost centres (machining, assembly). As shown in Figure 17.1, the allocation of the service cost centre costs involves selecting appropriate methods for allocating these costs to the production cost centres (e.g. maintenance might be allocated on the basis of maintenance man hours, stores on the number of store requisitions per department, etc.). At the conclusion of this second stage, both production and service overhead factory costs will have been accumulated to the production cost centres.

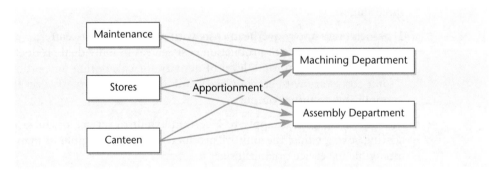

Figure 17.1

Example 17.1 The production process of Simplex Ltd is based on a machining department and an assembly department, which are supported by one service department which is a maintenance department. Consider the following cost information:

Departmental cost data

Direct (or allocated overheads)	Total	Machining	Assembly	Maintenance
	£	£	£	£
Materials	15,000	8,000	5,000	2,000
Labour	6,000	4,000	1,000	1,000
Depreciation of machinery	7,000	2,500	4,500	–
Total direct departmental costs	28,000	14,500	10,500	3,000
Indirect costs of departments				
Supervisory salaries	6,000			
Rates	10,000			
Total factory overhead costs	44,000			

From this information, the first step in the treatment of overhead factory costs has been completed, since those factory overhead costs which are 'direct to cost centre' have been assigned. In this connection, it should be mentioned that the material and labour which are direct to cost centre in this example remain indirect to the units of the product.

The next step is to allocate the indirect overhead factory costs (supervisory salaries and rates) between the three cost centres. It will be recalled that indirect factory overhead costs are those which cannot be directly assigned to individual cost centres, but are attached to the factory as a whole. Bases are needed, therefore, to allocate them to the three cost centres in question. These bases should reflect the benefits received by the three departments from these costs. For example, since rates are related to the area occupied by the factory, the area occupied by each cost centre may serve as a basis for allocating rate charges.

Simplex Ltd has adopted the following bases for the allocation of indirect factory overhead costs:

Basis of allocation	Total	Machining	Assembly	Maintenance
Number of employees	60	30	20	10
Square feet of floor space	100,000	50,000	40,000	10,000
Maintenance man hours	2,500	1,500	1,000	–
Direct labour man hours	10,000	5,000	5,000	–

Applying these bases to the allocation of indirect factory overhead costs to the three cost centres, the following distributions are obtained:

Allocation of indirect factory overhead costs to cost centres

Overhead costs	Basis	Total	Machining	Assembly	Maintenance
		£	£	£	£
Indirect materials	Direct	15,000	8,000	5,000	2,000
Indirect labour	Direct	6,000	4,000	1,000	1,000
Depreciation of machinery	Direct	7,000	2,500	4,500	–
Supervisory salaries	No. empl.	6,000	3,000	2,000	1,000
Rates	Square ft	10,000	5,000	4,000	1,000
		44,000	22,500	16,500	5,000
Apportionment of maintenance cost centre overheads	Maintenance hours		3,000	2,000	(5,000)
		44,000	25,500	18,500	–

It may be noted from the foregoing example that the final step in allocating factory overhead costs to production cost centres is the allocation of the service cost centre overhead costs. The basis used was the number of maintenance man hours expended in each of the production cost centres. Among other methods commonly used in respect of other service cost centres are the following examples:

Service cost centres	Basis of apportionment
Purchasing	Cost of materials purchased or number of orders placed
Stores	Cost of materials used, or the number of stores requisitions
Personnel/HR	Number of employees
Canteen	Number of employees
Building maintenance	Space occupied

The procedure for service organizations follows a similar pattern. For example, in the case of a hospital as distinct from a manufacturing firm, instead of 'Machining' and 'Assembly', there would be 'Paediatrics' and 'ENT Surgery' as cost centres. Similarly, service departments would be maintenance, stores (drugs, bedding, clothing, etc.) and a canteen. Other service departments might be 'X-ray', 'blood tests', 'ECG'. As in the case of manufacturing firms, the first step would be with overheads being classified as materials, labour and so on. The second step would be to assign these costs to direct service and indirect service departments. The third step would be to allocate the costs of the indirect service cost centres to the direct service cost centres.

The allocating of production cost centre costs to products

Difficulties arise where production cost centres produce more than one product or where service organizations provide more than one service. In such case, it is necessary to establish a method of allocating to each product or service an equitable proportion of the production cost centre's overhead costs. The method to 'recover' or 'absorb' these costs, to use cost accounting language, relies on the calculation of an 'overhead rate' that, in the case of manufacturing firms, is usually linked to one or more of three factors:

1 direct labour costs;
2 direct labour hours;
3 machine hours.

The overhead or charge-out rate for service organizations is linked to several factors depending on the organization. For example, a hospital will be linked to patients or patient days. A bus company will be linked to passenger miles.

A prerequisite for the calculation of the 'overhead rate' is the selection of an appropriate base for this purpose.

Example 17.2 Having completed the accumulation of factory overhead costs by the two production cost centres – machining and assembly – the next problem facing Simplex Ltd is to select an appropriate overhead base for allocating overhead costs to the products manufactured in these two centres. The following information relates to the machining cost centre:

	£
Direct labour costs	5,000
Direct labour hours	10,000
Machine hours	15,000

On the basis of this information, we are able to calculate three different 'overhead rates' for absorbing overhead costs into the full product costs of each unit of the different products manufactured by Simplex Ltd. The calculations are as follows:

Overhead rate based on direct labour costs

$$\frac{\text{Cost centre overhead costs}}{\text{Cost centre direct labour costs}} \times 100$$

$$= \frac{£25,500}{£5,000} \times 100$$

$$= 510\%$$

For each £1 of direct labour cost incurred by a unit of a product in the machining cost centre, that unit will also attract £5.10 of the cost centre's overhead costs. Given that the prime costs incurred by Product A in the machining cost centre are:

Prime costs of product A in the machining cost centre

	£
Direct labour costs per unit	1.00
Direct material costs per unit	2.00

The full product costs per unit of Product A at the end of processing through the machining department would be:

	£
Direct costs as above	3.00
Indirect costs – factory overhead costs	5.10
	8.10

Overhead rate based on direct labour hours

$$\frac{\text{cost centre overhead costs}}{\text{cost centre direct labour hours}}$$

$$= \frac{£25,500}{10,000}$$

$$= £2.55 \text{ per direct labour hour}$$

For every hour of direct labour spent on making a unit of a particular product in the machining department, the unit will attract £2.55 of the cost centre's overhead costs. Hence, if Product A needs $2\frac{1}{2}$ direct labour hours, the overhead costs allocated would be £6.375 per unit (£2.55 x 2.5).

Overhead rate based on machine hours

$$\frac{\text{cost centre overhead costs}}{\text{cost centre direct labour hours}}$$

$$= \frac{£25,500}{10,000}$$

$$= £2.55 \text{ per direct labour hour}$$

For every hour which is spent on machining a unit of a product in the machining department, the unit will attract £1.70 of the cost centre's overhead costs. Hence, if product A needs $3\frac{1}{2}$ hours of machining, the overhead costs allocated would be £5.95 per unit.

The choice of one particular basis for allocating overheads as against the others may substantially affect the amount of overhead costs allocated to a unit of product. Consequently, variations in full product costs may result simply from the manner in which the overhead base is selected and the overhead rate is calculated. The 'best' basis to use depends on the particular circumstances facing the firm.

The 'direct labour cost' base is easy to use since the necessary information is usually readily available. There may be no relationship, however, between direct labour costs and overhead costs. The direct labour base is not useful where increases in direct labour and increases in factory overheads are not related. Most factory overhead costs are incurred on a time basis and are not related to the labour payroll. A further problem resulting from the use of this overhead base is that there will be distortions in the absorption of overhead cost by different products, if the rate of pay for similar work is not comparable.

The 'direct labour hour' base is usually found to be a better method because most factory overhead costs are more related to time than any other factor. Where, however, there is a greater reliance on machinery rather than on labour, the 'machine hour' base may be the most suitable overhead base for absorbing costs into full-product costs.

Plant-wide versus department overhead recovery rates

In the discussion so far, we have examined methods of calculating departmental overhead rates related to departmental overhead costs and bases. For example, information for the machining department was used as a means of calculating an overhead rate for the absorption of its own factory overhead costs into the costs of various products processed in that department. The argument in favour of departmental overhead rates is that different departments have different total costs, different capital intensity (some use lots of labour, others lots of machines), are used very differently in the manufacture of different products, and the products themselves have similar diversity (some needing much labour, others much time on machines).

An easier and less complicated method would be to calculate a single plant-wide overhead rate for the entire factory: the factory overhead costs being divided by the chosen base to give a single overhead rate per direct labour hour or machine hour, as the case may be. However, a plant-wide overhead rate will not produce an accurate measure of departmental costs associated with each unit of product and may only be justified if all products use factory resources in a similar way. Departmental overhead rates, by contrast, lead to more accurate measurement, as may be seen from the following example.

Example 17.3 Eastlands Carburettors Ltd manufactures two types of carburettor, Type X and Type Y, both of which are processed in two departments – Department A and Department B. The following cost information is available:

	Type X	Type Y
Direct factory costs per unit	£8	£8
Direct labour hours		
Department A	4 hours	1 hour
Department B	1 hour	4 hours
Total hours	5 hours	5 hours

Overhead rates based on direct labour hours are given as follows:

Overhead rates	Per direct labour hour
Department basis	£
Department A	6
Department B	1
Plant-wide basis	
Department A	3
Department B	3

233

This information enables us to compare the costs per unit that would result from the use of a plant-wide overhead rate as against departmental overhead rates:

Unit costs using a plant-wide overhead rate

	Type X	Type Y
	£	£
Direct factory costs per unit	8	8
Add: Overhead charge per unit	15	15
(5 hours at £3.00)		
Manufacturing costs per unit	23	23

Unit costs using a plant-wide overhead rate

	Type X	Type Y
	£	£
Direct factory costs per unit	8	8
Add: Overhead charge per unit		
Department A @ £6/hour	24	6
Department B @ £1/hour	1	4
Manufacturing costs per unit	33	18

It is noteworthy that:

1 Product X, which spends more processing time in Department A which has the higher overhead rate, is undercosted by £10 when a plant-wide overhead rate is used.
2 Product Y, however, which spends more processing time in Department B, which has the lower overhead rate, is overcosted by £5 when a plant-wide overhead rate is used.

These wide differences highlight the dangers of using cost measurements that do not lead to accurate statements of unit costs. The absorption of factory overhead costs by means of departmental overhead rates rather than a plant-wide overhead rate yields a more accurate measurement of the costs incurred in manufacturing products. Management decisions requiring accurate cost measurements for such purposes as pricing policies and production mix decisions would be made incorrectly if a plant-wide rather than a departmental rate was employed.

The selection of an appropriate level of activity

So far, costs have been classified into two categories – direct costs and indirect costs. This classification helps to understand how costs are related to products for measuring unit costs of production. As mentioned earlier, different cost classifications are used for different purposes. A cost classification that distinguishes fixed from variable costs is needed to understand how costs are affected by changes in levels of activity. At the beginning of this chapter, we noted that for this purpose, fixed costs are defined as non-variable costs and include those costs that are more or less fixed for the year (rent and rates) and others that vary, but not directly and proportionately with changes in production volume (maintenance and repairs of machinery and plant equipment, heat, light and power).

Activity levels have a significant impact on the calculation of unit product or service costs. Fixed costs remain constant as output fluctuates within a predefined range, where variable costs will increase or fall as the activity level changes. For the purpose of calculating unit costs the greater the output, the lower will be the fixed cost per unit, whereas variable costs will remain constant per unit.

Example 17.4   Fixed costs for the period are £10,000, If 10,000 units are produced, the fixed costs cost per unit will be £1; if 5,000 units are produced, the fixed cost per unit will be £2. Fixed costs per unit will depend upon the total number of units produced. By contrast, variable costs per unit remain constant at all levels of activity, assuming always that prices remain stable. The relevant activity level has to be taken into account in providing information for management decisions.

The following table illustrates the behaviour of costs as volume changes:

Units produced	Total fixed cost £	Total variable costs £	Total cost £	Average fixed cost per unit £	Average variable cost per unit £	Average total costs per unit £
1	300	100	400	300	100	400
2	300	200	500	150	100	250
3	300	300	600	100	100	200
4	300	400	700	75	100	175
5	300	500	800	60	100	160

Current unit costs based on the actual level of activity are of little use for decisions regarding the future. Pricing decisions require a reliable view of full costs that takes account of fluctuating levels of output. Cost control implies that full unit costs incurred in one period are comparable with those of other periods. Comparisons based on actual levels of output are unreliable because fixed costs per unit vary at different output levels. Even for the purpose of inventory valuation, which is central to income measurement, calculations based on actual volume will introduce distortions. Finally, since the calculation of unit costs based on actual volume can be made only at the end of an accounting period, such unit costs are not relevant to decision problems that are concerned with future rather than with past costs.

Actual volume is not a satisfactory basis for calculating a fixed overhead rate which will be useful for the purposes mentioned, the following alternative bases may be considered:

1 theoretical capacity, which is the capacity of a particular department to maintain output at a 100 per cent level of rated capacity without interruption;
2 practical capacity, which is the result of making allowances against the theoretical capacity in respect of unavoidable interruptions to output such as time lost for repairs and holidays;
3 expected capacity as a short-run view of capacity needed, from forecasts of output levels in the immediate future;
4 normal capacity, which is an estimate of output capacity based on a period of time long enough to level out peaks and troughs of cyclical fluctuations.

The argument in favour of normal capacity is that it provides a fixed overhead rate that will be relatively stable over a number of years. It will be appreciated that there is an element of subjectivity in the assessment of normal capacity, and it will lead invariably to some under- or over-absorption of fixed factory overhead costs, depending on whether the actual level of activity is under or over the normal level. We will deal with this problem in Chapter 35. However, normal capacity may often provide a reliable and stable basis for calculating full product costs for decision-making purposes.

The arguments in favour of practical capacity are no less compelling. The idea is to distinguish between resources that are being consumed by products and those that are not. The latter constitute unused or spare capacity. Why should we believe that a product costs more to produce simply because we have spare capacity? At the heart of this dilemma lies a confusion of cost objects. A cost can be a perfectly legitimate factory cost without being used to make a car – spare capacity in the press shop would be a perfect example. According to the *Financial Times* of 26 February 2010, the car industry in Europe has the capacity to make 86 million cars per year. Forecast volumes are around 55 million, indicating that there is spare capacity of about 31 million cars, that is over 36 per cent. Do we want to say that cars cost 36 per cent more to produce than usual, or that they cost as much as before and we have 36 per cent spare capacity?

Limitations of full cost calculations

It is clear from the foregoing examination of the problems associated with overhead costs that full product costs cannot be measured accurately. To some extent, all methods used for allocating overhead costs are arbitrary, and are based upon assumptions which by their nature have to be subjective. The 'benefit received' should be the main criterion for allocating factory overhead costs to cost centres. It is difficult, however, to find bases that are suitable for this purpose. For example, the cost of the factory personnel department may be allocated to cost centres on the basis of the relative number of their employees, but this base assumes that all employees will benefit equally from the services of this department. This example is, of course, a gross simplification of the general problem of allocating overhead costs. Labour turnover and the difference in skills between different classes of employees will influence the time and the effort expended by the personnel department.

We have referred already to the element of subjectivity which enters into the choice of method for allocating overhead costs. This is exacerbated by the further subjectivity of having to choose the level of activity for recovering overhead costs. Indeed, two equally competent accountants may arrive at very different product costs simply because their views of what constitutes a 'normal level' of activity differ. This problem applies similarly to the allocation of administrative costs. The costs of operating the purchasing department cannot be related, for example, to any of the bases which we have mentioned.

It is clear that the main difficulty in computing full product costs stems from the presence of fixed overhead costs. The allocation of these costs to products on bases that are arbitrary renders the end result of doubtful accuracy. In some instances, incorrect decisions may result from the inclusion of fixed costs in product costs. For example, for the purpose of external financial reporting, we argue in Chapter 20 that more useful information may be provided if fixed overhead costs are not absorbed in output, but are treated as period costs. Moreover, their inclusion in product costs may give a misleading view of profits. It is often claimed that for the purpose of long-range planning, product cost information should reflect total costs. However, as we shall see in Chapter 30, there is a case for directing attention away from a narrowly conceived view of price determination based on markup percentages on costs to the broader implications of cost–volume–profit relationships. As we shall also see, because of the behaviour of fixed and variable costs over different volumes of output, product cost information based on full costs is irrelevant to the problem of control. A distinction has to be made, therefore, between fixed and variable cost information for control purposes.

It follows that the limitations inherent in full-cost computations should be appreciated by all those using such information for decision making. From an accountant's perspective, specific guidance from management is needed before they can decide how best to include fixed costs in product costs. Even then, a clear visibility should be maintained between fixed and variable components of product costs.

Costing systems

Costs are accumulated in costing systems. The development of costing systems reflects the manner in which accounting methods have been adapted to the needs of different forms of activity and technology, and also to the developments in advanced manufacturing techniques that have been much in evidence in recent years.

In effect, the objective of costing systems has remained constant in the sense that the accumulation of costs has the ultimate purpose of ascertaining product or service costs. However, the need to render this information relevant for decision making has shifted the emphasis from recording costs *incurred* to anticipating costs that *will be incurred* in producing goods and services in the future. The increasingly competitive nature of the markets in which goods and services are sold has placed further stress on the efficient management of costs, thereby reinforcing the need for costing systems to reflect how these forces will affect the business model. Management must anticipate the conditions under which their business can be successful in the future – initiatives such as outsourcing, or moving back office functions to a different country take time. The emphasis on what costs *should be incurred* by world class companies is an indispensable part of the process of remaining competitive.

Product costing systems

Product costing represents the classical tradition in cost accounting in the manner in which costs are analysed and recorded. Its objective is to allow product costs to be determined as accurately as possible to permit efficient management decisions in various areas, such as pricing and in seeking to improve efficiency in the use of scarce resources.

The identification of costs with products has focused attention on the classification of costs as direct and indirect. As we have seen, the major problem in determining full product costs is the need to find reliable allocation keys with which to allocate indirect costs to products, thereby accumulating direct and indirect costs into 'full product costs'.

The suitability of product costs is also a function of two other criteria:

1 the technology used for providing the goods or services, and
2 the time reference of the cost data itself.

Cost accounting systems for different technologies

Cost accounting systems allow full product costs to be accumulated in accordance with the type of technology employed. Five major costing systems commonly found are:

1 job order costing;
2 contract costing;
3 process costing;
4 operations costing;
5 service costing.

Job order costing and contract costing share the similarity that the product or contract is undertaken upon receipt of the client's order and is completed in accordance with the client's specifications. Costs are accumulated to the job or contract until it is completed. The essential difference between job order costing and contract costing lies in the time taken to fulfil the order. For this reason, job order costing is found where production is completed in the short term: contract costing is used where completion extends over one or more years. Accordingly, the major accounting problem associated with contract costing systems is the determination of periodic profit. This is because contract costing involves carrying forward substantial work-in-process costs across accounting year ends, until work is delivered to the client in accordance with the terms of the contract. For example, a major road construction contract may take two years to complete, during which only costs are incurred. Hence, at the end of the first year, the question is: can the contractor show a profit if he is not entitled to full payment for the work done in that year?

Process costing is a method of product costing used by manufacturing concerns engaged in the mass production of standardized products. Production is undertaken in anticipation of demand, and hence finished products are stored until sold. Process costing is used in such industries as cement, flour, sugar, oil and chemicals. Product costs are accumulated by reference to a standard quantity of a homogeneous product, expressed in a conventional cost unit, either by quantity, volume or weight, as the case may be.

Operations costing is a form of costing that lies somewhere in between job order costing and process costing. It is found in situations where the technology of production does not rely upon a job order specification, nor is process costing applicable by reason of the homogeneity of the product. It consists of accumulating product costs by reference to the cost of operations, as such, that batches of slightly dissimilar products undergo.

Service costing is a special application of process costing which is used where services rather than products are supplied: for example, computer services, transport, retailing, health, accountants, solicitors, etc. As mentioned earlier, the particular problems that are involved in setting up service costing systems are:

1 selecting cost units in relation to which the cost of services can be accumulated: for public transport a suitable cost unit might be cost per passenger mile; a hotel might use cost per room per day; a hospital might use cost per patient day, etc.;
2 selecting a charge-out rate for services.

Today there is considerable interest in developing more sophisticated costing systems in industries which previously were not particularly concerned about costs. The passenger service industry, the health industry and others have seen radical changes in the approach to costing systems. Many of the principles used for implementing management accounting systems in manufacturing industries are now being applied to service industries and there is significant growth in the development and implementation of these systems. The change in emphasis in some service organizations comes from management requesting information on service costs.

Costing systems and the time reference of cost data

Two different time references are used with respect to cost data. Costing systems that record invoiced product costs accumulate actual costs, defined in accounting as 'historic costs'. These costs are useful for financial accounting purposes, but have limited usefulness for the control of product costs. The development of the concept of 'standard' or 'predetermined' costs is associated with the concept of cost for control purposes. Standard costs reflect a desire to discover efficient product costs, as a basis for controlling product costs. Standard costs are discussed in Chapter 35.

Summary

Cost information is required for three main purposes:

1 for the measurement of reported income;
2 for making decisions;
3 for planning and control.

The type of cost information required may be different in each of these cases. This chapter has been concerned with the accounting problems involved in the measurement of unit costs of production. The major difficulty in the measurement of full product costs lies in the calculation and allocation of factory overhead costs. The process of allocating factory overhead costs to units of product occurs in the following stages:

1 allocating factory overhead costs to production cost centres and finding appropriate levels of activity for this purpose;
2 allocating the costs of production cost centres to units of product and finding appropriate methods for this purpose.

The measurement of unit costs of services was also discussed and is an emerging area in cost accounting. The steps used in the determination of unit costs of production could also be applied here.

The use of cost information for planning and control decisions implies that such cost information should reflect the future rather than the past. For this reason, standard costs – which are predetermined costs – are used. They not only reflect expectations about the costs which will be current in the period ahead, but are intended to deal with the uncertainties implicit in decision making.

Self-assessment questions

1 State the three purposes for which costs are collected.

2 Describe the three elements of product costs.

3 What is the significance for product costing of the difference between manufacturing and non-manufacturing costs?

4 What is meant by the term 'full product cost'?

5 What problems are involved in determining factory overhead costs per unit?

6 What methods are commonly used for recovering overhead costs?

7 What are the advantages of departmental rates, as against plant-wide overhead rates?

8 Describe four major types of product costing systems.

Problems *(* indicates that a solution is to be found in the Lecturer's Guide)*

1 As the accountant of the Northumberland Engineering Co. operating in a very competitive industry by means of special jobs to each customer's requirements, you are required to:
   (a) Calculate the (estimated) cost of job enquiry number 876, for which details are given below.
   (b) On the basis of your cost figures, indicate the price you feel should be charged to the customer for job 876; or, if you feel unable to do this, indicate what further information you would need in order to arrive at a price.

   All calculations should be clearly shown and figures justified.

   ### Job Enquiry Number 876

   (a) Estimated direct material cost: £1,000
   (b) Estimated direct labour input:

	Hours	Rate per hour (£)
Plating department	81	4.00
Welding department	14	3.00
Assembly department	10	2.00

   (c) Indirect departmental costs:

	Plating	Welding	Assembly
Total indirect costs:			
Last year's actual	£20,000	£8,000	£4,000
This year's budget	£22,000	£9,000	£5,000
(d) Activity levels (labour hours):			
Last year's actual	10,000	8,000	4,000
This year's budget	9,000	10,000	4,000

2* Byfokal Product Ltd uses a predetermined overhead rate for the purpose of job order costing. This rate is based on machine hours with regard to the machining department and on direct labour cost with respect to the assembly and finishing department.

   The following forecasts have been used to calculate the predetermined overhead rate for these two departments:

	Machining department	Assembly and finishing department
Machine hours	100,000	30,000
Direct labour hours	60,000	150,000
Direct labour cost	£500,000	£1,250,000
Factory overhead costs	£2,500,000	£2,000,000

The job order cost sheet for Job Number 35 showed the following information:

	Machining department	Assembly and finishing department
Direct materials used	£3,500	£1,000
Direct labour cost	£20,000	£28,000
Direct labour hours	2,400	3,360
Machine hours	4,000	672

Required:

(a) What is the predetermined overhead rate for each department?

(b) Calculate the total overhead cost for Job 35.

3 The managing director of Marco Fabrication is concerned about the reliability and relevance of the product unit costs which have been used to date for general purposes. Shortly after your appointment as the firm's accountant you are required to write him a report explaining your general approach to the use of cost accounts and in particular the problems of overhead costing. You derive the following information for this purpose:

The company has two producing departments, machining and assembly, and one service department, the canteen. Direct departmental overhead for the coming year is estimated as machining £50,000, assembly £40,000 and canteen £10,000. Details of estimated indirect overhead are as follows:

Rates	£1,000
Depreciation	£9,300
Light and power	£600

Departmental data

	Kilowatt hours	No. of employees	Cost of equipment	Square feet
Machining	600	20	£10,000	600
Assembly	1,100	10	£20,000	1,200
Canteen	300	5	£1,000	200

	Estimated direct labour hours	Estimated direct hours	Estimated machine
Machining	£10,000	18,000	8,000
Assembly	£15,000	12,000	20,000

The above activity levels are based on what could be attained if production was at full capacity. Expected activity for the coming year is estimated to be 70 per cent full capacity, and normal activity at 80 per cent.

4 A factory in Norfolk processes turkeys for sale. The production process is classified into four cost centres and the relevant forecast information for each of the cost centres is as follows:

	Total £	Cutting £	Cooking £	Canteen £	Maintenance £
Indirect labour	340,000	120,000	140,000	30,000	50,000
Consumables	82,000	24,000	32,000	20,000	6,000
Heating and lighting	24,000				
Rent and rates	36,000				
Depreciation	60,000				
Supervision	48,000				
Power	40,000				
	630,000				

The following information is also available:

	Total	Cutting	Cooking	Canteen	Maintenance
Floor space (sq metres)	60,000	20,000	24,000	6,000	10,000
Book value of machinery (£)	600,000	300,000	240,000	20,000	40,000
Number of employees	160	80	60	10	10
Kilowatt hours	20,000	9,000	8,000	1,000	2,000
Direct materials (£)		100,000	50,000		
Direct labour (£)		50,000	42,000		
Maintenance hours		8,000	6,000		
Labour hours		12,640	8,400		
Machine hours		15,700			

Required:

(a) An overhead cost statement which clearly shows the bases of apportionment.

(b) The labour hour overhead absorption rate for the Cutting Department and a machine hour overhead rate for the Cooking Department.

(c) How many alternative methods of overhead absorption might be used in this situation? What are the benefits and limitations with regard to using these rates at the company?

(d) The actual overhead figures for the year were:
   Cutting Department: £310,000; 12,000 labour hours.
   Cooking Department: £312,000; 15,810 machine hours.
   What is the under/over-absorption for each department?

Reference   Drucker, P.F. (1990) The emerging theory of manufacturing, *Harvard Business Review*, May–June.

CHAPTER 18

ABC and JIT

Setting the scene

Conventional wisdom having been challenged, new thought emerged: a company should understand its cost drivers – and apply these drivers to the cost of products in proportion to the volume of activity that a product consumes. This powerful thought became popularized under the name activity-based costing (ABC).

Over the last several years, professional literature has been filled with articles on ABC. Of more importance, many companies have adopted activity-based costing methodology. A private survey of Price Waterhouse clients indicates that more than half of American manufacturing companies list ABC as one of their current buzzwords. About one-third of service companies have experimented with the approach. In addition, the technique of activity-based costing is spreading quickly to Pacific Rim and European-based companies.

Learning objectives

After studying this chapter you should be able to:

1 define activity-based costing (ABC) systems;

2 explain how ABC systems are developed;

3 contrast traditional volume-based costing systems with ABC systems;

4 discuss how ABC systems are used in service organizations;

5 describe the features of just-in-time (JIT) production systems.

The product costing methods discussed in the previous chapter were developed and used over the past several decades. They were suitable for a particular type of decision environment and in a particular type of manufacturing technology. As we saw in the previous chapter, the traditional method of costing assigns production overheads to products using volume-based recovery bases. This is acceptable if a large proportion of overheads are product volume-related. However, an increasing amount of overhead costs relate to the number of 'transactions' taking place within the factory, e.g. machine set-ups, quality control, material handling, etc. Furthermore, the introduction of new technology and automation results in fixed costs becoming a very high proportion of total costs. In these circumstances the use of overhead rates using, say, labour hours, is often unrealistic and machine hours are used instead. Activity-based costing (ABC) has developed to address the issue of factory costs not being a function of product volume.

Developing an ABC system

The basic premise of ABC is that activities consume resources and products consume activities. ABC assumes that it is activities which cause cost, not products. In Chapter 17 we saw how traditional overhead costing first assigns (direct) and allocates (indirect) overhead costs to organizational units (e.g. departments) before they are allocated to products. In contrast, an ABC system first traces costs to activity centres and then to products. Activity cost centres are cost accumulations that are associated with a given activity, such as machine usage, inspections and production set-ups. Activity cost centres are allocated to products using cost drivers, which may be the number of production set-ups or the number of inspections involved in each product's manufacture. Although both ABC and the conventional methods finally allocate all overhead costs to products, ABC uses many cost drivers. Conventional methods typically use only one or two. As a result, it is expected that the ABC method will increase product-costing accuracy.

The steps for developing an ABC system are as follows:

Step 1: Analyse and define activities

Both service and production activities of an enterprise are identified, a process which decomposes an organization into elemental activities that are understandable and easy to manage. Activities are not necessarily traditional organizational segments such as departments. In some instances, activities may cross department boundaries. In other instances, a department may contain several activities.

Step 2: Determine the cost driver for each activity

The cost driver is that action or transaction that results in costs being incurred. In many instances the cost driver will be measured in terms of the volume of transactions undertaken. Therefore, if production scheduling cost is driven by the number of production set-ups, then set-ups would represent the cost driver for the cost of production scheduling. Examples of activities and cost drivers are given in the following table:

Activity	Cost driver
Maintenance	No. of breakdowns
Quality control	No. of inspections
Material procurement	No. of purchase orders
Material handling	No. of movements

Step 3: Identify activity centres

Activity costs which have the same cost driver are collected in activity centres.

Step 4: Allocate costs to products

The costs of activities in the activity centres are allocated to products/services based on cost drivers.

Comparison with traditional costing

The following example, which is adapted from the examinations of the Chartered Institute of Management Accountants (CIMA), illustrates the traditional and ABC methods of calculating product costs.

Example 18.1 Having attended a CIMA course on activity-based costing (ABC), you decide to experiment by applying the principles of ABC to the four products currently made and sold by your company. Details of the four products and relevant information are given below for one period:

Product	A	B	C	D
Output in units	120	100	80	120
Costs per unit (£):				
Direct material	40	50	30	60
Direct labour	28	21	14	21
Machine hours (per unit)	4	3	2	3

The four products are similar and are usually produced in production runs of 20 units and sold in batches of 10 units.

The production overhead is currently absorbed by using a machine hour rate, and the total of the production overhead for the period has been analysed as follows:

	£
Machine department costs (rent, business rates, depreciation and supervision)	10,430
Set-up costs	5,250
Stores receiving	3,600
Inspection/quality control	2,100
Materials handling and despatch	4,620
	26,000

You have ascertained that the 'cost drivers' to be used are as listed below for the overhead costs shown:

Cost	Cost driver
Set-up costs	Number of production runs
Stores receiving	Requisitions raised
Inspection/quality control	Number of production runs
Materials handling and despatch	Orders executed

The number of requisitions raised on the stores was 20 for each product and the number of orders executed was 42, each order being for a batch of 10 of a product.

Required:

1 Calculate the total costs for each product if all overhead costs are absorbed on a machine hour basis.

2 Calculate the total costs for each product, using activity-based costing.

3 Calculate and list the unit product costs from your figures in items 1 and 2 above.

Solution

1 Machine hour rate $= \dfrac{\text{total production overheads}}{\text{machine hours}} = \dfrac{£26,000}{1,300} = £20$

Product costs using machine hour rate

	A £	B £	C £	D £
Prime cost	68	71	44	81
Overhead (1)	80	60	40	60
Product cost	148	131	84	141
Total cost (£)	17,760	13,100	6,720	16,920

2 Activity-based costing

Cost	£	Driver	Number	Cost per unit of driver £
Set-ups	5,250	Production runs	21	250
Stores receiving	3,600	Requisitions	80	45
Inspection/quality	2,100	Production runs	21	100
Handling/despatch	4,620	Orders	42	110

The machine department costs are absorbed on a machine hour basis, viz. £10,430 ÷ 1,300 = £8.02 per machine hour.

Cost	A £	B £	C £	D £
Prime costs	8,160	7,100	3,520	9,720
Set-ups	1,500	1,250	1,000	1,500
Stores receiving	900	900	900	900
Inspection/quality	600	500	400	600
Handling/despatch	1,320	1,100	880	1,320
Machine dept costs	3,851	2,407	1,284	2,888
Total costs	16,331	13,257	7,984	16,928
Product costs	136.09	132.57	99.80	141.00

3 Comparison of unit product costs

	A £	B £	C £	D £
Costs from item 1	148.00	131.00	84.00	141.00
Costs from item 2	136.09	132.57	99.80	141.07
Difference	(11.91)	1.57	15.80	0.07

The example shows that ABC does not change the amount of overhead costs incurred; however, it does distribute those costs in a more equitable manner. Traditional cost accounting systems, presuppose that all factory costs, whether product volume related or not, do in fact vary with product volumes (because they use product volume drivers). This can lead to seriously distorted product costs being reported to management. Non-product volume-related factors such as set-up costs are included in the above example. Therefore, the ABC cost allocation better reflects the pattern of overhead consumption and is more accurate. Using only product volume-based cost drivers can lead to one product subsidizing another. In our example, ABC product costing reveals that the traditional method under-costs item C and over-costs item A.

ABC systems reveal that significant resources are consumed by low-volume products and complex production operations. ABC typically shifts a substantial amount of overhead costs from the standard, high-volume products, where those costs have been allocated under traditional methods, to premium, special-order, low-volume products.

The above example illustrates how ABC provides more visibility on the composition of overheads and cost. Under the traditional system costs are simply collected under the heading of 'total production overheads' and then allocated. The greater segmentation provided by ABC indicates the sources and purpose of resource consumption. This additional detail, together with the gathering of cost-driver information, suggests that management will be provided with valuable feedback which will aid the operational control of their manufacturing processes. Therefore, for performance measurement and control purposes, the information provided by ABC has substantial potential advantages over traditional methods.

Levels of activity and cost behaviour

Traditionally, cost drivers were viewed only at the unit level: how many hours of labour or machine time does it take to produce a product or render a service? While some costs are unit-level costs that are caused by the production or acquisition of a single unit of product or the delivery of a single unit of service, other costs occur at 'higher' levels of activity. ABC requires costs to be aggregated at these different levels. Only if costs are accumulated on the same level as the activity that generates them can an allocation base be selected that represents a cause/effect relationship between the cost and the cost centre. The 'higher' levels include batch, product and facility levels.

Batch-level activities are those that are performed each time a batch of products is produced, e.g. set-ups, inspections, production scheduling and materials handling. Product-level activities are those that are performed as needed to support the various products produced by a company, e.g. engineering charges, maintenance of equipment and product development. Facility-level activities are those that sustain a factory's general manufacturing process, e.g. plant management, building depreciation and security. Facility-level costs are common to many different activities and products or services and can be allocated to products only on an arbitrary basis. Therefore, facility-level costs theoretically should not be assigned to products at all. It is important to remember that random or arbitrary events do not contain any predictive information (other than their continued unpredictability). Consequently that part of product cost (or any other cost, for that matter) derived from an arbitrary process (cost driver), contains no information and is useless for decision making.

Accountants have traditionally assumed that if costs did not vary directly and proportionately with changes in production at the unit level, those costs were fixed rather than variable. This assumption was false. There is no such thing as a fixed cost: there are sticky costs that are difficult to change, there are costs that management would rather not change (their head offices in expensive parts of major cities, corporate jets), but there are no fixed costs in the sense that they cannot under any circumstances be changed. There are many illustrations of companies moving their headquarters out of expensive city centre location. In reality, batch, product and facility-level costs do vary, and may indeed be variable, but they do so for reasons other than changes in production volume. Therefore, to determine a valid estimate of product or service cost, costs should be accumulated at each of the higher levels. Since unit, batch and product-level costs are all associated with units of products, these costs can be aggregated to match with the revenues generated by aggregate product sales.

ABC moves away from the notions of short-term fixed and variable costs and focuses on the variability of costs in the medium and longer term. Advocates of ABC claim that all costs are ultimately variable and can be traced to products or other cost objects (customers, distribution channel, etc.) thereby enabling more accurate costs to be computed for decision making. While the proposition that all costs can be explained by something is obviously true, it is not correct to therefore assume that all costs are strictly variable with respect to its cost object. The salary of the managing director can be explained by the existence of a company to manage. But what causes the salary to vary? Moreover it would be a mistake to assume that a causal mechanism could be found that allocated this cost accurately to a unit of product (e.g. a light bulb).

ABC and service organizations

Although the discussion so far of ABC has focused on manufacturing, ABC can also be useful to service organizations. Since all organizations have activities and outputs, the concepts of ABC can be applied universally. However, there are fundamental differences between manufacturing and service organizations. First, the service sector is less homogeneous than the manufacturing sector. Manufacturing companies tend to perform many of the same types of activities in similar ways, but there is little similarity between the activities of an insurance firm, a hospital, a bank, a retail shop and a government department. Second, output in the service sector is less tangible and, therefore, harder to define. Yet output must be defined so that it can be costed. The intangible nature of service outputs makes costing more difficult.

Example 18.2 Consider the case of a hospital for which a product may be defined as a patient's stay and treatment. To illustrate the potential of ABC, we shall focus on one type of service provided to each patient: daily care. Daily care comprises three activities: hospitalization (admission and discharge), hotel services (accommodation and food) and nursing care. Output is defined as patient days. Traditionally, hospitals have assigned the cost of daily care by using a daily rate (a rate per patient day), which is computed by dividing the annual cost of hospitalization, hotel services and nursing care by the unit's capacity expressed in patient days.

Within each unit (e.g. intensive care unit and obstetrics unit) all patients are charged the same daily rate. However, the traditional method does not take account of the fact that the three activities may be consumed in different proportions by patients. This would imply product diversity and a possible requirement to use more than one activity driver to assign daily care costs accurately to patients. Hansen and Mowen (1995) provide an illustration of a private maternity unit for which the following activity and cost information applies:

Activity	Annual cost	Cost driver	Annual quantity
Hospitalization and hotel	£1,100,000	Patient days	11,000
Nursing care	£1,100,000	Hours of care	55,000

The activity pool rates are £100 per patient day and £20 per nursing hour.

The traditional approach for charging daily care would produce a rate of £200 per patient day (£2,200,000 ÷ 11,000). Every maternity patient, regardless of type, would pay the daily rate of £200. However, assume that within the maternity unit there are three levels of increasing severity: normal patients, Caesarean patients and patients with complications, and that they have the following annual demands:

Patient type	Patient days demanded	Nursing hours demanded
Normal	8,000	30,000
Caesarean	2,000	13,000
Complications	1,000	12,000
	11,000	55,000

Using the pool rates for each activity, a different daily rate is produced for each patient which reflects the different demands for nursing services:

Patient	Daily rate £
Normal	175[1]
Caesarean	230[2]
Complications	340[3]

[1] [(£100 × 8,000) + (£20 × 30,000)] ÷ 8,000
[2] [(£100 × 2,000) + (£20 × 13,000)] ÷ 2,000
[3] [(£100 × 1,000) + (£20 × 12,000)] ÷ 1,000

This example illustrates that ABC can produce significant product costing improvements in service organizations that experience product diversity.

Time-driven activity-based costing

Almost as soon as the first activity based costing models appeared in the literature (Schraeder Bellows, John Deere Component Works, etc.), anecdotes began circulating that the early adopters were delighted with the information the new models provided and horrified by the costs of developing, running and maintaining them. Rumours of companies held up as exemplars of the new approach abandoning them were rife. This did nothing to stem the steady flow of cases describing the development of ABC models in new settings (banking, insurance, defence ministries, hospitals, etc.).

In 2004, Kaplan published an article (Kaplan and Anderson, 2004), recognizing the difficulties with traditional ABC and proposing a simpler method of getting the source data on which the whole edifice reposes – unit costs and times for activities.

Traditional ABC proceeded more or less as follows:

(a) interview people to establish a list of the things that they did (called activities),
(b) ask them how much time (what proportion) went on each;
(c) divide the costs of the cost centre among the activities in strict proportion to the time;
(d) from records determine how many of each activity had been performed or produced in total;
(e) divide the costs of the activity by the number of occurrences to obtain the unit cost of the activity.

It should be reasonably obvious that this was a hugely labour intensive task (all those interviews), the data were contaminated (nobody ever volunteered that they were not fully occupied), and every reorganization of work flows or processes required more interviewing. Unit times and costs were determined in a manner analogous to processing costing – find the total cost of performing the activity and divide by the number produced.

Time-driven activity-based costing reverses the process. It establishes an allowed time for each occurrence of the activity (through time study or other means of direct observation), multiplies this by a cost per unit of time (at practical capacity), which gives a standard unit time of efficient operations at practical capacity. Changes simply require new standard times and costs for new activities; no repeat interviews of large swathes of the organization are needed. The new activity and its standard costs are inserted in the time equations and the model is ready for use. It may be noted that time-driven activity-based costing adopts a standard costing approach, with allowed times and costs per unit estimated directly.

Evaluation of ABC

A company is particularly suited for the use of ABC if:

1 it produces a variety of products or services which are targeted at, and modified for, different market segments;
2 it has high overhead costs that are not proportional to the unit volume of individual products;
3 it has a highly automated production system;
4 it has a highly complex production process with lots of activities and tasks not linked to production volume (production planning, machine set-ups, etc.).

In these circumstances ABC provides a better understanding of the cost of making a product or performing a service. Such insight could result in management decisions about expanding or contracting product variety, raising or reducing prices and entering or leaving a market, e.g. managers may decide to raise selling prices or discontinue production of low-volume speciality output, since that output consumes more resources than high-volume output. Furthermore, as we saw previously, ABC helps to make the behaviour of some costs far more visible, and therefore more controllable, than under traditional accounting methods.

ABC is not a general panacea to costing problems. It is not necessarily appropriate to all businesses. In some cases, especially where a simple product is produced, it may be appropriate to use more traditional methods of cost allocation. Hence, managers have to choose the technique which best suits management's requirements and the organizational environment. In addition, it is now accepted that it is not essential to apply ABC to all costs or to the entire accounting system. ABC can be used alongside a more traditional accounting system.

Activity-based management

The initial interest in ABC related to product or service costing – how to allocate overhead costs more accurately in order to compute the cost of delivered products or services? More recently, the emphasis on ABC has switched from product costing to improving business management. From a managerial perspective, an ABC system offers more than just more accurate cost information. It also provides information about the cost and performance of activities and resources and it can trace costs accurately to cost objects other than products, such as customers and channels of distribution. Knowing the cost of activities, their importance to the organization and how efficiently they are performed, allows managers to focus on those activities that might offer opportunities for cost savings. If activities are linked across departments forming cross-functional processes, the model structure of an organization is simplified and powerful information results. This 'process' view of ABC allows management to focus on value-added and non-value-added activities in order to reduce or eliminate those activities that are not adding value but are causing costs to be incurred. Activity-based management is considered further in Chapter 38.

Just-in-time production systems

Just-in-time (JIT) systems are concerned with reducing production costs by eliminating as far as possible inventories and production delays. Terms that describe just-in-time systems include MIPS (minimum inventory production systems), ZIPS (zero inventory production systems) and MANS (materials as needed systems). JIT systems are, in effect, manufacturing systems with zero inventories and constant production flows. Essentially JIT implies the firm produces only to demand, without the benefit and cost of buffer stocks. Production is dictated by demand and 'pulled' through the system rather than 'pushed'. JIT was developed by Toyota in the 1950s and 1960s and was adopted by other Japanese companies in the 1970s. US companies started adopting it during the 1980s since when it has been adopted by some UK companies.

Traditional manufacturing involves one or more sequential production processes. Raw material inventory exists as well as buffer inventories of work in progress and finished goods. An acceptable rate of defects is budgeted and feedback regarding these defective products is provided only at the end of the production period. Plant support services such as quality control or maintenance are usually centrally located within the plant.

JIT systems imply a radical change in the manufacturing environment, since their successful implementation requires an environment concerned with the following:

1 elimination of waste;
2 zero inventories;
3 zero idle production time:
4 constant production rate;
5 balanced capacity;
6 emphasis on zero waste/faulty work;
7 full employee involvement;
8 an emphasis on perfect quality.

These concerns highlight the role of JIT as a management philosophy and not simply as a toolbox of techniques. The aim of JIT is the elimination of waste from all parts of the manufacturing process, from product design to product delivery. Thus, JIT aims to eliminate activities which do not add value to the product and to use the minimum amount of material consistent with the market requirements of the product.

The concern with perfect quality implies that things are done correctly the first time. That involves three independent aspects: product design, process design and supplier quality. Design engineers need to establish and maintain close working relationships with customers. The whole production process must be designed with quality in mind. A JIT company will ensure incoming quality not by strict goods-inward inspection procedures but rather by careful selection of a limited number of suppliers with whom a long-term partnership will be established. Bulk deliveries are replaced by small, frequent deliveries from a small number of suppliers who participate in quality assurance programmes. The suppliers are viewed as a vital part of the production team and not an external factor to be treated in a confrontational manner.

Without the full involvement of all employees, the potential benefits of JIT will not be achieved. The implementation of the JIT philosophy requires major cultural change for companies. All employees need to be involved in a process of continued improvement.

As we saw earlier, traditional product costing systems define the objective of costing systems as being concerned with three elements of costs, namely raw materials, direct labour and overhead costs, which are recorded in three separate stock accounts, namely raw materials, work-in-process and finished goods.

The concern with the elimination of inventories implies a radical alteration in the tracking of inventories through inventory accounts, as seen in conventional product costing systems. Consequently, the control of materials focuses on the points of materials utilization, rather than on inventory control. The concern of JIT materials accounting is with the following two aspects of materials control:

1 estimating materials requirements for actual production;
2 eliminating usage variances at the point of usage.

JIT systems also imply radical changes in the tracking of direct labour costs as product costs. Since JIT systems aim to secure constant manufacturing conditions, many of the objectives involved in obtaining direct labour cost information have been superseded. For this reason, JIT direct labour accounting systems are also greatly simplified, and the significance attached to accounting separately for direct labour cost has also decreased. For example, conventional labour utilization and efficiency measures are largely redundant when emphasis is given to constant work flows.

In many industries, the proportion of direct labour costs in total production costs is decreasing. In some companies, the implementation of JIT has seen the introduction of the following methods of accounting for direct labour costs:

1 expensing direct labour at source;
2 recovering direct labour costs in the form of a product overhead rate, thereby eliminating direct labour costs as a separate cost element;
3 retaining direct labour as a separate production cost, but allocating such costs over time.

With the reduced significance of work in progress under JIT, there is less need to carry out detailed allocations of overhead.

In conclusion, JIT allows the use of 'leaner' accounting systems. Furthermore, it accentuates the importance of real-time performance feedback rather than periodic accounting variance reports. Instantaneous feedback permits the immediate identification of problem production areas, allowing corresponding action before entire defective batches of material are produced and cost revenues are incurred. This feedback can be provided by the use of non-financial measures of performance which reflect items like elapsed time, distance moved and space occupied. The role of non-financial measures of performance is discussed further in Chapters 37 and 38.

Summary

The first part of this chapter reviewed the use of activity-based costing as a means of increasing the accuracy of cost allocation for both manufacturing and service organizations. ABC assumes that it is activities which cause cost, not products. In certain circumstances ABC provides a better understanding of the cost of making a product or performing a service. More recently, the emphasis on ABC has switched from product costing to improving business management. JIT is essentially a management philosophy, not simply a toolbox of techniques. Its use has implications for management accounting systems both in view of the 'leaner systems' which are adopted and the role of non-financial measures of performance.

Self-assessment questions

1 What is activity-based costing? How does it differ from traditional product costing approaches?

2 Describe four general steps in using ABC.

3 What is a cost driver and how is it used? Give some examples of cost drivers.

4 What characteristics of a company would generally indicate that ABC might improve product costing?

5 What is JIT manufacturing?

6 In which ways does JIT manufacturing differ from traditional manufacturing?

7 How does JIT affect accounting systems?

Problem

1 Redmires Limited had identified the following overhead activities, costs and activity drivers for the coming year:

Activity	Expected cost £	Activity driver	Activity capacity
Set-up costs	60,000	No. of set-ups	300
Ordering costs	45,000	No. of orders	4,500
Machine costs	90,000	Machine hours	18,000
Receiving	25,000	No. of parts	50,000

Assume for simplicity that each activity corresponds to a process. The following two jobs were completed during the year:

	Job 600	Job 700
Direct materials	£750	£850
Direct labour (50 hours per job)	£600	£600
Units completed	100	50
No. of set-ups	1	1
No. of orders	4	2
Machine hours	20	30
Parts used	20	40

The company's normal activity is 4,000 direct labour hours.

Required:

(a) Determine the unit cost for each job using direct labour hours to apply overhead.
(b) Determine the unit cost for each job using the four cost drivers.
(c) Which method produces the more accurate costs? Why?

References   Hansen, D.R. and Mowen, M.M. (1995) *Cost Management*, South-Western College Publishing.

Kaplan, Robert S. and Anderson, Stephen R. (2004) Time-Driven Activity Based Costing, *Harvard Business Review*, November.

Keegan, D.P. and Eiler, R.G. (1994) Let's re-engineer cost accounting, *Management Accounting (USA)*, August.

CHAPTER 19

Cost–volume–income analysis

Setting the scene

The purpose of this study is twofold: (1) to understand the effect of cost in response to changing volume of activity, such as sales or production, and (2) to discern the resulting impact of cost on profitability. Thus the variables cost and volume can be manipulated appropriately and changes in profit determined before choosing a level of activity where operations are likely to result in optimal profit.

Cost–volume–profit (CVP) analysis is often called 'break-even' analysis, i.e. determining a level of activity at which an enterprise's total revenues equal total cost. The significance of breaking even stems from the fact that it is an important step forward towards survival and growth. But CVP analysis has much broader applications and its scope extends well beyond the determination of the break-even level of activity.

(Qureshi, 1978)

Learning objectives

After studying this chapter you should be able to:

1 determine the number of units that must be sold to break-even or to earn a target profit;

2 use a cost–volume–profit chart and a profit–volume chart to determine the break-even point and the volume necessary to achieve a target profit;

3 explain the impact of changing variables on CVP analysis;

4 calculate and interpret the impact of sales mix considerations in CVP analysis;

5 discuss the limitations of CVP analysis.

Cost–volume–profit (CVP) analysis is the systematic examination of the interrelationships between selling prices, sales and production volume, costs, and profits. It is a commonly used tool providing management with useful information for decision making. For example, CVP analysis may be used in setting selling prices, selecting the mix of products to sell, accepting special orders, choosing among alternative marketing strategies and analysing the effects of cost increases or decreases on the profitability of an enterprise.

Cost analysis and changes in output

The response of cost to a variety of influences is invaluable to management decision making. As we saw in Chapter 17 one important question is how do costs behave with respect to changes in volume? We stressed that contrary to popular usage, fixed costs are not costs that do not change with volume, but costs that are not variable. Moreover variable costs are not costs that vary, but those that vary in a very special manner – linearly – with respect to volume. In order to make the problem of modelling cost behaviour tractable, cost–volume–profit analysis abandons the complexity of the real world and makes simplifying assumptions that permit all costs to be divided into strictly variable and strictly fixed (those that do not change with volume). The division of costs into these two categories depends on a number of assumptions: there are four in all:

1 *Normal volume* – cost behaviour is explored within a predetermined range either side of what management believes to be the expected or normal volume of production and sales in the immediate future, frequently defined as 70–80 per cent of practical capacity.
2 *Range* – management has to decide over what range it wishes to model cost behaviour; typically this might be 20 per cent either side of normal volume.
3 *Capital intensity/technology* – the degree of capital intensity and the technology used are major influences on the division of costs between fixed and variable; consequently break-even analysis is performed for a given capital intensity.
4 *Time period* – the length of the time period is obviously a key factor in determining which costs vary with changes in volume: in the very short run only materials and utilities are variable costs; as the period lengthens direct labour becomes variable and so forth. In break-even analysis the time period is one year.

The question now becomes, which costs vary directly and proportionately with volume within a period of one year, given capital intensity, normal volume and range?

CVP analysis requires that these two classes of costs be segregated and calculated so that all costs may be divided into those that vary with respect to volume and those which do not. Hereinafter for the purpose of CVP analysis, we assume that this segregation can be achieved with an acceptable degree of accuracy.

One of the most important uses of the distinction between variable costs and fixed costs lies in the analysis of these costs at different levels of production.

Example 19.1 Duofold Ltd produces an article which it sells for £10. Fixed costs of production are £150,000 per year, and variable costs are £4 per unit. The present yearly volume of output is 40,000 units, but could be increased to 50,000.

Unit sales	40,000		50,000	
	Total	Unit	Total	Unit
	£	£	£	£
Revenue	400,000	10.0	500,000	10.0
Variable costs	160,000	4.0	200,000	4.0
Contribution margin	240,000	6.0	300,000	6.0
Fixed costs	150,000	3.8	150,000	3.0
Net profit	90,000	2.2	150,000	3.0

Problem: What will be the effect on total costs of the projected increase in output, and the impact of profit?

The analysis shows that total variable costs increase proportionally with output while unit variable costs are constant. Total fixed costs, however, remain constant at both levels of output so that unit fixed costs fall as output rises and vice versa. It is because unit fixed costs fall that total unit costs are less for an output of 50,000 units than for one of 40,000 units.

If we assume that selling prices remain unaltered, unit cost savings themselves will lead to increased profitability. The contribution margin is an important concept in cost–volume–profit analysis. As may be seen from the example above, the contribution margin is calculated by deducting variable costs from revenue. It is the first stage in calculating the net profit and measures the profit which is available to cover fixed costs. Since fixed costs are incurred irrespective of sales, a firm will make a loss if the contribution margin is insufficient to cover fixed costs. This occurs at low levels of output. As output increases, so does the contribution margin which will ultimately equal and then exceed fixed costs. The relation between fixed cost and the contribution margin is illustrated as in Figure 19.1. The critical point at which the contribution margin is equal to fixed costs is known as the break-even point which indicates that level of output (OA) at which the firm makes zero profits, that is, where total costs are equal to total revenues.

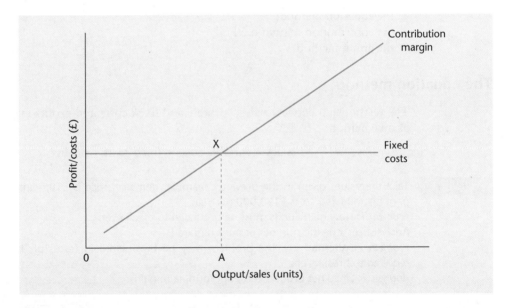

Figure 19.1

Break-even analysis

Break-even analysis focuses on the measurement of the break-even point. Before we attempt any calculations, it is necessary to make certain assumptions about the behaviour of costs and revenues. Thus, we assume that the behaviour of costs and revenues has been reliably determined and that they are linear over the range of output which is being analysed. These assumptions also imply that costs may be divided into fixed and variable; that fixed costs will remain constant; that variable costs will vary proportionally with volume of output; and that all other factors will remain constant, that is, that selling prices will remain unchanged, that the methods and the efficiency of production will not be altered and that volume is the only factor affecting costs. It is because these assumptions are difficult to maintain in 'real life' that break-even analysis cannot pretend to be anything but a rough guide. Its value to management lies in the fact that it highlights the relationships between the factors affecting profits, allowing management to explore the consequences of changes in these assumptions. Hence, break-even analysis is useful as a management decision model. For example, a small shop selling bathroom fittings, with five employees/owners had achieved sales of £80,000 in its first year of business. The company was making a loss at this sales figure. The sales value necessary to break-even was calculated and found to be £160,000. The owners decided that this could not be achieved and closed the business. Had the break-even sales figure been known at the outset, their approach to the business would have been different.

Calculating the break-even point

There are three methods commonly employed in solving break-even problems:

1 the equation method;
2 the contribution margin method;
3 the graph method.

The equation method

The relationship between sales, variable and fixed costs and profits may be expressed as an equation:

sales = variable costs + fixed costs + profits

Example 19.2 Take the values given in the previous example: unit sale price is £10, variable costs are £4 per unit and fixed costs £150,000 per year.
Problem 1: How many units must be produced to break even?
Analysis: Let x be the number of units required.
Problem 2: Alternatively, the problem may be formulated in terms of the sales revenue required to break-even.
Analysis 1: Since net profit is zero, our formula remains:

$$£10x = £4x + £150,000 + £0$$
$$\text{i.e. } £10x - £4x = £150,000 + £0$$
$$\text{so that } x = \frac{£150,000}{6}$$
$$= 25,000 \text{ units}$$

Analysis 2: Let the unknown level of sales revenue be x; given that variable costs are four-tenths of x, we can substitute:

$$x = \frac{4}{10}x + £150,000$$

$$x - \frac{4}{10}x = £150,000$$

$$\frac{6}{10}x = £150,000$$

$$x = £250,000$$

The break-even sales revenue can be derived from the break-even volume of sales (25,000 units at £10 = £250,000), but the calculations are intended to show that the results can be calculated directly.

The contribution margin method

This method makes use of the variable profit or contribution margin per unit of output which is required to cover fixed costs.

Example 19.3

Problem 1: On the basis that the unit sale price is £10, variable costs are £4 per unit and fixed costs total £150,000 a year, calculate the break-even volume of sales.

Analysis: Let x be the number of units required. We know that the unit contribution margin is the difference between unit sale price and unit variable costs. Our formula is:

$$x = \frac{\text{fixed costs} + \text{net profit}}{\text{unit contribution margin}}$$

$$x = \frac{£150,000 + 0}{(£10 - £4)}$$

$$= \frac{150,000}{6}$$

$$= 25,000 \text{ units}$$

Problem 2: Using the same values, calculate the break-even sales revenue.

Analysis: In this case, we make use of the contribution margin ratio to calculate the sales revenue required to cover fixed costs. The contribution margin ratio is:

$$\frac{\text{unit contribution margin}}{\text{revenue per unit}}\%$$

Our formula may be expressed as follows:

$$x = \frac{\text{fixed costs} + \text{net profit}}{\text{contribution margin ratio}}$$

Substituting the given values we have:

$$x = \frac{£150,000 + 0}{60\%}$$

$$= £250,000$$

Alternatively, the break-even revenue may be found from the following formula:

$$x = \frac{\text{fixed costs} + \text{net profit}}{1 - \dfrac{\text{total varible costs}}{\text{total sales revenue}}}$$

$$\frac{150,000}{1 - \dfrac{160,000}{400,000}}$$

$$= £250,000$$

It is clear that both the equation method and the contribution margin method can be applied to profit planning by the substitution of the net profit figure, which when analysing the break-even point is zero. Both methods are different ways of manipulating the same data.

The graph method

This method involves using a break-even chart. This description is not very satisfactory because it gives undue emphasis to the break-even point whereas other points on the graph are just as important.

A break-even chart is easy to construct, but the accuracy of the reading depends on the accuracy with which data are plotted. The output or sales in units are drawn on the horizontal axis and the vertical axis is used to depict monetary values.

Example 19.4 Using the values given for the previous examples, the stages in compiling the break-even chart are as follows:

1 Using suitable graph paper, draw a horizontal axis to measure total output of at least 50,000 units. Draw a vertical axis representing the monetary equivalent of this output at its selling price of £10 per unit (£500,000).
2 Draw the variable-cost curve as a straight line from the origin to the point whose coordinates are £200,000 (50,000 at £4) and 50,000.
3 Draw the fixed-cost curve parallel to the variable-cost curve but £150,000 higher, so that total costs including variable costs will be represented by the area below this curve.
4 Insert the total revenue curve from zero to £500,000 at 50,000 units.

Figure 19.2 vividly depicts the relationship between costs, revenues, volume of output and resultant profit. The area between the revenue curve and the variable cost curve represents the contribution to fixed costs and profit at each level of output. The point at which the revenue curve crosses the total cost curve is the break-even point. As output expands from zero, fixed costs are gradually recovered until the break-even point, and thereafter each additional unit of output contributes to profit.

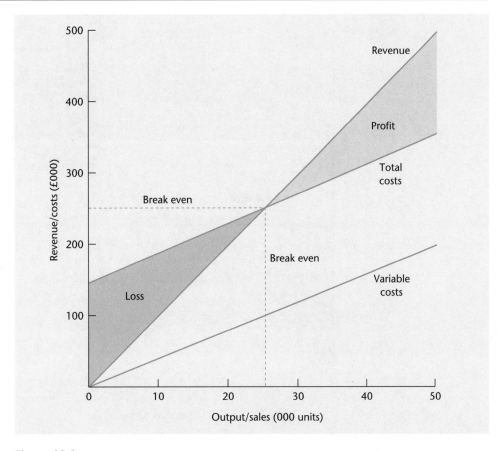

Figure 19.2

The excess by which actual sales exceed break-even sales amounts to £250,000, so that sales could be reduced by £250,000 before losses are incurred. This excess is known as the margin of safety. The margin of safety ratio is the percentage by which sales revenue may fall before a loss is incurred and is expressed as follows:

$$\text{margin of safety ratio} = \frac{\text{margin of safety revenue}}{\text{actual sales}}$$

Hence, in the example given, the margin of safety ratio is:

$$\frac{£250,000}{£500,000}$$

i.e. 50%

Clearly, the higher the margin of safety ratio, the safer the firm's position.

An alternative way of constructing the break-even chart is as in Figure 19.3. The disadvantage of this form of presentation is that unlike Figure 19.2, it does not emphasize the importance of the contribution margin to fixed costs.

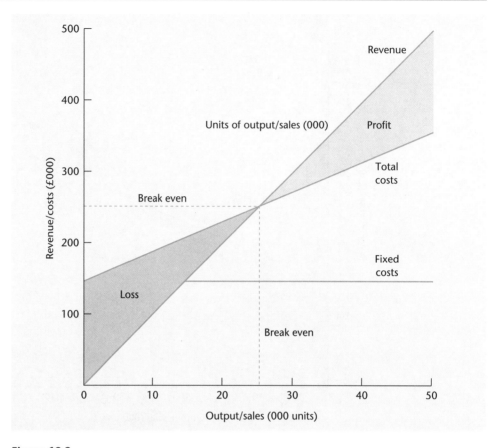

Figure 19.3

The profit–volume chart

The profit–volume chart is a special type of break-even chart. It is concerned with analysing profit and loss at different levels of activity. As in the break-even chart, the horizontal axis is used to measure the volume of output or sales in units, but the vertical axis is employed to measure the profit or loss at any given level of output or sales.

Using the same information as above, Figure 19.4 shows the profit–volume chart. Only three items are needed to plot this chart – the fixed costs, which are £150,000, and which must be recovered before a profit is made, the break-even point, which represents sales of £250,000 necessary to cover fixed costs, and the profit at an assumed level of activity (which in this case is 50,000 units yielding a profit of £150,000).

The profit–volume chart (Figure 19.4) is simply the conventional break-even chart rearranged to show changes in profit or loss which occurs through volume changes either of sales or of output. It is less detailed since it does not show separate curves for costs and revenues, but its virtue lies in the fact that it reduces any changes to two key elements – volume and profit. For this reason, the volume–profit chart is useful for illustrating the results of different management decisions.

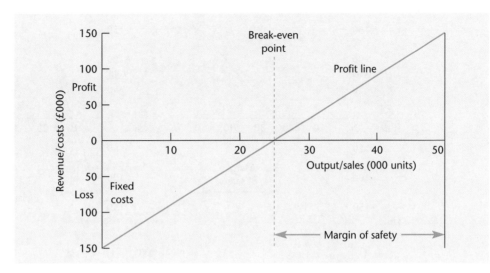

Figure 19.4

In so far as the volume–profit chart focuses simply on the relationship between volume and profit, it allows for an extended analysis of this relationship. Thus, the slope of the curve DA indicates the contribution margin ratio, which may be measured by AB/BE or DC/CE – either calculation giving the same results in this case (60 per cent).

The slope of the curve DA also indicates the rate at which changes in volume assist in the recovery of fixed costs and affect profit: the greater the slope the greater will be the effect of changes in volume on profits. Equally, the steeper the slope of the profit curve the quicker will the margin of safety be eroded and the break-even point reached as the volume of output or sales falls, as may be seen from the three cases in Figure 19.5.

Changes in the factors

Cost–volume–profit analysis is related to a consideration of four factors – fixed costs, variable costs, selling price and sales volume. Any change in one or more of these factors will affect profits. Cost–volume–profit analysis enables management to consider the effects of these changes.

Changes in fixed costs

Assuming that all other factors remain constant a change in fixed costs will affect only the break-even point.

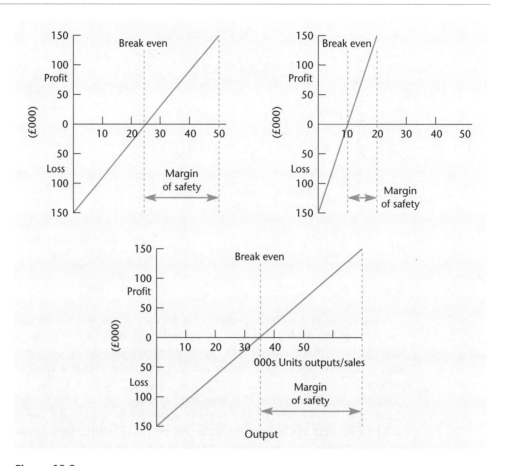

Figure 19.5

Example 19.5 The effect of an increase of £15,000 in head office costs on the break-even level is:

	Original	After increase in fixed costs
	£	£
Sales	500,000	500,000
Variable costs	200,000	200,000
Contribution margin	300,000	300,000
Fixed costs	150,000	165,000
Net profit	150,000	135,000
Contribution margin ratio	60%	60%

The new break-even point is:

$$\frac{\text{Fixed costs}}{\text{Unit contribution margin}} = \frac{£165,000}{£6} = 27,500 \text{ units}$$

Hence, a 10 per cent increase in fixed costs has resulted in a 10 per cent increase in the sales volume (and sales revenue) required to break-even from 25,000 units (£250,000) to 27,500 units (£275,000). Thus, additional sales of 2,500 units at £10 a unit are required to cover an increase of £15,000 in fixed costs. It should be noted that as the contribution margin ratio has remained constant, the change in fixed costs is the only factor affecting profit. The change is illustrated as in Figure 19.6.

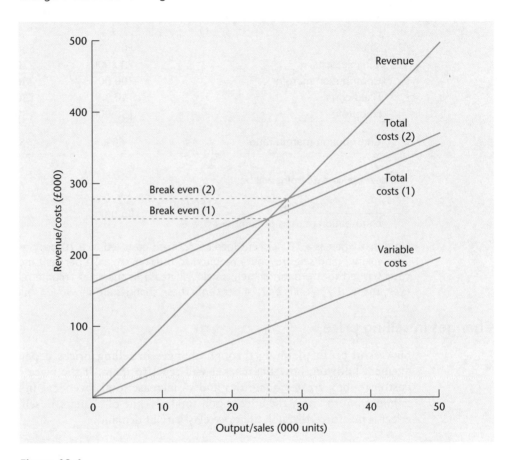

Figure 19.6

Changes in variable costs

A change in variable costs will have the immediate effect of changing the contribution margin ratio, and consequently the break-even point.

Example 19.6 It is decided to improve the quality of a product by incorporating more expensive materials. As a result, variable costs are increased by 10 per cent, and the effects on the break-even level are:

	Original	After increase in variable costs
	£	£
Sales	500,000	500,000
Variable costs	200,000	220,000
Contribution margin	300,000	280,000
Fixed costs	150,000	150,000
Net profit	150,000	130,000
Contribution margin ratio	60%	56%

The new break-even point will be:

$$\frac{\text{fixed costs}}{\text{contribution margin per unit}} = \frac{£150,000}{5.6} = 26,786 \text{ units.}$$

Note that whereas a 10 per cent increase in fixed costs led to a 10 per cent increase in the sales volume (and sales revenue) required to break-even, a 10 per cent increase in variable costs has led to a proportionately smaller increase in the sales volume required to break-even, that is, 1,786 units or 7.14 per cent. These changes are shown in Figure 19.7.

Changes in selling price

Successful profit planning through changes in selling prices depends upon management knowing how the market will react to them. If the price is reduced, will customers buy greater quantities and so increase total revenues? In other words, it is important to know the effect upon total revenue of changes in selling prices. This effect is measured through the price elasticity of demand.

Example 19.7 Let us assume that a 10 per cent increase in selling price leads to a 10 per cent reduction in the volume of sales. Assuming all other factors remain constant, the result of the price change will be:

	Original	After increase in variable costs	
Sales in units	50,000	45,000	
Sales revenue	£500,000	£495,000	(45,000 @ £11)
Variable costs	200,000	180,000	(45,000 @ £4)
Contribution margin	300,000	315,000	
Fixed costs	150,000	150,000	
Net profit	150,000	165,000	
Contribution margin ratio	60%	63.6%	

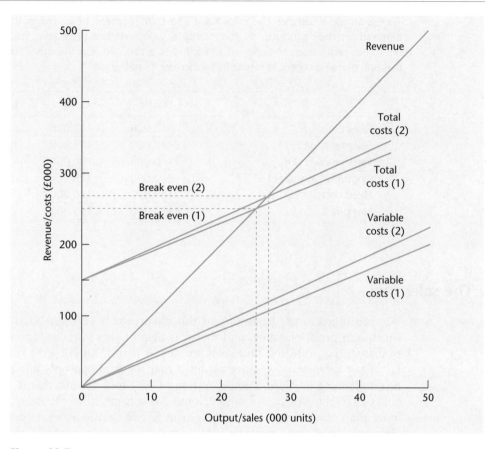

Figure 19.7

The break-even point will, as a result, be lowered from 25,000 units to 21,429 units as follows:

$$\frac{\text{fixed costs}}{\text{contribution margin per unit}} = \frac{£150,000}{£7} = 21,429 \text{ units}$$

Thus, a 10 per cent increase in the selling price has led to a much greater adjustment in the sales volume required to break even, that is, 3,571/25,000 or 14.3 per cent. We have assumed, however, that the elasticity of demand for the product was unity, that is sales volumes change by the same percentage as the change in price. In most situations this would be an unikely assumption to make. Knowledge of the slope of the demand curve for the product – its price elasticity of demand – is essential to assessing the impact of price changes on net profit. The different results that would be obtained by the same price change under three different demand conditions for the product might be as follows:

1 where the demand is *elastic*, i.e. elasticity is greater than unity: in this case a 10 per cent increase in selling price leads to a 20 per cent reduction in sales;
2 where the elasticity of demand is *unity*: in this case a 10 per cent increase in selling price leads to a 10 per cent reduction in sales;
3 where demand is *inelastic*: in this case a 10 per cent increase in selling price leads to a 5 per cent reduction in sales.

This example illustrates the importance to management of knowing the nature of the demand for their products. In the example, where demand is elastic, we witness a sharp fall in net profit from the original £150,000 to £130,000. On the other hand, a unitary or inelastic demand schedule results in an increase in net profit.

	Elastic	Unity	Inelastic
Sales units	40,000	45,000	47,500
Sales revenue (£11)	£440,000	£495,000	£522,500
Variable costs (£4)	160,000	180,000	190,000
Contribution margin	280,000	315,000	332,500
Fixed costs	150,000	150,000	150,000
Net profit	£130,000	£165,000	£182,500

The sales mix

We mentioned at the beginning of this chapter that CVP analysis is important to short-term profit planning, and that it is helpful also to the solution of other types of managerial problems. One such problem is that of selecting the best sales mix. So far in our discussion, we have assumed that the firm had only one product so that profit planning involved a consideration of only four factors, that is, fixed and variable costs, selling price and sales volume. Most firms, however, either produce or sell more than one product and management has to decide in what combination these products ought to be made or sold. It may be possible, for example, that by altering the existing sales mix by selling proportionately more of the product which has the highest contribution margin, the overall contribution margin and the break-even point is improved.

Example 19.8 Assume that Maximix Ltd has the following data concerning the three products:

Product	A	B	C	Total
	£	£	£	£
Sales	100,000	100,000	50,000	250,000
Variable costs	50,000	30,000	20,000	100,000
Contribution margin	50,000	70,000	30,000	150,000
Fixed costs				150,000
Net profit				Nil
Contribution margin ratio	50%	70%	60%	60%

If the firm could switch its sales so as to sell more of product B, which has a higher contribution margin ratio than the other two, it would improve its profitability. At the moment, the firm is just breaking even. Let us assume that it maintains the present total sales of £250,000, but that the sales mix is altered:

Product	A	B	C	Total
	£	£	£	£
Sales	50,000	175,000	25,000	250,000
Variable costs	25,000	52,500	10,000	87,500
Contribution margin	25,000	122,500	15,000	162,500
Fixed costs				150,000
Net profit				12,500
Contribution margin ratio	50%	70%	60%	65%

Hence the new product mix has raised the contribution margin ratio by 5 per cent, leading to a profit of £12,500 and a lowering of the break-even point from £250,000 to £230,769 as follows:

$$\frac{\text{fixed costs}}{\text{contribution margin ratio}} = \frac{£150,000}{65\%} = £230,769$$

The effect of the change in the product mix is depicted graphically as in Figure 19.8.

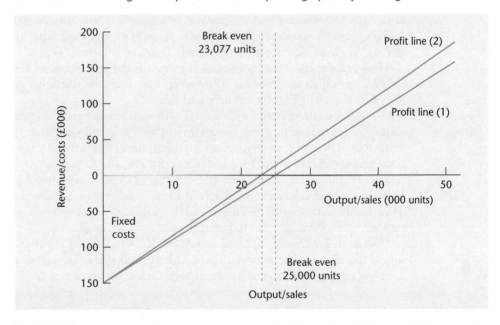

Figure 19.8

Cost–volume–profit analysis: some limitations

CVP analysis, though a useful tool for decision making, is based upon certain assumptions which are rarely encountered in practice. Hence the fragility of these assumptions limits the reliability of CVP analysis. For example, it is assumed that fixed costs are constant, and that both the variable cost and the revenue curves are linear over the relevant range. It is also assumed that volume is the only factor affecting costs, and that the price of inputs (materials, labour, etc.) and outputs remains unaffected by changes in volumes.

All these assumptions may be challenged. Fixed costs may not remain constant over the entire output range considered in the analysis, that being particularly true if the range is large. Fixed costs may indeed be constant over a small range, but then rise sharply and remain constant for another stage, as shown in Figure 19.9.

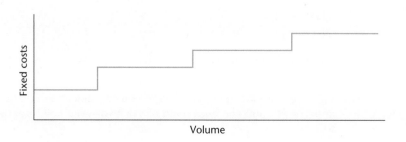

Figure 19.9

Equally doubtful is the assumption that the variable cost curve is linear so that variable costs change in direct proportion to changes in volume. As demand for input factors increase so eventually will their price, with the effect that the variable-cost curve is likely to increase proportionately faster as volume of output expands.

To overcome these limitations, and to retain the usefulness of CVP analysis, the range over which volumes are allowed to vary must be restricted accordingly. The relevant range will vary by industry and firm.

As regards the revenue curve, other things being equal, increasing sales will require a reduction in price, so a straight line is not an accurate portrayal of its behaviour. Therefore, computations are often needed at several price levels – several total-revenue curves are needed instead of just one.

Finally, the break-even chart presents an extremely simplified picture of cost–volume–revenue relationships. Each of these is subject to outside influences as well as each other. Above all, break-even analysis should be viewed as a guide to decision making, not a substitute for judgement and common sense.

Despite its limitations, the real usefulness of CVP is that it enriches the understanding of the relationship between costs, volume and prices as factors affecting profit, enabling management to test assumptions which assist short-run decision making.

Long-term variable costs

In the previous chapter we saw that activity-based costing moves away from the notions of short-term fixed and variable costs and focuses on the variability of costs in the longer term. It is appropriate to regard fixed costs as long-term variable costs because fixed costs are not fixed forever. Companies can, over the long term, through managerial decisions lay off supervisors and sell plant and equipment. As companies become less focused on production and sales volumes as cost drivers, they begin to recognize that 'fixed costs' exist only under a short-term reporting period perspective.

Summary

In the short run, the firm's capacity is fixed, so that its room for manoeuvre is limited. Given this condition, short-range decision making considers the most desirable actions for achieving a planned profit. Cost–volume–profit analysis (CVP) has an important role to play in short-run decision making by providing an insight into the relationships between costs, volume of output, revenue and profit. In particular, CVP analysis highlights the significance of the distinction between fixed and variable costs and how these behave with changes in the volume of output.

CVP analysis makes an important contribution to short-run decision making by providing an understanding of the conditions required to break-even. It does not assist in the discovery of the conditions required to maximize profits, in sharp contrast to economic theory which pays particular attention to this aspect of profit planning. Its usefulness lies in the insights it provides. Moreover, it deals with the most important consideration – the avoidance of losses. In this sense, CVP analysis reflects the assumption that decision makers are risk averse or at least want to understand the risks they run.

The limitations of CVP analysis derive from the assumptions it makes. Many of these can be challenged, for example, the linearity of the behaviour of costs and revenues over a range of output. Although some of the criticism of CVP analysis may be partially refuted, its real usefulness lies in the manner in which it enriches the understanding of the relationship between cost, volume of output and revenue for decision making purposes in the short run, thereby assisting management in making short-run decisions.

Self-assessment questions

1 Explain what is meant by CVP analysis.

2 Describe how CVP analysis is used in profit planning.

3 What is the significance of the break-even point?

4 Describe various ways in which the break-even point may be calculated.

5 What is a profit–volume chart?

6 List a number of possible ways in which short-term profitability may be improved.

7 What difficulties are implied in using CVP analysis for short-term decision making?

1   The Carbon Ink Company's profit statement for the preceding year is presented below. Except as noted, the cost and sales relationship for the coming year is expected to follow the same pattern as in the preceding year.

	£
Sales (2,000,000 bottles at £0.25)	500,000
Variable costs	300,000
Fixed costs	100,000
Total costs	400,000
Profit	100,000

Required:

(a)   What is the break-even point in sales value and units?

(b)   An extension to the factory will add £50,000 to the fixed costs and increase production capacity by 60 per cent. How many bottles would have to be sold after the extension to break even?

(c)   The management of the company feels that it should earn at least £10,000 on the new investment. What sales volume is required to enable the company to maintain existing profits and earn the minimum required on the new investment?

(d)   If the factory operates at full capacity after extension, what profit will be earned?

(e)   What are the weaknesses in the use of break-even analysis?

2* An accountant and an economist were having an argument. The economist accused the accountant of using a naive, over-simplified model of cost–volume–profit relationships by assuming linear patterns in variable costs. Since costs do not behave in this simplistic way, the accountant, argued the economist, should be more realistic in his assumptions.

The accountant countered by saying that the economist was just as bad, if not worse, because most economic models ignore variations in fixed costs. Although the accountant agreed that in the long run all costs are variable, a firm had to make decisions in the short run in order to survive. And, argued the accountant, in the short run some costs are definitely fixed.

The economist was becoming somewhat agitated and accused the accountant of not using a dynamic analysis for solving business problems. The economist claimed, for example, that the static nature of cost–volume–profit analysis often produced misleading information. The accountant thought this a case of the pot calling the kettle black, and accused the economist of using unrealistic models which never exist in practice.

Required:

Both the accountant and the economist turn to you for support; what would be your reply? Use the case below to illustrate your answer.

The Malplaquet Company cans fresh orange juice. The company's budget at 80 per cent capacity for 20X0 was as follows:

	£
Sales	250,000
Cost of oranges and other materials used	60,000
Cost of cans	30,000
Direct labour	60,000
Manufacturing expenses:	
Fixed	20,000
Variable	30,000
Administration, selling and other indirect expenses:	
Fixed	10,800
Variable	8,000

The directors of the company anticipate the following in costs during 20X1:

Price of oranges and other materials used	5% increase
Price of cans	No change
Rates for direct labour	10% increase
Manufacturing expenses: fixed	£800 decrease
Administration, selling and other indirect expenses:	
Fixed	No change

Manufacturing variable expenses will maintain the same ratio to wages paid, and administration, selling and other indirect variable expenses will vary only with quantity sold.

In 20X1 sales quantity and selling price are expected to remain constant.

3 The Brown Fox motel is owned and run by Billy Fisher. Fisher, a professional footballer, could earn £24,000 per annum as a full-time player, but prefers to play on a part-time basis (for £12,000) and run the motel.

The motel has 60 available rooms which are charged out at £30 per day. The variable costs of operation of the motel amount to £8 per room rental per day. This includes cleaning, laundry, coffee, tea, etc.

The fixed costs per annum are:

Reception/office staff	£65,000
Repairs/maintenance	£39,000
Depreciation	£75,000
Miscellaneous	£23,600

Fisher complains that business is not as good from October to March as it is from April to September, as illustrated below:

	April–September	October–March
Potential rentals	10,920	10,920
(60 × 26 × 7)		
Rooms rented	8,736	6,552

Required:

(a) Prepare a contribution break-even chart of the data for each six-month period, illustrating the margin of safety.

(b) Calculate the number of rooms per period which must be rented in order to break even.

(c) Calculate the number of rooms which would have to be rented to break even if the room charges were reduced from £30 to £25 from October to March.

(d) Assuming that it is impossible to cover the fixed costs during November and February, regardless of the price per room, should the motel be closed during these months? What would be the financial and non-financial effects of the closure? What are the limitations of using break-even analysis in short-term decision making? Illustrate by reference to the Brown Fox motel.

4* The Bolton Haulage company is a small to medium-sized removals firm with ten large removal vans. Following the deregulation of passenger transport, the owner of the business proposes to diversify into passenger transport using eight mini buses. The diversification will lead to greater use of the servicing facilities and the pool of drivers employed.

It is proposed to operate minibuses on four existing routes which were bid for by the company, and have now been awarded by the Passenger Transport Authority. The minibuses will also be available for private hire.

The company currently only prepares six-monthly accounts. The owner believes this is insufficient to run the proposed business.

The current expense headings (taken from the financial accounts) are: drivers' wages; fuel and oil; repairs and maintenance; servicing (three months or 20,000 miles); motor tax; insurance; mechanics' wages; depreciation of vehicles; rent and rates; electricity; and tyres.

A manager is currently responsible for running the removals business, and a transport manager is to be appointed to run the minibus side of the business. In addition to these staff, there is the owner of the business, and a general staff to cash-up, provide refreshments, clean the buses, etc. Their offices are on the same site as the garage.

Required:

(a) Design a draft operating cost statement to facilitate control of the removal vans and the minibuses. Justify your format and classification of expenses and the purpose and objectives of reporting such information.

(b) Design a draft management accounting information statement which will assist management in assessing the efficiency and effectiveness of both segments of the business.

(c) How will the statement meet the twin objectives of measuring efficiency and effectiveness?

Reference   Qureshi, M.A. (1978) Analysing Business Strategy: The Uses of Cost–Volume–Profit, *Analysis*, CIMA.

CHAPTER 20

Marginal costing

Setting the scene

One of the most progressive phases in the history of management accountancy – in the sense of distinguishing it from other sectors of the profession – was that in which marginal costing came to the fore.

It was, and remains, perfectly reasonable in financial accounts to use techniques of apportionment and absorption, so as to arrive at figures suitable for valuing stocks, and analysing profits by product.

What the marginal costers pointed out, however, was that such an approach did not reflect how profits are actually earned. In the real world, products make contributions (sales minus variable costs) to a pool from which fixed costs are defrayed. If, in aggregate, contribution exceeds fixed costs, the company makes a profit; if not, it makes a loss.

(Allen, 1993)

Learning objectives

After studying this chapter you should be able to:

1 explain the differences between marginal and absorption costing;

2 prepare the income statements based on a marginal costing approach;

3 discuss the advantages of a marginal costing approach over absorption costing.

Marginal costing is an invaluable management accounting tool used to provide management with information about cost, volume and profit relationships in a form that is easy to understand. The key advantage of marginal costing is that it facilitates decision making, cost management and profit planning. Cost–volume–profit relationships discussed in the previous chapter consider how aggregate costs change with volume Marginal costing focuses on the incremental changes in costs that result from marginal changes in production volume and looks at the difference between fixed costs (non-variable costs) and marginal manufacturing costs. This distinction is critical for many decision and control models that are used in management accounting. However, for financial reporting to external users the conventional method of product costing based on full or absorption costing is required under generally accepted accounting principles.

The case for marginal costing for inventory valuation

As we saw in Section 1 of this Part, periodic income measurement and the matching principle constitute the core of financial accounting. According to SSAP 2 'Disclosure of Accounting Policies' in the United Kingdom, later replaced by Financial Reporting Standard 18 'Accounting Policies', 'revenues and costs are matched with one another so far as their relationship can be established or justifiably assumed'. The International Accounting Standards Board IFRS 1 'First time adoption of international accounting standards' requires that entities adopting for the first time international accounting standards select accounting policies based on international accounting standards in force. International Accounting Standard 1 (IAS) 'Presentation of Financial Statements' requires that an entity must use the accrual basis of accounting in preparing financial statements (other than cash flow statements), which involves matching expenses with revenues, making the matching principle one of the cardinal rules for profit measurement in the global economy.

Different methods of matching

The logic behind the matching principle springs from a desire to provide a rule which will secure uniformity in the preparation of profit and loss accounts. Investors require uniformity in accounting practices if they are to be able to evaluate the performance of one firm against another. The development of accounting standards represents an attempt at ensuring these comparisons can be made. However, no set formula has been prescribed for valuing inventory, particularly work-in-progress and finished goods, so that there is a great deal of flexibility in the valuation of inventory. Terms such as 'at cost or net realizable value' and 'should include a proportion of factory overhead' are loose enough to allow significant variations in companies' methods. As far as the matching principle is concerned the problem is to develop suitable methods for matching costs to revenues. Two such methods have been developed: product costing and period costing.

Product costing

Accountants long ago recognized the product itself as a convenient vehicle for matching costs with revenues. Product costing involves attaching all costs, whether direct or overhead costs, to the product. In measuring the cost of goods produced and sold to be matched against revenues from sales, product costing requires the inclusion of those manufacturing costs which are incurred irrespective of production. Thus, costs such as rent, insurance and rates which are incurred on a time basis rather than on the level of production are recovered against the units produced.

The proponents of product costing as the only method of matching costs to revenues argue that all manufacturing costs are product costs, and that there is no such thing as a period cost because 'ideally all costs incurred should be viewed as absolutely clinging to definite items of goods sold or services rendered. . . . The ideal is to match costs incurred with the efforts attributable to or significantly related to such costs' (Paton and Littleton, 1940). They argue, therefore, that manufacturing costs are incurred solely to make possible the creation of a product.

Period costing

Period costing recognizes that certain costs are related to the passage of time, and that the benefit derived from these costs is not affected by the actual level of production during a period of time. Since rent, insurance and salaries are incurred on a time basis, the cash outflows associated with them are not influenced by the lack of revenue.

Period costing is a method of costing which conflicts with the traditional view expressed by product costing, and has given rise to the marginal costing controversy. The issue between the two schools of thought revolves round the question of whether fixed manufacturing costs, that is those costs incurred irrespective of production, should be charged as the costs of the product and included in the costs of inventories, or charged against the revenue of the period. According to the supporters of product costing, who employ absorption or full costing, all manufacturing costs should be absorbed by the product. Marginal costing assigns only the marginal costs, that is the costs which vary with the level of production, to the products, and fixed manufacturing costs are written off each year as period costs.

One advantage of marginal costing over absorption costing cited by its advocates is its superiority for management decision making. Because the distinction between fixed and marginal costs is 'built into' the accounting system, it assists profit planning, product pricing and control. However, the controversy which surrounds marginal costing is whether or not it should be used for external reporting. The advocates of absorption costing argue that figures prepared on a marginal costing basis for the use of management should be adjusted to an absorption costing basis before they are released to external users.

Both management and investors are concerned primarily with the future outcome of present decisions. Accountants who advocate the use of absorption costing for external financial statements deprive investors of a useful analytical device and make the task of interpreting the results more difficult.

Marginal costing emphasizes the behaviour of fixed and variable costs, which is of utmost importance to investors. Marginal costing helps to predict cash flows in relation to volume changes; the isolation of fixed costs in the profit statement permits more accurate forecasts of claims on cash in meeting current outlays on fixed expenses. Marginal costing also helps to correlate fluctuations in cash flows with fluctuations in sales volume.

We argued earlier that management should not receive the credit for increasing the net worth of business before the critical event has occurred, and we conceded that in almost every case, the sale was the critical event. Since profit should vary with a company's performance (which really means accomplishing the critical event) where profit is related to sales, it is logical that there should be a direct relationship between the two. Marginal costing should therefore be used in these cases. Absorption costing, being based on the product concept, does not provide this relationship between profit and sales, because under this method, profit variation is partly related to production.

Marginal costing also permits more accurate profit forecasts because net profit will have a direct relationship with sales, instead of confusing the picture with the impact of the two activities of producing and selling.

The treatment of overheads

International Accounting Standard 2 (IAS 2) Inventories states that the measurement of inventories should include all costs of purchase, of conversion (including fixed and variable manufacturing overheads) as well as other costs in bringing inventories to their present location and condition. It reflected the traditional accounting view stated by SSAP 9 'Stocks and Long-Term Contracts' in the United Kingdom that the aim should be to match costs and revenues 'in the year in which revenue arises rather than the year in which cost is incurred', cost being defined for this purpose as including 'all related overheads, even though some of these may accrue on a time basis'.

Absorption and marginal costing compared

Example 20.1 Let us assume the following basic data:

Total sales and production over 4 years (500 units per year)	2,000 units
Direct material costs per unit	£1
Direct labour costs per unit	£1
Marginal overhead costs per unit	£0.5
Fixed overhead costs	£1,000 p.a.
Sales price per unit	£6

Let us further assume that the volume of sales and of production are constant in time. The volume of production, sales and the level of stocks in units are as follows:

Year	1	2	3	4	Total
Opening inventory (units)	40	40	40	40	40
Production (units)	500	500	500	500	2,000
Sales (units)	500	500	500	500	2,000
Closing inventory (units)	40	40	40	40	40

The results under the two forms of costing would appear as follows:

Year	1	2	3	4	Total
Marginal costing	£	£	£	£	£
Sales	3,000	3,000	3,000	3,000	12,000
Cost of goods produced	1,250	1,250	1,250	1,250	5,000
Add: Opening inventory	100	100	100	100	100
Available for sale	1,350	1,350	1,350	1,350	5,100
Less: Closing inventory	100	100	100	100	100
Cost of goods sold	1,250	1,250	1,250	1,250	1,250
Contribution margin	1,750	1,750	1,750	1,750	7,000
Fixed overheads	1,000	1,000	1,000	1,000	4,000
Net profit	750	750	750	750	3,000
Absorption costing					
Sales	3,000	3,000	3,000	3,000	12,000
Cost of goods produced	2,250	2,250	2,250	2,250	9,000
Add: Opening inventory	180	180	180	180	180
Available for sale	2,430	2,430	2,430	2,430	9,180
Less: Closing inventory	180	180	180	180	180
Cost of goods sold	2,250	2,250	2,250	2,250	9,000
Net income	750	750	750	750	3,000

The above example illustrates the effects on profits of using absorption and marginal costing methods for a firm in which everything stayed exactly the same in four consecutive years. Therefore, sales and levels of production are constant in each period and both opening and closing inventories remain unchanged. Under these conditions income figures for each year remain the same under both methods of calculating income.

In reality, the effect on production of shortages of materials, or the effect on sales of credit squeezes and changes in indirect taxation, will distort the relationship between sales and production and inventory levels act as buffers. Inventory levels, therefore, are not stable; they are in fact very volatile. Moreover, modern methods of production require a constant rate of production, not only to maintain the efficiency of operations but also to prevent layoffs and so assist in the preservation of good industrial relations. Flexible inventory level standards are normally established for the purpose of planning for a reasonably uniform level of production.

We shall now examine the different results obtained under marginal and absorption costing under the following circumstances:

1 where sales fluctuate but production remains constant;
2 here sales are constant but production fluctuates.

Results where sales fluctuate but production is constant

As soon as the rate of sales begins to differ from the rate of production the use of different methods of allocating overheads to costs of production starts to affect profit calculations.

Example 20.2   Let us take the figures given in the earlier example, but keeping the level of production constant against varying levels of sales as follows:

Year	1	2	3	4	Total
Opening inventory (units)	40	140	340	240	40
Production (units)	500	500	500	500	2,000
Sales (units)	400	300	600	700	2,000
Closing inventory (units)	140	340	240	40	40

The results under the two methods of costing would appear as follows:

Year	1	2	3	4	Total
Marginal costing	£	£	£	£	£
Sales	2,400	1,800	3,600	4,200	12,000
Cost of goods produced	1,250	1,250	1,250	1,250	5,000
Add: Opening inventory	100	350	850	600	100
Available for sale	1,350	1,600	2,100	1,850	5,100
Less: Closing inventory	350	850	600	100	100
Cost of goods sold	1,000	750	1,500	1,750	5,000
Contribution margin	1,400	1,050	2,100	2,450	7,000
Fixed overheads	1,000	1,000	1,000	1,000	4,000
Net income	400	50	1,100	1,450	3,000
Absorption costing					
Sales	2,400	1,800	3,600	4,200	12,000
Cost of goods produced	2,250	2,250	2,250	2,250	9,000
Add: Opening inventory	180	630	1,530	1,080	180
Available for sale	2,430	2,880	3,780	3,330	9,180
Less: Closing inventory	630	1,530	1,080	180	180
Cost of goods sold	1,800	1,350	2,700	3,150	9,000
Net income	600	450	900	1,050	3,000

It becomes evident why there is a controversy between the two schools of thought as regards the measurement of income for the purpose of financial reporting for under the circumstances outlined above wide differences appear in net income figures. These differences may be illustrated graphically in Figure 20.1, and it may be seen that the income profile fluctuates more widely when overheads are excluded, as they are under marginal costing, than when they are included as under absorption costing.

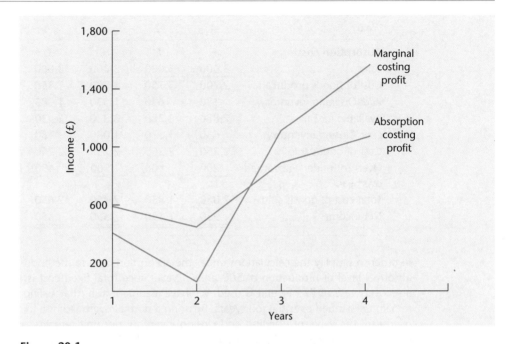

Figure 20.1

Results where sales are constant but production fluctuates

Example 20.3 Let us now keep the figures for sales constant, and compare results under the two methods of costing when levels of production vary.

Year	1	2	3	4	Total
Opening inventory (units)	40	140	340	240	40
Production (units)	600	700	400	300	2,000
Sales (units)	500	500	500	500	2,000
Closing inventory (units)	140	340	240	40	40

The results under the two methods would be calculated as follows:

Year	1	2	3	4	Total
Marginal costing	£	£	£	£	£
Sales	3,000	3,000	3,000	3,000	12,000
Cost of goods produced	1,500	1,750	1,000	750	5,000
Add: Opening inventory	100	350	850	600	100
Available for sale	1,600	2,100	1,850	1,350	5,100
Less: Closing inventory	350	850	600	100	100
Cost of goods sold	1,250	1,250	1,250	1,250	5,000
Contribution margin	1,750	1,750	1,750	1,750	7,000
Fixed overheads	1,000	1,000	1,000	1,000	4,000
Net income	750	750	750	750	3,000

Year	1	2	3	4	Total
Absorption costing	£	£	£	£	£
Sales	3,000	3,000	3,000	3,000	12,000
Cost of goods produced	2,700	3,150	1,800	1,350	9,000
Add: Opening inventory	180	630	1,530	1,080	180
Available for sale	2,880	3,780	3,330	2,430	9,180
Less: Closing inventory	630	1,530	1,080	180	180
Cost of goods sold	2,250	2,250	2,250	2,250	9,000
Over- (or under-) absorbed overhead	200	400	(200)	(400)	–
Total cost of goods sold	2,050	1,850	2,450	2,650	9,000
Net income	950	1,150	550	350	3,000

In order to simplify the calculations under the absorption costing method we have assumed a normal level of production of 500 units a year. Since total fixed cost is £1,000 per year, a recovery rate of £2 per unit is used. We have assumed, also, that selling prices and costs remain unchanged over the four years. By using a normal overhead rate for recovering fixed overhead, the value of opening and closing inventory per unit remains constant at £4.50 (£2.50 marginal + £2 fixed). In the first two years the normal output level is exceeded by 100 and 200 units respectively, with shortfalls in the last two years. The cost of goods sold is adjusted by the over- or under-recovery of fixed overhead resulting from those differences in deriving income under absorption costing.

In this example, where sales have remained constant but production has fluctuated, we note that profit results obtained under marginal costing remain constant, but those based on absorption costing show wide fluctuation – £1,150 in year 2 and £350 in year 4.

Marginal and absorption costing: their impact on income summarized

The various examples we have considered enable the following generalizations to be made on the impact on income of these two different methods of costing:

1 where sales and production levels are constant through time, income is the same under the two methods;
2 where production remains constant but sales fluctuate, income rises or falls with the level of sales, assuming that costs and prices remain constant, but the fluctuations in net income figures are greater with marginal costing than with absorption costing;
3 where sales are constant but production fluctuates, marginal costing provides for constant income, whereas under absorption costing, income fluctuates;
4 where production exceeds sales, income is higher under absorption costing than under marginal costing, since the absorption of fixed overheads into closing inventory increases their value thereby reducing the cost of goods sold;
5 where sales exceed production, income is higher under marginal costing. The fixed costs, which previously were part of inventory values, are now charged against revenue under absorption costing. Therefore, under absorption costing the value of fixed costs charged against revenue is greater than that incurred for the period.

The marginal costing controversy

We have seen in this chapter how income may be affected by the manner in which costs are matched against revenues, so that the selection of one accounting procedure rather than another may, according to prevailing circumstances, affect the outcome of income plans. Advocates of marginal costing base their case on the superiority of this method for planning and control purposes. It does so by clarifying the relationship between costs, volume and profit by identifying the contribution margin, that is the excess of sales revenue over marginal costs of production, linking income to the level of sales which is the most critical event affecting a firm's financial performance.

The arguments in favour of providing marginal costing information for assisting decision making by external users are overwhelming. Some opponents of marginal costing assert that it is incorrect to suggest that information which is useful for management decision making is relevant for all business purposes, although it is difficult to accept the contention that marginal costing information may be helpful to management but not to external users, for both management and investors are faced with the same task, that is, decision making.

Some accountants have been concerned by the fluctuations which are imported in income measurement by the exclusion of fixed costs, and to secure a certain stability in income, advocate the retention of the absorption costing method of valuing inventories. A further controversy arises from the effects of marginal costing on the balance sheet of omitting fixed factory overheads from inventory values. The real argument on this issue is whether the balance sheet should show inventories at actual cost or at a value to the current period of the resources transferred from the period just ended. Marginal costing is said to have an 'income statement', whereas absorption costing is said to have a 'balance sheet emphasis'.

The absorption costing method allows overheads to be carried into the next period, thus enabling a manipulation of the income figure. By carrying forward overheads, income is increased. Moreover if inventory value falls, income will fall, resulting in a strong temptation to keep the inventory figure increasing as this will almost always lead to an increase in income.

Marginal costing and ABC

The development of activity-based costing has provided support for the product concept. As we saw in Chapter 18, ABC aims to allocate all costs to products, including those that occur at the 'higher' levels. However, because some of these costs (e.g. facility-level costs) can only be allocated on an arbitrary basis, they should not be assigned to products at all. In the short term they remain period costs which are incurred on a time basis.

Summary

Accountants are more likely to agree on the nature of measurement if they agree on the purpose of accounting. If the central purpose of accounting is to make possible the periodic matching of costs and revenues, and if the matching principle is the 'nucleus of accounting theory', then clearly the absorption costers are correct in their view. But if, as we argue in this book, the prime objective of accounting is to provide information which is useful for decision making, then the case for marginal costing is very strong.

Self-assessment questions

1 What do you understand by marginal costing?

2 Explain the treatment of overhead costs under absorption costing and marginal costing.

3 Discuss the different profit results that are obtained using absorption costing and
   (i)   marginal costing under the following circumstances;
   (ii) where sales fluctuate but production remains constant;
   (iii) where sales are constant but production fluctuates.

Problems

1 Computer Limited was formed three years ago to produce a single product, the 'Mini'. The directors are receiving the financial results of the first three years presented by the company accountant, and are concerned with the decline in profits in the year 20X2 despite a substantial increase in sales.

Summarized results are shown below:

	20X0	20X1	20X2
Production: Budget (units)	1,000	1,000	1,000
Actual (units)	900	1,100	800
Sales (units)	800	800	1,000
Selling price per unit	£80	£80	£80
Marginal production cost per unit	£10	£10	£10
Fixed production overheads	£40,000	£40,000	£40,000
Fixed selling and administrative overheads	£20,000	£20,000	£20,000
Net profit	nil	£8,000	£2,000

Fixed overheads are absorbed on the basis of budgeted annual production. Under- or over-absorbed overheads are charged to cost of goods sold.

Required:

(a) Prepare a statement showing the profit figures derived by the company accountant.
(b) Prepare an income statement using a marginal costing approach.
(c) Reconcile the profits calculated in parts (a) and (b) above.
(d) Explain the rationale behind the approaches adopted in parts (a) and (b).

2 The Sherwood Co. Ltd is a single-product manufacturing company, which uses a marginal costing system for internal management purposes. The year-end external reports are converted to absorption costs. Variances are charged to the cost of goods sold.

The following data refers to the years ended 31 December 20X0 and 20X1:

	20X0	20X1
	£	£
Sale price per unit	80	90
Standard marginal costs per unit:		
Direct materials	21	23
Direct labour	19	22
Marginal factory overheads	8	10
Marginal selling and administrative expenses	2	3
Fixed factory overheads	170,000	180,000
	Units	Units
Opening inventory	1,500	2,000
Closing inventory	2,000	1,500
Sales	20,000	25,000

The normal volume used for the purpose of absorption costing is 28,000 units in both years.

Required:

(a) Prepare profit and loss accounts for the year ended 31 December 20X1 on a marginal costing and on an absorption costing basis.
(b) Discuss any differences which you may find between these two profit and loss accounts.
(c) State what advantages and disadvantages attach to the marginal costing approach for internal management purposes.

References Allen, D. (1993) A picture paints a thousand words, *Management Accounting* (UK), September.

Paton, W.A. and Littleton, A.C. (1940) *An Introduction to Corporate Accounting Standards*, Monograph 3, AAA.

CHAPTER 21

Costs for pricing

Setting the scene

Pricing is one of the key factors in selling products or services under competitive market conditions. However, the significance of pricing goes far beyond the simple question of determining profitability. The complex set of notions involved in pricing have their roots in the strategic decisions that are concerned with capital investment, as well as those that relate to the immediacy of current operating profitability. If a firm develops a pricing policy that affects its position in the market, there will be long-term implications, for any change in demand will affect the capital budgeting process. Similarly, pricing policy influences current market demand and given cost–volume profit relationships will also affect current profitability. The expansion of the global market economy has greatly stimulated foreign trade and the importance of export pricing.

Learning objectives

After studying this chapter you should be able to:

1   explain the nature of the pricing problem;

2   understand pricing theory in accounting and economics;

3   describe full-cost pricing and show how it differs from conversion-cost pricing;

4   explain return on investment pricing;

5   discuss the advantages of marginal-cost pricing;

6   explain target pricing;

7   discuss the issues involved in export pricing.

The purpose of this chapter is to discuss how accountants use costs to help develop prices for a variety of different recurring decisions. Since different costs are needed for different decisions, the first question has to be, 'What are the circumstances for which cost information is needed?' The circumstances in which pricing decisions are made are complex and allow alternative solutions and methods of measuring costs.

The nature of the pricing problem

The firm's long-term survival depends on its ability to sell products and services at prices that cover costs and provide a margin that ensures a reasonable rate of return to investors. This simple statement of the pricing problem suggests that the task of accountants is to measure costs, leaving management to add a margin that provides the required return on capital expected by investors.

The truth is that the pricing problem is much more complex than simply estimating costs. In the short term the firm's cost structure determines whether a given price makes a product profitable or not, but total profit is affected by other factors such as changes in aggregate demand, actions by competitors, the bargaining power of suppliers and customers. The sheer variety of possible circumstances calls for different pricing policies, implying alternative concepts and measurements of costs.

Pricing is only one of the ways a firm can influence demand for its products. Other possibilities are advertising, which increases sales and brand loyalty, as well as initiatives to increase market share, expand or rationalize the number of distribution channels, improve marketing techniques, and product presentation. Attempting to increase sales through lowering prices or otherwise altering pricing policy may not be the best way of expanding sales and improving profits. Equally, a fall in demand for a product may be remedied in ways other than simply reducing prices. Therefore, in focusing on pricing, we are only looking at one of the factors that influence sales.

Recent years have seen a remarkable shift in the relative importance of long-term rather than short-term considerations in developing pricing policies. Whereas traditional approaches to pricing in the US and Europe have taken a short-run perspective, enterprises in the Far East have viewed pricing as a long-term problem and have consequently developed new approaches.

Pricing theory in accounting and economics

As we saw in Chapter 7, accounting theory is founded on a set of concepts that define the nature and the practice of accounting. The entity and cost concepts determine the manner in which accounting theory deals with aspects of the pricing problem. In line with the entity concept, accounting theory is solely concerned with the business entity and its shareholders. The cost concept constitutes an empirical theory of costs as they appear in accounting records through invoices. These costs are analysed, classified, used and reported according to the specific circumstances for which cost information is needed.

Significantly, accounting has no concept of price and no pricing theory that would provide a basis for developing pricing policies for decision making that have normative prescriptions for profitability. Accounting theory has been concerned with the pricing problem solely from the viewpoint of supplying cost information relevant to the pricing decision at hand. Accounting theory views price as an exit value that is recognized in accordance with the realization concept, namely a number shown on a sales invoice giving the date and the amount.

The earliest interest in cost accounting may be traced to the Industrial Revolution in the United Kingdom, when many manufacturing firms went bankrupt because they had no knowledge of product costs when fixing market prices. The considerable expansion of mass-production in the United States at the beginning of the twentieth century increased the concern with pricing and marked the real birth of modern cost accounting.

In contrast, the theory of the firm in economics, which corresponds to the accounting theory based on the entity concept, places pricing in the context of profitability. Now the role of price is to maximize profits by bringing demand and supply into equilibrium. The price which maximizes profits is found at that level of sales where the extra revenue from selling one more unit (the marginal revenue) exactly equals the extra costs of producing it (marginal cost).

Example 21.1 Let us assume that a firm producing 'widgets' in large numbers has information about the quantities that would be sold at different prices. The accountant produces the following data:

Price per unit	Sales volume	Revenues	Variable cost per unit	Total variable cost	Fixed costs	Total costs	Profit
£	£	£	£	£	£	£	£
30	100,000	3,000,000	18	1,800,000	800,000	2,600,000	400,000
32	90,000	2,880,000	18	1,620,000	800,000	2,420,000	460,000
34	80,000	2,720,000	18	1,440,000	800,000	2,240,000	480,000
36	70,000	2,520,000	18	1,260,000	800,000	2,060,000	460,000
39	60,000	2,280,000	18	1,080,000	800,000	1,880,000	400,000
40	50,000	2,000,000	18	90,000	800,000	1,700,000	300,000

It is clear that the price of £34 a unit yields the maximum profit, and that is the price which the firm should establish. While it is not obvious from the figures in the table, it is also the price at which marginal revenue equals marginal costs. The calculation of these requires a bit of mathematics and the interested reader should consult more specialised textbooks (e.g. Noreen, Brewer and Garrison, 2008). The key relationships between revenues, costs and profits are shown in Figure 21.1 and make it clear why a price of £34 and volume of 80,000 maximize profits.

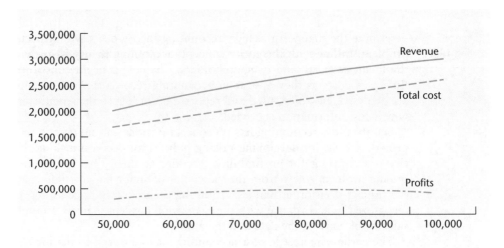

Figure 21.1

Accordingly, economic theory develops normative prescriptions aimed at maximizing profitability, whereas accounting theory has no such pretensions, leaving pricing decisions to the discretion of management. Studies tend to suggest that managers do not follow the advice of economists by setting prices such that marginal costs equal marginal revenues, either because the assumptions do not apply or because the data are not available (see Govindarajan and Anthony, 1983).

Unlike accounting theory, the theory of the firm in economics examines the pricing problem under different market conditions, namely perfect competition, imperfect competition and the existence of monopolies. These different conditions completely alter the circumstances under which pricing policies are developed. The existence of perfect markets that ensure perfect competition is a theoretical fiction that was inspired by the idealism that motivated early classical economists, such as Adam Smith and Jeremy Bentham. It remains influential in the theory of finance in the efficient market hypothesis which seeks to explain the pricing of financial instruments transacted on Stock Exchanges. In particular, the efficient market hypothesis assumes that prices accurately reflect all public information and therefore ensures the optimal allocation of capital in the economy.

The generalized presence of imperfect competition and natural monopolies has led to the creation of government agencies such as the monopoly commissions and industry regulators (OFWAT for the water and sewage industry) aimed at preventing unfair competition through such practices as price rings and agreements in restraint of trade.

Cost-based pricing theories

Traditions of conservatism and sound management have induced a reliance on knowledge of costs for setting minimum prices. Consistently selling below full costs will lead to insolvency and so long-term survival depends on the firm being able to sell at prices which not only cover all costs but yield a sufficient profit. How this is to be achieved depends very much on the industry in which a firm competes and its particular strategy and business model (think of Ryanair and BA).

In general, cost-based pricing theories are concerned with two elements of price. The first is the relevant costs which should be included in the price, and the second is the mark-up for the profit margin. The size of the profit margin will depend on the existence of close substitutes for the firm's products (commodities like sand have low profit margins, highly differentiated ones like luxury watches have big margins).

The relevance of costs to pricing decisions is influenced also by the firm's drive to meet strategic objectives such as earning a specified rate of return, increasing market share, or penetrating a new market. The firm's relative marketing position in a particular market may be a more dominant influence on pricing than its costs. Thus, a firm may be so strong as to be a price-maker and thus able to fix a price which other producers have to follow. Conversely, a firm may be a price-taker, unable to influence the overall market price and therefore obliged to align its own prices with the market.

Cost-based pricing theories have a moral quality, which economic theory does not reflect, in the notion that a cost-plus formula is 'fair'. This embodies the medieval notion of a 'just price' which was an important part of the teaching of such men as St Thomas Aquinas and which still dominates our own conception of fair trading. Business people are concerned with finding a 'fair' price which covers their own costs, generates a profit and provides value and satisfaction to customers.

Full-cost pricing

At first sight full-cost pricing appears to be an easy method of pricing, but difficulties begin to appear in the details. The first problem is defining what is meant by full costs.

Initially, the determination of full costs for pricing purposes depends on the nature of the firm's business. Where a firm is under contract to supply on a cost-plus basis, full costs are all those costs that are uniquely identified with the contract and include all assets and other expenses incurred for contract purposes. In all other cases where the firm sells a product or service in the market at large, complications arise in identifying full product (or service) cost per unit because of the number of different products and the complexity of the firm's business structure.

Full-cost pricing is based on the assumption that it is possible to establish a correct and equitable manner of recovering, over time, the totality of the firm's costs through the selling of individual products or services. Full costs therefore include a share of all the costs of creating and maintaining the infrastructure necessary to conduct the business: long-term assets (tangible and intangible), as well as all the activities involved in current operations (finance, administration, supply chain, information technology, etc.).

The difficulties involved can best be appreciated by considering a practical example. Electricité de France has a large number of nuclear power stations. These have a useful life of around fifty years, at the end of which they will have to be decommissioned. Dismantling will be hugely expensive and the parts that are radioactive will have to be stored somewhere safe for thousands of years. The tariffs used by EDF to charge current customers for electricity have to include a share of the costs of construction, periodic maintenance, decommissioning and storing radioactive material as well as the current running costs. This involves estimating the costs to be incurred many years in the future and finding a mechanism for allocating these fairly to current production. These difficulties in cost accounting have been discussed in earlier chapters and will not be further elaborated here other than by emphasizing that they are obviously non-trivial and frequently controversial.

Example 21.2 is a simplified illustration of full-cost pricing in which all costs, fixed and variable, of bringing the product to market are included in the selling price. Once full costs have been established, the agreed profit margin is added.

| Example 21.2 | High Speed Castings Ltd produces two castings, Type A and Type B. The total unit costs are as follows: |

	Type A	Type B
	£	£
Direct materials	4	12
Direct labour	6	4
Factory overheads:		
Variable	6	3
Fixed	4	1
Total manufacturing costs	20	20
Selling and administrative costs:		
Variable	2	3
Fixed	4	3
Full costs per unit	26	26

To calculate the selling price under this method, we simply add the required profit margin:

	Type A	Type B
	£	£
Full costs per unit	26	26
Add: Markup (50% on costs)	13	13
Selling price	39	39

Example 21.2 ignores that it may be difficult to identify all factory, administrative and marketing costs unambiguously with a particular cost centre. Furthermore, there is the problem of selecting an appropriate basis for allocating them to individual products. Under full-cost pricing, this problem is critical to the determination of the selling price. Product costs and therefore prices will be wrong to the extent that costs are incorrectly traced to cost centres and incorrectly allocated to products. Consider the previous example of High Speed Castings Ltd and let us assume that the demand for Product B is buoyant and that for Product A slack. In these circumstances, managers may be tempted to transfer a higher proportion of fixed costs to Product B, enabling the price of Product A to be lowered to encourage sales. Such arbitrary actions replace the traditional approach to full-cost pricing by the willingness of the customer to pay and the ability of the product to bear higher costs.

Example 21.2 also ignores that changes in activity levels impact the allocation of fixed costs to units of product. Changes in volume lead to changes in fixed costs per unit: if volumes go up fixed costs per unit go down and vice versa. This leads to unintended consequences: pernicious if volumes go down and favourable if they rise. An experiment reveals the danger: demand is weak and sales go down, fixed costs per unit go up and prices are raised, this causes sales to drop further. This is known as the 'death spiral'. Not only are the consequences dire and illogical, they are also contrary to common sense. If sales go down it means that demand is less than supply, in which case prices should be lowered to bring them back into equilibrium not raised under full-cost pricing which will only make the situation worse. A similar difficulty arises when capacity is expanded in anticipation of extra sales. Management will probably want to price below actual full cost in order to stimulate sales, which will make the investment profitable. The sooner they get there the more profitable the investment. If they are forced by company rules to base prices on actual full costs, at best they achieve their objectives more slowly and at worst they never achieve them.

Example 21.3 shows the impact on the relationship of fixed costs and volume changes on pricing. Given that the percentage markup remains constant, there is a range of selling prices which will cover costs corresponding to different sales volumes. Suppose the firm currently has a price of £6.60, a volume of 100,000 and capacity of 500,000.

Example 21.3

No. of units (thousands)	100	200	300	400	500
Variable cost per unit	£4.00	£4.00	£4.00	£4.00	£4.00
Fixed cost per unit	2.00	1.00	0.67	0.50	0.40
Full cost per unit	6.00	5.00	4.67	4.50	4.40
10% Markup	0.60	0.50	0.47	0.45	0.44
Selling price	6.60	5.50	5.14	4.95	4.84

It is interesting to note the total profits generated by these different prices.

No. of units (thousands)	100	200	300	400	500
Selling price	£6.60	£5.50	£5.14	£4.95	£4.84
Profit per unit (at 10%)	0.60	0.50	0.47	0.45	0.44
Total profit (£000)	60.00	100.00	141.00	180.00	220.00

Faced with these production and sales possibilities, management would wish to pursue an aggressive pricing policy which maximized total profits. As explained above, full-cost pricing would stand in the way of such a pricing policy because with a current volume of 100,000, a price of £4.84 gives a unit loss of £1.76 and a total loss of £176,000. If the firm does manage to increase sales to 500,000 units it will have to stabilize production or incur further capital expenditure on the expansion of productive capacity. This would involve the firm in a capital investment decision and a complete reconsideration of its pricing policy.

One method of avoiding the undesirable consequences of full costs based on actual volumes is to allocate fixed cost to units of product on practical capacity. This is defined as the output that could be maintained in the long run, with regular maintenance, normal quality and no excessive overtime. Use of practical capacity eliminates the potentially perverse consequences of actual volumes as denominators.

The fundamental merit of using practical capacity is that it distinguishes between those resources that are consumed and those that are not. The former are charged to products, the latter are not. The product (or cost object) should not be charged with the cost of resources it neither caused nor consumed. While costing at practical capacity is relatively new compared with using actual volumes, it comes with an excellent pedigree. Some textbooks advocate 'normal volumes' as an alternative to actual volumes. This fits a trend line to the forecast sales volumes for the next few years. The idea is to smooth out variations due to business cycles and prevent them having deleterious effects on full product costs. While this is an improvement on using actual volumes it still does not solve the problem caused by structural overcapacity. The arguments in favour of allocating fixed costs to units of products on the basis of practical capacity are unimpeachable.

Finally, having ascertained the full cost per unit, it remains to discuss how the markup percentage is determined, which, when added to full costs, yields the price. As already mentioned, there are a number of factors which must be borne in mind when deciding on the markup. First, there is the notion of the 'fair price', and business people will argue strongly that such-and-such a percentage is a 'fair profit' for a given trade. For example, there is a connection between the rate of inventory turnover and the markup percentage; it is normal to expect jewellers to impose higher markups on their goods than butchers. Second, the markup is influenced by the elasticity of demand for the product and market conditions generally. Third, the markup is influenced by the firm's long-term strategy. Many innovative high technology products are priced high initially (e.g. the iPhone), and then reduced in price as competitors enter the segment. Fourth, although business people argue that they seek a reasonable profit, it is evident that they mean the highest profit that they can 'reasonably' make. Finally, there is evidence in the pricing policies of large firms, and particularly state corporations, that the need to generate capital to finance expensive capital projects influences the profit markup, and hence the price. A flagrant example would be the rise in rail fares in the UK to finance new rolling stock. This is an abuse of oligopoly power, because customers should be charged for what they consume today – the current rolling stock – not what their children will consume in fifteen years time.

Alternative approaches to full-cost pricing that seek to reduce or eliminate some of its weaknesses include the use of total factory costs, conversion costs and marginal costs.

Total factory costs

Under this method of full cost pricing, full costs are determined at the factory level and not at the firm level. Accordingly, all costs that lie outside the factory gates are treated at the firm level and charged against total income and not against products or services.

Conversion costs

Conversion-cost pricing, unlike full-cost pricing, takes into account only the costs incurred by the firm in converting raw materials and semi-finished goods into finished products. One of the limitations of full-cost pricing is that where the firm is selling two products which require different degrees of effort to convert raw materials to marketable state, no distinction is drawn between them. That is to say all costs, irrespective of nature and provenance, are summed for determination of the markup. Conversion-cost pricing excludes direct materials and selling and administrative costs from the calculation of the markup. The data of Example 21.2 are used as illustration:

	Product A		Product B	
	£	£	£	£
Direct materials		4		12
Conversion costs:				
Direct labour	6		4	
Factory overheads	10		4	
		16		8
Total factory costs		20		20

Under full-cost pricing, both products were priced at £39 as follows:

	Product A	Product B
	£	£
Total factory costs	20	20
Selling and administrative costs	6	6
Full costs	26	26
Markup at 50%	13	13
Selling price	39	39

The objective of conversion-cost pricing is to provide a pricing policy which will relate the selling price of the product to the cost and effort expended by the firm to convert raw material into a marketable product. From the foregoing example, it is evident that Product A takes twice the effort to produce (£16) as Product B (£8). Hence, the firm should formulate a pricing policy which will encourage the expansion of Product B, two units of which may be produced for the same production effort as one of Product A. This may be achieved by conversion-cost pricing, which will establish a lower price for Product B than for Product A. Under conversion-cost pricing, the markup is calculated on the conversion costs, as shown below.

It will be recalled from Chapter 19 that in selecting an appropriate sales mix, other things being equal, the firm will prefer that mix of products which produces the best total profit. Conversion-cost pricing helps the firm to do this. If the demand for Product B were such that the firm could switch entirely to that product, the firm would simply cease manufacturing Product A. The firm is compelled to produce both products because demand for Product B is not enough to fill the factory and so the sales-mix problem arises. It is in these circumstances that conversion-cost pricing is most useful.

	Product A	Product B
	£	£
Conversion costs:		
Direct labour	6	4
Factory overheads	10	4
	16	8
Markup at 100%	16	8
	32	16
Other costs:		
Direct materials	4	12
Selling and administrative costs	6	6
Selling price	42	34

Marginal-cost pricing

Sometimes referred to as the contribution method of pricing, this method of pricing is related to the ideas which are discussed in Chapter 20. No one seriously disputes that in the long term a firm's pricing policy must cover full costs, whether these are interpreted as full production costs or the replacement of the capital invested, as well as providing an acceptable margin of profit. This is the main argument put forward by the supporters of full-cost pricing.

For short-term decisions, there are many situations in which a price that covers variable costs but not full costs and consequently makes a contribution to profits is acceptable. Where a firm is facing a fall in demand for its product due to a temporary weakness in the market and is operating at a loss, any sales at a price which is above marginal costs contributes to the recovery of fixed costs. Moreover, at any time when a firm has spare capacity and has covered its fixed costs at the price set for its regular customers, it may attempt to reach another market by selling the article at a lower price with a slight alteration to the product presentation. Price discrimination, as this practice is known, enables the firm to sell the same product in different markets at different prices. The firm's total profits will be greater as a result.

Marginal-cost pricing enables the firm to pursue special marketing policies, such as the penetration of a new market or the development of an export market, provided revenues in the main market segment recover all fixed costs. Marginal-cost pricing is useful, therefore, because it sets a lower limit for prices. For example, the variable costs and minimum prices of the two products of High Speed Castings Ltd are as follows:

	Product A	Product B
	£	£
Direct materials	4	12
Direct labour	6	4
Variable factory overheads	6	3
Variable selling and administrative overheads	2	3
Minimum price – variable costs	18	22

Although marginal-cost pricing is useful for dealing with temporary market difficulties or for exploiting new marketing strategies, there may be a danger that marginal-cost pricing becomes the established method of pricing. The firm should develop long-term and short-term pricing strategies and return to a long-term pricing strategy once the short-term situation has been resolved. Nevertheless, marginal-cost pricing also has advantages for the long term. Full-cost pricing may inhibit the firm from developing sales and production strategies which management considers desirable for maximizing total profits. Marginal-cost pricing takes account of the relationship between price, volume and costs, and in this sense enables better profit planning.

Going-rate pricing

Going-rate pricing reflects the view of market leaders about what the market will bear in terms of pricing. It represents the collective wisdom of the industry concerning the price that would produce a fair return on investment.

Going-rate pricing is commonly used where firms market homogeneous products in competitive markets and have little choice in setting prices. Their major challenge is to control production and distribution costs. Where the firm is faced with a 'going rate', the major problem for the firm is how much to produce. In these situations, the volume produced is determined by the firm's costs and its profit planned accordingly. The classic examples where firms are faced with the going rate are the various commodity markets. Producers try to solve the price uncertainty by selling in the 'futures market' that is, contracting now to supply say in three months' time at an agreed price.

Going-rate pricing is also found in oligopolistic markets dominated by few large firms and where the price is controlled either by the dominant firm or by collective agreements.

Target pricing and target costs

Until recently, the development of cost-based pricing theories has assumed that product cost measurements were needed as the starting point from which to build up prices by adding required profit margins. Accountants have been concerned with improving the accuracy of cost measurements. A significant innovation of this century was the shift from historic to standard costs. This enabled cost measurements to be predetermined by anticipation of changes in cost elements in the annual budgeting process.

As indicated earlier, the concept of target pricing is a radical development that seeks to improve price competitiveness by setting a target price that has been established in the long-range product planning process. The objective of target pricing is to seek the required profit margin through product cost economies. Hence, target costs are used to compress costs by designing costs out of the product (through standardization, elimination of parts, etc.) and by paying particular attention to production processes (through introducing complexity and variety as late as possible).

By making costs rely on selling prices rather than selling prices on costs, there is greater certainty that all costs incurred during production are necessary. Unnecessary costs should be eliminated without reducing value to the customer. One way to do this is to eliminate those activities that do not add value to the final product.

Return-on-investment pricing

The cost-based pricing theories which we have examined so far focus on costs of production. Although such costs will include depreciation, they exclude any consideration of the capital employed by the firm. The firm has profit objectives which are expressed in terms of a percentage markup on costs of production. Return-on-investment pricing attempts to link the markup to the capital employed. Research has shown that many firms have pricing policies which reflect a target rate of return. The formula used is:

$$\text{Selling price} = \frac{\text{total costs} + (\text{desired \% return on capital employed})}{\text{volume of output}}$$

Example 21.4 Let us assume that High Speed Castings Ltd, which produces the two products Type A and Type B, has a 'normal' output of Product A amounting to 20,000 units a year. Let us assume also that the capital employed by the firm is £1.5 million, of which £1 million is employed in the production of Product A. The product costs are given in Example 21.2. The desired rate of return which the firm has imposed on all its capital investment decisions is 20 per cent. Accordingly, the firm seeks a profit markup which reflects this objective. The selling price is calculated as follows:

	Product A
	£
Total costs of production (20,000 × £26)	520,000
Desired return on capital employed (20% of £1 m)	200,000
Expected sales revenue	720,000
Selling price per unit (£720,000 ÷ 20,000)	£36

The attraction of this method of establishing a markup on costs is that it relates the problem of pricing to financial objectives and integrates pricing decisions with the firm's overall planning objectives. From a rational point of view it is clearly superior from a rational point of view to simply deciding upon a percentage markup on the basis of what is considered to be 'fair'. At the same time, return-on-investment pricing has all the tendencies to rigidity which are the features of full-cost pricing.

Since pricing decisions are generally short-run in nature, their effects on long-range objectives require that these objectives be explicitly taken into account. A firm which has a long-range target rate of return may find that in attempting to apply such a target to short-run pricing it may be forced out of the market by competition. Thus, the firm may be compelled to price below its target rate of return to retain its share of the market: the result is below the original target but above what would have happened had it gone into the market at too high a price.

Return-on-investment pricing may, in practice, invert the relationship of costs to price, in that costs are tailored to fit selling policies. If market prices of competitors and the required rate of return on capital are known, the only 'variables' are total costs and capital employed. This requires more knowledge about the market, for example the likely size of the market and its sensitivity to quality and other elements of the marketing mix. In these circumstances, a firm may ensure that a specific rate of return on investment is obtained by selling a commodity at a price not exceeding a predetermined cost.

Costs for export pricing

The expansion of the global market economy has increased considerably the volume of foreign trade in raw materials, intermediate products and manufactured products, as well as international services of various kinds. In terms of economic theory, the justification for foreign trade is found in the law of comparative advantage, where individual countries enjoy competitive advantages over other countries. In the case of developed countries, these may take the form of technological, marketing, financial and other advantages resulting from their superiority in these areas, and especially highly developed credit and financial markets and related financial and professional skills. In the case of many developing countries, export trade is concentrated on raw materials, agricultural products and the export of manufactured products of industrial firms that have relocated to seek lower labour costs and tax rates.

Assuming that the exporting firm is a price-taker and not a price-maker, the initial attraction of exporting is expanding overall sales volume and revenue, with the possibility that export prices may be higher than domestic prices. There are substantial additional costs involved in exporting, notably packaging, transport, the margins of intermediaries such as agents, taxes and duties. The terms that normally apply to export contracts determine which costs are borne by the exporter and importer respectively. They are referred to as International Commercial Terms (incoterms) of which there are 14; Free on Board (FOB) and Cost, Insurance and Freight (CIF) being the best known. In FOB export contracts, the exporter delivers the goods free on board at the outward departure point. In CIF contracts, the exporter pays cost, insurance and freight to the stipulated destination. These additional costs have to be brought into account in determining the viability of exporting in terms of the net profitability of exporting sales. The upper limit to the export price will be that price which the best customer is willing to pay; in the case of a price-taker this is the going-rate price. The lower limit is either the full-cost or the marginal cost, depending on the circumstances facing the export firm when determining the acceptability of an export order.

Retrograde pricing

Retrograde pricing is a technique that consists of deducting from the ceiling export price all additional expenses, taxes, duties and margins applying to export sales: this gives a number that can be compared with the relevant ex-factory cost. The analysis of export prices may be conducted on a mark-up basis, where a CIF contract price is marked up to include all expenses to arrive at the price to customer. Retrograde pricing is the reverse and is conducted on a mark-down basis by deducting all expenses to arrive back at the CIF contract price.

Example 21.5

Price to customer		100%
Retail markup	50%	−33
Wholesaling price		67
Wholesale markup	25%	−14
Importer price		53
Importer's markup	35%	−13
Landed price		40
Customs duty	20%	−6
CIF price		33

Retrograde pricing provides a systematic way of comparing the incoterm price with ex-factory costs and evaluating the profitability of exporting by referring to the relevant export costs. On a long-term basis, relevant costs would be full ex-factory costs; a short-term decision would look at the contribution margin.

Summary

Pricing decisions form an integral part of the firm's planning process, and are related directly to its objectives. The nature of the firm's product, the market situation and the firm's short-term and long-term objectives are all factors relevant to pricing decisions.

Pricing policies must be examined in terms of the particular objectives they seek to achieve. Occasions may arise where a short-term objective requires a policy that would be unacceptable in the long term. Numerous examples exist of business objectives which require their own tailor-made pricing policies. The introduction of a new product may require a 'skimming price policy' by setting a high price initially and lowering the price as the product gains acceptance and popularity and permits the firm to expand the scale of production, so reducing its costs. Ballpoint pens, nylons and television sets have all undergone this process. 'Penetration price policies', on the other hand, have been a popular way of entering a foreign market and call for low prices to encourage rapid acceptance of the product.

For all these reasons, the only general rule that can be laid down is that unit costs provide a means of determining the lowest limit of an acceptable short-term price, while in the long term the price should cover all costs and provide the margin of profit required by management.

Self-assessment questions

1   Review briefly some of the business objectives involved in pricing policies.

2   Compare approaches to pricing in accounting and economic theory.

3   Explain the nature of cost-based pricing policies.

4   What do you understand by 'full-cost' pricing?

5   What kind of accounting information do you consider to be relevant to making full-cost pricing decisions?

6   Comment on the statement that 'since prices are determined by supply and demand factors, accounting data are irrelevant in determining a firm's pricing policy'.

7   Explain what is implied by:
    (a)   conversion-cost pricing;
    (b)   return-on-investment pricing.

8   What do you understand by 'marginal-cost' pricing? In what circumstances do you consider this method of pricing useful?

9   Explain the objectives of target pricing.

10   Discuss briefly the main problems involved in costing for export.

11   Consider the view that long-term factors are more significant than short-term ones in determining pricing policies.

Problems

1 Schlutz and Co Ltd manufactures a product which it distributes through its own branches in England and Wales. The managing director was recently approached by McTosh and Co Ltd, a Glasgow-based company interested in obtaining sole distributor rights in Scotland. McTosh proposes to purchase the product from Schlutz at a price of £32.50 and to offer it for sale to retailers in Scotland at £42.50 and would pay the transport charges to Scotland averaging £3.50 per unit. No commission would be payable to McTosh on these sales. Schlutz and Co undertook to consider this offer. Given the under-mentioned information (a) to (f), would you advise Schlutz and Co to accept the offer?

(a) The products are now sold to retailers in England and Wales at a price of £44 inclusive of delivery charges.

(b) Sales commissions paid to retailers are computed at 5 per cent of sales.

(c) Transport costs average £1.50 per unit.

(d) Other selling and administrative costs are regarded as fixed and amount to £4.50 per unit.

(e) Manufacturing costs amount to £29.50 per unit as follows:

Materials	£18.70
Labour	3.00
Variable overheads	3.30
Fixed overheads	4.50
	£29.50

(f) Manufacturing capacity is adequate to handle the increased volume which is estimated to amount to 1,000 units a month, but fixed factory overheads would probably increase by £1,500 a month.

2 A standard unit of the Whitmore Manufacturing Company contains the following marginal costs:

	Per unit
Direct materials	£5.60
Direct labour cost	1.50
Variable factory overhead	0.40
	£7.50

Fixed factory overhead is budgeted at £280,000 for a normal sales volume of 400,000 units. Factory capacity is 500,000 units. Distribution and administrative expenses are budgeted at £180,000.

Capital employed is considered to consist of 50 per cent of net sales for current assets and £450,000 for fixed assets.

Additional analysis indicates:

(a) Direct material prices will increase £0.40 per unit.
(b) An unfavourable direct labour variance of approximately 6 per cent has been experienced for the past two years.
(c) Customers' discounts average to about 2 per cent of the gross sales price.

Required:

Determine a sales price which will yield 16 per cent return on capital employed.

References

Claret, J. and Phadke, P.D. (1995) Pricing – a challenge to management accounting, *Management Accounting* (UK), October.

Govindarajan, V. and Anthony, R.N. (1983) How firms use cost data in pricing decisions, *Management Accounting*, July, 30–36.

Noreen, E.W., Brewer, P.C. and Garrison, R.H. (2008) *Managerial Accounting for Managers*, McGraw-Hill Irwin.

CHAPTER 22

Costs for short-run tactical decisions

Setting the scene

The concept of relevant costs for decisions is a pervasive one in accounting and economics. Simply stated, the relevant-cost approach requires that, for any decision, the cost which will change *as a result of the decision*, should be compared with the revenues which will be earned *as a result of that decision*. Costs which will not alter are not a relevant consideration in the incremental approach.

Where incremental revenue exceeds incremental cost it is recommended that the proposed course of action be followed as it will increase the wealth of the organization. Conversely, where there is an excess of incremental cost over incremental revenue it is recommended that the proposed course of action be rejected.

(Kennedy, 1995)

Learning objectives

After studying this chapter you should be able to:

1 define and explain the concept of relevant costs;

2 discuss the importance of the contribution margin in short-run decision making;

3 explain how opportunity costs affect decision making;

4 identify business situations in which relevant costs are appropriate;

5 explain the importance of qualitative factors in using the relevant cost decision model;

6 discuss the role of limiting factors in short-term decision making;

7 use linear programming to find the optimal solution to a problem of constrained resources.

We discussed in Chapter 19 the importance of the relationship between cost and volume of output for profit planning purposes. Cost behaviour is a crucial element in profit planning: it is also important for a whole range of other decisions which management has to make.

We may divide the accountant's task of providing information about costs for decision making into two parts. First, when planning the volume of output in the short term, the accountant has to provide information as to the behaviour of fixed and variable costs over the planned range of output. Second, for other decisions relating to alternative courses of action, such as the acceptance or rejection of a special order, s/he has to provide cost information which guides management towards making the best, that is the most profitable, decisions.

Decisions always involve choice among alternatives, even if one is the status quo or perhaps, in extreme instances, doing nothing at all. The insight behind relevant costs (and benefits) is that the merits of a particular decision can only be properly appreciated by comparison with the alternative (there may be more than one). The analysis of every decision therefore requires the explicit or implicit consideration of relevant costs.

Relevant costs are defined as all those costs that are affected by a particular decision, that is to say, they differ in total between the alternatives under consideration. They are of two types: those that change automatically (suppression of a product means suppression of the materials needed to make it), and those that management are prepared to make happen (reduction of headcount in the purchasing department due to lower volumes of vendor certification studies, fewer purchase orders, etc.).

The purpose of this chapter is to examine the nature of relevant costs, and the importance of the related concept of contribution margin in these areas of decision making.

The nature of relevant costs

The nature of the costs which are relevant for short-run tactical decisions will depend on the type of decision problem for which they are required. We shall examine several different types of decision problems, and in this way ascertain the type of cost information which ought to be supplied by the accountant. In general, however, relevant costs have two important characteristics:

1 They are future costs, that is, they are costs not yet incurred. This is a most important point, for it is easy to fall into the error of believing that costs which have already been incurred must be recovered. Past costs, that is sunk costs, are irrelevant: their only usefulness is the extent to which they may help the accountant estimate the trend of future costs.

Example 22.1 Excelsior Ltd has spent £5,000 on developing a new process. A revised estimate of further expenditure required to complete the development work shows an increase of 20 per cent on the original total estimate of £10,000. The cost which is relevant to the decision to continue with the development work is £7,000, that is, the future cost which will be incurred, and not the new estimate of total costs of £12,000. Hence, the costs already incurred are irrelevant to the decision to be made concerning the completion of the development work.

2 Relevant costs differ in total among the alternatives being considered. Consequently not all future costs are relevant costs. Those costs that are the same whichever alternative is chosen are by definition not relevant. The way to think about this is to remember that something that is the same whichever alternative is chosen cannot possibly help us choose between them.

Example 22.2 John Brown has decided to go to the cinema, and he is considering whether to go by bus or by car. The price of the cinema ticket is not a relevant cost, for it is not affected by the manner in which he travels to the cinema. Likewise, since cars tend to depreciate over time (rather than with small changes in mileage), the additional mileage on the car is also not a relevant cost. Although Brown's decision on his mode of travel will be influenced by his individual preference, the relevant cost is the difference between the cost of using the car, that is, petrol and parking, and going by bus. This cost difference is the relevant cost.

When considering decisions that involve variable and fixed costs (e.g. of products) it is easy to fall into the trap of believing that the former are always relevant and the latter irrelevant. Although in a given situation it may be true that variable costs are relevant and fixed costs irrelevant, it would be a grave error to assume it to be so. There are many situations in which costs that have been classified as variable by accountants are not in fact relevant (direct labour is frequently classified as a variable cost, but for small changes in volume and mix, is not relevant). There are also many occasions when costs classified as fixed are in fact relevant (factory overhead is usually considered fixed, at least in the short term, but management may be prepared to outsource some activities to third parties and reduce costs).

Thus not all variable costs are necessarily relevant, and not all fixed costs necessarily irrelevant. All depends on the decision and the context.

The importance of the contribution margin

Usually, short-run tactical decisions are aimed at making the best use of existing facilities. In these circumstances the contribution margin may be a good first approximation of relevant costs. The contribution margin is defined as revenues minus variable costs, and is available as a contribution towards fixed costs and profits. Profits, of course, will not be made until all fixed costs have been covered, but under certain circumstances the expectation of a contribution margin will be sufficient to justify a particular decision.

One decision with which businesses are frequently faced is the acceptance of a special order, which may be a large order at a price below the usual selling price, and sometimes even below total manufacturing costs.

Example 22.3 Minnies Kurt Ltd manufactures a garment which is sold under the trade name of Withitog. Its total productive capacity is 100,000 units in the current period, and actual production is running at 80 per cent of productive capacity. The product sells at £1.00 per unit, and the company's costs of production are as follows:

Fixed costs	£25,000
Variable costs	£0.50 per unit

The company receives a special order for 10,000 Withitogs from a mail order firm, subject to the company agreeing to sell the product at £0.60 per unit. The managing director is reluctant to accept the order because the selling price is well below the manufacturing costs, which he has calculated as follows:

Fixed costs per unit (allocated over 90,000 units)	
$\dfrac{£25,000}{90,000}$	£0.28
Variable costs per unit	0.50
Total manufacturing costs per unit	£0.78

The contribution margin approach to the solution of this decision leads to a different conclusion. The revenue per unit is £0.60, and the relevant costs associated with the decision are the variable costs of production only, that is £0.50 per unit. Hence, there is a unit contribution margin of £0.10 per unit, and on that basis, the company should accept the special order. The fixed costs are not relevant costs for two reasons: first some of them are probably sunk costs, that is they are not future costs, and second they are not affected by the decision to accept the special order.

The result of accepting the special order on the company's total profit may be seen from the calculations below.

It is clear, therefore, that it is advantageous for the company to accept the special order, since overall income will be improved by £1,000, which is the amount of the contribution margin resulting from the acceptance of that order.

It is evident, too, that the widespread belief that all costs should be covered may influence managers to make the wrong decision when considering special offers. Absorption costing is useful in determining the full costs of production, but leads to erroneous conclusions if indiscriminately applied.

	Without the special order (80,000 units)		With the special order (90,000 units)		Contribution margin –
	£	£	£	£	£
Sales revenue:					
80,000 units @ £1.00		80,000		80,000	
10,000 units @ £0.60		–		6,000	
		80,000		86,000	6,000
Manufacturing costs:					
Fixed costs	25,000		25,000		–
Variable costs @					
£0.50 per unit	40,000		45,000		
		65,000		70,000	5,000
Net income		£15,000		£16,000	£1,000

Example 22.4 Speedo Engineering Ltd manufactures an electrical component widely used in the motor industry. It is currently producing 5,000 units selling at £10 a unit. Its total productive capacity is 8,000 units, and budgeted costs at different levels of output have been estimated as follows:

Output (units)	5,000	6,000	7,000	8,000
Variable costs	£30,000	£36,000	£42,000	£48,000
Fixed costs	10,000	10,000	10,000	10,000
Total costs	£40,000	£46,000	£52,000	£58,000
Total costs per unit	£8.00	£7.67	£7.43	£7.25

The firm receives three offers for three lots of 1,000 units at selling prices of £8, £7 and £6.50 per unit respectively. Should these offers be accepted or rejected?

The unit costs of production under the absorption costing method may be calculated and compared with the respective offers, as shown below:

Output (units)	6,000	7,000	8,000
Total costs per unit	£7.67	£7.43	£7.25
Selling price per unit	8.00	7.00	6.50
Profit (loss) per unit	£0.33	£(0.43)	£(0.75)

From these calculations one might deduce that the firm should accept the order at £8 per unit, which will produce a profit of £0.33 per unit, but should reject the other two offers of £7 and £6.50 since they would result in losses.

An examination of the relevant costs leads to a different conclusion. The fixed costs are not relevant costs, since they will be incurred irrespective of the level of output. By comparing the relevant costs with the three offers, we may calculate the differential profits thus:

Output (units)	6,000	7,000	8,000
Differential units	1,000	1,000	1,000
Differential selling price	£8.00	£7.00	£6.50
Differential unit cost	6.00	6.00	6.00
Differential profit per unit	2.00	1.00	0.50
Differential total income	£2,000	£1,000	£500

These figures illustrate the misleading effect of using absorption costing methods for decision making, and the necessity for using the relevant cost analysis. Using this latter method, it is clear that all three offers should be accepted, for in each case they provide a contribution margin towards fixed costs and income.

Opportunity costs

Opportunity cost is defined as the value of the next best opportunity foregone, or of the net cash inflow lost as a result of preferring one alternative to the next best one. Opportunity costs are not recorded in the books of account, and although they are favoured by economists as appropriate costs for decision making, they are difficult to identify and to measure in practice. Hence, accountants prefer to record and use more objective measures of costs, such as past costs or budgeted future costs, as guidelines for decision making. However, there are a number of decision problems in which the only relevant cost is the opportunity cost. In cases where it is clear that the opportunity cost is necessary for evaluating the merits of a decision, the accountant is often able to attempt its measurement.

Example 22.5 The Nationwide Investment Corporation Ltd seeks to invest £1 million. It has selected two investment projects for consideration: project A which is estimated to produce an annual return of 15 per cent, and project B which is expected to yield 20 per cent annually.

On the basis of these facts it is clear that the Corporation will select project B. The additional gain resulting from that decision may only be measured in terms of the opportunity costs of sacrificing project A, as follows:

Estimated annual return from project B	£200,000
Less: Opportunity cost (the sacrifice of the estimated annual returns from project A)	150,000
Advantage of project B	**£50,000**

The opportunity cost is always a relevant cost when the problem facing the firm is a problem of choice: the measure of the cost of the decision must include the loss sustained by sacrificing the opportunity of the second best alternative. It is the opportunity cost which must be taken into account in calculating the advantage of choosing one alternative rather than the other.

The use of opportunity costs is illustrated in the following situations:

1 dropping a product line;
2 selling or further processing a semi-manufactured product;
3 operate or lease;
4 make or buy a product.

Dropping a product line

Invariably, the reason for wishing to drop a product line is that it is unprofitable, or it is less profitable than another product line to which the firm could switch resources.

Example 22.6 Mechanical Toys Ltd manufactures three products, whose contributions to total profits for the year just ended are:

Products	A	B	C	Total
	£	£	£	£
Sales	200,000	100,000	150,000	450,000
Variable costs	100,000	70,000	80,000	250,000
Contributions	100,000 (50%)	30,000 (30%)	70,000 (47%)	200,000 (44%)
Fixed costs	60,000	40,000	50,000	150,000
Net income (loss)	40,000	(10,000)	20,000	50,000

The company is considering dropping product B as it is showing a loss. Suppose that by dropping product B, fixed costs could be reduced by £10,000, and that the remaining balance of fixed costs of £30,000, being overhead fixed costs allocated to the product, would have to be reallocated to products A and C.

The only choice facing the company is to continue or to cease making product B, and the financial consequences of that choice may be shown as follows:

	Keep product B	Drop product B
	£	£
Sales	450,000	350,000
Variable costs	250,000	180,000
Contribution	200,000	170,000
Fixed costs	150,000	140,000
Net income	50,000	30,000

It is clear that although an overall loss appears to result from producing product B, the contribution which product B makes to the firm's fixed costs would be lost if the decision were made to drop product B. The net cost of dropping product B would be £20,000, that is, the contribution margin less the fixed costs of £10,000 incurred solely as a consequence of its production.

Expressed in terms of opportunity cost analysis, the company has the choice between a profit of £50,000 associated with a decision to keep product B, and a profit of £30,000 associated with a decision to drop product B. Clearly, it cannot have both: hence the cost of selecting the profit of £50,000 is the sacrifice of the opportunity of the alternative profit of £30,000. Hence, the opportunity cost of the decision to keep product B is £30,000, and the advantage of this decision over the alternative of dropping product B is £20,000.

There may be other alternatives open to the firm, of course, besides the two alternatives which we have discussed, such as replacing product B by a more profitable product. In such a case, all the available alternatives must be examined and their outcomes accurately estimated if the best decision is to be made.

Selling or further processing

On occasions, it is possible for a firm to bring a product to its semi-finished state and then sell it, rather than proceed to complete the production process and sell the finished article.

Example 22.7 Product A, which cost £4.80 per unit to produce, is sold as a refined petroleum product at £8 a unit. It could be put through a further processing stage after which it may be sold for £12 a unit. The costs associated with the further processing stage are estimated at £2 per unit.

The outcome of the two alternatives facing the firm, to sell or to further process the product, may be stated in the following terms:

	To sell	To process further
Revenues associated with the decision	£8.0	£4
Costs associated with the decision	4.8	2
Differential profit per unit	£3.2	£2

It is clear that if the firm decides to sell rather than to process further, it will lose the additional profit of £2 per unit. Hence, the opportunity cost of the decision to sell is £2 and the comparative advantage of selling over further processing is £1.20.

Operate or lease

The decision whether to operate or lease assets is another example of the importance of opportunity costs for decision making.

Example 22.8 Betashoes Ltd owns a desirable freehold in Puddingford High Street, which it uses as a sales outlet. The Managing Director receives an offer to lease the property to a local company willing to pay an annual rent of £30,000. The net contribution of the sales outlet in Puddingford to the group profits of Betashoes Ltd is £40,000, after deducting the expenses attributable to it. The information which is relevant to the decision to continue to use the sales outlet may be set out as under:

Contribution to group profits	£40,000
Less: Opportunity cost (rent)	£30,000
Net advantage of operating	£10,000

In the absence of other factors which may induce Betashoes to sell the site, the offer to lease the premises should be rejected and Betashoes should continue to use them as a selling outlet.

Make or buy

It is quite common for firms to subcontract the making of components to specialist firms. This practice does increase their dependence on outside suppliers and reduce to some extent their control on the quality of the components. The opportunity cost approach to this type of decision enables the firm to consider the advantages which could be obtained from alternative uses of the productive capacity released as the result of subcontracting the making of components.

Example 22.9 Highperformance Motors Ltd specializes in the manufacture of sports cars, making some of the components which are required and buying others. Alparts Ltd offers to supply a part currently made by Highperformance Motors Ltd at a price of £7. The costs incurred by Highperformance Motors in making the part are as follows:

Variable costs	£4
Traceable fixed costs	2
Allocated fixed costs	3
Total unit costs	**£9**

Let us assume for the moment that the productive capacity released as a result of accepting the offer will remain idle. On the basis of a monthly production of 5,000 units a month, the relevant monthly costs, that is, those which would be affected by the decision to buy the units, are as follows:

Variable costs	£20,000
Traceable fixed costs	10,000
Relevant costs	30,000
Cost of buying	35,000
Advantage in making	**£5,000**

The allocated fixed costs are irrelevant to the decision since they are not affected, and will continue to be incurred by Highperformance Motors irrespective of whether the parts are made or bought. Since the relevant costs of making are less than the costs of buying, the firm should reject the offer and continue to make the parts.

Let us now consider the possibility that if the firm accepted the offer, the productive capacity released as a result will not remain idle, and will be used to extend the production line of motor cars. It is calculated that an additional four cars a month could be produced, leading to an increase in profits of £10,000. The opportunity costs of not accepting the offer from Alparts, therefore, amount to £10,000. Hence, the information which is now relevant to the decision as to making or buying the part is as under:

Cost of making	
Relevant manufacturing costs	£30,000
Opportunity cost	10,000
	40,000
Cost of buying	35,000
Advantage of buying	**£5,000**

The introduction of the opportunity cost of not accepting the offer has altered the nature of the decision completely, and reversed the previous conclusion that it was advantageous to make the part.

Decision making in the face of limiting factors

In the examples examined so far, a course of action has been selected on the basis of seeking the most profitable result. Business enterprises are limited in the pursuit of profit by the fact that they have limited resources at their disposal, so that quite apart from the limitation on the quantities of any product which the market will buy at a given price, the firm has its own constraints on the volume of output. Hence at a given price, which may be well above costs of production, the firm may be unable to increase its overall profit owing simply to its inability to increase its output.

The limiting factors which affect the level of production may arise out of short-ages of labour, material, equipment and factory space to mention but a few obvious examples. Faced with limiting factors of whatever nature, the firm will wish to obtain the maximum profit from the use of the resources available. In making decisions about the allocation of its resources between competing alternatives, man-agement will be guided by the relative contribution margin which they offer. Since the firm will be faced with limiting factors, however, the contribution margins must not be calculated in terms of units of product sold, but should be related to the units of the most limited factor. The rule is: maximize the contribution per unit of scarce resource. A simple example will serve to explain this point.

Example 22.10 Multiproduct Ltd manufactures three products about which is derived the following data:

Product	Machine hours required per unit of product	Contribution margin per unit	Contribution margin per machine hour
A	3 hours	£9	£3.0
B	2 hours	£7	£3.5
C	1 hour	£5	£5.0

The three products can be made by the same machine, and on the basis of this information, it is evident that product C is the most profitable product, yielding a contribution of £5 per machine hour, as against product A, which shows the smallest contribution per machine hour. Hence, in deciding how to use the limiting factor the firm should concentrate on the production of product C, rather than products A and B. If there were no limits to the market demand for product C, then there would be no problem in deciding which product to produce – it would be product C alone.

Firms undertake the manufacture of different products because the market demand for any one product is limited, so that they seek to find that product mix which will be the most profitable. Let us assume that the maximum weekly demand for the three products and the total machine capacity necessary to meet this demand are as follows:

Product	Maximum demand in units	Machine hours equivalents
A	100	300
B	100	200
C	100	100
		600

Machine capacity is limited to 450 hours per week, so that the most profitable product mix is a function of both machine capacity and market demand. The following product mix would maximize profits:

Product	Output units	Machine hours	Contribution per machine hour	Total contribution
C	100	100	£5.0	£500
B	100	200	£3.5	£700
A	50	150	£3.0	£450
		450		£1,650

This product mix reflects the order of priority in allocating machine use to the products with the highest contribution margin per machine hour. Product C receives the highest priority, then product B, and lastly product A. If machine hours were further limited to 300 hours, the firm would cease to make product A.

Linear programming and decision making

Linear programming is a mathematical technique which seeks to make the best use of a firm's limited resources to meet chosen objectives, which in accounting terms may take the form of the maximization of profits or the minimization of costs. In those situations, for example, where a manufacturer has a limited plant capacity, the level and cost of output will be determined by such capacity.

Example 22.11 Blackamoor Steels Ltd manufactures two high-quality steel products in respect of which the following information is available:

	Product A	Product B
	£	£
Selling price per unit	30	20
Variable costs per unit	15	10
Contribution margin	15	10

Milling and grinding machines are used in the manufacturing process, and the total machine hours necessary to produce one unit of each product are:

	Product A	Product B
Milling	5 hours	$1\frac{1}{2}$ hours
Grinding	2	2
	7	$3\frac{1}{2}$

Both products are in great demand, and the only constraint on expanding output is machine capacity. The total machine hours available per month are:

Milling (3 machines at 200 hours a month)   600 hours
Grinding (2 machines at 200 hours a month)   400 hours

On the basis of the facts given above, the problem facing management is to ascertain that combination of output of products A and B which will maximize the total contribution margin to overheads and profits. At first glance, it would appear that the firm should maximize the production of product A since that product yields the highest unit contribution margin. Analysed in terms of the machine capacity limit, the total number of units of either product A or product B which could be manufactured is as follows:

Product A   600 hours ÷ 5 hours = 120 units
Product B   400 hours ÷ 2 hours = 200 units

These output limits are derived in the case of product A by the fact that output is limited to the capacity of the milling machines, for product A requires five hours of milling as against only two hours of grinding. Product B, however, is limited in output by the capacity of the grinding machines of which it requires two hours per unit, as against one and a half hours of milling time.

By relating the calculation of the contribution margin to the machine capacity limits, the total contribution to overhead costs and profits which will be obtained by the production of *either* A or B is as follows:

$$\text{Product A} \quad 120 \text{ units} \times £15 = £1,800$$
$$\text{Product B} \quad 200 \text{ units} \times £10 = £2,000$$

It follows, therefore, that given the option of making either product A or product B the firm should concentrate on the making of product B.

The approach to the solution of this problem under linear programming consists, first, of formulating the problem in simple algebraic terms. There are two aspects to the problem, the first being the wish to maximize profits and the second being the need to recognize the production limits. The two aspects may be stated algebraically as follows:

1 The objective is to maximize the contribution to fixed overheads and profit. This objective is called the objective function, and may be expressed thus:

$$\text{Maximize } C = 15A + 10B$$

where C is the total contribution and A and B are the total number of units of the two products which must be manufactured to maximize the total contribution. This equation is subject to the limits that:

$$A \geq 0$$
$$B \geq 0$$

for it is not possible to produce negative quantities of either A or B.

2 The constraints on production arising from the machine capacity limits of the milling department (600 hours) and of the grinding department (400 hours) may also be expressed in algebraic terms as follows:

$$5A + 1\tfrac{1}{2}B \leq 600$$
$$2A + 2B \leq 400$$

The first inequality states that the total number of hours used on milling must be equal to or less than 600 hours; the second inequality states that the total hours used on grinding machines must be equal to or less than 400 hours.

The problem may now be summarized in the form:

$$\text{Maximize } C = 15A + 10B$$

subject to the constraints:

$$5A + 1\tfrac{1}{2}B \leq 600$$
$$2A + 2B \leq 400$$
$$A \geq 0$$
$$B \geq 0$$

It is possible to solve the problem by means of a graph (Figure 22.1) showing the manufacturing possibilities for the two departments, as given in the following data:

Milling department:	
Product A	$600 \div 5 = 120$ units
or Product B	$600 \div 1\tfrac{1}{2} = 400$ units
Grinding department:	
Product A	$400 \div 2 = 200$ units
or Product B	$400 \div 2 = 200$ units

The shaded region in Figure 22.1 contains all the combinations of products A and B which are feasible solutions to the problem, hence its name – the feasibility region. The optimal solution, that is, the product combination of A and B which is the best of all the feasible solutions, lies at the intersection of the lines at point D, and may be read off as 85 units of A and 115 of B. It will be observed that the optimal solution lies on a tangent which is the furthest away from the point of origin. The graphical method of solving the problem is susceptible to error unless carefully plotted, and a more reliable answer may be obtained by solving the problem mathematically.

Figure 22.1

The optimal combination of products A and B may be found by solving the simultaneous equation given above, that is,

$$1 \quad 5A + 1\tfrac{1}{2}B = 600$$
$$2 \quad 2A + 2B = 400$$

The solution is obtained by multiplying (1) by 4 and (2) by 3 to give us the value of A, as follows:

$$20A + 6B = 2,400$$
$$\underline{-6A + 6B = 1,200}$$
$$14A = 1,200$$
$$A = 85\tfrac{5}{7}$$

Since we are concerned only with completed units of A, the optimal production of product A is 85 units. The optimal number of units of B may be calculated by inserting the known value of A into the equation, as follows:

$$(6 \times 85) + 6B = 1,200$$
$$\text{i.e.} \quad 510 + 6B = 1,200$$
$$6B = 1,200 - 510$$
$$B = 115$$

Hence, the optimal combination of products A and B is 85 units and 115 units respectively, in terms of the limited machine capacity which will be utilized as follows:

	Milling department (hours)	Grinding department (hours)
Product A – 85 units	425 (85×5)	170 (85×2)
Product B – 115 units	172.5 $(115 \times 1\frac{1}{2})$	230 (115×2)
Total hours used	597.5	400
Total hours available	600	400

The optimal combination will produce a total contribution to overheads and profits of £2,425 as follows:

Product A	85 units of £15 =	1,275
Product B	115 units of £10 =	1,150
		£2,425

We may verify that this combination of products is the optimal one in terms of profits and available machine capacity, as follows:

1 Altering the product combination from 85 units of A and 115 units of B to 84 units of A and 116 units of B, which would affect machine use as follows:

	Milling department (hours)	Grinding department (hours)
Product A – 84 units	420 (84×5)	168 (84×2)
Product B – 116 units	$174\frac{1}{2}$ $(116 \times 1\frac{1}{2})$	232 (116×2)
Total hours used	594	400
Total hours available	600	400

Hence, this combination is as efficient in the utilization of the grinding department but less efficient in the utilization of the milling machines. It is also less profitable, yielding a contribution of only £2,420 as against £2,425 as follows:

Product A	84 units at £15 =	1,260
Product B	116 units at £10 =	1,160
		£2,420

2 Altering the product combination from 85 units of A and 115 units of B to 86 units of A and 113 units of B, which would affect machine use as follows:

	Milling department (hours)	Grinding department (hours)
Product A – 86 units	430 (86×5)	172 (86×2)
Product B – 113 units	$169\frac{1}{2}$ $(113 \times 1\frac{1}{2})$	226 (113×2)
Total hours used	$599\frac{1}{2}$	398
Total hours available	600	400

Hence, whereas this combination is more efficient in the use of the milling machines than the optimal combination, it is less efficient in the use of the grinding machinery. Moreover, to keep within the capacity limits of the milling department we have had to forgo the production of two units of product B to expand the manufacture of product A by one unit. The consequential contribution to profits is also only £2,420 as against the optimal contribution of £2,425, which may be calculated as follows:

Product A	86 units of £15	=	1,290
Product B	113 units of £10	=	1,130
			£2,420

It is noteworthy, also, that the linear programming approach to the best product combination mix gives a solution which is more profitable than the one which relates the contribution margin to the machine capacity limits, which we discussed on page 312, and which suggested that only product B should be made so that 200 units of B would be manufactured to yield a contribution of £2,000.

We have so far discussed a simple case involving only two resource constraints. In real life, a firm may be faced with more than two constraints, but mathematical techniques exist for coping with larger numbers of limits. The Simplex Method, for example, which is based on matrix algebra, may be employed in such cases and it is ideally suited for solutions using a computer.

Summary

In addition to providing information for short-run decision-making purposes, the accountant also often has to provide information for a number of short-run tactical decisions such as dropping a product line or choosing between selling and further processing a semi-manufactured product. As in other areas of accounting, cost information plays an important role in short-run tactical decisions. The costs which are relevant for such decisions are future differential costs.

Although opportunity costs are not recorded in the books of account, there are a number of decision problems where opportunity costs must be considered and on some occasions are the only relevant costs. Opportunity costs may be defined as the value of the next best alternative forgone, or of the net cash inflow lost as a result of preferring one alternative rather than the next best one.

Limits placed on resources have to be recognized in decision-making. Product-mix decisions illustrate the nature of this problem and the manner in which the best use of limited resources may be made. In this connection, linear programming affords a useful technique for maximizing profits or minimizing costs in the face of constraints on resources.

Self-assessment questions

1 Define the nature of relevant costs.

2 State what you understand by the following terms:
    (a) future costs,
    (b) sunk costs,
    (c) differential costs.

3 Give examples of future, sunk and differential costs, and state the conditions required for such costs to be relevant costs.

4 Define the contribution margin.

5 What do you understand by 'opportunity costs'? Are opportunity costs also relevant costs?

6 Name four major classes of decisions, and review the impact of these decisions on the enterprise in the short and the long term.

7 Explain how opportunity costs may be relevant costs in the four major classes of decisions referred to in (6) above.

8 Define a limiting factor, and give four examples of limiting factors.

9 Explain how the contribution margin may be applied to decision-making in the face of a limiting factor.

10 What do you understand by linear programming? Explain the usefulness of this method in decision making.

Problems *(*indicates that a solution is to be found in the Lecturer's Guide)*

1 Heating Products Ltd has a division which manufactures radiators. The standard radiator is the Radwarm, but the company also produces radiators to customers' specification. Such radiators are described in the firm as Specials. The forecast results of the division for the year ending 31 December 20X0 are shown below:

	Radwarm	Specials	Total
	£	£	£
Sales	50,000	100,000	150,000
Materials	16,000	20,000	36,000
Labour	18,000	40,000	58,000
Depreciation	7,200	12,600	19,800
Power	800	1,400	2,200
Rent	2,000	12,000	14,000
Heat and light	200	1,200	1,400
Miscellaneous costs	1,800	800	2,600
	46,000	88,000	134,000
Net income	4,000	12,000	16,000

The expenses have been arrived at as follows:

(a) Depreciation is calculated on the book value of machinery used during production of each of the two groups of products.

(b) Rent is based on the space occupied in the division by each of the product lines. The building housing this division is rented at £14,000 p.a. on a ten-year lease.

(c) Heat and light for the building are apportioned on the basis of area occupied by the two groups of products.

(d) All other costs are traced directly to the product lines.

The divisional manager has received an order to supply 1,000 Special radiators. To accommodate this order, the division would have to switch half of its Radwarm production capacity. The customer has offered a price of £70 per radiator for these Specials and each radiator would take £20 of materials and £36 of labour.

A special press would need to be purchased for this order at a price of £4,000. There would be no further use for this once this order is finished and it would be discarded.

Required:

(a) Calculate
   (i)   the differential cost of the special order;
   (ii) the full cost of the order; and
   (iii) the opportunity cost of accepting this order.

(b) Write a report explaining whether Heating Products Ltd should accept the special order.

2 It is three months since William Wright was appointed accountant at Broomhill Manufacturing Company. During this period he has become increasingly dissatisfied with the company's accounting system. In particular, overheads are not analysed into fixed and variable elements. Wright believes that profit planning requires an understanding of the characteristics of cost and their behaviour at different operating levels. He resolved to write to the managing director and explain his new approach. To support his case Wright searched for examples which could be used to illustrate his arguments. One such example is given below.

Example

The income statement for 31 December 20X0, Wright believed, could be improved for making the predictions implied in the profit planning process. This showed the following results:

	£
Sales revenue	100,000
Cost of sales:	
Materials	15,000
Labour	20,000
Factory overheads	20,000
	55,000
Gross margin	45,000
Selling and administrative expenses	35,000
Net income	10,000

Wright estimated that fixed factory overheads amounted to £5,000 and fixed selling and administrative expenses to £25,000.

The accountant of Broomhill Manufacturing, previous to Wright's appointment, had analysed the results for 20X0 by product groups and this had led the managing director to consider eliminating Product B, a loss-making product. The analysis by product is given below:

	A	B	C
	£	£	£
Sales revenue	60,000	15,000	25,000
Cost of sales:			
Materials	10,000	2,000	3,000
Labour	11,000	4,000	5,000
Factory overheads	11,000	4,000	5,000
	32,000	10,000	13,000
Gross margin	28,000	5,000	12,000
Selling and administrative expenses	20,000	8,000	7,000
	8,000	(3,000)	5,000

Factory overheads were allocated to products at a rate of 100 per cent direct labour cost. Wright estimated that fixed factory overhead elements of the assigned costs were as follows:

A £3,000
B £1,000
C £1,000

Selling and administrative expenses had been assigned to products on an arbitrary basis. Wright estimated the fixed elements as below:

A £15,000
B £6,000
C £4,000

Required:

To what extent is Wright justified in seeking a reappraisal of the situation?

3* The Appleton Apparel Company manufactures and sells three types of outer-wear, a Basic, a Standard and a Superior waxed jacket.

The forecasts for the forthcoming year are as follows:

	Basic £	Standard £	Superior £
Selling price	56	120	225
Direct materials	20	40	100
Direct wages	16	30	40
Variable overheads	16	30	40
Fixed overheads (apportioned)	8	15	20
Sales (units)	3,000	2,000	1,500

The material price per metre varies according to each coat but the usage (4 metres per coat) is the same. Employees are paid at a rate of £2 per labour hour. The fixed overheads for the period are £84,000.

At the same time as the forecasts were completed a competitor in the same industry increased the wage rates to its employees and some Appleton Apparel employees secured jobs at the other company. This resulted in the workforce of Appleton Apparel falling by approximately 30 per cent. The total labour hours now stands at 60,000 hours.

Required:

(a) Prepare an income statement, using the original forecast, which provides meaningful accounting information to management.
(b) Given the reduction in labour hours, which product(s) should the company concentrate on? Calculate the net profit resulting from your suggestion.
(c) A comparable product could be imported. The buying-in prices for the three products are £62, £110 and £175 for the Basic, Standard and Superior respectively. What would be your advice?
(d) What other factors should be taken into consideration?

4 An electronics company produces many types of expensive components. A recent contract for a batch of components (KRS) was priced by the company's accountant. Although the company is short of work, the accountant has advised the managing director that the contract should not be accepted because it will result in a loss, as follows:

Contract: KRS	£	£
Contract price		100,000
Less:		
Materials	65,000	
Labour	49,000	
Depreciation	10,000	
Variable overheads	6,000	
Fixed overhead allocation	20,000	150,000
Loss		(50,000)

The following additional information is available:

£10,000 of material, for which there is no other use, is already in stock. If the contract does not go ahead, it will be disposed of at a cost of £1,000. A contract has been agreed for £5,000 worth of stock. The balance of the stock will also need to be purchased.

Labour costs include an allocation of supervisor's costs of £20,000. If the contract is not accepted, some of the workforce will be made redundant at a cost of £10,000.

It has just been realized that the machinery for the contract needs some modification at a cost of £3,000. If the machinery is not used in the contract it will be sold for £5,000.

The contract will take 3,600 direct labour hours.

Required:

(a) Should the contract be accepted or rejected? Justify your inclusion or exclusion of costs and state what other factors should be taken into account.

(b) Before a final decision is made, the company receives a new order for its products. The following information is available:

Per unit	£
Selling price	100
Direct materials	45
Direct labour	20
Allocated fixed costs	10
Variable cost	15

To make one unit takes five labour hours.

The company does not have the labour hours available to complete contract KRS and accept the new order. Should contract KRS or the new order be accepted? Explain your reasons and give supporting figures.

(c) 'Decision making is not concerned solely with costs and revenues.' Give some examples of non-financial considerations that may be taken into account when making various types of decision.

Reference   Kennedy, A. (1995) Activity-based management and short-term relevant cost: clash or complement?, *Management Accounting* (UK), June.

PART 3

Accounting information for decision making

Introduction to Part 3

The expansion of the global market economy has changed and continues to change the environment in which business corporations operate. New opportunities for trade bring with them new challenges for decision making in a complex economic, cultural and social context. By and large, the global market economy functions according to the legal, business and accounting principles and methods associated with the industrialized nations of the Western world. International institutions that have been established to promote international agreement for the regulation of international trade have been concerned with harmonizing the variety of regulations applying to business corporations. Financial markets and stock exchanges through which business corporations are able to raise capital and obtain credit also impose their own financial information and reporting requirements.

From an accounting viewpoint, business corporations are subject to the legal and accounting rules that apply to their country of origin, as well as other countries where they operate through permanent establishments. These rules constitute the basic rules. They are subordinated to international rules promulgated by international regulatory bodies, such as the International Accounting Standards Board for accounting rules and the 4th and 7th European Directives on Company Law for rules relating to financial reporting by corporations operating within the European Union.

At the same time, social regulations reflecting the social conscience continue to address the social conflicts that capitalism creates through discriminating in favour of financial capital in corporate decision making. Social accounting, green accounting and alternative business structures in the form of cooperative, mutual and co-ownership arrangements reflect the objectives of those promoting the ideals of a caring society and a fairer distribution of the benefits of economic progress achieved under capitalism. These ideals will remain a continuing demand for social progress and provide significant benchmarks for political action.

In this part, accounting information for decision making is examined from the perspective of the concepts that underpin the regulatory framework applying to corporate financial reporting. The debate concerning the extension of corporate accountability is discussed in terms of social objectives, the ultimate objective which is postulated being the common good.

This part goes on to discuss accounting information relevant to the scientific management of business corporations that is the hallmark of Western capitalism concerned with the efficiency of management of economic resources. Defining economic efficiency in terms of optimizing shareholder value in the long-term, the improvement of current profitability in the management of current operations is the basis of budgetary planning and control. At the same time, considerable gains in shareholder value have been realized through asset and risk management techniques that have improved balance sheet values.

Industry leaders are sensitive to the political and social aspects of corporate decision making. However, the highly competitive nature of international business and the pressure for continuous profit improvement from financial markets impedes the pursuit of social objectives that impact directly on costs. Improved profitability by the reduction of costs is blamed for much of the human misery of unemployment and the social deprivation resulting from the relocation of business in search of lower labour and tax costs.

The various management techniques used by business corporations and examined in this part are interesting from a scientific viewpoint. The logic of reason that provides rationality for business decisions has a unique valuation base. It defines the nature of information for corporate management and control. Money is the unique valuation base for corporation decision making and money measurement is the main vehicle for expressing meaning and driving action. Attempts to develop non-financial measurements for providing information about the wider social effect of business activities have been frustrated to some extent by the inability to integrate financial and non-financial measurement in a coherent manner, where business survival is the ultimate criterion and profitability the ultimate condition.

Financial reporting

CHAPTER 23

Companies: their nature and regulation

Setting the scene

Legal systems recognize two types of persons; physical persons and legal persons. Legal persons do not have a physical existence. Their existence is fictional and recognized only in law. Both types of persons enjoy virtually the same citizenship rights and obligations, which are acquired at birth and define the county in which they enjoy the benefits and protection of law. A company is 'born' in the country where it is created; a company registered in London is a British company. A company may carry on its own business, acquire assets, incur liabilities, enjoy the same legal rights and responsibilities under civil law and is punishable under criminal law for wrongful acts. Through merger and acquisitions, a company may create a family or group of companies, become a parent company, have children in the form of subsidiary companies, operate in and migrate to other countries and die through the legal process of dissolution. The only substantial right which companies do not have is the democratic right of voting in Parliamentary election. However, they have far greater influence on government and law-makers than ordinary citizens through political lobbying that perverts the democratic process and its agents.

Learning objectives

After studying this chapter you should be able to:

1 understand how companies are created, regulated and controlled;

2 understand the role of international accounting bodies as regulators;

3 explain how companies are managed and financed;

4 distinguish between share capital and loan capital;

5 explain 'leverage' and illustrate its significance for ordinary shareholders.

Companies are created and regulated by the law of the country in which they are created and have their legal identity. International companies do not have an international legal identity and are international only by virtue of their activities. The only exception to this rule is the *Societas Europea SE*, the European Company which is formed by registration in the European Commercial Register kept by the Court of the European Communities in Luxembourg.

In this chapter, we discuss the nature and the regulations applying to companies using the example of the United Kingdom. The Companies Act 1985 and 2006 effectively brought accounting law in the United Kingdom in line with other countries in the European Union by requiring companies to publish their financial reports in accordance with prescribed formats, thereby ensuring greater comparability with other countries. The Companies Act 1985 incorporated the requirements of the EEC Fourth Directive on Company Accounts, and the Companies Act 2006 unified company law throughout the United Kingdom to include Scotland and Northern Ireland. Furthermore, it restated the paramount objective of convergence with the international accounting standards of the IASB which were discussed earlier in Part 2, Chapter 9. Other countries in the European Union have followed a similar evolution under their respective Civil Code.

The nature of companies

By a legal fiction, the legal personality of a business enterprise established as a company is separate from the legal personalities of the various individuals having an interest therein, whether as owners, managers or employees. This means that, although a company has no physical life, it may nevertheless own property, enter into contracts, sue and be sued in a court of law and undertake any activity consistent with the objectives envisaged at the time of its creation. It acts through its directors with whom it enters into contracts of employment.

The owners of a company are recognized in law as being those persons owning its capital. The capital is divided into shares. Investors become shareholders on acquiring shares. As evidence of their legal title to the shares they own, shareholders are issued with share certificates. Shares are transferable property rights, and may be negotiated either privately or through a stock exchange. Stock exchanges have rules for granting permission for the shares of individual companies to be 'listed on the Stock Exchange', thereby allowing them to be traded on the Stock Exchange.

Companies are usually established by the formal registration of documents with a Public Registrar charged with enforcing statutory provisions in respect of enterprises operating as companies. In the United Kingdom, individuals wishing to incorporate themselves for the purpose of carrying on trade are called promoters, and it is their responsibility to arrange for the process of incorporation. This involves lodging a number of documents with the Registrar of Companies and paying the required fees. The two most important documents are the memorandum of association, which defines the powers and objectives of the companies, and the articles of association which contain the rules for its internal regulation. The name, objectives and the capital clauses are found in the memorandum of association. For our purposes, the capital clause is the most important, for it states the number, classes and nominal value of the shares which the company has power to issue. The authorized capital is stated in the capital clause, and it is the maximum capital which the company may raise. Subsequently, the capital clause may be altered by a formal process.

Initially, a company seeking to raise capital from the public at large issues a prospectus inviting investors to subscribe for shares at the stated price. They usually have to pay a portion of the purchase price on application and the balance when the shares have been formally allotted to them. The capital clause states the value of each share as a nominal figure. Thus, the authorized capital may be stated to consist of 1 million shares of £1 each, giving the company an authorized capital of £1 million. When a company offers shares for sale, however, it may set a price which is higher than the nominal value, and it need not offer for sale all the shares which it is authorized to sell. That portion of the authorized capital which is sold is called the issued capital.

Once shares have been issued, they become the property of the individual investors who have acquired them, and they are free to sell their shares to anyone. The sale price is negotiated between buyer and seller, and the deal may be transacted through a stock exchange if the shares are quoted shares. The seller transfers shares formally to the buyer by notice to the company, and the buyer is registered in the register of shareholders as the new shareholder. Shares transferred in this way are known as registered shares. An alternative type of shareholding, which is restricted by law in some countries, is known as a bearer share. A bearer share is more easily transferred than a registered share since the share certificate does not detail the name of the shareholder who is not registered in the register of shareholders. Consequently, bearer shares are transferable by hand.

A company receives only the issue price of a share. The legal effect of shareholding is to grant ownership rights in respect of the fraction of capital represented by the share, and a right to receive the appropriate portion of corporate net income distributed in the form of a dividend. Companies usually retain a portion of net income for reinvestment, and distribute the balance as dividends. We will consider shortly the accounting consequences of the distinction made between retained income and distributable income.

The distinction between ownership and management is one of the most distinctive features of corporate activity. As owners, shareholders may be considered as having ultimate control over the activities of the company through their right to appoint directors. The rights of shareholders to exercise control over the affairs of companies are defined by legislation. Once appointed, directors exercise day-to-day control of the company's affairs, and although they are accountable to shareholders, the diffusion of shares among many shareholders usually places directors in a very strong position *vis-à-vis* shareholders. Although they are treated as stewards of corporate assets on behalf of shareholders, the effective power to make decisions of major importance in respect of those assets lies almost entirely in their hands.

Social change is affecting the traditional method of regulating corporate enterprise in a number of ways. First, the recognition of the right of employees to share managerial responsibility is an important feature of the democratization of corporate control. Some European countries have already legislated for two-tier boards of directors. Seen in employee participation in the management of companies, this feature is an explicit admission that the interests of employees are as important as those of shareholders. Second, the concept of social accounting further broadens the classical notion of stewardship as a definition of the function of directors to include a responsibility to all sections of society having an interest in the activities of corporate enterprises. Consumers, as well as the local community, are included in the group of those having a vested interest in the nature of corporate activity.

Financial accounting implications of corporate status

Corporate status implies a distinctive treatment of the capital structure and of the allocation of the net as between dividends and retained income. The normal procedure for dealing with the financial accounting implications of corporate status is to establish a separation of functions between the accountant and the company secretary.

The former is usually concerned with the financial accounting procedures directed at recording business transactions: the latter usually maintains the register of shareholders, including such details as the record of shareholders' names and addresses, class and number of shares held, instructions regarding correspondence and payment of dividends. Much of the routine work of the secretary's department in this respect involves recording the transfer of shares and the payment of yearly dividends to shareholders. The specialized nature of share transfer work, as well as its sheer volume in some corporations, often requires a separate department under a share transfer registrar. In such cases, the share transfer registrar is a senior official of the company.

The financial accounting aspects of the share capital with which the accountant is concerned consist of the ledger records associated with shareholders, namely the share capital account, the dividend account, and those accounts retaining income in the form of capital or current reserves. These accounts are concerned with aggregate figures.

Example 23.1 Excel plc is a public company having a share capital of one million £1 shares held in different proportions by 20,000 individual shareholders. The detailed records of the individual shareholding are kept by the registrar, and the accountant will keep the following ledger record:

Share capital account

	Sundry shareholders	£1,000,000

The capital structure

The capital structure may consist of both share capital and loan capital. It represents the long-term finance available to the company, as distinct from the short-term finance represented by the credit facilities offered by trade creditors and bank overdrafts. Shareholders are regarded at law as owners. The share capital is at risk and in the event of business failure shareholders may lose all the capital invested, since they rank last as claimants on the residual assets of the corporation. By contrast, loan capital is made available by creditors on a long-term basis. A company may invite the public to supply loan capital for a period of, say, five years at a rate of interest of, say, 10 per cent. Individuals may offer varying sums, and receive from the company a debenture certificate. Debentures frequently involve the mortgage of specific corporate assets to the body of debenture-holders represented by a trustee for debenture-holders, and in the event of the company defaulting in any way on the conditions of the debenture instrument, the specified assets may be seized and sold on behalf of the debenture-holders. The charge on the corporate assets may be fixed, as we have mentioned, or floating, that is, not be specific as regards any particular assets but applying to all corporate assets. Debenture-holders are guaranteed, therefore, both repayment of loan capital and interest as specified in the conditions of issue. It is the duty of the trustee for the debenture-holders to act before any loss threatens debenture-holders. Very large and financially strong companies may be able to raise long-term loans without mortgaging their assets to lenders. They issue certificates of indebtedness described as unsecured notes, which also carry an obligation to pay interest and to redeem at the end of the stated period. Holders of unsecured notes rank as ordinary creditors in liquidation.

Shares, debentures and unsecured notes may all be quoted on Stock Exchanges and transacted between buyers and sellers. Appropriate registers of debenture-holders and holders of unsecured notes must be kept by the company.

The share capital may consist of different classes of shares, but the two most common classes of shares are preference shares and ordinary shares.

Preference shares give preferential rights as regards dividends, and often as regards the repayment of capital on winding-up. Preference shares may be issued as redeemable preference shares, that is, they may be redeemed and cancelled by the company. Preference shares may also be issued as cumulative preference shares, which means that if the net income of any particular year is insufficient to pay a dividend to preference shareholders of this class, the right to receive a dividend for that year is carried forward to the following year, and so on, until such time as the accumulated dividend entitlement may be declared and paid out of incomes. Preference shareholders are usually entitled to a fixed dividend expressed as a percentage of the nominal value of the share. A holder of 100 preference shares of £1 each carrying a fixed dividend rate of 8 per cent will be entitled to a total yearly dividend of £8. Preference shares may also be issued as participating preference shares, meaning that in addition to the fixed-dividend-rate entitlement, they participate in the remainder of the net income with ordinary shareholders. It is common for conditions to be imposed limiting the participating rights of such shares to allow for a minimum level of dividend for ordinary shareholders. A participating preference share may carry a right to a fixed dividend of 8 per cent and a right to participate in the remaining net income after the ordinary shareholders have received their dividend.

Ordinary shares provide the bulk of the share capital. In return for bearing the risk involved in financing corporate activities, ordinary shareholders enjoy the right to the whole of the net income – either as dividends or, if retained, as the increased value of net corporate assets – subject to the rights of preference shareholders. Some companies obtain the whole of the share capital in the form of ordinary shares. The reason for issuing a variety of shares – preference shares of different classes and ordinary shares – is to tap the funds held by investors with differing investment needs. A young person with money to invest will be looking for growth in the value of their capital and will be attracted to buying ordinary shares in a company having good prospects of expansion. A retired person, looking for a safe investment providing a steady income, may wish to hold some preference shares. Institutional buyers, such as pension funds and insurance companies, also have a wish to hold shares of different classes. Deferred shares are a separate class of shares to both preference and ordinary shares, and may be issued in restricted numbers to managers of the company. In such a case, deferred shares carry an entitlement to dividend only after the ordinary shareholders have received a specified dividend rate.

Leverage and the capital structure

The nature of the capital structure has important implications for financial management purposes, and the relative proportion of equity to debt in the capital structure is an important consideration. The leverage represents the amount of long-term debt used to finance a company's assets, as distinct from shareholder equity. Financial leverage, also known as 'gearing', is a financial analysis ratio that compares long-term debt to equity capital and is expressed in percentage terms.

The leverage expresses the relationship between the proportion of fixed interest (loan capital) and fixed dividend (preference share capital) to ordinary shares. A company with a large proportion of fixed-interest- and fixed-dividend-bearing capital to ordinary capital is said to be highly leveraged.

Example 23.2 Companies Alpha, Beta and Gamma have the same total capital which is issued as follows:

	Alpha	Beta	Gamma
	£	£	£
Share capital			
8% Preference shares of £1 each	40,000	10,000	–
Ordinary shares of £1 each	20,000	80,000	100,000
Loan capital			
7% Debentures of £100 each	40,000	10,000	–
	100,000	100,000	100,000

The leverage of these three companies may be calculated as follows:

1	Alpha	(40,000 + 40,000) :	20,000	or	4 : 12
2	Beta	(10,000 + 10,000) :	80,000	or	0.25 : 1
3	Gamma	:	100,000	or	0

Alpha is, therefore, the most highly leveraged company.

The importance of leverage is that fluctuations in net income may have disproportionate effects upon the return accruing to ordinary shareholders in the case of a highly leveraged company, and hence on the pricing of ordinary shares on the Stock Exchange. Directors looking for stability in the price of the company's ordinary shares will be swayed by this consideration when faced with raising further capital. The net cost of debenture interest may be lower than the net cost in dividends of further issues of ordinary shares. Similarly, fixed dividend preference shares may also cost less than issuing ordinary shares. The following example shows the effects of fluctuating net income levels on the return to ordinary shareholders, assuming that the available net income is wholly distributed.

Example 23.3 The consequence of fluctuations in net distributable income on ordinary shareholders in Alpha Company, Beta Company and Gamma Company geared in the ratios established in the example above may be judged as follows:

	Alpha		Beta		Gamma	
	£	£	£	£	£	£
Assuming net income of £15,000						
Net income		15,000		15,000		15,000
8% Preference shares	3,200		800		–	
7% Debentures	2,800		700		–	–
		6,000		1,500		
Available for ordinary shares		9,000		13,500		15,000
Maximum dividend for ordinary shareholders	$\frac{9,000}{20,000}$	= 45%	$\frac{13,500}{80,000}$	= 16.875%	$\frac{15,000}{100,000}$	= 15%
Assuming net income of £10,000						
Net income		10,000		10,000		10,000
8% Preference shares	3,200		800		–	
7% Debentures	2,800		700		–	–
		6,000		1,500		
Available for ordinary shares		4,000		8,500		10,000
Maximum dividend for ordinary shareholders	$\frac{4,000}{20,000}$	= 20%	$\frac{8,500}{80,000}$	= 10.625%	$\frac{10,000}{100,000}$	= 10%

Hence, in a highly leverage company such as Alpha, a fall of $33\frac{1}{3}$ per cent in net income has produced a fall of 56 per cent in the maximum dividend payable to ordinary shareholders, and in Gamma, a $33\frac{1}{3}$ per cent fall in incomes has produced a $33\frac{1}{3}$ per cent fall in dividends.

Accounting procedures applied to the capital structure

The share capital

We mentioned earlier that a distinction exists between the authorized capital and the issued capital. The former is the maximum limit in the total value of shares of different classes which a company is permitted to issue under the conditions of its registration; the latter is the nominal value of shares of different classes which have been issued. The reason why companies do not establish the value of the authorized capital greatly in excess of their anticipated requirement lies in the taxes imposed on the value of the authorized capital, which deter promoters from incurring unnecessary expenses.

The financial accounting procedures applied to the treatment of the share capital may be said to have two main objectives:

1 recording the issue of shares and the consideration received in respect of such shares;
2 providing information about the share capital in the balance sheet.

We do not propose to deal with the procedures applied to the redemption of redeemable preference shares, or those applied to the issue of bonus shares, since these procedures are not essential to this book. It may be mentioned, however, that bonus shares are commonly issued free of cost to existing shareholders in proportion to their shareholdings by way of distribution of accumulated incomes. They are also commonly distributed to directors and corporate staff as additional remuneration, enabling companies to recruit and keep highly skilled management personnel by paying a proportion of their remuneration in the form of bonus shares.

Recording the issue of shares

It has become the practice for companies seeking to make an issue of shares to the public to employ the services of merchant bankers, not only to act as advisers but also to deal with the details of the issue, such as issuing the prospectus advertising the offer of the shares for sale, recording the applications from investors and the monies received with the applications, the allotment of shares to individual shareholders, where an offer has been oversubscribed and arranging for the shares undersubscribed to be taken up by the underwriters who have acted as insurers in respect of the issue of the shares in return for a commission. The detailed accounting procedures for dealing with the issue of shares need not detain us, for they have become part and parcel of a rather specialized aspect of work.

The central financial problems relating to the issue of shares concern the nature of the shares to be issued, that is, whether to issue preference or ordinary shares, how many to issue and the price to be attached to such shares. All these are problems in respect of which a company will seek expert advice. The financial accounting procedures which we shall consider reflect merely the outcome of the decisions taken.

We mentioned earlier that shares are described in the memorandum of association as having a nominal value. This practice applies in the United Kingdom, although in United States, for example, it is the practice for shares not to have a nominal value, and they are issued as 'shares of no par value'. This means that the recorded issue value of the share capital reflects the price determined at the time of issue.

In the United Kingdom, the practice of attaching a nominal value to shares makes it possible for an issue of shares to be made:

1 *at par* – that is, a share having a nominal value of £1 is issued at a price of £1;
2 *at a premium* – that is, a share having a nominal value of £1 is issued at a price higher than £1;
3 *at a discount* – that is, a share having a nominal value of £1 may be issued at a price which is less than £1. In practice, legislation attaches very strict conditions to the issue of shares at a discount.

A number of considerations affect share issues, not the least of which is that the issue should be a financial success. This means that the company should receive a realistic price for the shares offered and that the issue should be wholly subscribed.

The following examples show the accounting procedures applied to the issue of ordinary shares at par and at a premium.

Example 23.4 The issue of ordinary shares at par

The Omega Co. Ltd has issued 2 million £1 ordinary shares at par. The purchase price has been paid on application and allotment and the company's cash book has been debited with the amount received. The entries in the company's accounts are as follows:

Ordinary share capital account

	Sundry ordinary shareholders £2,000,000

Sundry ordinary shareholders

Ordinary share capital	£2,000,000	Cash	£2,000,000

Cash book

Sundry ordinary shareholders	£2,000,000

The detailed list of individual shareholdings does not form part of the financial accounting system, but rather of the register of shareholders. Hence, the sundry ordinary shareholders account does not exist as such: it is represented by the register of shareholders. From a financial accounting viewpoint, only the ordinary share capital account and the cash book are significant.

Example 23.5 The issue of ordinary shares at a premium

The Onedin Co. Ltd has issued two million £1 ordinary shares at a premium of 50 pence, that is, at £1.50 a share. The purchase price has been paid on application and allotment and the company's cash book has been debited. The practice in the United Kingdom is to separate the par value of the shares from the share premium. Legislation permits adjustments to the share premium account, for example in redeeming preference shares at a premium.

The accounting entries are as follows:

Ordinary share capital account

	Sundry ordinary shareholders £2,000,000

Share premium account

	Sundry ordinary shareholders £1,000,000

Sundry ordinary shareholders

Ordinary share capital	£2,000,000	Cash	£3,000,000
Share premium	1,000,000		
	£3,000,000		£3,000,000

Cash book

Sundry ordinary shareholders £3,000,000	

As explained earlier, the sundry ordinary shareholders do not exist as a formal account, but are found in the register of shareholders. Consequently, the only accounts of significance are the ordinary share capital account, the share premium account and the cash book.

In the United States and Canada, the practice for the last fifty years has been to issue shares of no par value. This simplifies the accounting process, for there is no need to have a share premium account and the share capital account shows the amount actually received from the sale of shares. The case against shares of fixed nominal value is that they bear no relation to the real value of the issued shares, and hence the nominal value is virtually meaningless except as a measure of growth.

The procedures outlined above apply equally to the treatment of other classes of shares.

Loan capital

There is very little difference in the accounting treatment of loan and share capital. Registers of debenture-holders and of holders of unsecured notes are kept, and the method of issue is identical to that of shares in so far as the issuing process tends to be conducted on behalf of the company by merchant bankers. Debentures may be issued at par, at a premium or at a discount. Premiums received on the issue of debentures are regarded as capital incomes, and are usually transferred to a capital reserve account. Discounts allowed on the issue of debentures are treated as finance costs, as required by FRS 4, 'Accounting for Capital Instruments'.

Example 23.6 Hightrust Investment Company offers for sale 10,000 9 per cent debentures in units of £10 at a premium of 5 per cent. The debentures are repayable on 31 December 20X8. The accounting entries are as follows:

9% Debentures 20X8 account

	Sundry debenture holders £100,000

Capital reserve account

	Sundry debenture holders £5,000

Cash book

Sundry debenture holders £105,000	

As in the case of the issue of shares, details of individual debenture-holders would be found in the register of debenture-holders.

Distributable income

The distinguishing feature of an incorporated company is the manner in which periodic income is appropriated. Once the net income has been ascertained, the board of directors have to decide the proportion which should be paid out to shareholders as dividends and the proportion which should be retained. The amount of dividend declared from time to time should be determined by sound financial principles that ensure that income calculated as available for distribution has been established in accordance with accepted accounting principles and the relevant company law.

In considering the manner in which the net income should be appropriated, the following factors are important:

1 Adequate provision should be made in respect of corporation tax payable on the net income for the year. In this connection, under- or overprovisions in respect of previous years have to be taken into account.
2 Adequate provision should be made for anticipated expenditure on the replacement of non-current assets. During periods of inflation, in particular, the cost of replacing non-current assets exceeds amounts provided for depreciation.
3 Adequate provision should be made for capital expenditure which is to be financed out of earnings.

In the United Kingdom, the Companies Act 1980 introduced complex provisions that deal with distributed incomes. The Act provided that no company may make a distribution except out of accumulated realized income less accumulated realized losses. There is one exception to this rule. If a company has revalued a non-current asset, and subsequently calculates depreciation on the higher revalued figure, the depreciation attributable to the excess may be counted as a realized income.

It is quite common for companies to distribute only about half their after-tax income to shareholders. Usually an interim dividend is declared during the account period in anticipation of a final dividend, which is declared after the final results for the year have been ascertained.

The regulation of financial reporting

Financial reporting in the United Kingdom is regulated through company law, accounting standards and the Listing Agreement of the Stock Exchange. Company law provides a broad framework of legal regulations which is supplemented by the accounting standards provided by the accounting profession. The Listing Agreement augments disclosure requirements for companies whose shares are listed on the Stock Exchange. Other influences on financial reporting are three reports on corporate governance which appeared in the 1990s, and international considerations which are playing an increasing part in the setting of UK standards.

Legal regulations

Since the first general legislation on companies was enacted in 1844, numerous Companies Acts have introduced varying amounts of change into the legal requirements for accounting disclosure. The Companies Act 2006 marked a major development in modernizing company law. It amended and restated the provisions of the Companies Act 1985 that had made significant changes in financial reporting requirements. The current legal framework is the result of legislation over a period of over forty years beginning with the Companies Act 1948 which was added to by subsequent acts in 1967, 1976, 1980, 1981, 1985 and 1989.

The introduction of the Companies Act 1948 marked a radical departure from the approach adopted in previous legislation. For the first time emphasis was placed on the importance of providing information in financial reports to assist in investment decisions. Amongst the major provisions of the Act were: the subjection of the income statement to audit; the requirement for group accounts; a considerable extension in the requirements regarding individual items of information which should be disclosed; and, most importantly for subsequent developments in company financial reporting, the requirement that auditors report whether financial statements present a 'true and fair view' of the company's financial position and profitability. The criterion of a 'true and fair view' superseded that of a 'true and correct view' which first appeared in 1844. The Companies Act 1948 provided that the 'true and fair view' shall override all other requirements for the Companies Act as to matters to be included in a company's financial reports. This means that information not specifically required by law must be provided in order to give a true and fair view. Despite its overriding importance, the interpretation of the 'true and fair view' has not been without its difficulties.

In 1983 the Accounting Standards Committee (ASC) obtained a written opinion from counsel on the meaning of 'true and fair' with particular reference to the role of accounting standards. The ASC intended to take account of the opinion in all its future work. The opinion states that financial statements will not be true and fair unless the information they contain is sufficient in quantity and quality to satisfy the reasonable expectations of the readers to whom they are addressed. But the expectations of the readers will have been moulded by the practices of accountants because, by and large, they will expect to get what they ordinarily get and that, in turn, will depend upon the normal practices of accountants. Therefore, the courts will treat compliance with accepted accounting principles as prima-facie evidence that the financial statements are true and fair.

The opinion also states that since the function of the ASC was to formulate what it considered should be generally accepted accounting principles, the value of a Statement of Standard Accounting Practice to a court is:

1 as a statement of professional opinion as to what readers may expect in financial statements which are true and fair;
2 that readers expect financial statements to comply with standards.

The opinion concludes, therefore, that financial statements which depart from standards may be held not to be true and fair, unless a strong body of professional opinion opts out of applying the standard. The Companies Act 1989 introduced a requirement to state whether the accounts have been prepared in accordance with applicable accounting standards and to give details of, and the reason for, any material departures. According to a more recent legal opinion, the effect of the 1989 Act is to 'increase the likelihood that the courts will hold that, in general, compliance with accounting standards is necessary to meet the true and fair view requirement' (Arden, 1993).

Regulation by the accountancy profession

As noted in Chapter 9, the Accounting Standards Board (ASB) replaced the Accounting Standards Committee in 1990. The ASB has the power to issue accounting standards (Financial Reporting Standards or FRSs) on its own authority and is part of a larger structure as shown in Figure 23.1.

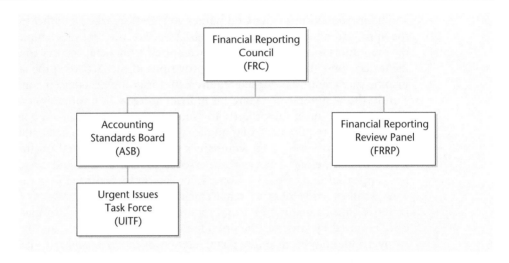

Figure 23.1

The Financial Reporting Council gives guidance to the ASB on priorities, work programme and issues of public concern, and acts as an instrument for promoting good accounting practice.

The Financial Reporting Review Panel examines accounts, either on its own initiative or in response to outside representations, in cases where departures from standard accounting practice have occurred, and an issue of principle is involved or the accounts do not give a true and fair view. The Review Panel may invite the company's auditors and directors to give evidence. If it concludes that the accounts need revision in order to give a true and fair view, it will notify the Stock Exchange and any other relevant professional body, and may publish its findings. In the last resort, the Review Panel may bring civil proceedings against a company which will not revise its accounts in order to give a true and fair view.

The aims of the ASB are as follows: to establish and improve standards of financial accounting and reporting, for the benefit of users, preparers and auditors of financial information. The ASB intends to achieve its aims by:

1 developing principles to guide it in establishing standards and to provide a framework within which others can exercise judgement in resolving accounting issues. These principles will be examined later in this chapter;
2 issuing new accounting standards, or amending existing ones, in response to evolving business practices, new economic developments and deficiencies being identified in current practice;
3 addressing urgent issues promptly.

The Accounting Standards Board's consultative process includes, first, the issue of Working Drafts for discussion (DDs); these then become Financial Reporting Exposure Drafts (FREDs); this process culminates in the publication of Financial Reporting Standards (FRSs).

The way in which the ASB addresses urgent issues promptly is through the Urgent Issues Task Force (UITF), which is a committee of the ASB. Its main role is to assist the ASB in areas where an accounting standard or a Companies Act provision exists, but where unsatisfactory or conflicting interpretations have developed or seem likely to develop. In such circumstances, it operates by seeking a voluntary consensus as to the accounting treatment that should be adopted. The UITF operates within the framework of the law and the principles established in accounting standards and other pronouncements of the ASB. UITF pronouncements, which are issued in the form of abstracts, are therefore intended to be complied with by companies when preparing financial statements.

The development of a conceptual framework

The main criticism levelled against the programme adopted by the Accounting Standards Committee was that it failed to establish objectives for financial reports. This resulted from the failure to develop the accounting standards programme within a framework which would have allowed that programme to proceed in a coherent manner. The ASB has aimed to remedy this defect by developing a clear Statement of Principles from which work on individual standards will derive, and providing a framework for the standards themselves. The ASB's intention is that accounting standards should be based on principles backed up by examples rather than on detailed *ad hoc* rules. The seven chapters making up the Statement were published as Discussion Drafts or Exposure Drafts in the period 1991 to 1994. In 1999 the ASB issued a new Exposure Draft which presented all the chapters together with minor changes. Two chapters which are most relevant to this introductory text are summarized below.

Chapter 1: The objective of financial statements

The Statement of Principles begins with the proposition that:

The objective of financial statements is to provide information about the reporting entity's financial performance and financial position that is useful to a wide range of users for assessing the stewardship of management and for making economic decisions.

The statement emphasizes that financial statements cannot provide all the information that users may need to make economic decisions, because they largely portray the financial effects of past events and do not necessarily provide non-financial information. Also, the information presented in financial statements is subject to various limitations. It is subject to uncertainty because it incorporates estimates, and because the effects of transactions are allocated to discrete reporting periods. Information that cannot be expressed in monetary terms cannot be reflected in the primary financial statements. Moreover, the information in financial statements is largely historical, in that it relates to the position at a point in time and performance for a prior period.

Seven potential user groups are identified.

1 Investors are interested in information that is useful in assessing the stewardship of management and in taking decisions about their investment or potential investment in the entity. They are, as a result, concerned with the risk inherent in, and return provided by, their investments, and need information on the entity's financial performance and financial position that helps them to assess its cash-generation abilities and its financial adaptability.

2 Lenders wish to determine whether their loans and the attached interest will be paid when due.

3 Suppliers wish to determine whether amounts owing to them will be paid when due.

4 Employees are concerned with their employer's stability and profitability, and with assessing the ability of the enterprise to provide the remuneration and retirement benefits.

5 Customers are concerned with the continuance of an enterprise.

6 Governments require information enabling them to regulate firms' activities, determine taxation policies and compile national statistics.

7 The public may be affected by enterprises in different ways. For instance, an enterprise may have a major effect on the local economy. Local residents will want information about the prosperity of the enterprise.

Some, but not all, information needs are common to all users. The Statement concludes that the provision of information meeting the needs of investors will satisfy most of the needs of other user groups.

The Statement identifies three different information requirements among users of financial statements; these are for information about the financial position of an enterprise, its performance and its financial adaptability.

1 *Financial position.* The financial position of an enterprise encompasses the economic resources it controls, its financial structure, its liquidity and solvency, and its capacity to adapt to changes in the environment in which it operates. Information on financial position is provided in the balance sheet.

2 *Performance.* The performance of an enterprise comprises the return obtained by the enterprise and the resources it controls, including the cost of its financing. Information on performance is provided in the income statement and in the statement of total recognized gains and losses.

3 *Financial adaptability.* Financial adaptability consists of the ability of an enterprise to take effective action to alter the amount and timing of its cash flows so that it can respond to unexpected events and opportunities. All the primary financial statements provide information that is useful in evaluating the financial adaptability of the enterprise.

Chapter 3: The qualitative characteristics of financial information

Qualitative characteristics are the characteristics that make the information provided in financial statements useful to users for assessing the financial position, performance and financial adaptability of an enterprise.

Some qualitative characteristics relate to the content of the information contained in financial statements; others relate to how that information is presented. The primary qualitative characteristics relating to content are relevance, reliability, comparability and understandability.

Figure 23.2, reproduced from the statement, summarizes the points dealt with in Chapter 3 of the Statement. Each of the numbered items in the figure is briefly explained below.

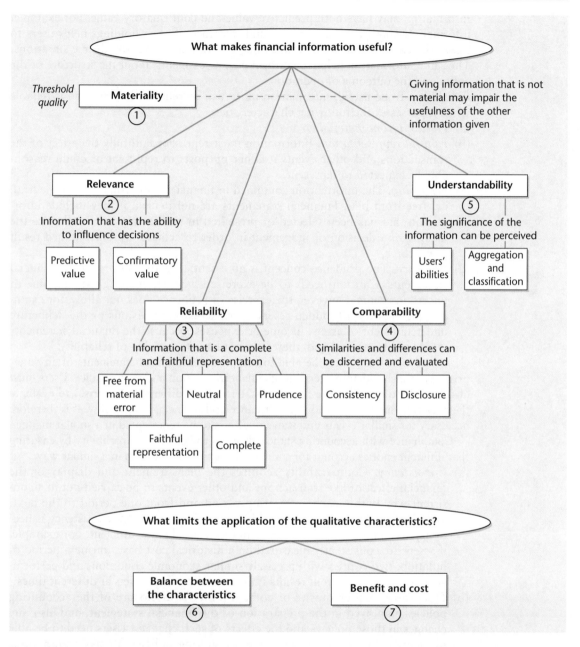

Figure 23.2

1 *Materiality*. Information is material if it could influence users' decisions taken on the basis of the financial statements.

2 *Relevance*. To be useful, information must be relevant to the decision-making needs of users. Information that is relevant has predictive value or confirmatory value.

   (a) *Predictive value* helps users to evaluate or assess past, present, or future events.

   (b) *Confirmatory value* helps users to confirm or correct their past evaluations and assessments.

Information may have both predictive value and confirmatory value. For example, information about the current level and structure of asset holdings helps users to assess the entity's ability to exploit opportunities and react to adverse situations. The same information helps to confirm past assessments about the structure of the entity and the outcome of operations.

3 *Reliability*. To be useful, information must also be reliable. Information is reliable when it possesses the following characteristics:

(a) *Freedom from material error.*

(b) *Faithful representation*. Information must represent faithfully the effect of the transactions and other events it either purports to represent or could reasonably be expected to represent.

(c) *Neutrality*. The information contained in financial statements must be neutral, i.e. free from bias. Financial statements are not neutral if they include information that has been selected or presented in such a way as to influence the making of a decision or judgement in order to achieve a predetermined result or outcome.

(d) *Prudence*. The prudence concept is an essential feature in preparing financial statements. Caution needs to be exercised when estimating the outcome of uncertain events. However, the exercise of prudence does not allow, for example, the creation of hidden reserves or excessive provisions or the deliberate understatement of assets, income or expenses, because the financial statements would not be neutral and, therefore, not have the quality of reliability.

4 *Comparability*. Users must be able to compare the financial statements of an enterprise over time to identify trends in its financial position and performance. Users must also be able to compare the financial statements of different enterprises to evaluate their relative financial position, performance and financial adaptability. It is therefore necessary for similar events and states of affairs to be represented in a similar manner.

Compliance with accounting standards helps to achieve comparability by ensuring that different entities account for similar transactions and events in a similar way.

(a) *Consistency*. Comparability requires the measurement and display of the financial effect of like transactions and other events to be carried out in a consistent way within each accounting period and from one period to the next, and also in a consistent way by different entities. Although consistency is necessary to attain comparability, it is not in itself always sufficient. For example, if assets are consistently measured on a historical cost basis during a period of inflation, two entities with precisely similar economic conditions and performance will report different results if they acquired their assets at different times.

(b) *Disclosure*. A prerequisite of comparability is disclosure of the accounting policies employed in the preparation of the financial statement, and also any changes in those policies and the effects of such changes. Users need to be able to identify differences between the accounting policies for like transactions and other events used by the same enterprise from period to period and by different enterprises.

5 *Understandability*. An essential quality of the information provided in financial statements is that it should be readily understandable by users. Whether information is understandable will depend on:

(a) *Users' abilities*. Those preparing financial statements are entitled to assume that users have a reasonable knowledge of business and economic activities and accounting and a willingness to study with reasonable diligence the information provided.

(b) *Aggregation and classification*. An understandable presentation requires that items are aggregated and classified in an appropriate way.

6 *Balance between characteristics*. One constraint is that a balancing, or trade-off, between qualitative characteristics is often necessary. For example, information that is more reliable is frequently less relevant and vice versa. Generally the aim is to achieve an appropriate balance among the characteristics in order to meet the objective of financial statements. The relative importance of the characteristics in different cases is a matter of judgement.

7 *Benefit and cost*. As a general principle, the benefits derived from the provision of information should exceed the cost of providing it.

Regulation by the Stock Exchange

A company wishing to obtain a full listing, that is a quotation on the Stock Exchange, must comply with the listing requirements in the rules issued under the authority of the Stock Exchange Council. These impose additional disclosure requirements such as the publication of interim reports and a statement that shows how much of a company's bank loans and other borrowings are repayable within one and two years, between two and five years and in excess of five years. Listed companies are also expected to comply with the provisions of accounting standards and companies are required to give reasons for any significant departures from standard accounting practice.

Corporate governance

The Combined Code on Corporate Governance (1998) was an important step in improving company reporting. It brought together the work of three committees which were set up because of the low level of confidence in financial reporting and auditing. A series of spectacular failures coupled with criticism of board accountability over matters such as directors' pay suggested that corporate governance required improvement.

The code establishes principles of good corporate governance related to a well-balanced board of directors and the information it receives from management, relations with shareholders, internal audit, and control and risk management. With regard to the last item, the board is required to disclose that there is an on-going process for identifying, evaluating and managing the significant risks faced by the company; that this process has been in place for the year under review and up to the annual report approval date; and that it is regularly reviewed by the board.

The London Stock Exchange requires UK listed companies to make a statement of compliance with the Combined Code in their annual report.

Summary

In this chapter, we have examined the nature of limited companies and the financial accounting implications of incorporation. These implications stem from the manner in which companies are capitalized and from the manner in which the net income is appropriated. We discussed particular financial problems such as leverage. The accounting procedures relating to the share capital are concerned principally with recording the issue of share capital, and with providing information about the share capital in financial accounting reports.

The accounting procedures applicable to periodic income are concerned with the manner in which the income is appropriated to various purposes. The size of the dividend is a matter of financial policy which directors have to consider in relation to capital requirements, its effect on the share price and the availability of other sources of finance.

We considered also the regulation of financial reporting in the UK and its three major means: company law, accounting standards and the Listing Agreement of the Stock Exchange. Also we considered the influence of international bodies. Finally, we examined two chapters of the ASB's Statement of Principles for Financial Reporting.

Self-assessment questions

1 Distinguish between share capital and loan capital.

2 Explain 'leverage'. Why is it significant for ordinary shareholders?

3 What is meant by issuing shares at a premium? How is this recorded in the accounts?

4 Explain the importance of a 'true and fair view'.

5 Distinguish between the roles of:
   (a) the Financial Reporting Council;
   (b) the Accounting Standards Board;
   (c) the Financial Reporting Review Panel;
   (d) the Urgent Issues Task Force.

6 How is financial reporting practice in the UK affected by international influences?

7 Explain the role of a conceptual framework. Distinguish between financial position, performance and financial adaptability.

8 What are qualitative characteristics?

9 Explain 'relevance' and 'reliability'. What makes information relevant and reliable?

Reference   Arden, M. (1993) *The True and Fair View Requirement*, Appendix to Foreword to Accounting Standards, Accounting Standards Board.

Published financial statements

Although companies utilise a wide variety of media to disseminate information to the investment community such as in-person briefing, interim publications and the Internet, financial reports have historically been the primary vehicle by which public companies communicate with shareholders, customers and a host of other stakeholders. Since the financial report supplements historical financial detail with information about a company's strategy, its management, current position and future prospects, it is not surprising that it should be relied on so heavily by investors and analysts to assess value.

(Price Waterhouse Coopers, 1999)

Learning objectives

After studying this chapter you should be able to:

1 prepare the financial statements of a limited company for publication;

2 explain how taxation is dealt with in the financial statements;

3 describe additional disclosure requirements.

T he purpose of this chapter is to examine the accounting and financial reporting implications of incorporation, and the rules applying to financial reporting that are peculiar to public as distinct from private companies. Public companies are defined as those private-sector companies in which the public at large may become shareholders. Generally, such companies have their shares quoted on stock exchanges. Private companies are those private-sector companies that do not issue shares to the public at large and restrict the issue to shares to participating persons. Their shares are not quoted on stock exchanges. The information disclosure rules are much less onerous for private companies than those applicable to public companies.

The law relating to the incorporation and the legal, accounting and financial rules are found in domestic law. In the United Kingdom, they are consolidated in the Companies Act 2006. International influences on the evolution of UK company legislation are seen in the convergence with accounting and financial reporting standards issued by the International Accounting Standards Board and the 4th and 7th EEC Directives on Company Accounts as they relate to member countries of the European Union.

With the exception of the European Company or Societas Europaea, there are no provisions in international law for the incorporation of international companies. As part of the evolution of the European Union, the European Council passed a resolution in 2001 providing for the creation of a European Company, the Societas Europaea, within the European Union. The Societas Europaea is a European public limited company. It may be created on registration in any one of the member states of the European Economic Area (EEA). Article 10 of the Regulation requires member states to treat a Societas Europaea as if it were a public limited company formed in accordance with the law of the member state in which it has its registered office. As from 2004, domestic laws in United Kingdom that apply to public limited companies also apply, in many respects, to Societas Europaeas registered in the United Kingdom (Article 9(1)(c)(ii) of the Regulation).

The post-war evolution of statutory requirements relating to the disclosure of financial information is seen in a series of statutes beginning with the Companies Acts 1948, 1967, 1976, 1980 and 1981. A major consolidation of these statutes was effected by the Companies Act 1985, as amended by the Companies Act 1989. The current legislation is foundf in the Companies Act 2006, fully effective as from October 2009, which now contains the overall legal framework. Many of the statutory requirements contained in these Acts have been enlarged as the result of the issue of UK accounting standards and the Companies Act 2006 has a section on the application of IAS regulation. In addition, companies listed on a stock exchange in Great Britain or Ireland must observe certain additional requirements.

The recent developments of accounting and financial reporting legislation

The Companies Act 1981 marked an important step in the international convergence of accounting and financial reporting rules through the implementation in the United Kingdom of the European Council's Fourth Directive on the Annual Accounts of Certain Types of Companies (78/660/EEC of 25 July 1978) aimed at harmonizing the accounts of member countries. This directive applies only to the accounts of individual companies in European Union member states. On 13 June 1983, the Council issued a Seventh Directive on the Consolidated Accounts of Companies with Limited Liability (83/349/EEC of 13 June 1983). The Companies Act 1981 required that group accounts shall be prepared as far as possible to comply with the accounting rules laid down for individual companies. Accounting for groups of companies is considered in Part 4.

The Companies Act 1981 introduced major changes in British company legislation:

1 Precise formats for the income statement and balance sheet are prescribed for the first time in United Kingdom law and they require disclosure of considerably more detail than was previously the case.

2 Fundamental principles (concepts) for the preparation of published accounts are prescribed:

    (a) the company is to be presumed to be carrying on its business as a going concern;

    (b) all accounting principles are to be applied consistently from one financial year to the next;

(c) the amount of any item is to be determined on a prudent basis and in particular only profit realized at the balance sheet date is to be included in the income statement;

(d) revenues and expenses are to be accounted for on an accruals basis;

(e) in determining the aggregate amount to be shown in respect of any item in the accounts the amount of each individual component asset or liability must be determined separately;

(f) amounts in respect of items representing assets or income may not be set off against amounts in respect of items representing liabilities or expenditure.

The first four principles are the fundamental accounting concepts discussed in Chapter 8.

If it appears to the directors of a company that there are special reasons for departing from any of these six principles in preparing the company's accounts then the particulars of the departure, the reasons for it and its effects must be given in a note to the accounts.

3 Historical cost and alternative accounting rules are prescribed. These rules do not differ from those generally followed in practice; they merely represent a shift from non-statutory to statutory regulation. They will be detailed later in this chapter. The alternative accounting rules allow assets to be valued at their current cost.

4 A distinction is drawn between the publicity and filing requirements of different companies according to their size. Small and medium-sized companies must present a full set of accounts to their shareholders. However, they may file modified reports with the Registrar of Companies. Details of the qualifying conditions and exemptions are considered later in this chapter.

The Companies Act 1985 was last major consolidated act prior to the Companies Act 2006, which incorporated many of its provisions.

The Companies Act 1989 introduced a requirement to state whether the accounts have been prepared in accordance with applicable accounting standards and to give details of, and the reasons for, any material departures. Small and medium-sized companies are exempt from this disclosure requirement.

The Companies Act 2006 was announced in a White Paper of 2002 as a modernizing act. It amends and restates many provisions of the Companies Act 1985. Significant changes are highlighted in Accounts and Reports Guidance BERR that provides guidance on the accounting and reporting requirements under the Companies Act 2006. They concern, in particular, the framing of the audit report and restate the requirement of the Companies Act 1985 for a business review that contains a fair review of the business and the company and a description of the principal risks and uncertainties facing the company. The business review requires the use of 'key performance indicators' (KPIs) that measure effectively the development, performance or position of the company. The selection of KPIs is left to the discretion of directors to decide exactly what information to include about their particular company, provided that the information is relevant to an understanding of the business. It leaves scope for abuse in that it leaves the selection of KPIs to those showing the company's performance in a favourable light. With respect to small companies, the intention of the Companies Act 2006 was to make company law more accessible, easier to understand and less restricting. For example, small companies are excluded from the business review requirement.

The current legislative framework for financial reporting

Company accounts contain five financial statements. These comprise:

1 an income statement;
2 a statement of total recognized gains and losses;
3 a balance sheet;
4 a reconciliation of movements of shareholders' funds;
5 a cash-flow statement.

These statements are examined in the remainder of this chapter and in Chapter 25.

The income statement

The Companies Acts provide two horizontal and two vertical formats for the presentation of the income statement. Essentially, the two formats may be distinguished by the way in which costs are analysed. Format 1 analyses costs by type of operation, while Format 2 analyses costs by type of expenditure. The vertical formats of these two different types of analyses are:

Income statement – Format 1

1	Turnover
2	Cost of sales
3	Gross income
4	Distribution costs
5	Administrative expenses
6	Other operating income
7	Income from shares in group companies
8	Income from shares in related companies
9	Income from other fixed-asset investments
10	Other interest receivable and similar income
11	Amounts written off investments
12	Interest payable and similar charges
13	Tax on income on ordinary activities
14	Income on ordinary activities after taxation
15	Extraordinary income
16	Extraordinary charges
17	Extraordinary profit or loss
18	Tax on extraordinary profit or loss
19	Other taxes not shown under the above items
20	Income for the financial year

Income statement – Format 2

1	Turnover
2	Change in inventory of finished goods and in work in progress
3	Own work capitalized
4	Other operating income
5	(a) Raw materials and consumables
	(b) Other external charges
6	Staff costs:
	(a) wages and salaries
	(b) social security costs
	(c) other pension costs
7	(a) Depreciation and other amounts written off tangible and intangible non-current assets
	(b) Exceptional amounts written off current assets
8	Other operating charges
9	Income from shares in group companies
10	Income from shares in related companies
11	Income from other non-current investments
12	Other interest receivable and similar income
13	Amounts written off investments
14	Interest payable and similar charges
15	Tax on income on ordinary activities
16	Income on ordinary activities after taxation
17	Extraordinary income
18	Extraordinary charges
19	Extraordinary profit or loss
20	Tax on extraordinary profit or loss
21	Other taxes not shown under the above items
22	Income for the financial year

The Acts require disclosure of the following items on the income statement although they do not appear in the formats:

1 income on ordinary activities before taxation;
2 transfers and proposed transfers to and from reserves;
3 the aggregate amount of dividends paid and proposed.

A company must adhere to the format it has chosen in subsequent accounting years, unless in the opinion of the board of directors there are special reasons for a change. Details of any decision to change the format must be given in the note to the accounts.

The income statement must be prepared in the order and under the headings given in the formats. Each item in the format is prefixed by an arabic number, which need not be shown in the published accounts. It is permissible to amalgamate certain items if the amount involved is not material, or if such an amalgamation facilitates the assessment of the company's affairs. It is also possible to adapt the title or to rearrange the position of certain items where the special nature of the company's business requires such alteration.

In addition to the items shown in the formats, and those noted above, the Companies Acts specify certain items of information which must be shown in the income statement or in notes to the accounts. In particular,

1 corresponding amounts for the preceding financial year must be shown for every item in the income statement and the notes thereon. Where a corresponding amount would not be comparable with the current-year item, an adjusted corresponding amount must be shown, particulars of the adjustment and the reasons for it being included;
2 the accounting policies followed by a company in determining the amount of income must be stated.

Turnover

Turnover means any amount derived by the company from the provision of goods and services in the context of its ordinary activities. The term turnover replaces the term sales previously used. It includes all receipts from these activities after deduction of traded discounts, value added tax and any other sales-based tax (e.g. excise duty).

Additionally, there must be disclosed in notes to the accounts the following information relating to the analysis of the turnover:

1 where the company carries on two or more classes of business which differ substantially from each other, the amount of the turnover attributable to each class;
2 where the company has traded in different 'markets' (defined by geographical boundaries), the amount of the turnover attributable to each market must be stated.

Expenditure

In calculating the cost of sales, distribution costs and administrative expenses (Format 1), the following must be included:

1 Provisions for depreciation or diminution in value of assets. Amounts written off investments must be shown separately.
2 Directors' and employees' emoluments. Additionally, notes to the accounts must show the following information:

In respect of directors, distinguishing between directors' fees and directors' salaries:
(a) aggregate emoluments, including fees and percentages, expense allowances charged to United Kingdom tax, pension contributions paid in respect of them and benefits in kind;
(b) aggregate of directors' and past directors' pensions, excluding pensions from schemes maintained by contributions;
(c) aggregate of compensation paid to directors or past directors for loss of office;
(d) prior-year adjustments arising from expense allowances being disallowed for tax purposes, or a director retaining emoluments for which he or she was previously accountable.

In respect of employees:
(e) the average number of employees, calculated by dividing the annual number of employees by the number of weeks in the accounting year. Where Format 1 is used, there must be shown in respect of all employees taken into account in determining the relevant annual numbers:

     (i) wages and salaries paid to employees,

     (ii) social security costs (being contributions by the company towards any state social security or pension scheme),

     (iii) other pensions costs (being contributions to company pension schemes and pensions paid);

  (f) the average number of employees for each category of employees, such categories being defined by the directors having regard to the manner in which the company's activities are organized.

3 Sums payable for the hire of plant and machinery, the sums so payable being shown in the notes to the accounts.

4 Auditors' remuneration, the total payable being shown in the notes to the accounts.

5 Sums paid in respect of any exceptional transactions, being defined as transactions falling outside the ordinary activities of the company.

Other operating income

Other operating income includes income from normal operations which does not fall under any other headings, e.g. royalties and rent received. Income from rents of land and buildings (net of outgoings) must be shown separately if this is a substantial part of a company's revenue.

Other investment income

The four Formats, that provide two income statement formats and two balance sheet format respectively, require income from other non-current asset investments and other interest receivable and similar income to be shown separately. Income from listed investments must be separately identified in the notes if not in the income statement.

Amounts written off investments

This item is required to be shown on the face of the income statement. Where a non-current asset investment has diminished in value a provision for the diminution in its value may be made. However, where the reduction in value of any non-current asset (including investments) is expected to be permanent, a provision for the diminution in value must be made. Consequently, no asset may be stated at a net value in excess of its estimated recoverable amount. Where the reasons for any provision for diminution in value no longer apply, the provision must be written back to the extent that it is no longer necessary.

Interest payable and similar charges

There must be shown in the notes to the accounts information relating to the interest charged in respect of the following:

1 Bank loans and overdraft and other loans made to the company which are either repayable otherwise than by instalment and fall due for repayment within five years from the end of the accounting year, or repayable by instalment, the last of which falls due for payment before the end of that period.

2 Loans of any other kind made to the company, i.e. those repayable wholly or in part after more than five years.

Income on ordinary activities before taxation

As previously stated, this item must be shown on the face of the income statement. The figure reported must represent the balance of all previously mentioned items including exceptional items (see below) that relate to the ordinary activities of the company, but excluding taxation and extraordinary items (see below).

Extraordinary items, exceptional items and prior year adjustments

The required formats for the presentation of the income statement provide headings for extraordinary income, extraordinary charges and tax on extraordinary income. The Companies Acts do not define extraordinary items. They were interpreted in the light of SSAP 6 'Extraordinary Items and Prior Year Adjustments' as 'those items which derive from events or transactions outside the ordinary activities of the business and which are both material and expected not to recur frequently or regularly. They do not include items which, though exceptional on account of size or incidence, derive from the ordinary activities of the business.' The importance of extraordinary items arose from the effect of their treatment on a company's earnings per share (EPS) which was defined in SSAP 3 as the 'profit in pence attributable to each equity share before taking into account extraordinary items'. SSAP 6 attracted much criticism. The facility it allowed for extraordinary items was much abused by companies which increasingly created such items to boost EPS.

FRS 3 'Reporting Financial Performance' (1992) supersedes SSAP 6 and amends SSAP 3. This standard made extraordinary items virtually extinct and reduced the emphasis on EPS as a single measure of performance. Much of this was achieved not by forcing companies to reveal new information, but by altering the presentation of what was already disclosed. The standard requires all income statement items down to operating income to be analysed between amounts attributable to continuing and discontinued operations, with new acquisitions being shown as a sub-category of continuing operations. Where an activity both starts and ceases in a period, it should be treated as discontinued. An illustrative example, which is a simplified version of the example in FRS 3, is given opposite.

The logic behind the distinction between continuing and discontinued operations is that where financial statements are used to assess the likely future performance of a company, then the results from those operations that the company no longer owns need to be excluded, because it is only the continuing operations that will affect the future. Similarly, if the actual results of a period are to be sensibly compared with forecasts made for that period, then the contributions from any operations acquired during the year need to be eliminated so that like can be compared with like. All exceptional items should be credited or charged in arriving at the income on ordinary activities and should be attributed to continuing or discontinued operations as appropriate. Where other exceptional items are involved (e.g. a large bad debt or inventory write-offs,) these should be included within one of the statutory headings in the income statement and disclosed in the notes to the accounts.

Prior period adjustments are those 'material adjustments applicable to prior periods arising from changes in accounting policies or from the correction of fundamental errors'. Such adjustments may be made through reserves.

Income statement

	Continuing operations		Discontinued operations	Total
	Existing	New acquisitions		
	£m	£m	£m	£m
Turnover	550	50	175	775
Cost of sales	415	40	165	620
Gross income	135	10	10	155
Distribution and administrative expenses	85	4	25	114
Operating income	50	6	(15)	41
Income from the sale of properties	29			29
Loss on sale of discontinued operations			(7)	(7)
	79	6	(22)	63
Interest payable				18
Income on ordinary activities before taxation				45
Taxation				16
Income on ordinary activities after taxation				29
Extraordinary items				–
Income for financial year				29
Dividends				8
Retained income for the financial year				21

Taxation

The requirements of the Companies Acts are twofold. First, the income account must disclose the net income on ordinary activities before taxation, and the taxation charge on those activities should be deducted to give the net income on ordinary activities after taxation. Second, the notes to the accounts must contain the following additional information:

1 the amount of the charge for United Kingdom corporation tax;
2 if that amount would have been greater but for double taxation relief, the amount it would have been but for such relief;
3 the amount of the charge for United Kingdom income tax;
4 the amount of the charge for taxation imposed outside the United Kingdom on profits, income and (so far as charged on revenue) capital gains.

These notes must also specify the base on which the charge to United Kingdom corporation tax and income tax is calculated, and give details of any circumstances affecting the liability to corporation tax, income tax and capital gains in the current and succeeding years.

Appropriation of income

The following items must be disclosed separately:

1 any amounts set aside for the redemption of share capital or the redemption of loans;
2 any amount set aside or withdrawn, or that is proposed to be set aside or withdrawn from reserves;
3 the aggregate amount of any dividends paid and proposed.

The statement of total recognized gains and losses

This primary statement, which was introduced in 1993 as part of FRS 3, must appear alongside the income statement, the balance sheet and the cash-flow statement. The ASB argued that such a statement is necessary because not all components of a company's financial performance are reflected in the income statement. As we saw in Chapter 8, the realization concept requires that the income statement include only realized sums which are determined by transactions resulting from sales that have been made. However, a company can make substantial income through the revaluation of non-current assets. These are recognized by increasing the value of the assets in the balance sheet, the double entry being to a revaluation reserve included in shareholders' funds.

The objective of the statement is to show the extent to which shareholders' funds have increased from any gains that the company has included in its accounts and, therefore, have been recognized in the period. Although such information has always been found in the accounts, in the note on reserves, it may not have been included by non-professional readers in their attempts to determine the company's financial performance during the period. FRS 3 puts the argument as follows:

> Statements of total recognised gains and losses contribute further to the purposes of financial reporting by:
>
> (a) combining information about operating and related performance with other aspects of a reporting entity's financial performance; and
> (b) providing information (jointly with the other primary statements) that is useful for assessing the return on investment in a reporting entity.

If a company has no recognized gains or losses other than income for the period, a statement to this effect should be shown immediately below the income statement.

An illustrative example, which is a simplified version of the example in FRS 3, is given below.

Statement of total recognized gains and losses

	£m
Income for the financial year (this is the income shown in income statement after charging tax and after allowing for extraordinary items if any)	29
Unrealized surplus on revaluation of properties	4
Unrealized loss on trade investment	(3)
Total gains and losses recognized since last annual report	30

This statement brings together information from the income statement and balance sheet. Its aim is to give the information a greater prominence and reduce the likelihood of misinterpretation.

The balance sheet

The Companies Acts provide two Formats for the balance sheet presentations, one vertical, the other horizontal. Once a company has chosen which format it intends to adopt, it may not alter that choice without giving an explanation to shareholders in a note to the accounts.

Note from the vertical format shown hereunder that the Acts provide for the classification of broad headings by a letter prefix. Major subdivisions are identified by roman numerals, minor subdivisions by arabic. These prefixes do not have to be shown on the published balance sheet, but are used to set out the manner in which accounting items have to be aggregated on the balance sheet, and the extent to which information has to be disclosed. In this regard, note particularly that any item shown on the format which is preceded by a letter or roman-numeral prefix must be disclosed in a company's published balance sheet.

A company's balance sheet may include any item not otherwise shown on the proposed format, and indeed may show any item in greater detail than is required by the Companies Acts. The following items may not, however, be treated as assets in any company's balance sheet:

1 preliminary expenses;
2 expenses and commissions relating to the issue of shares or debentures;
3 research costs.

With regard to the arrangement of items, it is provided that items preceded by arabic numerals on the format may be amalgamated if they are not material or if the amalgamation facilitates the assessment of the company's state of affairs. In the latter case, the individual items amalgamated must be disclosed by note. Furthermore, these items may be shown in a different order or may have their title adapted where the special nature of the company's business requires such alteration.

Balance sheet – Format 1

A	Called-up share capital not paid		
B	Non-current assets		
	I	Intangible assets	
		1	Development costs
		2	Concessions, patents, licences, trademarks and similar rights and assets
		3	Goodwill
		4	Payments on account
	II	Tangible assets	
		1	Land and buildings
		2	Plant and machinery
		3	Fixtures, fittings, tools and equipment
		4	Payments on account and assets in course of construction

III   Investments
1   Shares in group companies
2   Loans to group companies
3   Shares in related companies
4   Loans to related companies
5   Other investments other than loans
6   Other loans
7   Own shares

C   Current assets
I   Inventory
1   Raw materials and consumables
2   Work-in-progress
3   Finished goods and goods for resale
4   Payments on account

II   Debtors
5   Trade debtors
6   Amounts owed by group companies
7   Amounts owed by related companies
8   Other debtors
9   Called-up share capital not paid
10   Prepayments and accrued income

III   Investments
1   Shares in group companies
2   Own shares
3   Other investments

IV   Cash at bank and in hand

D   Prepayments and accrued income
E   Creditors: amounts falling due within one year
1   Debenture loans
2   Bank loans and overdrafts
3   Payments received on account
4   Trade creditors
5   Bills of exchange payable
6   Amounts owed to group companies
7   Amounts owed to related companies
8   Other creditors including taxation and social security
9   Accruals and deferred income

F   Net current assets (liabilities)
G   Total assets less current liabilities
H   Creditors: amounts falling due after more than one year
1   Debenture loans
2   Bank loans and overdrafts
3   Payments received on account
4   Trade creditors
5   Bills of exchange payable
6   Amounts owed to group companies
7   Amounts owed to related companies
8   Other creditors including taxation and social security
9   Accruals and deferred income

I Provisions for liabilities and charges
    1 Pensions and similar obligations
    2 Taxation, including deferred taxation
    3 Other provisions
J Accruals and deferred income
K Capital and reserves
    I Called-up share capital
    II Share premium account
    III Revaluation reserve
    IV Other reserves
        1 Capital redemption reserve
        2 Reserve for own shares
        3 Reserves provided for by the articles of association
        4 Other reserves
    V Income statement

As with the income statement, general disclosure rules for establishing the comparability of accounting numbers are provided. Thus, corresponding amounts for the previous year must be shown for all balance sheet items, and where, for example, due to a change of accounting policy the numbers are not comparable, adjustments must be made to the previous year to establish comparability. Equally, corresponding amounts must be given, and they must likewise be adjusted if necessary, in respect of every item stated in the notes to the balance sheet (other than amounts relating to the movements on fixed assets, reserves and provisions). Full amounts must be disclosed, and there should be no set off of items representing assets against items representing liabilities.

As stated previously, the Companies Acts prescribe historical cost and alternative accounting rules. The Acts acknowledge that the historical cost of purchase or production is the primary method of valuing assets. Purchase price is defined to include expenses incidental to acquisition. Production cost is defined to include all costs directly attributable to the production of the asset and may also include a reasonable proportion of indirect costs as well as any interest paid on money borrowed to finance the asset in question. The inclusion of distribution cost is specifically prohibited.

Non-current assets

Subject to any provision for depreciation or diminution in value, non-current assets are to be shown at purchase price or production cost, as the case may be. Non-current assets with limited useful economic life must be depreciated.

A provision for the diminution in value of a non-current asset investment may be made, and must be made in respect of any non-current asset where the reduction in value is expected to be permanent. The non-current assets so reduced are shown at their reduced amount on the balance sheet, and the provision for reduction in value is disclosed in a note to the accounts or shown on the income statement.

While maintaining historic cost valuations as the normal basis for balance sheet purposes, the Companies Acts allow alternative valuation bases provided that the items affected and the basis of valuation are shown in a note to the accounts. This permits companies to revalue assets or to use current cost valuations. The amount of income arising from the adoption of an alternative accounting valuation must be credited or debited, as the case may be, to the revaluation reserve.

The Companies Acts require the following information to be disclosed in respect of each non-current asset item:

1 the aggregate purchase price, production cost or alternative accounting valuation at the beginning and end of the accounting reference period, showing the effect of acquisitions, disposals or transfers or any revaluation during this period;
2 the cumulative provision for depreciation, or diminution of value as at the beginning and end of the accounting reference period, showing the annual provision arising from the disposal of any asset and any other adjustment to the provision.

Example 24.1 The requirements of the Companies Acts would be satisfied by the following presentation:

	Freehold land and buildings	Plant and machinery	Total
	£000	£000	£000
Cost:			
At 1 January	1,000	200	1,200
Additions	30	40	70
Disposals	–	(20)	(20)
	1,030	220	1,250
Accumulated depreciation	£	£	£
At 1 January	200	50	250
Depreciation for the year	20	24	44
Disposals	–	(19)	(19)
At 31 December	220	55	275
Net book values	£	£	£
At 31 December	810	165	975

With regard to *intangible assets*, these must be included on the face of the balance sheet under this main heading, with the following subheadings included either on the face of the balance sheet or in a note: development costs; concessions, patents, licences, trade marks and similar rights and assets; goodwill; and payments on account. The Acts make the following provisions:

1 *Development costs* (but not research costs) may be capitalized, but only in 'special circumstances'. In practice, this treatment must be read in conjunction with SSAP 13 'Accounting for Research and Development', discussed in Chapter 15, which defines the special circumstances that must exist before development costs may be capitalized. Where development costs are capitalized and shown on the balance sheet, the Companies Acts require that notes must be appended disclosing (a) the period over which the costs are being written off and (b) the reason for capitalizing the development costs.
2 *Concessions, patents, licences, trademarks, etc.* may be shown on the balance sheet only if they have been acquired by purchase and are not required to be shown under goodwill, or if they were created by the company itself.
3 *Goodwill* may be shown as an asset on the balance sheet only if it was acquired by purchase. In such a case, it must be written off over a period which does not exceed its useful economic life.

Investments

The formats show that investments may be reported either in the category of non-current assets or of current assets. Investments intended to be retained by a company on a continuing basis should be treated as non-current assets, while any other investments should be listed under current assets. When investments are of a long-term nature then they must be classified under the following headings:

1 Shares held in group companies, where the company is a member company in a group of companies.
2 Loans to group companies. Group companies are discussed in Part 4.
3 Shares in related companies, where the company is related to another company in which the relationship involves at least 20 per cent shareholding by one company in another.
4 Loans to related companies.
5 Other investments other than loans, for example shares in companies which are neither group nor related companies.
6 Other loans.
7 Own shares, where – as allowed by the Companies Acts – a company is allowed to purchase its own shares.

The valuation of investments poses particular problems, where there is no stock exchange quotation for shares or debentures. The Companies Acts do not require unquoted investments to be valued, and the requirements would be satisfied by the conventional historical cost of such investments. Where investments are listed on a recognized stock exchange, the aggregate market value must be disclosed where this value differs from the value at which they were stated on the balance sheet.

Current assets

The value to be placed on any current asset is the lower of the purchase price or production cost and the net realizable value. The Companies Acts requires inventories to be subdivided into the following categories:

1 raw materials and consumables;
2 work-in-progress;
3 finished goods and goods for resale;
4 payments on account.

Inventories may be valued using any of the recognized valuation methods, namely FIFO (first in first out), LIFO (last in first out), or weighted average cost.

As noted in Chapter 15, SSAP 9 'Stocks and Long-Term Contracts' does not recommend the use of LIFO. Any material difference between the value of the inentory shown on the balance sheet and its replacement cost, or, if more appropriate, the most recent purchase price, must be disclosed for each category of inventory.

Debtors must be disclosed as a main heading on the balance sheet and the following items must be disclosed either on the face of the balance sheet or in the notes thereto: trade debtors; amounts owed by group companies; amounts owed by related companies; other debtors; called-up share capital not paid; prepayments and accrued income. Additionally, the amounts falling due after more than one year must be shown separately for each item.

Creditors

The Companies Acts require creditors to be shown under the following sub-headings either on the face of the balance sheet or in the notes thereto: debenture loans, bank loans and overdrafts; payments received on account; trade creditors; bills of exchange payable; amounts owed to group companies; other creditors including taxation and social security; and accruals and deferred income. The amounts falling due after more than one year must be shown separately for each item.

Provisions for liabilities and charges

FRS 12, discussed in Chapter 15, defines provisions as 'liabilities of uncertain timing or amount' and lays down the conditions that must be fulfilled before a provision can be included in the financial statement totals.

Share capital

The share capital issued and the amount called up must be shown separately. Where the company has issued shares of different classes, the number and aggregate nominal value of each class must be given by name on the balance sheet. Where redeemable shares have been issued, the following information must be given:

1 the earliest and latest dates on which the company has power to redeem the shares;
2 whether those shares must be redeemed in any event, or are liable to be redeemed at the option of the company;
3 whether any premium (and if so, what) is payable on redemption.

Moreover, if there has been an issue of shares during the financial year, the following information must also be given:

1 the reason for the issue;
2 the class of shares issued;
3 in respect of each class of shares issued, the number issued, their aggregate nominal value and the consideration received by the company.

Reserves

The Companies Acts do not give a general definition of a 'reserve' but it is generally accepted that the term 'reserve' does not include the following:

1 a provision for depreciation, renewal or diminution in value of assets;
2 a provision for a known liability;
3 a provision for undue fluctuations in charges for taxation.

Any share premium account and any revaluation reserve must be shown separately under 'reserves', and any other reserve built up by the company must be shown under an appropriate heading. The income statement balance must be shown separately.

In the event that there has been any transfer to or from the reserves shown as separate items during the accounting period, there must be shown by way of note to the balance sheet the following information:

1 the amount of reserves at the beginning of the year;
2 the amounts transferred either in or out, and the source and application of such amounts;
3 the amounts of reserves at the end of the year.

Guarantees and financial commitments

The following information, if not included in the accounts, must be given in the notes:

1 particulars of any charge on the assets of the company to secure the liabilities of any person, indicating where practicable, the amount secured;
2 the estimated amount of future capital expenditure;
3 pension commitments, both provided for and not provided for;
4 particulars of other financial commitments which are not provided for in the accounts but which are relevant to assessing the company's state of affairs.

Other disclosure requirements

Among other disclosure requirements to be noted are the following:

1 there must be disclosed in a note to the accounts the accounting policies used by the company in determining the amounts shown as items in these accounts;
2 the basis of translation of any item originally denominated in foreign currencies and translated into sterling must be shown.

Three additional requirements are examined below. These are:

1 reconciliation of movements in shareholders' funds;
2 note of historical cost income;
3 segmental information.

Reconciliation of movements in shareholders' funds

The income statement and the statement of total recognized gains and losses are intended to measure the performance of the company during the period. However, there might be other changes in the shareholders' funds (for example, movements on share capital) which are important to understanding the changes in the company's financial position. Shareholders' funds consist of the share capital plus all the various reserves that may exist. Examples of reserves are:

1 the share premium account, which represents the extra premium paid, over the nominal value, for the shares that have been issued by the company;
2 the revaluation reserve, which represents the amount by which shareholders' interest in a company rises when assets are revalued upwards;
3 the income statement, which shows the balance of the retained income at the balance sheet date. This is the only distributable reserve.

FRS 3 requires that a reconciliation of the movement in shareholders' funds be given where there have been any such changes which are not included in the statement of total recognized gains and losses. Items that would appear in such a reconciliation include:

1 dividends for the period;
2 capital contributions from shareholders or repaid to shareholders during the period;
3 goodwill that has been written off during the period.

An illustrative example is given below.

Reconciliation of movements in shareholders' funds

	£m
Income for the financial year	29
Dividends paid and proposed	(8)
	21
Other recognized gains and losses (net)	(1)
New share capital subscribed (total received)	20
Goodwill written off	(25)
Net addition for shareholders' funds	15
Opening shareholders' funds as at beginning of year	365
Closing shareholders' funds	380

Note of historical cost income

As we saw at the beginning of this chapter, the Companies Act 1981 allowed companies to draw up their accounts on either a historical cost basis or one of the alternative bases. An alternative basis that is widely used by companies which wish to make their accounts more realistic is historical cost modified by the revaluation of certain assets. Where a company produces financial statements on any basis other than historical cost, then FRS 3 requires that they include a note showing the historical cost income, and reconciling this amount to the actual income if the difference is material.

Two reasons for disclosing the income for a period on the unmodified historical cost basis of accounting are commonly cited. The first of these is to report the income of different companies on a more comparable basis. Where a company revalues an asset, depreciation is based on that increased value. Therefore, the reported income is less than it would have been if the revaluation had not taken place. The second reason is the wish of some users to assess the income on the sale of assets that is based on the historical cost of the assets sold rather than on the revalued amount. An illustrative example, adapted from FRS 3, is given below.

Note of historical cost income

	£m
Reported income on ordinary activities before taxation	45
Realization of property revaluation gains of previous years	9
Difference between a historical cost depreciation charge and the actual depreciation charge of the period calculated on revalued amounts	5
Historical cost income on ordinary activities before taxation	59

It is necessary to point out that since many of the non-current assets that are commonly revalued are those with long useful economic lives the effect of the cost concept is usually immaterial with regard to reported income (although it may be material with regard to the balance sheet).

Segmental information

A feature of business development that began in the 1960s has been the growth of diversified companies in which different segments of the operations are subject to significantly different notes of profitability, degrees of risk and opportunities for growth. The disclosure of segmental information for diversified companies is necessary in order to provide the user with a better basis for the assessment of the enterprise's past performance and future prospects.

The statutory requirements for disclosure of segmental information are contained in the Companies Act 1985. These were alluded to earlier in this chapter when we examined the disclosure requirements for turnover. These requirements were extended by SSAP 25 'Segmental Reporting' which was issued in 1990. Two types of segment are recognized:

1 class of business, the identification and designation of which is entirely a matter on which the directors must exercise their judgement;
2 geographical segments. Such a segment may consist of a single country or a group of countries in which the business operates or to which it supplies products or services.

SSAP 25 requires the segmental disclosure of:

1 turnover;
2 income before interest and tax;
3 net assets.

The purpose of the net assets disclosure requirement is that it enables the turnover and profit/loss of each segment to be related to the net assets which generate them.

Example 24.2	Sloan Products plc

Report and accounts for the year ended 31 December 20X0

The following illustration conforms with the requirements of the Companies Acts for the publication of income statements and balance sheets except that comparative figures are omitted for the sake of clarity. The illustration does not take account of the supplementary disclosures required by accounting standards such as earnings per share information nor of the Stock Exchange Listing Agreement. In the illustration the income statement and the balance sheet follow Format 1.

Sloan Products plc
Income statement for the year ended 31 December 20X0

Notes		£000
2	Turnover	22,340
	Cost of sales	(15,782)
	Gross income	6,558
	Distribution costs	(1,801)
	Administrative expenses	(1,972)
3	Operating income	2,785
6	Investment income	18
	Interest payable and similar charges	(210)
	Income on ordinary activities before taxation	2,593
7	Tax on income on ordinary activities	(808)
	Income for the financial year	1,785
8	Dividends paid and proposed	(900)
	Retained income for the year	885

Sloan Products plc
Balance sheet at 31 December 20X0

Notes		£000	£000
	Non-current assets		
9	Intangible assets		30
10	Tangible assets		7,828
11	Investments		150
			8,008
	Current assets		
12	Inventory	1,574	
13	Debtors	1,436	
14	Investments	68	
	Cash at bank and in hand	63	
		3,141	
15	**Creditors**: amounts falling due within one year	(1,840)	
	Net current assets		1,301
	Total assets *less* current liabilities		9,309
16	**Creditors**: amounts falling due after more than one year	360	
17	**Provisions for liabilities and charges**	134	(494)
			8,815
	Capital and reserves		
18	Called-up share capital		6,000
	Share premium account		123
19	Revaluation reserve		104
20	Income statement		2,588
			8,815

Sloan Products plc
Statement of total recognized gains and losses

	£000
Income for the financial year	1,785
Unrealized surplus on revaluation of properties	104
Total gains and losses recognized since last annual report	1,889

Sloan Products plc
Reconciliation of movements in shareholders' funds

	£000
Income for the financial year	1,785
Dividends paid and proposed	(900)
	885
New capital subscribed (total received)	200
Goodwill written off	(10)
Net addition to shareholders' funds	1,075
Opening shareholders' funds at the beginning of year	7,740
Closing shareholders' funds	8,815

Sloan Products plc
Notes to the accounts at 31 December 20X0

1 Accounting policies

(a) Basis of accounting
The accounts have been prepared under the historical cost concept, modified by the revaluation of properties.

(b) Depreciation
Depreciation is provided on all tangible non-current assets, other than freehold land, at rates calculated to write off the cost or valuation, less estimated residual value, of each asset evenly over its expected useful life, as follows:

| Freehold buildings | 40 years |
| Plant and machinery | 10 years |

(c) Goodwill
Goodwill acquired for cash relating to a business purchased by the company is amortized over five years. In the opinion of the directors this represents a prudent estimate of the period over which the company will derive a direct economic benefit from the products acquired as part of the business.

(d) Research and development expenditure
This is written off in the year in which it is incurred.

(e) Inventory and work-in-progress
These are stated at the lower of cost and net realizable value. In general, cost is determined on a first in, first out basis and includes transport and handling costs; in the case of manufactured products cost includes all direct expenditure and production overheads based on the normal level of activity. Net realizable value is based on estimated selling price less further costs expected to be incurred to completion and disposal.

(f) **Foreign currencies**

Assets and liabilities in foreign currencies are translated into sterling at the rates of exchange ruling at the balance sheet date.

(g) **Pensions**

Retirement benefits to the present employees of the company are funded by contributions from the company and employees. Payments are made to pension trusts, which are financially separate from the company, in accordance with calculations made periodically by consulting actuaries. The cost of these contributions and of providing pensions to some former employees is charged against the profits of the period.

2 Segmental information

	Turnover £000	Profit £000	Net assests £000
Class of business			
Domestic appliances	16,004	2,053	7,300
Water sports	6,336	732	1,515
	22,340	2,785	8,815
Geographical analysis			
United Kingdom	7,673	756	2,715
United States	2,342	359	864
Europe	12,325	1,670	5,236
	22,340	2,785	8,815

3 Operating income

Operating income is stated after charging:	£000
Depreciation	1,052
Amortization of goodwill	10
Hire of plant and machinery	43
Auditors' remuneration	11
Exceptional bad debt	7

4 Employee information

(a) **Number employed**

The average number of employees during the year was as follows:

Office and management	70
Domestic appliances	231
Water sports	68
	369

(b) **Payroll costs**

The aggregate payroll costs were:	£000
Wages and salaries	3,912
Social security costs	455
Other pension costs	188
	4,555

5 **Directors' emoluments**

	£000
Fee	37
Other emoluments	282
Pensions to past directors	16
	335

The chairman received emoluments of £42,000 and the highest-paid director £46,000. The emoluments of the other directors were within the ranges:

£15,001 – £20,000	2
£20,001 – £25,000	4
£30,001 – £35,000	7

6 **Investment income and interest payable**

	£000
Income from listed investments	18
Interest payable on bank loans, overdrafts and loans:	
repayable within five years	17
on other loans	141
	158

7 **Tax on income on ordinary activities**

	£000
Corporation tax at 30% on taxable profit for the year	756
Deferred taxation	52
	808

8 **Dividends**

		£000
Ordinary dividend:		
interim (paid)	5.0p per share	300
final (proposed)	10.0p per share	600
	15.0p	900

9 **Intangible non-current assets**

	£000	£000
Goodwill		
Cost		50
Accumulated amortization at 1 January 20X0	10	
Provision for the year to 31 December 20X0	10	20
Net book value at 31 December 20X0		30

10 Tangible assets

| Cost or valuation | Freehold | | Plant and | |
	Land	Buildings	machinery	Total
	£000	£000	£000	£000
Cost:				
At 1 January 20X0	204	1,146	9,250	10,600
Revaluation surplus	–	104	–	104
Additions	32	87	800	919
Disposals	(15)	(100)	(280)	(395)
At 31 December 20X0	221	1,237	9,770	11,228
Depreciation:				
At 1 January 20X0	–	480	2,083	2,563
Provision for year	–	32	1,020	1,052
Disposals	–	(75)	(140)	(215)
At 31 December 20X0	–	437	2,963	3,400
Net book values:	–			
At 31 December 20X0	221	800	6,807	7,828

Part of the buildings were revalued on 1 June 20X0 by Wheeler and Wright, chartered surveyors and valuers. It was valued on 'an open-market existing-use basis' and resulted in a revaluation surplus of £104,000. This has been credited to a revaluation reserve in the balance sheet.

11 Investments

Cost:	£000
At 1 January 20X0	125
Additions	25
Disposals	–
At 31 December 20X0	150

	£000
Listed investments	140
Unlisted investments	10
	150

Valuation:	£000
Listed investment at market value	210

The unlisted investment comprises £10,000 ordinary shares in Vesta plc, representing 15 per cent of the issued share capital of that company. Vesta plc was incorporated in Great Britain which is the principal country of operation. Taxation of £7,500 would be payable if the investments were sold at valuation.

12	Inventories	£000
	Raw materials	407
	Work-in-progress	283
	Finished goods	884
		1,574

Current replacement costs exceed costs of the above items as follows:

	£000
Raw materials	6
Work-in-progress	4
Finished goods	12
	22

13	Debtors	£000
	Trade debtors	1,082
	Other debtors	298
	Prepayments and accrued income	56
		1,436

14	Investments	£000
	Short-term deposits	68

15	Creditors: amounts falling due within one year	£000
	Bank loans and overdrafts	42
	Trade creditors	286
	Taxation and social security	1,105
	Accruals	7
	Proposed dividends	400
		1,840

16	Creditors: amounts falling due after more than one year	£000
	11% debentures	360

The debentures are secured by a floating charge over the company's assets. They are repayable at the company's option between 20X4 and 20X9 with a final redemption date of 31 December 20X9.

17	Provisions for liabilities and charges	£000
	Pensions and similar obligations	55
	Taxation, including deferred taxation	79
		134

	£000
18 Called-up share capital	
Allotted, issued and fully paid:	
Ordinary shares of £1 each	6,000
Authorized 8m ordinary shares of £1 each	8,000

	£000
19 Revaluation reserve	
At 1 January 20X0	–
Revaluation of buildings	104
Balance at 31 December 20X0	104

	£000
20 Income statement	
At 1 January 20X0	1,703
Retained for year	885
	2,588

	£000
21 Capital commitments	
Contracted for but not yet provided	72
Authorized by directors but not yet contracted for	230
	302

Additional disclosures

In addition to the financial statements and notes to the financial statements, certain other information is disclosed in a corporate report. The nature of this information has been affected, in recent years, by two events. The first was the publication of 'a statement of best practice', called *Operating and Financial Review*, by the ASB in 1993. This aimed to provide a framework for directors to discuss and analyse the business's performance and the factors underlying its results and financial position, in order to assist users to assess for themselves the future potential of the business. The second event was developments in corporate governance. As we saw earlier in this chapter, good corporate governance informs financial report users how the directors are running an organization to ensure its resilience. The Combined Code encourages companies to review the effectiveness of their governance procedures and to provide sufficient disclosure so that investors and others can assess company performance and governance practice and respond in an informed way.

In summary form, 'best practice' would include the following disclosures:

Chairman's statement

This statement comments on the overall financial results and the dividend recommended. Praise is normally heaped on the hard work of the staff which made the results possible. The outlook for the business is examined.

Operating review

The principal aim of the operating review is to enable the user to understand the dynamics of the various lines of business undertaken – that is, the main influences on the overall results, and how they interrelate. In particular, it should explain:

1 the dynamics of the business;
2 investment for the future;
3 income for the financial year, total recognized gains and losses, dividends and earnings per share;
4 accounting policies.

Financial review

This should explain:

1 the capital structure of the business and treasury policy;
2 taxation;
3 cash flows from operating activities;
4 current liquidity;
5 company resources and strengths not reflected in the balance sheet.

Board of directors

This report gives a brief biography of each director – their age, qualifications, date they were appointed, previous jobs and other directorships.

Report of directors

The directors' report normally deals with the following matters in particular:

1 principal activities of the company during the period and any significant changes in those activities;
2 significant developments during the year, e.g. acquisitions;
3 research and development, giving an indication of activities in this area;
4 significant changes in non-current assets;
5 post balance sheet events, particularly important events affecting the company which have occurred since the end of the year;
6 major shareholders, disclosing companies which hold 3 per cent or more of the company's share capital, in accordance with the Companies Act 1985;
7 charitable and political contributions;
8 employment policies;
9 employee participation.

Corporate governance

This statement outlines how the company has applied the principles set out in the Combined Code on Corporate Governance:

1 the board of directors – the structure of the board, directors' responsibilities, the provision of information to them;
2 board committees – the role of the audit, remuneration and personnel committees;
3 internal financial control;
4 risk management;
5 relations with shareholders.

Remuneration report

The aim of the Remuneration Committee is to determine the company's policy on remuneration, and in particular:

1 to consider and make recommendations to the board on remuneration arrangements including bonuses, share options, pension rights, service contracts and compensation payments;
2 to review employee share schemes;
3 to disclose the remuneration received by each director during the year;
4 to disclose directors' interests in ordinary shares and share options.

Statement of directors' responsibilities

Company law requires directors to prepare accounts for each financial year which give a true and fair view of the state of affairs and the profit and loss for the company. This statement confirms that the directors have:

1 used appropriate accounting policies, consistently applied;
2 made judgements and estimates that are reasonable and prudent;
3 ensured that all applicable accounting standards have been followed; and
4 prepared the financial statements on the going concern basis.

Report of auditors

The auditor give an opinion on whether the accounts give a true and fair view of the state of affairs of the company and of the profit and loss and cash flows for the year.

Notice of meeting

This statement gives notice of the location, time and agenda for the Annual General Meeting.

Small and medium-sized companies

The Companies Act 2006 allows small and medium-sized companies to file modified accounts with the Registrar of Companies, although they must still prepare accounts in full form for presentation to their members. A company qualifies to be treated as small or medium-sized for a financial year if, both for that year and the preceding year, it satisfies any two or more of the following conditions:

	Small	Medium
Turnover not exceeding	£5.6m	£22.8m
Balance sheet total not exceeding	£2.8m	£11.4m
Employees less than	50	250

Small and medium-sized companies benefit from modification or exemption from filing requirements applying to large companies. These are more extensive for small companies that do not need a full auditor's report, directors' report and income statements and need only publish abbreviated balance sheets. Medium-sized companies are exempted from the obligation of a full auditor's report, but must publish a directors' report, full balance sheet and an abbreviated income statement with relevant notes and accounting policies. Until recently, all companies were required to follow accounting standards, with a few exceptions, in spite of the fact that most have been developed particularly with the needs of large listed companies in mind. The FRSSE (Financial Reporting Standard for Small Entities), issued in 1997 and amended in 1999, is an optional standard which collects together in a simplified form the requirements from other accounting standards that are applicable to smaller entities.

Taxation in company accounts

There have been several changes to the UK tax system over the last few years, the most important of which were the abolition of repayment of tax credits to pension schemes and UK companies in 1997 and the abolition of advance corporation tax (ACT) in 1999. These changes made a significant proportion of SSAP 8 'The Treatment of Taxation under the Imputation System in the Accounts of Companies' redundant. SSAP 8 has been superseded by FRS 16 'Current Tax', which is applicable to accounting periods ending on or after 23 March 2000, although earlier application is encouraged.

The main principles under FRS 16 are:

(a) Current tax should be recognized in the income statement for the period. The only exception is where a gain or loss is recognized directly in the statement of total recognized gains and losses. In these cases the related tax should also be recognized in that statement.

(b) Dividends, interest and any other payables or receivables should be recognized –
  (i) net of any available tax credit or other taxes not payable wholly on behalf of the recipient;
  (ii) grossed up for any withholding taxes payable wholly on behalf of the recipient. Such taxes normally arise on overseas dividends.

This inclusion of dividends net of any tax credit, i.e. recording the income at the actual dividend received, is a significant departure from the old SSAP 8, provisions. Under SSAP 8, dividends received from UK companies were grossed up for ACT tax credits. The net effect of the abolition of ACT, and of the consequential introduction of FRS16, is that pre-tax income for a company that receives UK dividend income will be reduced.

Example 24.3 A company with taxable income of £80,000 declares a dividend of £21,000. The rate of corporation tax is assumed to be 30 per cent.

	£
Income before tax	80,000
Corporation tax at 30%	24,000
	56,000
Dividend	21,000
Retained income	35,000

Computing taxable income

Financial accounting, which is governed by a 'true and fair' presentation of financial position and the results of operations, does not share in all respects the principles which govern the computation of taxable income. Differences between 'book' and tax accounting originate from the following:

1 Some items which appear in the income statement are not allowed for tax purposes. These include entertaining expenses and certain types of donations and subscriptions.
2 Dividends received from other companies resident in the UK do not incur corporation tax.
3 Timing differences. The first two categories give rise to permanent differences where, because of legislation, particular revenues or expenses are omitted from the computation of taxable income. A timing difference, on the other hand, arises when an item is includable or deductible from income for tax purposes in one period, but in income for general reporting purposes in another. The different treatment of non-current assets creates timing differences because depreciation is not an allowance deductible for tax purposes, capital allowances being granted instead.

Example 24.4 A company has accounting income of £150,000, depreciation of £50,000, entertaining expenses and donations of £10,000, dividend received of £10,000 and capital allowances of £100,000. Taxable income is calculated as follows:

	£	£
Accounting income		150,000
Add: Depreciation		50,000
Add: Entertaining, etc.		10,000
		210,000
Less: Capital allowances	100,000	
Less: Dividend received	10,000	110,000
Taxable income		100,000

Deferred taxation

The provision for deferred taxation originates from the timing differences which we discussed above. Deferred tax arises because certain types of income and expenditure are not included in the calculation of taxable income at the same time as they are reflected in accounting income. When such timing differences arise, the tax assessed for the year is not regarded as the full liability for that year. Deferred tax is recorded to adjust the tax charge for the year to the amount that will be payable over time on the income shown in the accounts.

SSAP 15 requires deferred tax to be provided for using the 'partial provision' method. Provision is made only to the extent that the timing differences at the balance sheet date are expected to reverse without being replaced in the future.

Example 24.5 A company buys a machine for £50,000 which it intends to use for five years. Using the straight-line depreciation method, £10,000 would be written off each year. Although this is not currently available, we make the simplistic assumption that the system of capital allowances for tax purposes allows the entire cost of the machine to be written off in the first year. We assume accounting income is £200,000. Deferred taxation for the year is calculated as follows:

	£
Accounting income	200,000
Add: Depreciation	10,000
	210,000
Less: Capital allowances	50,000
Taxable profit	160,000
Tax on accounting income (30% of £200,000)	60,000
Tax on taxable income (30% of £160,000)	48,000
Deferred taxation	12,000

The income statement would be debited with the full amount of tax of £60,000 described as follows:

Corporation tax (including £12,000 credited to deferred taxation account)	£60,000

The deferred taxation account balance of £12,000 would be shown as a separate item in the balance sheet.

The 'partial provision' method required by SSAP 15 is criticized primarily because of its subjectivity (relying heavily on management expectations about future events) and is inconsistent with other areas of accounting. For these reasons, it has lost favour internationally. Other major standard setters and the International Accounting Standard IAS 12 now require deferred tax to be provided in full. In 1999, the ASB published an Exposure Draft of a new accounting standard for deferred tax which would require entities applying accounting standards to account for deferred tax on a 'full provision' basis, thereby bringing the UK more into line with international practice.

Summary

A public company that is listed on the Stock Exchange is required to present an annual report to its shareholders. The annual report consists of a number of statements. We have considered four financial statements, namely the income statement, the statement of total recognized gains and losses, the reconciliation of movements of shareholders' funds and the balance sheet and, in addition, certain other information which is disclosed in a corporate report. These disclosure requirements have been determined mainly by company law, accounting standards and the Listing Agreement. They have developed in an ad hoc fashion with no obvious, overriding rationale for the disclosure of information. We return to this topic in Part 4.

Problems (*indicates that a solution is to be found in the Lecturer's Guide*)

1* The partnership of Black, White and Grey are considering forming a limited company to obtain the benefits of limited liability. However, they are uncertain as to whether the capital of the company should be in shares or debentures and are also unsure of the method of appropriating income.

At 31 December 20X0 the capital accounts of the partners were:

	£
Black	44,000
White	36,000
Grey	48,000

Interest of 10 per cent per annum is allowed on the capital accounts.

Black is the managing partner and receives a salary of £20,000 p.a. White works part-time but does not receive a salary. Grey takes no active part in the business. The balance of income is shared equally.

The budgeted income for 20X1 is £260,000 before any appropriation to the partners.

Required:

(a) Advise the partners on the difference between debentures and ordinary shares and suggest the most appropriate capital structure for the new company.

(b) Advise the partners on a suitable method of rewarding themselves when the company is formed. Prepare an income appropriation account for year ended 31 December 20X1 on the assumption that the company is formed on 1 January 20X1, and your re-commendations are accepted. Assume a corporation tax rate of 30 per cent.

(Problem supplied by A J Naughton)

2 Scheid and Sons Ltd are considering expanding their operations. Several alternative strategies are being discussed for financing this expansion. The latest balance sheet of the company as at 31 December 20X0 is as follows:

Scheid and Sons Ltd
Balance sheet at 31 December 20X0

	£	£
Non-current assets		
Land and buildings		40,000
Plant and equipment		90,000
		130,000
Current assets		
Inventory	50,000	
Debtors	40,000	
Cash	5,000	
	95,000	
Creditors: amounts falling due within one year	25,000	
Net current assets		70,000
Total assets less current liabilities		200,000
Creditors: amounts falling due within one year:		
12% loan repayable 20X6		90,000
		110,000
Share capital and reserves		£
8% cumulative preference shares of £1 each		30,000
Ordinary shares of £1 each		50,000
Income statement		30,000
		110,000

The board of directors has identified the following possible alternative ways of obtaining the additional £50,000 required during the following year:

(a) Issue additional ordinary shares
(b) Issue additional 8 per cent preference shares
(c) Raise an additional long-term loan at 12 per cent.

Discuss the company's existing capital structure in terms of its gearing, and examine the advantages and disadvantages of each alternative method of financing the expansion plan.

3 The Huby Haulage Company Ltd produced the following trial balance at the end of December 20X0. Using this and the additional information following prepare an income statement, appropriation account and balance sheet for the year ended 31 December 20X0.

	£	£
£1 ordinary shares fully paid		200,000
Retained income		70,000
10% Debenture		50,000
Sales		365,000
Bank and cash	20,000	
Motor lorries – at cost	360,000	
– accumulated depreciation		110,000
Freehold property	165,000	
Repairs and renewals	22,000	
Drivers' wages	60,000	
Maintenance wages	15,000	
Parts and consumables	70,000	
Licences and insurance	20,000	
Administration salaries	20,000	
Sundry administrative expenses	12,000	
Drivers' overnight expenses	6,000	
Directors' salaries	25,000	
	795,000	795,000

(a) Drivers' claims for £150 relating to overnight expenses had not been taken into account.

(b) The parts and consumables account included parts valued at 1 January 20X0 at £15,000. Inventory taken on 31 December revealed that parts valued at £18,000 were held at that date.

(c) It was estimated that there was a prepayment of £4,000 with regard to licences and insurance at the end of 20X0.

(d) Depreciation of £62,500 is to be charged on vehicles for the year to 31 December 20X0.

(e) Tax is estimated at £22,400.

(f) There is a proposed dividend of £20,000.

4 Nether Edge plc, a retailing company, has an authorized share capital of 700,000 ordinary shares of £1 each. The following trial balance was extracted from the books of account as at 31 December 20X0.

	Dr	Cr
	£000	£000
Issued share capital		560
Share premium account		140
Income statement		180
10% Debentures		100
Furniture and fittings at cost	400	
Depreciation to 1 January 20X0		200
Cash balances	118	
Trade creditors		120
Trade debtors	500	
Inventory at 1 January 20X0	400	
Hire charges (distribution, vehicles, etc.)	680	
Purchases	1,000	
Administrative expenses	300	
Deferred taxation		80
Distribution costs	200	
Accrued expenses		50
Auditors' remuneration	40	
Interim dividend (paid on 1 July 20X0)	14	
Trade investments at cost (market value £170,000)	140	
Debenture interest (gross)	10	
Dividends received (on 1 December 20X0)		30
Turnover		2,400
Prepaid expenses	58	
	3,860	3,860

You are also given the following information:

(a) Turnover excludes value added tax.
(b) Inventory at 31 December 20X0 was valued at £600,000.
(c) Depreciation of £80,000 is to be charged on the furniture and fittings for the year to 31 December 20X0.
(d) Administration includes directors' emoluments of £110,000.
(e) The corporation tax payable (based on the profits for the year to 31 December 20X0 at a rate of 30 per cent) is estimated to amount to £100,000.
(f) The company proposes to pay a final ordinary dividend of 10 per cent.

Required:

Prepare financial statements for publication, together with relevant notes. (Work to the nearest £1,000.)

5* The following data has been extracted from the records of Purple plc at 31 March 20X1:

	£
Turnover	18,108,488
Cost of sales	16,471,616
Distribution costs	864,531
Administrative expenses	1,494,228
Surplus on sale of fixed assets	11,054
Interest receivable	21,721
Losses due to seizure of imported sugar	351,890
Overdraft interest	139,001
Loan interest (loan repayable 31 March 20X9)	162,299
Corporation tax for the year	8,101
Dividends (interim 0.25p per share)	17,292
Transfer from reserves	1,389,105

You are also given the following information:

(a) Number of ordinary shares in issue during the year: 7,192,380.
(b) Turnover excludes value added tax.
(c) Distribution costs and administrative expenses given above include the following items:

	£
Depreciation	365,928
Directors' emoluments	105,773
Auditors' remuneration	26,020
Hire of plant and machinery	3,084

You are required to prepare an income statement for publication, together with any notes required. It should comply with the Companies Acts.

Reference   Price Waterhouse Coopers (1999) *Value Reporting Forecast 2000.*

CHAPTER 25

Statement of cash flows

Setting the scene

As the value of intangible assets such as intellectual property or bonds increases as a proportion of the company's total value, while conversely the amount of long-term (i.e. non liquid) assets decreases, the correlation between book value and market value lessens. This increases the importance of cash flow as a key metric for judging company performance. If the company provides sufficient cash to shareholders through dividends or if management invests it in ways that investors approve, markets typically show their gratitude by increasing the company's share price.

(Price Waterhouse Coopers, 1999)

Learning objectives

After studying this chapter you should be able to:

1　appreciate the advantages of statements of cash flows;

2　prepare a statement of cash flows for publication;

3　identify the factors that cause a company's cash flow position to change.

In 1991 the Accounting Standards Board's first standard, FRS 1 'Statement of Cash Flows', revised in 1996, introduced the requirement for medium and large companies to prepare a statement of cash flows as part of their general financial statements. The International Accounting Standards Board followed suit in 1992 with IAS 7 'Statement of Cash Flows', revised in 1977 and in 2007 with the name changed to Cash Flow Statements.

As we saw in Chapter 7, the purpose of a statement of cash flows is to report the cash receipts and payments of an accounting period. The method of reporting cash flows in the United Kingdom differs from that recommended by the IASB. This difference was discussed briefly in Chapter 7, emphasis being given to the practice in the United Kingdom. This chapter elaborates further on the nature and preparation of statements of cash flows. The commitment of regulators is to seek convergence between national and international accounting rules. In view of this commitment, the practice of presenting statements of cash flows in the United Kingdom will ultimately converge towards IAS 7 'Statement of Cash Flow'. Accordingly, this chapter presents the recommendation for the preparation of the statement of cash flows prescribed by the IASB and compares the present practice in the United Kingdom based on FRS 1 with the practice that would result from convergence with IAS 7.

Advantages of the statement of cash flows

As with all financial reports, the importance of the statements of cash flows relates to the needs of users. The major report user groups were identified in Chapter 3. The purpose of financial reporting is to enable users to make decisions about the reporting entity. Finance theory postulates that these decisions will be influenced by assessments of future cash flows. It is argued that historical cash flows give relevant information about future cash flows because they illustrate how the entity generates cash and how it is spent. An entity may be considered as a cash-generating machine: cash flow information should help to show how the machine works (Lee, 1984; Lawson, 1978; Heath, 1978).

Historical cash flow information may assist users of financial statements in making judgements on the amount, timing and degree of certainty of future cash flows. It gives an indication of the relationship between profitability and cash generating ability and of the quality of the profit earned. Additionally, users of financial information often develop models to assess and compare the present value of the future cash flows of entities. Historical cash flow information could be useful to assess the accuracy of their previous predictions for that period.

A statement of cash flows, in conjunction with a balance sheet, provides information on liquidity, viability and financial adaptability. The balance sheet provides information about an entity's financial position at a particular point in time including assets, liabilities and equity and their relationship with each other at the balance sheet date. The balance sheet is often used to obtain information on liquidity, but the information is incomplete for this purpose as the balance sheet is drawn up at a particular point in time. Because statements of cash flows provide incomplete information for assessing future cash flows they should normally be used in conjunction with income statements. Some cash flows result from transactions that took place in an earlier period and some cash flows are expected to result in further cash flows in a future period.

Understanding changes in cash

In Chapter 7 we explained how cash flows are inextricably linked with the income statement and balance sheet. In Chapter 11 we examined the accounting equation (Capital + Liabilities = Assets) and explained how successive transactions maintain the accounting equation on which the balance sheet rests, though its constituent elements would vary. The accounting equation can be expanded to include both the short-term (less than one year) and long-term (more than one year) elements:

non-current assets + current assets = long-term creditors +
short-term creditors + capital and reserves

We can disaggregate current assets and isolate cash, and rewrite the equation as follows:

cash = long-term creditors + short-term creditors +
capital and reserves – non-current assets – inventory – debtors

This equation may be used to illustrate how changes in the various elements on the right-hand side of the equation affect changes in cash.

Cash inflows (i.e. increases in cash) result from:

1 increases in long-term creditors, short-term creditors and capital and reserves; and
2 decreases in non-current assets, inventory and debtors.

Cash outflows (i.e. decreases in cash) result from:

1 decreases in long-term creditors, short-term creditors and capital and reserves; and
2 increases in non-current assets, inventory and debtors.

For example, if short-term creditors (say, trade creditors) increase, cash increases because less cash is required to finance short-term creditors and this cash can be used for other purposes. Conversely, an increase in inventory causes an outflow (or a decrease) in cash because more cash is required to pay for extra inventory. Similarily, an increase in debtors is financed by an outflow of cash.

Reporting cash flows

The objective of IAS 7 'Statement of Cash Flows' is to require the presentation of information about the historical changes in cash and cash equivalents of an enterprise by means of a statement which classifies cash flows during the period according to operating, investing, and financing activities. All enterprises that prepare financial statements in conformity with IFRSs are required to present a statement of cash flows.

According to IAS 7, cash and cash equivalents comprise cash on hand and demand deposits, together with short-term, highly liquid investments that are readily convertible to a known amount of cash, and that are subject to an insignificant risk of changes in value. IAS 7 amplifies the classification of corporate cash flows as follows:

1 *operating activities* are the main revenue producing activities of the enterprise that are not investing or financing activities and include cash received from customers and cash paid to suppliers and employees;
2 *investing activities* relate to the acquisition and disposal of long-term assets and other investments that are not considered to be cash equivalents;
3 *financing activities* are activities that alter the equity capital and borrowing structure of the enterprise.

It is interesting to note that these three broad classes are directly related with the income statement and the balance sheet, thereby allowing these two documents to be reconciled on a cash flow basis through the statement of cash flows. The income statement reports on operating activities in calculating periodic net income; the asset side of the balance sheet reports on changes in the asset structure and the equity and liabilities side of the balance sheets portrays changes in the financing structure. The logic of the structure underlying the statement of cash flows, as stated in IAS 7, is to convert and integrate changes in these three areas of corporate management into their overall cash flow impact.

The classification of cash flow adopted by IAS 7 leaves open the manner in which interest, dividend and taxation cash flows should be reported. Interest and dividends received and paid may be classified as operating, investing, or financing cash flows, provided that they are classified consistently from period to period. Cash flows arising from taxes on income are normally classified as operating cash flows, unless they can be specifically identified with financing or investing activities. The lack of clarity is avoided in the classification adopted in the United Kingdom by FRS 1 'Statement of Cash Flows', which groups cash flows in terms of their nature rather than the function with which they are identified, as shown in the following classification:

1 operating activities,
2 returns on investments and servicing of finance;
3 taxation;
4 capital expenditure;
5 asset acquisitions and disposals;
6 dividends paid;
7 management of liquid resources;
8 financing.

Reporting on operating activities

In general, cash flows from operating activities are the cash effects of transactions and other events relating to operating or trading activities. Net cash flow from operating activities represents the net increase or decrease in cash resulting from operations shown on the income statement in arriving at operating income. Cash flows in respect of any provision for operating items such as the costs or redundancy or reorganization should also be included in this section.

A reconciliation between the operating income (for non-financial companies normally income before interest) reported in the income statement and the net cash flow from operating activities should be given either in the statement of cash flows or as a note. The reconciliation should disclose separately the movements in inventory, debtors and creditors related to operating activities and other differences between cash flows and results.

IAS 7 recommends the use of the direct method of reporting on operating activities, but allows the use of the indirect method. FRS 1 also allows a choice between two methods of presenting operating cash flows: the indirect and direct methods, the former being used generally in the United Kingdom. In the United States, where a similar choice between the indirect and direct methods is allowed, the vast majority of companies also use the indirect method (Kronquist and Newman-Limata, 1990).

The direct method shows each major class of gross cash receipts and gross cash payments (including, in particular, cash receipts from customers, cash payments to suppliers and cash payments to and on behalf of employees), aggregating to the net cash flow from operating activities. The indirect method adjusts accrual basis income before tax for non-cash charges and credits to reconcile it to the net cash flow from operating activities.

The format for reporting operating cash flows under the direct and indirect methods respectively is as follows:

Operating cash flows under the direct method:

Cash receipts from customers	……..
Cash paid to suppliers	……..
Cash paid to employees	……..
Cash paid for other operating expenses	……..
Interest paid	……..
Income taxes paid	……..
Net cash from operating activities	……..

Operating cash flows under the indirect method:

Income before interest and income taxes		....
Add back depreciation		....
Add back amortization of goodwill		....
Increase in receivables		....
Decrease in inventories		....
Increase in trade payables		....
Interest expense	....	
Less interest accrued but not yet paid	....	
Interest paid		....
Income taxes paid		....
Net cash from operating activities		....

Example 25.1 XYZ Limited is a United Kingdom company. It complies with FRS 1 and not IAS 7 in preparing the following statement of cash flows:

Statement of cash flows for the year ended 31 March 20X1

	£000
Net cash inflow from operating activities (see 1 below)	6,889
Returns on investments and servicing of finance (see 2 below)	2,999
Corporation tax paid	(2,922)
Capital expenditure (see 3 below)	(1,525)
	5,441
Equity dividends paid	(2,417)
	3,024
Management of liquid resources (see 4 below)	(450)
Financing (see 5 below)	57
Increase in cash (see 6 below)	2,631

1 Reconciliation of operating income to net cash inflow from operating activities under the indirect method

	£000	£000
Operating income		6,022
Depreciation charges		893
Loss on sale of tangible non-current assets		6
Increase in inventory		(194)
Increase in debtors		(72)
Increase in creditors		234
Net cash inflow from operating activities		6,889

2 Net cash inflow from operating activities under the direct method:

	£000	£000
Cash received from customers	98,524	
Cash payments to suppliers	(53,673)	
Cash paid to employees	(37,962)	
Cash flow from operating activities		6,889

The principal advantage of this method is that information about operating cash receipts and payments may be useful in assessing future cash flows.

3	Returns on investments and servicing of finance		
	Interest received	3,011	
	Interest paid	(12)	
			2,999

4	Capital expenditure		
	Payments to acquire intangible non-current assets	(71)	
	Payments to acquire tangible non-current assets	(1,496)	
	Receipts from sales of tangible non-current assets	42	
			(1,525)

5	Management of liquid resources		
	Purchase of treasury bills	(650)	
	Sale of treasury bills	200	
			(450)

6	Financing		
	Issue of ordinary share capital	211	
	Repurchase of debenture loan	(149)	
	Expenses paid in connection with share issues	(5)	
			57

7	Reconciliation of net cash flow to movement in net debt		
	Increase in cash in the period	2,631	
	Cash repaying debenture	149	
	Cash paid to increase liquid resources	450	
	Change in net debt*		3,230
	Net debt at 1 April 20X0		(2,903)
	Net cash at 31 March 20X1		327

* In this example all changes in net debt are cash flows.

8 Analysis of changes in net debt

	At 1 April 20X0	Cash flows	At 31 March 20X1
	£000	£000	£000
Cash in hand, at bank	42	847	889
Overdrafts*	(1,784)	1,784	
		2,631	
Debt due within one year	(149)	149	
Debt due after one year	(1,262)		(1,262)
Current asset investments	250	450	700
Total	(2,903)	3,230	327

*Assume that the overdraft is repaid

Returns on investments and servicing of finance

These are receipts resulting from the ownership of an investment and payments to providers of finance. They include: interest received, including any related tax recovered; dividends received (disclosing separately dividends received from equity accounted entities), net of any credits; interest paid (whether or not the charge is capitalized), including any tax deducted and paid to the relevant tax authority; the interest element of finance lease rental payments.

Taxation

The cash flows included under the heading taxation are cash flows to or from taxation authorities in respect of the reporting entity's revenue and capital profits. Taxation cash inflows include cash receipts from the relevant tax authority of tax rebates, claims or returns of overpayments. Taxation cash outflows are cash payments to the relevant tax authority of tax.

Capital expenditure

The cash flows included in 'capital expenditure' are those related to the acquisition or disposal of any non-current assets, and any current asset investment not included in liquid resources.

Cash inflows from 'capital expenditure' include receipts from sales or disposals of non-current assets other than trades, businesses or entities, and receipts from sales of investments in other entities. Cash outflows from capital expenditure include payments to acquire non-current assets and payments to acquire investments in other entities.

Dividends paid

The cash outflows included in 'dividends paid' are those related to dividends paid on shares.

Management of liquid resources

To assist users to assess the liquidity and financial adaptability of companies, statements of cash flows reflect the way that liquid resources are managed to ensure the availability of cash to carry on or expand the business. Each company has a particular policy on which current asset investments it uses as a store of liquid resources, although an investment must be a readily disposable current asset to qualify (debtors, therefore, do not qualify). The 'management of liquid resources' section could, therefore, include cash flows related to a wide range of investments and each company should explain its policy on liquid resources and any changes to it.

Cash inflows in management of liquid resources include sales of government securities, debt instruments of other entities held as current assets, derivative instruments held as liquid resources and highly liquid equity investments held as liquid resources. Cash outflows in management of liquid resources include purchases of government securities, debt instruments of other entities held as current assets, derivative instruments held as liquid resources and highly liquid equity investments held as liquid resources.

Financing

Financing cash flows comprise receipts from or repayments to external providers of finance of amounts in respect of principal amounts of finance.

Financing cash inflows include: receipts from issuing shares or other equity instruments; receipts from issuing debentures, loans, notes and bonds and from other long- and short-term borrowings (other than overdrafts).

Financing cash outflows include: repayments of amounts borrowed (other than overdrafts); the capital element of finance lease rental payments; payments to re-acquire or redeem the entity's shares; payments of expenses or commissions on any issue of shares.

The amounts of any finance cash flows received from or paid to equity accounted entities should be disclosed separately.

Reconciliation of net debt

A note reconciling the movement of cash in the period with the movement in net debt should be included either at the end of the statement of cash flows or in a note. The reconciliation is not part of the statement of cash flows: if included at the end of the statement of cash flows, it should be clearly labelled and kept separate. The objective of the reconciliation of cash flows to the movement in net debt is to provide information that assists in the assessment of liquidity, solvency and financial adaptability.

Net debt is defined to include liabilities in relation to borrowings less assets comprising the entity's store of liquidity because movements of net debt so defined are widely used as indicating changes in liquidity, and therefore assist in assessments of the financial strength of the entity. The definition excludes non-equity shares of the entity because, although these have features that may be similar to those of liabilities in relation to borrowings, they are not actually liabilities of the entity. The definition also excludes debtors and creditors because, while these are sources of finance to the entity, their main role is as part of the entity's trading activities. This reconciliation will enable users to assess the cash flows of the entity in the wider context of the information given in the other financial statements.

Exceptional and extraordinary items

Where cash flows relate to items that are classed as exceptional items in the income statement, these exceptional cash flows should be shown under the appropriate standard headings, according to the nature of each item. Sufficient disclosure of the nature of cash flows relating to exceptional items should be given in a note to the statement of cash flows to allow a user of the financial statement to gain an understanding of the effect on the reporting entity's cash flows of the underlying transactions.

Where cash flows relate to items that are classed as extraordinary items in the income statement, these extraordinary cash flows should be shown separately under the appropriate standard headings, according to the nature of each item. In the extremely rare circumstances where it is inappropriate to include a cash flow relating to an extraordinary item under one or more of the standard headings within the statement of cash flows the cash flows should be shown within a separate section in the statement. Sufficient disclosure of the nature of cash flows relating to extraordinary items should be given in a note to the statement of cash flows, to allow a user of the financial statements to gain an understanding of the effect on the reporting entity's cash flows of the underlying transactions.

Converting from FRS 1 Statement of cash flows to IAS 7 Statement of cash flows

Using the example from XYZ Limited, a statement of cash flows presented according to IAS 7 would appear as follows:

XYZ Limited Statement of cash flows for the year ended 31 March 20X1

Cash flows from operating activities	
Net Income	6,099 [6,022 + 2,999 – 2,922]
Adjustments to reconcile net income to cash provided by operating activities:	
Depreciation	893
Loss on sale of asset	6
Increase in inventories	(194)
Increase in debtors	(72)
Increase in creditors	234
Net cash provided by operating activities	6,966
Cash flows from investing activities	

Purchase of intangible assets	(71)
Purchase of tangible assets	(1,496)
Sale of assets	42
Purchase of treasury bills	(650)
Sale of treasury bills	200
Net cash used by investing activities	(1,975)
Cash flows from financing activities	
Issue of ordinary share capital	211
Repurchase of debenture loan	(149)
Expenses of share issue	(5)
Dividends	(2,417)
Net cash used by financing activities	(2,360)
Increase/(decrease) in cash	2,631

Example 25.5 The draft balance sheets of Stannington plc as at 31 December 20X0 and 31 December 20X1 are as follows:

	20X0		20X1	
	£000	£000	£000	£000
Non-current assets				
Land and buildings at cost		2,400		3,000
Aggregate depreciation on buildings		(450)		(525)
Plant and equipment at cost		3,000		5,100
Aggregate depreciation on plant		(1,350)		(1,875)
		3,600		5,700
Current assets				
Inventory	900		1,125	
Debtors	450		675	
Cash	300		–	
	1,650		1,800	
Current liabilities				
Creditors	300		450	
Taxation	375		450	
Dividends	225		225	
Overdraft	–		75	
	900		1,200	
Net current assets		750		600
		4,350		6,300
Capital and reserves				
Ordinary share capital		3,000		4,500
Share premium		300		600
Retained income		750		1,200
10% debentures repayable 31/12/20X1		300		–
		4,350		6,300

Extracts from the income statement for the year ended 31 December 20X1 are as follows:

	£000	£000
Income before taxation		1,350
Taxation for the year		525
		825
Dividends for the year		
Interim dividends paid	150	
Final dividend proposed	225	375
Retained income for the year		450
Retained income at 1 January 20X1		750
Retained income at 31 December 20X1		1,200

Further information:

- Depreciation charge for the year amounted to £900,000.
- An item of plant was disposed of during the year for £225,000. It had cost £450,000 when new and had a depreciated value of £150,000.

Stannington plc.
Statement of cash flows for the year ended 31 December 20X1

	£000	£000
Net cash inflow from operating activities		1,905
Returns on investment and servicing of finance		
Interest paid (W1)		(30)
Corporation tax paid (W2)		(450)
Capital expenditure		
Payments to acquire fixed assets (W3)	(3,150)	
Receipts from sales of fixed assets	225	
Net cash outflow from the capital expenditure		(2,925)
		(1,500)
Dividends paid		(375)
		(1,875)
Financing		
Issue of ordinary share capital (W4)	1,800	
Repurchase of debenture loan	(300)	
Net cash inflow from financing		1,500
Decrease in cash		(375)

Notes to the statement of cash flows

1 Reconciliation of operating profit to net cash inflow from operating activities

	£000
Operating income (1,350 + 30)	1,380
Depreciation charges	900
Profit on sale of fixed assets	(75)
Increase in inventory	(225)
Increase in debtors	(225)
Increase in creditors	150
Net cash inflow from operating activities	1,905

2 Reconciliation of net cash flow to movement in net debt

	£000
Decrease in cash in period	£375
Cash repaying debenture	£300
Change in net debt	(75)
Net debt at 1.1.20X1	–
Net cash at 31.12.20X1	(75)

Workings

1 Interest paid

10% × £300,000 = £30,000

2 Tax and dividends payable

	Tax	Dividends
	£000	£000
Opening balances	375	225
Appropriations for year	525	375
Total liability for the year	900	600
Closing balances	450	225
	450	375

3 Non-current asset acquisitions

	Land/buildings	Equipment
	£000	£000
Opening balances	2,400	3,000
Less: cost of disposals	–	450
	2,400	2,550
Closing balances	3,000	5,100
Acquisitions during year	600	2,550

4 Share issues

	£000
Increase in share capital	1,500
Increase in share premium account	300
Total cash received	1,800

Stannington plc.
Statement of cash flows for the year ended 31 December 20X1 (converting from FRS 1 Statement of cash flows to IAS 7 Statement of cash flows)

Cash flows from operating activities	
Net income	825
Adjustments to reconcile net income to cash provided by operating activities:	
Depreciation	900
Profit on sale of asset	(75)
Increase in inventories	(225)
Increase in debtors	(225)
Increase in creditors	150
Tax due	525
Tax paid	(450)
Net cash provided by operating activities	1,425
Cash flows from investing activities	
Purchase of land and buildings	(600)
Purchase of equipment	(2,550)
Sale of assets	225
Net cash used by investing activities	(2,925)
Cash flows from financing activities	
Issue of ordinary share capital	1,800
Repurchase of debenture loan	(300)
Dividends	(375)
Net cash used by financing activities	1,125
Increase/(decrease) in cash	(375)

Summary

It is the ability to generate cash that determines the success of an entity. Therefore the major user groups of financial statements use an assessment of future cash flows on which to base their economic decisions about entities.

Historical cash flow information may assist users of financial statements in making judgements on the amount, timing and uncertainty of future cash flows. It gives an indication of the relationship between profitability and cash generating ability and thus of the quality of the profit earned.

Statements of cash flows are important for financial planning purposes. In this context, they are associated with budget forecasts. The particular importance of the cash flow budget is to highlight the financial consequence of budgets and predict the cash surpluses and deficits which will occur periodically through the planning period.

Problems (*indicates that a solution is to be found in the Lecturer's Guide*)

1 The following information relates to South Ltd for the year ended 31 December 20X0:

	£000
Cash and cash equivalents	
at 1 January 20X0	8,952
at 31 December 20X0	10,043
Operating income	4,100
Depreciation charges	1,080
Increase in working capital	165
Proceeds of sale of tangible assets (book value £116,000)	96
Issue of ordinary share capital	400
Expenses in connection with share issue	10
Purchase of intangible non-current assets	150
Purchase of tangible non-current assets	2,540
Corporation tax paid	2,460
Dividends paid	1,570
Interest received	2,290

Required:

Prepare a statement of cash flows for the year ended 31 December 20X0 in accordance with FRS 1 Statement of cash flows.

2 Set out below are the condensed balance sheets for Walkley Ltd for 20X0 and 20X1, and an income statement for the year ended 31 December 20X1.

Balance sheets

	20X0 £000	20X1 £000
Ordinary share capital (£1 shares)	740	940
Revenue reserves	531	864
Share premium account	–	100
Loans	320	150
Trade creditors	152	141
Proposed dividends	140	170
Current taxation	470	602
Bank overdraft	–	766
	2,353	3,733

Plant and machinery		
Cost	2,700	3,831
Accumulated depreciation	748	1,125
	1,952	2,706
Inventory	203	843
Debtors	147	184
Cash at bank	51	–
	2,353	3,733

Income statement for the year ended 31 December 20X1

	£000	£000
Income before tax		1,195
Corporation tax		602
Income after tax		593
Ordinary dividends		
Paid	90	
Proposed	170	260
		333

Notes:

1 The only new loan raised during the year was a five-year bank loan amounting to £65,000.
2 Depreciation charged during the year amounted to £401,000.
3 During the year, plant which originally cost £69,000 was disposed of for proceeds of £41,000.
4 During the year, the company offered 200,000 shares by way of rights to existing shareholders.

Required:

Prepare a statement of cash flows for 20X1 in accordance with FSB 1 Statement of cash flows.

3* The balance sheets for Jobin & Co Ltd for the years ended 20X0, 20X1 and 20X2 are as follows:

Jobin & Co Ltd
Balance sheets at 31 December

	20X0 £000	20X1 £000	20X2 £000
Non-current assets			
Plant and equipment	13,200	16,110	16,410
Current assets			
Inventory	2,190	2,280	2,490
Trade debtors	2,040	2,100	2,430
Short-term investments	4,200	1,800	1,290
Cash at bank and in hand	1,920	1,650	2,160
Creditors: amounts falling due within one year			
Short-term loans	(2,340)	(2,580)	(2,550)
Trade creditors	(2,760)	(2,610)	(2,670)
Taxation	(360)	(420)	(530)
Net current assets	5,460	5,610	5,750
Net current assets	4,890	2,220	2,620
Total assets less current liabilities	18,090	18,330	19,030
Capital and reserves			
Called-up share capital	4,500	4,500	4,500
Share premium account	9,000	9,000	9,000
Other reserves	3,280	4,060	4,570
Income statement	1,310	770	960
	18,090	18,330	19,030
Other data			
Income before tax	960	1,020	1,590
Tax on annual profit	360	420	530
Tax paid during the year	300	360	420
Annual depreciation	645	780	900
Dividends declared and paid	360	360	360

In 20X1, equipment was sold at a loss of £210,000. New plant in 20X1 cost £5,100,000 and in 20X2 cost £1,200,000. Income transferred to other reserves in 20X1 and 20X2 amounted to £780 and £510 respectively.

Required:

Prepare a statement of cash flows for 20X1 and 20X2 in accordance with FSR 1 and show how they would be presented under IAS 7.

4 Set out below are the condensed balance sheets for Zepf and Co Ltd for 20X0 and 20X1, and an income statement for the year ended 31 December 20X1.

Comparative balance sheets at 31 December 20X0 and 20X1

	20X0		20X1	
	£000	£000	£000	£000
Non-current assets				
Land and buildings at cost	240		240	
Accumulated depreciation	30		40	
		210		200
Plant and machinery at cost	262		694	
Accumulated depreciation	42		84	
		220		610
Motor vehicles	60		60	
Accumulated depreciation	30		34	
		30		26
		460		836
Current assets				
Inventory	204		234	
Trade debtors	360		432	
Cash at bank and in hand	276		10	
	840		676	
Creditors: amounts falling due within one year:				
Trade creditors	(144)		(192)	
Taxation	(60)		(80)	
Proposed dividend	(16)		(20)	
	(220)		(292)	
Net current assets		620		384
Total assets *less* current liabilities		1,080		1,220
Creditors: amounts falling due after one year:				
7% debenture loans		140		200
		940		1,020
Capital and reserves				
Called-up share capital		600		600
Share premium account		100		100
Other reserves		80		100
Income statement		160		220
		940		1,020

Summarized income statement for the year ended
31 December 20X1

	£000	£000
Turnover		1,324
Cost of sales		936
Gross income		388
Distribution costs	98	
Administrative expenses	100	
		198
Income on ordinary activities		190
Taxation on ordinary activities		80
		110
Loss on the sale of assets		10
Income for the financial year		100
Ordinary dividend proposed		(20)
Transfer to reserves		(20)
Retained income for the financial year		60

Plant and machinery recorded at cost of £28,000 and at written-down value of £16,000 was sold for £6,000.

Required:

Prepare a statement of cash flows for the year ended 31 December 20X1 under FSB 7 and show how it would be presented under IAS 7.

5* Kashvlow Limited has the following balance sheets for the years ended 31 December 20X0 and 31 December 20X1.

Kashvlow Limited
Balance sheet as at 31 December 20X0

	£	£		£	£	£
					Accumulated	
Capital			**Non-current assets**	Cost	depreciation	
Ordinary shares		350,000	Buildings	310,000		310,000
Redeemable		150,000	Plant	431,000	195,000	236,000
preference shares						
Income statement		210,000	Vehicles	196,000	85,000	111,000
		710,000		937,000	280,000	657,000
Long-term liabilities						
Debentures		50,000	Investment in associate			120,000
Current liabilities			**Current assets**			
Taxation	70,000		Stock	100,000		
Dividend	40,000		Debtors	120,000		
Creditors	110,000		Bills receivable	20,000		
Bank overdraft	40,000		Cash in hand	3,000		
		260,000				243,000
		1,020,000				1,020,000

Kashvlow Limited
Balance sheet as at 31 December 20X1

	£	£ Non-current assets		£ Cost	£ Accumulated depreciation	£
Capital						
Ordinary shares		350,000	Buildings	250,000		250,000
Capital redemption reserve fund		150,000	Plant	460,000	287,000	173,000
Income statement		139,000	Vehicles	220,000	100,000	120,000
		639,000		930,000	387,000	543,000
Long-term liabilities						
Debentures		100,000	Investment in associate			140,000
			Loan to associate			40,000
Current liabilities			**Current assets**			
Taxation	80,000		Inventory		120,000	
Dividend	60,000		Debtors		170,000	
Creditors	140,000		Bank balance		5,000	
			Cash in hand		1,000	
		280,000				296,000
		1,019,000				1,019,000

Notes:

1   During the year a building was sold for £90,000 and motor vehicles costing £90,000 were sold for £40,000, a book loss of £10,000. New vehicles were bought for £114,000.
2   Depreciation is 20 per cent straight-line for plant, and 25 per cent straight-line for vehicles.
3   A £15,000 premium on the redemption of preference shares was written off to P & L in the year.

Required:

(a)   Reconstruct the company's income statement for 20X1.
(b)   Prepare a statement of cash flows in the formats required under FSB 1 and IAS 7 respectively.

References

Heath, L.C. (1978) *Financial Reporting and the Evaluation of Solvency*, Accounting Research Monograph 3, American Institute of Certified Public Accountants.

Kronquist, S.L. and Newman-Limata, N. (1990) Corporate cash flows, *Management Accounting* (USA), July.

Lawson, G.H. (1978) The rationale of cash flow accounting, in C. van Dam (ed.), *Trends in Managerial and Financial Accounting*, Martinus Nijhoff.

Lee, T.A. (1984) *Cash Flow Accounting*, Van Nostrand Reinhold.

Price Waterhouse Coopers (1999) *Value Reporting Forecast 2000*.

CHAPTER 26

Interpreting and comparing financial reports

Setting the scene

Financial statements generally provide users with essential information that heavily influences their decisions. They are an excellent model for capturing and organising financial information. They package information in a structured fashion that permits analysis of a wide range of trends and relationships among the data. These trends and relationships, in turn, provide considerable insight into a company's opportunities and risks, including growth and market acceptance, costs, productivity, profitability, liquidity and many others.

(AICPA, 1994)

Learning objectives

After studying this chapter you should be able to:

1 conduct a ratio analysis using the contents of the financial statements of a commercial organization;

2 discuss the limitations of the analytical techniques used;

3 examine the ability of published financial statements to predict business failure.

Financial reports combine facts and personal judgements. In attempting to interpret the information disclosed in financial reports, it is necessary to be aware of the limitations imposed by accounting concepts and methods of valuation.

Aggregate figures are always of differing orders of magnitude and do not facilitate comparisons. Ratio analysis is the most widely used technique for interpreting and comparing financial reports. Ratios are useful for summarizing relationships and results that are significant as critical business indicators of performance, for example, the ratio of net profit to assets employed. Ratios are particularly useful for analysing how the performance of a given company evolves through time and for comparing one company with another. Companies differ from each other in many ways. By themselves, ratios do not provide sufficient information about a company to reach definitive conclusions and financial analysts use other sources of market information. The role of ratio analysis is to help focus the questions on key issues that need further investigation.

On a systematic basis, ratio analysis allows trends to emerge, and throws into relief the significance of changes indicated by current events. Since the future is uncertain, the analyst has to rely substantially on past behaviour in indications of future changes. Trends developed from ratios are very useful for making predictions.

One important use of ratio analysis is to make comparisons that assist in forecasting future events. The fact that Ada Ltd has a ratio of net income to assets employed of 10 per cent in the year 20X0 is meaningless by itself. To be meaningful, that ratio must be compared with the ratios obtained from the results of previous years, and may be made even more meaningful by comparing it with those of its competitors.

In the United Kingdom, the Centre for Inter-Firm Comparisons Ltd, a non-profit-making organization established in 1959 by the British Institute of Management in association with the British Productivity Council, has greatly facilitated inter-firm comparisons. It collects a large amount of management accounting information from its subscribers. Maintaining a high level of confidentiality, it computes a whole range of ratios which are reported back to subscribers together with the best, worst and average ratios.

The nature of ratio analysis

In this chapter, discussion focuses on a number of important ratios dealing with two critical areas. They are the ability of the firm to survive and grow and the efficiency of its financial performance. They relate directly to the two central postulates of a normative theory of financial reporting discussed in Chapter 6. Both postulates are interrelated and interdependent. The first postulate is the maintenance and increase of the value of invested capital and the second is the level of income which investors expect to derive from invested capital.

Maintaining the value of the capital invested depends on the ability of the firm to survive. Solvency is the most important criterion of survivability. It is defined as the ability of the firm to meet its debts as they fall due for payment. Solvency is a matter of both fact and law. If a creditor presses a claim for payment of the amount due, and the firm is unable to pay this is a fact; that is to say it is a state of affairs that can be objectively verified and confirmed by independent auditors if necessary. The firm may have substantial assets which cannot be realized immediately. Its prospects may not necessarily be bad in terms of its future, or even its present, ability to generate income. Its insolvency is determined by the fact that it has insufficient liquid resources in cash or near cash to meet individual claims and has no further credit facilities available.

Solvency becomes a question of law by the formal process in which the creditor seeks the recovery of a debt through a court of law, and the issuance of a court order for payment against the defaulting firm. The firm is declared insolvent if at the end of the period of notice determined by the court, it still has not made the payment. The legal procedure for the firm's liquidation by winding-up ensues with the appointment of a liquidator by the court.

The second postulate concerns the level of income which investors expect to derive from their investment. This depends, firstly on the firm's current financial performance, and secondly on its prospects for future growth. Ratios of financial performance are one way that the market assesses the performance and prospects of a company. Shareholder income consists of a stream of dividend flows. Over the long term, dividends are related to the level of corporate earnings, and are reflected in the market value of the shares. Ratio analysis provides a view on the efficiency of current financial performance by relating net income to such indicators as net assets or share prices and on the attractiveness of the investment for shareholders by relating dividends to corporate net profit and to share prices. For companies with a market quotation, reported financial performance is a major factor in the determination of share price and assessing shareholder value.

Example 26.1 The ordinary shares of Ada Ltd are priced currently at £2 each. The Income Statement for the year ended 31 December 20X0 shows the following information:

Ada Ltd
Income Statement for the year ended 31 December 20X0

	£
Turnover	350,000
Cost of sales	208,000
Gross income	142,000
Distribution costs	80,000
Administrative expenses	30,000
Interest on long-term loan	4,000
Income on ordinary activities	28,000
Tax on ordinary activities	14,000
After-tax income on ordinary activities	14,000
Preference dividend	2,000
Income for the financial year	12,000
Ordinary dividend	5,000
Retained income	7,000

Ada Ltd
Balance sheet at 31 December 20X0

	£	£
Non-current assets		
Tangible assets at cost less depreciation		130,000
Current assets	£	
Inventory (opening £35,000)	45,000	
Debtors	40,000	
Cash	7,000	
	92,000	
Creditors: amounts falling due within one year:		
Trade creditors	23,000	
Other liabilities	28,000	
	51,000	
Net current assets		41,000
Total assets *less* current liabilities		171,000
Creditors: amounts falling due after more than one year:		
Debenture loans		40,000
		131,000
Capital and reserves		
80,000 £1 ordinary shares		80,000
20,000 10% preference shares		20,000
Undistributed income		31,000
		131,000

The analysis of solvency

Ratio analysis makes a limited contribution to assessing solvency for the following reasons:

1 The firm's total current liabilities and total current assets at the end of the last accounting period may indicate that its financial stability is precarious, but solvency happens in the present and not in the past. A firm may be perfectly solvent on the last day of the accounting period, and may now be insolvent by reason of the sudden withdrawal of a credit facility upon which it relied.

2 The balance sheet does not reveal sources of credit which the firm may tap, or the willingness of creditors and investors to see the firm through a difficult period.

3 The information disclosed in financial reports is incomplete with respect to other facts affecting solvency. It is important to have a good idea of a company's pattern of receipts and payments in interpreting solvency. For example, a supermarket will be able to generate funds from inventories much more quickly than a manufacturing company.

4 Companies may window-dress their balance sheets to make their performance appear better than it really is. As far as solvency is concerned the possibilities are: getting distributors to accept delivery of more products than they really need (on a sale or return basis), thereby reducing inventories and increasing accounts receivable (improving the acid-test ratio); paying back a short-term loan just prior to the year end and then reinstating it again immediately at the beginning of the following financial year (this improves the current ratio).

Short-term solvency

In the face of a deteriorating financial situation, long-term creditors and short-term creditors exhibit different behaviours. Long-term creditors, such as debenture-holders, may attempt to realize their security by selling specific assets mortgaged under the debenture instrument or they may be willing to wait for a viable rescue operation. In the first case they precipitate bankruptcy proceedings by depriving the firm of a necessary asset. In the second case they play a wait-and-see game. However, short-term creditors, such as trade creditors, are generally unwilling to allow credit to a firm which is running into financial difficulties, and usually precipitate insolvency.

Small firms in difficulties perish quickly. Large firms create losses not only for short-term creditors but also for financial institutions that may have extended large loans and credit facilities. For these reasons, financial institutions are usually unwilling to provoke large scale insolvencies and will even extend credit to prevent insolvency crystallizing. Indicators of short-term financial stability are particularly important for companies listed on stock exchanges. Two types of ratios are useful in this respect:

1 Ratios that relate current assets to current liabilities and indicate an imbalance between the burden of immediate debts in relation to the firm's ability to meet such debts.

2 Ratios that indicate the rate at which short-term assets are utilized, thereby giving a measure of the elasticity with which they are transformed into cash.

Ratios of current assets to current liabilities

Two ratios in common use are:

1 the current ratio;
2 the acid test (or quick) ratio.

The *current ratio* is the ratio of current assets to current liabilities expressed as follows:

$$\frac{\text{current assets}}{\text{current liabilities}}$$

Ada Ltd has current assets valued at £92,000 and current liabilities amounting to £51,000. The current ratio is 1.8:1. It will be recalled that current assets minus current liabilities measures working capital, that is, the long-term funds conventionally regarded as being devoted to financing current operations.

Using the current ratio as a predictor of financial stability presents a number of problems. First, since current assets include inventory and trade debtors as well as cash, an element of subjectivity is introduced into this ratio by methods of valuing inventory (LIFO, FIFO, Average) and the assessment of the likelihood of bad debts. Second, an efficient business that has a high rate of cash flow from current operations may be able to reduce inventory and debtor levels without affecting its financial stability. Its current ratio may be relatively low, but it remains a viable concern. Some businesses, such as cash retailers, have a rapid inventory turnover and few debtors. In such a case, a very low current ratio is normal (for some supermarkets it is actually negative). By contrast, a firm with a high current ratio represented by high levels of inventory, debtors and cash may be a very inefficient firm. The current ratio may conceal a poor rate of funds generation, and a very unstable situation. For this reason, Glautier (1971) has argued that the current ratio is not a useful indicator of solvency from a theoretical viewpoint. Nevertheless, it should be said that what is considered a normal current ratio is peculiar to each industry, and financial analysts tend to look for current ratios falling within acceptable limits for the company's particular sector.

The *acid test* ratio is based on a stricter view of liquidity by excluding inventory from current assets and including only liquid current assets. The motive is that it may not be possible to turn inventories into a known amount of cash quickly. It is calculated as follows:

$$\frac{\text{current assets} - \text{inventory}}{\text{current liabilities}}$$

This ratio attempts to compare potential sources of short-term funds with potential needs for short-term funds. It assumes that inventory will be unavailable as funds to meet immediate liabilities. While the acid test ratio is a stricter indicator of solvency, it suffers from the same disadvantages which affect the current ratio. It ignores the importance of cash flows from current operations and by emphasizing cash and debtors tends to put the less efficient firm in a more favourable light. It would be an inappropriate measure of solvency for such a business as a supermarket but might be appropriate for a manufacturing company with high levels of credit sales.

In general terms, there is a risk of insolvency if a company does not have sufficient assets convertible into cash during the normal credit period. Assume that Ada Ltd will have to find £51,000 to meet current liabilities and has only £47,000 in debtors and cash. The potential shortfall of £4,000 translates into a ratio of 0.92 to 1 and indicates a potential shortfall.

While intuition suggests that the acid ratio should be greater or equal to 1, there is nothing magical about this threshold. Many large reputable companies have acid ratios less than 1, but not by too much. As for the current ratio it should be remembered that bigger is not better. Current assets are tied up in the operating cycle; they are not a source of income. Revenues and eventually profits are earned when products are sold, but having lots of products waiting to be sold incurs costs, it does not generate income. Thus it should be noted that there is no universally desirable ratio; 'rules of thumb' like 2:1 current ratios and 1:1 acid test ratios may be misleading and it would be unwise to place too much emphasis on a single ratio.

Ratios of the cash elasticity of current assets (i.e. activity ratios)

We noted that the firm's ability to meet current liabilities depends upon the rate at which cash flows into the firm from current operations. Since sales is the critical event in this respect, the rate at which inventory is sold is crucial. Where a substantial proportion of sales are credit sales, the credit period allowed is also crucial. For these reasons, the following ratios are good indicators of the cash elasticity of current assets:

1 average inventory turnover;
2 collection period of trade debts.

Average inventory turnover

The average inventory turnover is calculated as follows:

$$\frac{\text{cost of goods sold during the period}}{\text{average inventory held}}$$

For Ada Ltd the average inventory turnover is as follows:

$$\frac{£208,000}{(£35,00 + £45,000)/2} = 5.2 \text{ times}$$

This ratio means that the average length of time that inventory is held prior to sale is 365 days/5.2, that is, 70 days.

The average inventory turnover ratio is only a crude measure of the inventory turnover rate for the purpose of comparing the cash elasticity of inventory of different enterprises. Businesses face different market situations. A business selling perishable foodstuff has a much higher inventory turnover rate than one selling luxury goods. Alternative methods of inventory valuation also distort the significance of inter-firm comparisons. It is also important to recognize that average inventory as calculated above is only an approximation and that seasonal fluctuations, or increased sales and inventory during the year, may seriously distort this figure. A company with significant seasonal sales, such as a fireworks manufacturer could show wildly differing average inventory figures if calculated at different times of the year.

Nevertheless, the average inventory turnover ratio may give a useful indication of trading difficulties facing a particular firm by comparing it with the average inventory turnover ratio of previous periods. A fall in the average inventory turnover may indicate stiffening competition, adverse marketing circumstances or a degree of obsolescence in the firm's products. At the same time, firms operating in similar markets may be expected to have roughly similar average inventory turnover ratios. For this reason, even a crude ratio of comparability may be a useful indicator for investors.

Collection period of trade debts

An important measure of the cash elasticity of debtor balances may be obtained from the average collection period of trade debtors by using the following formula:

$$\frac{\text{trade debtors} \times 365}{\text{credit sales}}$$

While the formula might not look intuitively obvious in this form, it calculates the proportion of the year's sales that are tied up in trade debtors, i.e. the cash has yet to be received, and expresses this as a number of days by multiplying by 365. Assume that Ada Ltd sells all its goods on credit, the average collection period is as follows:

$$\frac{£40,000 \times 365}{£350,000} = 42 \text{ days}$$

These calculations show that 42 days is the approximate time required to collect trade debts outstanding at 31 December 20X0. This ratio allows analysts to determine if the average collection period for debtors is too slow. A rough rule of thumb which is sometimes used by credit agencies assumes that the average age of trade debts should not exceed $1\frac{1}{3}$ times the net credit period. If a firm gives 30 days' credit for payment, the average collection period should not exceed approximately 40 days. Information about credit terms is not included in corporate financial reports. Also, the calculation of days' sales in debtors is an approximation which assumes more or less consistent sales levels during the year. If a company experienced relatively high sales in the period immediately before the accounting year-end, this would have the effect of increasing the collection period, since a high current sales level would be compared to a lower average level for the year. Companies will have accurate information available internally through real-time computerized analysis of the average collection period for debtors plus detailed aged debtors lists.

Other factors affecting short-term solvency

In addition to the ratios mentioned above, other factors which should be taken into account when evaluating short-term solvency include:

1 *The level of operating costs*. Neither the income statement nor the balance sheet reveal the cash required to meet current operating costs such as payroll, rent and other expenses. Where a firm has very few liquid assets in its balance sheet, and it is faced, for example, with very large payroll obligations, it may be extremely short of cash.
2 *Bank credit*. A firm which has sufficient credit facilities may have lower current and acid test ratios.
3 *Seasonal patterns of trade*. Where firms normally experience seasonal patterns of trade, there will be distortions in the solvency ratios arising from seasonal build-up of inventory, trade debtors and cash depletions during the time interval across the peak season as mentioned above. Where such seasonal patterns of trade exist, they must be taken into account when making inter-firm comparisons.

Long-term solvency

Solvency is the ability to meet current liabilities as they fall due for payment. The long-term financial stability of the firm may be considered as dependent upon its ability to meet all liabilities, including those not currently payable.

Two ratios which are considered important in this respect are:

1 the shareholders' equity ratio;
2 the interest coverage ratio.

Shareholders' equity ratio

This ratio is considered by many analysts to be equal in importance to the current ratio as an indicator of financial stability. It is computed as follows:

$$\text{shareholders' equity ratio} = \frac{\text{shareholders' equity}}{\text{total assets}} \times 100$$

Substituting figures from Ada's accounts:

$$\frac{£111{,}000}{£222{,}000} \times 100 = 50\%$$

It is generally felt that the larger the proportion of the shareholders' equity, the stronger is the financial position of the firm. This is related to the notion of 'leverage' discussed in Chapter 23. By increasing long-term borrowing, the firm may increase its current assets, thereby creating a more favourable current ratio. At the same time, however, it reduces the shareholders' equity, signalling a possible over-dependence on outside sources for long-term financial needs. This creates a problem associated with high levels of leverage, namely that where net profit tends to fluctuate, a high level of fixed interest payments may greatly impair the ability of the company to make dividend payments and will certainly magnify the variations in earnings attributable to shareholders and hence share prices.

Although no explicit rules of thumb exist regarding desirable shareholders' equity ratios, financial analysts may have a general idea of the appropriate financial structure of a particular company by considering the stability of its profit. The less variable a company's underlying business activities and profits, the more safely it can use long-term debt. The total risk of a company is made up of business risk (risk inherent in the type of business) and financial risk (through borrowing). If a company has low business risk, it will generally be able to carry more financial risk.

Interest coverage ratio

The ability of a firm to meet its debt service costs out of current earnings is a rough indicator of its long-term solvency. Long-term loans which are usually in the form of debentures carry interest charges which must be paid regularly. The inability to meet such interest charges places the firm's solvency in jeopardy. The interest cover ratio is calculated as follows:

$$\text{interest coverge ratio} = \frac{\text{earnings before interest and tax}}{\text{periodic interest charges}}$$

$$= \frac{£32{,}000}{£4{,}000} = 8 \text{ times}$$

Generally speaking, a firm which can cover its debt service costs several times over by its operating profit even in a poor year would be regarded as a satisfactory risk by long-term creditors. The level of safety required would, however, depend on the company's level of business (inherent) risk.

The analysis of financial performance

Financial performance may be assessed by reference to its ability to generate profit. Ratios of financial efficiency in this respect focus on the relationships between profit and sales and profit and assets employed. Financial performance is also assessed in terms of the value of its shares to investors. In this regard, ratios of financial performance focus on earnings per share, dividend yield and price/earnings ratios.

The analysis of earning power

The overall measure of earnings performance is the return on capital employed. This ratio is made up of several components, two of the most important of which are the asset turnover ratio and the return-on-sales ratio.

Return on capital employed

There are several ways of expressing this ratio, and care must be taken in making inter-firm comparisons that the basis used is the same. The return on capital employed may be expressed as follows:

$$\text{return on net assets} = \frac{\text{operating profit (before interest and tax)}}{\text{total assets less current liabilities}}$$

$$\text{return on shareholders' equity} = \frac{\text{profit (after interest and tax)}}{\text{shareholders' equity}}$$

Note that interest is excluded to enable comparisons of operating efficiency between firms that have different leverage.

Return on net assets indicates the efficiency with which management used the resources to earn profit. For Ada Ltd it is computed as follows:

$$\frac{£32,000}{£171,000} \times 100 = 18.7\%$$

Return on shareholders' equity measures the return which accrues to the shareholders after interest payments to creditors and taxes are deducted. It does not measure the efficiency with which available resources are used, but rather the residual return to the owners on their investment in the business. For Ada Ltd the return on shareholders' equity is calculated as follows:

$$\frac{£12,000}{£111,000} \times 100 = 10.8\%$$

When comparing the ratios of different companies it is necessary to adjust the data for differences in accounting policies. However, it will be difficult for an outsider to assess the effects of such differences. Also, these ratios are based on historic costs and do not reflect the current value of corporate assets.

The factors which affect the return on capital employed may be broken down into the following ratios:

Figure 26.1

These ratios may be further subdivided, for example, by a closer analysis of the components of current assets, that is, inventories and debtors, and the elements of direct and overhead expenses.

The ratio of return on capital employed (ROCE) is generally expressed as follows:

$$\text{ROCE} = \frac{\text{sales}}{\text{capital employed}} \times \frac{\text{net profit}}{\text{sales}} \times 100$$

Asset turnover ratios

The first component of the formula for calculating the ROCE is an asset utilization ratio. It is intended to reflect the intensity with which assets are employed. If the firm has a low ratio of sales to assets, it implies that there is some substantial underutilization of assets, or alternatively that assets are not being efficiently employed. This ratio focuses, therefore, on the use of assets made by management. Because it is a measure of past managerial efficiency in this respect, it is thought to provide a reasonable basis for forecasting management's future efficiency. It is considered to be a prime determinant of the level of future income flows.

The following ratios may be used and the data for their calculation are derived from the accounts of Ada Ltd.

$$\text{total assets turnover} = \frac{\text{turnover}}{\text{total assets}}$$

$$= \frac{£350,000}{£222,000} = 1.6 \text{ times}$$

$$\text{non-current assets turnover} = \frac{\text{turnover}}{\text{non-current assets}}$$

$$= \frac{£350,000}{£130,000} = 2.7 \text{ times}$$

$$\text{working capital turnover} = \frac{\text{turnover}}{\text{net current assets}}$$

$$= \frac{£350,000}{£41,000} = 8.5 \text{ times}$$

The ratio of net income on sales

This is the second component of the formula for calculating the ROCE. It seeks to assess the profitability of sales, that is, the efficiency of sales as a critical event in generating income.

The ratio of net income on sales varies widely from industry to industry and should be used solely for comparing similar companies in the same industry, or in assessing the performance of the same company over a period of time. Some companies may operate in an industry characterized by low profit margins and high levels of turnover, for example, the manufacture and distribution of foodstuffs.

In considering the relevance of ratios of performance, conventional accounting measurements introduce limitations. Current, or fair, value accounting removes at least two basic difficulties. First, the effect of timing differences in the acquisition of assets, which results in the aggregation of assets of differing money values being removed, and similar values are added together. Second, the use of historical cost measurements results in arbitrary allocations, e.g. LIFO and FIFO allocations of inventory to the cost of sales. Replacement cost accounting increases the usefulness of ratio analysis by providing uniformity in cost allocations, since all costs are allocated at their replacement price.

For Ada Ltd the ratio is calculated as follows:

$$\frac{£32,000}{£350,000} \times 100 = 9.1\%$$

The analysis of investment decisions

Investors seek to make the best allocation of their investment funds when buying shares of a particular company. Several ratios used by investors appraise corporate financial performance in terms of share prices and yields.

Earnings per share

In the United Kingdom, FRS 14, which superseded SSAP 3, requires that all companies listed on a recognized stock exchange show in their published accounts the earnings per share (EPS) for the accounting period and for the previous period. EPS is the profit in pence attributable to each equity share after deducting preference dividend and extraordinary items, divided by the weighted average number of ordinary shares outstanding during the period. The EPS for Ada Ltd is calculated as follows:

$$EPS = \frac{£12,000}{80,000} = 15 \text{ pence per share}$$

The Institute of Investment Management and Research (1993) in the United Kingdom sets out a 'headline' definition of earnings which states:

1 All the trading income for the year, including abnormal items, should be included in the earnings number.
2 Income arising in operations discontinued at some point during the year, or in operations acquired at some point during the year, should remain in the earnings figure. The income on the sale or termination of a discontinued operation should be excluded.

3 Income from the sale of non-current assets or of businesses, or on their permanent diminution in value or write-off, should be excluded.

EPS is an important ratio for two reasons. First, the trend in EPS is a useful indicator to investors in the company of the profitable use of their money. Second, EPS is related by investment analysts to the market price of the shares to derive the price/earnings ratio. (See below.) For these reasons, it is important that EPS should be calculated and disclosed on a comparable basis from year to year and between one company and another.

The International Accounting Standards Board IAS 33 'Earnings Per Share' 1997 and revised 2003 has the objective of prescribing principles for the determination and presentation of earnings per share (EPS) amounts in order to improve performance comparisons between different enterprises in the same period and between different accounting periods for the same enterprise. IAS 33 applies to entities whose securities are publicly traded or that are in the process of issuing securities to the public. They are required to present, on the face of the income statement, basic and diluted earnings per share. Basic EPS is calculated by dividing profit or loss attributable to ordinary equity holders by the weighted average number of ordinary shares outstanding. Diluted EPS is calculated by adjusting the earnings and number of shares for the effects of dilutive options and other dilutive potential ordinary shares. Dilution occurs as a reduction in earnings per share or an increase in loss per share resulting from the assumption that convertible instruments are converted, that options or warrants are exercised, or that ordinary shares are issued upon the satisfaction of specified conditions.

Price/earnings ratio

This ratio indicates the number of years it would take to recover the share price out of the current earnings of the company. It is calculated by dividing the market price of the ordinary shares of a company by the EPS figure described above. For Ada Ltd the price/earnings ratio is calculated as follows:

$$\text{price/earnings ratio} = \frac{£2}{15 \text{ pence}} = 13.3$$

This means that if £2 is paid for these shares, then 13.3 years of current earnings of 15 pence per share are being bought. Because the current market value of a share reflects the expectations of investors concerning the future profits of a company, the ratio is effectively measuring the market's anticipations for future earnings compared to the current performance of the company. Therefore, the price/earnings ratio is an indicator of the confidence that the stock market has in the company. A low price/earnings ratio suggests a lack of confidence in the company's ability to maintain earnings, while a high price/earnings ratio suggests a belief that the company is expected to increase earnings in the future. However, as with all ratios, interpretation must allow for differences between companies. A high risk company will be expected to generate higher returns than a 'safe' one and this will be reflected by a relatively lower price/earnings ratio.

Dividend yield

The dividend yield focuses closely on the value of the declared dividends to an investor. It is calculated as follows:

$$\text{dividend yield} = \frac{\text{dividend per ordinary share}}{\text{market price per ordinary share}}$$

In the case of Ada Ltd the dividend per ordinary share is:

$$\frac{£5,000}{80,000} = 6.25 \text{ pence}$$

The dividend yield is:

$$\frac{6.25 \text{ pence}}{£2} = 3.1\%$$

The dividend yield shows the return currently earned in the form of dividends from an investment in shares. Future returns will be affected by changes in the rate of dividend and movement in the share price.

Dividend cover ratio (or payout ratio)

The ability of a company to continue to pay current dividend levels in the future may be forecast by the dividend cover ratio, which may be calculated as follows:

$$\text{dividend cover} = \frac{\text{net income, taxation and preference dividend}}{\text{ordinary dividend}}$$

The dividend cover ratio indicates the proportion of earnings retained by the company and the level of risk in future years attached to the ability to maintain the same dividend flow, should earnings decline. Interpretation of dividend ratios is difficult because some investors will prefer low payout (dividend) companies and others high payout companies. Other things being equal, a lower payout leads to greater growth in the value of the company which can then be realized by investors in the form of capital gains through the sale of shares. It is not at all clear whether high or low payout policies will have any effect on share prices and returns, but it is likely that investors will prefer companies to adopt a consistent policy.

Cash flow ratios

We noted in Chapter 25 that the cash flow statement is designed to aid users in making judgements on the amount, timing and degree of certainty of future cash flows. It also enables ratios to be developed which relate the cash flow statement to items in the income statement and balance sheet. Two such ratios are explained below.

Cash return on capital employed

This ratio is expressed as a percentage and is calculated as follows:

$$\frac{\text{net cash flow from operating activities}}{\text{capital employed}} \times 100$$

To many users of financial statements it is cash return on investment rather than the income-based return on investment that is of greater meaning and value.

Operating cash flow/total debt

This ratio indicates a firm's ability to cover total debt with the yearly cash flow. The higher the ratio, the better the firm's ability to carry its total debt.

Ratios as predictors of business failure: empirical studies

Empirical studies have been undertaken to determine the extent to which financial ratios may be used to predict business failure. The ability to predict company failure is particularly important from both the private investor's viewpoint and the social viewpoint, as it is an obvious indication of resource misallocation. An early warning signal of probable failure would enable both management and investors to take preventive measures.

In a study using more powerful statistical techniques than used by his predecessors, Beaver (1966) found that financial ratios proved to be useful in the prediction of failure in that such failure could be predicted at least five years before the event. He concluded that ratios could be used to distinguish correctly firms which would fail from those which would not, with much more success than would be possible by random prediction. One of his significant conclusions was that the most effective predictor of failure was the ratio of both short-term and long-term cash flow to total debt. The next best was the ratio of net income to total assets. One of Beaver's most surprising findings was that the current ratio was among the worst predictors of failure. Turnover ratios were found to be at the bottom of the list of effective predictors. Generally, Beaver found that 'mixed ratios', which had income or cash flows compared to assets or liabilities, outperformed short-term solvency ratios which had been believed traditionally to be the best predictors of failure.

In a later study, Beaver (1968) suggested that business failure tends to be determined by permanent factors. He argued that if the basic financial position of a company was sound and income prospects were good, it would recover from a temporary shortage of liquid assets, but that if the long-term prospects in these areas were not good, business failure could not be prevented by a good liquid position.

Altman (1968, 1983) extended Beaver's univariate (single-variable) analysis to allow for multiple predictors of business failure. He used a multiple discriminant analysis for the purpose of developing a linear function of a number of explanatory variables to predict failure. Altman used twenty-two financial ratios based on data obtained one year before failure, and selected five financial ratios for the purposes of establishing his final discriminant function. These five financial ratios were:

1 working capital/total assets as an indicator of liquidity;
2 retained earnings/total assets as an indicator of the age of the firm and its cumulative profitability;
3 earnings before interest and tax/total assets as an indicator of profitability;
4 market value of the equity/book value of debt as an indicator of financial structure;
5 sales/total assets as an indicator of capital turnover.

Altman's five-variable model correctly identified 95 per cent of the total sample of companies tested for bankruptcy. This percentage rate of success in predicting failure fell to 72 per cent when the data used was obtained two years prior to failure. As earlier data was used in testing the model, so its predictive ability became more unreliable.

Taffler and Tisshaw (1977; Taffler, 1983) applied Altman's multiple discriminant analysis to companies in the United Kingdom. They tested the predictive value of eighty different ratios in a variety of combinations. The best results were found when four ratios were combined in accordance with weighting which reflected their significance to the analysis of business failure.

The ratios used by Taffler and Tisshaw and the weightings which they were given were as follows:

1 Income before tax/current liabilities (53 per cent), which 'is a profitability measure indicating the ability of an enterprise to cover its current liabilities through its earning power. If it has a low or negative value, its downside risk is clearly greater than that for the average company.'
2 Current assets/total liabilities (13 per cent), which 'is related to the conventional current ratio, and is a measure of the working capital position of the firm. The greater the ratio, the sounder the enterprise.'
3 Current liabilities/total assets (18 per cent), 'which measures the company's current liabilities position and is a financial leverage ratio. The greater its magnitude, the more serious the problems the company has to face in financing the cost of its debt and the acquisition of new debt.'
4 Immediate assets minus current liabilities/operating costs minus depreciation (16 per cent), which 'calculates the time for which the company can finance its continuing operations from its immediate assets, if all other sources of short-time finance are cut off, and is a ratio relatively new to the accounting literature . . . and is akin to the acid test.'

All these empirical studies present evidence to support the conclusion that firms which avoided failure had stronger ratios in areas of significant analysis than firms which failed. The measures used by Altman and Taffler and Tisshaw are expressed by a number known as a 'Z score'. Scores such as these are now available through online data services such as 'Datastream'.

Morris (1998) has drawn attention to the limitations of financial ratio analysis which restrict the usefulness of financial ratios for predicting business failure. In particular, he argues that most failure prediction models probably tell potential users little they don't already know. Furthermore, case study research shows that corporate failure is usually the result of an unfortunate and unforeseeable conjunction of events, and the underlying causes of financial distress differ at varying stages of the economic cycle. However, it seems likely that decision makers will continue to refer to failure prediction models.

Summary

Ratio analysis provides the most commonly used indicators to assess and compare the financial performance of companies, both over time and as between different companies. However, unless ratios are collected in a systematic and uniform manner, comparisons may be very misleading. For this reason, they are most useful when collected and developed by such organizations as the Centre for Inter-Firm Comparisons.

It is very important that external users of financial reports should understand the limitations of ratios based on conventional accounting measurements; otherwise, their analyses will not be sound and their interpretations invalid. The conclusion which may be drawn from our examination of ratio analysis is that its general usefulness and relevance to investors would be enhanced by increasing the uniformity of financial reporting practices and adopting current (fair) value accounting.

Considerable interest exists in the possibility of using financial ratios as predictors of business failure. Several studies have been conducted that show that there exist ratios and combinations of ratios which are significant in this regard. Nevertheless, caution is required in accepting the conclusions suggested by financial ratios as regards business failure.

Problems (*indicates that a solution is to be found in the Lecturer's Guide)

1 The following information relates to the operations of the East Lancashire Trading Company for the three-year period ended 31 December 20X2:

Income statements

	20X2	20X1	20X0
	£	£	£
Net sales	1,000,000	900,000	800,000
Cost of goods sold	600,000	550,000	545,000
Gross income	400,000	350,000	255,000
Selling and administrative expenses	300,000	275,000	220,000
Net income before tax	100,000	75,000	35,000
Tax at 50%	50,000	37,500	17,500
Net income after tax	50,000	37,500	17,500
Dividends	30,000	25,000	10,000
Net increase in retained earnings	20,000	12,500	7,500

Balance sheets

	20X2	20X1	20X0
	£	£	£
Assets			
Land and buildings	500,000	450,000	425,000
Plant and equipment (net)	450,000	500,000	410,000
Inventory (at cost)	635,000	600,000	520,000
Debtors	425,000	410,000	440,000
Bank balance	40,000	55,000	63,000
	2,050,000	2,015,000	1,858,000
Shareholders' equity and liabilities	£	£	£
Ordinary share capital £1 shares fully paid	600,000	600,000	600,000
Share premium account	125,000	125,000	125,000
Retained earnings	532,000	512,000	500,000
12% debentures 20X9	200,000	200,000	200,000
Creditors	496,000	493,000	390,000
Accrued expenses	15,000	17,000	9,000
Taxation	52,000	43,000	24,000
Provision for dividends	30,000	25,000	10,000
	2,050,000	2,015,000	1,858,000

Required:

From the foregoing information, calculate the following ratios for the years 20X1 and 20X2 (assume that all sales are on a credit basis and the year is 360 days):

(a) The current ratio
(b) The acid test ratio
(c) The average inventory turnover
(d) The average collection period for debtors
(e) The shareholders' equity ratio
(f) The return on capital employed
(g) The earnings per share.

Evaluate the liquidity position of the company at the end of 20X2 as compared with 20X1.

2* Evaluate the usefulness of financial ratio analysis in assessing the financial state of an enterprise. Use the case below to illustrate your answer.

Case

A summary of the results of Sandygate Enterprises Limited for the last three years is as follows:

	Year ended 31 December		
	20X0	20X0	20X0
	£	£	£
Sales	480,000	560,000	690,000
Income before tax	63,000	70,000	74,000
Tax	23,000	25,000	28,000
Income after tax	40,000	45,000	46,000
Dividends	30,000	30,000	36,000
Retained income for year	10,000	15,000	10,000
	£	£	£
Share capital (600,000 £0.25 shares)	150,000	150,000	150,000
Retained income	85,000	100,000	110,000
Shareholders' funds	235,000	250,000	260,000
10% debentures	65,000	150,000	150,000
Capital employed	300,000	400,000	410,000
Market price per share at 31 December	£1	£1.50	£1.25
Debt interest	£6,500	£15,000	£15,000

3 Jack and Jill each carry on business as wholesalers of the same product. Their respective accounts for the year ended 31 December 20X0 are as follows:

Income statements

	Jack		Jill	
	£	£	£	£
Sales		144,000		140,000
Cost of sales:				
Opening inventory	28,000		3,200	
Purchases	124,000		121,600	
	152,000		124,800	
Closing inventory	32,000	120,000	4,800	120,000
Gross income		24,000		20,000
Selling expenses	7,200		2,800	
Admin expenses	8,160	15,360	9,500	12,300
Net income		8,640		7,700

Balance sheets at 31 December 20X0

	Jack	Jill
	£	£
Freehold property	20,000	14,000
Fixtures and fittings	21,750	13,840
Motor vehicles	12,000	6,000
	53,750	33,840
Inventory	32,000	4,800
Debtors	28,800	11,200
Bank	8,950	11,360
	123,500	61,200
Capital	108,000	30,800
Creditors	15,500	30,400
	123,500	61,200

Notes:

(a) All sales are on credit.
(b) The amounts of debtors and creditors have not changed significantly over the year.
(c) All non-current assets are net of accumulated depreciation.

Required:

Compare the profitability and financial position of the two businesses by:

(a) calculating suitable ratios for each business;
(b) commenting on the significance of the results of your calculations.

4 You are financial adviser to a retailing company, Us Ltd. You obtain the accounts of its main competitor operating in the same market, Them Ltd, and extract the comparison shown below:

Balance sheets as at 31 March 20X0

	Us Ltd			Them Ltd		
	£000	£000	£000	£000	£000	£000
Non-current assets						
Land and buildings		381			286	
Fixtures and fittings		342			218	
Vehicles		62			59	
			785			563
Current assets						
Inventory	96			122		
Trade debtors	166			124		
Cash	9			6		
		271			252	
Current liabilities						
Overdraft	20			21		
Trade creditors	132			97		
Accruals	48			42		
		200			160	
			71			92
			856			655
Shareholders' funds						
Share capital		470			350	
Capital reserves		35			65	
Income statement		287			185	
			792			600
10% debentures			64			55
			856			655

Income statements for the year ended 31 March 20X0

	Us Ltd		Them Ltd	
	£000	£000	£000	£000
Sales (on credit)		570		747
Cost of sales				
Opening inventory	92		102	
Purchases (on credit)	381		588	
	473		690	
Closing inventory	96		122	
		377		568
Gross income		193		179
Distribution costs	60		64	
Administration costs	29		31	
		89		95
		104		84
Interest charges		8		9
Net income		96		75
Taxation		45		37
		51		38
Dividend		37		24
Retained profit for the year		14		14

Upon analysing this information, you observe that it reveals significant differences between the companies.

Required:

(a) Calculate and identify the key differences in profitability and in working capital management as between the two companies.

(b) Based upon the analysis at (a) above, recommend actions which the management of Us Ltd should consider in order to improve their financial performance.

(c) State any reservations you may have about drawing conclusions from the comparative analysis of the two companies.

References

AICPA (1994) *Improving Business Reporting*, American Institute of Certified Public Accountants.

Altman, E.I. (1968) Financial ratios, discriminant analysis and the prediction of corporate bankruptcy, *Journal of Finance*, No. 7.

Altman, E.I. (1983) *Corporate Financial Distress*, Wiley.

Beaver, W.H. (1966) Financial ratios as predictors of failure, *Journal of Accounting Research*, No. 4.

Beaver, W.H. (1968) Alternative accounting measures as predictors of failure, *The Accounting Review*, January.

Glautier, M.W.E. (1971) Towards a reformulation of the theory of working capital, *Journal of Business Finance*, Spring.

Institute of Investment Management and Research (1993) *The Definition of Headline Earnings*, Statement of Investment Practice No. 1.

Morris, R. (1998) Forecasting bankruptcy: how useful are failure prediction models?, *Management Accounting*, May.

Taffler, R.J. (1983) The assessment of company solvency and performance using a statistical model – a comparative UK-based study, *Accounting and Business Research*, Autumn.

Taffler, R.J. and Tisshaw H. (1977) Going, going, gone – four factors which predict, *Accountancy*, March.

Introduction to Section 1b

The process of attaching money measurements to accounting events and items is essentially a process of valuation. Valuation enters into accounting measurements in two senses. First, the money standard of measurement is itself unstable through time. One pound today does not have the same value as one pound yesterday, or one pound tomorrow, since the purchasing power of money over goods and services changes. Second, the use of money measurements in accounting implies a choice between one of several different valuation bases. It is possible to represent the original cost of acquisition of an asset by the enterprise as a representation of a past financial effort. Equally, it is possible to represent the value of an asset to the enterprise in terms of the future net benefits it represents.

Accounting for changes in the value of money is a subject which has long occupied the attention of accounting researchers. It was not until 1975, however, with the publication of the Sandilands Report, that the subject received attention from accountants generally. The ensuing lively debate illustrated the problem of producing a consensus regarding the best method of dealing with price level changes. One reason for the controversy which characterized the inflation accounting debate was due to the failure of accountants to reach agreement on the objectives of financial reports.

The importance of understanding the interaction and interdependence between valuation and measurement is apparent in such important areas of accounting as income determination and asset valuation. In this sense, the notions of capital and income are largely dependent on valuation concepts.

In this part, seven valuation concepts are discussed:

1 *Historical cost*, as we saw in Part 2, is the conventional valuation concept used in accounting. Resources are valued in accordance with their cost of acquisition by the enterprise. The historical cost valuation concept poses many difficulties under price level changes.
2 *Present value* is a concept which relates the value of an asset to the decision to hold it and to derive its utility from using it in the production of income. It is defined as the sum of the future expected net cash flows associated with the use of the asset, discounted to their present value.
3 *Current purchasing power* is basically an adjusted historical cost concept, in which adjustments are made to recorded historical cost values for changes in the purchasing power of money by means of a consumer price index.
4 *Current replacement cost* is where the value of an asset is determined by the current cost of replacing it, and using the replacement to maintain the same service to the enterprise. It requires current market price data as a basis for preparing financial reports.
5 *Net realizable value* estimates the value of an asset to the enterprise as the amount which would be realized from its sale, after adjusting for selling expenses.

6 *Current value accounting* is a valuation concept which combines the concept of current replacement cost and net realizable value in determining whether selling (exit) or buying (entry) prices should be used for the purposes of establishing the value of an asset to the business.

7 *Fair value accounting* applies to assets and liabilities for which a fair value is required for reporting purposes. The fair value of an asset is the amount at which that asset could be bought or sold in a current transaction between willing parties, other than in a liquidation. The fair value of a liabilitiy is the amount at which that liability could be incurred or settled between willing parties, other than in a liquidation. If available, a quoted market price in an active market is the best evidence of fair value. If a quoted market price is not available, fair value is to be estimated using the best information available in the circumstances. Fair value accounting is based on the principle of mark-to-market.

Chapter 27 'Capital, value and income', deals with the conceptual problems involved in the valuation of the enterprise and the measurement of income. Chapter 28, 'Accounting and economic concepts of income and value', considers two different approaches to income measurement and valuation. Chapter 29, 'Accounting under monetary instability and market volatility', examines alternatives to the traditional historical cost accounting model under monetary instability and market volatility that limit the usefulness and relevance of historical cost measurements based on entry-values for decision making.

CHAPTER 27

Capital, value and income

Setting the scene

Current financial reporting suffers from a number of deficiencies. It concentrates on the legal form of transactions more than on their economic substance and frequently does not reflect economic reality, it concentrates on the past rather than the future, it concentrates on cost rather than value and it leads to too much attention being paid to 'profit' and not enough to wealth and changes in it.

(ICAS Research Committee, 1988)

Learning objectives

After studying this chapter you should be able to:

1 discuss the significance of capital maintenance and describe the different concepts that have been postulated;

2 explain the relationship between capital and income;

3 identify the purposes for which businesses require income measurements.

We stated in Chapter 2 that the objectives of financial reporting to investors should be found in the decisions which investors have to make about their investment in companies. Hence, we argued, financial reporting should be concerned with the provision of such information as is required for making those decisions. We assumed, also, that investors were principally concerned with the worth of their investments in two senses. First, they are concerned with maintaining and increasing the value of their capital. Second, they are concerned with maintaining and increasing the income which is derived from that capital. Financial reporting ought to be concerned, therefore, with the valuation of shareholders' capital and income. In accordance with the stewardship concept of financial reporting, feedback information is required in order that investors may ascertain the current value of share capital and income. The decision-making concept of financial reporting asserts that financial reports should contain information which is useful in assisting investors to predict future changes in capital and income.

Three main concepts involved in financial reporting are capital, value and income. Together they provide the focus for this part. The purpose of this chapter is to introduce and explain the nature of these three concepts.

Capital

To the economist, the term 'capital' relates to those assets which are used in the production of goods and services. The capital of the firm is represented by the firm's stock of assets, and investment by the firm occurs when the stock is increased. From the point of view of society, the term 'capital' is restricted similarly to those assets which produce goods and services. Capital includes, therefore, physical assets in the form of buildings, plant and machinery, housing, hospitals, schools, etc. as well as intangible assets such as technology, human skills (human capital), etc.

In accounting theory, a person's capital is increased by the amount of his periodic income which he has not consumed. Financial accounting procedure effects this transfer by crediting the net profit to the capital account, and if the level of consumption, or drawings, is less than that profit, the capital is increased by the difference. In the case of companies, dividends are analogous to drawings, and retained profit is added to the total of the shareholders' equity. One of the important implications of profit measurement in the case of companies lies in calculating what may be safely distributed as dividends.

Early writers on bookkeeping recommended, as a first step in the record-keeping process, the preparation of an inventory or statement of capital showing all the personal and real property, as well as debts due and owing on the first day of business. Paciolo in 1494 advised the businessman to prepare his inventory in the following way:

> *First of all, he must write on a sheet of paper or in a separate book all his worldly belongings, that is, his personal or real property. He should always begin with the things that are more valuable and easier to lose. . . . He must then record all other things in proper order in the Inventory.* (Gene Brown and Johnston, 1963, p. 27)

It is evident that at this stage of development, accounting made no distinction between personal capital and business capital. In the course of subsequent developments, however, a distinction emerged between total wealth and wealth committed to business activities. Whereas in Paciolo's time capital was taken to mean the entire amount of what was owned, the capital account became ultimately a device which described and quantified that portion of private wealth invested in a business enterprise.

The development of the entity theory of accounting, as distinct from the proprietary theory, which culminated in the appearance of the joint stock company, gave expression to two important notions. First, as we saw in Part 2, an enterprise could be separated from its owner by a legal fiction and used by the owner as a vehicle for conducting business. Second, the fictional life granted to the enterprise by accounting practice, and additionally in the case of corporations by law, was to serve limited purposes. The capital account was to remain the umbilical cord linking the enterprise to its owner or owners. In line with this view, the enterprise continued to be regarded as an asset and this view has important implications for the valuation of capital and income.

From the foregoing, it is evident that there are some fundamental differences between economists and accountants in the manner in which the notion of capital is conceptualized. As Littleton (1961, p 244) points out, the balance sheet presentation of 'capital' emphasizes its legal rather than its economic aspect, for capital is shown as a liability, whereas in economics, capital refers to assets. The assets held by a business and actively employed by it are usually greater in value than the so-called 'capital'. In the light of modern interests, we may say that the terminology of financial reports in this respect is misleading. However, supposing that the total assets employed by an enterprise were to be redefined as its 'capital', there remain a number of problems:

1 the valuation of business capital;
2 the valuation of investors' financial interests, that is, personal capital;
3 the methods selected for these valuations;
4 the manner in which these valuations are to be communicated.

From our previous discussion of the objectives of financial reporting, we may say that investors are interested primarily in the valuation of their shareholding and this valuation is dependent on the valuation of business capital.

Capital maintenance

We stated earlier in this chapter that investors are concerned with maintaining the value of their capital. The concept of capital maintenance is central to discussions regarding price level adjustments. There is general agreement that income is a residue available for distribution once provision has been made for maintaining the value of capital intact. Difficulties begin to emerge when discussion turns to the consideration of the meaning of 'capital maintenance'. Several alternative interpretations of this concept have been offered and are considered below.

The money amount concept

The aim of this concept is to maintain financial capital in money terms. Consequently, the measurement of periodic profit should ensure that the monetary value of the shareholders' equity is maintained intact. In effect, the profit of the period amounts to the increase in monetary terms in the shareholders' equity measured between the beginning and the end of the period. It is this amount which may be distributed to ensure that the money capital is maintained intact. The money amount maintenance concept is reflected in historical cost accounting.

The financial capital concept

The objective of this concept is to maintain the financial capital of an enterprise in real terms by constantly updating the historical cost of assets for changes in the value of money. The translation of historical asset cost is effected by a retail price index, and results in the representation of asset values in common units of purchasing power. This concept of capital maintenance purports to show to shareholders that their company kept pace with general inflationary pressures during the accounting period, by measuring profit in such a way as to take into account changes in the price levels. In effect, it intends to maintain the shareholders' capital in terms of monetary units of constant purchasing power. The use of a retail price index based on a range of goods and services restricts adjustments for changes in the purchasing power of money to those changes which would be experienced by consumers.

The operating capability concept

The financial capital concept of capital maintenance views the capital of the enterprise from the standpoint of the shareholders as owners. Hence, it reflects the proprietorship concept of the enterprise as regards both income and capital, and seeks valuation systems which fit this view. By contrast, the operating capability concept of capital maintenance views the problem of capital maintenance from the perspective of the enterprise itself, thereby reflecting the entity concept of the enterprise.

The operating concept states that the productive (operating) capacity of the enterprise should be maintained as a prime objective in the course of profit measurement. The operating capability concept of capital maintenance asserts that income is a residue after provision has been made for replacing the resources exhausted in the course of operations. In this view, 'there can be no recognition of profit for a period unless the capital employed in the business at the beginning of the period has been maintained. . . . The starting point will be the various items making up the capital' (Goudeket, 1960). The criteria imposed on income measurement by the operating concept are reflected by the system of replacement cost accounting, in which assets are valued at their replacement cost to the firm. Replacement cost accounting takes into account changes in the prices of commodities specific to the enterprise, either directly or by using specific price indices to measure changes in the prices of similar commodities.

The disposable wealth concept

Whereas all previous concepts of capital maintenance envisage the enterprise as a going concern, the disposable wealth concept suggests that the maintenance of capital should be viewed from the perspective of the realizable value of the assets of the enterprise. Accordingly, the measurement of periodic income is required to take into account changes in the realizable value of the net assets attributable to the shareholders' equity. At the beginning of the accounting period, the shareholders' equity, defined as the capital of the enterprise, is valued by reference to the realizable value of assets, after deducting realization expenses. A similar valuation of the net amount which would accrue to shareholders from the realization of assets is made at the end of the accounting period.

The disposable wealth concept of capital maintenance is based on the proprietorship theory of the enterprise. However, it interprets this theory in terms of the 'exit' rather than the 'entry' values of enterprise assets.

Income

The concepts of capital and income are closely related. Irving Fisher expressed their relationship in 1919 as follows: 'A stock of wealth existing at a given instant of time is called capital; a flow of benefit from wealth through a given period of time is called income' (Fisher, 1919, p 38).

An analogy may be found in the relationship between a tree and its fruit – it is the tree which produces the fruit, and it is the fruit which may be consumed. Destroy the tree, and there will be no more fruit: tend the tree with care and feed its roots and it will yield more fruit in the future.

Once the concept of value is introduced into the relationship between capital and income, however, the exact nature of this relationship becomes clearer. According to Fisher (1969, p. 40),

It would seem . . . that income must be derived from capital; and, in a sense, this is true. Income is derived from capital goods, but the value of the income is not derived from the value of the capital goods. On the contrary, the value of the capital is derived from the value of the income. . . . Not until we know how much income an item will probably bring us can we set any valuation on that capital at all. It is true that the wheat crop depends on the land which yields it. But the value of the crop does not depend on the land. On the contrary, the value of the land depends in its crop.

Economic and accounting theory are both concerned with the relationship between capital and income and the implications of this relationship. There is agreement between accountants and economists on a number of aspects of the relationship and considerable disagreement as regards the valuation of capital and income. There is agreement, for example, that only income should be available for consumption, and that in arriving at a measure of income, it is necessary to maintain the value of capital intact. Since the ultimate aim of economic activity is the satisfaction of wants, it follows that income is identified as a surplus which is available for consumption. The valuation of income in this analysis is subject to a fairly conservative criterion which Hicks expressed as follows: 'The purpose of income calculations in practical affairs is to give people an indication of the amount which they can consume without impoverishing themselves' (Hicks, 1946).

Income plays a central role in many business and personal decisions, since it is based essentially on the notion of spending capacity. As Hicks pointed out, income should be an operational concept providing guidelines to spending. As applied to business corporations, Hicks's definition of income has been interpreted as the 'amount the corporation can distribute to the owners of equity in the corporation and be as well off at the end of the year as at the beginning' (Alexander, 1962, p. 139). It is evident, however, that income is used for other purposes as well. For this reason, we examine the objectives of income measurements before proceeding to the analysis and selection of appropriate concepts.

The objectives of income measurement

Income as a measure of efficiency

Income is used as a measure of efficiency in two senses. First, the overall efficiency of a business is assessed in terms of income generated. Hence, income tends to provide the basic standard by which success is measured. There are clearly problems in focusing upon financial efficiency to the detriment of other concepts of business efficiency – such as the effectiveness of the business as a social unit and its efficiency in developing and using new ideas and processes. Nevertheless, those who support the use of income as a measure of business efficiency argue that in the last analysis all other aspects of efficiency converge on income. Second, shareholders assess the efficiency of their investments by reference to reported income. Hence, the allocation of investment funds, the selection of portfolios and the operations of the financial system depend upon income as a standard by which decisions are taken.

Income as a guide to future investment

The selection of investment projects is made on the basis of estimates of future cash flows. These estimates are self-sufficient to the extent that risk and uncertainty have been sufficiently discounted in the decision-making process. In a more general way, however, current income acts to influence expectations about the future. This is particularly so as regards investors who have to rely on financial reports and whose willingness to hold and to subscribe for further shares will be affected by reported income.

Income as an indicator of managerial effectiveness

Management is particularly sensitive about the income which is reported to shareholders since the effectiveness of managers both as decision makers and as stewards of resources is judged by reference to reported income. It is in this respect that auditors play a key role in ensuring that the statements placed before shareholders reflect a 'true and fair' view of the financial results. What is 'true and fair' is a contentious problem for accountants. Nevertheless, what is evidently neither true nor fair rarely avoids comment.

Income as a tax base

The tendency of most governments to take a substantial share of corporate income in the form of taxation means that the basis on which corporate tax is assessed is critically important to shareholders and management. Although taxation legislation does not define 'income', it does specify what is taxable and what is deductible in arriving at a measure of taxable income. Much litigation in this area has revolved around the meaning of words, but the taxation authorities accept accounting profit as the base from which to assess taxable profit.

Income as a guide to creditworthiness

A firm's ability to obtain credit finance depends on its financial status and its current and future income prospects. For this reason, credit institutions and banks require assurances of a firm's ability to repay loans out of future income and look upon current income levels as a guide in this respect.

Income as a guide to socio-economic decisions

A wide range of decisions take into account the levels of corporate income. Thus, price increases tend increasingly to be justified in terms of income levels, and wage-bargaining procedures usually involve appeals by both sides to their effects on corporate income. Government economic policies are guided by levels of corporate income as one of the key economic indicators.

Income as a guide to dividend policy

The distinction between capital and income is central to the problem of deciding how much may be distributed to shareholders as dividends. A series of important legal cases have been concerned with the concept of capital maintenance, and rules have been established for the measurement of distributable income with a view to protecting the interests of creditors. Thus, there is a rule which provides that losses in the value of current assets should be made good, whereas in arriving at the measure of distributable income, there is no need to make good losses in the value of fixed assets.

Nowadays, however, dividend policy is directed towards establishing the proportion of current income which should be retained and the proportion which should be distributed. This is because companies expect to finance part of their investment needs from retained income.

Income concepts for financial reporting

The application of different accounting valuation concepts to asset valuation and income measurement offers a variety of alternative bases for drawing up financial reports. In this part, we examine the implications of reporting to shareholders on the basis of the six alternative accounting valuation concepts listed in the introduction to this part, namely historical cost, present value, current purchasing power, replacement cost, net realizable value and current value.

Two criteria – relevance and feasibility – are highly significant in this regard. The stewardship concept of financial reporting is identified with historical cost accounting. This concept focuses on safeguarding assets rather than on presenting measurements useful for decision making. Clearly, financial reports should provide some safeguards against the misuse of assets by management, but they should also provide measurements to shareholders indicative of the efficiency with which assets have been employed. The latter type of measurement is relevent for decision making by shareholders and investors. It has become apparent that when applying the criterion of relevance to users' information needs, historical cost measurements fail to satisfy those needs. Feasibility embraces such aspects of the measurement problem as objectivity and ease of understanding, as well as considerations of costs of implementation.

Unfortunately, the selection of accounting measurements on the basis of the two criteria of relevance and feasibility does not rely on a simple set of accept/reject decision rules. To some extent each measurement currently available meets both criteria, but meets them at different levels of quality. For example, an accounting method which utilizes a measurement which scores highly for relevance may not score well for feasibility.

A second problem which will be examined in this part stems from alternative definitions of capital maintenance. There is some controversy about the manner in which concepts of capital maintenance may be made operational for financial reporting purposes. For example, the debate which followed the Sandilands Report illustrates that the operating capacity concept of capital maintenance does not immediately suggest agreement about the choice of an accounting valuation system which would satisfy the objectives of such a concept.

Summary

The purpose of this chapter was to examine the implications for financial reporting of three concepts – capital, value and income. Two meanings may be attached to the concept of capital. First, capital may be seen as the totality of enterprise assets which give rise to income. Second, capital may be seen as the investment made by shareholders in the equity of the enterprise and from which they expect to derive income in the form of dividends. Investors are concerned not only with the interdependence of the value of their shareholdings and the value of enterprise assets, but also with maintaining the value of that capital. The value of capital and the measurement of income are also interdependent in the sense that income is the difference between the value of capital at two points in time. Therefore, a central issue in the measurement of periodic income is the notion of capital maintenance. Difficulties arise in reporting income due to the different concepts of capital maintenance discussed in this chapter.

Further problems arise in financial reporting from the application of different valuation concepts to asset valuations. The combination of different capital maintenance and asset valuation concepts lies at the heart of much of the controversy in financial reporting. The problem of selecting a financial reporting framework requires the evaluation of alternative accounting valuation systems in terms of criteria of relevance and feasibility.

Self-assessment questions

1 How do accountants define capital?

2 Compare the accountants' definition of capital with the definition used by economists.

3 Discuss the significance of the concept of 'capital maintenance'.

4 Explain briefly the different concepts of capital maintenance that have been postulated.

5 Identify which of these concepts of capital maintenance would be most appropriate to the following two groups of decision makers, with brief explanations of your reasons:
  (a) corporate shareholders;
  (b) management.

6 Explain briefly how accountants measure business income.

7 Review the various purposes for which businesses require income measurement.

8 Explain what you understand as 'value'.

9 'Valuation is a process by which value is established. However, since there are different approaches to valuation, it follows that there are different values.' Comment on this statement.

10 In the light of Question 9, consider the significance of alternative values to the measurement of capital and income.

References

Alexander, S.S. (1962) revised by Solomons, D. Income measurement in a dynamic economy, in Baxter, W.T. and Davidson, S. (eds) *Studies in Accounting Theory*, Sweet & Maxwell.

Fisher, I. (1919) *Elementary principles of economics*.

Fisher, I. (1969) Income and capital, in Parker, R.H. and Harcourt, G.C. (eds) *Readings in the Concept and Measurement of Income*, Cambridge University Press.

Gene Brown, R. and Johnston, K.S. (1963) *Paciolo on Accounting*, McGraw-Hill.

Goudeket, A. (1960) An application of replacement value theory, *Journal of Accountancy*, July.

Hicks, J.R. (1946) *Value and Capital* (2nd edn), Oxford University Press.

ICAS Research Committee (1988) *Making Corporate Reports Valuable*, Kogan Page.

Littleton, A.C. (1961) *Essays on Accounting*, University of Illinois Press.

CHAPTER 28

Accounting and economic concepts of income and value

Setting the scene

The adoption of a value basis of accounting would remove many of the difficulties which we have identified in relation to the present income statement. It would obviate the need for a depreciation charge when assets were gaining in value, although assets which were losing value would still need to be written down to their current value. There will be those who think that revenue should bear a charge for the consumption of assets used in earning it: this would mean, under our suggestion, the results of the period including the write-up for any increase in the worth of an asset and a write-down to provide for consumption. This makes sense if one accepts the matching concept of measuring income, but it is rather cumbersome. If the comparison of financial wealth from period to period is accepted as the basis for judging results, we are of the opinion that the double step is unnecessary.

(ICAS Research Committee, 1988)

Learning objectives

After studying this chapter you should be able to:

1 appreciate the effects of the cost and realization concepts on the measurement of income;

2 explain the essential differences between the accounting and economic approaches to income measurement;

3 describe the relation between income and value in the measurement of economic income;

4 discuss the difficulties of applying economic concepts of income and value to accounting measurements.

Accounting concepts

Accounting concepts of income and value have been influenced mainly by two concepts – the cost concept and the realization concept. These concepts have received much criticism in recent years on the ground that they restrict the usefulness of financial accounting reports for decision-making purposes.

The effects of the cost concept

The historical cost method of valuation seriously distorts the measurement of income when the value of money is changing. This distortion results from the difference between the historical cost and the current cost which, as we shall see later, is a function of the time gap between the acquisition and the utilization of assets committed to earning periodic revenues. For items such as wages and other current expenses, this difference may be very small, but for inventory and non-current assets there may be a substantial difference between the acquisition cost and the current cost when those assets are charged against revenue under the matching concept. Under conditions of rising prices, the historical cost may bear no resemblance to the current cost of assets, with the result that income is overstated. Conservative asset values on the balance sheet are combined with optimistic income measurements in the income statement.

The historical cost method of valuation creates a particular problem in periods of inflation when money units of different values are brought together in the accounting process as though they were money units of the same value. Such arithmetic is quite incorrect, for it involves adding together amounts expressed in different measurement scales. Accordingly, historical cost values are not additive during periods of changing money values.

Example 28.1 A firm constructed a building at a cost of £100,000. Ten years later, a similar building was constructed at a cost of £200,000. In accordance with the concepts of historical cost accounting, these two items were added together in the balance sheet to show a total historical cost of £300,000. Clearly, the two buildings are not comparable in the sense that the second is either twice as large as the first or more costly, in real terms, to build. In effect, no such conclusions could be drawn. Adding together pounds which represent units of different purchasing power is similar in nature to adding together pints, quarts and gallons without converting them to a common denominator. Consider what the effect would be of such arithmetic on the depreciation provision for the buildings. If we assume that the buildings are in fact identical, an annual rate of depreciation of 5 per cent would provide depreciation at the rate of £5,000 for the first building, and £10,000 for the second building. Therefore, it may be concluded that the entire arithmetic underlying the balance sheet representation of asset values would be incorrect under inflation, when assets purchased at different times are added together in asset totals.

The main advantage which is claimed for historical cost valuation is that it is verifiable. The stewardship approach to financial reporting theory is the major factor which supports this method of valuation. It may be argued, however, that if it is objectivity which accountants are seeking, they should restrict themselves purely to counting cash, since this asset is virtually the only one in respect of which complete objectivity is possible. As soon as accountants move away from cash, they are dealing with subjective factors. For example, there are many alternative measures available for valuing stocks, calculating depreciation, allocating overheads and providing for bad debts. Consequently, 'true' objectivity under historical cost valuation is not possible.

The effects of the realization concept

In accordance with the realization concept, the accountant does not recognize changes in value until they have crystallized following a transaction. Until a right enforceable at law comes into existence, gains in book values are ignored for the purpose of income measurement.

It has been suggested that there are two principal reasons which favour the practice of measuring income on realization rather than on value added. The first is that a sale affords an objective measure of a change in value, and the second is that the sale is generally considered to be the most decisive and significant event in the chain of transactions and conditions making up the stream of business activity.

By focusing on realized gains and ignoring unrealized gains, the realization concept can lead to absurd results.

Example 28.2 Two investors each have £1,000 to invest. Each invests £1,000 in the shares of Texton plc. The shares of Texton plc double in value by the end of the accounting period. On the last day of the accounting period, the first investor sells his shares for £2,000 and places this sum in the Homestead Building Society. Hence, one investor has £2,000 in the building society and the other holds shares in Texton valued at £2,000. They are both equally well-off, yet, under the realization concept, the investor who has sold his shares is seen as having realized income of £1,000, whereas the investor who has held on to his shares is shown as having no income from this source.

Economic concepts

The process of valuation is central to all aspects of decision making. For example, capital budgeting decisions require forecasts to be made about the present value of streams of future net cash receipts associated with investment projects. Similarly, investors may also be regarded as exchanging current assets, namely cash or cash equivalents, for a stream of future income in the form of cash dividends or increments in the value of their shares.

This approach values capital on the basis of discounted future net receipts. It is directly relevant to the information needs of shareholders and investors. The value of the firm to the shareholder is computed in such a way as to facilitate the investment decision, which is to seek that investment which will yield the highest value.

In economics, the value of capital is derived from the value of income. The economic concept of income relies on Hicks's definition of income as the amount which a man can consume during a period and still remain as well off at the end of the period as he was at the beginning (Hicks, 1946, p. 172). This concept of income was adopted by Alexander to define the income of a company as the amount the company can distribute to shareholders and be as well off at the end of the year as it was at the beginning (Alexander, 1962). It is measured by comparing the value of the company in terms of the present value of expected future net receipts at two points in time.

The economic concept of income treats assets of all kinds as representing future receipts expected to flow from them to the firm. The main measurement problem lies in comparing the capitalized value of the future net receipts expected both at the beginning and at the end of the accounting period. The difference represents income, that is, what may be consumed, under the Hicksian criterion. Hicks recognized the problems of measurement involved in his criterion in the following terms:

> At the beginning of the week the individual possesses a stock of consumption goods, and expects a stream of receipts which will enable him to acquire in the future other consumption goods . . . Call this Prospect I. At the end of the week he knows that one week out of that prospect will have disappeared; the new prospect which he expects to emerge will have a new first week which is the old

second week . . . Call this Prospect II. Now if Prospect II were available on the first Monday, we may assume that the individual would know whether he preferred I to II at that date: similarly, if Prospect I were available on the second Monday he would know if he preferred I to II then. But to enquire whether I on the first Monday is preferred to II on the second Monday is a nonsense question; the choice between them could never be actual at all; the terms of comparison are not in pari materia.

(Hicks, 1946)

Hicks was making a very crucial point regarding the measurement problem of his criterion; comparative states of well-offness at Prospect I and Prospect II must be established in order to know how much may be spent. Neither points nor prospects are comparable in reality, for they exist at different times.

The economic concept of income based on Hicks's criterion is an estimate since, in deciding how much may be spent, Prospect II must be estimated from the standpoint of Prospect I. In view of this problem two concepts of economic income have evolved. The first concept is called ex-ante income, and compares Prospect II with Prospect I from the time perspective of Prospect I. The second concept is called ex-post income, and compares Prospect II with Prospect I from the time perspective of Prospect II. Neither concept overcomes the fundamental difficulty which Hicks pointed out, namely, that one cannot compare alternatives which are not available together at the same time in making decisions requiring a concept of income. Despite this difficulty, income ex-ante and income ex-post have become established as central concepts in the theory of economic income.

It is important to remember that both income ex-ante and income ex-post are based on estimates of future expected net receipts both at Prospect I and Prospect II. The valuation of income is inseparable, therefore, from the valuation of assets, since assets are valued in terms of the present value of the sum of future expected net receipts associated with their use by the firm. The valuation of income and capital in economics is therefore based on predictions.

Estimation of ex-ante income

The nature of ex-ante income may be seen from the following example.

Example 28.3 Seeking to maximize the return on its funds, Excel Ltd plans to invest in the purchase of assets, which at 1 January 20X0 are expected to produce the following future net receipts at year-end:

Year	Amount
	£
20X0	10,000
20X1	10,000
20X2	10,000
20X3	10,000

This stream of expected future net receipts represents a return on investment of 10 per cent, which may be assumed to be the best return obtainable by Excel Ltd. Accordingly, the present value of those future net receipts discounted at 10 per cent may be calculated as follows:

Year	Expected net receipts at end of year	Present value on 1 January 20X0	
	£	£	
20X0	10,000	10,000/1.10	= 9,091
20X1	10,000	10,000/(1.10)^2	= 8,264
20X2	10,000	10,000/(1.10)^3	= 7,513
20X3	10,000	10,000/(1.10)^4	= 6,831
Present value of expected future net receipts at 1 January 20X0			31,699

Since the present value of expected future net receipts associated with the purchase of those assets is £31,699, Excel Ltd would be unwilling to pay more than this sum for those assets. Hence, we may say that the economic value of those assets is £31,699 at 1 January 20X0.

The present value of the funds already received plus the expected future net receipts one year later on 1 January 20X1, may be calculated as follows:

	£
Cash received at end of year 20X0	10,000
Present value of future new receipts:	
End of year 20X1	9,091
End of year 20X2	8,264
End of year 20X3	7,513
Present value of the assets in terms of actual	34,868
and future expected net receipts on 1 January 20X1	

The two estimates of the present value of the assets enable us to calculate ex-ante income as follows:

		£
Present value of assets at 1 January	20X1	34,868
	20X0	31,699
Ex-ante income for the year	20X0	3,169

Note that since the income of £3,169 represents the expected increase in the value of the assets during the year, given an expected rate of return on investment of 10 per cent, it also represents 10 per cent of the initial value of those assets estimated at £31,699 on 1 January 20X0.

Estimation of ex-post income

In the foregoing example, the income for the year 20X0 has been calculated on the basis that the expected future net receipts at the end of the year 20X0 remained the same as those at the beginning of the year. Under such conditions, ex-ante and ex-post income would be the same.

If, however, the present value of expected future net receipts at the end of the year 20X0 is different from the present value of those expected receipts at the beginning of the year, the ex-post income is different from the ex-ante income. The ex-ante income refers to the estimated income from the perspective of the beginning of the year, and the ex-post income refers to the estimated income from the perspective of the end of the year.

Example 28.4 Let it be assumed that the revised estimates of the future net receipts on 1 January 20X1 are as follows (the estimates at 1 January 20X0 are in brackets):

Year	Expected net receipts at end of year as at 1 January 20X1		Present value of expected receipts as at 1 January 20X1	Expected net receipts at end of year as at 1 January 20X0	Present value of expected receipts as at 1 January 20X0
	£	£	£	£	£
20X0	10,000		10,000	(10,000)	(9,091)
20X1	9,000	(9,000/1.10)	8,182	(10,000)	(8,264)
20X2	9,000	$(9,000/(1.10)^2)$	7,438	(10,000)	(7,513)
20X3	9,000	$(9,000/(1.10)^3)$	6,762	(10,000)	(6,831)
Present value of expected future net receipts on 1 January 20X1			32,382		(31,699)

Ex-post income for the year 20X0, based on the revised estimates established on 1 January 20X1, is as follows:

			£
Estimated present value on 1 January	20X1		32,382
	20X0		31,699
Ex-post income for the year	20X0		683

The ex-post income for the year 20X0 is made up of the following components:

	£
Ex-ante income	3,169
Ex-post adjustment [34,868 – 32,382]	2,486
Ex-post income	683

The subjective nature of economic income

The net present value method of valuation presents a number of measurement problems. Accuracy of measurement depends upon the degree of certainty under which the forecasts of expected future cash flows are made. Ideally, the size of the net future cash flows should be estimated with reasonable accuracy as should the time profile of these future cash flows. This is because a sum of money in two years' time is worth more than the sum of money in three years' time. We discuss this problem further when we examine capital budgeting decisions.

The net present value concept also requires that the discount rate selected for reducing the future cash flows to their present value should reflect accurately the time value of money. If interest rates are going to fluctuate during the time period considered for using the asset, it follows that the present value of the asset will be distorted because the correct discount rate has not been applied.

Because the future cash flows and discount rate cannot be determined with certainty, Edwards and Bell (1961) call economic income 'subjective income', and dismiss the concept on the grounds that it cannot be satisfactorily applied on an operational basis. They echo, therefore, Hicks's own dissatisfaction with the concept, mentioned earlier in this chapter.

We mentioned in Part 2 that because of uncertainty surrounding the valuation of a firm, it is not the accountant's function to value the firm for the shareholder or investor. On the contrary, it is for the investor to establish the firm's value as an investment and to bear the risk implied in such a valuation. The role of the accountant is to furnish information which is useful for this purpose. The usefulness and relevance of the information provided in financial reports lies in the effectiveness with which it allows the investor to formulate valuations with some degree of accuracy. In the face of uncertainty, accuracy can never be guaranteed, but information about past and current performance may be used as a basis of developing projections and estimates of likely future trends. The adequacy of the accountant's presentation of information for this purpose and the clarity and sufficiency of disclosure are the central problems facing the accounting profession in this area. Investors should use the information provided to make their own estimates of future net receipts, and taking into account their assessment of the degree of uncertainty involved in those estimates, they should discount those estimated net receipts by an appropriate discount rate to arrive at a valuation of the firm. This valuation will retain a high degree of subjectivity, for the discount rate will vary from individual to individual depending upon their respective risk preferences. Therefore, the concept of well-offness is really a matter of an individual's personal preferences. For all these reasons, the concept of economic income has little applicability to the practical problems of financial reporting.

However, it has uses in focusing our attention on aspects of financial reporting that will be of interest to investors, and on the problems that require attention (e.g. future cash flows and the risks of those cash flows).

Summary

Conventional accounting concepts of income and value are of little use for decision making, because of the limitations inherent in the historical cost and realization concepts which govern the measurement of accounting income. Under conditions of inflation, conservative asset values on the balance sheet contrast with optimistic income measurement in the income statement. Changes in value are not reported as they occur. Changing money values also undermine the stability of the unit of measurement in accounting.

Under conditions of certainty, economic income provides an ideal concept for financial reporting purposes. The value of the firm's future net receipts may be capitalized, thereby providing the investor with a basis for decision making.

The presence of uncertainty, which is the general rule, precludes the use of economic income because of its essentially subjective nature. Future cash flows and discount rates cannot be estimated with certainty. For this reason, the accountant does not attempt to value the firm. Instead, financial reports are concerned with past performance, and investors are required to make their own valuations from the information made available.

Despite these practical limitations, the importance of economic concepts of income and value lies in the emphasis they place on the measurement of value and and in changes of value rather than on historical costs. Moreover, they stress the limitations of accounting concepts such as the realization concept for financial reporting purposes, and emphasize the importance of the concept of capital maintenance to income measurement.

Self-assessment questions

1 Analyse the effects of the cost concept on the measurement of accounting income.

2 Analyse the effects of the cost concept on accounting valuations.

3 Discuss the modifications that could be made to historic cost accounting that would improve the quality of accounting information for financial reporting purposes.

4 Explain the significance of the realization concept with respect to accounting information. Are accountants justified in their commitment to the realization concept?

5 Explain the essential differences between the accounting and economic approaches to income measurement.

6 Comment briefly on Hicks's definition of income.

7 Comment briefly on Alexander's definition of business income.

8 Explain briefly the relation between income and value in the measurement of economic income.

9 Explain the difference between 'ex-ante' and 'ex-post' income. What are the implications of these two approaches for the measurement of economic income?

10 Comment briefly on the difficulties that could be found in applying economic concepts of income and value to accounting measurements.

References

Alexander, S.S. (1962) revised by Solomons, D. Income measurement in a dynamic economy, in Baxter, W.T. and Davidson, S. (eds) *Studies in Accounting Theory*, Sweet & Maxwell.

Edwards, E.O. and Bell, P.W. (1961) *The Theory and Measurement of Business Income*, University of California Press.

Hicks, J.R. (1946) *Value and Capital* (2nd edn), Oxford University Press.

ICAS Research Committee (1988) *Making Corporate Reports Valuable*, Kogan Page.

CHAPTER 29

Accounting under monetary instability and market volatility

Setting the scene

Stewardship accounting characterized by accounting concepts and relying on data drawn from invoices of past transactions is founded on a control paradigm that has its legitimacy in the law of contract in providing a record of legal rights and obligations arising from business transactions. There is a universal obligation under business law, company law and tax lax of all jurisdictions to keep proper accounting records of transactions and to prepare annual reports therefrom. Over the years, financial reports based on these accounting and legal traditions have been criticized for not meeting market needs for information relevant to decision making. It has moved the debate about accounting theory towards the adoption of a new paradigm that has its legitimacy in decisions relating to the management of economic resources and, in particular, the information needs of investors and financial markets. It has not changed by one iota the fundamental reasons why businesses must maintain proper records of all transactions, as evidenced in invoices and prepare annual reports from these records.

In effect, there now exist two accounting paradigms that are fundamentally different; the first focuses on the past, the second focuses on the future. The requirement that the veracity of accounting information is an essential part of 'truth' that is the basis of legal rights, is opposed by the view that objectivity should be judged by usefulness and relevance to favour value judgements that facilitate decisions about the future. Traditional accounting is seen as having its Achilles heel in its commitment to historic cost and its necessary assumption that monetary and market values are constant through time, thereby ensuring the stability of its measurement base as defined in the cost convention. Monetary instability and market volatility deny this assumption and put into question those accounting concepts that determine the nature, purpose and scope of accounting theory as a social context defined in terms of a stewardship (management) responsibility. If those concepts and accounting standards from which they are derived are abandoned or significantly modified by fair value accounting, a considerable extension of the regulatory framework may be needed that recognizes the inescapable social function of accounting, in which truth and trust are essential criteria.

After studying this chapter you should be able to:

1 understand the significance of the control paradigm and the valuation paradigm in financial reporting;

2 appreciate the distinctive roles of historic cost versus current cost as a valuation base;

3 relate the discussion of accounting under monetary instability and market volatility to ethical values for ensuring truth and trust in financial reports;

4 convert money measurements recorded at historical cost into their current purchasing power equivalent in calculating periodic income and stating financial position;

5 appreciate the objectives of asset value accounting and explain its different forms;

6 explain the concept of 'value to the firm';

7 explain the accounting entries necessary to record foreign invoices received and settled under fluctuating exchange rates;

8 understand the meaning of fair values in the context of financial reporting;

9 compare the US proposal for fair value accounting proposed under FAS 157 Fair Value Measurement with that stated by the exposure draft on Fair Value Measurement issued in 2009 by the IASB.

The evolution of business accounting had its roots in the necessity to maintain proper records of business transactions as they occur in a methodical and permanent form to enable owners of businesses to exercise control through the assessment of periodic performance and to have an on-going and clear knowledge of business assets and liabilities. In searching for an appropriate paradigm through which to discuss the role of accounting, the control paradigm is the most obvious (Glautier, 1983). Seen in the context of stewardship accounting, the control paradigm implies an information system that accumulates knowledge of the continuous flow of business transactions. Double-entry bookkeeping reflects entirely this paradigm, relying on historical data about transactions, assets and liabilities that create legal rights and obligations expressed and measured in money terms.

The most important accounting activity to this day remains the orderly and systematic recording of business facts in money terms that are summarized in financial accounting statements and audited by professional auditors. Once recorded at their entry value into the accounting system, historical accounting facts have a constant and unchanging monetary value in book terms. This is the fundamental nature of historical cost accounting. Moreover, insofar as they arise out of legal contracts, historical money values are acknowledged as enforceable legal values. For example, a liability is a sum of money originating in a legal contract enforceable at law at the contract value. It is not susceptible of being indexed to correct for changes in the value of money arising from monetary instability or market volatility with respect to traded value of such liability. The same rule applies to assets.

The control paradigm that validates historical cost accounting has a perspective that looks to the future insofar only as the analysis of past transactions reveals corrections needed to be made to attain desired future improvements. However, as Popper (1972) has convincingly argued, the past in not a reliable guide to the future and this knowledge is widely accepted in accounting.

445

The second paradigm reflects the demand of financial markets for information relevant and useful to investor decision making. It assumes that the role of financial reports should reflect valuations based on market values and not historic entry costs. Historical cost measurements that form the database of accounting systems are deemed irrelevant for valuation models on which investors make decisions. Accordingly, the valuation paradigm renders conventional accounting information redundant and looks to market values for information relevant to decision making. The principle of 'mark-to-market' becomes the relevant accounting information source and data obtained from invoices are relegated to the necessary audit control function.

In response to pressures from financial markets for information relevant to decision making by investors in the form of current values rather than historical costs, there has been considerable progress over the years in financial reporting methods and practices. Manufacturing and service companies switched to reporting production information in the form of standard costs, rather than actual costs. Companies accepted the need to modify the reported values of assets and liabilities through the process of year-end accounting revaluations of historical cost values. Significantly, quoted companies have responded to stock exchange requirements to publish budget forecasts and to shorten reporting period through short-term interim financial statements.

During this period of evolution of financial reporting theory and, in the face of the debate on fair value accounting that has crystallized in the wake of the credit crisis, traditional accounting concepts have continued to act as ethical bulwarks acting for truth and trust in accounting and reflecting judgements about 'what is right'. In particular, and exceptionally by reason of the need for year-end accounting adjustments, no information should enter the accounting system otherwise than through invoicing and no gains should be recognized that have not been realized, Entry costs should be measured by reference to contracted money values representing the actual financial effort engaged at that time. Current market values may be used to modify recorded values only in exceptional cases. Market values must not be merely opinions or beliefs, but must be susceptible of verification by reference to market values. In accordance with the principle of prudence, holding gains should not be reported as income, but anticipated losses should be recognized as incurred and deducted from income. It is fundamental accounting doctrine that manipulation of all sorts should be prevented and proscribed to ensure truth and trust in financial reporting. Ethical standards embedded in accounting theory insist that balance sheets should not be made the instrument for inflating shareholder value and spinning poor income results. Non-current assets that have not been purchased should not be admitted on balance sheets, but where market values are higher than historic cost, it is permissible to revalue such assets and in the reverse case, to write them down. As regards current assets, unrealized gains should not be recognized and such assets must continue to be valued at historic cost. However, should market values be lower than historic costs, unrealized losses should be recognized and balance sheet values modified accordingly.

The foregoing considerations serve to heighten the debate concerning the control and the valuation paradigms in accounting theory; the means by which the legitimate aims of accounting may be attained in supplying relevant and useful information under both paradigms, and the moral imperatives embedded in accounting conventions that represent ethical standards of accounting responsibility for truth and trust defined by the knowledge of what is right. Monetary instability and market volatility are distinct phenomena. They relate to different circumstances affecting the market economy. Monetary instability has been ingrained in history of money from its very origins by reason of the pervasive dishonesty that its importance in society engenders. Ranging from clipping gold coins to the infinite ways in which market operators seek to gain through representing and manipulating traded values, both money values and market values are never constant but evolve continually. The control paradigm fixes on money measurement at one point in time, namely the entry money value, which is its timeless and stable value in a control perspective. The valuation paradigm recognizes the risks imported into decision making by different circumstances and different time horizons in which money values are determined by constantly fluctuating market values, whether they are affected by money markets or other markets.

Accounting under monetary instability

Monetary instability affects accounting measurements when the domestic value of money fluctuates as against the value of goods and services and when the international value of a currency fluctuates against other currencies. Both forms of monetary instability are discussed in this section.

Domestic monetary instability

Domestic fluctuations may result from inflation or deflation and are seen in the falling or rising purchasing power of money associated usually with changes in the level of aggregate demand for goods and services in the economy. They may also result from changes in monetary policy that affects the supply of money or credit. It maybe noted that the recent credit crunch had a marked deflationary impact on demand, restricted the supply of credit and led to changes in monetary policy in favour of massive monetary expansion to counter these effects. This massive monetary expansion eventually will have to be re-absorbed, if it is not to lead to high levels of inflation as the economy recovers.

By and large, economic growth tends to have inflationary effects because it increases disposable incomes in a climate of increased supply of money and credit, even though accompanied by increases in the gross national product. However, economic growth may also stall under inflationary conditions, leading to what has been described as stagflation.

Inflation, rather than deflation, is the normal condition that affects accounting measurements and has highlighted the shortcomings of historic cost values for financial reporting purposes. Zero inflation would validate historic cost values, mild inflation would only have a slight and acceptable consequence and hyper-inflation would destroy the meaning of historical cost values as well as the value of money itself and results in a flight to other assets.

Monetary instability as observed in price changes may be seen as having general and specific effects. General price changes reflect increases or decreases in the value of money. In this case, general price changes are measured by an index showing difference in the value of money in relation to goods and services through time. For example, if £15 is needed today to buy what £10 would have bought on an earlier date, it may be said that the price level has increased, the purchasing power of money has fallen and the economy is in a period of inflation. By contrast, specific price changes occur for several reasons. Changes in consumer tastes, technological improvements and speculation by buyers are all reasons found at the root of specific price changes.

Adjusting for the effects of price changes may take the following forms:

1 General adjustments: based on current purchasing power accounting.
2 Specific adjustments based on current values:
   (a) replacement cost accounting – which is based on the current acquisition value of assets, so that in affect they are valued at their current entry price;
   (b) realizable value accounting – which is based on the current realizable value of assets – that is, their current exit price;
   (c) current value accounting – which is concerned with the value to the firm of assets. While, in many cases, this value would, in fact, be the replacement cost, in some circumstances it would be the net present value of the future income from the asset or its net realizable value.
3 A combination of (1) and (2).

Current purchasing power accounting

Reacting to high levels of inflation occurring early in the 1970s, accounting regulators recommended that a supplementary statement should be attached to the financial reports of companies showing the conversion of the figures in the financial reports in terms of their current purchasing power (CPP) at the closing day of the accounting period. In the UK, they recommended that the Retail Price Index (RPI) should be used to effect the conversion of historical cost values into current purchasing power equivalents (SSAP 7, 'Accounting for Changes in the Purchasing Power of Money' 1974, withdrawn 1978).

CPP adjustments are limited to dealing with changes in the general purchasing power of money that occur during periods of inflation or deflation. It takes the view that the purpose of price level adjustments is to show each item in financial reports in terms of a common monetary unit of the same purchasing power. The RPI is assumed to reflect the general movement in price of all goods and services. Thus, the doubling of the RPI from 100 to 200 between two points in time would mean that the purchasing power of money had fallen by half during that time interval.

Historical cost accounting is based essentially on the maintenance of financial capital in money terms. Such a concept asserts that all funds available to the firm in excess of the original contribution of funds by shareholders make the firm better off. High levels of inflation undermine the validity of this assertion. CPP accounting attempts to deal with this problem by adjusting historical cost measurements for the effects of inflation to maintain the purchasing power held by the firm. The income after CPP adjustments is stated as gains arising during the accounting period which may be distributed to shareholders, so that the purchasing power of the shareholders' interest in the company is the same at the end of the year as it was at the beginning. However, this adjustment cannot of itself ensure the maintenance of the productive capacity of the assets held by the company, which is a different concept. The price level adjustment alone ignores the fact that capital may be dispersed through changes in individual prices, if those relevant to the individual firm rise at a rate faster than the rate of change in the price level. Equally, real capital will increase if the relationship is reversed.

Monetary and non-monetary items

For the purpose of CPP accounting it is necessary to distinguish between two classes of items – monetary and non-monetary items.

Monetary items may be defined as those fixed by contract or by their nature and are expressed in money terms regardless of changes in the price level. They include monetary assets such as cash, debtors and loans, and exist as money or as claims to specified sums of money. Holders of monetary assets suffer a loss in the general purchasing power of their assets during periods of inflation. Thus, if one holds money in the form of a bank deposit and the yearly rate of inflation is 25 per cent, the loss in the purchasing power of that money by the end of the period will be 25 per cent.

They also include monetary liabilities such as creditors, bank overdrafts and long-term loans. As the value of money falls during a period of inflation, the value of such liabilities similarly falls, which is a purchasing power gain to the debtor. Consequently, holders of monetary liabilities gain at the expense of creditors during periods of inflation, as they will settle these liabilities with money having less purchasing power than when incurred.

Non-monetary items are assets and liabilities such as non-current assets, inventories and shareholders' equity, which are assumed neither to lose nor to gain in value by reason of inflation or deflation. This is because price changes for these items will tend to compensate for changes in the value of money. For example, if inventories on hand at the beginning of the year remain unsold at the end of the year, there will be no purchasing power loss since one assumes the sale price when they are sold would be adjusted upwards to take account of the fall in the value of money.

If £100,000 was used to purchase land on a date when the RPI stood at 100, and it now stands at 150, the assumption underlying this movement in prices is that £150,000 in today's money has the same purchasing power as £100,000 when the RPI stood at 100. Hence, to report on the purchasing power invested in the land, its acquisition cost should be stated as £150,000. This value says nothing about the present market value of that particular piece of land. Property values may have increased more or less than the general movement in prices indicated by the RPI. The particular piece of land mentioned in this example may now be worth £300,000 or only £90,000. Hence, the figure of £150,000 represents only the historical cost of acquisition adjusted for the decrease in the general value of the pound.

The acceptance of the need to adjust accounting measurements for inflation is recognition of a fundamental proposition in income theory, namely maintaining the value of capital is a prerequisite for measuring income. There can be no recognition of income for a period unless it has been established that the purchasing power of the capital employed in a firm is the same at the end of the accounting period as it was in the beginning.

A simple example serves to explain the nature of adjustments which are required to financial reports based on historical cost measurements in order to remove the effects of general price level changes.

Example 29.1 Bangored Supplies plc was formed on 1 January 20X0, with a share capital of £75,000 which was fully subscribed in cash on that date. On the same day, equipment was purchased for £45,000, of which £20,000 was paid immediately, the balance of £25,000 being payable two years thence. The price level index was 100 on 1 January 20X0.

Goods were purchased in two instalments prior to commencing business as follows:

1st purchase in the sum of £44,000, when the price level index was 110;
2nd purchase in the sum of £45,000, when the price level index was 120.

All sales were made when the price level index was 130, and expenses of £16,000 were also incurred at the same index level. Stocks were valued on the FIFO method and the closing stock was valued at £29,000. The price level index at 31 December 20X0 was 130.

The income statement and balance sheet in respect of this year, prepared on a historical cost basis, were as follows:

Balance sheet as at 31 December 20X0

	£	£
Non-currrent assets		45,000
Less: Accumulated depreciation		4,500
		40,500
Current assets		
Inventory	29,000	
Debtors	19,000	
Bank balance	39,500	
	87,500	
Less: Current liabilities	33,500	
Net current assets		54,000
		94,500
Share capital		75,000
Retained earnings		19,500
		94,500

Income statement for the year ended 31 December 20X0

	£	£
Sales		100,000
Cost of goods sold		60,000
Gross operating income		40,000
Expenses	16,000	
Depreciation (10% of £45,000)	4,500	
		20,500
Net operating income		19,500

Required:
(a) Calculate the purchasing power gain or loss on the monetary items.
(b) Prepare an inflation-adjusted income statement account for the year ended 31 December 20X0.

Prepare an inflation-adjusted balance sheet as at 31 December 20X0 when the price level index was 130.

(a) Calculation of purchasing power gain or loss on short-term monetary items during the year ended 31 December 20X0

	Unadjusted monetary items	Conversion factor	Adjusted monetary items
	£		£
Net current monetary items on			
1 January 20X0 (cash invested)	75,000	130/100	97,500
Add: Sales	100,000	130/130	100,000
	175,000		197,500
Less:			
Purchases of equipment	20,000	130/100	26,000
Purchase of goods			
(i) index at 110	44,000	130/110	52,000
(j) index at 120	45,000	130/120	48,750
Expenses	16,000	130/130	16,000
	125,000		142,750
Net current monetary items on	50,000		54,750
31 December 20X0			
Unadjusted net current monetary items on 31 December 20X0			50,000
Purchasing power loss for the year ended 31 December 20X0			4,750

(b) Preparation of inflation-adjusted income statement for the year ended 31 December 20X0

	Unadjusted	Conversion factor	Adjusted
	£		£
Sales	100,000	130/130	100,000
Cost of goods sold			
At index 110	44,000	130/110	52,000
At index 120	16,000	130/120	17,333
Expenses	16,000	130/130	16,000
Depreciation	4,500	130/100	5,850
	80,500		91,183
Net income	19,500		8,817

(c) Preparation of inflation-adjusted balance sheet as at 31 December 20X0

	Unadjusted	Conversion factor	Adjusted
	£		£
Non-current assets	45,000	130/100	58,500
Less: Accumulated depreciation	4,500	130/100	5,850
	40,500		52,650
Current assets			
Inventories	29,000	130/120	31,417
Debtors	19,000	130/130	19,000
Bank balance	39,500	130/130	39,500
	87,500		89,917
Less: Current liabilities	33,500	130/130	33,500
Net current assets	54,000		56,417
Total assets	94,500		109,067
Share capital	75,000	130/100	97,500
Retained earnings	19,500	–	8,817
Accumulated purchasing power gain			2,750
	94,500		109,067

Calculation of accumulated purchasing power gain:

Gain on unpaid balance of purchase price of equipment	
Adjusted balance (£25,000 × 130/100)	32,500
Unadjusted balance	25,000
	7,500
Less: Loss as computed on short-term monetary items	4,750
Net accumulated purchasing power gain	2,750

An appraisal of CPP accounting

CPP can be applied with a high degree of objectivity required of accounting valuation as it does not depart in principle from historical-cost-based measurement. Price level adjustments are verifiable by reference to the index used to measure changes in the purchasing power of money, and result in alterations to historical cost measurements which are themselves objective. Therefore, both criteria of objectivity and verifiability are satisfied in CPP accounting.

An objection to CPP accounting is raised by some authorities who believe that there is no such thing as generalized purchasing power (Gynther, 1974). Organizations and people do not see themselves as holding general purchasing power when they hold money; rather, they see themselves as holding specific purchasing power in respect of those relatively few items which they wish to purchase. Hence, the purchasing power of money should be related to those items on which money is intended to be spent. A unit of measurement which relies for its validity on the purchasing power of money assessed by reference to a set of goods and services will not be equally useful to all individuals and entities.

Moreover, the concept of income on which these adjustments are based is not one which maintains the service potential of capital. A general price index, particularly a consumer price index, is a weighted average of the price change occurring in a wide variety of goods and services available in the economy. Adjusting financial data for the effects of inflation is not the same as reporting current values. Price-adjusted data still represents costs, or funds, committed to non-monetary items: these costs are merely translated into the equivalent costs in terms of today's pounds.

General price indices assume that the movements in the price of all goods correspond with each other. However, only by coincidence will a change in the general price index correspond with the change in the price of any particular good or service during the same period. Indeed, there is no reason why they may not move in opposite directions. A general price index will not be relevant to any business entity which needs to make adjustments to asset valuations in order to maintain the value of its capital in the long term.

Controversy surrounds the treatment of gains and losses arising on monetary items. By our approach in Example 29.1, the gain or loss on net monetary items is disclosed separately and is not included in income from continuing operations. It is treated as a capital adjustment. The 'gains' resulting from these adjustments do not increase sums available for distribution as dividends to shareholders, since they are purely accounting adjustments. They could be distributed only by drawing on existing cash resources or by borrowing. Hence, if the net 'gains' on monetary items are regarded as available for distribution, the users of adjusted financial reports could be seriously misled.

Although CPP accounting has serious limitations, many writers have argued the need to adjust accounting income for general inflation. According to Baxter (1984):

> *Hitherto we have found little fault with statistical tables (e.g. of national income) in constant prices; we do not decry the indexing of tax allowances; most of us would accept indexed investments as a godsend. Admittedly the retail price index does not reflect precisely the consumption patterns of wealthy shareholders; but the divergence does not seem to be big. No system of inflation accounting will be perfect, and correction of income by a general index seems the least bad of the possibilities.*

Replacement cost accounting

The basic concept underlying replacement cost accounting is that the firm is a going concern, which is continuously replacing its assets. Therefore, the cost of consuming such assets in the profit generation process should be equivalent to the cost of their replacement. Replacement cost accounting differs from current purchasing power accounting in that it is concerned with the manner in which price changes affect the individual firm. It focuses on the specific commodities and assets employed by the firm taking into account changes in the price of such commodities and assets reflected in specific price indices or price indices of groups of similar commodities and assets. It became on important issue in the UK in the form of current cost accounting, which followed the publication of the Sandilands Report (Report of the Committee on Inflation Accounting 1975). It resulted in the issue of SSAP 16 'Current Cost Accounting' 1980 that required large companies to publish supplementary CCA disclosure with their annual financial statement based on historic costs. It was withdrawn in 1988. In the USA, FAS 33 introduced a similar requirement that was also withdrawn about the same time.

Replacement cost accounting is addressed to the concept of capital maintenance, interpreted as maintaining the operating capacity of the firm, and involves:

1 calculating current operating income by matching current revenues with the current cost of resources exhausted in earning those revenues;
2 calculating holding gains and losses;
3 presenting the balance sheet in current value terms.

Components of replacement cost income (RCI)

The treatment of the two components of replacement cost income (RCI), namely current operating income and holding gains and losses, is a controversial matter in the literature of accounting.

Current operating income results from operating activities and is calculated by matching revenues with the current cost of resources exhausted in these activities. Holding gains and losses result from holding rather than operating activities.

According to the method of replacement cost accounting suggested by Edwards and Bell (1961), holding gains and losses should be reported together with current operating income in the measurement of RCI. In identifying holding gains as they arise, thereby distinguishing these gains from gains occurring on realization, the pattern of income recognition differs under replacement cost accounting from that associated with conventional accounting income, as may be seen from the following example.

Example 29.2 During the year ended 31 December 20X0, an asset was acquired at a cost of £40. By 31 December 20X0 its replacement cost had risen to £60. It was sold during the year ended 31 December 20X1 for £100, and at the time of sale its replacement cost was £65.

For the purpose of measuring accounting income, the profit arising from the sale of the asset (assuming no depreciation) would accrue in the year ended 31 December 20X1 and would be calculated as follows:

$$\text{accounting profits} = \text{revenue} - \text{historical cost}$$
$$= £100 - £40$$
$$= £60$$

For the purpose of measuring RCI, three distinct gains are recognized which occur as follows:

1 A holding gain in the year ended 31 December 20X0, measured as the difference between the replacement cost at 31 December 20X0 and the acquisition cost during the year, that is, £60 – £40 = £20.
2 A holding gain in the year ended 31 December 20X1, measured as the difference between the replacement cost at 31 December 20X0 and the replacement cost on the date of sale, that is, £65 – £60 = £5.
3 An operating gain resulting directly from the activity of selling, measured as the difference between the realized sale price and the replacement cost at the date of sale, that is, £100 – £65 = £35.

These differing timings of income recognition may be compared as follows:

Year ended 21 December	20X0	20X1
	£	£
Accounting income	–	60
Replacement cost income holding gains	20	5
Current operating gain	–	35

It is clear from this example that the RCI concept provides more detailed information than the accounting income concept for the purpose of evaluating the results of activities. Moreover, RCI indicates whether the sales proceeds are sufficient to cover the replacement cost of the resources sold, that is, whether the activity of selling itself is efficient. Where the goods sold are manufactured by the firm, current operating income indicates whether the manufacturing process is profitable, for the input factors of production are valued at their current replacement cost. Hence, from a long-term point of view, it affords a means of evaluating the firm as a going concern.

Income measurement under historical cost and replacement cost compared

The extent of the differences between these two concepts of income are revealed by a more comprehensive example.

Example 29.3 The financial position of Preifat Ltd, as revealed by the balance sheet as at 31 December 20X0 using historical cost measurements, is as follows:

	£		£
Share capital	1,400	Non-current asset	1,000
		Inventory	400
	1,400		1,400

The non-current asset shown on the balance sheet was acquired on 31 December 20X0 and has an estimated life of five years, with no scrap value.

Data recorded in respect of the year ended 31 December 20X1 is as follows:

	£
Sales	2,000
Purchases at historical cost	700
Closing inventory: at historical cost	200
at replacement cost	250
Cost of goods sold at replacement cost	1,000

It was also estimated that the replacement cost of the non-current asset had risen to £1,200 by 31 December 20X1.

On the basis of this information, the accounting income for the year 20X1 may be computed as follows:

Accounting income for the year ended 31 December 20X1

	£	£
Sales		2,000
Cost of goods sold:		
Opening inventory	400	
Purchases	700	
	1,100	
Closing inventory	200	
		900
		1,100
Depreciation (£1,000 ÷ 5)		200
Accounting income		900

By contrast, the calculation of the components of replacement cost income gives a more comprehensive analysis of the nature of operating and holding gains, as follows:

Replacement cost income for the year ended 31 December 20X1

	£	£	£
Sales			2,000
Cost of goods sold (at replacement cost)			1,000
			1,000
Depreciation (£1,200 ÷ 5)			240
Current operating income			760
Holding gains			
Realized through use during the year			
Non-current assets	40		
Inventory	100		
		140	
Unrealized at the end of the year			
Non-currrent assets	160		
Inventory	50		
		210	
Total holding gains			350
Current operating income plus holding gains			1,100

Notes:

1 Depreciation is calculated on the replacement cost of the non-current assets (£1,200) rather than on the historical acquisition cost (£1,000). By this means, the depreciation provision is more realistic in relation to the current cost of resource utilization.
2 Inventory is charged against sales at their current replacement cost at the time of sale.
3 Holding gains are of two kinds:

(a) Realized holding gains which result from the application of replacement cost values to the input of resources to the income generation process. In the example, depreciation charged under replacement cost accounting is £40 greater than that charged under historical cost accounting. Similarly, the cost of goods sold under replacement cost is £100 greater than that charged under historical cost accounting. Both amounts represent holding gains realized by reason of the use or the sale of assets.

(b) Unrealized holding gains which result from the increased value of assets held by the firm and remaining unused or unsold at the end of the accounting period. In the example, the unrealized holding gains are calculated as follows:

(i) assets: unallocated value at the end of the accounting period:

Under replacement cost	£1,200 – 240 = £960
Under historic cost	£1,000 – 200 = 800
Unrealized holding gain	160

(ii) Inventory: unsold at the end of the accounting period:

Under replacement cost	£250
Under historical cost	200
Unrealized holding gain	50

Historical cost and replacement cost balance sheets compared

The effect of applying historical cost and replacement cost valuations to balance sheets is seen in the following balance sheet drawn from data given in the example.

Balance sheet as at 31 December 20X1 (assuming that all sales and purchases were paid in cash)

	Historical cost	Replacement cost
	£	£
Non-current assets	1,000	1,200
Less: Accumulated depreciation	200	240
	800	960
Current assets		
Inventory	200	250
Cash	1,300	1,300
	2,300	2,510
Share capital	1,400	1,400
Retained income		
Accounting income	900	
Current operating income		760
Revaluation reserve		350
	2,300	2,510

457

Note:
Cash balance is calculated as follows:
Sales £2,000 – Purchases £700 = Cash £1,300
As may be observed, the application of replacement cost values attempts to reflect economic reality by maintaining the value of asset balances in line with changes in the value of money and changes in the specific value of the assets concerned.

The treatment of holding gains

One of the controversial issues in the debate about replacement cost accounting is whether holding gains constitute income. There is little doubt that current operating income satisfies the accounting convention relating to realization, and at the same time is directed to the maintenance of capital, which is a basic principle in the measurement of economic income.

How holding gains are treated depends on one's view of capital maintenance. Proponents of the maintenance of financial capital in money terms (i.e. the original amount of money invested in the assets of the entity) view the holding gains as an item of income. Income is considered to be the total gain arising during the period which could be distributed in full while still maintaining capital, in the sense of the original financial investment, at the level which existed at the beginning of the period. Advocates of the operating capability concept, however, argue that increases in the price of items that a firm must have if it is to continue in business are not an element of income, but a capital maintenance adjustment to be placed directly in the owners' equity. This is the amount which is necessary for replacing assets. This is the view taken in the above example.

An evaluation of replacement cost accounting

As a method of financial reporting, replacement cost accounting provides a concept of income which can be assessed against the criteria of relevance and feasibility which were discussed earlier.

Replacement cost income is more relevant to investors than accounting income for the purpose of decision making. First, it provides for the maintenance of the service potential of capital by charging against revenue the cost of replacing the assets exhausted in earning revenue. Second, an important distinction is made between operating income and holding gains, thereby allowing investors to appraise the firm as a going concern. Third, it recognizes changes in the value of assets, since they are related to current market prices. For these reasons, investors are provided with information which is more relevant than accounting income for evaluating the business, and they are placed in a better position to predict the future. By providing more accurate valuations of assets in use, replacement cost accounting is likely to lead to a more efficient allocation of financial resources than that afforded by conventional accounting methods. A further argument in favour of replacement cost accounting lies in the diversity of values found in conventional accounting due to the employment of a variety of valuation methods, such as LIFO, FIFO or average cost. With replacement cost accounting, however, values are uniformly derived from the current replacement cost of specific assets, so that comparisons are much more meaningful.

Criticisms are sometimes advanced against replacement cost accounting on the ground that the measurements involved are subjective. There exist, however, government indices which relate to non-current assets of various kinds which may be employed for the purpose of calculating the replacement cost of specific non-current assets. The Sandilands Committee recommended that the Government Statistical Service should publish as soon as possible a new series of price indices specific to particular industries for capital expenditure on plant and machinery. Such a series of indices should be designed to provide a 'standard reference basis' for making reasonable approximations of current replacement costs. The derivation of replacement costs for inventory could present problems. However, when the various different methods of valuing inventory at the present time are considered, it appears that replacement cost provides a more objective measure.

A major problem arises during periods of rapid technological change. Most authorities argue that since a measure of the profitability of existing operations is required, current replacement costs should be measured in terms of the market prices prevailing for the actual non-current assets which are exhausted in producing income. Some authorities are opposed to this view, since it seemingly ignores the effect of technological change. They argue that the replacement cost of new-generation assets should be used, because 'the primary interest is in the long-run prospects of the firm, and there seems to be no particular reason why these long-run prospects would be indicated by the prospects of the present mode of production, when becoming obsolete'. Accordingly, if the firm is using a second-generation computer made obsolete by the development of third-generation computers, they argue that the current replacement cost should be based on the current market price of third-generation rather than second-generation computers.

Realizable value accounting

Both historical cost and replacement cost accounting employ entry values, that is, they are based on the acquisition cost of assets. By contrast, realizable value accounting employs exit values, that is, it is based on the realizable price of assets.

The distinction between entry and exit values leads to two different concepts of income – realized and realizable income. Realized income arises only upon sale, so that unsold assets are valued at cost. By contrast, realizable profit is based on the current selling price of the assets, thereby indicating the revenue which could be obtained should the assets be sold. As a result, unsold assets are valued not at cost, but at realizable value.

The case for realizable value accounting

The realizable value model is based on the concept of opportunity cost, that is, value is expressed in terms of the benefit lost in holding assets in their present form rather than in the next-best alternative form. For example, as regards closing inventory, the next best alternative to holding stocks is selling them, so that on an opportunity cost basis, the value of closing inventory is what they would realize if sold.

Chambers and Sterling have argued in favour of realizable value accounting. According to Chambers, for example, the most important characteristic of the firm is its capacity to adapt to a changing environment, and in this way, to ensure its survival. The survival of the firm depends, therefore, on its ability to acquire goods and services, which is related to the realizable value of its existing assets. Chambers coined the term 'current cash equivalent' to indicate the realizable value of the firm's currently held assets, that is, the cash represented by those assets and available, if sold, for investing in market alternatives and consequently redeploying its resources (Chambers, 1966; Sterling, 1970).

By contrast, replacement cost accounting reflects a relatively static situation, and does not inform investors about the economic sacrifice made in holding resources in their current form.

Another argument in favour of realizable value accounting is that realizable value income is an acceptable surrogate for economic income, for it indicates minimum future cash flows which may result from the realization of currently held assets. As argued in Chapter 27, the present value of future cash flows associated with the holding of assets is the most relevant concept of value from the point of view of investors. Backward-looking concepts, such as historical cost and replacement cost values, are poor surrogates as predictors of future cash flows. Finally, a further argument in favour of realizable value lies in its relevance to the needs of creditors for information about the market value of the assets held by a company to which they have extended credit facilities, particularly if the security for loans and other forms of credit is represented by liens or mortgages over such assets.

Components of realizable income

Realizable income reflects the periodic change in the value of enterprise capital measured in terms of resale price. It consists of two components:

1 realized gains resulting from the sale of assets during the accounting period, which are measured as the difference between the actual realized revenue from sale and the realizable value estimated at the beginning of the period;
2 unrealized gains resulting from changes in the realizable value of assets which have remained unsold at the end of the accounting period.

Example 29.4 During the year ended 31 December 20X0 an asset was acquired for £40. At 31 December 20X0, its estimated realizable value was £85, and it was sold during the year ended 31 December 20X1 for £100. The realizable income for the years ended 31 December 20X0 and 20X1 is as follows:

	20X0	20X1
Realizable income		
Unrealized gain	£85 – 40 = £45	
Realized gain		100 – 85 = £15

We noted in our earlier discussion of holding gains arising under replacement cost accounting that such gains could not be treated as part of replacement income. The reason for this view is to be found in the capital maintenance criterion to which replacement cost income is directed. By contrast, the realizable value concept of income is directed towards measuring the firm's ability to adapt to a changing environment, and for this purpose profit is required to measure changes in the firm's command over goods and services. This may be measured by reference to both realized gains and unrealized gains which result, as we mentioned earlier, from changes in the realizable value of assets during the year. Hence, under realizable value income, no distinction is maintained between current operating income and holding gains. Assets are shown on the balance sheet at their realizable value.

Limitations of exit values

Exit values imply a short-run approach to the analysis of business operations because they entail disposition and liquidation values being shown on the balance sheet. Hence, business operations resulting in realizable income only indicate that it is worth staying in business in the short run, not that it is worth replacing assets and staying in business in the long term. Realizable value accounting values all assets at exit prices even though many assets are not held for resale.

It has been argued that the crucial test of the usefulness of exit values in financial reports lies in the treatment of highly specific assets, which may have very little value for anyone except the present owner for whom they were constructed. The most extreme example of such assets are mineshafts, which, being large holes in the ground, have no exit value. Such assets may be presumed to have been worth as much to the firm as their acquisition or construction costs. Otherwise, it is clear that they would not have been acquired or constructed. The question is, what would be the sense of writing such assets down to their current realizable value?

Another limitation of exit values lies in their anticipation of operating income, before the critical event giving rise to revenue has occurred. It has been argued, for example, that:

> If profit is to be recognized at a moment of time, we must select that moment. The economist gives a clue in the formulation of entrepreneurship as the function of directing a business, bearing the risks and reaping the rewards of the business. This suggests that profit is earned at the moment of making the most crucial decision or of performing the most difficult task in the cycle of a complete transaction.

(Myers, 1973)

Where production is the critical event and sale presents no problem, the valuation of products at net realizable value gives a better indication of managerial performance than does replacement cost. Where selling is the main difficulty, the sale is the critical event which must occur before managerial performance may be correctly evaluated, for without a contract of sale or an active quoted market for the product, the accountant has little evidence of managerial accomplishment. The accountant must assume, in these circumstances, that the product will be sold for at least the break-even price, so that replacement cost is the most suitable measurement of value in these circumstances.

Current value accounting

Current value accounting is a modification to historical cost income to arrive at the surplus after allowing for the impact of price changes on the funds needed to continue the existing business and to maintain its operating capability, whether financed by shares or borrowings.

Current value accounting utilizes two important theoretical concepts:

1 operating capability, and
2 value to the firm.

Operating capability

Operating capability is assumed to be represented by net operating assets that include not only physical assets, such as fixed assets and stocks, but also the net monetary working capital.

Value to the firm

The concept of 'value to the firm' should determine whether exit or entry values should be used in the valuation process. One way of determining 'value to the firm' is to reverse the opportunity cost concept, and to define opportunity value as the least costly sacrifice avoided by owning the asset. This approach to the valuation of an asset to the firm has been adopted by a number of economists. Bonbright (1937, p. 71), for example, defined opportunity value in the following terms: 'The value of a property to its owner is identical in amount with the adverse value of the entire loss, direct and indirect, that the owner might expect to suffer if he were deprived of the property.'

In no sense may historical cost be measured as the value of an asset to the firm because it is not related to the amount which would have to be paid for the asset, the amount that might be gained from disposing of it or the amount to be gained by holding it. It remains to consider, therefore, the other three bases of valuation which were listed in the introduction:

1 the current purchase price (replacement cost) of the asset (RC);
2 the net realizable value of the asset (NRV);
3 the present value of expected future earnings from the asset (PV).

It has been argued (Parker and Harcourt, 1969, p. 17) that six hypothetical relationships exist between these three values:

	Correct valuation basis
(a) NRV > PV > RC	RC
(b) NRV > RC > PV	RC
(c) PV > RC > NRV	RC
(d) PV > NRV > RC	RC
(e) RC > PV > NRV	PV
(f) RC > NRV > PV	NRV

In (a) and (b) above, NRV is greater than PV. Hence, the firm would be better off selling rather than using the asset. The sale of the asset necessitates its replacement, if the NRV is to be restored. We may say, therefore, that the maximum loss the firm would suffer by being deprived of the asset is RC. In (c) and (d) above, PV is greater than NRV, so that the firm would be better off using the asset rather than selling it. The firm must replace the asset in order to maintain PV, so that the maximum loss the firm would suffer by being deprived of the asset is again RC.

The general statement which may be made, therefore, in respect of the first four cases (a) to (d) is that, where either NRV or PV, or both, are higher than RC, RC is the appropriate value of the asset to the business. As regards a current asset such as inventory, RC will be the current purchase price (entry value). In the case of a non-current asset, RC will be the written-down current purchase price (replacement cost), since the value of such an asset will be the cost of replacing it in its existing condition, having regard to wear and tear.

As regards cases (e) and (f), RC does not represent the value of the asset to the firm, for if the firm were to be deprived of the asset then the loss incurred would be less than RC. Case (e) is most likely to arise in industries where assets are highly specific, where NRV tends to zero and where RC is greater than PV, so that it would not be worth replacing the asset if it were destroyed, but it is worth using it rather than attempting to dispose of it. The conclusion which may be reached as regards non-current assets is that except in the rare occurrence of case (e) non-current assets which are held for use should be valued at RC if such assets are to represent their value to the firm.

Case (f) applies to assets held for resale, that is, where NRV must be greater than PV. If RC should prove to be greater than NRV, such assets would not be replaced. Hence, it implies that they should be valued at NRV or RC, whichever is the lower. This recommendation, despite its superficial resemblance to the lower of cost or market value is not a concession to the convention of conservatism, but represents an attempt to measure the value of assets to the business. If RC exceeds NRV, stocks will not be replaced, so that NRV represents their value to the firm. Conversely, where NRV exceeds RC, inventory is worth replacing, so that their value to the firm is determined by RC.

Recent developments

The IASB's views on dealing with monetary instability followed the concern that existed with respect to double-digit inflation during the 1970s. In 1983, it issued IAS 15 Information for Reflecting the Effects of Changing Prices that required companies to restate historic cost financial reports in either CPP or RC costs. By 1989 these mandatory requirements were relaxed in view of falling inflations rates and in 2003 IAS 15 was withdrawn. IAS 29 Financial Reporting in Hyperinflation Economies 1989 applies only to economies exposed to hyperinflation rates.

Elsewhere, the inflation accounting debate has subsided, but remains in existence, since inflation is always a perspective that is considered under monetary policy and is a major consideration within the European Union, as regards the limits of permissible levels of public debts that are not allowed to exceed 3 per cent of GNP. The remit given to the European Central Bank to aim for monetary stability for the euro is a bone of contention in those countries desirous of seeking growth as the prime objective of policy.

In the UK, the Accounting Standards Committee issued in 1988 a document *Accounting for the Effects of Changing Prices: A Handbook* with the objective of specifying the limitations of historical cost accounting and examines various remedies. The *Handbook* argues for current costs as the method of valuing assets, combined with a financial capital maintenance system (based on CPP type measurements) which maintains shareholders' funds in 'real terms'.

In 1993, the Accounting Standards Board published a Discussion Paper, *The Role of Valuation in Financial Reporting* that acknowledges the superiority of a current value approach over a historical costing approach. According to the *Statement*,

> *The current value based on the value to the firm model ... allows users to observe current operating margins and gives a better guide to future potential performance than the historical cost profit which combines operating margins and any gains or losses from holding assets. Thus, the use of current values for both assets and liabilities provides the information that is most relevant to the decisions of users.*

Interest in inflation accounting virtually disappeared as companies stopped revaluing non-current assets and reported financial assets at market values, where such assets were held as current assets. The concern with current value accounting revived following the credit crunch and financial institutions found themselves holding toxic financial assets that had no market value. It caused a furore in financial markets and among accounting regulators. The debate about historic cost-based financial reporting took new vigour in favour of fair value accounting, which we discuss in the next section.

Instability of currency exchange rates

International trade presents accounting problems in several ways and at distinct levels of importance. In the simplest case, a domestic company that only has a commercial relationship with a foreign company will record its transactions with that company at the invoiced value. If invoiced in the domestic currency, the transaction is recorded in the same way as a domestic transaction. If invoiced in the currency of the foreign company, it has to be translated into the domestic currency at the rate of exchange ruling at the invoice date. Where settlement at a subsequent date results in a higher or lower value, when translated into the domestic currency, the resulting difference is treated separately as an exchange loss or gain and recorded in a separate account. In this way, the commercial transaction is isolated from any instability in foreign exchange rates. Where domestic companies have a substantial volume of foreign business, the exchange rate risk may be handled separately by recourse to forward rates markets or through centralized foreign currency bank accounts managed by specialist staff. Alternatively, the growing importance of foreign trade may be treated as organic growth and hived off structurally through the creation of foreign branches or a foreign subsidiary company, which are distinct and separate accounting entities. Accounting for currency rate instability for international entities will be discussed in Part 4 in relation to the process of accounting consolidation necessary to preparing financial statement by international groups. In this section, we are concerned solely with the treatment of accounting balances held in foreign currencies that have to be restated in the domestic currency at the accounting year-end.

In the United Kingdom, SSAP 20 'The Effects of Changes in Foreign Exchange Rates' 1983 provided that the result of each transaction should be translated in a company's local currency using the exchange rate at the date at which the transaction occurred. It provided rules also for the treatment of exchange gains and losses arising on the settlement of a transaction or where a transaction is unsettled at the year-end. It was replaced by FRS 23 'The Effect of Changes in Foreign Exchange Rates' corresponding to IAS 21 'The Effect of Changes in Foreign Exchange Rates'. In accordance with IAS 21, it allows a presentation currency different from a company's functional currency and when translating assets and liabilities requires the use of spot rates at the relevant dates or period ends. Hence, foreign exchange gains and losses are to be calculated by reference to accounting differences stemming from different spot exchange rates at settlement or year-end in the case of unsettled transactions.

Example 29.5

Chamley Limited is a UK company that imports directly from a Cheascott Inc. a US company that invoices in dollars. On 1 February 200X, Chamley receives an invoice in the amount of $100,000, when the exchange rate between sterling and the dollar was £1: $2. Chamley Limited's functional currency is sterling. On 1 February 200X, this invoice is entered in its books, as follows:

	Purchases a/c	Cheascott Inc. a/c	
Cheascott	£50,000	Purchases	£50,000

On 28 February 200X, the amount owing to Cheascott Inc. is paid by bank ransfer. On that date, the sterling/US dollar exchange rate was £1:$1.80. The credit balance standing in

favour of Cheascott Inc. remains at £50,000 in sterling, but Chamley Limited is required to pay the invoice at its dollar value, which is $100,000. The 10 per cent fall in the exchange rate of sterling against dollar since receiving the invoice means that Chamley now has to pay an additional 10 per cent in sterling to clear the Cheascott Inc. a/c, that is, £55,000. The payment will be recorded in Chamley Limited's book on 28 February 200X as follows:

(1) Cheascott Inc. a/c	Bank a/c
Bank a/c £50,000	Cheascott £50,000
(2) Exchange gains and losses a/c	Bank a/c
Bank a/c £ 5,000	Exchange gains/losses a/c £5,000

It will be noted that nothing has changed in the dollar amount owing to Cheascott Inc., which was recorded as £50,000 on invoice date. The historic cost shown in purchases has not altered. The sole reason why it has cost £55,000, that is £5,000 more to clear the outstanding invoice, is the exchange rate loss of 10 per cent against sterling, which needs to be recorded separately as an expense to be deducted in the calculation of income.

(3) Exchange gains and losses a/c	
Bank a/c £5,000	Income statement £5,000

Income statement
Dr Exchange gains and losses a/c £5,000

These entries show that, under conventional historic cost accounting, the gains and losses arising from the instability of exchange rates are segregated from the results of ordinary business and charged separately as expenses against current income. Under existing accounting rules, year-end balances exposed to exchange rate instability are treated as current financial assets and liabilities and are translated into the functional currency at the year-end spot rate of exchange. Differences between the exchange rate at invoice date and at the year-end appear as exchange gains or losses and shown on the income statement. It follows that conventional accounting rules deal appropriately with the instability that arises from international trade by bringing into line the accounting treatment of international trade with that applying to domestic trade.

Currency exchange risk is one of the most significant problems for large international groups of companies operating in many different countries by reason of the legal requirement for such groups to publish annual consolidated income statements and balance sheets. Exchange gains and losses will impact directly onto the reported group financial performance and balance sheet values and will be discussed in Part 4.

Accounting for market volatility

Monetary instability may be considered as a factor in market volatility defined as fluctuations in the demand for goods and services showing up as price increases or price falls. Changes in aggregate demand that are influenced by changes in disposable income due to changes in economic activity, credit conditions, tax changes, as well as speculative factors driving demand in particular sectors, may also be considered to be at play in market volatility. In both the USA and in the UK, a long period of low interest rates, coupled with an excessive growth of bank credit led to excessive increases in property prices and speculative buying both of residential properties and corporate assets that created boom conditions. Banks and mortgage companies recklessly lent money that grossly exceeded a prudent ratio of lending with respect to the income levels of sections of the population that constituted the hard core of subprime lending. Frenzied merger and acquisition activity hoisted corporate valuations on the expectation of continued boom conditions, greatly increased corporate indebtedness and leverage levels, leaving the corporate sector exposed to the risk of financial collapse in the face of an economic downturn. Consumer demand was also boosted by an unsustainable level of credit card debt. The financial hazards that these merry-go-round conditions created did not alarm governments or regulatory authorities as they showed up in consistent increases in GNI, bank profits and excessive executive remuneration in the form of massive bonuses paid by financial sector institutions. During the entire period prior to the credit crunch, the collapse of bank lending and sudden perception of the dangerous level of toxic assets that stopped dead inter-bank lending, the level of monetary instability was relatively low and it was market volatility, particularly in property prices, that dominated the financial landscape.

The sudden fragility of most financial institutions that had abandoned all notions of probity in seeking high income and high risk business, threatened the economic collapse of the entire financial sectors in the USA and the UK and widespread bankruptcy in both countries. In the USA, huge losses by financial institutions on subprime assets caused the collapse of several very large financial sector companies and led to a heated debate over the implementation of SFAS 157 'Fair Value Accounting' issued in 2006 in circumstances where markets collapsed and reference prices were either not available or manifestly distressed. Banks, mortgage companies and investment banks had to reduce the value of mortgages and mortgage-backed securities to reflect current prices that had declined severely with the collapse of credits markets and mortgage defaults. Regulators were faced with the problem of how to prepare financial statements that were completely illusory in the light of economic reality. Financial assets composed of newly invented financial instruments, such as CDIs traded as money value equivalents and, in effect, securitized irrecoverable mortgage debts bundled together to finance an active market in inter-bank lending. They were accepted at face value, apparently by word of mouth and without any verification of underlying values. For balance sheet purposes, assets and liabilities had values that were largely fictional, although they were required to be stated at historical cost, where that convention applied, namely historic cost for non-current assets and liabilities, the lower of cost and market value for inventory and market value for current monetary assets and liabilities.

Ethical considerations entered the debate after a long period of absence, having been superseded by the valuation paradigm and identified Wall Street and the banks as 'bad guys' that had defrauded Main Street. For several years, legislation in the UK and the USA had alluded to 'fair values' in various statutes, as did several accounting and financial reporting standards of the IASB, the FASB in the USA and the ASB in the UK. Tax legislation applying to transactions between associated companies within a group are required to be priced on an 'arm's length' basis, as would be the case in an open market situation. In a sense, references to ethical considerations in valuation may be considered to reflect a social conscience that had not lost sight entirely of the doctrine of the 'just price' that can be traced back to Aristotle and St Thomas Aquinas.

Both the FASB in the USA and the IASB concur that the fair value of an asset is the best price at which that asset could be bought or sold in a current transaction between knowledgeable willing parties, other than in liquidation. Similarly, the fair value of a liability is the amount at which that liability could be incurred or settled in a current transaction between knowledgeable, willing parties, other than in a liquidation. If available, a quoted market price is the best evidence of fair value and should be the basis of measurement. If a quoted market price is not available, an estimate must be made of the fair value using the best information available in the circumstances. By definition, fair values expressed in this context represent exit values, whereas conventional historic cost values are entry values.

Countries that are members of the IASB are committed to establishing convergence between their own standards and those of the IASB, the controversy over fair value accounting may therefore be summarized, as follows:

(a) Historic cost accounting remains the basis of accounting records and is the source of information shown in year-end financial statement that has its objectivity in historic cost values. This information is verified through audit and consists of legal facts. Financial reports based on historic cost will continue to be issued to investors, along with financial reports based on fair value measurement.

(b) Where there is existing legislation or accounting standards requiring the use of fair values and market values do not exist, fair values should be estimated in the best possible manner.

(c) Where financial markets represent a large sector in the economy, such as the USA and the UK, the valuation paradigm reflects a strong view that financial statements should enable investors to have knowledge of current values for the purpose of making buy or sell decisions. In these countries, the credit crunch was particularly severe and reinforced an already strong demand for greater transparency in financial reporting and a view that mark-to-market, as fair values, should be the universal measurement basis for all balance sheet values. This was especially true in the USA, where FAS 157 'Fair Value Measurements' (FASBB, 2006) determined that fair values should be applied to financial assets and to non-financial assets that are recognised, or disclosed, at fair value on a recurring basis. Beginning in 2009, SFAS 157 applied to other non-financial assets, where fair values are required under other authoritative accounting pronouncements.

Those countries with economies that focus on industrial and commercial rather than financial activities and which have a bureaucratic tradition of government, attach more importance to the control paradigm and to the audit tradition based on historic cost records. They have been correspondingly less affected by the banking crisis and less severely affected by toxic assets by reason of tighter credit regulations, particularly as regards the granting of mortgages.

In its Exposure Draft 'Fair Value Measurement' issued on 28 May 2009, the IASB marked its difference with the FASB as regards the extension of fair values within a general valuation framework. It provided guidance on how fair value should be measured in all standards in terms of a single, unified definition, as well as its application in inactive markets. It did not extend its use in any way. Consequently, the rules applying to balance sheet values would remain much the same as at present:

non-current, non-financial assets are valued at historic costs; current non-financial assets are valued at the lower of cost and market value; financial instruments are to be classified as to their fundamental characteristics. Where cash flows are stable and predictable (loan or government bonds), instruments are to be valued at cost and impaired, if necessary. Where cash flows are volatile (or securities are being traded) they must be marked to market. Sir David Tweedie, Chairman of the IASB commented as follows:

> *This exposure draft is an important milestone in our response to the global financial crisis. The proposed guidance proposes clear and consistent guidance for the measurement of fair value and also addresses valuation issues that arise in markets that have become inactive. This guidance is consistent with the report of the Expert Advisory Panel and with US GAAP and would achieve overall convergence with US GAAP.*

Fair values and the need for truth, objectivity and trust in financial reporting

The contradictions between the control and the valuation paradigms with respect to the use of historic costs have been a central issue of debate in accounting theory for many decades. It surfaced in the 1970s in the debate in favour of current cost accounting that led the UK to issue SSAP 16 'Current Cost Accounting' in 1980. It proved to be a fiasco and was withdrawn in 1988. It re-surfaced again in the aftermath of the credit crunch in 2006 in proposals for fair value accounting and the need not only for relevance but for transparence in financial reports.

Many years ago, R.S. Edwards (1962) referred to the strongly held view among accountants that 'accounting is not essentially a process of valuation, as some writers on accounting and some economists conceive it to be . . . Primarily accounting is historical in its approach, with valuation entering into it at times as a safeguard. The emphasis is on cost . . .' It may be worth recalling at this time when the pressure is on the accountant to refer to fair value, rather than historic costs, that the entire tradition that explains the social role of accounting focuses on costs and, correspondingly, that valuation is not within the competence of accountants.

The control paradigm is concerned with truth and trust as ethical values in giving significance to accounting information. It relies on the truth that resides in historical cost information that is verifiable and accepted as evidence in legal proceedings addressed to the discovery of truth. Historic costs are objective by nature, whereas valuations are subjective in nature and strongly associated with beliefs and opinions. As a basis for measurement, valuations are volatile and as unstable as the opinions on which they depend, provoking daily changes in market values. The chief executive of a French insurer refused to talk about fair values, insisting that the standards mandate 'immediate values' (*Financial Times*, 2009). The current debate on the use of fair values in financial reporting is reminiscent of the earlier debate about current cost values and may prove to exacerbate the problems that it seeks to solve, namely, the inability of regulators to prevent the abuses that resulted in the credit and banking crisis.

Truth disappears when it is substituted by opinion. Truth is indivisible and cannot be qualified. Yet, in the tradition of Anglo-Saxon countries, truth and fairness co-exist and are juxtaposed in the requirement that financial reports should reflect a true and fair view at the balance sheet date of the financial situation of a business and of the income earned during the reported accounting period for the business entity in question. In this accounting philosophy, truth is perceived as also needing to satisfy the criterion of fairness, which is not a quality of truth. Indeed, fairness is a matter of opinion and not an aspect of truth. During the negotiations preceding the issue of the 4th Directive of Company Accounts by the European Union (then the EEC), the truth and fair requirement in the certification of annual accounts in the United Kingdom was preferred to the alternative certification used in France that insisted on the criteria of fidelity and sincerity, the term 'fidelity' referring to the observance of accounting conventions and regulations.

Accordingly, fairness has become an accepted ingredient of the meaning of truth that modifies the nature of truth to include opinions as to fairness into relevant truths for valuation purposes. This corruption of the concept of truth is necessary to allow opinion to inform those valuations that are relevant to decision making.

The concept of fairness, as modified truth, carries a hidden threat: unless those opinions that are taken into account when establishing fair values can be validated, financial reports will not create necessary trust in users. In other words, fair value accounting could destroy or significantly reduce trust in financial reports, unless very strict criteria are developed and applied to ensure the reliability of fair value judgements. FAS 157 'Fair Value Accounting' provides a hierarchy of three levels of input data for determining the fair value of an asset or liability. In themselves, they point to the difficulties that may eventually undermine fair value accounting as a practicable alternative to historic cost accounting.

Level 1 are quoted prices for identical items in active, liquid and visible markets such as stock exchanges.
Level 2 is observable information for similar items in active, liquid and visible markets, such as two similarly situated buildings in a downtown real estate market.
Level 3 are unobservable inputs to be used in situations where markets do not exist or are illiquid such as the recent credit crisis. At this level, fair values are highly subjective.

Summary

It is axiomatic that stability is one of the most important qualities expected of any standard of measurement, whether physical or monetary. The selection of the appropriate measurement base is of utmost importance for giving meaning to the phenomenon that it is sought to describe and explain. The use of historic cost measurement or other measurement base in accounting must be evaluated by reference to the paradigms that are relevant to the purpose for which accounting information is needed. In this chapter, two basic paradigms are distinguished and discussed, namely the control paradigm and the valuation paradigm. They refer to fundamentally different measurement systems that provide different descriptions, explanations and meanings to information used for financial reporting purposes. Conflict between two different paradigms explains the debate in accounting theory about the use of historic cost measurement as distinct from market values as fair values.

Historic cost measurement assumes that monetary values are constant. Monetary instability and market volatility deny this assumption, but do not invalidate the use of historic costs for control purposes. Advocates of mark-to-market or fair value accounting insist that transparency is the most relevant criterion for users of accounting information concerned with decision-making. The debate about valuation cannot be conducted separately from that about the uses of accounting information. This chapter attempts to place the former in the context of the latter. As discussed in Chapter 1, accounting measurement should be judged in terms of ethical values since they are used in a broad social context in which both economic and social decisions are made. The most important ethical values in accounting are truth, trust, objectivity and transparency It is argued that the debate about the most appropriate accounting measurement base either in terms of the control paradigm or the valuation paradigm can only be properly conducted by reference to these ethical values.

Self-assessment questions

1 What do you understand by monetary instability and market volatility respectively?

2 Discuss briefly how these two distinct phenomena impact on accounting information.

3 What do you understand by the control paradigm and the valuation paradigm?

4 Review briefly the possible effects of monetary instability on accounting data.

5 State what is meant by current purchasing power accounting.

6 Describe how you would convert money measurements recorded at historic cost into their current purchasing power equivalent in calculating periodic income.

7 Describe how you would convert money measurements accumulated on balance sheets into their current purchasing power equivalent for preparing a year-end balance sheet.

8 Describe how exchange rate instability as a form of monetary instability impacts accounting information.

9 State the objectives of mark-to-market in fair value accounting.

10 Explain the intentions of the IASB's Exposure Draft on Fair Value Measurements.

11 Comment on FAS 157 Fair Value Measurements 2006 and the different position that it takes from the IASB's position on fair value based financial reports.

12 Explain why truth, trust, objectivity and transparence are important to accounting information disclosed in financial reports.

13 What are the likely difficulties of obtaining fair value measurements that satisfy the ethical criteria postulated in question 12 above.

Problems (*indicates that a solution is to be found in the Lecturer's Guide)

1 Vitex plc was created on 1 January 20X0 with a share capital of £150,000, fully paid in cash on that date. The price level index at that date was 100. The following transactions were recorded:

Purchased equipment for £90,000, £40,000 paid when the index was 100, and payment of the balance being deferred for 18 months.

Purchased goods for £88,000 when the index was 100.

Purchased goods for £90,000 when the index was 110.

Sold goods for £200,000 when the index was 120, the cost of sales amounting to £120,000.

Cash expenses amounted to £32,000, and a depreciation provision of 10 per cent on historic cost of equipment was made at year end.

Additional information as at 31 December 20X0 was as follows:

Trade debtors	£36,000
Bank balance	£81,000
Creditors	£67,000

Closing inventory was valued at £58,000 on a FIFO basis.
The index at year end was 120

Required:

(a) Calculate the purchasing power gain or loss on the monetary items.
(b) Prepare an inflation-adjusted income statement for the year ended 31 December 20X0.
(c) Prepare an inflation-adjusted balance sheet as at 31 December 20X0 when the price level index was 130.

2* ABC Ltd has traded for several years. Its accounts are kept on a conventional historical cost basis.

Balance sheet

	31.12.X0	31.12.X1		31.12.X0	31.12.X1
	£	£		£	£
Capital	38,100	38,100	Plant	100,800	100,800
Retained income	8,490	19,260	*Less:* Depn	37,800	44,800
	46, 590	57,360		63,000	56,000
Loan	27,000	27,000	Inventory	4,290	7,560
Creditors	3,600	8,600	Debtors	9,000	24,000
Cash				900	5,400
	77,190	92,960		77,190	92,960

Indices	General	Stock	Plant
	£	£	£
Date capital acquired	50		
Date plant acquired	80		70
Date opening inventory acquired	85.8	110	
1 January 20X1	90	120	100
30 June 20X1	100	130	115
30 September 20X1	105	135	122
31 December 20X1	110	140	130

No purchases or sales of plant took place during the year. No dividends have been paid or proposed. Ignore taxation.

Closing inventory was valued at 30 September prices.

Required:

Prepare a balance sheet as at 31 December 20X1 on a CPP basis and on an RC basis.

3* Keaton Ltd started business 1 January Year 1. Set out below is the balance sheet on a historical cost basis as at 31 December:

		Year 1		Year 2
		£000		£000
Land		110		110
Plant cost	40		40	
Depreciation	4	36	8	32
Inventory		90		120
Debtors		30		50
Bank		60		50
		326		362
Creditors		50		80
		276		282
		£		£
Share capital		250		250
Retained earnings		26		32
		276		282

The realizable value of the assets is as follows:

	£	£
Land	150	160
Plant	25	22
Stocks	130	170

The income statement for Year 2 on a historical cost basis is:

	£
Sales	130
Cost of sales	90
	40
Depreciation	4
	36
Dividend	30
Retained earnings	6

Required:

Prepare balance sheets at the end of Years 1 and 2 on the basis of realizable value accounting.

(Problem supplied by A.J. Naughton)

References

Arnold, J., Boyle, P., Carey, A., Cooper, M. and Wild, K. (1991) *The Future Shape of Financial Reports*, ICAEW.

Baxter, W.T. (1984) *Inflation Accounting*, Philip Allen.

Bonbright, J.C. (1937) *The Valuation of Property*, McGraw-Hill.

Chambers, R.J. (1966) *Accounting, Evaluation and Economic Behaviour*, Prentice Hall.

Edwards, E.O. and Bell, P.W. (1961) *The Theory and Measurement of Business Income*, University of California Press.

Edwards, R.S. (1962) The Nature and Measurement of Income, in Baxter, W.T. and Davidson, S. *Studies in Accounting Theory*, Sweet and Maxwell Ltd, p. 76.

Financial Times (2009) Axa chief attacks accounting rules switch, 28 September.

Financial Accounting Standards Board (FASB) (2006) FAS 157 Fair Value Measurements 2006.

Glautier, M.W.E. (1983) Searching for accounting paradigms, *Accounting Historians Journal*, Vol. 10, No. 1, Spring, 51–68.

Glautier, M.W.E. (2007) *The Social Conscience*, Shepheard-Walwyn Publishing Ltd.

Glautier, M.W.E. (forthcoming) *The Caring Society*.

Gynther, R.S. (1974) Why use general purchasing power? *Accounting and Business Research*, Spring.

HMSO (1975) Report of the Committee on Inflation Accounting (Sandilands Report).

Myers, J.H. (1973) The critical event and recognition of net profit, in Zeff, S.A. and Keller, T.F. (eds) *Financial Accounting Theory*, McGraw-Hill.

Parker, R.H. and Harcourt, G.C. (1969) *Readings in the Concept and Measurement of Income*, Cambridge University Press.

Popper, K.R. (1972) *Objective Knowledge: An evolutionary approach*, Oxford University Press.

SSAP 7 (1974) Accounting for Changes in the Purchasing Power of Money', London, withdrawn 1978.

Sterling, R.R. (1970) *Theory and Measurement of Enterprise Income*, University of Kansas Press.

SECTION 1c

Extending the boundaries of corporate accountability

Introduction to Section 1c

The scope of accounting was defined in Part 1 as being 'to provide information which is potentially useful for making economic decisions and aims to assess the impact of an organization or company on people both inside and outside'. This definition of the scope of accounting was followed by a discussion of the development of accounting theory, where several approaches to accounting theory (e.g. descriptive, decision-usefulness, normative and empirical, welfare) were discussed. It was seen, in particular, that the current state of accounting knowledge depended substantially on a descriptive approach to accounting theory. This emphasized observations of the practices of accountants as a major source of accounting knowledge. It was for this reason that Part 2 was devoted to an analysis of the knowledge provided by a descriptive approach to accounting theory. Part 3 considers adjustments necessary to historical cost accounting by reason of the instability of the monetary standard of measurement and market volatility. This instability and volatility affect not only the measurement of periodic income but also the valuations which are significant in financial reports.

The problem which must be considered is the relevance of accounting information in the context of the needs of users for decision making. This problem, which was posed in the definition of accounting given in Part 1, has only been touched on in that Part. At the beginning of Part 3, in Chapter 23 we saw that the ASB's 'Statement of Principles', which adopts a decision-usefulness approach, forms a framework for the future development of financial reporting. The ASB's intention is that accounting standards should be based on principles rather than *ad hoc* rules. In this section we consider how such principles may be applied in extending the boundaries of corporate accountability.

Tomorrow's Company, a study by The Royal Society for the Arts (1996), examined the kinds of companies likely to succeed in tomorrow's business climate. The study concluded that tomorrow's company would form deeper relationships with key stakeholders as a means of achieving financial success. These key stakeholders are the groups of people with an interest in a business organization, which we considered in Chapter 3. In this view the company which ignores its stakeholders does so at its peril, and similarly those which take them into account are more likely to prosper.

Chapter 30 examines the nature of the information needed by investors and Chapter 31 examines the concept of social accounting and extends the discussion of corporate social responsibility to defining the responsibilities of a caring society having a fuller engagement towards the common good.

Reporting to investors

Setting the scene

The long-standing debate on the needs of investors for financial reports, which are useful for decision making and the limitations of traditional financial statements based on the accounting concepts and on historic cost information, seems to have reached a defining moment with the publication in the USA of FAS 157 'Fair Value Measurements' 2006 and the IASB's 'Exposure Draft Fair Value Measurement' 2009. Arguing for a generalization of the use of fair values, as defined by the mark-to-market valuation rule, rather than entry costs defined by the transaction and cost concepts, the debate implies that the criteria of usefulness and relevance are met only through fair value measurements. From this perspective, historic costs are seen as redundant to the needs of investors.

The debate contrasts the control paradigm and the valuation paradigm. The former, which underpins stewardship accounting, was and remains the main purpose for maintaining accounting records. The latter is of more recent origin and assumes that financial reports should reflect market values at publication date that are not found in accounting records. These two paradigms co-exist and both are necessary for reporting to investors, as will be argued in this chapter.

Learning objectives

After studying this chapter you should be able to:

1   understand the significance of the control paradigm and the valuation paradigm to financial reporting;

2   understand the reality of being a shareholder in a business corporation;

3   recognize the limitations of current financial reporting procedures from a decision usefulness perspective;

4   explain the advantages which could accrue from improved long-term disclosures;

5   discuss the advantages of, and the objections to, the disclosure of company forecasts;

6   identify the perceived advantages of adopting fair value in financial reporting;

7   discuss the advantages to the investor of quarterly reporting by public companies;

8   explain what is meant by 'the efficient market hypothesis' and consider its implications for financial reporting.

What investors want to know and the role of the IASB and the ASB

The two most obvious questions that summarize the concerns of investors about any business enterprise may be stated simply as:

How well is the enterprise managed?
How much is it worth?

These two questions open up the entire range of issues which financial reports need to address. The first question relates to assessing the relevant areas of management performance in an objective manner and on the basis of substantive evidence that may be verified. The relevant paradigm is control and verification is effected through audit of recorded facts. The second question is situated in the context of decision making; whether to maintain, increase or sell an investment in an enterprise in the search for the most profitable option. The relevant paradigm is valuation and involves formulating an opinion about each of the three mutually exclusive alternatives. Valuations cannot be other than opinions or beliefs that can only be validated by subsequent events. They are always subjective and speculative. Nonetheless, investors do need information that is useful to making decisions on their investments. Information about performance provided in year-end published financial reports is widely used by investors and analysts in efforts to understand the underlying factors that help explain performance and in identifying strengths and weaknesses. The usefulness of this information is limited in that it concerns the year just ended. It does not provide insights into management's plans for the future to sustain or improve performance.

To appreciate the implication of the foregoing two questions about performance and worth in relation to financial reporting, it is necessary to understand the context defining the nature of the relationship between shareholders and business corporations.

Company legislation under which business corporations are created as separate legal persons grants proprietary status to shareholders, but gives extensive powers of management and control to boards of directors. Shareholders have very limited legal powers over the general conduct of business. The legal rights of shareholders are exercised through annual general meetings or special meetings and are restricted to the business which such meetings are authorized to conduct. Shareholders must approve the appointment of directors and auditors, and they also have to approve the payment of dividends, increases in authorized share capital and financial reports. Their approval is also necessary for actions that affect the business structure, such as mergers and acquisitions. While company law and accounting standards boards, such as the IASB and the FASB (USA) and the ASB (UK), give limited recognition to the proprietary concept through the notion of ultimate shareholder control, they have all accorded primacy to the entity concept through which business corporations are recognized as having their own distinct identities and interests.

Accordingly, it is only through the proprietary concept and stewardship accounting that shareholders could be considered as having a primary concern with the notion of control implied in the first question, namely, how well is the business managed?

There is a curious paradox in that, until recently, legislation, regulatory bodies and accepted theories of economics, finance and management all accepted that the primary business objective is the optimization of shareholder value. Its overwhelming influence stems from it being the fundamental hypothesis of the theory of finance and the assumptions on which trading is conducted in financial markets and corporate decisions are made. This seeming unity of purpose is denied in practice by the extensive powers granted to management to divert to themselves, virtually at will, whatever proportion of annual corporate earnings they deem themselves to have earned. It is noteworthy that the reality of the relationship between the enterprise and shareholders has the semblance of fiction; management is able and has the legal right to appropriate corporate profits by awarding themselves excessive remuneration, substantial bonuses and share options; whereas the profits belong in law to shareholders. The reality is that management assumes that legal control is akin to legal possession and akin to 9/10ths of the law. This understanding holds good with respect to public companies and, in particular quoted companies. In the case of small and medium-sized companies whose shares are privately held, shareholder control is the reality to the extent that there is unity and consensus between shareholders in dealing with management.

In quoted companies with very diffused shareholders, the market is seen as the meeting point between corporate management and investors, who merely provide funds for a rate of return which is market determined. While large institutional investors can exercise considerable influence on boards of directors, frequently behind the scenes, by and large they all form part of the same constituency that has effective financial control of the business sector and create a virtual concordat to this end. In the last few years shareholders have become more vociferous and forced companies to listen to them although motions at annual general meetings may still pass thanks to proxy votes, the hostility of those present makes for bad publicity and can lead to a change in policies.

Evolving and expanding legislation shows how far statutory control has replaced ownership control as the effective authority over corporate management. From the obligation to maintain proper accounting records, to publishing audited financial statements and reports, to the list of supplementary information that corporations progressively are required to publish, the state now exercises considerable control over corporate entities. Corporate managers are personally liable under civil and criminal law for wilful wrongdoing as well as negligence in the exercise of their management responsibility. The impressive array of senior executives who have been found guilty of criminal conduct and sentenced to long terms of imprisonment is testimony to the rigorous nature of statutory control. Likewise, the authority of national regulators and of the IASB through the issue of authoritative accounting standards constitute an expanding body of rules with which management must comply.

In practice, shareholders have proprietary rights only over the shares they personally own. It is for this reason that they are principally concerned with the second question, namely, how much are the shares worth? It explains the significance of the valuation paradigm and its influence on initiatives to revise accounting standards and to develop the objectives framework for accounting and financial reporting standards issued by the IASB.

This chapter draws heavily on the analyses and conclusions of several major studies. These include *Making Corporate Reports Valuable* (The Research Committee of the Institute of Chartered Accountants of Scotland, 1988); *Guidelines for Financial Reporting* (Solomons, 1989); *The Future Shape of Financial Reports* (Arnold *et al.*, 1991); *Improving Business Reporting – A Customer Focus* (American Institute of Certified Public Accountants, 1994); *Report of the CICA Task Force to Review the Recommendations of the AICPA Special Committee on Financial Reporting* (Canadian Institute of Chartered Accountants, 1995); and *Value Reporting Forecast 2000* (PricewaterhouseCoopers, 1999).

The case for a decision usefulness approach

In Chapter 24 we saw how disclosure requirements have been determined mainly by company law, accounting standards and Listing Agreements. They have developed in an *ad hoc* fashion with no obvious, overriding rationale for the disclosure of information. Consequently, they are not user-oriented and have severe disadvantages for an investor who is concerned primarily with estimating the dividends and risks associated with an investment. In particular:

1 The present system based on the control paradigm is essentially backward-looking; it involves the measurement of past performance and current position. It is of limited help to those concerned with future performance.
2 Much emphasis is placed on a single measure of earnings, namely earnings per share (EPS). In an increasingly complex world it is unlikely that any single number can capture the variety of facets which contribute to the changes in an enterprise's worth during a period.
3 It reports measures of performance and financial position which are based largely on the original or historical costs of resources used by the reporting entity. Little account is taken of the current costs or values, which are likely to be more relevant in the measurement of efficiency and in the prediction of future performance.

The argument in favour of fair value accounting reflects the idea that decision-usefulness requires financial reports to provide information that helps investors make predictions about future performance: these predictions are concerned with long-term as well as short-term profitability. In extending the boundaries of financial reporting to include decision-usefulness fair value accounting is claimed to have the following advantages:

1 More useful and relevant information will lead to better corporate valuations and enable financial markets to achieve better allocations of capital.
2 Corporate accountability to shareholders and investors will be enhanced through the improved transparency of the impact of management actions on shareholder wealth.
3 Although investors will still have to make their own judgements about the past, present and future corporate performance, they will be provided with more and better information on which to base their decisions.
4 Investors will be better able to identify those corporations that are likely to achieve and maintain high levels of performance in the future.

Possible solutions

This chapter considers some suggestions for enabling financial reporting to provide information to help investors make predictions about corporate performance:

1 adopt a forward-looking perspective;
2 include profit warnings;
3 report high-level operating data;
4 report fair value information;
5 extend background information;
6 extend interim financial reporting.

Adopting a forward-looking perspective

The provision of additional forward-looking information is one of the most significant proposals for new information made by the Jenkins Committee (AICPA, 1994) which concluded that financial reports should include the following:

1 information about a company's broad objectives and related business strategies;
2 details of opportunities and risks limited to those that have been identified and considered by management in operating the business. Knowledge of what management thinks about opportunities and risks helps users understand where management plans to lead a company;
3 management's plans, including critical success factors, i.e. those factors or conditions that must be present for the plans to be successful;
4 a comparison of actual performance with previously disclosed opportunities, risks and management plans.

The Jenkins Report (AICPA, 1994) did not include a requirement for a forecast in its consideration of forward-looking information. This contrasts with the conclusions of the Research Committee of the ICAS (1988) in *Making Corporate Reports Valuable (MCRV)* which argued for forecasts of financial performance for the coming year, although the period could be longer if management so decided. It also asserted that the major assumptions on which such forecasts were based should be disclosed and that management should provide explanations for differences between the forecast for the previous year and the actual results of the current year.

It may be argued that the disclosure of corporate forecasts of future profits or cash flows would be very advantageous to investors. The advantages cited for such disclosures are:

1 Since investment decisions by management are made in the context of their expectations of the profitability of future operations, the disclosure of their forecasts would provide essential information needed by investors to help them gauge their confidence in the expected oucomes. Research conducted by Backer (1970) showed that the procedure employed by security analysts for forecasting profits closely parallels that used internally by companies. This procedure starts with a projection of sales; then profit margins are examined, and other significant operating ratios are compiled from published income statements. These ratios are adjusted for anticipated changes in sales volume, prices and costs, and are then applied to the sales forecasts to obtain profit forecasts.
2 The disclosure of corporate forecasts would provide investors with an insight into management's own assessment of corporate operations and their future propects.
3 The publication of information relevant to investors' needs would help reduce the incidence of corrupt practices, grossly excessive managerial remuneration and abuses in many forms revealed by the recent banking and financial crisis.
4 The disclosure of corporate forecasts would provide investors with a better basis for evaluating managerial performance.

Numerous objections have been made to the proposition that forecasts should be published. The four major objections are:

1 they are uncertain and may mislead investors;
2 they may be manipulated by unscrupulous managers;
3 they are difficult to audit;
4 if made known to competitors they may be harmful to the interests of the enterprise, and therefore to those of its investors.

481

Each of these objections has merit, but neither individually nor collectively do they amount to compelling arguments against publication:

1 It is true that forecasts are uncertain. This uncertainty stems from the unpredictable nature of the different elements that constitute the forecasts. However, this does not render forecasts valueless. Budgetary control implies the necessity of forecasting, as do a host of management decisions regarding production, personnel, product development and so forth. Forecasts made and used by management are of critical importance to the quality of decision-making. Such forecasts will be treated as reliable to the extent that they have been carefully researched and prepared. In most cases management forecasts are likely to be of higher quality than those which could be attempted by outsiders. This explains why it has been the practice for more than a decade to publish profit forecasts in prospectuses and in circulars issued in the course of mergers and acquisitions. The real question is not whether forecasts are sufficiently reliable in an absolute sense, but whether users of financial reports are likely to find such reports more useful if accompanied by forecasts. As the Trueblood Report stated, 'the important consideration is not the accuracy of management forecasts themselves, but rather the relative accuracy of users' predictions with and without forecasts in financial statements' (AICPA, 1973).

2 It is also true that forecasts may be manipulated by unscrupulous management. However, if management had to explain differences between forecasts and actual outcomes, this would restrain any tendency to making wild or unsubstantiated forecasts.

3 It may also be true that forecasts are more difficult to audit than actual results. Auditors have been reluctant to get involved in the audit of forecasts, and the position of auditors as regards forecasts is confused, particularly in the United States, where the danger of legal action against auditors is considerably greater than in the United Kingdom. The resistance of the accounting profession to the inclusion of forecasts in annual reports has diminished since the publication of the City Code and the Institute of Chartered Accountants' statement on the matter.

The requirement to report publicly was initially accepted with reluctance at the insistence of the Panel. However, when asked if they would report publicly, if it were not for the Panel, an overwhelming number of accountants said 'yes', they would report publicly. Many pointed out that they had been reporting privately on profit forecasts for some time and they felt that public reporting was not that different.

(Adelburg, 1976)

The difficulty of verifying corporate forecasts through auditing is a very controversial subject. Although accountants should have knowledge of forecasting techniques, they are not experts in this field. Moreover apart from knowledge of techniques, forecasting requires expert knowledge of the industry and the markets in which the firm operates. These obstacles could be overcome by using consultants who are experts in the field of business forecasting to provide second opinions. Consequently, the auditor would not be legally liable for the forecasts and would be responsible merely for verifying the opinions of the experts concerned. However, it is not clear that moving the legal liability from the auditor to consultants would solve the fundamental problem; namely no one wants to accept responsibility for expressing an expert opinion on management's forecasts at a price the companies are willing to pay.

The problem of verification becomes more complex when forecasts covering several years are involved. Forecasts for the year immediately ahead merely provide an extended view of current performance. Ideally, investors would need to be provided with forecasts covering a longer period. There would seem to be no reason why five-year rolling forecasts should not be adopted as a framework for disclosure, thereby enabling investors to appraise current performance and plans in relation to the attainment of long-term goals. It would be difficult to propose standard procedures that would ensure the required objectivity for audit purposes. The longer the period of the forecast, the greater the possibility of legitimate differences of opinion between management and expert forecasters with respect to the numbers that should be disclosed.

The ICAS recognized the problems posed by its advocacy of the use of corporate forecasts. It suggested the involvement of non-accountants in what it called the 'independent assessment teams' that would be responsible for ensuring the quality of financial statements. It recognized that the work of the independent assessor would be more judgemental than that of the present-day auditor. The report produced would need to be longer and more explicit than the present audit report, and tailored to the circumstances of the individual client rather than following a predetermined format.

4 The argument that the disclosure of corporate forecasts to competitors would be harmful to the interests of the enterprise and its shareholders is the same argument which has been advanced for years against the increased disclosure requirements of the company legislation, the Stock Exchange and the Statements of Standard Accounting Practice. Profit forecasts are currently made public during merger and acquisition procedures or for the issue of shares. Were corporate forecasts to be made mandatory for all comparable companies, it is difficult to see how an unfair advantage could be gained by a competitor. The only user likely to gain from having such information is the one who is better able to compare and evaluate the prospects of different firms.

Profit warning

A profit warning is a profit forecast by a company that projects the next set of earnings to be below the previous comparative period, or below what the company had previously forecast, or below the consensus estimate of securities analysts.

(Financial Times Lexicon)

The Listing Rules for quoted companies on stock exchanges in all major financial centres include the obligation to issue a profit warning concerning the immediate future when this is likely to affect the value of a company to investors. Under paragraph 9.1–9.38 of the London Stock Exchange Listing Rules, there is a general obligation of disclosure whenever a major development in a company's sphere of activity that is not public knowledge may substantially affect the price of its listed securities. Under paragraph 9.2, the company must notify the Company Announcement Office whenever the directors are aware of changes in the financial condition, or the performance of its business, or the company's expectations of its performance, and where general knowledge of this would likely lead to a significant movement in the price of its listed securities. Experience shows that the percentage change in share price is greater than the percentage downgrade in profits as a result of the warning. The market appears to overreact, at least in the short term.

Reporting high-level operating data

The Research Committee of the ICAS (1988) in *Making Corporate Reports Valuable (MCRV)* concluded that the information needed by investors is the same as that needed by management. Similarly, the Jenkins Committee indicated that users believe they would benefit by greater access to the high-level operating data and performance measurements management use to manage the business. One aspect of high-level operating data concerns operating costs.

As we noted in Part 2, operating costs fall into categories that behave differently under changing activity levels. Variable production costs tend to vary in direct proportion to production levels; programmed costs that are budgeted annually, for example advertising and research and development costs are relatively sticky over the budgeted period; long-run fixed costs change little in total with changes in output.

Investors require some knowledge of a company's cost structure if reliable forecasts are to be made that take account of the impact of changing output levels on income. Financial reports omit this crucial information. This problem was discussed in Chapter 15, where the effects of SSAP 9 'Stocks and Long-Term Contracts' on investment decisions was discussed.

Reporting fair value information

As we saw in Chapter 29, fair value reporting provides better information on current performance and the financial position of the business and thus enables users to make better predictions.

As early as 1973, the Trueblood Report had stated, 'of primary importance for predicting the risk associated with the firm's cash flows (but also for assessing returns) is the degree of flexibility and maneuverability that the management possesses in employing its resources'. One alternative use of a firm's resources is to dispose of them. This alternative may be quantified by using market exit values. Clearly, the easier it is to convert the firm's resources into cash and the greater their realizable value, the greater the degree of flexibility and manoeuvrability management has over the employment of resources. If market exit values are low, the alternative uses of resources will be more restricted. Consequently, the best utilization of resources inside the firm will be highly dependent on the marketability of the specific assets of the enterprise.

More recently in 1988, the Research Committee of the ICAS in *Making Corporate Reports Valuable* strongly advocates the adoption of net realizable value (NRV) in reporting. It argues that NRV has a number of advantages:

1 It is based on values which may be readily observed in the marketplace.
2 It is readily understandable by investors.
3 It removes the need for depreciation calculations.
4 It produces values which are additive because they are all expressed in the same monetary units.
5 It provides a useful measure of an entity's liquidity.
6 Its use would improve the comparability of financial statements between entities and between different periods.

Extending background information

Price Waterhouse's study (Coleman and Eccles, 1999) questioned more than 200 financial analysts and fund managers with the aim of assessing their satisfaction with companies' financial reporting. This report identified an information gap between the needs of analysts and the information provided by companies. Seven measures which the analysts considered valuable were not adequately reported, namely market share, employee productivity, new product development, customer retention, product quality, research and development and intellectual capital.

Both the Jenkins Committee and the ICAS recommended extending disclosure of the background information about a company giving users a better understanding of the business environment. For example, *MCRV* suggests that the following information about the economic environment should be published:

1 *The marketplace.* Every entity requires information on various aspects of its market. That information would come mainly from outside the entity. The major divisions are (a) the size of the market, (b) balance of demand and supply, (c) market share, (d) economic facts likely to affect the market, (e) political factors likely to affect the market, and (f) actions of major competitors.
2 *Competitive operational statistics.* Benchmarking is now a regular preoccupation of management: both internally across units to identify and share best practice and externally to identify their company's standing in the industry. Making this information available to analysts and shareholders would help them understand the challenges facing the company.

Extending interim financial reporting

Interim financial reports provide financial information for a period of less than one year. In the United Kingdom quoted companies have to deliver a six-monthly report of profitability and financial position to their shareholders. In the United States the disclosure requirement is on a quarterly basis. Interim reports are not audited.

One normative characteristic of the process of reporting to users discussed previously was that of timeliness. The aim of interim reports is to provide users with more timely information about companies so as to alleviate the disadvantages of the significant time lag between annual reports. American experience indicates that a more extensive use of interim reports in the United Kingdom would enhance the predictability of company reports.

When the Jenkins Committee reported in 1994 users in the United States believed strongly that quarterly reporting by public companies should be retained. They provided three main reasons:

1 Quarterly reporting helps users with a longer-term focus. Interest in recent developments is not inconsistent with a longer-term view. It is critical that the user with a longer-term focus detect, on a timely basis, changes in long-term trends. Quarterly reporting helps provide that information.
2 Quarterly reporting provides for an orderly dissemination of reliable information. In its absence investors may base trading decisions on less reliable information, such as rumour.
3 Quarterly reporting reduces problems of trading on inside information. Quarterly reporting provides a vehicle for companies to disseminate information so market participants have equal access to reliable information about a company on which to trade freely.

While these reasons are plausible, financial market professionals are less convinced than they used to be about the merits of quarterly reports. GE's legendary ability to maintain a smooth and rising trend in reported earnings during Jack Welch's tenure was the result of capital gains on asset sales from its significant holdings of real estate. The gap between guidance and operations was miraculously filled at the last moment by a judiciously timed sale of an asset. Another perverse incentive to smooth earnings in the short term at the expense of the long came from fund managers who are regularly ranked against their peers. If a company in which they had significant holdings did not meet analyst's expectations the share price would fall and their ranking suffer.

The efficient market hypothesis

The efficient market hypothesis supports the case for extending the disclosure of information to investors. The efficient market hypothesis assumes the following:

1 Investors, and particularly analysts, react to new information in such a way as to cause the price of shares traded on the Stock Exchange to change instantaneously. Therefore, an item of information disclosed in a footnote to the financial report will be impounded in the share price just as surely as if it had been included in the main body of the report.
2 The price of shares traded on the Stock Exchange fully reflects all publicly available information.
3 Abnormal returns cannot be earned by investors, that is, no investor can expect to use published information in such a way as to increase the benefits accruing to him/her as against those accruing to other investors. Each investor can expect to earn the return on a security commensurate to its risk class.

The assumptions of the efficient market hypothesis initially received considerable support from research findings. These findings show that accounting information does have economic significance in that share prices react to new accounting information. Moreover, research indicates that the Stock Exchange reacts almost immediately to the public release of information. Research also shows that sharp price changes occur on the announcement of new information, but little discernible price movements thereafter, since the adjustment made at that time removes the possibility of future abnormal returns to individual investors. This observed behaviour is consistent with the behaviour of an efficient market.

A further condition required of an efficient market is that it should be able to interpret accounting information correctly. A number of research studies have examined the share price reaction to reported earnings reflecting a change in accounting policy. An interesting example of the market's ability to understand changes in accounting policy is illustrated by Sunder's (1975) research into share price reactions to switches in the basis of stock valuation from FIFO to LIFO and from LIFO to FIFO. The expected results on earnings of these changes were discussed in Chapter 12. It will be recalled that firms switching from FIFO to LIFO will report lower earnings which will coincide with an improvement in economic earnings resulting from a reduced tax bill. Conversely, firms switching from LIFO to FIFO will report higher earnings and will hope that the market will respond positively to this information, thereby compensating for the negative impact of the increased tax bill that would result from the change. While such changes are not permitted in the United Kingdom, they are allowed in the United States and the American research experience of the impact of changes in accounting policy reflected in stock valuation changes is illuminating. In effect, research evidence shows that firms switching from FIFO to LIFO did not encounter any adverse price reactions from the market. On the contrary, average share prices rose by an average of 5 per cent more than would have been expected, taking account of market movements during the year when the change in accounting policy occurred. Sunder's research also indicated no market reaction to switches from LIFO to FIFO. In effect, it appeared that such an attempt to improve share prices was both fruitless and expensive in the context of the increased tax bill resulting from the change.

Indeed, many other studies have shown results similar to those produced by Sunder, and it may be concluded from these studies that the market does not respond to earnings increases that result from cosmetic changes in accounting policies (Beaver, 1981).

Finally, it does appear that there has been no major readjustment of share prices in the United Kingdom since companies began to publish inflation-adjusted accounts in varying forms several years ago (Brayshaw and Miro, 1985). These findings are consistent with the view that the market made its own assessment of the effects of inflation on company profits, and had already made the necessary adjustments for these effects.

The following inferences may be drawn from research conducted in the area of financial reporting:

1 Where there is controversy over which of two alternative measurements should be reported to external users, and no additional costs are involved in reporting both measurements, the solution to the controversy lies in reporting both measurements. Use could be made of footnotes to the financial report for this purpose, and the market may be left to interpret the importance of such additional information.

2 As there is evidence of a direct relationship between the price of a share and its risk, concern for the ordinary investor is ill-founded. Naive investors are price-takers, and any additional disclosure will be to their advantage. Increased disclosure to sophisticated investors will improve the predictions which they are able to make, and to hereby reduce the speculative and destabilizing influences associated with the uncertainties of stock market behaviour. As ordinary investors are likely to be naive investors, and to be price-takers, they have an interest in share prices behaving in an orderly manner.

The efficient capital market theory has come under increasing attack, forcing its proponents into distinguishing between strong and weaker forms of the theory. The strong version maintained that markets knew everything immediately and correctly and instantaneously incorporated this information into prices, that there were no trends or patterns that could be exploited by investors and that process moved as a random walk. Commenting on these propositions, Warren Buffet is quoted as saying that 'observing correctly that the market was frequently efficient, they (academics, investment professionals and corporate managers) went on to conclude incorrectly that it was always efficient. In an article in the *Financial Times*, 7 October 2009, John Kay noted that Mr Buffet has made his money not from that part that is frequently efficient, but from that which is infrequently efficient. Weaker versions acknowledge that there are too many anomalies and that there have been too many large abrupt corrections to market indices for the strong theory to be tenable any longer.

Confirming Buffet's view, as evidenced in fractal geometry, the French mathematician Benoît Mandelbrot made perhaps the most telling criticism of the efficient market hypothesis in its failure to take account of the 'wild randomness' that drives markets and shows up in freak occurrences. These deny the validity of the basic assumptions on which the efficient market hypothesis relies (see Benoit Mandelbrot and Richard L. Hudson, *The (Mis)behavior of Markets*). For the same reason, Mandelbrot equally faults random walk theory that assumes with respect to movement in share prices that the price at any given moment depends on what it was the moment before.

The efficient market hypothesis is about how markets react to information, but does not necessarily imply that markets promote economic efficiency in a wider sense. Confidence in the market economy, and in financial markets particularly, was so badly shaken by the credit and banking crisis that doubts began to be expressed about the sustainability of the capitalist system and free markets generally. It has created a widespread view in public and political opinion favouring much greater regulatory control not only in the surveillance of financial markets, but significantly with respect to stricter conditions applying to financial reporting and information disclosure. We discussed in Chapter 1 the importance of truth, trust, care and transparence as basic moral values in accountability and for accounting methods. These values are manifestly present in the social conscience and are finding their expression in public opinion.

The costs of increasing disclosure

So far in this chapter we have considered the benefits of increasing disclosure but not the costs, the most important cost being that of competitive disadvantage. If too much of what is known to the directors and other insiders is made public, the company itself may suffer as a result of competitors and others making use of sensitive information. This would clearly be to the detriment of the investors. According to *MCRV* the subset of the internal information has to be carefully tailored so that the maximum useful knowledge is available to the external groups with a right to such knowledge without giving so much that the entity and its owners will be prejudiced.

However, as the Jenkins Report points out, every company that could suffer competitive disadvantage from disclosure could gain competitive advantage from comparable disclosure by competitors. There cannot be competitive disadvantage for one company without one or more others gaining competitive advantage. Assuming it is required, competitors would have access to each other's disclosures. This creates the concept of net competitive disadvantage from disclosure. It would vary from company to company and from time to time, could be positive or negative, and could therefore also be called net competitive advantage from disclosure.

Summary

The debate on the information needs of investors involves defining the nature of the decisions for which information is needed. Accepting the criteria that user-oriented information must be both useful and relevant for decision making, it is important to understand the reality of the relationship of business corporations and investors. Two paradigms are relevant to this debate – the control paradigm that assumes the investors have proprietary interest in the business and have both legal and effective authority over management decisions and the valuation paradigm that assumes that they do not have that authority and have only a proprietary interest in the shares they own. The purpose of this chapter is to examine the case for providing investors with financial reports relevant to their needs as shareholders. The solutions considered were: adopting a forward-looking perspective, reporting high-level operating data, reporting fair value information, extending background information and extending interim financial reporting.

Self-assessment questions

1 Why has financial reporting attracted criticism from a decision usefulness perspective?

2 What advantages could accrue from improved long-term disclosures?

3 What are the advantages of publishing company forecasts?

4 Examine the case for adopting net realizable value in financial reporting.

5 Discuss the advantages to the investor of quarterly reporting by public companies.

6 What do the findings of efficient market research show?

References

Adelburg, A.H. (1976) Forecasting and the US dilemma, *Accountancy*, October.

AICPA (1973) *Report of the Study Group on Objectives of Financial Reporting* (The Trueblood Report), American Institute of Certified Public Accountants.

AICPA (1994) *Improving Business Reporting – A Customer Focus* (The Jenkins Report), American Institute of Certified Public Accountants.

Arnold, J., Boyle, P., Carey, A., Cooper, M. and Wild, K. (1991) *The Future Shape of Financial Reports*, ICAEW.

Backer, M. (1970) *Financial Reporting for Security Investment and Credit Decisions*, NAA.

Beaver, W.H. (1981) *Financial Reporting: An Accounting Revolution*, Prentice Hall.

Brayshaw, R.E. and Miro, A.R.O. (1985) The information content of inflation-adjusted financial statements, *Journal of Business Finance and Accounting*, Summer.

Canadian Institute of Chartered Accountants (1995) *Report of the CICA Task Force to Review the Recommendations of the AICPA Special Committee on Financial Reporting*.

Coleman, I. and Eccles, R. (1999) *Pursuing value: Reporting Gaps in the United Kingdom*, PricewaterhouseCoopers.

Institute of Chartered Accountants of Scotland, Research Committee (1988) *Making Corporate Reports Valuable*, Kogan Page.

Kay, J. (2009) Markets after the Age of Efficiency, *Financial Times*, 7 October 2009.

Mandelbrot, B. and Hudson, R.L. (2004) *The (Mis)behavior of Markets: A Fractal View of Financial Turbulence*, New York: Basic Books.

Pricewaterhouse Coopers (1999) *Value Reporting Forecast 2000*.

Solomons, D. (1989) *Guidelines for Financial Reporting*, ICAEW.

Sunder, S. (1975) Accounting changes in inventory valuation, *The Accounting Review*, April.

CHAPTER 31

Social accounting and the caring society

Setting the scene

The role of business in society implies fundamental issues about the nature of society itself, its structure, the values that it embodies, its effectiveness in raising living standards, ensuring social cohesion and placing the common good at the heart of social, economic and political action. A schism exists today between those who defend the values of a market economy and others who would promote the values of a caring society. Should the enterprise be a place of conflict between competing interests resulting in a divided society, or should it be a place where common purpose inhibits conflict, ensures social cohesion and leads to an integrated society? This debate echoes Keynes' perception of the need for Government policy to reconcile and promote three distinct objectives, namely economic efficiency, social justice and individual freedom (Keynes, J.M., *The End of Laissez-Faire*, p. 133). It addresses two fundamental questions. 'Can a caring society exist in a market economy? Is a market economy sustainable if it denies man's fundamental nature and needs, as they are expressed in caring and sharing, which is the experience of a family-based society and the moral values that it enshrines?'

(Glautier, M.W.E. (2007) *The Social Conscience*, p. 23)

Learning objectives

After studying this chapter you should be able to:

1 discuss the relationship of business and society;

2 understand social accounting as an accounting responsibility;

3 discuss three approaches to the concept of social responsibility;

4 discuss employee reporting as an aspect of social accounting;

5 explain how partnerships for the common good reflect the values of a caring society;

6 identify six areas in which social objectives may be found;

7 explain recent trends in corporate social reporting in the UK;

8 appreciate the implications for accounting of the increasing concern with green issues;

9 discuss whether a caring society can exist in a market economy.

Business accounting and social accounting

Until recently business accounting was considered as concerned exclusively with recording, classifying and summarizing in terms of money, transactions and events of a financial character, and interpreting the result thereof in the form of periodic financial reports to shareholders. We noted in Chapter 30 that this narrow definition remains valid for reporting to investors and, in a significant manner, provides the terms of reference for the International Accounting Standards Boards in developing international accounting and reporting standards. Latterly this definition has been relaxed to include other users and as being 'the provision of information about the reporting entity's financial performance and financial position that is useful to a wide range of users for assessing the stewardship of management and for making economic decisions' (ASB, 1999).

The claim that business accountability should extend beyond those having financial interests, such as shareholders, investors, creditors, managers and financial markets generally, reflects an evolving social conscience in the call for information potentially useful for making economic decisions and 'aims to assess the impact of an organisation or company on people both inside and outside' (Gonella et al., 1998). It is a claim for change in the relationship between business and society going much beyond the responsibilities of business, as they are currently determined under company law, the law of contract, employment law, industrial relations, product liability and many forms of negligence arising from the ordinary course of business activity.

The approach adopted in this chapter addresses the two questions stated at the outset, namely, can a caring society exist in a market economy and is a market economy sustainable in the light of mankind's need for caring and sharing in the context of a family-based society? First, in line with the extant literature, we discuss the reconciliation of business and society through the extension of corporate social responsibility in its different meanings. Second, we discuss the sustainability of the market economy through structural adjustments to the relationship of capital and labour susceptible to eliminating the social conflict at the workplace, with the objective of combining economic efficiency with social justice, resulting in enhanced social cohesion.

The debate about social accounting has been about corporate social responsibility and accountability. It raises fundamental issues about the relationship between business and society:

1 Is economic efficiency, defined as optimizing shareholder value compatible with social justice defined as 'fair shares' for all who participate in its activities?
2 Is the search for profit that drives the market economy and private investment in business, compatible with that level of awareness of others that would incite investors to share that profit?
3 Is individual freedom compatible with the rights of others and with the concept of social justice?

One definition sees social accounting as an extension of traditional financial accounting in the 'application of double-entry bookkeeping system to macro-economic analysis, also called national income accounting. It is a tool used to measure the economic performance of a nation. It also involves such areas as health and education, and their measurement by a double-entry system' (*Dictionary of Accounting Terms*, Barron's Educational Series Inc., 2005). The French Government has extended the Plan Comptable Général (Accounting Chart) to regulate not only business accounting, but also governmental accounting, using the same principles and method.

Social accounting is more commonly formulated as a very broad extension of corporate accountability, referring to such notions as social and environmental accounting, corporate social accounting, corporate social responsibility reporting, non-financial reporting, sustainability accounting and green accounting. As we noted in Chapter 2, social accounting draws attention to the gulf existing between the interests represented in conventional business accounting and its focus on profit, and the need to see the social role of business organization in the context of all those affected by its activities. The recent debate on 'triple bottom line' (TBL) reporting that focuses on sustainable development calls for the publication of economic, environmental and social information that reflects activities and outcomes across these three dimensions of a company's performance.

The basic differences between business accounting and social accounting relate to their legitimacy, objectives, compatibility, methods and measurements. Significant considerations of this debate stem from the role of the accounting profession in corporate reporting, its established methods and standards that define its responsibilities, the specialization of accountants in the area of financial information, and the universal use of the money standard of measurement in providing a unique standard for the rationalization of decision making in optimizing economic efficiency, defined as profitability.

Social responsibility and accountability

Social relationships create duties, impose responsibilities, require accountability and determine the content of accounting. The social context that leads to the existence of duties and responsibilities is a complex network of relationships that define the nature of society itself. The Enlightenment freed European society from the shackles that religion had imposed on science and society. Capitalism triumphed over religion, science made possible the Industrial Society, Adam Smith found moral justification for free markets in his *Theory of Moral Sentiments* and, eventually, a new social order based on democracy and individual freedom was proclaimed. In the process, individual freedom motivated self-interest and created a divided society; selfishness led to exploitation; wealth was the privilege of the few; the poor inherited injustice and lived its unfairness. The consequences are seen today in a profound schism between those who defend capitalism and a social conscience concerned with social justice and the ideals of a caring society. The debate has polarized between capitalism and socialism as mutually exclusive alternative social structures.

This polarization is unfortunate and premature since it risks being seen as an attack on a man of straw – capitalism 'red in tooth and claw' – that has no defenders. There have been several debates over the years, some are now settled at least for the time being, others are on-going. Two, that used to be conflated, are communism and centrally planned economies versus democracy and market-based economies. The context between the second pair in each dyad has been settled: markets allocate resources better than centrally planned economies. Examples are Cuba, North Korea, the Soviet Union, China before the Great Leap Forward and East Germany. The countries that have abandoned central planning for market-based economies have seen dramatic growth in their economies. Whether democracy will prevail as a superior political system over communism is not yet settled. Communist China before long will be the most powerful economy in the world despite the fact that its citizens do not enjoy the same freedoms as those in the West.

While markets have prevailed, there is widespread, if not universal recognition that they do not always function as they ought: they suffer from market failure. Obvious examples are natural monopolies, like the distribution networks of utility companies, oligopolies, and the more recent examples of the banks that have become too big to fail. In these instances, governments need to establish a 'level playing field' by law, and perhaps set up regulatory frameworks to minimize market imperfections.

At a meeting of centre-left heads of government in London during February 2010, the debate was not about how to turn the clock back, but how to make financial capitslism work better. The headlines of the report of this meeting said it all, 'Centre-left fails to make capital from economic train wreck (Beattie, 2010).

As we noted in Chapter 1, social accounting assumes that there exists a theory about the social role of business in modern society that defines its duties, responsibility and accountability necessary to determining appropriate accounting methods with the same clarity as business accounting. Business accounting strongly reflect the ideals and purposes of a capitalist society in defining those duties, in terms of management (stewardship) responsibility and accountability exclusively to shareholders. The classical view of the social responsibility of business was stated by Milton Friedman (1962, p. 133) in the following terms:

> There is one and only one social responsibility of business – to use its resources and engage in activities designed to increase its profit, as long as it stays within the rules of the game, which is to say, engages in open and free competition, without deception or fraud . . . Few trends could so thoroughly undermine the very foundations of our free society as the acceptance by corporate officials of a social responsibility other than to make as much money for their shareholders as possible.

Social accounting implicitly reflects the values of a caring society. Those values are found in a society founded on family values, expressed in caring and sharing and which, motivated by a sympathetic awareness of others, seeks 'what is right' for the common good (Glautier, M.W.E. *forthcoming)*. The social conscience ensures social cohesion through moral values that are universally accepted in individual conscience and expressed in law. It may be defined as 'a shared conscience, which embodied in each one of us, is the collective of all individuals seeking to do 'what is right'. Its force resides in consensus, its strength in the moral values that it claims as it own and that endow it with unique and permanent authority. It is this Unity of Conscience that is the significant symbol of identity' (Glautier, M.W.E., 2007).

Responsibility and accountability cement social relationships, ensuring their stability and permanence. They are essential elements to social order, defined in rules of conduct recognized, accepted and enforced in law. In a very precise sense, the law embodies and asserts the moral values by which behaviour is to be regulated. Business responsibility and accountability is strictly laid down and enforced in law. For example, business enterprises are liable in law for various offences, such as allowing the escape of dangerous substances, failing to provide adequate safety precautions for employees, etc. Equally, the law provides very clear rules for the manner in which the accountability of business firms to investors is to be met. There is a continuing debate about the role of business in society, but business firms and governments are committed to an enlarged concept of corporate social responsibility.

The nature of corporate social responsibility

The concept of corporate social responsibility introduces new dimensions and new problems. The extension of the accountability of business enterprises based on capitalism to include social responsibilities has been stated in normative terms and as additional to existing laws. Almost everyone agrees that business should be socially responsible, though it may be argued that such a view is merely an extension of the universally accepted doctrine that individuals, either singly or in groups, should weigh the impact of their actions on others. As yet, there does not appear to be a generally accepted concept of the social responsibility of business.

Three approaches to the concept of corporate social responsibility may be distinguished:

1 As stated earlier classical economic theory considers that the firm has one and only one objective, which is to maximize profit. By extension, the objective of a corporation should be to maximize shareholder value. It is asserted that in striving to attain this objective within the constraint of the existing legal and ethical framework, business corporations are acting in the best interests of society at large.

2 The second approach developed in the 1970s recognizes the significance of social objectives in relation to the maximization of profit. In this view, corporate managers should make decisions which maintain an equitable balance between the claims of shareholders, employees, customers, suppliers and the general public. The corporation represents a coalition of interests, and the proper consideration of the various interests of this coalition is the only way to ensure that the corporation will attain its long-term profit maximization objective. This 'stakeholder' approach received much publicity in Britain when it was adopted by the opposition Labour Party in 1996. In the party's draft manifesto for the general election it was described as a 'different economic approach . . . which means opportunities for all – our vision of stakeholder Britain'.

3 The third approach regards profit as a means to an end, and not as an end in itself. In this view, 'the chief executive of a large corporation has the problem of reconciling the demands of employees for more wages and improved benefit plans, customers for lower prices and greater values, shareholders for higher dividends and greater capital appreciation – all within a framework that will be constructive and acceptable to society' (Committee for Economic Development, 1971). Accordingly, organizational decisions should be concerned with the selection of socially responsible alternatives. Instead of seeking to maximize profit generally, the end result should be a satisfactory level of profit which is compatible with the attainment of a range of social goals.

The change from the second to the third approach to corporate social responsibility is characterized as a move from a concept of the business corporation based on shareholders' interests to one which extends the definition of 'stakeholder'. The former concept views the business enterprise as being concerned with making profits for its shareholders, and treats the claims of other interested groups, such as customers, employees and the community, as constraints on this objective. The latter concept acknowledges that the business enterprise has a responsibility to all stakeholders, that is, those who stand to gain or lose as a result of the firm's activities.

The third approach that 'organizational decisions should be concerned with the selection of socially responsible alternatives' requires clarification of the meaning of 'socially responsible alternatives'. It is evident that unless firms are able to develop clear views of society's preferences and priorities, they will be unable to plan activities which will make a social impact, much less report in a meaningful way on their social performance. Therefore, without a precise knowledge of such preferences and priorities, much of the discussion of what is socially desirable must pass for subjective judgements, or at worst pure guesswork.

It has been argued that both from a theoretical standpoint and from the standpoint of welfare economics, it is impossible to make public decisions about the common good. According to Arrow's general impossibility theorem, 'if we exclude the possibility of inter-personal comparisons of utility, then the only method of passing from individual tastes to social preferences which will be satisfactory and which will be defined for a wide range of sets of individual orderings are either imposed or dictated' (Arrow, 1963).

At the operational level, there is the problem of the ever-changing nature of the ordering of social preferences, were such ordering ever possible. Social costs, as well as social benefits, are a function of social perception of what is bad and good about business activity. As a result, the nature of corporate social responsibility is not a static concept. Rather, it is concerned with moving targets, many of which are the subject of government action. Such action may take three forms:

1 Legislation which outlaws undesirable social activities. Many examples exist of public concern with undesirable features of business activity, and of legislation to suppress such activities. One early example in the United Kingdom was the legislation relating to child labour in the nineteenth century which was made illegal.

2 Licensing systems may be employed to limit the extent of activities which are useful to society, but present a potential social problem. The licensing of lorries, for example, has been made the subject of certificates of road-worthiness, and attention is now paid to the control of exhaust emission. Thus, licensing may be qualitative as well as quantitative.

3 It has been argued that taxation is a convenient manner of internalizing external social costs of activities having negative effects on society. The objective is to impose taxes on the firm equal in magnitude to the damage sustained by society from the firm's activities. The obvious purpose of such taxes would be to encourage firms to abate the effects of such activities, or alternatively to finance public programmes for controlling these effects. According to some advocates of the taxation approach to dealing with social costs, business firms would be free to choose between abating the social nuisance and avoiding tax, or continuing as before and paying the tax. According to other advocates of this approach, there should be a tariff of taxes designed to encourage firms to locate in areas where their methods of production would do least harm to the environment. Many environmentalists would probably argue, however, that such by-products as pollution do harm wherever they occur, and that suppression through legislation is the only appropriate course of action for society to take.

From the foregoing discussion of the nature of externalities and the role of government in solving social problems, it is apparent that corporate social responsibility is difficult to define. The question may be asked – to what extent should business enterprises be responsible for dealing with all social problems left unsolved by government? Should they concentrate on solving some of these problems? Or should firms merely operate within a strict interpretation of the letter of the law, and if so, would this adherence to the letter of the law frustrate any claim that their behaviour towards externalities could be antisocial?

In the absence of a clear definition of corporate social responsibility by legislation, individual firms must decide for themselves the nature of their social responsibility as a management concept and constraint. The only guidelines available to a firm in this respect are legislation on the one hand and public opinion and pressure on the other. Subject to these constraints, it is evident that corporate social responsibility may be broadly or narrowly defined, and that individual firms have a fair margin of choice as to the standard of corporate social responsibility which they may be willing to accept.

Social accounting and employee reporting

Having discussed in Chapter 30 the information needs of investors as users of financial reports, it is interesting to examine the information needs of employees for similar information. In both cases, it is necessary to focus upon their needs as users rather than upon their wants.

1 The information needs of employees are more complex than those of investors, because employees require additional information on matters of special interest, for example matters of safety. At the same time, the information deemed in Chapter 30 to be relevant to investors is also relevant to employees (Clark and Craig, 1991).

2 In both cases, the disclosure of information has been regulated by law. In the United Kingdom, the Companies Act 1985 prescribed the minimum level of information which should be disclosed to shareholders and the Employment Protection Act 1975 placed an obligation on employers to disclose information to trade unions for the purpose of collective bargaining.

3 In both cases, traditional financial reports have limited usefulness. If anything, the timing, presentation and content of corporate financial reports are less relevant to the needs of employees than they are to investors and do not deal with matters of importance to employees, such as explanations of reductions in the amount of overtime pay and the effects of streamlining the product range.

4 The impact of management decisions falls more obviously and directly on employees than on investors. Shareholders who dislike current management policy have the possibility of selling their shares. Employees do not have such a simple choice, for they may find it difficult to transfer their labour elsewhere.

5 The role of the auditor has been traditionally to protect the interests of shareholders by ensuring that the financial reports present a true and fair view. The presentation of information to employees does not require auditing in the same sense. Reports to employees are devised and presented by management, and consequently may be discredited (Nay, 1991; Cullinan and Knoblett, 1994).

6 One important difference between investors and employees in the area of financial reporting lies in the historical background to the different treatment accorded to these two groups. Financial reporting to investors originated in the nineteenth century, whereas there was very little interest in reporting to employees before 1970.

The accountant has been involved in the process of reporting to employees in two distinct ways:

1 direct reporting to employees in the form of employee accounts;
2 reporting as part of the process of collective bargaining.

Direct reporting

The main aim of reporting directly to employees is to promote goal congruence by explaining how the interests and efforts of employees relate to those of the firm. The intention is to improve employees' understanding of the manner in which the firm is being managed in the interests of all participants in the context of a general communicative and consultative philosophy of the corporate environment in which they work. Many companies have embarked upon the practice of informing employees about matters of which management believes they should be aware (Cullinan *et al.*, 1994).

Another aim of reporting directly to employees is to improve public relations. Management realizes that employee reports have effects which extend beyond the firm. Employee reports are read by persons outside the firm, by members of employees' families, and friends. They not only have public relations implications, but also may be helpful in the recruitment of personnel.

Reporting for collective bargaining

In the past, the release of information for collective bargaining purposes has depended on the strengths and abilities of the parties involved in the collective bargaining process. In the United Kingdom, the Employment Protection Act 1975 altered this situation radically by placing a general duty on employers to disclose information for collective bargaining purposes.

The construction of a normative theory of financial reporting relevant to pay bargaining between employers and employees and their representatives ought to be based on the criteria suggested by the ASB's Statement of Principles. The information which may be assumed to be most relevant to pay bargaining is related to two factors:

1 The minimum acceptable settlement which is based on considerations of equity, and is made up of a combination of factors including the cost of living, comparability with other industries and value added. Given the sensitivity attaching to the term 'profit', *The Corporate Report* (Accounting Standards Committee, 1975) suggested that 'the simplest and most immediate way of putting profit into proper perspective *vis-à-vis* the whole enterprise as a collective effort by capital, management and employees is by the presentation of a statement of value added'. Many companies are introducing value-added concepts into wage incentive schemes in order to improve productivity.
2 The ability to pay, which determines whether the firm is in a position to afford to meet a pay claim without endangering profitability (Cullinan, 1992). The ability of the firm to meet a pay claim is defined as the distributable operating cash flows less the minimum required by those who have provided the capital. Productivity data is an important aspect of the definition of the firm's ability to pay. Management may be amenable to arguments that link pay increases to increases in productivity, for pay increases may be absorbed by increased productivity without affecting the firm's pricing policy.

Partnerships for the common good

The drive for economic efficiency enabled the market economy to be remarkably successful in creating wealth. The major criticism of the free market economy that remains unanswered lies in Adam Smith's optimistic expectation that man 'led by an invisible hand and pursuing his own interests, frequently promotes that of society, an end that was no part of his original intentions' (Smith, A., *An Inquiry into the Nature and Causes of the Wealth of Nations*). The recent credit and banking crisis brought nations to the brink of bankruptcy and raised doubts about the sustainability of capitalism and free trade. Seeking high returns through high risk lending, banks succeeded in passing huge losses to taxpayers. Corporate managers are awarding themselves large bonuses, even when profits fall, and expropriating profits due to shareholders. The pursuit of higher profits, often through labour cost savings and the relocation of business, not only perpetuates the conflict between management and labour, but heightens tension between business and society. The evolution of modern financial capitalism has created a three-fold conflict between shareholders, management and labour, and increased public hostility, particularly against financial institutions. A general consensus now favours imposing strict regulatory controls of business in the public interest.

Essentially, the enduring conflict between capital and labour resides in the perception of an unfair distribution of business income, often manifested during labour disputes in demands for 'a fair day's wage for a fair day's work'. The history of the process of conciliation of the conflicting interests between capital and labour is seen in the development of such business structures as mutual and cooperative companies, in which ownership is defined by membership and profit is distributed to members. Mutual and cooperative companies are found in a wide variety of business activities, including insurance, banks, manufacturing, agriculture, wholesale and retail businesses. These forms of business organizations define the common good in terms of the interests of their members, capital being obtained from financial institutions on a commercial basis. At the same time, improvements in industrial relations have been achieved through the eventual acceptance of employee participation in management decision-making and, in some counties, by representation at board level.

The John Lewis Partnership Limited in the United Kingdom is an outstanding example of a large and very successful commercial company that operates under employee ownership and control. It is a unique example in the United Kingdom of a corporate management model which offers an opportunity to successfully reconcile economic efficiency with social justice through the principle of sharing thereby ensuring its sustainability. (See Glautier, M.W.E. (forthcoming) *The Caring Society*, Chapter 6 Partnerships for the Common Good, for a more complete discussion of the philosophy and description, analysis and evaluation of the management model under employee ownership and control as adopted by the John Lewis Partnership Limited.) Its founder, John Spedan Lewis was moved by the unfairness of the distribution of income to labour in the family business to observe 'the profit, even after ten thousand pounds had been set aside as interest at 5% upon capital, was equal to the whole of the pay of the staff, of whom there were about three hundred (MacPherson, H. (1985), pp. 9–10). According to Lewis, the primary purpose for transferring ownership and control to employees was 'securing the happiness of employees by sharing gain, knowledge and power'. This business philosophy places employees at the centre of corporate concern and their collective endeavour as the main driver.

Corporate social objectives

Zadek *et al.* (1997) have identified several areas in which corporate social objectives may be found:

1 environmental protection;
2 energy savings;
3 fair business practices;
4 human resources;
5 community involvement;
6 product.

Environmental protection

This area involves the environmental aspects of production, covering pollution control in the conduct of business operations, prevention or repair of damage to the environment resulting from processing of natural resources and the conservation of natural resources.

Corporate social objectives are to be found in the abatement of the negative external social effects of industrial production, and in adopting more efficient technologies to minimize the use of irreplaceable resources and the production of waste.

Energy saving

This area covers conservation of energy in the conduct of business operations and increasing the energy efficiency of the company's products.

Fair business practices

This area concerns the relationship of the company to special interest groups. In particular it deals with the employment and advancement of minorities; the use of clear English in legal terms and conditions with suppliers and customers; and the display of information on its products, etc.

Human resources

This area concerns the impact of organizational activities on the people who constitute the human resources of the organization. These activities include:

1 recruiting practices;
2 training programmes;
3 experience building job rotation;
4 job enrichment;
5 wage and salary levels;
6 fringe benefit plans;
7 congruence of employee and organizational goals;
8 mutual trust and confidence;
9 job security, stability of workforce, layoff and recall practices;
10 transfer and promotion policies;
11 occupational health.

Community involvement

This area involves community activities, health-related activities, education and the arts.

Products

This area concerns the qualitative aspects of the products, for example their utility, life-durability, safety and serviceability, as well as their effect on pollution. Moreover, it includes customer satisfaction, truthfulness in advertising, completeness and clarity of labelling and packaging. Many of these considerations are important already from a marketing point of view. It is clear, however, that the social responsibility aspect of the product contribution extends beyond what is advantageous from a marketing angle.

Corporate social reporting in the UK

Companies are required by law to disclose the following information:

1 *Fair business practices*: companies with more than 250 employees are required to state the policy regarding the employment, training, career development and promotion of disabled people.
2 *Human resources*:
   (a) For companies which employ 100 or more, the Directors' Report is required to state the average number of UK employees and their related remuneration during the year.
   (b) The Health and Safety at Work Act 1974 provides for regulations to be made requiring companies to disclose information about 'arrangements in force for securing the health, safety and welfare at work of employees of the company and its subsidiaries'.
   (c) The Directors' Report is required to include action with regard to informing employees, consulting employees, encouraging involvement (e.g. share ownership schemes).
3 *Charitable and political gifts*: these must be disclosed in the Directors' Report.

Several surveys have been undertaken in the UK in order to establish the nature and extent of social disclosures in the annual accounts. Maunders (1982) surveyed the published accounts of 300 large companies for 1981/82. Mirza (1987) examined the annual reports of 131 top companies for 1984/85. Gray (1989) conducted a longitudinal survey of 200 large companies for 1978/87. All three surveys raise the issue of the possible measurement levels that are feasible in relation to social reporting:

1 identification and description of efforts (e.g. general policy statements);
2 physical but non-financial quantification (e.g. employee hours in training); and
3 financial quantification (e.g. expenditure on pollution control).

Most social reporting was found to be of the first type with the exception of human resource information. Gray (1989) found that the trend of mandated disclosure is upward, reflecting an increased response to legislation. No such conclusion could be drawn from the voluntary disclosures, although over 60 per cent of the companies surveyed made voluntary disclosures of some sort.

Maunders (1982) found that the voluntary disclosures by his sample of companies for 1981/82 by categories of information were as follows:

	%
Human resources	40
Fair business practice	19
Energy	15
Community involvement	12
Product-related	10
Environmental	9

The largest incidence of voluntary disclosure is in the category of human resources which includes items such as employee training and development. Fair business practice concerns the disclosure by companies of information about women and persons of various ethnic groups in their employment. Mirza (1987) found that 15 per cent of his sample included information about environmental protection including the reporting of activities like treatment of effluent water, following stringent nuclear safety standards, restoration of mining areas and maintenance of trees. However, Gray (1989) showed that there had been no significant increase in environmental and energy disclosures during the five years following the Maunders' survey.

The two categories where voluntary disclosures appear to have shown an upward trend in recent years are 'community involvement' and 'product-related'. According to Gray's (1989) sample, product safety disclosures had increased over the nine years in question and community involvement disclosures had increased to nearly 40 per cent. Recent years have witnessed an increasing accounting interest and political debate about corporate social and environmental reporting,

The greening of accounting

In this section we extend our consideration of the environment as an area in which corporate social objectives may be found. This reflects the growing concern in recent years over natural resource depletion, unacceptably high levels of pollution, global warming, acid rain and deforestation, among other issues. The environmental crisis has intensified the debate about social accounting and the role that accounting can play in mitigating or reversing the crisis.

Long-term environmental strategies at national and international level were proposed by the World Commission on Environment and Development in 1987 (the Brundtland Report). The centrepiece of the Report was sustainable development that 'meets the needs of the present without compromising the ability of the future to meet its own needs'. The concept of 'stakeholders' is thus extended to include future generations. Sustainability was at the heart of *Blueprint for a Green Economy* (Pearce *et al.*, 1989). This report, which was commissioned by the Department of the Environment, stresses the need to account for the use of environmental resources and the use of substances which may damage the environment. An effective form of intervention, according to Pearce, was the 'polluter pays principle', which requires those who produce products or services to bear the cost of achieving agreed standards of environmental quality. The report distinguished between two types of capital, namely man-made and natural, and the need to strike a balance between the two to ensure that each generation passed the same value of capital on to future generations. Man-made capital has been growing very significantly, but this growth has been at the expense of a decline in natural capital.

Environmental legislation

Growing concern about the environment, and in particular sustainability, has prompted legislation at the national and European level. The Environmental Protection Act 1990 takes the first steps towards piecemeal implementation of the principle that the polluter pays through a system of integrated pollution control. The Act provides for levies on certain categories of companies to fund the regulatory and control bodies which were to enforce it. Controls were to be placed on emissions and industrial processes and there would be more public disclosure on the operations of polluting companies. Of significance for the accounting function is the legal obligation imposed to minimize waste production utilizing what is called the 'best available technology not entailing excessive cost' (BATNEEC) principle.

Developments at the European level are, of course, having an ever increasing influence on UK business practices. Again, the main thrust behind these initiatives has been the issue of sustainability. In 1992, the so-called Fifth Action Plan introduced a long-term strategy together with objectives to be achieved in the medium and short term. This recognizes the finite nature of raw materials and the need to change consumption and behaviour patterns. The aim of the Plan is to promote cooperation between national and local governments, and companies and consumers, in achieving environmental targets in defined areas, for example pollution control, waste reduction and the sustainable use of resources. EU-inspired environmental legislation is set to have an increasingly significant impact on all industrial and commercial activity in the future.

Challenges facing accountants

Accountants have begun to define the ecological issue as falling within their range of skills. For example, a study by the Chartered Institute of Management Accountants argued that 'the forward-thinking management accountant should be taking an active role in environmental management, as he or she has key skills to apply to the process' (CIMA, 1997).

The basic financial accounting model is an impediment to change because it only records and employs the data which arise from transactions which generate a price. Prices are only generated when property rights are transferred. The majority of the matters that are of concern in ecology are things over which property rights do not exist. As a result, the basic financial accounting model ignores them (Gray, 1993). Therefore, although there is an active and essential role that accountants can play in the development of sound environmental and reporting procedures, much work must be done to develop more comprehensive reporting systems involving both quantitative and qualitative techniques.

The accountant can make a considerable contribution in developing:

1 financial reporting practice; and
2 environmental management systems.

Financial reporting practice

Recent accounting research has focused on the demand for data on the environmental performance of an entity and the obligation which accountants have to provide information to shareholders and other users on the costs and benefits involved (Bell and Lehman, 1999). There is also a business case for greater responsibility and accountability. One study has found a positive link between environmental and financial performance, and specifically that over two-thirds of green companies perform better than their non-green counterparts in 1,200 direct comparisons of green and non-green companies (Edwards, 1998).

The United Nations Environment Programme has directed its attention to issues of environmental disclosures. Recommendations have been made for companies to disclose the following (Adams, 1998):

1 key environmental issues facing the company and plans for addressing these;
2 progress in addressing changes required by future legal requirements;
3 actual and projected levels of environmental expenditure;
4 energy use, material use, emissions and waste disposal routes;
5 financial estimates of savings and benefits flowing from pro-environment efforts;
6 an independent audit statement.

The UK has no formal requirements that organizations should publish statements of their environmental performance. The preference has been to avoid regulated reporting and to encourage companies to experiment with voluntary disclosure. However, UK companies generally give a low priority to the reporting of environmental information. A survey found that only 32 per cent of the top UK companies produced a separate environmental report (KPMG, 1999). Only 14 of these reports included quantifiable targets and only 19 reported on poor performance. The slow response on the part of UK companies towards heightened public concern over environmental issues is unfortunate in view of the fact that external reports are extremely valuable as a means of promoting public accountability, the need for which is central to the emerging green agenda.

The approach of increasing environmental disclosure is still rooted in conventional accounting measurement. It does not deal with the need to recognize the importance of environmental capital and guard against its depletion. An approach which meets this objective involves the requirements for organizations to calculate and disclose sustainable costs. Sustainable cost can be defined as the amount an organization must spend to put the biosphere at the end of the accounting period back into the state (or its equivalent) that it was in at the beginning of the accounting period (Adams, 1999). Such a figure would be a notional one, and disclosed as a charge to a company's profit and loss account. Thus, we would be presented with a broad estimate of the extent to which accounting profits had been generated from a sustainable source. This would have the effect of reducing the organization's profit and thus reducing the amount it could distribute to the shareholders – while maintaining natural capital. The reader will note the parallel with current value accounting, discussed in Chapter 29.

According to one research study, voluntary disclosure has not been successful, either in terms of its extent or nature, partly because organizations lack experience of social accounting (Adams, 2000). Guidance is needed on the definition of goals and targets, the measurement of progress made against the targets, the auditing and reporting of performance, the feedback mechanisms. Accountability 1000 (ISEA, 1999) provides guidance on all these issues. It is a private voluntary standard designed for experimentation and to help users develop innovative social responsibility and sustainability strategies. It also provides a means by which to evaluate the quality of social reports.

Environmental management systems

The focus of an environmental management system (EMS) is prevention of environmental damage rather than detection and amelioration after occurrence. This role was identified by the British Environmental Management System Standard, BS 5750 (British Standards Institute, 1994) which states that an EMS should:

1 identify and assess the environmental effects arising from the organization's existing or proposed activities, products or services;
2 identify and assess the environmental affects arising from incidents, accidents and potential emergency situations;
3 identify the relevant regulatory requirements;
4 enable priorities to be identified and pertinent environmental objectives and targets to be set;
5 facilitate planning, control and monitoring, auditing and review activities to ensure both that the policy is complied with, and that it remains relevant;
6 be capable of evolution to suit changing circumstances.

Although implementing an EMS that meets these objectives is a team effort, because expertise in a variety of disciplines is needed, accountants should be in a position to play a major role (Willits and Guitini, 1994). Indeed, many writers view this possible role as being a logical development of the accounting profession in a world where natural resources, as well as monetary capital, are limiting factors (Birkin, 1996).

Environmental issues permeate all aspects of business, from product design to manufacturing and delivery, in all ways that directly impact on the bottom line. When environmental issues are translated into financial terms, they are more likely to be included in the decision-making process. It is suggested that accountants, the primary recipients, analysts and providers of financial information, can play a pivotal role in bringing this about (Bell and Lehman, 1999).

Adapting management accounting

Management control techniques, discussed in this part will need to be adapted to embrace environmental issues. For example, budgeting can, if properly applied, bring financial discipline into the organization as targets are agreed and managers are held accountable for their performance in achieving them. It should be possible to allocate environmental responsibilities and targets to managers in addition to purely financial goals, with rewards and penalties incorporated (Gannon and Rowell, 1995). Accountants could also encourage the inclusion of environmental objectives as mandatory in capital investment appraisals.

Summary

The concept of corporate social responsibility emerged in the 1960s when changing social values and expectations gave rise to a debate about the role of business in society. This debate focused on the nature of corporate social responsibility and gave rise to the possibility that this responsibility could be discharged through a method of social accounting. It was argued that such a method of accounting would indicate the nature and the manner of the firm's social contributions or outputs.

The comparison between investors and employees as users of financial reports indicates a similarity of needs for information for decision making. Changes in the social environment and political attitudes in favour of human rights through greater democracy and employee participation in decision making, extending to industrial democracy and employee ownership and control, make possible the reconciliation of economic efficiency with social justice, thereby ensuring the sustainability of the market economy.

Corporate social objectives may be found in six areas of enterprise activity. Most social reporting disclosures are descriptive in nature. Although the trend of mandated disclosure in the UK has been upwards in recent years, no such conclusions can be drawn from voluntary disclosures. The recent concern for environmental issues may have a dramatic effect on future corporate environmental and management systems.

Self-assessment questions

1 'There is as yet no generally accepted concept of the social responsibility of business enterprises.' Discuss.

2 How do the needs of employees for financial information compare with those of investors?

3 What issues are involved in direct reporting to employees and supplying information for collective bargaining?

4 How do partnerships for the common good differ from businesses financed by shareholders?

5 What do you understand by employee ownership and control. Refer your comments to the the corporate management model used by John Lewis Partnership Limited.

6 What areas in which corporate social objectives may be found were identified by Zadek *et al.*?

7 Examine recent trends in corporate social reporting.

8 What are the implications for accounting of the increasing concern with green issues?

9 Can a caring society exist in a market economy?

References

Accounting Standards Board (ASB) (1999) *Statement of principles for financial reporting*, ASB Publications.

Accounting Standards Committee (1975) *The Corporate Report*, Institute of Chartered Accountants in England and Wales.

Adams, C.R. (1998) Going green, *The Accountant*, April.

Adams, C.R. (1999) Performance indicators for sustainable development, *Accounting and Business*, April.

Adams, C.R. (2000) Ethical reporting: past and future, *Management Accounting*, February.

Advisory Conciliation and Arbitration Service (1977) *Disclosure of Information to Trade Unions for Collective Bargaining Purposes*.

Arrow, K.J. (1963) *Social Choice and Individual Values*, Yale University Press.

Beattie, A. (2010) Centre-left fails to make capital from economic train wreck, *Financial Times*, 22 February 2010.

Bell, F. and Lehman, G. (1999) Recent trends in environment accounting, *Accounting Forum*, June.

Birkin, F. (1996) Environmental management accounting, *Management Accounting*, February.

British Standards Institute (1994) BS 5750: *Specification for Environmental Management Systems*, BSI.

505

CIMA (1997) *Environmental Management: the Role of the Management Accountant*, Chartered Institute of Management Accountants.

Clark, F. and Craig, R. (1991) Juridical perceptions of the relevance of accounting data in wage fixation, *British Journal of Industrial Relations*, vol. 29, no. 3.

Committee for Economic Development (1971) *Social Responsibilities of Business Corporations*.

Confederation of British Industry (1975) *Guidelines for Action – The Provision of Information to Employees*.

Cullinan, C.P. (1992) *The role of accounting information in models of the collective bargaining process*. In Proceedings of the Twenty-Third Annual Meeting of the Midwest Decision Sciences Institute.

Cullinan, C.P. and Knoblett J.A. (1994) Unionization and accounting policy choices: an empirical examination, *Journal of Accounting and Public Policy*, Spring.

Cullinan, C.P., Clark, M.W. and Knoblett, J.A. (1994) Accounting information and collective bargaining, *Journal of Accounting Literature*, vol. 13.

Crowther, D. (2000) Social and Environmental Accounting, *Financial Times*, Prentice Hall.

Edwards, D. (1998) *The Link Between Company Environmental and Financial Performance*, Earthscan.

Friedman, M. (1962) *Capitalism and Freedom*, University of Chicago Press.

Gannon, J. and Rowell, S. (1995) Are accountants ready for the green revolution?, *ACCA Students' Newsletter*, August.

Glautier, M.W.E. (2007) *The Social Conscience*, Shepherd-Walwyn Publishing Ltd.

Glautier, M.W.E. (forthcoming) *The Caring Society*.

Gonella, C., Pilling, A. and Zadek, J. (1998) *Making Values Count*, Association of Certified Accountants.

Gray, R.H., Owens, D.L. and Maunders, K.T. (1987) *Corporate Social Reporting: Accounting and Accountability*, Prentice Hall.

Gray, R.H. (1989) *Corporate Social Reporting by UK Companies: a Cross-Sectional and Longitudinal Study*, Draft Working Paper, December.

Gray, R.H. (1993) *Accounting for the Environment*, Paul Chapman.

Institute of Social and Ethical Accountability (1999) *Accountability 1000*.

Keynes, J.M. (1926) *The End of Laissez-Faire*, Macmillan, p. 133.

KPMG (1999) *International Survey of Environmental Accounting*, 1999.

MacPherson, H. (1985) General Editor, *John Spedan Lewis 1885–1963: Remembered by some of his contemporaries in the centenary year of his birth*, John Lewis Partnerships Ltd.

Maunders, K.T. (1982) Social reporting and the employment report, in Skerratt, L.C.L. and Tonkin, D.J. (eds) *Financial Reporting 1982–83: A Survey of UK Published Accounts*, The Institute of Chartered Accountants in England and Wales.

Mirza, A.M. (1987) Social reporting by the UK companies, *Business Graduate Journal*, April.

Nay, L.A. (1991) The determinants of concession bargaining in the airline industry, *Labour Relations Review*, January.

Newell, G.E., Kreuze, J.G. and Newell, S.J. (1990) Accounting for hazardous waste, *Management Accounting*, USA, May.

Pearce, D.W., Markandya, A. and Barbier, E.B. (1989) *Blueprint for a Green Economy*, Earthscan.

Willits, S.D. and Guitini, D. (1994) Helping your company go green, *Management Accounting*, USA, February.

Zadek, S., Pruzan, P. and Evans, R. (1997) *Building Corporate Accountability*, Earthscan.

SECTION 2

Management control

Introduction to Section 2

In Part 2, we examined the nature and the role of accounting information as originating in business transactions recorded on an on-going basis in accounting records,
known as 'books'. In accordance with the concept of stewardship accounting, these
records are used to prepare financial reports in the form of income statements, balance sheets and cash-flow statements to enable proprietors to exercise effective
control and evaluate managerial performance. The financial reports of incorporated companies are the subject of regulatory controls in the form of legislation and
accounting standards that define their meaning and content in the context of their
use and relevance for decision making by shareholders and investors.

We noted also that the information which is recorded into the accounting system is
also used in traditional cost accounting to enable management to develop product and
service cost information relevant to pricing and other management decisions through
a separate cost accounting system. Both the financial and cost accounting systems are
integrated because they share the same historic cost-based data that have originated
in invoices. This integration of the two systems continues through the transfer of full-
product costs of finished goods from the cost accounting system into the financial
accounting system, where it shows up ultimately in the cost of sales in the calculation
of periodic income. Consequently, accounting concepts and standards automatically
apply to cost accounting information that is used for financial reporting purposes.
This is particularly true with respect to valuation rules applicable to inventories.

The context of management control calls for accounting information that is ori-
ented towards management decision making rather than external users. The need
is for accounting information relating to product, service and activity costing in the
context of pricing decisions and profit management. Budgetary planning and control and the variety of decisions implied in the efficient management of resources
demand information that has its usefulness in dealing with future events rather
than conventional accounting information that relates to the past. The evolution of
cost accounting in providing information useful and relevant to the management of
business enterprises has been remarkably innovative in seeking its inspiration from
such fields as economics, decision science and the behavioural sciences. Free from
the concepts and standards that have constrained financial accounting and reporting practices by regulations seeking to impose comparability of information and
uniformity of methods, cost and management accounting have been enriched by the
freedom to experiment, to borrow ideas from other areas of knowledge and adopt
new methods and procedures for management decision making and control.

These two different cultures cohabit in the necessity to find common purpose in
the optimization of shareholder value through the profitable management of business
operations and the efficient management of corporate resources. Whereas 'fair value
accounting' has dominated the debate over the relevance and usefulness of financial
reports for investors needing current rather than historic values, industrial companies

have long been using standard costs, defined as expected future costs of production for valuing inventory. By substituting in cost records standard costs for historic costs, such companies are effectively already using the equivalent of 'fair values' for financial reporting purposes and are using historic costs purely for internal control and evaluation of performance.

These two different cultures have followed very different paths with respect to the defined scope of subject matter, the identification of their respective problems and the methods that they have developed.

CHAPTER 32

Budgeting for planning and control

Setting the scene

While some proposed management accounting techniques seem to be little used in practice, this cannot be said of budgeting. Surveys have shown that 99 per cent of all companies in Europe operate formal budgeting systems. Most management accountants spend a considerable amount of time preparing, revising and monitoring budgets and most organisations have clear and well proven budgeting routines.

(Kennedy and Dugdale (1999) Getting the most from budgeting, *Management Accounting* (UK), February)

Learning objectives

After studying this chapter you should be able to:

1   explain how strategic planning relates to budgeting;

2   identify the budgets that make up the overall budget;

3   prepare operating budgets for a manufacturing enterprise;

4   describe zero-based budgeting;

5   appreciate the difference between traditional budgeting and activity-based budgeting.

The process of budgeting focuses on the short term, normally one year, and provides an expression of the steps which management must take in the current period if it is to fulfil organizational objectives. However, many organizations prepare three-year plans, with a detailed budget covering the first year, and a summarized one covering each of the following two years. The focus of this chapter is on the preparation of the budget for the first year.

Objectives of budgeting

Long-range planning involves the selection of the mission statement (i.e. the reason for the organization being in business) and the determination of a suitable plan for attaining its objectives. Budgets are the quantitative expressions of these plans stated in either physical or financial terms or both. Therefore, the long-range plan is the guide for preparing the annual budgets and defines actions that need to be taken now in order to move towards long-term objectives. Indeed, the budget represents the first one-year span of the long-range plan. Budgeting is part of the management control process discussed in Chapter 16.

The reader will recall that one important feature of planning is the coordination of the various activities of an enterprise, and of its departments, so that they are harmonized in the overall task of realizing corporate objectives. For example, if the marketing function were to increase sales massively over a short period of time, the manufacturing function would have to increase output substantially – probably through the use of costly overtime labour, or by buying goods from an outside supplier at high prices. Conversely, excessive production may force the marketing function to sell at unrealistically low prices in order to avoid excessive investment in stock. The function of budgeting is to coordinate the various activities of an organization in order to achieve company rather than divisional or departmental objectives. Therefore it is necessary to establish objectives for each section of the organization which are in harmony with the organization as a whole.

As a plan of action, budgets can be used to control by comparing actual outcomes as they happen with the planned outcomes. If the actual differs significantly from the planned, actions can be taken to put the plan back on track if necessary.

The need for flexibility

Because business conditions are always changing, it is necessary to view the budgeting process as a guide to future action, rather than a rigid plan which must be followed irrespective of changing circumstances. The latter approach may place the manager in a straitjacket in which he or she is forced to take decisions which are not in accordance with company objectives. For example, a departmental manager may find, due to changing conditions, that he has not spent all his budget on a particular item. In order to spend all his budget allowance, so as to prevent the possibility of a cut in his allowance next year, he may squander funds which could have been put to better use in other sections of the organization. This used to be the case in government organizations, in that if money was not spent, the next year's budget would be reduced regardless of whether the money was needed that year. Towards the end of the government financial year, many managers would ensure that any expense heading which was under-spent was spent by the year end.

More importantly, management must plan for changing business conditions, in order that appropriate action may be taken to deal with changes that may occur should any of the assumptions underlying plans be affected by such changes. This implies that contingency plans should be available to deal with changes which were unforeseen at the time when the budget was originally prepared.

Some firms relate their budgets to changing conditions by means of a rolling budget which is prepared every quarter, but for one year ahead. At the end of each quarter the plans for the next three quarters are revised, if this is necessary, and a fourth quarter is added. By this process the budgets are kept continually up-to-date.

Flexibility is also required if budgetary control is to be effective. Indeed the type of budget which may be suitable for planning may be inappropriate for control purposes. Therefore, budgets should be established for control purposes which reflect operating conditions which may be different from those envisaged in the planning stages. This is essential if individual managers are to be held responsible only for those deviations over which they have control. Such a requirement is called for by the use of a responsibility accounting system, which is discussed in Chapter 33.

The organization of budgeting

The budgeting process itself requires careful organization. In large firms, budgeting is often in the hands of a budgeting committee which acts through the budget officer whose function it is to coordinate and control the budgeting process for the whole organization. Departmental budget estimates are requested from divisional managers, who in their turn collate this information from estimates submitted to them by their own departmental managers. Hence, budget estimates are based on information which flows upwards through the organization to the budget committee. The budget committee is responsible for coordinating this information, and resolving any differences in consultations with the managers involved. The final budget proposal is presented to the board of directors for its final approval.

Steps in budgeting

The first stage of a budgeting exercise is the determination of the 'key' factors or constraints which impose overall limits to the budget plan. Among these factors are the productive capacity of the plant, the finances available to the firm, and, of course, the market conditions which impose a total limit on the output the firm is able to sell. Normally from a management point of view, the critical question is 'what is the firm able to sell in the budget period?', and this question summarizes all the limits to the budget plan. It is for this reason that the sales budget is at once the starting point and the fulcrum of the budgeting process.

Figure 32.1 illustrates how the various resources and activities of an enterprise are coordinated. A similar exercise would be carried out in a non-manufacturing organization or service organization. The areas which would not feature in some service organizations would be finished goods stock budget, material usage budget, raw materials budget and materials purchases budget. It is necessary to adapt the budget process to the industry and type of organization. For example in the health service, each service (acute, maternity, diagnostic and paramedic, etc.) would prepare an expense budget based on staff and the forecast of patients to be treated. Some materials costs would be incurred (drugs, bed sheets, etc.) but the major expense would be salaries. Next, the service costs would be accumulated into an expenditure budget while concurrently the money available to run the service would be cascading from the Department of Health downwards towards the area health authorities and then down to the hospitals. Ultimately a master budget would be prepared and submitted to the governing body.

The arrows indicate the flow of relevant information. Once the level of sales is established, selling and distribution cost may be ascertained. The production budget itself is determined by the sales forecast, the desired level of stock of finished goods and plant capacity. From the production budget may be estimated the production costs, and the cost schedules for materials, labour and overheads.

In addition, the budgeting process for capital expenditure reflects decisions taken in developing the long-range plan. The capital expenditure budget is concerned with expenditure during the budget period on the maintenance and improvement of the existing productive capacity. Associated with this budget are research and development costs for improving methods of production and product improvement as well.

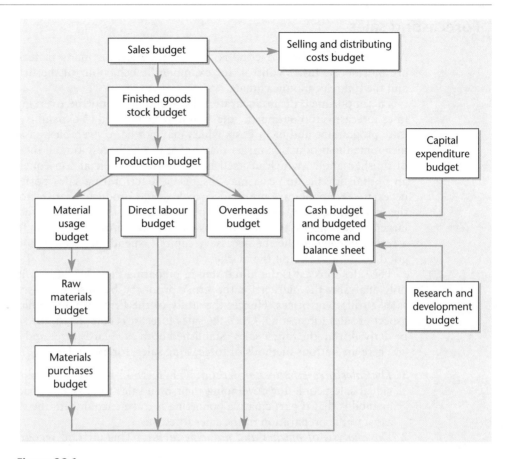

Figure 32.1

From a financing point of view, the cash surplus or deficits arising out of the overall budget are revealed by the cash budget which incorporates all cash revenues and cash expenditures. This enables the firm to arrange its financial needs accordingly.

Finally, the projected results in terms of the overall net profit and the changes in the structure of the firm's assets and liabilities are expressed in the budgeted profit and loss account and the budgeted balance sheet at the end of the budget period.

This description of the manner in which the budget coordinates the various activities of the firm is a simplified one. Budgetary planning is an activity which is of critical importance to the firm, and the problems involved are often complex and difficult ones to resolve. A firm's sales policy, for example, cannot be considered in isolation from its pricing policy and its cost structure. The firm's planned costs in relation to the required output may be too high to reach the profit target. If this should be the case, pricing and advertising policies may require further scrutiny, both planned and development costs may have to be reduced, and the final product itself may have to be modified. The role of the budget committee is, therefore, a very important one: not only has it to harmonize all the divisional budgets into an overall planning framework, but it has to deal with the numerous adjustments which may have to be made if the overall budget fails to meet some of the firm's stated objectives. Hence, the role of the budget committee is not only important in a practical sense: it affects important and sensitive areas of policy making and management.

Forecasting sales

A major problem in budgeting is forecasting sales, for many factors affecting sales are outside the firm's control, for example the behaviour of the firm's competitors and the future economic climate.

The importance of an accurate sales forecast cannot be overemphasized. If the sales forecast is too optimistic, the firm may be induced to expand its capital expenditure programme and incur costs which may not be recoverable at a later date. In the meantime the production target may be set too high, resulting in the pile-up of stock of finished goods, which in itself has important financial consequences. Moreover, an optimistic sales forecast may disguise a deteriorating sales position, so that the necessary economies are not made which would produce a satisfactory profit. If, on the other hand, the sales forecast is pessimistic, the firm will miss the opportunity of larger current profit and may be misled as to its future prospects. The firm may, as a result, not undertake the necessary capital expenditure which would place it in a good position to exploit the market.

The sales forecast is the initial step in preparing the sales budget. It consists of not only analysing the market for the firm's products, but also forecasting the levels of sales at different prices. Hence, the study of the firm's pricing policy is an integral aspect of sales forecasting. Once the sales forecast is completed, the sales budget may be derived from the target sales established both as regards price and sales volume.

There are various methods of forecasting sales, for example:

1 *The salesforce composite method.* This method places responsibility upon individual salespeople for developing their own sales forecasts. The advantage of this method is that if participative budgeting is to be encouraged, the sales staff should assist in the preparation of the sales forecast.
2 *The analysis of market and industry factors.* This method recognizes the importance of factors not within the knowledge of the salesforce, such as forecasts of the gross national product, personal incomes, employment and price levels, etc. The salespeople's estimates are modified by the information so obtained.
3 *Statistical analysis of fluctuations through time.* Sales are generally affected by four basic factors: growth trends, business cycle fluctuations, seasonal fluctuations and irregular variations in demand. A time series analysis of sales is a statistical method of separating and analysing the historical evidence of the behaviour of sales to identify these several effects and their impact on sales. The results of this analysis are applied to the sales forecast, and are means of testing the quality of the forecast.
4 *Mathematical techniques for sales forecasting.* Of recent years, mathematical techniques have been applied to the study of the relationship between economic trends and a firm's sales pattern through time, to arrive at a projection of future sales. These techniques usually involve the use of computers. One such technique is known as exponential smoothing, which is really a prediction of future sales based on current and historical sales data, weighted so as to give a greater importance to the latest incoming information.

An illustration of the budgeting process

Once the sales forecast is known, a firm may begin to prepare the budget. We believe that the reader will obtain a better understanding of budgeting if we work through a simple example. In the following example, we focus on the technical problems of budget construction, and we assume that the problem of changing price levels is not present. This assumption allows us to treat asset values as remaining constant.

Example 32.1 The Edco Manufacturing Co Ltd manufactures two products, A and B. A formal planning system had been introduced some time ago as a means of steering the company into more profitable levels of operation. Considerable progress had already been made in streamlining production and reducing costs. The budgeting process normally began in October, prior to the end of the accounting year on 31 December.

The Edco Manufacturing Co Ltd
Forecast results for the year ending 31 December 20X0
Income statement

	£
Sales	135,000
Cost of goods sold	80,000
Gross margin	55,000
Selling and administrative expenses	25,000
Income before tax	30,000
Tax at 40%	12,000
Income after tax	18,000

Balance sheet

	Cost £	Depreciation £	£
Non-current assets			
Plant and machinery	250,000	30,000	220,000
Current assets			
Inventories:			
Raw materials		1,650	
Finished goods		6,025	
		7,675	
Debtors		20,000	
Cash		5,325	
		33,000	
Less: Creditors: amounts falling due within one year			
Creditors	5,000		
Tax	12,000		
		17,000	
Net current assets			16,000
Total assets *less* current liabilities			236,000
Capital and reserves			
Called-up share capital			210,000
Income statement			26,000
			236,000

The expected results for the current year ending on 31 December 20X0 were as shown above. From these forecast results, the expected performance for the current year may be calculated as follows:

$$\text{return on stakeholders' equity: } \frac{£18,000}{£236,000} = 7.6\%$$

$$\text{return on capital employed: } \frac{£30,000}{£236,000} = 12.7\%$$

The following additional information was obtained for the purpose of preparing the budget for the year ending 31 December 20X1.

The sales forecast

	Product A	Product B
Expected selling price per unit	£11	£14
Sales volume forecast		
1st quarter	1,500 units	2,000 units
2nd quarter	1,000	2,000
3rd quarter	1,000	2,000
4th quarter	1,500	2,000
Total for the year	5,000	8,000

Factory costs forecast

Two departments are concerned with production: the preparation department and the machining department. The following analysis relates to the production of these departments:

1 Direct costs

	Direct labour required per unit of product (in labour hours)		Departmental wage rate	Direct labour cost per unit of output	
	A	B		A	B
Preparation department	$\frac{1}{5}$	$\frac{1}{2}$	£2 per hour	£0.40	£1.00
Machining department	$\frac{1}{2}$	$\frac{1}{2}$	£2 per hour	£1.00	£1.00
				£1.40	£2.00

2 Raw material requirement forecast

The standard quantities of the two raw materials, X and Y, which should be used in the manufacture of the two products, and the prices of these raw materials have been estimated as follows:

Standard quantities:
Raw material X – 2 units for each unit of product A
Raw material Y – 3 units for each unit of product B

Estimated costs:

Raw material X – £0.50 for each unit of X

Raw material Y – £0.30 for each unit of Y

3 Overhead costs

Factory overheads are classified into fixed and variable costs. The fixed overhead costs are deemed to be incurred in equal amounts quarterly for the purpose of allocation, whereas the variable overheads vary according to the level of production. The following estimates are available:

Fixed overheads:

Depreciation	£10,000 per annum
Rates and insurances	4,000
Supervisory salaries	6,000
	£20,000

Variable overheads

	Cost per unit of output	
	A	B
	£	£
Indirect labour		
Indirect material		
Repairs and maintenance	£0.50	£1.00
Power		

Using activity-based costing, some of the fixed and variable overheads may be allocated on the basis of cost drivers, as mentioned in Chapter 18, instead of on the basis of cost per unit, or cost per labour hour.

Inventory forecasts

Finished goods

Product A – estimated opening inventory:	750 units
Product B – estimated opening inventory:	1,000 units

It was planned that the closing inventory level at the end of each quarter should be maintained at a level equal to half the expected sales for the next quarter for both products.

For the purposes of calculating the expected income, the closing inventory is to be valued on a variable costing basis, as follows:

	A	B
Raw materials	£1.00	£0.90
Direct labour	1.40	2.00
Variable overheads	0.50	1.00
Total variable costs per unit	£2.90	£3.90

Raw materials

Raw material X – estimated opening inventory: 1,500 units

Raw material Y: 3,000 units

Administrative and selling costs forecast

	£	£
1 Administrative costs		
Office salaries	18,000	
Stationery	1,000	
Other	1,000	
		20,000
2 Selling costs		
Salaries	15,000	
Advertising	5,000	
		20,000
Total		40,000

Cash flow forecast

1 Sales receipts

50 per cent of sales received in cash during month of sales
50 per cent of sales received in cash in the following month

2 Cash expenditure

(a) *Production costs*: Direct labour, direct materials and variable overheads paid in the month in which incurred. Fixed overheads paid in equal amounts quarterly.
(b) *Administrative and selling costs*: Paid in equal amounts quarterly.
(c) *Other costs*: Tax outstanding amounting to £12,000 will be paid off in equal instalments quarterly over the year.

Capital expenditure: Expenditure on the acquisition of assets is planned as follows:

	£
1st quarter	10,000
2nd quarter	15,000
3rd quarter	8,000
4th quarter	20,000
	53,000

Sundry creditors balance

The amount outstanding to sundry creditors will remain constant at £5,000 throughout the year.

PREPARING THE BUDGET FOR THE YEAR ENDING 31 DECEMBER 20X1

The task of preparing the overall budget involves a sequence of steps:

Step	1	The sales budget
	2	The production budget
	3	The direct materials usage budget
	4	The materials purchases budget
	5	The budgeted direct labour costs
	6	The overhead costs budget
	7	The closing inventory budget
	8	The selling and administrative costs budget
	9	The capital expenditure budget
	10	The cost of goods sold budget
	11	The cash budget
	12	The budgeted income statement
	13	The budgeted balance sheet

Step 1 The sales budget

The sales budget is prepared from the sales forecast as follows:

	1st quarter	2nd quarter	3rd quarter	4th quarter	Total
Units					
Product A	1,500	1,000	1,000	1,500	5,000
Product B	2,000	2,000	2,000	2,000	8,000
Value					
Product A (£11)	£16,500	£11,000	£11,000	£16,500	£55,000
Product B (£14)	28,000	28,000	28,000	28,000	112,000
	£44,500	£39,000	£39,000	£44,500	£167,000

Step 2 The production budget

The production budget is designed to plan the resources required to produce the output envisaged by the sales forecast. A precondition for an agreement as to the size of the sales budget is the adequacy of the productive capacity of the plant to provide the required output. If existing capacity is inadequate, decisions will have to be made as to the advisability of introducing overtime working, of subcontracting production, or of hiring or purchasing additional plant and equipment. If, on the other hand, the sales forecast falls short of productive capacity, sales promotion schemes may be considered as a means of closing or reducing the gap. With the tendency of business people to use inventory levels as buffers to insulate an efficient rate of production from variations in sales, the production budget is also dependent upon the planned levels of closing inventory.

Using the information given in our example, the following production budget may be prepared:

	1st quarter	2nd quarter	3rd quarter	4th quarter	Year
Product A					
Desired closing inventory (units)	500	500	750	750	750
Add: Sales	1,500	1,000	1,000	1,500	5,000
Total required	2,000	1,500	1,750	2,250	5,750
Less: Opening inventory	750	500	500	750	750
Production required	1,250	1,000	1,250	1,500	5,000
Product B					
Desired closing inventory (units)	1,000	1,000	1,000	1,000	1,000
Add: Sales	2,000	2,000	2,000	2,000	8,000
Total required	3,000	3,000	3,000	3,000	9,000
Less: Opening inventory	1,000	1,000	1,000	1,000	1,000
Production required	2,000	2,000	2,000	2,000	8,000

Step 3 The direct materials usage budget

The rate of usage of raw materials is known, so that the direct materials usage may be budgeted by multiplying the usage rate by the production required.

	1st quarter	2nd quarter	3rd quarter	4th quarter	Year
Material X (2 units for A)	2,500	2,000	2,500	3,000	10,000
Material Y (3 units for B)	6,000	6,000	6,000	6,000	24,000

Step 4 The materials purchase budget

The purpose of this budget is to determine both the quantities and the values of raw material purchases necessary to meet the production levels stipulated in the production budget. The information required for this budget is found in the direct materials usage budget, inventory forecasts and raw materials purchase prices.

	1st quarter	2nd quarter	3rd quarter	4th quarter	Year
Raw material X					
Desired closing inventory	1,000	1,000	1,500	1,500	1,500
Add: Material usage (Step 3)	2,500	2,000	2,500	3,000	10,000
Total required	3,500	3,000	4,000	4,500	11,500
Less: Opening inventory	1,500	1,000	1,000	1,500	1,500
Purchases required (units)	2,000	2,000	3,000	3,000	10,000
Price per unit	£0.50	£0.50	£0.50	£0.50	£0.50
Total purchases (value)	£1,000	£1,000	£1,500	£1,500	£5,000

	1st quarter	2nd quarter	3rd quarter	4th quarter	Year
Raw material Y					
Desired closing inventory	3,000	3,000	3,000	3,000	3,000
Add: Material usage (Step 3)	6,000	6,000	6,000	6,000	24,000
Total required	9,000	9,000	9,000	9,000	27,000
Less: Opening inventory	3,000	3,000	3,000	3,000	3,000
Purchases required (units)	6,000	6,000	6,000	6,000	24,000
Price per unit	£0.30	£0.30	£0.30	£0.30	£0.30
Total purchases (value)	£1,800	£1,800	£1,800	£1,800	£7,200
Total purchases (X plus Y)	£2,800	£2,800	£3,300	£3,300	£12,200

Step 5 Budgeted direct labour costs

This budget is based upon calculations of the labour requirements necessary to produce the planned output. The direct labour costs are computed by multiplying the labour requirements by the forecast of wage rates payable during the budget period.

	1st quarter	2nd quarter	3rd quarter	4th quarter	Year
Production (Step 2 – units)					
Product A	1,250	1,000	1,250	1,500	5,000
Product B	2,000	2,000	2,000	2,000	8,000
Labour hours					
Preparation department					
Product A $(\frac{1}{5})$	250	200	250	300	1,000
Product B $(\frac{1}{2})$	1,000	1,000	1,000	1,000	4,000
Total	1,250	1,200	1,250	1,300	5,000
Machining department					
Product A $(\frac{1}{2})$	625	500	625	750	2,500
Product B $(\frac{1}{2})$	1,000	1,000	1,000	1,000	4,000
Total	1,625	1,500	1,625	1,750	6,500
Direct labour costs					
Preparation department					
Labour hours	1,250	1,200	1,250	1,300	5,000
Wage rate/hour	£2	£2	£2	£2	£2
Direct labour cost	£2,500	£2,400	£2,500	£2,600	£10,000
Machining department					
Labour hours	1,625	1,500	1,625	1,750	6,500
Wage rate/hour	£2	£2	£2	£2	£2
Direct labour cost	£3,250	£3,000	£3,250	£3,500	£13,000
Total direct labour cost	£5,750	£5,400	£5,750	£6,100	£23,000

Step 6 The overhead costs budget

Having disposed of the direct costs of production in the form of materials and direct labour, we now come to the preparation of the estimates of the overhead costs of production. These costs are divided into the two categories mentioned earlier. We are told that the fixed overheads are incurred in equal amounts quarterly, and we may calculate the total variable costs per quarter by multiplying the expected variable costs per unit by the planned quarterly output.

	1st quarter	2nd quarter	3rd quarter	4th quarter	Year
Production (Step 2)					
Product A (units)	1,250	1,000	1,250	1,500	5,000
Product B (units)	2,000	2,000	2,000	2,000	8,000
Variable costs					
Product A (£0.50 per unit)	£625	£500	£625	£750	£2,500
Product B (£1.00 per unit)	2,000	2,000	2,000	2,000	8,000
Total	2,625	2,500	2,625	2,750	10,500
Fixed costs					
Depreciation	2,500	2,500	2,500	2,500	10,000
Rates and insurance	1,000	1,000	1,000	1,000	4,000
Supervisory salaries	1,500	1,500	1,500	1,500	6,000
Total	5,000	5,000	5,000	5,000	20,000
Total overhead costs	£7,625	£7,500	£7,625	£7,750	£30,500

Step 7 The closing inventory budget

The closing inventory budget consists of an estimate of the value of planned closing inventory of raw materials and planned inventory of finished goods. It is arrived at by calculating the budgeted unit cost of inventory and multiplying the result by the planned inventory level.

1 Budgeted closing raw material inventory

Raw material	X	Y	
Closing inventory (units)	1,500	3,000	
Cost per unit	£0.50	£0.30	
Value of closing inventory	£750	£900	
Total			£1,650

2 Budgeted finished goods inventory

We are told that the accountant values the inventory of finished goods on a variable costing basis, and that the unit cost of Products A and B has been calculated to be £2.90 and £3.90 respectively. These values are applied to the budgeted closing inventory figures as follows:

Product	A	B	
Closing inventory (units)	750	1,000	
Cost per unit	£2.90	£3.90	
Value of closing inventory	2,175	3,900	
Total			£6,075

Step 8 The selling and administrative expenses budget

Selling expenses		
Salaries	£15,000	
Advertising	5,000	£20,000
Administrative expenses		
Office salaries	18,000	
Stationery	1,000	
Other expenses	1,000	20,000
Total		£40,000

Step 9 The capital expenditure budget

We devote Chapter 36 to a discussion of capital budgeting as an aspect of long-range planning and control. The annual capital expenditure budget must be seen, therefore, as a one-year slice of the long-term capital budget. The purpose of the annual capital expenditure is to make provision in the current budget for the planned capital expenditure in the current year. This information has been provided as follows:

Capital expenditure	
1st quarter	£10,000
2nd quarter	15,000
3rd quarter	8,000
4th quarter	20,000
Total for the year	£53,000

Step 10 The cost of goods sold budget

The reader will recall that all the previous budgets mentioned have dealt with the various aspects of the production process, in unit and value terms, including the expenses associated with selling and administration and the valuation of closing stock. The purpose of this budget is to bring all these items together to arrive at an estimate of the cost of the goods sold. This estimate will be used in the budgeted profit and loss account. It is compiled as follows:

Opening raw materials inventory (balance sheet 31.12.20X0)	£1,650
Add: Materials purchases (Step 4)	12,200
Raw materials available for production	13,850
Less: Planned closing inventory of raw materials (Step 7)	1,650
Cost of raw materials to be used in production	12,200
Cost of direct labour (Step 5)	23,000
Factory overhead costs (Step 6)	30,500
Cost of goods to be manufactured	65,700
Add: Opening inventory of finished goods (balance sheet 31.12.20X0)	6,025
	71,725
Less: Planned closing inventory of finished goods	6,075
Budgeted cost of goods sold	£65,650

Step 11 The cash budget

The cash budget consists of the estimates of cash receipts and cash payments arising from the planned levels of activities and use of resources which are considered in the various budgets we have examined. The cash budget is a complete survey of the financial implication of expenditure plans of both a current and a capital nature during the year. Moreover, by comparing the anticipated outflows of cash with the expected inflows, the cash budget enables management to anticipate any deficits so that the necessary financing arrangements may be made, and to decide upon a policy for placing any cash surpluses.

As its name implies, the cash budget deals only with 'cash' flows – it excludes expenses of a non-cash nature, such as depreciation. The cash budget is one of the last budgets to be prepared because it depends upon the other budgets which form part of the budgeting process.

Note that the cash budget is planned through time: the time profile of cash receipts and cash payments is critical to the analysis of a firm's cash needs at any given point of time.

In practice, determining the level of cash which is required at any point in time may not be an easy matter. The dilemma of cash management lies in the conflict of liquidity with profitability. If a firm holds too little cash in relation to its financial obligations, a liquidity crisis may occur and may lead to the collapse of the business. On the other hand, if a firm holds too much cash it is losing the opportunity to employ that cash profitably in its activities. Idle cash balances usually earn very little profit for the firm. A reasonable balance must be found, therefore, between the financial objectives of maintaining a degree of liquidity and of minimizing the level of unproductive assets. The problem of ascertaining optimal balances of physical stocks has for long attracted the attention of operational researchers, and certain of the ideas which they have developed may have applicability as regards the holding of optimal cash balances. Such techniques include just-in-time (JIT) inventory purchase systems, developing supply chains, where there is a direct link between suppliers and purchasers so that inventory needs are known almost immediately. Boots Company installed a computer system costing £75 million which saves £400 million per annum on inventory. It does this by linking the sales system to the inventory system to the resupply system so that only the relevant amount of inventory is resupplied.

	1st quarter	2nd quarter	3rd quarter	4th quarter	Total
	£	£	£	£	£
Opening cash balance	5,325	10,900	11,450	15,275	5,325
Receipts					
Debtors (balance sheet)	20,000	–	–	–	20,000
50% of current sales (Step 1)	22,250	19,500	19,500	22,250	83,500
50% of previous quarter (Step 1)	–	22,250	19,500	19,500	61,250
Total receipts	42,250	41,750	39,000	41,750	164,750
Total cash available	47,575	52,650	50,450	57,025	170,075
Payments					
Purchases (Step 4)	2,800	2,800	3,300	3,300	12,200
Direct labour (Step 5)	5,750	5,400	5,750	6,100	23,000
Factory overheads (Step 6) (excluding depreciation)	5,125	5,000	5,125	5,250	20,500
Selling and administrative expenses (Step 8)	10,000	10,000	10,000	10,000	40,000
Capital expenditure (Step 9)	10,000	15,000	8,000	20,000	53,000
Tax (balance sheet)	3,000	3,000	3,000	3,000	12,000
Total payments	36,675	41,200	35,175	47,650	160,700
Closing cash balances	10,900	11,450	15,275	9,375	9,375

The effects of inflation on business enterprises are manifested in a growth in monetary terms, which may be in some direct relationship with the rate of inflation, while at the same time undergoing no growth at all in real terms, or even shrinking in profitability and value. The financing problem resulting from the monetary growth associated with inflation lies in the need to finance higher levels of inventory and debtors. If a firm is unable to finance the higher level of working capital required from adjustments to its prices and sales revenues, it must either borrow or reduce its level of activity. In effect, the rapid inflation which business firms experienced in the 1970s caused severe liquidity problems and many cases of insolvency.

The problems of cash budgeting under conditions of inflation require that special attention be given to the timing of cash inflows and outflows, which should be adjusted for changes in specific price changes affecting the firm. In this connection, adjustments to budget figures for changes in the general purchasing power of money will not reflect the impact of inflationary changes as they affect individual firms.

Among the special problems associated with budgeting under conditions of inflation is the loss of purchasing power exhibited by holdings of net monetary assets. This implies that losses in the value of net monetary items should be minimized in a manner consistent with the overall objectives of the firm by the reduction of holdings of net monetary assets. In effect, particular attention should be given to cash and debtor balances, and the impact of changes in selling prices on cash inflows should be carefully monitored. At the same time, gains resulting from the impact of inflation on creditor balances should encourage more aggressive borrowing policies.

Step 12 The budgeted income statement

The purpose of the budgeted income statement is to summarize and integrate all the operating budgets so as to measure the end result on the firm's profit.

	£
Sales (Step 1)	167,000
Cost of goods sold (Step 10)	65,650
Gross income	101,350
Selling and administrative expenses (Step 8)	40,000
Net income before tax	61,350
Tax (40%)	24,540
Net income after tax	36,810

Step 13 The budgeted balance sheet

The final stage is the projection of the budgeted results on the firm's financial position at the end of the year. The following balance sheet reflects the changes in the composition of assets and liabilities as a result of the planned activities:

Budget balance sheet as at 31 December 20X1

Non-current assets	Cost	Depreciation	
	£	£	£
Plant and machinery	303,000	40,000	263,000
Current assets			
Inventory			
Raw materials	1,650		
Finished goods	6,075		
		7,725	
Debtors		22,250	
Cash		9,375	
		39,350	
Less: Creditors: amounts falling			
Due within one year			
Creditors	5,000		
Tax	24,540		
		29,540	
Net current assets			9,810
Total assets *less* current liabilities			272,810
Capital and reserves			
Called-up share capital			210,000
Retained earnings			62,810
			272,810

Evaluating the budget proposals

As a means of comparing the planned performance for the coming year with the results of the current year, the planned performance may be interpreted as follows:

Return on shareholders' equity: £36,810 ÷ £272,810 = 13.5% (previous 7.6%)
Return on capital employed: £61,350 ÷ £272,810 = 22.5% (previous 12.7%)

It is evident, therefore, that the firm is expected to make considerable improvements in the forthcoming period. If the budgeted results are considered to be satisfactory, the final stage is a recommendation that the budget proposal be accepted by the board of directors as its policy, and as conforming with its view of the future.

Budgeting systems

In this section we consider briefly three budget approaches: (1) zero-based budgeting; (2) feed-forward control; and (3) flexible budgeting.

Zero-based budgeting

The traditional approach to budgeting is the incremental approach which starts with the previous year's budget and adds or subtracts from that budget to reflect changing assumptions for the coming year. For example, if the previous year's budget expenditures for a department were £1 million, the department might request a 5 per cent increase (£50,000) to provide the same level of service for the coming year. The typical justification for increased expenditures is the increased cost of inputs (labour and materials, and so on). Any inefficiencies in the previous year's budget tend to be perpetuated by this almost automatic acceptance of that document as the starting point of the new plan.

One method developed to overcome the shortcomings of incremental budgeting is zero-based budgeting, by which all levels of management start from zero (a clean sheet of paper) and estimate the resource requirements to fund the year's activities. Managers must defend their budget levels at the beginning of each year. Thus, unlike incremental budgeting, the zero-based approach requires past budget decisions to be re-evaluated each year. Thus resource requirements are more likely to be adjusted to changing business conditions.

Feed-forward control

Feedback systems aim to highlight deviations from the budget plan as soon as possible so that remedial action may be taken. A feed-forward system differs from a feedback system in that it seeks to anticipate, and thereby to avoid, deviations between actual and desired outputs. The aim is to improve forecasting procedures. Therefore, once effective forecasting procedures have been established, the significant comparisons are no longer between planned and actual costs, but between forecasts, as follows:

1 *Latest forecast vs previous forecast.* This comparison becomes the prime action mover, and leads to the following questions:
   (a) Why has the forecast changed?
   (b) How does the latest forecast affect the net cash flow?
   (c) What actions should be taken to improve the situation?

2 *Actual vs previous forecast.* This comparison leads to the following questions being asked:
   (a) Was the previous forecast effective as regards identifying the events now facing the firm?
   (b) If not, why was the previous forecast wrong?
   (c) Are the errors in forecasting due to excessive pessimism or optimism, and can these errors be corrected?

Flexible budgeting

So far, we have discussed functional budgets and cash budgets. Another type of budget which takes into account changes in the volume of activity is the flexible budget. Most budgets assume a certain level of activity and this level of activity is used in the preparation of the budget. For example, in the Edco Manufacturing case above it was assumed that 1,250 units of output would be produced in the first quarter. However, actual production might be greater or less than 1,250 units. To compare the actual costs of, say, 1,300 units with the budgeted costs of 1,250 units would render the comparison meaningless. In a situation where the actual production was greater than budget, this would tend to show overspends on variable costs as these costs would increase with activity, but the budgeted value of these costs would remain at the 1,250 units level. Conversely, if no production was produced, then the financial report would show a saving on the variable costs as these would be set at the 1,250 units level, whereas the actual costs would be zero.

To overcome this weakness in reporting, flexible budgets are prepared which reflect the changes in production levels by multiplying the variable costs per unit by the actual activity levels. These are then compared with the actual costs and a meaningful variance is calculated. Any fixed costs are isolated in the report and shown separately. Flexible budgets are considered further in Chapter 34

Activity-based budgeting (ABB) and activity-based management (ABM)

We saw in Chapter 18 that the initial interest in activity-based costing (ABC) related to product or service costing, but that an ABC system offers more than just accurate product-cost information. It also provides information about the cost and performance of activities and resources. Activity-based management (ABM) is a term which has developed from the early approaches to ABC, and is designed to denote much wider use of the concept by management than just for product costing. Having undertaken ABC for product costing the information can be used for ABM. ABM is based on the premise that since people are involved in activities, and activities consume resources, the control of activities allows the control of costs at their sources. Activity-based budgeting (ABB) is an important element of ABM. It is a planning and budgetary tool which provides an understanding of the linkages between the drivers behind the activities. ABB defines the activities underlying the financial figures in each function and uses the level of activity to determine how much resource should be allocated, how well it is managed and how to explain variances from budget.

Traditional budgeting systems tend to view the organization vertically in functional blocks of cost and focus on resources bought by function or department. Most cost reports typically show wages, salaries, rent and so on by department in line with the functional organization structure. These reports reveal little about how the resources are being used to add value to the customer, what drives the level of resources required and whether the right amount of resources is in place. Alternatively, a business can be viewed as a series of linked activities, or processes, which ultimately add value to the customer. In adopting this view, ABM helps management to understand the activities, their cost and how they link together to form a simple chain of value-creating activities for a business. In doing so, ABM focuses on activity outputs rather than resource inputs.

ABB provides the foundation for a more effective control of overhead. We saw in Chapter 18 that ABC product costs give enhanced visibility to the components of overhead, providing greater segmentation and one which indicates the sources and purpose of resource consumption. This additional detail, together with the gathering of cost-driver information, provides management with valuable feedback which will aid the operational control of their manufacturing processes. ABM and ABB take the unit cost driver rates and multiplies by activity volume to give a spending amount: budget volumes for budgeted spending and actual volume for actual spending. Example 2 below indicates the type of report which can be produced with ABB, showing both budgeted and actual activity volumes and spending at those volumes. This activity-based budget report directs attention at the use of resources in the overhead area. It shows differences from budget for both expenditure and cost-driver levels. It highlights areas for investigation (Innes and Mitchell, 1993).

Example 32.2

Budget report

Activity	Cost driver	Unit cost	Original budget volume	£000	Actual budget volume	£000
Purchasing	Orders	£25/order	1,000	25	1,200	30
Set-ups	Set-ups	£150/set-up	200	30	300	45
Handling	Movements	£250/movement	400	100	500	125
Inspection	Inspections	£140/inspection	500	70	550	77
				225		277

Note: Great care must be taken in constructing and using activity-based budgets, because the *units costs/cost driver* assume that all the costs are stictly proportional to volume. This is certainly not true in the short term, and probably not completely true, either, in the long term.

In view of the fact that activities are linked across departments forming cross-functional processes, ABB permits managers to recognize the horizontal flow of products, services and activities through an organization by focusing attention on the organization as a whole. ABB ensures that there is an optimum allocation of scarce resources across the business. For example, consider the case of a conflict between two departments of a firm, the purchasing and warehouse functions. The purchasing department was buying from a supplier which delivered weekly, and the warehouse section held high staff levels solely to cater for this event. Although the change to smaller daily deliveries caused an increase in purchase prices, it eased the workload on staff in the warehouse and provided overall a substantial cost saving to the company.

In providing an understanding of the costs of activities, their importance to the organization and how efficiently they are performed, ABM allows managers to focus on those activities that might offer opportunities for cost savings. The process view of organizations allows management to focus on value-added and non-value-added activities that are not adding value, but are causing costs to be incurred. These issues will be considered further in Chapter 35.

Summary

Budgeting is an activity which should be seen as being concerned with the implementation of a yearly segment of the long-range plan. The budget expresses this plan in financial terms in the light of current conditions.

We have seen that the process of budgeting can be applied to any organization, such as retailing, local government, health service, leisure, banking, insurance and farming, to name but a few. Some steps (finished goods stock) are not relevant but the process is fundamentally the same. Budgets may be evaluated by means of financial ratios such as the return of shareholders' equity and the return on capital employed.

Activity-based budgeting directs cost control to the source of overhead costs (the activities) rather than their consequences (the production).

Self-assessment questions

1 Outline the series of steps that are implied in orderly budgeting.

2 Discuss the importance of the sales forecast.

3 State the various methods used for forecasting sales.

4 Examine the relationship between the sales budget and the production budget.

5 Comment on the significance of the cash budget.

6 Describe (a) zero-based budgeting; (b) feed-forward control; and (c) flexible budgeting.

7 How does an activity-based budgeting system differ from a traditional system?

1 Dafa Ltd is a trading company dealing in a single product. It is preparing its annual budget for the twelve months ending 30 June 20X1. So far, the following budgets have been prepared:

	July–Sept	Oct–Dec	Jan–Mar	April–June
Sales (at £3 per unit)	15,000	18,000	21,000	12,000
Purchases (at £2 per unit)	12,000	14,000	10,000	8,000
Sundry expenses				
Distribution	500	800	1,100	200
Administration	1,000	1,000	1,000	1,000
Depreciation	500	500	500	500
	2,000	2,300	2,600	1,700

Notes:

(a) Sales are made on one month's credit. It may be assumed that debtors outstanding on sales at the end of each quarter are equivalent to one-third of sales in that quarter, and that this is received the following quarter.
(b) All purchases are for cash. No credit is received.
(c) Distribution and administration expenses are paid in cash as incurred.
(d) The company has no expenses apart from those given.
(e) Opening balances at 1 July 20X0 are:

Debtors   £3,000
Cash   £2,000
Inventory 1,000 units

Required:

Complete Dafa Ltd's annual budget by preparing:

(a) a debtors' budget
(b) a cash budget, *and*
(c) an inventory budget to show the number of units in inventory at the end of each quarter.

2 A small private company, after several years of unprofitable trading, was taken over by a new management on 31 December.

The accounts for the following year were summarized thus:

	£
Direct materials	78,000
Direct wages	31,200
Variable overheads	15,600
Fixed overheads	30,000
Income	1,200
Sales	156,000

The balance sheet as at the end of the first twelve months of trading was as follows:

	£	£	£
Non-current assets			24,000
Current assets			
Inventory		26,000	
Debtors		26,000	
		52,000	
Less: Creditors: amounts falling due within one year			
Bank overdraft	26,500		
Creditors	19,500		
		46,000	
Net current assets			6,000
Total assets *less* current liabilities			30,000
Capital and reserves			
Called-up share capital			40,000
Income statement			(10,000)
			30,000

The budgeted sales for the second year of trading are as follows:

	£
1st quarter	42,000
2nd quarter	45,000
3rd quarter	48,000
4th quarter	51,000

It is anticipated that the ratios of material consumption, direct wages and variable overheads to sales are unlikely to change; that the fixed overheads (incurred evenly during the year) will remain at £30,000 per annum; and that creditors can be held at three months' direct material usage. Both inventory and debtors can be maintained at two months' sales.

Bank interest and depreciation, the latter at 10 per cent per annum on fixed assets, are included in the overheads.

Required:

Prepare quarterly budgets for the second year of operation to indicate to management:

(a) Whether the results are likely to be satisfactory.
(b) Whether the overdraft facilities (which are normally limited to £25,000) are sufficient, or whether further capital must be introduced.

3* Jones is considering whether to open up his own wholesaling business. He makes the following estimates about the first six months' trading:

(a) Sales on credit	– For first two months £50,000 per month.
	– Thereafter £80,000 per month.
	– One month's credit allowed to customers.
(b) Gross margin	– The cost of goods bought for resale is expected to be 75 per cent of the selling price.
(c) Closing inventory	– £75,000.
(d) Purchases creditors at end	– £50,000.
(e) Wages and salaries	– Paid for period £40,000.
	– Owing at end of period £2,500.
(f) Warehouse expenses	– Cash paid for rent, rates, lighting, heating, etc. £50,000.
	– In addition £5,500 of warehouse expenses will be owing at end of six months.
	– Of the cash paid, however, £3,500 will be rent and rates paid in advance.
(g) Furniture, fixtures and fittings	– Amounting to £50,000 to be purchased on opening of business and will be subject to 10 per cent p.a. depreciation.
(h) Delivery vehicles	– Three vans costing £2,000 each will be purchased at once and will be subject to 25 per cent p.a. depreciation.
(i) Loan interest	– Long-term loans can be raised at an interest rate of 10 per cent p.a.
(j) Jones	– Expects to draw from the business accounts his own 'wages' at a rate of £300 per month.

Required:

(a) A budgeted cash account for the period on the basis of the above information (see part (c) below).

(b) Budgeted income statement for the period and balance sheet as at the end on the basis of the above information (see part (c) below).

(c) Advise Jones as to how much capital should be introduced initially into the business. Jones, however, has only £50,000 available as capital. Complete the accounts on the assumption that he accepts your advice.

(d) Jones asks you whether the business appears to be a worthwhile one. Give a brief reply to this question.

4 The Astra leisure complex is a medium-sized company specializing in the leisure industry. The complex comprises a swimming pool, a diving pool, a leisure pool, a sauna, a sports hall (suitable for basketball, five-a-side football, etc.) and a conference hall. The complex also has a bar and a restaurant.

The managing director of the business, who has been recently appointed, is surprised to discover that there is no budgeting system at the complex.

Required:

(a) List five main reasons why a formal system of budgeting should be introduced.

(b) Identify which functional budgets will be required. For each functional budget named, propose which member of the organization should be responsible for its preparation and justify your choice. Draw an organization chart to illustrate your answer.

(c) Explain how computer applications could be used to advantage in the proposed budgeting system.

5* Rutland Furnishings Company is a small carpet and upholstery cleaning business with both commercial and domestic customers.

The balance sheet of the company at 31 October 20X0 was:

Non-current assets (NBV)			**£**
Freehold premises			32,000
Fixtures, fittings, equipment			4,000
Motor vehicles			12,000
			48,000
Current assets			
Inventory		3,200	
Debtors		20,000	
		23,200	
Current liabilities			
Creditors	4,000		
Bank overdraft	8,200	12,200	
Net working capital			
			11,000
			£59,000
Capital			£59,000

The company allows credit to its commercial customers but domestic customers are expected to pay cash. On the basis of past performance, the company expects sales in the coming six months to be:

November	December	January	February	March	April
£16,000	£16,000	£20,000	£40,000	£12,000	£12,000

The proportions of cash and credit sales are usually:

Month of sale	Cash sales (%)	Credit sales (%)
November	30	70
December	45	55
All other months	20	80

Customers who are on extended credit normally pay in the month following sale. The company's invoice price is made up of 55 per cent wages, 25 per cent materials and 20 per cent profit. Wages are paid in the month incurred.

Half the materials purchased each month are subject to a 3 per cent cash discount for immediate payment and it is company policy to take advantage of this discount. The firm pays the remainder of the purchases, without discount, in the month after purchase. Goods are normally purchased in the month they are sold except December when owing to a supplier's shut-down, half December's goods are purchased in November.

Expenditure on petrol and other expenses is £2,600 per month. Additionally, the fixtures, equipment and motor vehicles are depreciated at 25 per cent per annum on a reducing balance basis.

Required:

(a) Prepare a cash budget for the six months November to April.
(b) Prepare an income statement for the same period.
(c) Prepare a balance sheet at 30 April 20X1.
(d) The company proposes to purchase a new industrial cleaner costing £10,000 in January. Given the overdraft facility is £9,500, what action should the management take?

References   Innes, J. and Mitchell, F. (1993) *Overhead Cost*, Academic Press.

Kennedy, A. and Dugdale, D. (1999) Getting the most from budgeting, *Management Accounting* (UK), February.

CHAPTER 33

Organizing for control

Setting the scene

As organisations grow in size and complexity, top management find themselves unable to make all the decisions. In such circumstances authority for certain types of decision-making is delegated to subordinate managers and decentralisation takes place. Total decentralisation could occur whereby a division operated in complete autonomy. Of course, such a situation is unlikely. Certain types of decisions invariably are retained by central management. Decentralisation improves local decision-making, flexibility, motivation and training for divisional management. At the same time it relieves central management of making lower level, routine decisions. Therefore, if properly organised and controlled, it makes the enterprise as a whole more efficient.

(Kam-por, 1994)

Learning objectives

After studying this chapter you should be able to:
1. understand the relationship between planning and control;
2. appreciate why firms choose to decentralize;
3. identify the differences among the four types of responsibility centre;
4. explain the role of transfer pricing in a decentralized firm;
5. discuss the methods of setting transfer prices;
6. explain and compare return on investment and residual profit.

The integration of planning and control

We mentioned in Chapter 16 that control is closely related to planning since its purpose is to ensure that the organization's activities conform with its plans. Control is a distinct activity which should affect every aspect of the organization. The planning and control cycle is shown in Figure 33.1. Since an organization cannot be 'all things to all men' (and women) choices have to be made which determine the allocation of the organization's resources. The planning and control cycle is a process for making these choices, starting at the broadest level and working down through the organization to individual cost and projects. The role of planning is to allocate resources (financial, human, technological, etc.), that of control to make sure they went where they were supposed to, and achieve what was intended.

The planning and control cycle has eight stages:

- *Stage 1 Determine objectives and goals.* The language may differ, but every organization needs a mission – an articulation of fundamental purpose – and a vision – the description of a desired future state. Many organizations also include a statement of values – the beliefs and behaviours that will underpin relationships with all its constituencies.

- *Stage 2 Develop a long-range plan.* Long-range or strategic planning is concerned with telling a story about what the company intends to do and why. The annual report of IBM for 2008 contains what could be a preamble to its new strategy: the big trends in the world economy; the big changes in computing architecture; the new requirements of their customers. These led them to change their product offerings (mix of business), change the geographical spread and integration of their businesses (high growth, high profits and global integration); and hence the allocation of resources. The strategic plan typically covers a period of between 3 and 5 years and varies with the sector. Utilities have to plan over very long periods indeed – the life of a nuclear power station is in the region of 45 to 50 years, fashion companies such as Zara are presumably at the shorter end.

- *Stage 3 Develop an annual plan.* The annual plan or budget is a more detailed version of the first year of the strategic plan. Whereas the strategic plan stays at a high level of aggregation – division, country, company – the budget goes down to cost centres and individual products. They confer authority to engage resources and a commitment to produce certain results. Negotiations around budgets are intense: managers know that they will be expected to stay within budget on expenses and attain or exceed targets in terms of results.

- *Stage 4. Determine required resources and performance standards.* While shown as a separate stage, this really overlaps with budgeting in Stage 3. However it is a distinct process. The purpose of this stage is to develop the action plans that will deliver stretch targets imposed by top management and expected by shareholders and analysts. The trend in performance over the last few years provides a base-line of what can be expected if management does nothing new – the momentum of the organization – now the question is, 'what are the new things you are going to do to improve on this base-line performance?' Action programmes typically require investments and so feed into the planning and approval of capital expenditure.

- *Stage 5 Commence operations.* The approval of the strategic plan and the budget are invariably set piece occasions involving the usual cast of senior executives: presentations, debate, negotiation, and targets against which performance will be measured. With the budget and action programmes agreed managers now set about the serious business of implementation.

- *Stage 6 Compare actual performance with annual plan and required standards of performance.* Most companies experience seasonal variations in demand for their products and services – a notable exception is disposable diapers (nappies), for obvious reasons – consequently the budget should not be split into 13 identical 4-week periods (nor indeed into 12 calendar months of equal run rates). Each period should reflect the activity levels and costs of its season modified by any action programmes under way or recently completed. Control reports are concerned with whether operating expenditures are being incurred and capital investments (and projects) implemented as intended and also whether they are having their promised effects. In all these dimensions, actual will be compared with budget and management will have to explain, and propose remedial actions to correct, significant adverse variances. These remedial actions give rise to the first major reappraisal of action programmes and targets spelt out in Stage 5. In Chapter 32 the distinction was made between feedback and feed-forward aspects of control systems. The comparison of actual with budget is an example of the former, and the reappraisal of action programmes an example of the latter. The feedback loops occur every month, but are particularly important at the end of each quarter, when, combined with feed-forward loops, management has to decide whether the present trajectory is consistent with meeting year-end targets. Control reports typically contain comparisons for the current month, for year-to-date and the best estimate of the year end. They may also include comparisons with the same period in the previous year.

- *Stage 7 Compare results with long-range plan*. Besides having implications for the current year, information on actual performance contains valuable insights – sales, competitors, economic trends and so forth – for the longer term. The timing of this reflection on the long-term consequences of short-term performance will obviously be coordinated with the long-term planning process.
- *Stage 8 Compare goals achieved with the desired goals and organizational objectives*. At the end of the year there is always a post mortem of what happened and why, the lessons to be learned and, of course, the evaluation of the performance of managers and businesses.

Figure 33.1

The planning and control model illustrates the multidimensional nature of the process, and the manner in which the control and the planning processes are related and therefore integrated. The proposition that without planning it is impossible to exercise control was best expressed by The Cheshire Cat, 'If you don't know where you want to get to, it doesn't matter which way you go' (Lewis Carroll). If control without planning is impossible, planning without control is foolhardy, to say the least.

Control is exercised at different levels: overall control measures progress against the organization's objectives and strategies; management control is a subordinate activity concerned with the efficient use of resources committed to the realization of these organizational goals; finally operational control ensures that the tasks defined in the operational plan are carried out effectively. Specific performance standards are attached to these tasks, and information feedback allows actual performance to be compared with the required performance.

From the foregoing, it follows that control standards are embedded in the planning process. They are used as indices by which the effectiveness and the result of organizational activities are assessed. Moreover, since plans spell out the activities of different parts of the organization in terms of what they are supposed to achieve and the resources at their disposal, the plans themselves constitute performance standards (for business units, costs, products, etc.).

Both plans and controls presuppose an organizational unit that will carry out the plans and a manager responsible for its oversight: where in the organization are the resources going and who is exercising stewardship over them? Plans and controls both require a system of responsibility accounting which provides a clear definition of the controllable elements at every level of responsibility.

Responsibility accounting

The tasks to be performed and the decisions to be made when running a modern corporation are numerous, diverse and cover a wide area of expertise (some are specific to the sector – aeronautical engineering – some are generic – accounting). The only way to handle this is to draw up an organization chart that enumerates the major tasks, specifies who is responsible for each of them and shows the reporting relationships. A typical example is shown in Figure 33.4 on page 543. Each of the boxes defines a domain of responsibility, specialization and hopefully expertise of the respective manager. Each box is a responsibility centre.

The choice of organizational structure and responsibility depend on many factors – sector, size of organization, geographical spread, strategy – but also on the personalities and management style of senior executives.

As organizations grow, top management has to decide:

1 how to divide up tasks, activities and responsibilities;
2 and, having divided tasks up, how then to ensure a proper degree of coordination between subunits.

The dilemmas can best be illustrated by reference to Figure 33.4. This shows a functional organizational structure in that the first split of tasks and responsibilities is by function – marketing, production, etc. Now, while each manager is charged with oversight of his or her domain of responsibility, none can do this without a fairly detailed knowledge of the intentions of the others. For example, suppose Marketing is responsible for the publicity campaign that will accompany the launch of a new product. Without knowledge of its specification and attributes, Marketing will not know how to pitch the campaign. Moreover, Marketing needs target dates of its release from Research and Development to Production as well as the date when the factory will be able to make it in commercial quantities. This degree of coordination cannot be left to the initiative of individual managers, nor can it be left to chance. A formal and fairly elaborate process is needed to design coordination into the life of the organization at every level.

Interdependencies between responsibility centres place constraints on the autonomy of individual managers. These constraints are embedded in formal systems, for coordination and spelt out in procedures, place limits on what a manager can do on his own initiative without consulting colleagues or obtaining approval from superiors. Procedures govern such things as hiring, salary structures, spending limits on operating expenditure and on capital investments, and so forth. The effect of the organization structure coupled with the systems and procedures determine who is responsible for what and the freedom they have to act on their own volition. These choices of which decisions are made where are critical to the overall effectiveness of an organization. There is a celebrated occasion in which the front page of a paper carried an interview with the president of a major European electronics multinational in which he stated that the company would never enter the personal computer market. On page 3 of the same edition was a full-page advertisement announcing the launch of a new personal computer by one of the divisions. Clearly something important had gone wrong. The company gave a considerable degree of autonomy to the divisions and corporate management was apparently unable to impose its wishes. This was a minor hiccup rather than a major disaster as the sums of money were not large. But it is inconceivable that a company like EADS would let Airbus decide to pursue the development of the A380 without approval of the main board. Developing the A380 and the Dreamliner by Airbus and Boeing respectively, were decisions that 'bet the company' and had to be made at the centre.

The main alternative to the functional structure depicted in Figure 33.4 is one in which the first split of responsibilities is by division and then within each division by function. Each division functions as a semi-autonomous business: semi-autonomous because although they have many of their own specialized and dedicated functions, they do not have all of them. There will be some shared services that are provided by the centre and used by all divisions (central human resources and information technology platforms); there will be other services performed by the centre on behalf of the company as a whole (shareholder relations, annual reports). The divisional form of organizational structure is used when a company's activities span different sectors – healthcare, consumer lifestyle, lighting – or are within a broad sector with distinct subdivisions – cars, trucks, buses, tractors. The divisional structure is illustrated in Figure 33.2.

These decisions on structure, responsibilities and decision-making autonomy are critical, for although not set in stone, clearly cannot be changed frequently. They reflect strategy, cause major disruptions to the manner in which tasks and responsibilities are divided out among managers and have a profound impact on the careers of managers themselves. It is not unusual for big reorganizations to lead to the voluntary departure of senior executives who have 'lost out' in some way or other.

One aspect of the responsibility centre manager's job is to be answerable for financial performance. There are four types of financial responsibility:

1 *Cost centre*. The manager is only responsible for the costs of his activity.
2 *Revenue centre*. The manager is responsible for revenues minus the costs of selling but not the costs of producing the product or service.
3 *Profit centre*. The manager is responsible for revenues and costs of the product or service.
4 *Investment centre*. The manager is responsible for profits and the assets needed to generate them.

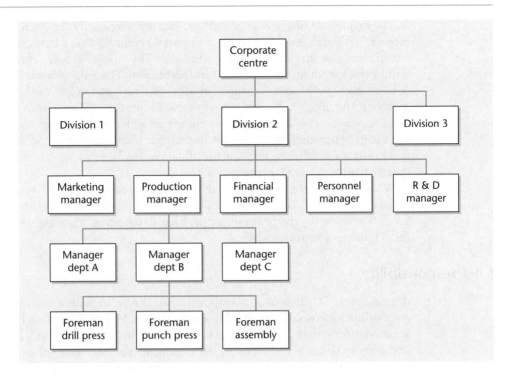

Figure 33.2

The relationship between the four types is shown in Figure 33.3.

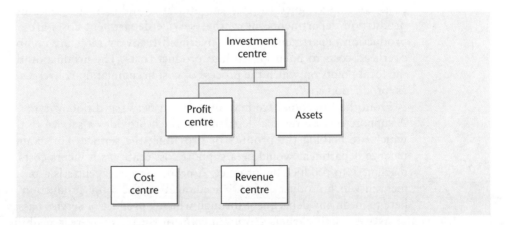

Figure 33.3

While responsibility for costs is a common element of all four (all responsibility centres have costs, even if it is only that of personnel), what is included will depend on the choices of the particular company. Some responsibility centres are only charged with their own direct costs, others are charged with some indirect costs (their share of central support functions, such as information technology and human resources that they consume), but not corporate overheads, and others are charged with a share of all costs.

The magnitude of the responsibilities, but not necessarily the degree of autonomy, increase with each successive type of financial responsibility; a cost centre is the most constrained, an investment centre the least. The role of a cost centre is to remain within the spending limits defined in the budget. The role of an investment centre is to so manage the relationships between revenues and costs on the one hand and assets on the other, as to achieve or surpass a predetermined return on investment. Thus, costs can exceed the original budget provided that the increase in revenues is sufficiently large that the return on investment (including any concomitant increase) is not impaired. Clearly, the courses of action available to an investment centre are greater than those available to a cost centre.

While this chapter discusses the different types of financial responsibility the behavioural aspects of control are discussed in Chapter 37. For the time being, we focus attention on the accounting problems stemming from the establishment of these four types of responsibility.

Cost responsibility

A cost centre is defined as a responsibility centre in which the manager is held responsible for costs. They are ubiquitous: the fundamental building block of all cost accumulation systems – costs are traced (direct costs of the cost centre) and allocated (indirect) to where they belong in the organization. They may subsequently be real-located to other cost centres and eventually to products, but their first resting place is always a cost centre which causes them to be incurred. It will be recalled that in Chapter 17, we drew a distinction between the accumulation of costs for product costing purposes and that for control purposes. In product costing, we noted that costs are first assigned (direct) and allocated (indirect) to service departments and production departments; next, that service department costs are allocated to the production departments; finally, overhead recovery rates are computed to enable overhead costs to be absorbed into product costs. The production departments are the focal points on which the process of cost accumulation converges and are known as 'production cost'.

From the foregoing, we may distinguish between different types of cost centre. A support cost centre is a department which provides a service to the departments which are making the product or providing the service. For example, the maintenance department would be a support cost centre as it incurs costs in maintaining machinery to produce the product. A production cost centre is a production department in which product costs are accumulated. The term 'production' is used loosely here to mean any department through which a product or service passes.

As we stated earlier, a prerequisite for an effective responsibility accounting system is the establishment of an organization chart which defines the formal reporting relationships which link the different executive roles in the organization. Levels of responsibility may be delineated for foremen, departmental managers, works managers and upwards to director level. Figure 33.4 is an organizational chart for a functional organization and shows that the three foremen are responsible to the manager of department B, who in turn reports to the works manager. The works manager reports to the managing director who is responsible to the board.

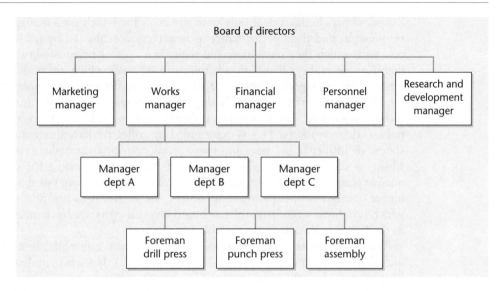

Figure 33.4

An important facet of a comprehensive planning and control system are reports incorporating comparisons of actual performance against planned performance for individual responsibility throughout the enterprise. These reports are a vehicle by which the costs of responsibility are identified with individual managers, who have authority over them and responsibility for them. The nature of the relationship existing between various levels of management and the flow of information between these levels is illustrated in Figure 33.5.

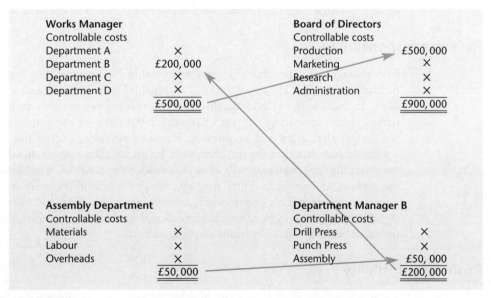

Figure 33.5

Responsibility budgets deal only with the costs for which each manager is to be held responsible, and their performance as managers is evaluated by reference to the success with which they have managed their own area of responsibility. It is important, therefore, to make a distinction between those costs which are under the control of a particular manager and those for which other managers are responsible. For example, the foreman of the assembly department may be responsible for the amount of direct labour used, but he will certainly not be responsible for the wage rate which is paid to these workers. This is determined by collective bargaining and is outside his sphere of influence. In assessing managerial performance under systems of responsibility accounting, managers should not be held responsible for costs which are outside their control. An inference which may be drawn from our diagram is that the higher one ascends the pyramid of control, the greater is the proportion of total costs which is defined as controllable: at board level all costs are by definition controllable as the board is ultimately responsible for all costs.

There are conflicting views as to whether non-controllable costs should be included in performance reports. One view is that if they are included, managers will be informed of all the costs incurred by the organization, even if they only personally control a small part. Their inclusion also enables department managers to appreciate the size and the costs of the organizational support upon which their department depends. If non-controllable costs are included in performance reports, they should be distinguished from the costs which fall within the manager's responsibility, that is, those costs which are defined as controllable.

Managers in charge of support cost centres have the responsibility for seeing that the costs incurred by their departments do not exceed the limits contained in the budgets. Clearly, their ability to control costs will be an important consideration in the evaluation of their effectiveness as managers. It follows, therefore, that the use of budgets for evaluating the performance of managers has implications for the manner in which budgets are organized. We discuss this problem in the next chapter.

Revenue responsibility

The manager of a revenue centre is responsible for revenues but not the costs of a product or service. However, there is responsibility for department costs. These are likely to include the salesforce, distribution, tactical promotions and perhaps advertising. Since the manager is not charged for the costs of the products sold, there is the danger that sales will be pursued provided revenues exceed the costs of selling – a disastrous situation for the company. To prevent the pursuit of sales 'at any cost' (not literally: the manager will always consider the costs of generating extra sales), the actions of a revenue centre manager will be monitored closely in terms of average price, volumes, sales promotion, advertising, headcount, etc. However, there are significant advantages to having a professional in charge of generating sales revenues, unencumbered by considerations of product costs.

Profit responsibility

As organizations grow in size the problem of control that this creates has encouraged the devolution of authority through organizational structures based upon the concept of 'divisions'. The rationale underlying this process of decentralization is founded on the belief that divisionalization enhances overall corporate profitability. Several reasons are advanced for this belief. First, responsibility for decision making is transferred to executives who are 'on the spot' and directly concerned with and well informed about the particular problems of the division. Moreover, they are able to devote all their energies to these problems, whereas under systems of centralized decision making and control, top management has less time to devote to the problems of individual divisions. Second, it is considered that the greater degree of freedom and the increased responsibilities enjoyed by divisional executives, increase their motivation towards the attainment of organizational goals, and in particular the profit goal. Third, since each division is a semi-autonomous business, it is easier to measure the contribution each makes towards the profit goal of the corporation, revealing areas of weakness and suggesting possibilities for profit improvement. Finally, decentralization of the decision-making process provides a training ground for managers as they progress up through the organization to higher levels of responsibility.

Investment responsibility

Many organizations have substantial investments in non-current assets (plant and equipment) and working capital (accounts receivable, inventories minus accounts payable). Who should be held responsible for them and how should they be managed? Cost, revenue and profit are not concerned with the cash tied up in physical assets and working capital although their decisions may well affect them.

Investment centres represents the ultimate stage in the decentralization of the decision-making process. Divisional managers are responsible not only for costs, revenues and profits, but also for elements of the capital invested in the division. However, while investments centres are frequently associated with high degrees of decentralization, their freedom of manoeuvre can be very limited and they do not have to be given a high level of autonomy. The fundamental purpose of the different types of financial responsibility is to change the trade-offs managers make, not the magnitude of their decisions. Thus, a cost centre minimizes costs; a profit centre is not concerned with costs in isolation, but with changes in costs versus changes in revenues.

Investment extends the principles underlying profit centres by associating divisional income with the capital invested in the divisions. The criterion most commonly employed for assessing the financial performance of investment centres is the return on capital employed (ROCE). It is a comprehensive measure of financial performance which enables comparisons to be made between companies and divisions for the purpose of evaluating the efficiency with which assets are utilized. The ROCE is calculated as follows:

$$\text{ROCE} = \frac{\text{earnings before interest and tax}}{\text{average capital invested}} \times 100$$

This formula may be extended to incorporate the ratio of earnings to sales, and the ratio of sales to capital employed (the rate of asset turnover).

$$\text{ROCE} = \frac{\text{EBIT}}{\text{sales}} \times \frac{\text{sales}}{\text{average capital invested}} \times 100$$

The expanded formula is useful for focusing attention on the important elements which affect the ROCE. It implies that profitability may be improved in the following ways:

1 increasing the volume of sales;
2 reducing total assets;
3 reducing costs;
4 improving the profit markup, for example by raising selling prices or improving the product mix.

The asset turnover will be improved by 1 and 2 and the profit margin by 3 and 4.

Example 33.1 The following table compares the sales, earnings and capital employed for three divisions of a large organization. Their profit contribution is £50,000 in each case.

	Division A	Division B	Division C
Sales	£500,000	£500,000	£1,000,000
Earnings before interest and tax	£50,000	£50,000	£50,000
Capital employed	£250,000	£500,000	£500,000
Return on sales	10%	10%	5%
Asset turnover	2	1	2
ROCE	20%	10%	10%

It is clear that Division A has the most effective financial performance since its ROCE of 20 per cent is higher than the ROCE of the other two divisions. Division B's return on sales, that is its profit margin, is equal to that of Division A, but its asset turnover is half as high as A's, implying that it employs twice as much capital to earn the same income. This suggests that sales could be improved or that excessive capital is being carried by Division B; perhaps investments in plant and inventory could be reduced. Division C has the same ROCE as Division B. Its margin on sales, however, is inferior to that of the other divisions, suggesting that selling prices are too low or operating costs too high.

The foregoing example shows that an ROCE analysis helps isolate factors requiring investigation. These levers of performance are illustrated in Figure 33.6, known as a Dupont Chart, after the American company that invented and popularized it.

Problems associated with ROCE measurements of performance
Three major problems arise as a result of employing ROCE for assessing divisional performance. They stem from the following factors:

1 the measurement of income and capital employed;
2 the allocation of costs and assets among divisions;
3 the limitations inherent in ROCE.

The measurement of income and capital employed
The use of ROCE for comparing the performance of similar divisions requires measurements of income and capital employed which are free from accounting bias. Thus, uniform accounting procedures should be established for valuing inventory, and charging against income such costs as depreciation, research and development and advertising. If comparisons are to be meaningful, the effect of price level changes should also be eliminated from accounting measurements. Moreover, income and capital employed as measured by conventional accounting tend to reflect a much better rate of return than is the case. When assets are recorded in the accounts at

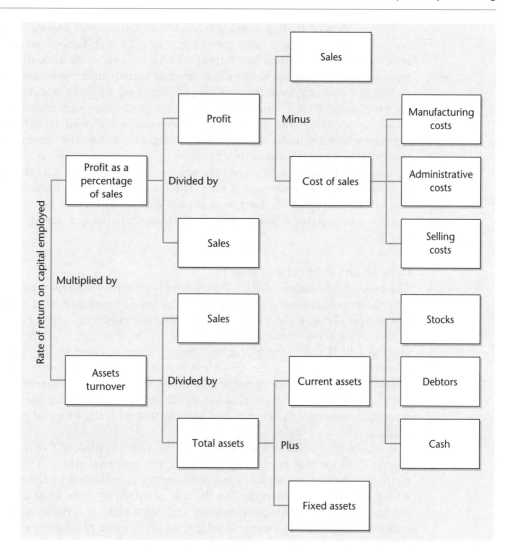

Figure 33.6

historical cost summing them involves adding together different monetary units. It follows that the same problem applies to the measurement of costs applied to current revenues for income calculation.

In order to overcome these problems, therefore, current operating revenues should be associated with the current costs of earning them, and the current value of the assets comprising the capital employed in current operations.

The allocation of costs and assets among divisions

In circumstances where factory buildings, production facilities, office, canteen and other facilities are shared by more than one division, the problem arises of allocating the costs of these facilities and the value of the investment which they represent. In any event, certain facilities (e.g. warehouses) will invariably be managed by the organization on behalf of all the divisions, and allocations may have to be made for head-office costs, management and technical services, etc.

The problem of finding suitable bases for allocating such costs and assets among divisions bears a strong resemblance to that of allocating factory overheads to products, which we examined in Chapter 17. As we saw, such allocations tend to be arbitrary, and seldom are the methods selected entirely immune from criticism.

There is a strong case for avoiding allocations, whether of costs or assets, for the purpose of ROCE calculations. In accordance with our definition of responsibility accounting, the evaluation of performance should recognize only those elements which are under the divisional manager's control. The incorporation of non-controllable items with controllable ones in performance reports is admissible for information purposes, so long as they are distinguished from each other, and the fundamental principles enshrined in responsibility accounting are maintained. It follows that divisional reporting statements should clearly distinguish between controllable and non-controllable expenses and possibly controllable and non-controllable assets and liabilities.

Limitations inherent in ROCE

The main disadvantage of ROCE measures is that they contain a conceptual weakness that stems from the fact that different investments will have different ROCE percentages. Thus, if the ROCE for the whole organization is 10 per cent, some divisions will be above this and others below it. The manager of an investment centre earning a ROCE of 15 per cent will be unwilling to consider any project offering a lower rate of return, even though it would benefit the organization as a whole. This is because his performance will be evaluated in terms his current ROCE. Hence, the use of ROCE for the evaluation of divisional performance may well motivate divisional managers to act in a way inconsistent with the financial objectives of the organization as a whole.

It was to deal with this difficulty that the General Electric Company introduced the residual income method of performance appraisal in the 1950s. Under this method, the performance of investment centres is evaluated by the residual income which remains after charging for the use of different types of assets. Because the residual income is an absolute number and not a ratio, a division which is trying to improve its residual income will undertake investment programmes even where the expected rate of return is less than the current ROCE.

Example 33.2 The net assets (total assets – current liabilities) of a division are valued at £1,000. The company has decided that a return of 10 per cent on these net assets is an appropriate target. The division's income statement for the current year is:

Revenue	£1,000
Less: Costs	700
	300
Less: Taxes	150
Income after taxes	150
Capital charge (10%)	100
Residual income	£50

If the manager of this division were evaluated on the ROCE basis, s/he would not invest in a project which produced a return of below 30 per cent, i.e.

$$\frac{£300}{£1,000} \times 100$$

However, if s/he were evaluated on residual income s/he would invest in a project which gives a return above 10 per cent because this would increase residual income. This action would be beneficial to the company.

Transfer pricing

In the manufacturing sector materials, components and products flow from one part of the organization to another. These subunits may be cost, profit or investment centres. For example, in the pharmaceutical sector a plant (cost centre) making active ingredients will send them to another plant (cost centre) where they are mixed with other compounds, pressed into pills, packaged and shipped. In manufacturing, a plant making gearboxes will ship these to the final assembly plant. These transfers between cost centres are common. A similar situation occurs in the financial sector as funds flow from one subunit to another. These transactions are purely internal, no third party is involved, but the question arises how they should be priced. How much should the receiving unit be charged and the supplying unit be credited for the transaction? The pricing of these internal transfers of goods and services comes under the generic name of 'transfer pricing'. The evaluation of managerial performance requires that the transfer price should reflect the value added to the final product by the selling centre. If it is set too high, it will reflect too favourably on the selling centre and too unfavourably on the buying centre, and vice versa. Hence, financial results may be heavily biased by the prices adopted for the transfer of intermediate goods and services. Defects in the transfer price mechanism may not merely fail to produce the right decisions: they may actively promote wrong ones.

In Chapter 21, we examined pricing as a means of regulating the exchange of the firm's products with the outside world. In this chapter, we examine transfer pricing as a method of controlling the activities of responsibility centres within the firm. Hence, we see that the distinction between pricing and transfer pricing lies in their different purposes.

Transfer prices should satisfy the following three criteria:

1 They should promote goal congruence within the organization by harmonizing the interests of individual responsibility centres with the interest of the organization as a whole, by preventing managers optimizing their own financial performance at the expense of the rest of the organization.
2 They should make possible reliable assessments of responsibility centre performance for the following purposes:
   (a) making predictions for decision-making purposes;
   (b) appraising managerial performance;
   (c) and when appropriate, evaluating divisional contribution to corporate income.
3 They should ensure that the autonomy of individual responsibility centres is respected, so that their performance is not dependent upon the actions of other parts of the organisation.

Transfer pricing methods

There are three main methods for establishing transfer prices:

1 market-based transfer pricing;
2 cost-based transfer pricing;
3 negotiated pricing.

Market-based transfer pricing

Where external markets exist for the selling centre's products (or services), it is preferable to use market prices rather than cost-based prices. This is because the market price is a better guide to the value of products than a cost-based price which may include operating inefficiencies and an unreasonable profit element. If the external market is competitive and interdependence between the units is minimal, the market price generally leads to optimal decisions within the organization, that is, decisions which satisfy the three criteria stipulated above. Where market prices can be used with a large measure of confidence, transfer prices reflect arms-length relationships.

When using market prices, it is essential that the transfer price for a captive internal customer should be no higher than the buying centre would have to pay on the open market. Otherwise, conflicts will be created between the interests of the selling and the buying centres. The existence of an independent market price imposes an upper limit to the transfer price, since the selling centre is able to sell at that price, the buying centre should be compelled to buy internally rather than to purchase from external suppliers.

A number of problems arise from the use of the market price as the basis for the transfer price. Thus, changes in supply may lead to large price changes, which in turn cause large variations in the transfer price. The performance of the buying unit will be affected and the control system will now have to highlight how much was due to changes in input prices and how much to operating (in)efficiencies. Further problems are associated with the weight which should be attached to different market prices available during the transfer period, and to other factors such as quantity discounts, distribution channel differentials, and transportation and delivery allowances. The market price also reflects the result of a bargain. The effects of relative bargaining positions on the market price have implications for the transfer price selected.

Hence the determination of a fair market price for establishing a viable transfer pricing system, which satisfies the three criteria calls for a solution to the various problems mentioned above. As a last resort, the solution may be arrived at only after appeal to an independent arbitrator. This process immediately undermines the third criterion – the preservation of the autonomy of individual units – and results in the establishment of a negotiated price.

Cost-based transfer pricing

In many cases, the transfer of products between responsibility centres involves intermediate goods for which an external market does not exist. In such cases, it is necessary to use cost-based transfer prices.

A common problem with cost-based transfer prices is that they may conceal inefficiencies in the activities of the selling centre. It is essential, therefore, that the transfer price should be based on standard costs rather than actual costs. As we shall see in the following chapter, the standard cost represents what an item should cost to produce rather than what it does cost, that is it excludes inefficiencies which have arisen in production. Hence, the use of standard costs prevents inefficiencies which have occurred in one responsibility centre from being transferred to another.

As we mentioned in Chapter 21, there are different kinds of cost-based prices. Two commonly used cost-related prices are full-cost and marginal-cost prices.

Full-cost transfer pricing

The major disadvantage of using full cost, or rather full cost plus a profit percentage, as a transfer price is that this method may encourage managers to make decisions which are not in the interest of the firm as a whole.

Example 33.3 Profit centre A sells to profit centre B at full cost plus a profit percentage and both units have spare capacity:

Profit centre	A	B
	£	£
Variable costs	10	30 + 10
Fixed costs	10	10
Markup (50%)	10	25
Total unit cost	30	75

Profit centre B treats the input of £30 from profit centre A as a variable cost. Hence, before profit centre B is able to have a contribution margin (defined, it will be remembered, as the excess of sales revenue over variable costs which contributes to fixed costs and income), it must be able to sell its products at £40 a unit. It is clear, however, that as far as the firm as a whole is concerned, total variable costs per unit are only £20. Given that both profit centres have spare capacity, it is in the firm's interest that profit centre B should produce and sell if it can obtain a price of £20 or over per unit for its output. If it regards £40 as its minimum acceptable price, the firm will lose the benefit of a contribution margin which otherwise it would have had.

In addition to the limitations of full-cost transfer pricing illustrated by the previous example, the use of full costs as a basis for transfer pricing may cause rigidities which contradicts the rationale for establishing profit centres. Managers should be able to control, or at least influence, all the determinants of income (selling price, volume, fixed and variable costs) if they are to be held responsible for profit. Thus, in the example given above, the manager of profit centre A may feel that its output, and therefore profit, is constrained by the obligation to sell to profit centre B at a transfer price of £30 a unit. Furthermore, its production is dependent upon the sales volume attained by profit centre B. This volume may be too low to enable profit centre A to achieve a satisfactory profit, and the manager may well wish to sell surplus production outside the firm, if that is possible, at prices other than he is charging B.

Therefore, there are circumstances when the rigidity caused by the inflexibility of a full-cost transfer pricing system does not provide a sound basis for the delegation of decisions to profit centres.

Marginal-cost transfer pricing

Transfer prices based upon marginal cost are designed to overcome some of the problems stemming from the use of full-cost measurements. Thus, in the above example, profit centre A would have transferred to profit centre B at a unit price of £10. In the short run, when both profit centres have surplus capacity, this would enable B to adopt a price that maximized income of the organization as a whole. Use of marginal-cost transfer pricing only works when two conditions are fulfilled: first the downstream unit, in this case B, chooses that combination of price, volume and costs (over which it has control) that maximize the profits of the whole organization; second a fair mechanism exists for dividing up this profit equitably between A and B. If B is not provided with information on A's relevant costs, or goes for market share rather than profit maximization, or does not share the total profits fairly, then the system obviously breaks down. As the capacity utilization in A and B approaches full capacity, the relevant costs get closer and closer to full costs. In the long run, transfer prices should converge on long-run relevant costs which may be approximated by full costs.

We saw in Chapter 21 that pricing policies should be based on differential costs and revenues of the company as a whole in order that profit planning decisions be well grounded. Transfer pricing should play a key role in communicating differential costs from the upstream unit to the downstream one. This implies that decisions about the output volume of interdependent divisions cannot be determined independently, thereby constraining the autonomy of individual divisions.

Negotiated pricing

Whatever method the firm adopts for determining transfer prices, it is evident that some form of negotiated price must be agreed between the managers of profit centres if the transfer pricing system is to operate satisfactorily. Thus while it is better to have a rules-based system, there will inevitably be occasions when recourse has to be made to negotiations. It is assumed that with good faith on both sides, independent negotiations between managers will produce results which are beneficial to the firm as a whole, and that the resolution of conflicts of interests will not reflect systematic bias in favour of any particular groups. These assumptions are probably questionable for a number of reasons. First, transfer price negotiations are very time-consuming, and the time and effort devoted to them detract from the other work that needs management's attention. Second, conflicts will undoubtedly occur and may lead to recriminations and the involvement of top management as arbitrators.

The advantages of transfer pricing

The various transfer pricing systems we have examined seem fraught with problems and drawbacks. Nevertheless, these difficulties should be weighed against the fact that without them profit centres and investment centres could only exist in autonomous business units. Equally, these difficulties do not amount to a substantial case for abandoning the practice of assigning transfer prices to interdivisional products. Some value must be found and attached to each element of input and output for the purpose of effective organizational control. Without some form of transfer pricing, the whole structure of intradepartmental analysis and control would collapse.

Very few aids for planning and control are perfect. This is certainly true of transfer pricing. It should be recognized that no available transfer pricing system is likely to serve all the purposes for which it is needed. The limitations found present in any transfer pricing system should be recognized, and any results obtained should be interpreted in the full knowledge of those limitations.

Summary

Planning and control are integrated processes which affect every aspect of organizational activity, including the determination of objectives and the development of long-range and short-range plans. The comparison of actual performance with the goals stipulated in these plans discloses the extent to which they have been attained.

Responsibility accounting underpins the control process, and requires the establishment of responsibility throughout an organization. A responsibility centre is a subunit of an organization where an individual manager is held responsible for the subunit's performance.

Responsibility may take four forms:

1 *cost*: the manager has no control over revenue but is able to control expenditure;
2 *revenue*: the manager is responsible for revenues minus the costs of selling;
3 *profit*: the manager has control over both revenue and costs of production;
4 *investment*: the manager has responsibility not only for revenues and costs but also for the capital invested.

The control problem is made more complex by the size of business organizations and the flow of products (intermediate and finished) between various subunits. While this situation occurs in many, if not most organizations, it is particularly prevalent in those non-diversified companies that have adopted divisional structures. The assessment of subunit performance requires transfer prices for the intermediate and finished products that flow from upstream units to downstream ones. Transfer prices can be rules-based (market or cost) or negotiated. However, not even the rules-based ones come up with a single unambiguous number. Consequently for transfer pricing systems are to operate smoothly, some form of negotiated pricing mechanism must be agreed by divisional managers. Investment centres pose additional problems as regards the assessment of financial performance. The ROCE is a comprehensive measure of performance, but its limitations should be understood.

Self-assessment questions

1 State what you understand by 'control'.

2 Examine the nature of the control process.

3 What is meant by 'responsibility accounting'?

4 What is the difference between an 'a support centre' and a 'production cost centre'?

5 Discuss the significance of the distinction between 'controllable' and 'non-controllable' costs.

6 What is meant by a profit centre? Give some examples of organizational subunits that would be able to function as profit centres.

7 State what criteria are relevant for evaluating transfer pricing policies.

8 Review four main methods used for establishing transfer prices.

9 What is meant by an 'investment centre'? Identify types of organizational subunits that would be able to function as investment centres.

10 'ROCE is a comprehensive measure of performance, but its limitations should be understood.' Discuss this statement.

Problems (*indicates that a solution is to be found in the Lecturer's Guide*)

1 Electrical Products Company consists of four operating divisions. Divisional managers are granted considerable discretion in setting employment, sales and production policies. For some time, the Chairman, Ronald Jackson, has been concerned with the method of evaluating divisional performance. On 1 June 20X0, he wrote the following letter to Miles French, a management consultant:

Dear Mr French

We have been trying to develop a system which will provide an incentive to our division managers and act as a basis for evaluating their effectiveness. Originally we used profit as an index for evaluation. Then we realized that, in order to be meaningful, profit should be related to another index such as profit of prior periods. After giving the matter much thought I have now become convinced that only a composite index, as shown below, will give equal weights to the three principal objectives of a division.

Composite index for evaluating division performance

Objective	Criterion	Last year	This year	% change
Minimize capital	Capital turnover	1.5	1.7	+13
Profitability	Return on sales	10.0%	9.0%	−10
Growth	Share of market	15.0%	15.6%	+4
	Net composite change			+7%

I propose to offer each division manager a bonus of £200 for each one per cent increase in the composite index. I aim to present this proposal to the board at the October meeting, and, if approved, start the system next year.

Please let me have an evaluation of this plan in writing.

Yours sincerely,

Ronald Jackson

Required: Assuming you are the consultant, write a letter to Mr Jackson evaluating the proposal.

2* The Akroid Corporation Ltd is a divisionalized enterprise manufacturing specialized equipment for the construction industry. Division A makes one of the basic components – the Spikron – which is used by Division B in the manufacture of the Akroid Scraper, which is then sold as a final product. Division B absorbs about three-quarters of the total output of Division A. The Spikron has other applications, and Division A has been selling the remaining 25 per cent of its output to outside firms. The annual output of Spikrons is 16,000 units. The Spikron is transferred at £350 to Division B, and is sold at £400 to outside firms.

The following costs are associated with the Spikron produced in Division A:

	£
Variable costs at £300 per unit	4,800,000
Fixed costs	200,000
Total costs	5,000,000

A German company makes a similar product to the Spikron, which could be adapted for integration into the Akroid Scraper, and has offered to supply Division B with the adapted product at a cost of £320 per unit.

The manager of Division B wishes to buy the German product as this will substantially reduce his costs, and make his own product more competitive on the market. The manager of Division A argues that he would not be able to expand his sales of the Spikron to outside firms, and that, as a result, the profitability of his division would be seriously affected.

Required:

Discuss the implications of the German offer from the point of view of the Akroid Corporation Ltd and of both divisions.

Reference   Kam-por, Y (1994) The influence of divisionalisation on an effective internal accounting system, *ACCA Students' Newsletter*, June.

CHAPTER 34

Standard costs and variance analysis

Setting the scene

Cost control can only come from comparing actual cost incurred with some preconceived idea of how much costs should be. The comparison can be with similar costs of a previous period, but the usefulness of that is limited. Previous costs will not reflect expected price increases, improved methods of production, different output levels and so on. It is also possible that past and present costs both reflect inefficiencies so that they are not revealed by the comparison. Much more effective control can be exercised by comparing actual cost with a standard cost taking into account expected inflation, levels of output, and objective assessments of reasonable efficiency levels.

It should not be assumed that standard costing is a useful technique to be applied to ALL costs in ALL organisations. It is likely that standard costing will be most usefully employed in mass production process costing type industries.

(Smith, 1990)

Learning objectives

After studying this chapter you should be able to:

1 explain why standard cost systems are adopted;

2 describe the basic concepts underlying variance analysis and explain when variances should be investigated;

3 calculate materials and labour variances and explain how they are used for control;

4 describe the purpose of flexible budgeting;

5 calculate variable and fixed overhead variances and explain their meanings;

6 calculate and explain the variances which are applied to the analysis of sales;

7 discuss the limitations of standard costing.

We turn now to a consideration of an important method of establishing standards of performance by the use of standard costs. The difficulty about using data recorded in the financial accounting system for planning purposes is that they relate to the past and although managers are interested in the results of previous decisions, they are primarily concerned with decisions which will affect the future.

For control purposes, historical costs are of little use: in times of inflation past experience will not inform management whether an operation, a job or a department costs too much. Indeed, what management wishes to know is not what costs were in the past but what they ought to be in the present. Once it has been determined what these costs ought to be, actual costs can be compared with them and any difference analysed.

Standard costing has been developed to meet this need. It relies upon predetermined costs, agreed to be acceptable under specified operating conditions.

Standard costs and budgeted costs

The principal differences between standard costs and budgeted costs lie in their scope. Whilst both are concerned with laying down cost limits for control purposes, budgeted costs impose limits to total costs for the firm as a whole, for departments or for functions for the budget period, whereas standard costs are attached to products and to individual manufacturing operations or processes. For example, the production department's budget for the period ahead may envisage a total production of 100,000 units at a cost of £10 a unit, so that the production department will be allocated an expenditure ceiling of £1 million. The unit cost of £10 will have been based upon the established standard costs relating to material usage and price, labour usage and rates as well as allocated overhead costs. Standard costs are revised when it is clear that they have ceased to be realistic in terms of current circumstances.

The relationship between budgeted costs and standard costs is clear: the setting of standard costs as performance standards for control purposes implies that they must be used as a basis for drawing up budgets in general and calculating budgeted costs in particular, for otherwise there can be no confidence in their use as a basis against which actual performance may be measured.

Applications of standard costing

Standard costing is a useful method of control in a number of ways. First, it allows management to focus on performance that deviates from predetermined standards: aptly called management by exception. More often than not, management is confronted with large amounts of feedback information and has to decide what information is significant and relevant to the control problem. Management by exception overcomes this difficulty by highlighting only the important control information, that is significant variances between the standard and the actual result. This process allows management to focus their attention and energy on correcting important situations which are falling out of control.

Second, a standard costing system provides opportunities for cost reductions. The development of standard costs presupposes that someone has determined how the product will be made (what materials, what operations on which machines, etc.). Production engineers will obviously choose the most efficient and cost-effective way leading to a simplification in the production process, a reduction in the amount of scrap material, etc. Apart from cost reductions on the shopfloor standard costs also make possible the simplification of clerical procedures such as inventory control. All similar items of inventory may be recorded in the accounts at a uniform price; this eliminates the need which arises under historical costing for recalculating a new unit price whenever inventory purchase is made at a different price.

Third, standard costs are used as a basis for determining selling prices. Standard costs represent what the product should cost, and are a much better guide for pricing decisions than historical costs which may contain purchasing and production inefficiencies which cannot be recouped in competitive markets.

Finally, perhaps the most important benefit which may be derived from a standard costing system is the atmosphere of cost consciousness fostered among executives and foremen. Each individual is aware of the costs and output measurements for which responsibility exists and in respect of which action is necessary should significant variances occur. If the philosophy of top management is positive and supportive, standard costing may work as an incentive to individuals to act in the best interest of the firm. Moreover, a standard costing system that allows subordinates to participate in setting the standards fosters a knowledge of costing on the shopfloor, and assists in decision making at all levels. Thus, if a foreman has to decide whether to scrap or rectify spoilt work, a knowledge of costs will enable him to make the best decision.

Setting cost standards

To be effective for the purpose of cost control, standard costs should reflect demanding and attainable standards of performance. This cannot be achieved without a great deal of sharing of information and discussions between the engineers setting the standards and the foremen supervising those doing the work.

Setting standard costs therefore implies:

1 establishing procedures for setting standards with respect to the price at which resources are acquired and their usage. This suggests the employment of specialist engineers and consultants for determining levels of cost efficiency that should be within the firm's reach;
2 establishing procedures for allowing participation by cost centre managers in setting attainable standards. This raises the possibility of resistance to cost standards that are too difficult and the need for some system of arbitration.

Cost standards are set for all categories of costs and for all cost centres. Setting cost standards for direct costs, such as direct material and direct labour, focuses upon price and usage as the two key cost components.

Setting cost standards for indirect costs is relatively more difficult, since there is no direct output against which standard costs can be set. This problem is resolved by a surrogate measure of output to which overhead costs can be related. Thus, overhead costs are considered to vary with activity levels expressed in standardized measures, such as standard labour hour, standard machine hour or standard labour cost.

Further problems associated with standard overhead costs are:

1 an appropriate overhead rate must be selected for allocating standard variable and standard fixed costs per unit;
2 in the case of fixed overhead costs, the overhead rate selected must be calculated by reference to a standard activity level for the budget period.

Setting standard costs for direct material and direct labour

Setting standard costs for direct material and direct labour involves two aspects:

1 quantifying an efficient input of resources;
2 acquiring that input at the best price.

Standard direct material costs

The quantity of raw material required for a standard unit is determined by engineers. The standard quantity should include an appropriate allowance for normal wastage in production.

Responsibility for purchasing rests with the purchasing department. The standard price should reflect the best price that the purchasing department can obtain, and be the price expected to be paid during the budget period.

Standard direct labour costs

Before standard labour costs can be set, operatives have to be graded according to standardized categories of skills. Labour time standards are set by time and motion study engineers. The standard wage rates are those that are expected to be paid during the budget period.

Variance analysis for direct costs

The control of direct costs through variance analysis is based on two principles:

1 *Management by exception.* Actual expenditure is assumed to be in line with standard costs, unless this is contradicted by information showing that variances are occurring between the budget allowance, based on standard costs, and actual expenditure being recorded in the financial accounts.
2 *Accounting responsibility.* Responsibility for the control of costs is located with the manager having the responsibility for the cost centre in question.

The first sign that standard costs are not being respected is the appearance of a *budget variance* on direct material or direct labour. A budget variance is defined as *a difference between the budget allowance for the output achieved and actual spending on the output achieved.* It requires further analysis before its causal factors may be identified, investigated and, if possible, corrected.

The analysis of the budget variance necessitates splitting it into the two components of standard costs, namely quantity and price. As a result, it is possible to attribute the problem to the occurrence of excessive usage or excessive price, or both.

Variances fall into two categories:

1 *Unfavourable variances* arise when the standard allowance is exceeded by actual expenditure.
2 *Favourable variances* arise when actual expenditure is less than the standard allowance.

Clearly, management will be more immediately concerned with possible inefficiencies arising as a result of *unfavourable* variances. *Favourable variances* may arise out of fortuitous events occurring in the firm's favour, for example, a fall in market prices for raw materials. However, *favourable variances* may also indicate that standards should be adjusted upwards to reflect actual performance more accurately. The truth remains that, under ideal conditions, neither favourable nor unfavourable variances should occur if standards have been correctly set.

Direct material variances

The analysis of the direct material variance begins by identifying the direct material budget variance. The material budget variance is *the difference between the actual expenditure and budgeted expenditure*. It provides a measure of the overall difference that has to be investigated. It is composed of two elements:

1 *price variance* that explains the proportion of the budget variance that is caused by paying more or less than the standard price for actual purchase;
2 *usage variance* that explains the proportion of the budget variance that is due to using more or less material than the standard quantity.

The principle of accounting responsibility means that responsibility for the price variances rests with the purchasing department, whereas responsibility for the usage variance lies with the manager of the appropriate production cost centre.

Example 34.1 Ragon Ltd is a small manufacturing company making a product known as Platron. It has a standard costing system, and standard direct material costs per unit of Platron have been set for the budget year 20X1 as follows:

Standard material quantity per unit	3 kilos
Standard price per kilo	£0.50

During the month of January 20X1, 4,000 units of Platron were produced. This was the budgeted volume. The following information was obtained by the costing department:

Quantity used during January	11,000 kilos
Quantity purchased during January	15,000 kilos
Budgeted expenditure for January	£6,000
Actual expenditure for January	£8,250

The analysis of the direct material budget variance into its two components is as shown in Figure 34.1.

It should be noted that the effect of the price variance has been magnified due to excessive purchasing over usage. Responsibility for the price variance falls on the purchasing department, which may well have acted rationally and in the best interests of the firm in stocking up in anticipation of rising prices: in which case while the unfavourable variance needs investigation it does not reflect poor performance. Responsibility for the usage variance rests with production cost centres (in this instance they did a good job).

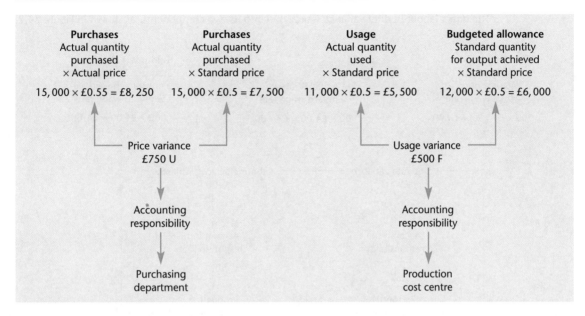

Figure 34.1 Analysis of direct material variances

Direct labour variances

The analysis of the direct labour variance begins by determining the *direct labour budget variance* defined as *the difference between the actual payroll and the standard labour cost of actual production*. The major difference between the analysis of direct material and direct labour variances is in the stocking of direct materials in excess of usage. The terminology is slightly different, though the same meaning is retained. The notion of price is expressed in the labour wage rate; and the notion of usage is stated in labour efficiency. Accordingly, once the direct labour budget variance has been calculated, it is split into *the direct labour wage rate variance and the direct labour efficiency variance*.

Standard direct labour costs established by Ragon Ltd for the 20X1 budget year were as follows:

Standard direct labour hours per unit	0.25 hour
Standard direct labour rate per unit	£4.00 per hour

The actual output for the month of January 20X1 was 4,000 units of Platron. This corresponded to the budgeted volume. The following additional information is given:

Actual hours	900
Actual expenditure	£3,690

The direct labour budget variance is analysed into its two components, as shown in Figure 34.2.

Figure 34.2 Analysis of direct labour variances

Setting standards for overhead costs

Setting standard overhead costs poses more difficult and complex problems than the setting of standard direct costs in the following respects:

1 setting cost standards for the multitude of activities that constitute manufacturing overhead and which are only loosely connected to production volumes;
2 selecting an overhead rate for both standard fixed and variable overhead cost allocation;
3 determining the standard volume for the purpose of recovering standard fixed overhead costs.

Setting cost standards

The single and perhaps most surprising fact about setting cost standards for overheads is that essentially it is no different from setting them for direct material and labour. There are two components: price and quantity. Establishing the standards for overheads is more complicated because some of the overheads are fixed and some variable and because there are many more types of costs involved (power, rent, maintenance, supervisors salaries, etc.). Despite the complications the task is the same: set demanding but achievable targets for price and quantity.

Getting the price right is more complicated because more departments are involved and more prices have to be negotiated: purchasing is responsible for everything that comes from outside the organization, while personnel (or human resources) is responsible for all the people related costs. The prices used in budgets must reflect these myriad negotiations with suppliers, unions, employee representatives, etc., and their likely evolution over the budgeted period.

Getting the quantity right is also complicated: the main reason being the tenuous linkages between changes in the level of activity and resources needed to support it. Some of these resources do indeed vary with changes in activity levels, others are more fixed in nature (at least within the range of fluctuations in output being envisaged and within the budgeted period of twelve months). Given these circumstances, how do the engineers determine an efficient amount of each resource consumed by a unit of product and by the cost centres that constitute manufacturing overhead?

Selecting a standard overhead rate

The difficulty in establishing an appropriate level of activity in relation to variable and fixed costs lies in that overhead costs are not directly related to output expressed as units of product. As discussed earlier in Chapter 17, an overhead rate has to be selected for the purposes of allocating standard variable and fixed overheads to products.

The most convenient overhead rate is the *standard hour* defined as *a unit of measurement representing the quantity of a product or service which can be produced or performed in one hour by any process, machine or operative.*

The standard hour is not a measure of time but a measure of performance in a period of one hour.

Example 34.3 If the estimated time required to write 200 letters is 20 hours, a standard hour represents 10 letters. Similarly, if 48 units of product A can be produced in 12 hours, a standard hour of that product represents 4 units.

The standard hour not only constitutes a convenient base for establishing standard overhead rates, but can also be applied to all types of cost centres where it is useful to have a common measure through which the output of diverse products can be expressed.

The standard hour may also be used to develop overhead rates both for variable and fixed overheads.

Three production control ratios are derived from the standard hour:

1 The *efficiency ratio* measures the efficiency of direct labour:

$$\text{Efficiency ratio} = \frac{\text{Standard hours of production achieved}}{\text{Actual direct working hours}} \times 100$$

2 The *production volume ratio* compares actual output with budget:

$$\text{Production volume ratio} = \frac{\text{Standard hours of production achieved}}{\text{Budgeted standard hours}} \times 100$$

3 The *capacity ratio* compares actual hours with budgeted hours:

$$\text{Capacity ratio} = \frac{\text{Actual hours worked}}{\text{Budgeted hours}}$$

Example 34.4 Tafel Ltd manufactures tables and chairs. It is estimated that two hours are required for one table and 1 hour for one chair. In March, 20X0, actual production was 50 tables and 150 chairs. Budgeted production for the period was 40 tables and 160 chairs. Actual hours worked were 230 and actual output in terms of standard hours was:

Tables: 50 units × 2 hours per unit =	100 hours
Chairs: 150 units × 1 hour per unit =	150 hours
	250 standard hours

Budgeted production in terms of standard hours was:

Tables: 40 units × 2 hours per unit =	80 hours
Chairs: 160 units × 1 hour per unit =	160 hours
	240 standard hours

$$\text{Efficieny ratio} = \frac{250}{230} \times 100 = 108.79\%$$

$$\text{Production volume ratio} = \frac{250}{240} \times 100 = 104.2\%$$

$$\text{Capacity ratio} = \frac{230}{240} \times 100 = 95.8\%$$

These results may be checked as follows:

Production volume ratio = Capacity ratio × Efficiency ratio

$$104.2\% = \frac{230}{240} \times \frac{250}{230}$$

Determining the standard volume for fixed overhead cost recovery

Variable overhead costs vary directly with output. Hence, if the output is expressed in standard hours, variable overheads will be applied to actual output in accordance with the predetermined rate.

Fixed costs, however, do not vary with output. Hence, a normal or standard output must be budgeted to enable a fixed overhead rate to be calculated. The standard fixed overhead rate will be applied to the number of standard hours fixed in the budget.

The term *fixed budgeting* refers to budgets prepared on the basis of a standard output for the purposes of establishing budget allowances throughout the firm. Under fixed budgeting, standard fixed overheads will be over- or under-applied whenever actual output is greater or less than the standard output, giving rise to favourable or unfavourable volume variances.

Firms will need always to plan their financing requirements on the assumption that they will attain the budgeted output level. In this sense, the financial budget will always be a *fixed budget*. The disadvantage of using the fixed budget for control purposes lies in the inability to control costs under fluctuating output conditions.

Flexible budgeting

Flexible budgeting is intended to overcome the difficulties posed by fixed budgeting for controlling overhead costs. Flexible budgeting does not replace fixed budgeting for planning the financing requirement purposes. It only replaces fixed budgeting for control. The particular difficulties that make fixed budgeting redundant for control are:

1 overhead allowances are budgeted in respect of only one output volume, namely the standard output;
2 fixed overheads will generally be under- or over-applied, but responsibility for volume variances cannot be attributed to cost centre managers, since they are not responsible for output variations.

Flexible budget allowances

Flexible budgeting allows fluctuations in output levels to be taken into account for cost control purposes by means of flexible budget allowances.

Example 34.5 Jobin Ltd is a small manufacturing company that has a budgetary planning and control system based on the fixed budgeting principle. The fixed budgeted overhead allowance for assembly cost centre A is £20,000 for a period of one month during which the standard output was equivalent to 5,000 standard hours. The following table shows the fixed budgeted allowance as well as what it would look like under flexible budgeting:

	Fixed budget	Flexible budget Variable	Flexible budget Fixed
	£	£	£
Indirect material	5,000	5,000	
Indirect labour	2,500	2,500	
Repairs and maintenance	5,000	3,000	2,000
Insurance	1,500	1,000	500
Rates	3,000		3,000
Depreciation	3,000		3,000
	£20,000	11,500	8,500

The overhead costs per unit are:

$$£20,000 ÷ 5,000 = £4 \text{ (£2.3 variable, £1.7 fixed)}$$

The firm has experienced severe fluctuations in demand for its products over several months. As a result, actual costs have diverged significantly from budget allowances. It has now decided to introduce flexible budgeting making it possible to match actual output with a corresponding budget allowance. During the month of June, actual activity level of cost centre A was 4,000 standard hours, for which the following flexible budget allowance was calculated:

	Variable costs	Fixed costs	Total budget allowance
	£	£	£
Indirect material	4,000		4,000
Indirect labour	2,000		2,000
Repairs and maintenance	2,400	2,000	4,400
Insurance	800	500	1,300
Rates		3,000	3,000
Depreciation		3,000	3,000
	9,200	8,500	17,700

If this flexible budget of £17,700 for 4,000 standard hours is recalculated for 5,000 standard hours, the budget allowance is £20,000; i.e. the data in the flexible budget are entirely consistent with those in the fixed budget. Therefore spending £20,000 to produce 5,000 standard hours under the fixed budget represents the same degree of operational efficiency as spending £17,700 to produce 4,000 under the flexible budget.

Flexible budgeting improves the control of overhead costs by establishing a flexible budget allowance for each output level. In effect, cost centres are allowed to incur overhead costs at a predetermined standard rate. Control is applied routinely for each management reporting period, usually monthly, when the flexible overhead allowance for the actual output achieved is calculated.

Example 34.6 Jobin Ltd has a fixed financial budget of £20,000 providing for a monthly output of 5,000 units as in Example 34.5. On this basis, each cost centre has been given a monthly budget allowance corresponding to predetermined standard costs per unit. Jobin Ltd uses flexible budgeting for cost control. During the month of July, actual output was 4,500 units. Actual overhead costs incurred amounted to £19,150. The following overhead cost control report was prepared.

	(1) Actual cost of production	(2) Total budget allowance	(3) Original budget	(4) Variation from original budget	(5) Variation from budget allowance
Units produced	4,500	4,500	5,000	(1) – (3)	(1) – (2)
Indirect materials	£4,700	£4,500	£5,000	£300 F	£200 U
Indirect labour	2,400	2,250	2,500	100 F	150 U
Repairs and maintenance	4,600	4,700	5,000	400 F	100 F
Insurance	1,450	1,400	1,500	50 F	50 U
Rates	3,000	3,000	3,000	–	–
Depreciation	3,000	3,000	3,000	–	–
	£19,150	£18,850	£20,000	£850 F	£300 U

In this table column (2), Total budget allowance, uses the same fixed costs and the same variable costs per standard hour as in Example 34.5. The only difference is that the output is now 4,500, whereas previously it was 4,000. The variations in column (5) are due entirely to expenditure as the quantities produced in columns (1) and (2) are identical. However the variations in column (4) are partly due to expenditure and partly to volumes: for indirect materials the total of £300 F is made up of £500 F due to lower volumes and £200 U due to higher expenditures.

Variance analysis for overhead costs

The analysis of overhead cost variances fall into two parts:

1 the analysis of variable overhead costs;
2 the analysis of fixed overhead costs.

Variable overhead cost variance

The analysis of the variable overhead cost variance begins by identifying the variable overhead budget variance, which is the difference between the actual expenditure and budgeted expenditure. It provides a measure of the overall difference that has to be investigated. It is composed of two elements:

1 *Expenditure variance* explains the proportion of the budget variance that is caused by differences in the price paid for services charged as overhead costs:

**Expenditure variance = actual overheads –
(actual hours × standard variable overhead rate)**

2 *Efficiency variance* explains the proportion of the budget variance that is due to difference in the usage of services charged as overhead costs:

**Expenditure variance = (actual hours − standard hours of actual production) ×
standard variable overhead rate**

Example 34.7 Jobin Ltd's assembly cost centre A has budgeted for an output of 5,000 standard hours. The total budget allowance is £20,000 of which the variable component is £11,500 (this can be checked from the data in the flexible budget representation of Example 34.5). The following additional information is given for August:

(a) actual hours worked	4,800
(b) variable costs incurred	£11,600
(c) standard variable overhead rate per standard hour	£2.3
(d) budgeted allowance (5,000 hours × £2.3)	£11,500

The expenditure and efficiency variances are calculated as shown in Figure 34.3.

Figure 34.3 Analysis of variable overhead variances

Fixed overhead cost variances

Fixed overhead cost variances fall into two types:

1 *Expenditure variances*, calculated as follows:

> **Fixed overhead cost expenditure variance = actual fixed overheads –
> budgeted fixed overhead costs**

2 *Volume variances*, calculated as follows:

> **Fixed overhead cost volume variance = budgeted fixed overheads –
> (standard fixed overhead rate × standard hours in the output achieved)**

Example 34.8   Refer to Examples 34.5 and 34.7, where the assembly department is budgeted for an output of 5,000 standard hours with fixed costs of £8,500 and actual hours worked in August were 4,800. The following fixed overhead cost information is given for the department:

	£
(a) actual fixed overhead costs	8,900
(b) budgeted fixed overhead costs	8,500
(c) standard fixed overhead rate per standard hour	1.7

The expenditure and volume variances are calculated in Figure 34.4.

Under flexible budgeting the manager responsible for the assembly department is only responsible for the expenditure part (£400 U) of fixed overhead cost variances (£700 U). The fact that production volumes were only 4,800 standard hours instead of 5,000 is not his fault nor his responsibility. The volume variance of £340 U will go to some central account. As mentioned earlier, the use of fixed budgeting will lead to the appearance of a fixed overhead cost volume variance, since the fixed overhead

Figure 34.4 Analysis of fixed overhead variances under fixed budgeting

rate used for recovering fixed overheads will have been determined on the basis of a fixed output level. The manager of the assembly department will see and be required to explain the total overhead variance, presumably accepting responsibility for the expenditure part and arguing that the volume part is beyond his control. The reader should note that the under- and over-absorption of overheads which we discussed in Chapter 17 results in expenditure and volume variances.

Sales variance analysis and the control of revenue

In general terms, the procedures appropriate for the control of revenue are similar to those applied to the control of costs:

1 the establishment of a sales plan;
2 the prompt determination and reporting of variances between actual and planned performance;
3 the investigation and analysis of variances so as to ascertain their causes and those responsible for them;
4 the implementation of appropriate corrective action.

The determination of the sales plan has both long-range and budgetary aspects. Long-range planning will be concerned with establishing revenue objectives and goals, from which may be derived specific sales targets and prices for the budget planning period. Since the level of demand for most products exhibits a seasonal pattern, the annual sales plan should be divided into shorter periods so that responsibility accounting is based on a meaningful comparison of actual and planned performance.

So far, we have discussed the control of revenue in terms of analysing the difference between actual and planned sales. However management is not so much concerned about sales as the profit from them. Sales variance analysis has been developed to measure the effects on profits of variances between actual sales and planned sales, and not the effect of such variances merely on revenue.

Three different variances are commonly applied to the analysis of sales:

1 sales price variance;
2 sales volume variance;
3 sales mix variance.

Sales price variance

It is quite common for actual selling prices to differ from the planned selling price. Numerous factors may be responsible for sales price variances, such as the need to adjust prices to meet competition, or to implement a new marketing strategy. However, by far the largest factor is the discretion allowed to individual sales managers to adjust prices to meet particular circumstances, such as price reductions for slightly spoiled goods, to secure the goodwill of a client, or to clear excessive inventories of slow moving goods.

The sales price variance is similar to the price variances already discussed. It may be calculated from the following formula:

Sales price variance = units unsold × actual contributions per unit less the standard contribution

It indicates, therefore, the total effect on income of differences between set prices and the prices at which goods were actually sold.

Sales volume variance

This variance discloses the effect on profits of differences between the planned sales volume and the actual volume of sales. It is calculated as follows:

**Sales volume variance = standard contribution per unit ×
(actual number of units sold – budgeted units of sales)**

Sales mix variance

A change in the product mix will change profitability if the products have different contribution margins, leading to a variance between planned and actual profits. This variance may be computed as follows:

**Sales mix variance = standard contribution per unit of each product ×
(actual quantities of units sold –
actual total sales of units in budgeted mix proportions)**

Example 34.9 | **Example of all three variances**
The following data relate to products X and Y sold by Biproducts Ltd during the quarter ended 31 December 20X0:

Budgeted sales:
   X 5,000 units at £10 (standard variable cost £6 and contribution margin £4)
   Y 5,000 units at £5 (standard variable cost £3 and contribution margin £2)

Actual sales:
   X 4,000 units for £44,000 (i.e. £11 per unit)
   Y 8,000 units for £32,000 (i.e. £4 per unit)

These data may be tabulated as follows:

	(a) Actual contribution	(b) Actual quantity	(c) Standard contribution margin	(d) (b) × (c) Value	(e) Actual quantity in standard proportions	(f) Standard contribution margin	(g) (e) × (f) Value	(h) Budgeted margin
	£	Units	£	£	Units	£	£	£
X	20,000	4,000	4	16,000	6,000	4	24,000	20,000
Y	8,000	8,000	2	16,000	6,000	2	12,000	10,000
	28,000	12,000		32,000	12,000		36,000	30,000

Notes:
1 Column (a) is derived from the following formula:
actual contribution for X
= actual sales less (actual units × standard cost)
= £44,000 – (4,000 × £6)
= £20,000

and similarly for Y

= £32,000 – (8,000 × £3)
= £8,000
2 Column (e) is derived by taking total actual sales of 12,000 units and applying the budgeted mix proportions. According to the budget, 50 per cent of X and 50 per cent of Y should be sold. Total sales were 12,000 units, which expressed in budgeted mix proportions amount to 6,000 units of X and 6,000 units of Y.
3 Column (h) is simply the budgeted sales times the standard contribution margin: 5,000 units times £4/unit for X and 5,000 units times £2/unit for Y.

The variances which may be extracted from these data are as follows:

Sales price variance

S_p = units sold × (actual contribution per unit less standard contribution)
= column (a) – column (d)
= £28,000 – £32,000
= £4,000 U

The sales price variance is unfavourable by £4,000 because an extra 3,000 units of Y (8,000 – 5,000) were sold at a price which was £1 lower than the standard (£4 – £5), while 1,000 units fewer of X (4,000 – 5,000) were sold at a price which was £1 higher than the standard price (£11 – £10).

Sales volume variance

S_v = standard contribution per unit × (actual number of units sold less budgeted units of sales)
= column (g) – column (h)
= £36,000 – £30,000
= £6,000 F

This variance reflects the fact that 12,000 units were actually sold as against a budgeted volume of only 10,000 units. Its value is the contribution which the extra 2,000 units would have brought if they were at standard price and mix.

Sales mix variance

S_m = (standard contribution per unit of each product $\times$ the actual quantities of units sold)
    – (standard contribution per unit of each product $\times$ actual total sales in budgeted mix proportions)

= column (d) – column (g)

= £32,000 – £36,000

= £4,000 U

This variance discloses the reduction in budgeted income caused by selling a greater proportion of units having a lower contribution margin than the standard.

Responsibility for variances

Under responsibility accounting, only those costs incurred by a responsibility centre over which it can exercise control may be used as a basis for evaluation. In variance analysis, it is necessary to determine the precise cause of a variance and to trace the cause to the individual responsible. It is the function of the individual in charge of each responsibility centre to act promptly upon reports of variances within his or her control. Variances are not ends in themselves. Rather, they raise the questions: 'Why did the variance occur? What must be done to eliminate them?' Obviously the importance of these questions depends on the significance of the deviations. We see how the significance of a variance is determined in the next section.

The material usage and labour efficiency variances respectively reveal whether the quantities of material and labour used in production are more or less than planned, depending on whether they are unfavourable or favourable. If more material is being used than planned, the cause may lie elsewhere than in the production department, for example in the purchase of inferior materials by the purchasing department. The fault may lie in the production department and be due to careless supervision, or the use of untrained staff, or faulty machines. An unfavourable labour efficiency variance may be due to poor control by the foreman, bad labour relations, health and safety factors, production delays, inferior tools and badly trained staff. Again, the responsibility for the variance should be tracked down. For example, if due to badly trained staff, this may be caused by inefficiency on the part of the personnel department, but if, on the other hand, the variance is caused by economic conditions causing a shortage of specialized labour, the variance is considered to be uncontrollable. Some of the variances may be interrelated. For example, if cheaper materials are purchased, this will result in a favourable materials price variance. It may also result in an adverse material usage variance if the quality of the material is poor; this may in turn lead to an adverse labour efficiency variance. Conversely, the use of higher grade labour may cause an adverse labour rate variance but may cause a favourable materials usage variance and a favourable labour efficiency variance. Finally, an adverse (or favourable) labour efficiency variance will affect the variable overhead efficiency variance and the fixed overhead efficiency variance.

Price and wage rate variances may not be controllable by the firm, and this is particularly true of raw material prices and wages agreed nationally with trade unions. On the other hand, variances may occur in the negotiation of contracts for materials which are the responsibility of the purchasing department. The purchasing department controls prices by getting several quotations, taking advantage of economic lots and securing cash discounts. Inefficiency in these areas will reveal unfavourable variances for which that department should be held responsible.

With regard to overhead variances, spending variances are usually the responsibility of the department head by whom they are usually controllable. The volume variance is not normally controllable by the departmental manager; it is usually the responsibility of the sales department or production control.

The investigation of variances

Managerial time is too valuable to be wasted on the indiscriminate checking of performance. When standard costs are properly established, they provide an automatic means of highlighting performance variances upon which management should concentrate their attention. Thus, the investigation of variances should focus on significant deviations from the established standards.

The investigation of a variance is a three-stage process consisting of:

1 an investigation to determine whether the variance is significant;
2 if it proves to be significant, an investigation into its causes;
3 if the variance can be corrected, action is taken to ensure that it will not occur in the future.

The determination of the significance of a variance in itself may be problematic. If its definition is left to managerial judgement and experience, inconsistencies may arise in the treatment of different variances solely by reason of behavioural factors affecting a manager's judgement. Thus, pressure of work in itself may lead the manager to perceive the significance of a variance as less important than it really is. Moreover, there is unlikely to be complete agreement between different managers about the investigation of borderline cases.

It is necessary, also, to distinguish 'chance' or 'random' variances from significant ones requiring investigation. By viewing the standard as an arithmetical mean about which fluctuations occur, it is possible to distinguish random from significant variances. Investigation of variances shows that random variances are inherent in standard costing systems. Such variances assume the shape of a 'normal distribution' about the standard – small variations are frequent, bigger ones less frequent and large ones rare. Therefore there are combinations of size of variation and frequency with which they occur that are to be expected – they are normal. Statistical control charts enable a manager to determine whether or not the size and frequency of a particular variation is significant. It defines the limits within which random or normal variances occur, so that those variances which fall outside these limits may be assumed to be abnormal and, therefore, significant and worthy of investigation.

Statistical control charts have been used for many years for the purpose of quality control, but it is only recently that this technique has been applied to the control of standard cost variances. Statistical control charts help managers decide whether a particular variation is random and therefore normal or non-random and in need of attention.

Figure 34.5

The use of statistical control charts requires that upper and lower limits of acceptable variation be laid down with precision. This is done by analysing variances for a representative period and calculating the mean and standard deviation of the sample. Management then has to decide how many standard deviations from the mean an observation has to be to signify that something is amiss. These limits are illustrated in Figure 34.5.

The figure shows the values for consecutive weeks in terms of standard deviations from the mean. While the first five observations are clearly within the control limits and therefore taken individually do not warrant any investigation, the trend suggests that all is not well. It looks as if something is drifting out of control. Weeks 6 and 7 are reassuring, while 9 and 10 suggest something untoward is going on, confirmed by week 11 which now is manifestly a significant variance. Investigation and remedial action bring the next observation for week 12 within the control limits. As the discussion shows, besides individual values, control charts provide interesting information concerning trends and patterns, all of which can trigger investigations.

Limitations of standard costing

Standard costing was developed to meet the needs of a traditional manufacturing environment. In a 'world-class manufacturing' environment the use of standard costs for performance evaluation has been questioned.

Firms that advocate continuous improvement may find that the use of standards demotivates the search for further improvements. In other words, once the standard performance is reached, there will be no incentive to improve the process any further. Standard costing, therefore, tends to reflect the status quo. In pursuit of continuous improvement, standard costs can be replaced by target costs. The former represents what ought to be achieved as far as current circumstances are concerned, whilst the latter represents what must be achieved to enjoy competitive advantage. Alternatively, standard costs can be replaced by actual costs which are tracked from period to period in the expectation of continuous cost reduction. Under this approach, last period's actual cost becomes this period's standard.

Standard costing encourages those responsible for their achievement to produce favourable variances. But the pressure to meet standards may create dysfunctional behaviour. The reporting of material price variances may be inappropriate where firms have just-in-time purchasing techniques. For example, purchasing officers may acquire materials of low quality, or in large lots, in order to produce a favourable materials price variance. As a consequence scrap (the number of defective units and the amount of rework activity) may increase or raw material inventory may be excessive. These outcomes run contrary to the objectives of total quality control and zero inventory. JIT companies will wish to focus on performance measures which emphasize quality and reliability rather than material price variances which direct attention away from these key factors. Similarly, efficiency variances may encourage workers to produce more than needed to achieve targeted efficiency levels or to avoid an unfavourable volume variance. But producing more product than needed is diametrically opposed to the JIT goal of zero inventory. In a JIT environment idle workers (in the short run) are not necessarily viewed as bad; keeping workers busy by over-producing can be much more costly than keeping them idle.

In an advanced manufacturing environment it is necessary to supplement standard cost information with non-financial measures for guiding operational performance. Non-financial measures such as lead time, number of line stops, and number of units scrapped are used in place of cost information for day-to-day decisions because non-financial data are a better description of the physical reality and can be produced much faster than accounting data. Transposing physical data into monetary units takes time, involves costs and is a poor reflection of what is actually happening on the shop floor. Therefore, conventional accounting data are better suited for the longer term and overall performance summaries of an operation, whilst non-financial information provide more timely and focused performance information. This applies particularly to computer-controlled manufacturing equipment with its immediate contemporaneous information feedback to the production manager. The control cycle is generally more effective with this non-monetary data than converting production data in monetary units at intervals for inclusion in periodic variance reports.

Summary

Standard costing underlies most manufacturing activities. The cost of a product must be ascertained prior to production for pricing and control purposes. Standard costing may also lead to cost reductions. Perhaps the most important benefit which results from a standard costing system is the atmosphere of cost consciousness fostered among managers.

Standard cost data are compared with actual cost data for the purpose of ascertaining variances. Such variances are normally broken down into two basic components – quantity and price. The control of overhead costs as distinct from direct costs requires a method which takes into account the possibility of changes in the level of production during the period. Flexible budgeting affords such a method, and provides for each department a series of budget allowance schedules for various volume levels within the normal range of operations.

The ascertainment of variances is only the first stage in assessing results. Variances should be analysed in order to establish whether they are significant, whether they are controllable and if so where responsibility lies. At the same time, the analysis of variances enables established standards to be validated and methods for establishing standards in the future to be improved.

Self-assessment questions

1 Distinguish standard costs and budgeted costs.

2 State some applications of standard costing.

3 Examine the problems of setting cost standards.

4 Explain what is meant by a budget variance.

5 What is the formula for calculating:
   (a) direct material price variance,
   (b) direct material usage variance,
   (c) wage rate variance,
   (d) labour efficiency variance?

6 What problems are involved in setting overhead cost standards?

7 Distinguish between fixed and flexible budgeting.

8 What is the formula for calculating:
   (a) variable overhead expenditure variance,
   (b) variable overhead efficiency variance,
   (c) fixed overhead expenditure variance,
   (d) fixed overhead volume variance?

9 State three variances that can be applied to the analysis of sales.

10 Comment briefly on the problems that are implied in the investigation of variances.

Problems (*indicates that a solution is to be found in the Lecturer's Guide)

1 For March 20X0 the master budget and actual results for Dept A of a firm were as follows:

	Master budget	Actual
Output – Units A	600	500
Units B	400	500
	£	£
Costs: Materials	13,200	13,300
Direct labour	7,000	8,400
Machining	9,600	9,450
Overhead costs	4,400	4,400
	34,200	35,550

The master budget was constructed on the following production specifications:

(a) Material required per unit – A, 4 kg; B, 5 kg.

(b) Direct labour hours required per unit – A, 1 hour; B, 2 hours.
(c) Machining costs include a variable element of £4 per machine hour. Machining time required per unit – A, 0.5 hours; B, 0.25 hours.
(d) Overhead costs include a variable element of £1 per direct labour hour worked.

Required:

(a) Construct a flexible budget for the actual output and show any variances.
(b) If it is known that in fact 1,400 direct labour hours were worked in March, what further information about the direct labour variance can be given?

2* The Vitrox Manufacturing Co Ltd is a single-product company and employs a standard absorption costing system. The standard cost per unit is calculated as follows:

	£
Direct labour 4 hours at £3.00	12.00
Direct materials 10 kg at £1.00	10.00
Overhead	10.00
Total standard cost per unit	32.00

The standard volume of output is 10,000 units per month. The variable overhead cost component is £1.00 per standard direct labour hour.

The following information is available for the month of December 20X0:

	£
Units completed	8,000
Direct materials used 83,000 kg at £1.05	87,150
Direct labour hours recorded 33,000 hours at £3.10	102,300
Variable overhead costs incurred	32,500
Fixed overhead costs incurred	65,000

Required:

(a) Analyse the following variances:
   – direct material variances;
   – direct labour variances;
   – variable overhead variances;
   – fixed overhead variances.
(b) Explain possible reasons for the appearance of these variances.

3 K Kiely makes and sells apple tarts which are sold in packs of ten. The company operates a standard costing system and the standard cost of a box of apple tarts is as follows:

Direct materials	2 kg at £1 per kilo
Direct labour	2 hours at £2.20 per hour
Variable production overheads	£1 per direct labour hour

The actual figures for the month of October were:

Production	8,200 boxes
Direct materials	
Opening inventory	1,000 kg
Closing inventoriy	2,500 kg
Purchases	9,000 kg at 98p per kg
	12,000 kg at 86p per kg
Direct labour	15,800 hours costing £36,340
Variable production overheads	£14,250

The company operates a standard marginal costing system.

Required:

(a) Calculate the variances for materials, labour and variable overheads in a form which would be useful to management.

(b) Comment on the purpose of variances.

(c) On being presented with the statement of variances, K Kiely offers the following reasons as to why they have arisen:

   (i) Although we used experienced employees, they were less efficient.

   (ii) The standard wastage allowance which was set for the apples was significantly exceeded.

   (iii) The projected increase in the labour rate of 4 per cent, turned out to be 2 per cent.

   (iv) The increased quantities of apples purchased. Because the market had a surplus, the buyer was able to negotiate a substantial discount in price.

   (v) The excessive electricity costs (included in the variable overheads) caused by cooking the tarts for longer than usual, resulted in the expense being higher than forecast.

Match the variance to the reasons and consider whether the explanation is acceptable.

Reference   Smith, R. (1990) Standard setting – objectives and limitations, *ACCA Students' Newsletter*, June.

CHAPTER 35

The control of managed costs

Setting the scene

The question is, 'What is the most effective way of controlling period costs?' The answer is through exactly the same techniques as are used for direct material and direct labour, that is, changing the design specifications of the job description to eliminate inefficiency, redundant, and unnecessary work elements. The difference is that cost analysts and administrators make the design changes rather than engineers and buyers.

In any cost control or reduction activity, the one fundamental fact that must be kept in mind is that all costs are results, not causes. Costs can be reduced or eliminated only by attacking their causes. Simply firing people to attack the salary expense line is likely to be offset by increases in overtime premiums and temporary help lines.

(Byrum, 1990)

Learning objectives

After studying this chapter you should be able to:

1 appreciate the nature of managed costs;

2 describe six methods for controlling managed costs;

3 indicate the main problems in controlling administrative costs;

4 discuss the main issues concerned with the control of marketing costs.

Traditionally, accountants have been concerned with the control of those manufacturing costs where clear-cut input–output relationships may be established. These relationships are used by engineers to design products and select production processes and thereby to determine product costs: the costs are being engineered into the product. Consequently they are referred to as engineered costs and, when the volume warrants it, give rise to the development of standard costs. The name explains the motivation: the specification of the product and the choice of production technology make it possible to predetermine what the product should cost, if all goes well.

Engineered costs comprise direct product costs (material and labour) and some manufacturing overheads that are engineered into the product by the choice of production process and technology (a numerically controlled machine, a robot welding line), the rest are what we might call support functions. In their pioneering article Miller and Vollman (1985) pointed out that the costs that were visible on the shop-floor, were dwarfed by the invisible part in the support functions (indirect labour, general and administrative expenses, facilities and equipment costs, engineering costs and material costs). Moreover, while the visible part had been studied in depth (allowed times, material usage, scrap rates, etc.), the invisible and largest part had largely escaped serious scrutiny.

Besides these manufacturing overheads that are not engineered into products, there are very significant amounts of cost incurred outside the factory gates. Once again, the absence of clear-cut input–output relationships make them difficult to plan and control. Collectively these different categories and instances of non-engineered costs are called managed or discretionary costs. Their growing significance has underlined the importance of developing effective methods of cost control for them. In this chapter, we review some of the methods that are applied in the control of managed costs.

The nature of managed costs

Essentially, managed costs concern the support functions in manufacturing and all non-manufacturing activities. Their level is determined at the discretion of management, and for this reason, they are often referred to as 'discretionary costs'.

There are four major categories of managed costs:

1 *Administrative costs*, incurred in providing the administrative structure. Unlike engineered costs, they are not strictly defined in terms of short-term output. For this reason, they are considered relatively fixed. Administrative costs include not only management salaries, but also costs associated with the provision of a host of administrative, accounting and secretarial services.

2 *Research and development costs*, incurred in developing new products and processes. Research and development costs are treated as operating expenditures, although in nature they are similar to an investment, and for this reason are related to long-term planning. There are two reasons why research and development costs are difficult to control:

    (a) given the speculative nature of research, returns from it are uncertain. Consequently, research spending is no indicator of the effectiveness of a research department or as a means of evaluating research projects;

    (b) there is a long lead time between incurring costs and obtaining results, even when research is successful.

3 *Marketing costs*, incurred in maintaining and increasing market share for the firm's products and services. Marketing costs include a variety of costs, such as advertising, market research, selling, warehousing, distribution, etc. Some of these costs, such as advertising, are concerned with introducing new products or extending market share and are like investments in that their benefits last several years: others, such as selling costs, benefit the current period. However, despite the differences in the duration of their likely benefits, both are treated as operating expenditures for accounting purposes. These costs may be difficult to control for the following reasons:

    (a) some costs, such as advertising, are acknowledged to have an impact on sales, but the relationship between cost and benefit is not easy to ascertain. Furthermore, the long-term and short-term nature of these benefits cannot be measured with accuracy;

(b) Other costs may be susceptible to input–output analysis, for example, warehousing costs, but most of them, such as salespeople's salaries and sales administration costs, lack accurate performance measurement standards.

4 *Training costs*, incurred in the development and improvement of staff, include costs of courses, training department salaries, the loss of production time, etc. These costs are easy to control, but deceptively difficult to justify in terms of quantitative benefits as there are very few measures of success.

In service organizations, as opposed to manufacturing, discretionary costs are much more important. For example, in the health service the inputs to the process (salaries and expenses) can be measured, the outputs (patients) are more difficult; additionally in the public sector, there are no profit figures to provide a relative measure (although hospitals are reimbursed according to a 'price list'). Attempts have been made recently to measure key performance indicators such as: outpatient waiting time, average length of stay, successful surgeries of critical diseases, but there is a long way to go before these indicators match the accuracy of standard costs.

The control of managed costs

The discretionary nature of managed costs implies that budgeted amounts of spending are not analysed in terms of expected output. Nonetheless, despite the difficulties of applying an input–output analysis to discretionary costs, there are implicit assumptions as to the volume and especially to the quality of the activity and services that such costs are expected to provide. In effect, the benefits associated with managed costs are both qualitative and quantitative.

Two main methods that have been developed for controlling managed costs are:

1 *Work study measurements*, that are similar in nature to work engineering studies in which tasks are analysed in terms of workloads, techniques used and number of people required to perform the work efficiently. Work study measurements rely on establishing key control factors to apply to particular activities. Examples of control factors are:

Activity	Control factor
Purchasing	Number of orders placed
Typing	Number of letters typed
Receipting cheques	Number of cheques received

Work study measurements are more suitable for controlling routine activities. For instance a clerical work measurement database exists providing standard times for clerical tasks. However, they are not useful for controlling non-routine activities that characterize management and specialist functions, in which qualitative factors are critical to success.

2 *Budgetary controls* in which discretionary costs are controlled in terms of departmental spending budgets. This approach to the control of discretionary costs is an application of the methods used to control variable and fixed overhead manufacturing costs discussed in Chapter 34.

The key to the control of discretionary costs under this method lies in designating people who have clear and unambiguous responsibility for budgets. If things go well or badly, the system must be capable of identifying who is responsible. The initial problem to be resolved is whether the discretionary costs are variable or fixed for budgeting purposes.

A variable-costing approach to the development of departmental budgets rests on the assumption that there is a cost–volume relationship in which costs rise directly and proportionately with the volume of activity, and that the relationship is quantifiable.

A fixed-cost approach treats discretionary costs as fixed during the budget period. This approach reflects the assumptions made by large organizations that existing organizational structures, with which discretionary costs are typically associated, are not changed in the short term, even if they are reviewed from time to time.

3 *Activity based costing (ABC)* was born out of an attempt to understand what the Miller and Vollman 'hidden factory' was doing. It organized its investigation around three intuitively obvious and compelling questions: (a) what are people doing? (called 'activities'), (b) why are they doing it? (called 'cost drivers'), and (c) how much does it cost? (the 'it' was measured in the same units as the cost driver i.e. cost/unit of cost driver). Everything hinged on whether the answer to the first question was sufficiently homogeneous and repetitive.

Having discovered that the support functions of manufacturing were amenable to being described by ABC, academics and consultants turned their attention to discretionary costs that lay outside the factory and then outside manufacturing industry. A vast literature describes the results of these endeavours. Obviously there are some jobs and job descriptions that lie outside the scope of ABC: the Board, the managing director, perhaps even a whole department such as 'Legal'.

4 *Overhead value analysis (OVA)* was less prescriptive in its methods than ABC, but no less convinced that the cause was noble, namely identification of those overhead activities and their associated discretionary expenditure that added value and those that did not. Each consulting company developed its own method of performing the analysis, but the need for it was not in question. A McKinsey article (Nimocks *et al.*, 2005) reported that 90 per cent of companies that had undertaken cost reduction programmes were back where they started after three years.

5 *Outsourcing* is another avenue that companies explore for reducing the costs of support functions. Favourites include information technology, keeping the books of account, call centres and even the management of human resource functions. The possibilities range from getting a third party to provide the service from your own premises to moving everything lock, stock and barrel offshore (for example, to India with its highly educated and intelligent labour force). Interestingly, companies are beginning to have second thoughts about moving to offshore locations and anecdotes are emerging of companies bringing customer-facing operations back home, as customers react against people with foreign accents being unable to provide technical advice about products.

6 *Benchmarking* is a systematic process for comparing the performance of the target organization with a similar one either in the same company or outside it. The purpose is to identify areas of potential performance and profit improvement. While the idea is appealing, the practice is fraught with difficulties. It is tempting for senior management to find the lowest unit cost for some administrative task, such as settling insurance claims, and then calculate the total savings if all countries achieved

this level of performance. Country managers will be quick to point out differences in their respective charts of accounts, differences in social security payments, lack of economies of scale because they have grown through acquisition rather than organically, and so forth. The rigour with which the studies have to be performed in order for the results to have any validity should not be underestimated. Done well, it can draw management's attention to areas worthy of further investigation.

Control of administrative costs

These costs are relatively fixed in the short run irrespective of the level of business activity. As yet, the detailed costing procedures used in manufacturing for engineered costs have not been applied to administrative activities. Management would certainly argue that administrative functions are not susceptible to work-study methods. Nevertheless, certain tasks, such as clerical ones, are susceptible to work study, and some organizations have attempted to establish standards of efficiency by which to determine staff requirements. Examples of the control factors employed were mentioned in the previous section.

Generally, administrative services are rendered indirectly to many different departments, and it is practically impossible to establish input–output relationships, which would enable overall evaluations to be made. Hence, the control of administrative costs is one of the most difficult areas of management control.

To some extent, budgets can assist in exercising control over them. The budgetary control of such costs requires that responsibility be clearly identified with particular managers. Financial requirements must be submitted, reviewed and approved becoming the standard against which expenditure is assessed.

The difficulty in using this method of controlling administrative costs lies in determining whether the initial budget is reasonable for the proposed level of activity. Clerical work measurement methods and ABC are helpful, but these are expensive to design, install and maintain. OVA and benchmarking are substantial undertakings, but probably not done every year, as the gestation period for implementation takes two or three years. Outsourcing is more radical, taking a considerable amount of time to work through the transition period and settle down with appropriate service level agreements. In the absence of these initiatives administrative cost budgets must be based largely on executive judgement and experience.

Control of research and development costs

There are two main reasons why research and development costs are difficult to control. First, research tends to be speculative and the link to products tenuous; so while a product may be an undoubted success tracing its specification back to all the enabling technologies could be time consuming, controversial (which laboratory did what) and ultimately not very illuminating. Development, being somewhat closer to new products and new processes, is not so difficult (either the new product exceeds expectations or not – the Senseo did). Whenever there is little connection between research costs and their benefits, research spending is no indicator of the effectiveness of a research department, or indeed of a research project. Second reason, there is a long lead time between costs incurred and benefits received.

Research and development is an activity directly related to long-range planning. The effectiveness of research and development expenditure may be assessed only in relation to the attainment of goals specified in the long-range plan. These goals should be selected by top management as crucial areas to which major research effort should be directed. Consequently research expenditure should be concentrated on specific projects which form part of the research effort in a particular area. The control of such expenditure may be exercised by reference to the progress made towards the completion of projects rather than a simple minded comparison of actual and budgeted expenditure.

In fact, recent research (Loch, 2008) suggests that significant benefits can be derived from cascading business strategy and its associated technology strategy down into the research and development department in a manner that encourages dialogue. Business strategy places demands on technology strategy, which in turn imposes constraints and proposes opportunities to business strategies. The dialogue that ensues should be managed to achieve: (a) clarity of what the organization wants to achieve through its business strategy, and (b) creative negotiations between the key actors which fosters motivation and commitment. The benefits of the latter should not be underestimated. If the cascading is undertaken in a spirit of dialogue and fair process between the business and the department of R&D, and between different hierarchical levels in the latter, this can offer a framework for empowerment and a licence to innovate. This common understanding and culture of collaboration facilitate sustained innovation. A number of tools are proposed for managing the process.

Control of marketing costs

Marketing costs have become significant elements in total costs, owing to the rising burden of such costs as advertising and market development. It follows that attention should be directed towards developing the most efficient cost control methods in this area to provide marketing managers with information which will enable them to make the best decisions from the firm's point of view.

Marketing costs cover a wide range of activities, including obtaining sales orders, warehousing and distribution, handling returns and after-sales service. They may be analysed from three different perspectives – the nature of the cost, the function performed and the appropriate sector of the firm's business, as follows:

1 *Classification as to the nature of costs*
Salespeople's salaries and commission
Travelling
Advertising
2 *Classification as to function*
Selling
Advertising
Transportation
Credit collection
Warehousing
Invoicing

3 *Classification as to business sector*
  Territory
  Product
  Marketing channels
  Operating divisions
  Customers

The analysis of marketing costs is helpful in providing information for a number of purposes, such as:

- determining the profitability of sales territories;
- evaluating the profitability of product lines;
- setting selling prices;
- evaluating salespeople's performance;
- determining the importance of individual customers;
- analysing order size profitability.

It is evident from the description of the range of decisions for which information is required, that the analysis of marketing costs is concerned essentially with profitability, which is a function both of revenue control and cost control.

Determining the profitability of sales territories

Most marketing activities are organized on a territorial basis. As a first stage in the analysis of territorial profitability, it is necessary to distinguish direct and indirect marketing costs. Direct costs are those incurred in respect of a single territory: indirect costs are those incurred for all the various sales territories. Direct costs will be controllable by territorial sales managers: indirect costs are only partially controllable (the quantity consumed but not the tariff) or beyond their control (an arbitrary allocation). Nevertheless, despite difficulties in effecting accurate allocations of indirect costs, they serve the useful purpose of providing regional managers with information on the services which support their own activities and from which they derive identifiable benefits. These allocations should be made, provided that they are distinguished from controllable items on reports.

Table 35.1 shows how the analysis of the profitability of sales territories may be made. Its purpose is to locate territories where weaknesses and problems exist. Once they have been located, prompt and intelligent managerial action is required, which may include such decisions as an increase in the number of salespeople operating in the area, or an improvement of the services provided. It will be recalled that the existence of a positive contribution margin warrants the continuance of operations in the short run even though conventional calculations indicate a loss.

Table 35.1 Income analysis by territories

	Territory 1	Territory 2	Territory 3	Total
Sales	£500,000	£300,000	£100,000	£900,000
Direct costs by territories				
Cost of goods sold	250,000	160,000	40,000	450,000
Transport and outside warehousing	30,000	20,000	10,000	60,000
Regional office expenses	50,000	30,000	20,000	100,000
Salesforce's expenses	25,000	15,000	6,000	46,000
Other regional expenses	15,000	10,000	5,000	30,000
Total direct cost by territories	370,000	235,000	81,000	686,000
Contribution to headquarters' overheads and income	130,000	65,000	19,000	214,000
Indirect costs				
Central administration	50,000	22,000	8,000	80,000
Central warehousing	20,000	8,000	2,000	30,000
Advertising	30,000	15,000	5,000	50,000
Total indirect costs	100,000	45,000	15,000	160,000
Net income	30,000	20,000	4,000	54,000
Percentage of net income	56%	37%	7%	100%
Percentage of sales	56%	33%	11%	100%
Contribution/sales %	26%	22%	19%	24%

Determining the profitability of products

The analysis of the profitability of different products is useful to management in a number of ways. It indicates not only the relative profitability of different products, but also areas of strength and weakness which should be noted in the development of corporate strategy. The application of techniques such as contribution margin analysis may assist in deciding whether or not to drop a product line. Pricing decisions may also be based on profitability analysis.

The selection of appropriate bases for the allocation of indirect costs is always problematical, especially when significant sums of money are involved. In Table 35.1 they come to 17.8 per cent of sales, quite big enough for errors to change management's conclusions about the profitability of territories.

Table 35.2 shows how the analysis of product profitability may be conducted. It indicates that product C is the least profitable product in the product range, for although it makes a contribution of £78,000 to fixed expenses and income, it generates a net loss of £28,000. Management's first task should be to seek reassurance that the fixed expenses have been allocated correctly. It should also investigate why the variable costs of goods sold is so high. However the message is clear. Until a better alternative comes along, product C is significantly better than nothing. In the meantime action should be taken to try and improve its profitability in the future.

Controlling marketing costs

Marketing costs may be classified into order-getting and order-filling costs. The former are associated with such activities as advertising, sales promotion and other selling functions: the latter are incurred after the order has been obtained, and cover such costs as packing, warehousing, delivering and invoicing finished products.

Table 35.2 Profitability analysis by product

| | Product | | | |
	A	B	C	Total
Sales	£350,000	£300,000	£250,000	£900,000
Variable costs of goods sold	90,000	85,000	125,000	300,000
Gross contribution	260,000	215,000	125,000	600,000
Variable marketing costs				
Transport and warehousing	15,000	12,000	13,000	40,000
Office expenses	30,000	30,000	20,000	80,000
Salesforce's salaries	20,000	15,000	10,000	45,000
Other expenses	6,000	5,000	4,000	15,000
Total variable marketing expenses	71,000	62,000	47,000	180,000
Contribution to fixed expenses and income	189,000	153,000	78,000	420,000
Fixed expenses				
Manufacturing	55,000	50,000	45,000	150,000
Administration	30,000	25,000	25,000	80,000
Marketing	50,000	50,000	36,000	136,000
Total fixed costs	135,000	125,000	106,000	366,000
Net income (loss)	£54,000	£28,000	£(28,000)	£54,000
Contribution/Sales %	54%	51%	31%	47%

Order-getting costs

The effectiveness of such costs may only be satisfactorily assessed by relating them to sales revenue. Many factors which affect sales, however, are outside the control of the sales department. For this reason, it is difficult to establish standards of performance that are relevant to the problem of maintaining and increasing the effectiveness of order-getting activities. Budgetary control may be used to determine the limits of expenditure, but it is not possible to use budgetary control methods, such as flexible budgeting in respect of advertising expenses. Flexible budgeting is designed to control expenditure by relating it to changing levels of activity: advertising is incurred in order to increase the level of activity. It would be nonsense, therefore, to attempt to apply flexible budgeting to the control of advertising expenditure.

The search for suitable methods of controlling order-getting costs continues. Objective measures may be too limited in their scope to be useful. Firms are using such objective measures as selling costs per order, selling costs per call, or calls per day to control selling costs. These measures should be used with care, for they do not necessarily reflect difficulties in selling to different markets at different times.

Advertising costs, in particular, involve such large financial commitments that their effectiveness must be assessed. Market research departments are better equipped than accountants to assess the effectiveness of advertising, since its effects go beyond the expansion of immediate sales to helping build the brand.

Order-filling costs

It is somewhat easier to control order-filling costs than order-getting costs, since order-filling costs are associated with internal procedures. These procedures are of a standard form and repetitive nature making them susceptible to standard control methods: the costs of invoicing, packaging and despatching can be controlled by reference to such objective standards as number of invoices dealt with, number and size of packages, etc. Moreover, unlike order-getting costs, flexible budgeting may be applied to the control of order-filling costs, so that more volume justifies more costs. Order-filling costs are also amenable to modelling through ABC.

Example 35.1 Bloxwich Ltd has a sales budget of 100,000 units of its product in the current year. Budgeted delivery costs are based on a standard cost of £1 per unit which are assumed to be strictly variable with volume. If only 80,000 units were sold and delivered by the end of the year at a cost of £90,000, it would be evident that the unfavourable delivery costs variance of £10,000 would require investigation.

Summary

In manufacturing, it is common to distinguish between those costs that are engineered into products and those that are not. The latter comprise the support functions of manufacturing overhead and are frequently a large percentage of total manufacturing costs. There are also a significant amount of activities and costs outside the factory gates. Those beyond the factory gates fall into three categories – administrative, research and development and marketing costs. The support costs of manufacturing and the costs beyond the factory gates are referred to as 'managed' or 'discretionary costs' since they are incurred at the discretion of management. These costs are the only ones found in non-manufacturing industries (banking, hotels, transport, etc.) as there are no engineered costs in these industries.

The difficulty of controlling managed costs is caused by the absence of a method for determining appropriate cost levels, since it is not possible to relate accurately and in financial terms the benefits associated with such costs. Moreover, it is not possible to determine whether a change in managed costs represents an improvement in performance. For example, providing product specifications are maintained, a reduction in manufacturing costs represents an improvement in performance. No such inference may be drawn from a reduction in managed costs.

In view of the rising proportion of managed costs as a percentage of total costs, the analysis and control of such costs is important and means should be found of overcoming the problems caused by the inability to establish rigorous standards.

A number of different methods or tools have been developed to help management make sure that the activities that constitute these managed costs are necessary and are being performed efficiently.

Self-assessment questions

1 What do you understand by managed costs?

2 Explain the problems implied in the control of managed costs.

3 Examine the process of budgetary control as applied to managed costs.

4 Discuss the problems associated with the control of administrative costs.

5 Review the problems of controlling research and development costs.

6 Indicate some of the considerations implied in the control of marketing costs.

7 Review three perpectives from which marketing costs may be analysed.

References

Byrum, A.J. (1990) The right way to control period expense, *Management Accounting* (UK), September.

Loch, C.H. (2008) *Mobilizing an R&D Organization Through Strategy Cascading*, Industrial Research Institute, Inc.

Miller, J.G. and Vollman, T.E. (1985) The hidden factory, *HBR*, September–October, pp. 142–150.

Nimocks, S.P. Rosiello, R.L. and Wright, O. (2005) Managing overhead costs, *The McKinsey Quarterly*, No. 2, 106.

CHAPTER 36

Capital investment decisions

Setting the scene

It needs to be stressed that the very features of the traditional accounting model, which make it appropriate as a basis for measuring short-term performance, make it totally inappropriate as a basis for making decisions affecting long-term financial health. Financial managers are concerned, not with the static concept of whether or not a profit can be declared on the basis of a selected convection of capital maintenance, but with the dynamic one of whether enough wealth will be created to justify the commitment of funds necessary to support the aspirations of the enterprise. Specifically, their quantifications of their team's judgements are likely to be expressed in terms of projected cash flows, discounted at the cost of capital.

(Allen, 1992)

Learning objectives

After studying this chapter you should be able to:

1 explain what is meant by a capital investment decision and why it is important;

2 compute the payback period and accounting rate of return for a proposed investment and explain their role in capital investment decisions;

3 compute the present value of future cash flows;

4 use net present value analysis to determine whether an investment is acceptable;

5 use the internal rate of return to assess the acceptability of an investment;

6 explain the impact of inflation on the capital investment decision;

7 appreciate the problem of high-tech investments.

Probably the most significant factor affecting the level of profitability in a business is the quality of managerial decisions affecting the commitment of the firm's resources to new investments within the firm. The reasons which render such strategic decisions so important are:

1 They involve the commitment of substantial sums of money.

2 This commitment is made for a long period of time, and the element of uncertainty is therefore much greater than in the case of decisions whose effects are limited to a short period of time.

3 Once made, capital investment decisions are almost impossible to reverse should they appear subsequently to have been wrongly made.

4 Occasionally, the success or the failure of a firm may depend upon a single decision. In all cases, the future profitability of the firm will be affected by the decision.

5 Not only is capital expenditure policy of major importance to a firm, but it is of great significance to an industry as well as to the national economy.

Types of capital investment decisions

A capital investment may be defined as an investment which yields returns during several future time periods, and may be contrasted with other types of investments which yield all their return in the current time period. Capital investment decisions may concern the following:

1 The acquisition or replacement of long-lived assets, such as buildings and plant.

2 The investment of funds into another firm from which revenues will flow.

3 A special project which will affect the firm's future earning capacity, such as a research project or an advertising campaign.

4 The extension of the range of activities of the firm involving a capital outlay, such as a new production line or indeed a new product.

Capital investment decisions encompass two aspects of long-range profitability. First, estimating the future net increases in cash inflows or net savings in cash outlays which will result from the investment. Second, calculating the total cash outlays required to effect the investment.

The analysis of capital investment proposals

In the analysis of capital investment proposals, many of the important facts are uncertain. The first problem is to reduce the area of uncertainty before a decision is made. The second problem is to ensure that all known facts are correctly assessed and quantified. Both known and uncertain facts are estimated in cash terms, and methods of capital investment appraisal focus on cash flows.

The selection of investment projects involves choosing between alternative ways of using the firm's scarce capital. This is done by quantifying the cash inflows and the cash outlays of the various alternatives and then discounting them.

Example 36.1   Wall Street Finance Ltd is offered the opportunity of selecting two investments, each of which will yield £500,000 yearly. Investment A requires a total cash outlay of £5,000,000 – hence it promises a rate of return of 10 per cent. Investment B requires a total cash outlay of £50,000,000 – and therefore offers a rate of return of 1 per cent per annum. The firm would prefer investment A. However, if the firm has a minimum acceptable rate of return of 15 per cent, neither project would be acceptable.

We may conclude, therefore, that there are four major factors affecting capital investment decisions:

1 The net amount of the investment required, expressed as the total cash outlay needed to support the project during its entire life.

2 The net returns on the investment, expressed as the future expected net cash inflows.

3 These may be actual cash flows, or cash savings.

4 The rate of return on investment, expressed as a percentage. The determination of the lowest acceptable rate of return on investment will be influenced by a number of factors, among which are the firm's rate of return on its other investment opportunities and the cost of capital to the firm.

The relevant cash flows

Before we proceed to examine the methods of selecting investment projects, let us briefly define the meaning of the terms which we shall be employing.

Net investment outlays

These consist of initial investment outlays required to establish the project, and any subsequent investment outlays which are envisaged at the outset, and are distinguishable from operating cash outlays. Thus, initial investment outlays may comprise expenditure on equipment, installation costs, training, working capital, etc. Subsequent investment outlays may include 'second stage' developments, plant extensions, etc. The analysis of a capital project is in terms of net cash costs to the firm, so that where tax credits are allowable, these credits must be deducted from the total cash costs to obtain the relevant cash outlay.

Net cash inflows

These are the operating cash flows associated with the investment over the period of its useful life. They are calculated after deducting operating cash expenditure and taxation. Since there may be year-to-year variation in the profile of these net cash flows, and since their periodic pattern is not known with certainty, they are the most difficult cash flows to quantify.

All cash flow calculations are made over the estimated useful life of the investment, which is defined as the time interval between the acquisition or commencement and the time at which the combined forces of obsolescence and deterioration justify the retirement of the asset or project. The useful life of the investment may be shortened by market changes which will diminish its earnings.

Methods of appraising capital investments

The more commonly used methods of evaluating capital investment proposals are:

1 The payback period.

2 The accounting rate of return.

3 The discounted cash flow (DCF) techniques, of which there are two main forms:
  (a) the net present value method (NPV);
  (b) the internal rate of return (IRR).

The payback period

This method calculates how long it will take for the expected net cash inflows to pay back the net investment outlays. The payback period is calculated as follows:

$$\text{payback period (years)} = \frac{\text{net investment outlays}}{\text{average net cash inflows}}$$

Example 36.2 Northend Engineering Co Ltd is considering the acquisition of machinery which will considerably reduce labour costs. The following are the relevant facts:

Net investment outlays	£200,000
Estimated annual cash savings (after tax)	60,000
Estimated useful life	5 years
Salvage value	nil

The payback period is as follows:

$$\frac{£200,000}{60,000} \text{ i.e. } 3\frac{1}{3} \text{ years}$$

The payback method has the advantage of simplicity. By advocating the selection of projects by reference only to the speed with which investment outlays are recovered, it recommends the acceptance of only the safest projects. It is a method which emphasizes liquidity rather than profitability, and is really a measure of risk rather than return. Its limitations are:

1 It lays stress on the payback period rather than the useful life of the investment, and ignores the cash flows beyond the payback period. Any salvage value or decommissioning costs are ignored. Hence, it focuses on breaking even rather than on profitability.
2 It ignores the pattern of cash flows before the payback period, attaching the same weight irrespective of when it occurred. This method therefore treats all cash flows through time as having the same value, so that in the example given, the value of £200,000 invested now is equated with £200,000 of net cash inflows over $3\frac{1}{2}$ years.

These problems may be illustrated as follows.

Example 36.3 Multiplexed Ltd is considering four different investment projects each costing £20,000. The following information relates to these projects:

Project No.	1	2	3	4
	£	£	£	£
Initial investment outlay	20,000	20,000	20,000	20,000
Cash inflows				
Year 1	9,000	11,000	3,000	10,000
Year 2	11,000	9,000	6,000	6,000
Year 3	–	–	8,000	4,000
Year 4	–	–	10,000	4,000
Year 5	–	–	10,000	3,000
Payback period (years)	2	2	$3\frac{1}{3}$	3

A crude application of the payback method would select projects 1 or 2 but would be unable to decide between these two projects. Moreover payback ignores that project 3 has inflows of £37,000 and 4 of £27,000.

The accounting rate of return

The accounting rate of return method expresses the average estimated yearly net income as a percentage of the net investment outlays. Instead of deriving net income from the profit and loss statement, it can also be calculated by subtracting depreciation from yearly net cash inflows. This is the approach adopted here. The formula is expressed as follows:

$$R = \frac{C - D}{I}$$

where R = the accounting rate of return
C = average yearly net cash inflows
D = depreciation
I = net investment outlays

Substituting the figures given in Example 36.2, the accounting rate of return would be calculated as follows:

$$R = \frac{£60,000 - £40,000}{£200,000} \times 100$$

$$= 10\%$$

It may be argued, however, that the recovery of depreciation over the useful life of the investment reduces the value of the net investment outlays through time. Assuming an average depreciation expense of £40,000 per year, the average net investment over the estimated useful life of five years is £100,000, calculated from the arithmetic mean as follows:

$$\text{Average lifetime investment} = \frac{£200,000}{2}$$

$$= £100,000$$

The average lifetime investment may be calculated graphically as shown in Figure 36.1.

In the light of this argument, the accounting rate of return on investment should express the annual net cash inflows minus the annual depreciation charge as a percentage of the average annual net investment outlays, so that, substituting the values given in our example, the average return on investment is:

$$R = \frac{£60,000 - £40,000}{£100,000} \times 100\%$$

$$= 20\%$$

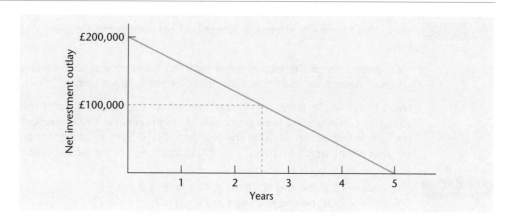

Figure 36.1

This method of evaluating investment projects overcomes the disadvantage of the payback method in that it attempts to calculate the profitability of the various projects under study over their entire life. Its main disadvantage is that it fails to consider the time value of money; i.e. it treats the value of £1 in the future as equal to £1 today. Moreover, it also ignores differences in the annual net cash inflows (by averaging them). In both these senses, it suffers from the same defects as the payback method. Furthermore, there is a lack of agreement about a single method of calculating the accounting rate of return.

Discounted cash flows

The methods of investment appraisal we have just examined are generally regarded as producing misleading results in terms of decisions to accept and reject projects and the order in which accepted projects should be ranked. The DCF method has gained widespread acceptance, for it recognizes that the value of money is subject to a time preference, that is, £1 today is preferred to £1 in the future. The principal reason for this preference is what Irving Fisher, the American economist, called 'impatience' and John Maynard Keynes 'liquidity preference'. The possession of a sum of money today provides choices of when to spend and on what to spend it. Money to be received in the future means foregoing those choices until a later date. This delay in consumption has a price; we need to be compensated for it. Notice that this compensation has nothing to do with inflation, nor with risk. There is an inflation-free, risk-free rate of interest. Inflation and risk are additional to it.

In simple terms, the DCF method attempts to evaluate an investment proposal by comparing the present value of the net cash flows accruing over the life of the investment with the value of funds about to be invested. Thus, by comparing cash flows that have been adjusted for the time value of money it is possible to calculate the rate of return on the investment in a realistic manner.

To find the present equivalent value of £1 receivable one year hence, one applies the rate of interest to discount £1 to its present value. This is the same thing as asking 'what sum of money invested today at the rate of interest would increase in value to £1 a year hence?'

Example 36.4 Given that the rate of interest is 10 per cent per annum the following calculations may be made:

£1 invested now at 10 per cent will amount to £1.10 in a year. Conversely, the value of £1.10 a year's hence is worth £1 now if the rate of interest is 10 per cent.

Using this principle, tables may be constructed for the value of £1 over several time periods ahead by compounding the interest rate through time, i.e. £1.00 invested for 1 year at 10 per cent will be worth £1.10 at the year end, £1.10 then reinvested for another year at 10 per cent will be worth £1.10 + 0.11 = £1.21 at the end of the second year.

Example 36.5 The value of £1 at the end of 1 year at 10% is (£1+ 0.10) = £1.1
The value of £1 at the end of 2 years at 10% is $(£1.1)^2 = £1.21$
The value of £1 at the end of 3 years at 10% is $(£1.1)^3 = £1.331$
The value of £1 at the end of 4 years at 10% is $(£1.1)^4 = £1.464$
The value of £1 at the end of 5 years at 10% is $(£1.1)^5 = £1.611$

Conversely, the present value of £1 receivable at a future date is as follows:

£1 receivable in 1 years' time is	$\dfrac{£1}{1.1}$	=£0.9091
£1 receivable in 2 years' time is	$\dfrac{£1}{1.21}$	=£0.8264
£1 receivable in 3 years' time is	$\dfrac{£1}{1.331}$	=£0.7513
£1 receivable in 4 years' time is	$\dfrac{£1}{1.464}$	=£0.6831
£1 receivable in 5 years' time is	$\dfrac{£1}{1.611}$	=£0.6208

The value of money is, therefore, directly affected by time, and the rate of interest is the method used to express how the passage of time affects it. Compound interest tables and discount tables are available which show the value of money at different interest rates over a number of years, making it a simple matter to apply the DCF method to the evaluation of an investment.

The net present value

This method is based on an assumed minimum rate of return acceptable to the investor. Ideally, this rate should be the average cost of capital to the firm (see p. 601 below) and it is this rate which would be used to discount the net cash inflows to their present value. The net investment outlays at the beginning of the project are subtracted from the present value of the net cash inflows leaving a residual figure, which is the net present value. A decision is made in favour of a project if the NPV is positive. The method is universal being applicable to all investment decisions.

The rule may be stated as follows:

Accept the project if:

$$\frac{a_1}{(1+i)^1} + \frac{a_2}{(1+i)^2} + \ldots + \frac{a_n}{(1+i)^n} > A$$

where A is the initial project cost
a are the net annual cash inflows
i is the cost of capital (or interest rate)
n is the expected life of the project

Example 36.6   Corween Ltd is considering a project which has a life of five years and which will produce an annual inflow of £1,000. The investment outlay is £3,000 and the required rate of return is 10 per cent.

Year	Inflow	Discount factor (at 10%)	Present value of inflow
1	£1,000	0.9091	£909.1
2	£1,000	0.8264	£826.4
3	£1,000	0.7513	£751.3
4	£1,000	0.6831	£683.1
5	£1,000	0.6208	£620.8
Present value of net inflows			£3,790.7
Cost of investment outlay			£3,000.0
Net present value of the project			£790.7

Since the net present value of the cash inflows (a) is greater than the present value of the cash outlay (A), the project should be accepted.

The internal rate of return

This method requires us to calculate the rate of interest which reduces the net present value of a project to zero. This enables us to compare the internal rate of return (IRR) with the required rate (sometimes called the cut-off rate).

The rule may be stated as follows:

Accept the project if the solution to the following equation:

$$A = \frac{a_1}{(1+r)} + \frac{a_2}{(1+r)^2} + \ldots + \frac{a_n}{(1+r)^n}$$

and $r > i$
where A is the initial project cost
a are the net annual cash inflows
r is the solution discount rate
i is the required rate of return

Example 36.7 Let us return to the example given above and assume that Corween Ltd applies the internal rate of return analysis to the project under consideration. The analysis would be as follows:

Year	Inflow	Discount factor at 19%	Present value at 19%	Discount factor at 20%	Present value at 20%
	£		£		£
1	1,000	0.8403	840.3	0.8333	833.3
2	1,000	0.7062	706.2	0.6944	694.4
3	1,000	0.5934	593.4	0.5787	578.7
4	1,000	0.4987	498.7	0.4823	482.3
5	1,000	0.4190	419.0	0.4019	401.9
Present value of net inflow			3,057.6		2,990.6
Cost of investment outlay			3,000.0		3,000.0
Net present value of the project			+ 57.6		– 9.4

We can see that the IRR is almost 20 per cent. (It is possible to approximate the true rate more closely by assuming a linear relationship and interpolating between the two nearest points.) We now compare the project's IRR with the required rate of return on investment by the company. If the cut-off rate is 15 per cent, then the project should be accepted.

Net present value and internal rate of return compared

When dealing with simple investment appraisal projects, that is, those involving a once-and-for-all investment outlay followed by a stream of cash inflows, both the NPV and the IRR methods produce the same YES or NO decisions. While these simple projects do exist, it is much more common for firms to be confronted by a series of projects from which to choose.

The NPV method has a number of characteristics that make it superior to IRR. We will leave detailed discussion to corporate finance texts, but give a brief summary here.

1 *NPV gives a result in monetary amounts.* While percentages may be familiar and intuitively appealing, the IRR contains significant traps for the unwary, discussed below. The advantage of NPV's monetary amount is that it is easy to interpret (a positive number is good news, negative bad).

2 *NPVs of different projects are additive.* Provided the different projects use the same discount rate their NPVs can be added. IRRs are not additive, if a project is modified in any way the percentage rate has to be recalculated.

3 *NPVs measure the impact of a project on the value of a firm.* Since the value of a firm is the present value of its expected future cash flows, the present value of any new project measures the amount by which the value will change as a result of the project.

4 *Traps with IRR.* There are four pitfalls associated with the use of the IRR. They can all be finessed if caught in time but require constant vigilance.

   (i)   There are circumstances in which the IRR method produces more than one result. While the circumstances are well known, working out whether it matters is tedious, correcting it is time consuming and explaining what you have done to capital expenditure appropriation committees is difficult. Moreover, when it does occur the results are not nearly the same, they are wildly different. For the curious, there is one IRR for every change of sign in the sequence of annual cash flows.

(ii) The interpretation of an IRR depends on whether it involves borrowing or lending (what is the sign of the initial cash flow?). If we are borrowing money low rates of interest are good news; conversely if we are lending high rates are good news. The issue here is not the calculation of the IRR but its interpretation.

(iii) Management is frequently faced with choice of the best way of doing something: labour intensive versus capital intensive, big lorry versus two smaller lorries, etc. These are mutually exclusive investments: management must choose one and refuse the other. In these circumstances the IRR rule can be misleading. Suppose one project has a higher IRR, the other a higher NPV, both are acceptable. Here intuition comes to our help: a large percentage return on a small amount of money is not as interesting as smaller, but acceptable, returns on larger sums of money – we spend cash, not per cents. In these situations the rule is simple: either go with the NPV on the individual projects, or calculate the IRR on the incremental cash flows of the larger project minus the smaller one.

(iv) The IRR assumes that the opportunity cost of capital is the same for all time periods. However, when short-term rates are lower than long-term rates (the normal situation according to the term structure of interest rates) then the IRR rule can lead us astray.

Example 36.8 Norwell Industries Ltd is studying two projects, each of which requires a net investment outlay of £3,000. Both have a useful life of five years, and the estimated profile of the net cash inflows is:

End of year	Project A	Project B
	£	£
1	500	2,000
2	1,000	1,500
3	1,500	1,500
4	2,000	1,000
5	2,000	500
	£7,000	£6,500

The desired minimum rate of return is 10 per cent.

Analysis – net present value

The present value of the two projects may be calculated by using the desired minimum rate of return as a discount factor.

End of year	Discount factor 10%	Project A	Present value	Project B	Present value
		£	£	£	£
1	0.9091	500	454.6	2,000	1,818.2
2	0.8264	1,000	826.4	1,500	1,239.6
3	0.7153	1,500	1,073.0	1,500	1,073.0
4	0.6830	2,000	1,366.0	1,000	683.0
5	0.6209	2,000	1,241.8	500	310.5
Present value of total cash inflows			£4,961.8		£5,124.3
Less: Net investment outlay			£3,000.0		£3,000.0
Net present value			£1,961.8		£2,124.3

Both projects are acceptable to the firm, and if a choice has to be made between them, Project B would be selected since it produces the highest net present value. The time profile of the net cash inflows is seen to be a determining influence on the result, for although the total cash inflows before discounting are higher with Project A (£7,000), the cash flows associated with Project B (£6,500) are concentrated in the earlier years and, when discounted, have a higher net present value than A's.

Analysis – the internal rate of return

For Project A, the rate which will discount the net cash inflows to £3,000 is found once again by trial and error. Using discount tables, we find that the discount rate lies between 28 per cent and 29 per cent, as follows:

Cash inflows	Discount factor at 29%	Present value at 29%	Discount factor at 28%	Present value at 28%
£		£		£
500	0.7752	387.7	0.7813	390.7
1,000	0.6009	600.9	0.6104	610.4
1,500	0.4658	698.7	0.4768	715.2
2,000	0.3611	722.2	0.3725	745.0
2,000	0.2799	559.8	0.2910	582.0
Original investment outlay		£2,969.3		£3,043.3
		£3,000.0		£3,000.0
		– 30.7		+ 43.3

Using the same approach, the IRR for Project B is 39 per cent.

   The crucial test upon which the final acceptance of a project depends is whether or not the IRR compares favourably with the required rate of return. If the required rate of return is 20 per cent then both projects qualify.

One of the problems of comparing rates of return on projects is that direct comparisons between two percentages are meaningless unless referred to the initial outlays, so that their true dimensions may be perceived. The best way of handling these scale differences is to calculate their respective NPVs.

With more complicated investment problems, for example those which require that cash surpluses be set aside to meet an obligation arising at the end of the project's life, both methods assume that those cash surpluses are reinvested at the appropriate rate of return. Thus, where a loan has been raised to finance the project, the IRR method envisages that the cash surpluses will be reinvested at the IRR, whereas the NPV method envisages that they will be reinvested at the minimum acceptable rate of return used in that method. (The simplifying assumption which we are making for the purpose of illustrating the point is that the firm's finances are linked to specific investment projects, which in reality is not perhaps the case.) In these situations the NPV method makes more realistic assumptions about reinvestment opportunities.

More complex problems arise when applying the IRR method to investment projects which do not have the simple pattern of cash flows of the above examples, but we regard these problems as beyond the scope of this text.

Taxation and other factors

In order that DCF calculations should lead to correct results, it is important that all factors affecting the calculations of cash flows should be taken into account. One important factor is taxation. Indeed, we have assumed from the outset that the cash flow figures were net after tax. Apart from the direct effects of taxation, we should also adjust figures for indirect aspects of taxation, such as investment grants, and the reader will recall that in calculating the net investment outlay, any recoveries in the form of investment incentives must be deducted from the amount brought into the DCF calculation. The effects of these incentives vary from project to project.

The cost of capital

The evaluation of an investment project by DCF analysis requires a firm to calculate its cost of capital. This is true in selecting the discount rate for appraisal by means of the net present value method, or for establishing the acceptability of the internal rate of return.

A full discussion of the concept of the 'cost of capital' is beyond the scope of this book; indeed, the subject is perhaps the most difficult and controversial topic in the whole theory of finance. Our discussion will be elementary, but adequate to provide the reader with some understanding of investment planning.

The first problem in discussing the cost of capital lies in different meanings which the term has acquired. From a lender's point of view, the cost of capital represents the cost to them of lending money which may be equated to the return they could have obtained by investing in a similar project having similar risks. This concept of the cost of capital is founded on its 'opportunity cost'. The opportunity cost approach to the assessment of the cost of capital is one which a firm must always consider when evaluating an investment project. A firm may find, for example, that investing funds outside the firm may produce higher returns than an internal project.

The main obstacle to a more widespread use of the opportunity cost concept is that of identifying investments of equal risks that can be used as a benchmark.

Another concept in use is the actual cost incurred by a firm in securing access to capital. A firm may obtain funds in a variety of ways, and each way has a different cost attached to it. Here we are only going to consider two ways: it can raise capital by issuing debt or equity. The cost of debt is the interest it incurs and that of equity the dividend payments. The cost of capital is the weighted average of the amounts from these two sources of finance.

Thus, the weighted average cost of capital, or WACC as it is known, can be written:

$$\text{WACC} = \text{Cost of debt} \times \frac{\text{Amount of debt}}{\text{Debt + Equity}} + \text{Cost of equity} \times \frac{\text{Amount of equity}}{\text{Debt + Equity}}$$

Since interest is tax deductible, its cost must be expressed on an after-tax basis by multiplying the cost by $(1 - T_c)$, where T_c is the corporate tax rate.

$$\begin{aligned}
\text{If} \quad & D = \text{amount of debt} \quad \text{and } k_D = \text{cost of debt} \\
\text{And} \quad & E = \text{amount of equity} \quad \text{and } k_E = \text{cost of equity}
\end{aligned}$$

$$\text{WACC} = k_D (1 - T_C) \frac{D}{D + E} + k_E \frac{E}{D + E}$$

When working out the weighted average cost of capital, it is important to use market, not book, values and we are concerned with target future capital structures and not historical ones.

Estimating the cost of debt is relatively simple: look up market rates for companies in the same sector, with a similar geographic spread of business and the same credit rating and compare with the information contained in the annual report of the company in question. It is possible that the historical numbers are a reasonable approximation of current market conditions. Good places to go to look for information are: *The Wall Street Journal*, *The Financial Times* and the site www.nasdbondinfo.com.

The cost of equity is more complex. We give one, relatively simple, method here: the reader is strongly advised to consult a finance text on the subject.

In theory the price of a share (P_0) is the present value of the stream of dividends $(\text{Div}_1, \text{Div}_2, \text{etc.})$ discounted at shareholders' required rate of return (k_E):

$$P_0 = \frac{\text{Div}_1}{(1 + k_E)^1} + \frac{\text{Div}_2}{(1 + k_E)^2} + \frac{\text{Div}_3}{(1 + k_E)^3} + \dots$$

If the dividend stream is constant in perpetuity, this can be simplified to:

$$P_0 = \frac{\text{Div}_1}{k_E}$$

The advantage of this formula is that it eliminates the requirement to forecast dividends for an infinite period – a tedious and thankless task.

If instead of being constant, dividends were to grow at a constant rate the formula becomes:

$$P_0 = \frac{\text{Div}_1}{k_E - g}$$

Since the current share price (P_0), recent earnings and dividend policy are all known, it is relatively easy to estimate the next dividend payment (Div_1), the formula can be used to calculate the required rate of return of shareholders. This is done by expressing k_E as a function of the other variables:

$$k_E = \frac{Div_1}{P_0} + g$$

It must be emphasized that this formula makes some heroic assumptions: the next dividend can be estimated with reasonable accuracy, the current share price reflects neither exuberance nor despair, and that dividends will grow at a constant rate for eternity. There are not many companies for which these would be remotely plausible: the obvious exception is utility companies, especially in regulated markets, such as water, gas and electricity. For companies not part of this select band other methods must be used for determining the cost of equity.

Example 36.9 Suppose a large multinational company has 1,382,000,000 shares and the current share price is $129.88. It also has $52,249,000,000 of interest bearing liabilities (debt) at a weighted average interest rate of 3.97 per cent.

Equity 1,382,000,000 shares at $129.88 gives $179,494 m
Debt $52,249 m at a weighted average rate of 3.97%
Corporate tax rate 28%
Dividends per share in 2008 $1.90
Growth rate in dividends 10.57%

Cost of equity

$$k_E = \frac{1.90}{129.88} + 10.57\%$$

$$k_F = 12.03\%$$

The weighted average cost of capital is:

$$WACC = 3.97\% \ (1 - 0.28) \left[\frac{52,249m}{52,249 \ m + 179,494m} \right] + 12.03 \left[\frac{179,494m}{52,249 + 179,494m} \right]$$

$$WACC = 9.96\%$$

Leverage and the cost of capital

It will be recalled from Part 2 that the distribution of a firm's capital structure as between equity and debt is known as the leverage. A firm which is highly leveraged has a higher ratio of fixed-interest debt to equity capital. By changing its leverage, a firm will alter its average cost of capital.

Example 36.10 Suppose that the share price is at its 52 week low of $79.68 and the debt amounts to $75,000m and the weighted average rate is 3.97 per cent. The weighted average cost of capital then becomes:

$$k_E = \frac{190}{79.68} + 10.57\%$$

$$k_E = 12.95\%$$

$$\text{WACC} = 3.97\% \, (1 - 0.28) \left[\frac{75,000 \text{ m}}{75,000m + 110,117m} \right] + 12.95\% \left[\frac{110,117m}{75,000m + 110,117m} \right]$$

$$\text{WACC} = 8.86\%$$

The change is in the right direction, but perhaps not as big as we might have expected. Debt is cheaper than equity, because the interest rate is lower and is then lowered even further by being tax deductible.

It should be noted that financial theorists have argued that it is due only to the influence of a corporation tax system which allows loan interest as a tax deductible expense that leverage is of any significance. However, this ignores the risks and costs of bankruptcy, which complicate matters.

Financial planning requires a firm to give very serious consideration to its capital structure and to its leverage. Very complex issues are involved in planning an appropriate capital structure. Circumstances may make it advantageous to attempt to increase the proportion of debt, that is increase the leverage, such as the tax deductibility of loan interest which we have already mentioned. There is an upper limit to debt finance, however, for not only are there obvious dangers in the presence of large fixed-interest charges against corporate income, but there are practical limits to the amount of funds which may be borrowed for long-term purposes.

Investment appraisal and inflation

As the cash flows associated with a particular project may span a considerable period of time, it is evident that the level of inflation during that time will affect considerably the profitability of the project. We pointed out in Chapter 17 that estimates of future events should take inflation into account, and in Chapter 29 the distinction between general price level and specific price changes was discussed. We indicated the need to adjust cash flow forecasts for specific price changes which would affect the enterprise, so as to maintain its operating capability. Accordingly, it is the inflation adjusted cost of specific items which are to be taken into account in investment appraisal. The cost of these specific items will be subject to different inflation rates, as will the prices of the products which will depend on the specific items that make up their costs. In effect, the existence of a lag between increases in cost and increases in prices may considerably reduce the profitability of a project under conditions of inflation. As the rate of inflation increases, so this problem becomes more acute. For this reason, firms entering into fixed-price contracts extending over a long period of time should arrange for cost-escalation clauses to mitigate the impact of inflation.

The most appropriate method of incorporating the effects of inflation into DCF calculations is to adjust cash flow forecasts for specific price increases. Such adjusted cash flows are then discounted by the inflation adjusted cost of capital.

Example 36.11 In the earlier example (p. 597), Corween Ltd had annual net cash flows of £1,000 for a period of five years, and the discount rate was given as 10 per cent. It may now be assumed that the annual net cash flows were derived as follows:

	£	£
Cash inflows from sales		5,000
Cash outflows:		
Materials	3,000	
Labour	1,000	
		4,000
Annual net cash flow		1,000

The impact of inflation is considered in the following terms:

1 Sales revenues are expected to be adjusted for price changes at the rate of 15 per cent per annum.
2 Material costs are expected to increase at the rate of 18 per cent per annum.
3 Labour costs are expected to increase at the rate of 10 per cent per annum.

	Annual rate of change	Year 1	Year 2	Year 3	Year 4	Year 5
	%	£	£	£	£	£
Sales revenue	15	5,750	6,613	7,605	8,746	10,058
Materials	18	3,540	4,177	4,929	5,816	6,863
Labour	10	1,100	1,210	1,331	1,464	1,610
Net cash flows (adjusted)		4,640	5,387	6,260	7,280	8,473
		1,110	1,226	1,345	1,466	1,585

These annual expected future net cash flows may now be discounted at the appropriate discount rate. For simplicity, if it is assumed that the discount rate is 10 per cent, these annual net cash flows have a present value of £5,017, as follows:

Year	Net cash flow	Discount factor at 10%	Present value
	£	%	£
1	1,110	0.9091	1,009
2	1,226	0.8264	1,013
3	1,345	0.7513	1,010
4	1,466	0.6831	1,001
5	1,585	0.6208	984
			5,017
Less: Initial investment outlay			3,000
Net present value of the project			2,017

The foregoing example shows the manner in which inflation adds a new dimension to the problem of calculating present values. More calculations are involved, and the degree of uncertainty is increased. Many accountants feel that, under conditions of rapid and high inflation, the task of forecasting cash flows over the lifetime of a project covering several years seems somewhat academic. Research suggests that the payback method is popular when inflation or uncertainty is high. When times are normal, IRR is the most popular, closely followed by NPV, payback is a distant third.

High-tech investments

Many of the long-term strategic effects of investing in advanced manufacturing technology (AMT) in a technologically competitive and changing production environment are simply not known or are very difficult to identify. As such, strategic considerations do not readily lend themselves to traditional capital investment appraisal. In many situations, strategic positioning becomes an overriding consideration. For example, if one company in an industry adopts AMT that enables it to offer greater product heterogeneity, more customized service, greater product liability and shorter lead time, it is likely that the others will follow suit irrespective of what their discounted cash flow models say. If they do not adopt the technology they will cease to be players in the marketplace.

A second item of consideration in regard to high-tech investments is that such projects are not free-standing, i.e. many high-tech investments are interrelated, integrated parts of a whole and should not be viewed as individual projects. Many benefits will invariably appear in departments other than where the investment is made. As they were not forecast or quantified in the original project proposal, when they do occur sometime later, they will appear as an unplanned variance which will not be attributed to the project.

Third, qualitative benefits may outweigh quantitative factors in advanced technology investment decisions. These intangibles are numerous. Beyond its quantifiable labour savings, AMT, for example, may lead to improved design and fewer product parts. The former would improve revenues and the latter production costs and product reliability. While these numbers are very difficult to quantify, they are probably more material then the actual labour cost savings.

Following Chalos (1992) quantitative and qualitative capital investment decisions are summarized in Figure 36.2. Once the numbers indicate whether or not an investment is worth while, qualitative factors should be addressed, in conjunction with the strategic implications for the firm.

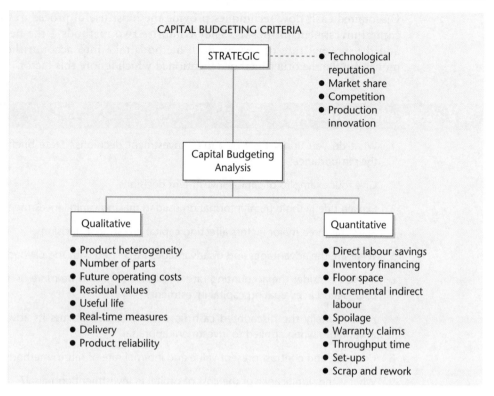

Figure 36.2

Summary

Preparing the capital expenditure plan is part of the long-range planning process. The quality of managerial decisions committing the firm's resources to new investments is probably the most significant factor affecting the level of future profitability.

Capital investment decisions encompass two aspects of the long-range profit plan – first, estimating the future net increases in cash inflows or net savings in cash outlays which will result from an investment; second, calculating the total cash outlays required to carry out an investment.

There are three well-known techniques for appraising investment proposals from a financial viewpoint:

1 *the payback method*, which emphasizes the length of time required to recoup the investment outlay;
2 *the accounting rate of return*, which seeks to express the average estimated yearly net inflows as a percentage of the net investment outlays for the purpose of assessing the profitability of a proposed investment;
3 *discounted cash flow methods*, which evaluate an investment proposal by comparing the present value of the net cash inflows accruing over the life of the investment with the present value of the funds to be invested.

Discounted cash flow techniques provide the most useful procedures for evaluating capital investment proposals. They comprise two methods – the net present value and the internal rate of return. Both methods take into account the time value of money, unlike the other methods mentioned which ignore this factor.

Self-assessment questions

1 What do you understand by capital investment decisions? State briefly the reason for their importance.

2 Give four examples of capital investment decisions.

3 Explain briefly the type of information used in making capital investment decisions.

4 State the three major factors affecting capital investment decisions.

5 What are the advantages and disadvantages associated with the payback period?

6 Do you consider the accounting rate of return method to be more useful than the payback period in evaluating capital investment?

7 Explain briefly the discounted cash flow method, and discuss its advantages and disadvantages when applied to investment appraisal.

8 Compare and contrast present value and internal rate of return methods.

9 What is the significance of the cost of capital in investment appraisal?

10 Suggest possible ways in which inflation may be taken into account in making capital investment decisions.

Problems (*indicates that a solution is to be found in the Lecturer's Guide)

1 The purchase of a machine is contemplated and the relevant facts concerning two possible choices are as follows:

	Machine A	Machine B
Capital expenditure required	£50,000	£60,000
Estimated life – years	3	4
Residual value	nil	nil
Cash flow after taxation – constant each year at	£25,000	£24,000

Assume a rate of interest of 10 per cent for which the reciprocals are:

Year 1	0.9091	Year 2	0.8264
Year 3	0.7513	Year 4	0.6830

Required:

Set out calculations illustrating and comparing the following methods of evaluating the return from these investments:

(a) payback period;
(b) accounting rate of return;
(c) discounted cash flow.

Comment on the results.

2 Jazz Ltd is considering replacing three of its record-pressing machines with one machine which has just come on to the market. The three existing machines are two years old and cost £1,500 each. They are being depreciated on a straight-line basis over twelve years. It was expected that their final scrap value would be £600 each. Their replacement is being considered because a fault has developed in their operation which can only be corrected at a total cost of £5,000 for the three machines. The current second-hand market value of the machines is £1,000 each.

The annual operating costs of the existing and new machines are as follows:

Existing machines: costs per machine

	£
Materials	60,000
Labour: one operator at 1800 hours	1,350
Variable expenses	925
Maintenance (excluding exceptional items)	2,000
Fixed expenses:	
Depreciation 75	
Fixed overheads absorbed 2,700	2,775

New machine

	£
Materials	162,000
Labour: two operators at 1,500 hours 3,000	
one assistant at 1,500 hours 900	3,900
Variable expenses	2,275
Maintenance	4,500
Fixed expenses:	
Depreciation 9,550	
Fixed overheads absorbed 7,800	17,350

The new machine's estimated life is 10 years and it will cost £100,000.

The company's cost of capital is 10 per cent.

Required:

(a) Advise the management of Jazz Ltd on the most profitable course of action to undertake.

(b) Comment on the method you have used and the other factors which might influence the decision.

3 Barry has invented an electronic executive toy which can be activated to emit various noises on selection of one of six buttons. The toy is pocket-sized and it is anticipated that it will retail for £10. Barry is keen to exploit the toy and with the help of his business partner, Bryn, they consider the following possibilities:

(i) Sell the exclusive rights to the game to a major toy manufacturer for £110,000.

(ii) Sell the rights to the manufacturer for £10,000 but receive an annual payment of £35,000 for the next five years (the payment being made at the end of each year).

(iii) Set up a manufacturing and selling operation. The best estimates for the next five years are:
   – Initial capital expenditure: £30,000.
   – Residual value at the end of year 5: £5,000.
   – Net working capital required to start up: £10,000.

Year	Sales (units)	Sale price/ unit	Variable costs/ unit	Fixed costs p.a.*
1	20,000	£10	£8	£45,000
2	40,000	£10	£8	£45,000
3	100,000	£10	£8	£45,000
4	60,000	£10	£8	£45,000
5	40,000	£10	£8	£45,000

Note: Including depreciation of £5,000 p.a.

Required:

(a) Evaluate the proposals, given that the required rate of return is 20 per cent, and recommend the optimum proposal. Justify the reasons for your selection.

(b) What factors would influence your choice of a required rate of return?

(c) Would you advise the use of the cash payback method? Justify your answer with appropriate calculations.

4* David and Ruth are the joint owners of Whirlow Farm with an average turnover of £180,000. The annual proposed target rate of return is 15 per cent. Ruth has recently attended the local agricultural show and seen the latest models in tractors. She believes that their current tractor should be replaced by a new one so that operating costs will be reduced. The details are as follows:

● The tractor is eight years old and has a net book value of £9,500. It cost £19,100 when new and has been depreciated at £1,200 per annum. The tractor could be disposed of for £2,100 to Neil, the local second-hand machinery dealer.

● The new tractor will cost £38,000 and will last for seven years. It will have a residual value of £6,500 at the end of the period.

● The maintenance costs of the new machine will increase by £3,000 for the first two years; and then reduce by £400 for the remaining five years.

● In addition, the operating costs will reduce by £6,000 per annum.

David believes that there is nothing to be gained from replacing the current tractor and he produces the following schedule to support his view:

	£
Cost of new tractor	38,000
Net increase in maintenance costs	
(2 years × £3,000 less 5 years × £400)	4,000
Loss on old machine £9,500 – £2,100	7,400
	49,400
Savings (7 years × £6,000)	42,000
Loss on investment	(7,400)

Required:

(a) Using discount tables calculate the net benefit (or cost) at the target rate of return if the old machine is sold and a new one purchased. Advise Ruth on whether they should proceed with the investment and discuss any other factors which should be borne in mind.
(b) Comment on the part played by the following factors in a decision of this kind: (i) book value of old equipment; (ii) cost of new equipment; (iii) gain or loss on disposal of old equipment; (iv) disposal value of old equipment; (v) disposal value of new equipment.
(c) Critically evaluate the schedule prepared by David.

References   Allen, D. (1992) The cost of capital: the criterion for sound financial management, *Management Accounting* (UK), December.

Chalos, P. (1992) *Managing Cost in Today's Manufacturing Environment*, Prentice Hall.

CHAPTER 37

Behavioural aspects of performance evaluation

Setting the scene

Do management accounting and control systems benefit organizations? Nobel Laureate Herbert Simon and his colleagues, among others, say they do. Such systems, they believe, play three roles: score-keeping, attention-directing and problem-solving. Robert Simons, writing in the March 1992 *CA Magazine* concurs. Management accounting, he says, consists of 'identification, measurement, accumulation, preparation, interpretation, and the communication of information that helps executives in filling organizational objectives'. In fact, most writers agree that financial controls, such as budgeting systems, aid in planning, co-ordinating and controlling any organization's complex flow of inter-related activities, and in motivating workers. But research also suggests there is a dark side to management accounting, that the system can do more harm than good.

(Mackintosh, 1994)

Learning objectives

After studying this chapter you should be able to:

1 explain what is meant by 'management style';

2 contrast 'Theory X' with 'Theory Y';

3 describe possible management reactions to budgets;

4 identify three possible levels of cost performance;

5 define 'management by objectives';

6 explain what is meant by 'contingency theory'.

Traditionally, accountants have followed economists in assuming the main organizational problem to be the maximization of profits and the optimization of resource allocation to this end. Consequently, accountants have tended to regard organizations in purely technical terms, subjecting human resources to the same analysis as that applied to other economic resources in the search for maximizing productivity and profits.

For more than two decades, social progress, political change and the internationalization of corporate organizations have created a strong awareness of the uniqueness of human resources, and in particular, of the way in which the behaviour of both management and workers affects the realization of organizational objectives. Both management and workers are recognized as having variable performance patterns depending directly on management styles and organizational culture. Much of the early work in this area was concerned with the evaluation of managerial performance, and the reaction of workers to management style and organizational culture. In the 1970s and 1980s the success of Japanese organizations was attributed to characteristics of national and corporate culture which exerted a strong influence on how organizations worked. This prompted research into the influence of organizational culture on business performance.

In this chapter, we review briefly some of these developments.

Managerial style and organization culture

According to Horngren and Foster (1987) managerial style is 'the set of behaviours exhibited by key managers in an organization'. Of particular interest is the contrast between authoritarian as against participative management styles in relation to decision making and the context in which performance is evaluated.

Again, according to these authors, organization culture is 'the set of beliefs and values shared by members of the organization'. This encompasses the prevalent interpersonal relationships and other significant constraints on social behaviour.

The considerable success of Japanese industry has underlined the importance of culture as a key factor, and points to a definition of this concept in an organizational setting that arguably is much broader than the definition adopted by Horngren and Foster. In effect, culture may be deemed to determine the manner in which both workers and management interact, and also the manner in which management decisions are made. Accordingly, management style may be viewed as subsumed in the concept of organization culture.

Much of the international comparison of the relative success of business organizations made currently tends to find substantial cause for disparity precisely in different national cultures as they find their expression in business enterprises. How far this may be substantiated as against the weight of other success factors is an open question. Nevertheless, the existence of the belief is in itself symptomatic of the importance attached to culture.

Despite all the research, there is considerable controversy about the influence of culture as an organizational success factor. Moreover, something that works in one culture may not work in another. There was considerable surprise when Carlos Ghosn succeeded in restoring the fortunes of Nissan despite conspicuously ignoring some of the hallowed traditions of Japanese corporate culture. For these reasons, we shall concern ourselves with the traditional accounting concern of evaluating management performance, as expressed in the literature of the English-speaking nations.

The objectives of performance evaluation

The objectives of performance evaluation may be stated as follows:

1 to assess how effectively the responsibilities assigned to managers have been carried out;
2 to identify areas where corrective actions should be taken;
3 to ensure that managers are motivated towards achieving organizational goals;
4 to enable comparisons to be made between the performance of different units of an organization, to discover areas where improvements may be made.

In our analysis of the process of control, we have so far discussed two important prerequisites for performance evaluation:

1 identifying areas of responsibility over which individual managers exercise control (responsibility accounting), and
2 the setting of standards of performance to be used as yardsticks for the evaluation of performance.

In this chapter, we address ourselves to some of the behavioural problems of budgets as measures for evaluating performance.

Leadership styles and the problem of control

There is a tendency for firms to expect desired results merely from the use of appropriate techniques, thereby failing to recognize that success in organizational control depends upon the actions of responsible individuals and their appreciation of the importance of sound interpersonal relationships McGregor has characterized the two extremes of interpersonal relationships or management styles as 'Theory X' and 'Theory Y' (McGregor, 1960). According to McGregor, these extremes are conditioned by the manager's view of mankind.

Theory X

The Theory X view of man, as summarized below, is supportive of an authoritarian leadership style:

1 Management is responsible for organizing the elements of productive enterprise – money, materials, equipment and people – in activities directed to economic ends.
2 As regards people, management is concerned with directing their efforts, motivating and controlling their actions, and modifying behaviour to fit the needs of the organization.
3 Without this active intervention by management, people would be passive – and even resistant – to organizational needs. Therefore, they must be persuaded, rewarded, punished, controlled. In short, their activities must be directed, and therein lies the function of management. This view is often summed up by the assertion that management consists of getting things done through other people.

Theory Y

By contrast, Theory Y is supportive of a more democratic and participative leadership style:

1 Management is responsible for organizing the elements of productive enterprise – money, materials, equipment and people – in activities directed to economic ends.
2 People are not by nature passive or resistant to organizational needs. They appear to have become so as a result of negative experiences of organizational needs.
3 The motivation, the potential for development, the capacity for assuming responsibility, the readiness to direct behaviour towards organizational goals are all present in people. Management does not put these qualities in people. It is the responsibility of management to make it possible for people to recognize and develop these human characteristics.

4 The essential task of management is to arrange organizational conditions and methods of operation so that people can achieve their own goals best by directing their efforts towards organizational objectives.

There is evidence that the Theory X leadership style is widely prevalent and clearly operational. Those who prefer the assumptions of Theory Y claim that the Theory X leadership style has a human cost in the frustration and the lack of personal development which result from its application to people. The trend in behavioural research suggests that benefits may be derived from leadership and organizations based on the assumptions of Theory Y. These assumptions recognize, in particular, that the basic motivating forces affecting people at work include biological, egoistic and social factors.

As people, employees at whatever organizational, level have certain needs which condition their own objectives. They are seeking *compensation* for their efforts to enable them to provide some desired standard of life for themselves and their families. They need outlets for their physical and intellectual energies which provide both *stimulation* and *satisfaction*. They seek *self-realization* in a sense of their own worth and usefulness. They are pursuing further *growth* and greater *personal effectiveness*. They seek the *recognition* of their fellows, whether their organizational equals, superiors or subordinates. They appreciate their *identification* with a worthwhile and successful undertaking.

In order to maximize employees' contribution to organizational activities, it follows that these personal needs and goals should be capable of realization in the tasks in which they are employed. An awareness of the nature of personal needs, therefore, is an important aspect of control.

The effects of budgets on people

Research suggests that there is a great deal of mistrust of the entire budgetary process at the supervisory level (Argyris, 1953). There is a tendency for traditional budgets to provide the following responses.

Reactions to pressure

The evaluation of a manager's performance in terms of the departmental budget is one of the few elements in performance appraisal which is based on concrete standards. There is little room for manipulation or escape if results are not going to turn out as expected in the budget. If budget pressure becomes too great, it may lead to mistrust, to hostility and eventually to poorer performance levels as reaction sets in against budgetary control.

The problem of distinguishing between controllable and non-controllable costs is an important cause of tension among managers. The task of the manager of a department or expense centre, for example, is to attain goals with the minimum cost. One of the initial difficulties which arises in evaluating performance applies to all levels of management, namely, the treatment of factors beyond their control. This problem is aggravated when the responsibility for an activity is shared by two or more individuals or functions. Labour inefficiency, for example, may be due to excessive machine breakdowns (maintenance function), inferior materials (purchasing function), defective materials (inspection function) or poor-calibre personnel (personnel function).

Establishing standards of performance in itself is not an easy task. It demands the clear definition of goals and responsibilities, the delegation of authority, the use of satisfactory surrogates for the activities concerned, effective communication of information and an understanding of the psychology of human motivation.

Overemphasis on the short run

One of the dangers facing organizations which evaluate the effectiveness of managers in terms of profit is that too much emphasis is given to achieving short-term profitability at the expense of the long term. Short-term increases in profits gained at the expense of reductions in research and development or the failure to maintain adequate standards of maintenance are two examples of short-term cost savings which are detrimental to the firm in the long term.

Poor-quality decision making by top management

Excessive reliance on the profit performance of divisions may also affect the quality of decisions made by top management. If the managerial competence of divisional managers is assessed mainly on the basis of their ability to hit agreed profit targets, they may be motivated to make wrong decisions. For example in order to reduce IT costs charged by a centralized department, a manager may decide to acquire his own server. He now makes no demands on the central IT facility and so receives no charge; his own performance is improved; since no savings are made in the budget of the central service provider the performance of the total company is worse. Moreover, if reported profits are used as part of an early-warning system, it may trigger action by top management which is not warranted. Therefore, although profit budgets are indispensable for planning purposes, great care should be taken in utilizing them for control. The attainment of profit targets is dependent on many factors, some of which are entirely outside the control of a divisional manager. The uncertainty attached to profit forecasts, in particular, limits the usefulness of profit targets for the evaluation of the performance of a divisional manager. The process of formulating the divisional profit forecast also introduces bias in the evaluation of performance. Divisional profit targets are usually based on the divisional manager's forecast of future events. Therefore, it is the ability to forecast the future successfully, rather than the ability to manage successfully, which forms the basis on which that manager's performance is evaluated. This consideration also affects the validity of comparisons between the performance of different divisions. For example, it is easier to determine an attainable profit goal for a division whose major constraint is productive capacity, where sales are limited only by output, than for a division which sells in a highly competitive market.

Another problem arising from the use of profit budgets in evaluating divisional performance stems from the fact that an annual budget covers too short a period in which to obtain a realistic picture. The effects of decisions in some instances may take several years before being reflected in profits. Thus, the decision to introduce a new product is one of several decisions whose impacts on divisional profits are not fully realized for some years. The more complex and innovative the division the longer will be the time period necessary for the evaluation of performance. In the light of these considerations, the use of annual profits may give a completely inaccurate view of divisional performance.

Poor communication

Where a Theory X style of management exists, negative attitudes may be generated against organizational goals leading to the falsification of budget results and an unwillingness to transmit information – the hiding of bad news. Managers will feel that their own survival justifies these tactics.

The prevalence of negative behaviour in an organization which practises management by domination may be aggravated by the response of top management, when it is realized that information which is needed for decision making is not transmitted. Their immediate reaction may be to impose even tighter controls, which reinforces the negative attitudes held by subordinate managers leading to the transmission of even less accurate and useful information. The progressive tightening of the managerial reins may well result, therefore, in a progressive deterioration of the information flow.

The communication of information is of central importance to the processes of planning and control, as it provides the link between various levels of management and the various decision points. Any reluctance on the part of subordinate managers to communicate information is a serious impediment to the efficiency with which planning and control decisions are made. It is not a sufficient condition for success that an organization should have accounting control systems and that it should have stipulated standards of performance. These control methods will not operate successfully and standards of performance will not be attained if the style of management adopted fails to secure a high degree of motivation and goal congruence within the organization.

Departmental focus

The budget process which involves defining areas of responsibility, measuring and comparing performance, concentrates the manager's entire attention on his/her own department. This narrow departmental focus obscures important relationships between departments, so that interdepartmental dependencies are ignored or overlooked in the quest for optimizing departmental results. Consequently, economies which would result from greater interdepartmental collaboration are lost to the organization.

The stifling of initiative

The planning and control aspects of budgeting may be overemphasized with the result that opportunities for the exercise of personal initiative are excluded. Budgets which appear to be straitjackets discourage managers from deviating from budget commitments even when circumstances indicate that opportunities for new actions exist.

Bias in budgeting

In the last analysis, the process of setting targets involves making subjective judgements. As a result, bias may inevitably be found in the budgeting process in a conscious or unconscious form. Managers may inflate costs and reduce expected revenues when setting budget targets, thereby making them easier to achieve. In this way, the introduction of conscious bias is a deliberate means of ensuring that their performance as managers will be highly evaluated.

The introduction of bias into estimates that find their way into budgets typifies the behavioural responses of individuals to organizational pressures. Take the example of a salesman threatened with the possibility of redundancy as a result of falling sales. He may negotiate sales targets that are at the low end of expected outcomes so that the chances of exceeding them are good. Whereas a stretch target might have encouraged him to do even better.

The presence of bias in setting budgets may be met either through the process of counter-biasing, which leads to gamesmanship in budgeting, or by reducing ignorance about the objectives of the firm in relation to personnel. The reduction of conflict between the firm's objectives and the objectives of managers and personnel is discussed later in this chapter, in the context of the system known as management by objectives.

Budget information and performance evaluation

According to Hopwood (1974), budget information may be used in three different ways for the purposes of assessing managerial performance:

1 Budget-constrained evaluation, where the manager's performance is primarily evaluated on the basis of the ability to continually meet budgets on the short-term basis.
2 Profit-conscious evaluation, where the manager's performance is evaluated on the basis of the ability to increase the general effectiveness of the operations of his/her unit in relation to the long-term objectives of the firm. In this case, budget information will be used with a degree of flexibility.
3 Non-accounting evaluation, where budget information plays a relatively small part in the evaluation of the manager's performance.

A summary of the effects of these different styles of managerial evaluation on managerial behaviour is given below:

	Budget-constrained	Profit-conscious	Non-accounting
Involvement with costs	High	High	Low
Job-related tension	High	Medium	Medium
Manipulation of accounting reports	Extensive	Little	Little
Relations with supervisor	Poor	Good	Good
Relations with colleagues	Poor	Good	Good

The need for several measures of performance

While the use of standard costs and flexible budgets plays an important role in the control of activities and in the evaluation of performance, undue attention to cost control tends to diminish the importance of other goals. For example, non-financial goals for a factory manager might include productive efficiency, the quality of the product, production schedules, the maintenance of satisfactory relations with employees. What importance will be given to these if the budget requires him to minimize costs?

The evaluation of performance therefore requires both financial and non-financial measures of performance. It is evident that some organizational and departmental goals may conflict, such as, for example, the need to minimize costs and to maintain product quality. Emphasis on specific goals will therefore mean that other goals may not be attained. The objectives of performance evaluation, which we have stipulated, require a balanced view of performance covering the various areas of managerial responsibility. If management uses only conventional measurement of revenues, expenses, profit, cost variances and output, it is possible that short-run economic gains may be achieved at the expense of long-run goals. The failure to appreciate the impact of control techniques on individuals responsible for organizational activities may adversely affect employee morale, loyalty, trust and motivation.

The importance of participation

The active participation by managers in the planning process not only enhances their personal sense of involvement in the organization, but improves the efficiency of the planning process. Moreover, such participation establishes a common understanding of purpose, and promotes the acceptance of organizational objectives and goals at all levels. Likewise, the control process is aided by the active participation of managers in the investigation of variances, the evaluation and selection of appropriate solutions and the development of related policies.

The degree of effort expended by members of an organization in attempting to achieve designated goals is particularly dependent upon their personal aspiration level. The aspiration level may be defined as that level of future performance in a familiar task which individuals explicitly undertake knowing their past performance level. For example, a manager's aspiration level as regards costs is the spending level which s/he accepts as realistic and with which s/he will strive to comply. Hence, we may identify three potential levels of cost performance:

1 the budgeted level;
2 the aspiration level;
3 the actual level.

Since the aspiration level is the real inner goal acceptable to the manager, the purpose of participation is to bring the aspiration level in harmony with the budgeted level (or vice versa). Clearly, a budgeted level significantly at variance with the aspiration level will have a negative effect on managerial behaviour.

It follows that managers should be motivated and not pressurized into achieving their budgetary goals. This may be achieved by recognizing the importance of aspiration levels in the planning stage and the timely communication of results as a basis for improving performance, where necessary. The purpose of participation in the control process is, therefore, to motivate managers and to generate in each participant the desire to accomplish or even improve his/her level of performance.

Management by objectives

From the foregoing discussion of the problem of controlling the activities of an organization and evaluating managerial performance, it follows that several conditions must be satisfied if the accounting function is to play a useful role.

1 Divisional and departmental goals must be clearly identified and defined, and appropriate measurements selected by which to express them and evaluate managerial performance. Where objectives are too vague or too ambiguous to be susceptible to clear definition in conventional terms, surrogates should be sought which will enable them to be defined and measured.

2 There should be participation by all levels of management in the control process, thereby ensuring good communication between supervisor and subordinate.

3 A style of management is required which pays particular attention to the human element in organizations, and in so doing provides an environment conducive to the effective employment of all resources.

The aim of management by objectives is to provide a framework for administering a control system which embraces these three conditions. By translating organizational objectives and goals in such a way that they become the personal objectives and goals of all management personnel, management by objectives seeks to create a high degree of goal congruence within an organization. The unity of personal and organizational objectives encourages managers to take actions which are in the best interest of the organization.

Some organizational goals are too remote from individual managers, and therefore have little significance for them, for example, goals relating to the return on capital employed or overall growth targets envisaged in the long-range plan. Management by objectives seeks to establish personal targets at all levels as a means of overcoming this problem. Relating personal goals to department and divisional goals and thence to organizational goals, achieves integration between them which may be depicted as follows:

Personal goals → Divisional goals → Organization goals

Management by objectives involves the following processes:

1 The review of long-term and short-term organizational objectives and goals.

2 The revision, if necessary, of the organizational structure. An organizational chart is required to illustrate the titles, duties and the relationships between managers.

3 Standards of performance necessary to fulfil key tasks are set by individual job holders in agreement with their immediate supervisors. Unless job holders participate in setting performance standards, they will not feel committed to them. The standards of performance which result from systems of management by objectives are not 'ideal', nor are they minimum acceptable levels of performance. They indicate what are agreed to be 'satisfactory' levels of performance. As far as possible, they should be expressed in quantitative terms. The purpose of management controls is to make it possible for supervisors to offer help and guidance to their subordinates rather than acting as watchdogs. A divisional profit goal in this sense is not only a target for the divisional manager, for it may also act as a means whereby top management may help to solve divisional problems should they become apparent through the failure to reach a stipulated figure.

4 Results are measured against goals. An important aspect of this stage is the use of periodic performance appraisal interviews, in which supervisor and subordinate jointly discuss results and consider their implications for the future. The performance appraisal interview is essentially a discussion between manager and subordinate about objectives and their achievement. Performance appraisal should

evaluate managers not merely in terms of current performance as expressed in tangible results; it should also enable their performance as managers, their personal qualifications and character and their potential for advancement to be assessed. It is an integral part of the process of managing by results by which both parties to the interview assess their efficiency as managers. The managers assess their own role as coaches to the subordinates; the subordinates consider their role in supporting the managers.

5 Long- and short-term organizational goals are reviewed in the light of current performance.

These stages in management by objectives are illustrated in Figure 37.1.

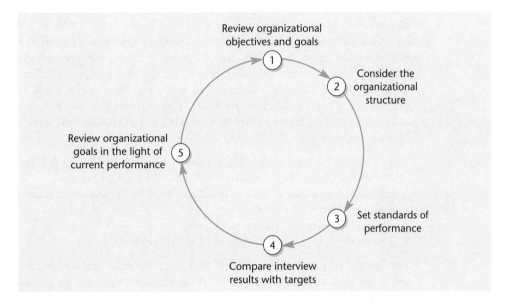

Figure 37.1

Organization theory

Some of the assumptions upon which we have so far relied have been necessary for the purpose of facilitating the examination of the basic aspects of accounting for planning and control. If an accounting system is to be effective in providing information for planning and control purposes, it should be capable of adapting to organizational and environmental factors peculiar to individual enterprises. Different enterprises may require different methods of control, depending on the internal and external influences affecting their own activities. Hence, some assumptions may be more applicable to some organizations than to others. In this respect, organization theory attempts to provide a framework for understanding the influences which bear upon organizations and is important, therefore, for clarifying issues of importance to the accountant.

Approaches to organization theory

By regarding the organization as a logical and rational process, the classical approach focuses in some detail on the organizing function of management. Hence, the classical theory is concerned with the structure of organizations and the determination of the tasks necessary to attain organizational objectives. By contrast, the human relations approach stresses people rather than structures, their motives and behaviour rather than the activities which need to be harnessed for achieving organizational goals. This approach originated in the Hawthorne experiments, which revealed that social and human factors in work situations were often more important than physical factors in affecting productivity. This series of experiments, first led by Harvard Business School Professor Elton Mayo at the Hawthorne Plant of the Western Electric Company in Cicero, Illinois from 1927 to 1932 started out by examining the physical and environmental influences of the workplace (e.g. brightness of lights, humidity) and later, moved into the psychological aspects (e.g. breaks, group pressure, working hours, managerial leadership). The ideas that this team developed about the social dynamics of groups in the work setting had lasting influence – the collection of data, labour–management relations, and informal interaction among factory employees. Four general conclusions were drawn from the Hawthorne studies:

1 The aptitudes of individuals are imperfect predictors of job performance, the amount produced being strongly influenced by social factors.
2 Informal organization affects productivity. The Hawthorne researchers discovered a group life among the workers.
3 Work-group norms affect productivity.
4 The workplace is a social system of interdependent parts.

The human relations theory asserts that since the most important factors are individual needs and wants, the structure of organizations should be geared to individuals rather than the individual being geared to the structure.

Finally, there has developed the contingency approach which starts with the premise that there is no single organizational design that is best in all situations. According to this approach, there are four factors or forces of particular significance in the design of an organizational structure: forces in the manager; forces in the environment; forces in the task; and forces in the subordinates.

1 *Forces in the manager*. This refers to factors relating to the personalities of managers and their influence on the design of the organizational structure. Managers tend to perceive organizational problems in a unique way, which is a function of background, knowledge, experience and values. These factors shape organizational decisions in such areas as strategy, organizational structure and style of management. Accordingly, organizations do not have objectives – only people have objectives. In this analysis, these objectives will differ from manager to manager.
2 *Forces in the environment*. Some studies suggest that the most effective pattern of organizational structure is that which enables the organization to adjust to the requirements of its environment (Burns and Stalker, 1961). These studies indicate that organizations with less formal structures are best able to cope with uncertain and heterogeneous environmental conditions. Conversely, highly structured

organizations will be more effective in stable environmental conditions. Hence, bureaucratic structures, as implied in classical theory, are more appropriate to stable conditions, whereas more democratic and participative structures are required to enable organizations to adapt to a changing environment.

3 *Forces in the task.* Empirical studies indicate that technology has an important impact on the design of an organizational structure. For example, Woodward (1965) has found that organizational structures varied according to the technology involved. According to Woodward, fewer managers are required under systems of unit production than under systems of mass production. The technology associated with unit production systems may also require relatively higher levels of operative skill, and there is evidence to suggest that skilled workers feel more involved in their jobs and are more anxious for an opportunity to participate in decision-making relating to their jobs than unskilled workers. This makes it possible to delegate more authority to lower levels in an organization and has important implications for devising schemes based on 'management by objectives'.

4 *Forces in the subordinates.* This refers to the psychological needs such as the subordinate's desire for a measure of independence, for the acquisition of skills and the motivation for assuming responsibility. The desire to participate in decision-making is not uniform among employees, and as implied earlier it is much stronger among skilled workers and employees with a professional background than it is among unskilled workers. Hence, organizations employing relatively more skilled than unskilled employees will be faced with a greater desire for a democratic structure.

Agency theory

According to Antle (1989), agency models are highly stylized logical tools for discovering basic relationships. They extend the traditional intellectual boundaries of accounting by assuming that its problems have psychological, sociological, economic and political dimensions. Heretofore, these problems have been recognized to some extent in articles dealing with the behavioural aspects of performance evaluation, which have been discussed earlier in this chapter.

Specifically, agency theory re-examines extant basic assumptions about human behaviour in organizations, by considering behaviour in terms of a model in which protagonists are acting out a principal and agent relationship. This relationship grants the agent delegated powers to act on behalf of the principal. The theory considers how to structure the relationship so that the agent acts in the best interests of the principal.

Agency theory is claimed to be particularly relevant when focusing on financial reports generated by agents whose performance is in part evaluated on the basis of those reports. If the choice of accounting method rests with the agents, as is normally the case in so far as management information systems are concerned, agency theory assumes that the information reported through these systems will reflect management preferences over what is reported.

Williamson's (1964) seminal work on the existence of managerial discretion as highly significant in organizational decision making shed new light on the manner in which personal interests influenced decisions. Williamson's thesis conflicted with the traditional view assumed in accounting theory that the interests of shareholders and managers are joined in the maximization of shareholders' wealth. Agency theory addresses the problem of information reporting for assessing managerial behaviour where management holds private information and does not communicate it, or communicates only the information that it wants to communicate.

From the foregoing, it is evident that agency theory considerably extends the debate over the assessment of managerial performance. It shifts this debate from one in which performance is seen as a reactive problem to be examined in the light of managerial styles to the much wider issue of the vested interests that exist in organizations and that are not adequately recognized in extant theories of the firm.

Summary

The budget process alone is not sufficient to maintain adequate management control. Too often, organizations tend to expect results from budgetary control and fail to recognize its behavioural implications. As a result, pressures are created leading to mistrust, hostility and actions detrimental to the long-term prospects of an organization. It follows that accountants should work more closely with behavioural scientists and that they should learn more about the behavioural implications of organizational control.

Participation schemes may be introduced into organizations with due consideration for the psychological problems entailed. One such scheme is management by objectives. Management by objectives differs from the conventional budgetary control theory in that it enables the precepts of Theory Y to be put into practice by creating an environment which allows employees to develop as individuals and to exercise responsibility through self-control. Self-control is found to induce stronger work motivation, for by giving individual managers greater freedom of action, it affords them a greater measure of satisfaction and pleasure which a sense of accomplishment confers.

Being concerned with the provision of information for planning and control, the accountant should find a knowledge of organization theory particularly useful in understanding the internal and external influences which affect the nature of organizational activities and the environment in which decisions are made. These influences have implications for the design of control systems, and the significance of contingency theory lies in the identification of their sources.

New considerations in the assessment of managerial behaviour have been inspired by protagonists of agency theory, which looks at the impact of discretionary managerial behaviour on management information.

Self-assessment questions

1 State what you understand by 'managerial style'.

2 What is meant by 'organization culture'?

3 List the objectives of performance evaluation.

4 Explain 'Theory X'.

5 Contrast 'Theory X' with 'Theory Y'.

6 Comment on possible managerial reactions to budgets.

7 Describe three possible levels of cost performance.

8 Define 'management by objectives'.

9 What do you understand by 'contingency theory'?

1* The following extract is taken from a conversation between the chairman of Westway Engineering Company and James Brown, accountant, on the day Brown took up his appointment with the company.

> Chairman: 'We apply a system of payment by results to foremen as well as to operatives. For each department, budgeted allowances are set for the expenditure which should be incurred over varying levels of output. The greater the saving on budgeted expenditure for a department, the greater the bonus received by the foreman concerned. For example, this report shows how the bonus the foreman of our assembly department had built up suffered a severe jolt last month.'

He hands the following report to Brown.

Westway Engineering Company – Assembly Department Foreman: W Rodgers

| | | | For month | Year to date |
	Budget allowance	Actual	(Over) under budget	(Over) under budget
	£	£	£	£
Direct material	4,000	5,000	(1,000)	(3,000)
Direct labour	10,000	12,000	(2,000)	(3,500)
Indirect labour	5,000	4,500	500	1,000
Indirect material	2,000	1,700	300	(1,000)
Power	6,000	6,500	(500)	(2,000)
Maintenance	7,000	10,000	(3,000)	4,000
Depreciation	5,000	4,000	1,000	2,000
Insurance	100	80	20	500
General expense	10,000	8,500	1,500	4,500
			(3,180)	2,500

> Chairman: 'Since the new accounting system was installed a year ago, there appears to have been a general deterioration in morale. The relations between a number of staff certainly need improving. Two months ago an error was made on an order, and the goods were returned for correction, a process which cost £700. None of the departmental foremen were prepared to accept the cost of the error, which was finally charged to general factory loss. Because of the incident two foremen stopped talking to each other.'

Required:

Discuss what improvements should be made in the accounting system in operation at Westway's.

References

Antle, R. (1989) Commentary on intellectual boundaries in accounting research, *Accounting Horizons*, June 1989.

Argyris, C. (1953) Human problems with budgets, *Harvard Business Review*, January–February.

Burns, T. and Stalker, G.M. (1961) *The Management of Innovation*, Tavistock Publications.

Hopwood, A. (1974) *Accounting and Human Behaviour*, Accountancy Age Books.

Horngren, C.T. and Foster, G. (1987) *Cost Accounting: A Managerial Emphasis*, 6th edn, Prentice Hall.

McGregor, D.M. (1960) *The Human Side of the Enterprise*, McGraw-Hill.

Mackintosh, N.B. (1994) *CA Magazine*, September.

Williamson, E.O. (1964) *The Economics of Discretionary Behaviour: Managerial Objectives in a Theory of the Firm*, Prentice Hall.

Woodward, J. (1965) *Industrial Organization: Theory and Practice*, Oxford University Press.

CHAPTER 38

Managing profitability

Setting the scene

The financial management of a business enterprise may be seen as involving three distinct areas of knowledge and accounting responsibility, namely creating and managing the capital structure that is most efficient for financing the enterprise; selecting and managing the asset structure that is most appropriate to the realization of business objectives in the long, medium and short-term; achieving defined financial objectives by effective operational management of corporate resources.

Financial markets consider shareholder value to be the appropriate measure for evaluating overall financial performance that integrates asset and debt management with operating performance. For this reason, the assessment of overall business performance has shifted attention from profitability to shareholder value as the reference standard. Profitability, as the reference standard for operating performance, also directly affects shareholder value. However, gains from asset and debt management by themselves may lead to improved shareholder value as well as improved profitability through gains in the management of structural costs.

As terms of reference, shareholder value and profitability serve to underline different approaches to increasing wealth. Financial institutions operating in financial markets, such as equity funds, seek gains through squeezing out shareholder value in the process of buying and selling stakes in business corporations acquired solely in a short-term trading context. Industrial, commercial and service corporations look to operating profitability in an on-going and long-term context, albeit subscribing to shareholder value as the main concern of their shareholders. This is reflected in management decision-models that focus on profitability.

This chapter is concerned with the management of operating profitability within a given asset and financial structure. It examines factors that directly affect operating profitability, such as competition, customers and products, as well as market conditions affecting demand.

After studying this chapter you should be able to:

1 discuss the nature and problems that are the concerns of enterprise financial management;

2 explain the significance of shareholder value for the evaluation of financial performance. How does it compare with the notion of profitability?

3 understand the scope of strategic planning;

4 discuss the nature of strategic management control and its role in managing profitability;

5 relate strategic management control with traditional management control planning;

6 discuss the objectives of activity analysis;

7 describe competitor analysis;

8 explain 'market-led accounting';

9 appreciate the role of non-financial measures of performance;

10 discuss the problems involved in managing profitability under conditions of growth, inflation, recession and deflation.

Profit is commonly understood as the difference between income and the cost of doing business, whether that business is a one-off deal or an on-going activity. Profitability is an index that expresses the gain over the cost involved. The uncertainty attached to the possibility of realizing gains in competitive markers heightens the need for the knowledge of costs. It explains the importance of cost accounting information in managing profitability and reducing the risk of loss. It is seen in the emergence of cost accounting, as an extension of financial accounting that corresponded with the role of accountants in collecting, recording, analysing and producing information derived from invoices, thereby providing information about actual costs.

By contrast, knowledge about gains is speculative and unknown until a transaction is completed. Accounting practice restricts information about revenues to that obtained from sales invoices. The reliability of accounting information is establishing through its objectivity and verifiable as fact. It has resulted in an accounting culture that has attracted criticism as being too narrow and inward-looking. It is argued that if the only information that is produced by management accountants is about internal costs, managers will tend to concentrate mainly on operational issues rather than on overall policy and the direction of the organization (Clarke, 1995). This view has found its expression in the need for strategic management accounting, or market-orientated, or even market-driven accounting, which emphasises competitors, customers and products and seeks to produce a range of information about these three concerns (Roslender *et al.*, 1998).

In recent years, the expansion of a deregulated global market economy, fuelled by an unregulated credit expansion, has significantly increased market competition and financial risk. It has important implications for management information that is outward-looking and concerned with competitive market forces under high growth levels and increased financial risk.

It follows that managing profitability, defined as the management of current and on-going operations, requires accurate and reliable knowledge both of internal costs and of market conditions that affect the costs of resource inputs as well as the demand for products and services. These include factors that are specific to the enterprise, namely, competitors, customers and products and more general conditions affecting demand that relate to economic growth, inflation and recession. In earlier chapters, we examined the role of cost information for product costing and discussed the reliance on management control systems, such as standard costing and budgetary planning and control, for managing profitability. This chapter extends the discussion to include such factors as competition, customers and products and explores the challenge of managing profitability under growth, inflation and recession.

Managing profitability through strategic management control

Strategic management control is directly related to strategic planning as part of a systematic attempt to influence the medium- and long-term future of an enterprise and to manage change. It involves the determination of corporate objectives and goals as well as the development of broad policies and strategies by which they may be achieved. Its main objective is to enable the enterprise to acquire and maintain a competitive advantage in its chosen marketplace, enabling it to earn supernormal profits (i.e. above normal rate of return) on its operations.

Porter (1985) argued that rather than being an outgrowth of the enterprise's own products and markets, strategic planning should be seen primarily in terms of its competitive environment. The structural analysis of industries involves consideration of five forces and the interplay between them: rivalry among existing competitors; the threat of new entrants to its market and the barriers to their entry; the threat of substitute products; the bargaining power of suppliers; and the bargaining power of customers. These relationships are shown in Figure 38.1.

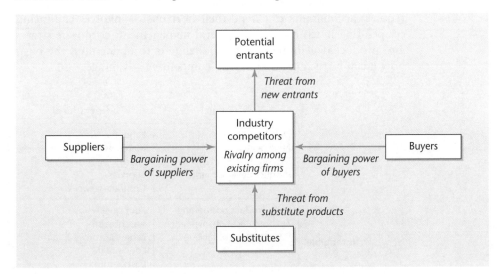

Figure 38.1 Forces driving industry competition

Source: adapted with the permission of the Free Press, a division of Simon & Schuster, Inc., from *Competitive Advantage: Creating and Sustaining Superior Performance* by Michael E. Porter. Copyright © 1985, 1998 by Michael E. Porter. All rights reserved.

The thrust of competitive strategy formulation is to identify the competitive advantage that the enterprise enjoys; to build on that advantage by denying existing or potential competitors the opportunity to match it. It relies heavily on information about the environment. This requires management:

1 To remain sensitive to the needs and demands of customers. Market research, market segmentation and customer targeting are now accepted as essential inputs to the process of strategic analysis. Such inputs permit the enterprise to remain close to its customers.
2 To identify the forces which shape competitive rivalry within a business sector. The company can only set objectives and strategies in the context of the firm's position relative to its key competitors. Products (goods and services) can be viewed as a bundle of attributes or characteristics which are on offer to potential customers. These characteristics are crucial to the formulation of the firm's strategies and include a variety of elements such as price, quality, performance and after-sales service.
3 To understand the nature and interaction of the various environmental forces bringing pressure to bear on industries and enterprises. This requires scanning the environment for technological developments, population trends and changing social and political attitudes.
4 To adopt a strategic perspective to internal data. In addition to the increased focus on external information, it is necessary to take a strategic view of internal information. This implies that cost and management accounting information traditionally used for internal control purposes should be seen also in the light of its strategic relevance.

The difference between a strategic and traditional approach to cost categorization is illustrated by Richardson (1988) in Figure 38.2. Accountants have always been concerned with the operational matters illustrated in the top right-hand quadrant. A comprehensive view embraces strategic and tangible and intangible items and requires accountants to extend their horizons. It involves embracing new skills and cooperating much more with general management, corporate strategists, marketing and product development. The challenge is to understand the business model and how it can be reconfigured to gain competitive advantage.

	Strategic	Operational
Tangible	Debt charges New plants Market development Product development	Labour Materials Energy Supplies Contract services
Intangible	Poor product positioning Technological obsolescence Poor location of facilities	Poor quality Absenteeism Labour turnover Low morale Lost output Late delivery

Figure 38.2

To be successful, world-class enterprises stress the following:

1 activity analysis,
2 customer profitability and analysis,
3 competitor analysis,
4 market-led accounting,
5 development of non-financial measures of performance.

Activity analysis

Porter (1985) suggests that firms can be viewed as a series of activities performed to provide products or services to customers. Above-average performance can be achieved by concentrating on two key variables: the distinctiveness of your products (differentiation) and your organization's level of costs (cost leadership). These two variables are important because Porter focuses on the ability of activities to add value. The best performing companies in any industry are those which add value either cheaply or distinctively.

We noted in Chapter 18 that ABC offers more than better information on product costs. It also provides information about the cost and performance of activities. If activities are linked together across departments into cross-functional business processes, management has a much better idea of how they combine to create competitive advantage. Activity-based management (ABM) focuses attention on how activities contribute to the value received by a customer and the profit generated by providing it. This process view of ABM enables management to judge each activity as value-added or non-value-added.

Value-added activities contribute something that is worthwhile to customers and therefore to the enterprise. If the activity were not performed the utility of the product for customers would be diminished. Such activities are essential to the enterprise's success. Where an activity increases the worth of a product or service to the customer, the customer is willing to pay for the performance of the activity and it is, therefore, value added. For example distributing a product faster than anyone else will add value if customers are prepared to pay more than the extra costs of providing quicker service. Also, you might try to add distinctiveness to your basic product with special features, superior customer service or clever advertising. The test of whether these unique differences add value is the willingness of customers to pay a premium over and above the extra cost of providing them.

Non-value-added activities represent waste; these activities can be reduced or eliminated without decreasing the enterprise's ability to compete and meet customer demands. Obvious examples are poor quality, inefficient work practices, slow after-sales service. Armed with a list of non-value-added activities, the organization can create teams to find innovative ways to eliminate, reduce, or re-engineer those activities. One of the costliest things a company can do is to invest in equipment and people to make non-value-added activities more efficient. The objective is to eliminate them altogether or subject them to a major overhaul, not to make them more efficient.

Inspection of incoming raw materials is a non-value-added activity that can be eliminated without diminishing the value received by the enterprise as customers do not value inspection; they value high quality. If a supplier of raw materials makes a commitment to supply high-quality materials, then inspection is no longer required, and buying testing equipment and hiring more people to inspect the incoming raw materials would waste time and money. Non-value-adding activities are not necessary for a firm to remain in business. Thus, the challenge of activity analysis is to find ways to produce the goods or services without using any of these activities. While the distinction appears intuitively appealing, in the real world things are not so clear cut. Is the legal department value-added or not, and what about the office of the president and the corporate jet?

Customer profitability analysis

In increasingly competitive markets, it is critical to know profitability of customers, markets and channels of distribution as well as that of products. Companies need to be able to quantify and report the profits generated by different trading relationships so that they can add real value to commercial decisions. Such an approach should answer key questions which conventional accounting fails to address, such as:

1 Does selling to company X meet profitability criteria? Can it ever? If so, how?
2 Which customer or market segment generates the greatest profit contribution? How best can we protect it?
3 What are the maximum discounts or after-sales servicing packages that may be allowed in the next round of negotiations?
4 Do our largest accounts earn reasonable contributions, or are the advantages of volume offset by the costs of promotional activity, distribution and discounts?
5 Should a customer or customer group be dropped?

Whereas product costs are determined from manufacturing costs (the rule is all manufacturing costs, but only manufacturing costs), costs of serving customers include technical support, distribution, marketing and sales costs that are incurred before and after the product is manufactured. These costs are considered period costs for generally accepted accounting principles. As a result, conventional management reporting typically follows financial reporting requirements and avoids allocating these costs or analysing them further. For decision-making purposes, activity-based approaches may be used to allocate these pre- and post-manufacturing costs to customers. Allocating these costs reflects the different ways in which customers consume resources. For example, one customer may frequently call on a company's technical support because they have no in-house technical staff, while another may not because they do have in-house staff. Differences such as these have an overall impact on the profitability of serving different customers. The table below lists examples of other activities for which customers may have different resource demands.

Activity	High-cost customer	Low-cost customer
Inventory-carrying requirements	Customer requires safety inventory close to their plants	Customer does not require safety inventory
Post-sales technical support	Customer requires specialized training to use product	Customer provides their own in-house training to use product
Promotional support	Customer requires promotional displays	Customer requires no promotional displays
Credit taken	Customer pays accounts 15 days	Customer pays accounts in 15 days

Example 38.1 Simon Electronics employs technical support personnel whose cost is £300,000. During the year, the technical support staff estimate they will receive 600 requests for technical assistance from customers. Simon Electronics has hundreds of customers generating total revenues of £1,200,000 and a gross profit of £400,000. Assume that customers X, Y and Z each purchase a single piece of test equipment from Simon Electronics for a price of £3,000. The cost of goods sold for each piece of equipment is £2,000. Customer X requires no technical assistance because it employs in-house technical staff. Customer Y made one technical request to the technical centre, while Customer Z made five requests to the centre. A customer report for these three customers is shown below.

Simon Electronics
Partial customer profitability report

	X	Y	Z	
	£	£	£	
Sales	3,000	3,000	3,000	
Cost of goods sold	2,000	2,000	2,000	
Gross income	1,000	1,000	1,000	
Technical support*	0	500	2,500	
Income (loss)	1,000	500	(1,500)	

*£300,000 ÷ 600 requests = £500 per request.

Customer profitability can be seen to vary with the amount of technical support used by the customer. Simon Electronics could use this information to adjust its customer strategies. For example, Simon Electronics could drop Customer Z, or they could price technical services separately.

Without accurate customer profitability information, a company may make strategic errors. For example, if Simon Electronics did not allocate technical support costs to customers according to their use of this activity, they would be unable to charge customers for the services they consumed. Failure to price differences in service levels provides incentives for customers to use what appear to be 'free' services leaving the cost to be borne by someone else.

According to Howell and Soucy (1990), who argue that customer profitability is as critical as product profitability,

Few companies have management information that provides managers with a clear understanding of which customers and markets are profitable. As services (sales, general and administrative costs) become a more significant part of companies' competitive advantage and cost structure, the management tools must respond.

Competitor analysis

A competitive analysis starts with identifying actual and potential competitors. There are two very different ways of identifying current competitors. The first takes the perspective of the customer who must make choices among competitors. In this case, substitute products can be relevant competitors. For example, rice and pastas are very real competitors to the makers of granulated potato buds which are used by institutions and restaurants for making mashed potatoes. Competitors are grouped according to the degree to which they compete for a buyer's choice. The second attempts to place competitors into strategic groups on the basis of their competitive strategy. The concept of a strategic group provides a very different approach towards understanding the competitive structure of an industry. A strategic group is a group of firms that:

1 over time pursue similar competitive strategies (e.g. the use of the same distribution channel and heavy advertising);
2 have similar characteristics (e.g. size, aggressiveness);
3 have similar assets and skills (e.g. quality, image).

The conceptualization of strategic groups can make the process of competitor analysis more manageable. Numerous industries contain many more competitors than can be analysed individually. Often it is simply not feasible to consider thirty competitors to say nothing of hundreds. Reducing this set to a small number of strategic groups makes the analysis compact, feasible and more useable. Further, little strategic content and insight will be lost in most cases, because firms in a strategic group will be affected by, and react to, industry developments in similar ways. Thus, in projecting future strategies of competitors, the concept of strategic groups can be helpful.

After competitors are identified the focus shifts to attempting to understand them and their strategy. What are the competitors' objectives? What strategies are being pursued by competitors and how successful are they? What are the competitors' strengths and weaknesses? The identification and evaluation of competitors' strengths and weaknesses is at the very heart of a well-developed competitive strategy. Competitive strengths and weaknesses are based upon the existence or absence of assets or skills. Thus, an asset such as a well-known name or prime location could represent a strength, as could a skill, such as the ability to develop a strong promotional programme. Conversely, the absence of an asset or skill can represent a weakness. It involves finding answers to questions such as 'Why are successful businesses successful?' and 'What are the key customer motivations?' It also involves an examination of competitors' innovative ability and financial, management and marketing skills.

Competitor analysis enables the anticipation of competitors' moves. This allows an enterprise to plan for the defence of its territory and to take advantage of opportunities that result from competitors' mistakes and weaknesses. According to Bromwich and Bhimani (1989),

> The need to consider the firm's comparative advantages relative to competitors and the benefits for which customers are willing to pay and their costs, is the main theme of strategic management accounting. Providing the relevant accounting information configured in a way in which it can be used for strategy is thought by many commentators to be a major contemporary challenge to accountants.

Accounting for market-led design

According to Hiromoto (1988), Japanese companies tend to use their management control systems to support their manufacturing strategies. He found that a more direct link existed between management accounting practices and corporate goals in Japanese companies than in their Western counterparts. Japanese companies use accounting systems more to motivate employees to act in accordance with long-term manufacturing strategies than to provide senior managers with precise and essentially short-term data on costs, variances and profits. Hiromoto claims that Japanese accounting plays more of an 'influencing' role than an 'information' role in the managerial process.

When estimating the cost of new products, for example, many Japanese companies do not rely on prevailing engineering standards. Instead, they establish target costs derived from estimates of a competitive market price. These target costs are usually well below those currently achievable by the firm. Managers are then set benchmarks to measure their progress towards meeting the target cost objectives by means of design and technology improvements. This amounts to a market-led approach whereby operating costs and efficiencies are designed to achieve a desired state of competitiveness.

A good example of market-led accounting practice is provided by Hiromoto's (1988) description of the Daihatsu Motor Company. The process begins when a product development manager instructs the functional departments to submit the features and performance specification that they believe the car should include.

The next stage is cost estimation. However, management does not simply present the development specification to the accountants to determine what it should cost to build the car based on existing engineering standards. Instead, Daihatsu establishes a target selling price, based on what it believes the market will accept, and specifies a target profit margin that reflects the company's strategic plans and financial projections. The difference between these two figures represents the allowable cost per car.

Throughout the design process, which usually lasts for three years, the design engineers frequently liaise with staff from other functional areas (purchasing, shop floor, sales, etc.) who will implement the final design. As the process unfolds, the participants compare estimated costs with the targets. The variances are fed back to the product developers, and the cycle repeats: design proposals, cost estimates, variance calculations, value engineering analysis to include desired features at the lowest possible cost. The cycle ends with the approval of the final design that meets the target cost.

The market-led philosophy at Daihatsu and other Japanese companies helps to explain why standard costing systems are used less extensively in Japan than in Britain. Standard costs reflect an engineering-led approach where the goal is to minimize variances within existing technological constraints. Market-driven management, on the other hand, emphasizes doing whatever is necessary to achieve a desired performance level under market conditions. How efficiently a company should make a product is less important to the Japanese than how efficiently it must be able to build it for success in marketplace.

Hiromoto highlights a central principle that seems to guide management accounting in Japan – accounting practices are subservient to corporate strategy and not independent of it.

Non-financial measures of performance

In recent years, world-class manufacturing companies have introduced dramatic changes to their manufacturing processes. These changes are intended to make radical improvements in the companies' competitiveness by improving quality, reducing lead times, reducing costs and enhancing production flexibility. These changes brought in their wake new measures to track progress. These new measures were predominately non-financial for two reasons. Firstly, financial measures are by their nature a transposition into monetary units of events in the physical world (units of time, number of breakdowns, number of defective parts, number of line stops, number of units scrapped, number of late deliveries) and therefore an abstraction of what is really going on. Secondly, financial measures are calculated and reported some time after the events have occurred and by then the problem should have been identified and resolved. Because of their immediacy and relevance to problem solving these non-financial measures became as important as financial ones. The day-to-day control of manufacturing and distribution operations soon came to rely on non-financial measures.

Whether the chosen strategy was differentiation or cost leadership non-financial measures played a critical role in providing fast feedback. This enabled the detection and resolution of problems as they occur, instead of waiting for several days while reports are produced. Many problems can be detected on the spot by the operators if they are provided with training and equipment that enables them to monitor quality, rate of flow, set-up time, etc. Performance measured in non-financial units can be produced with a rapidity unachievable by financial measures.

This preoccupation with non-financial measures has been formalized by Kaplan and Norton into a new managed tool, the Balanced Scorecard (BSC). The fundamental purpose of the BSC is to tell a story about how the company is going to compete; as such it is much more than an ad hoc collection of interesting performance metrics. The metrics are derived from the strategy and organized into four perspectives: financial (shareholder perspective); customer; internal processes, innovation and learning. Besides telling a story about competitive advantage, the metrics also explain how this is to be achieved, by being related to each other through cause-and-effect relationships. Consequently an action programme to improve a metric in one perspective will cause improvements in other metrics in other perspectives at a later date.

The Kaplan and Norton scorecard is balanced in a number of important ways:

(a) Four perspectives. Instead of focusing primarily on the financial perspective, the scorecard is a visible reminder that financial results are just that; they are the consequence of doing some other things as well as or better than competitors, and it is these other things that drive competitive advantage and ultimately financial performance. Vigilance is required to maintain critical levels of performance in all four perspectives: failure to do so inevitably ends in tears.

(b) Leading and lagging indicators. While the financial perspective contains lagging indicators – what was achieved last quarter, last month, the other perspectives are leading indicators. A rise in customer complaints or a fall in customer satisfaction this period may herald increased customer churn with attendant increases in costs and decrease in revenues next period. Failure to invest in human capital (innovation and learning perspective) may mean that personnel are ill equipped to explain product features to customers or cannot operate customer database information efficiently and so forth.

(c) Financial and non-financial. Events in organizations are principally non-financial: physical metrics are much more useful than their financial equivalents. Instruments in cars give fuel in gallons, not euros; speed in kilometres per hour not the fine for being 20kph over the speed limit.

(d) Short-run and long-run. One of the most difficult trade-offs is that between short-run and long-run performance. The balanced scorecard with its three non-financial perspectives of metrics derived from strategy keep management's attention focused on creating competitive advantage. An endeavour that takes years to accomplish and a fraction of that time to destroy.

The classic form of the balanced scorecard is shown in Figure 38.3.

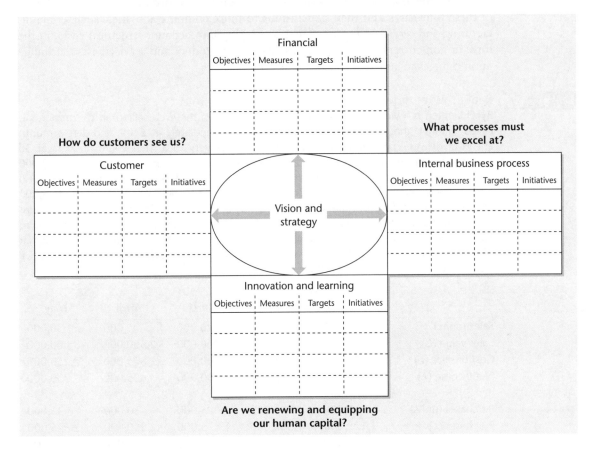

Figure 38.3 Balanced scorecard

(Adapted from Robert S. Kaplan and David P. Norton. Using the Balanced Scorecard Management System, *Harvard Business Review*. January–February 1996)

Managing profitability under growth, inflation, recession and deflation

Growth, inflation, recession and deflation are four distinct market phenomena that have their own characteristics and require a clear understanding of their implications for profitability management. Growth and recession result from changes in demand that impact activity levels and financing requirements. Income flows and cash flows are brought together in the management of profitability. Inflation and deflation are monetary phenomena. While they often impact directly upon activity levels, they are caused by changes in the value of money as against other things. As we saw in Chapter 30, they result from monetary instability, as well as instability in currency exchange rates.

For the purpose of obtaining a clear view of the nature and implications of these four phenomena, the following examples are based on simplifying assumptions, notably in choosing a simple trading business with no structural costs. Growth and inflation often occur together, as do recession and deflation. For simplicity and clarity, we assume that they are distinct and unconnected occurrences. The extrapolation of these four cases and their conclusions to more complex activities, such as manufacturing and service companies, involves taking into account structural costs, in the form of non-current assets, as well as changes in product and service costs that hinge upon changes in activity level and unit product costs.

Example 38.2 **Real growth under constant prices**

Bycel Limited is a virtual trading company operating on the Web selling an IT component, called 'Gadget' that it imports at £75 and resells immediately at £100. It orders a month ahead of delivery, pays with order and resells on delivery to a small client network at 30 days credit. Activity volume in a narrow market has been constant for some time at 10,000 units a month under stable price conditions. A considerable increase in market demand has led the company to raise its forecast sales volume for the immediate future by 5,000 units monthly, holding the sale price constant at £100. There will be no volume discount on purchased components. On 1 January 20X0, imports for January deliveries amounted to 10,000 units costing £750,000, receivables were £1,000,000 and the bank balance stood at £700,000. The increased volume of trade was due to start on 1 February. Figures for the five months beginning 1 January 20X0 were as follows:

	January	February	March	April	May
Sales (units)	10,000	15,000	20,000	25,000	30,000
Sales value (£)	1,000,000	1,500,000	2,000,000	2,500,000	3,000,000
Cost of sales (£)	750,000	1,125,000	1,500,000	1,875,000	2,250,000
Net income (£)	250,000	375,000	500,000	625,000	750,000
Purchases (units)	15,000	20,000	25,000	30,000	35,000
Purchases (£)	1,125,000	1,500,000	1,875,000	2,250,000	2,625,000
Receivables (£)	1,000,000	1,000,000	1,500,000	2,000,000	2,500,000
1/1 Cash balance	700,000	575,000	75,000	(300,000)	(550,000)
Receivables	1,000,000	1,000,000	1,500,000	2,000,000	2,500,000
Purchases	1,125,000	1,500,000	1,875,000	2,250,000	2,625,000
31/1 Cash balance	575,000	75,000	(300,000)	(550,000)	(675,000)

These figures are shown graphically in Figure 38.4.

Managing profitability under real growth, assuming zero monetary inflation, indicates that the only restriction to increased profitability is financing the expansion in the activity volume. Given that the company is a credit-giver to its clients, but cannot obtain credit from suppliers that would compensate the deficit, the question is 'how much growth can we afford?' The financing deficit appears as a short-term phenomenon that is absorbed as the growth in income translates into cash.

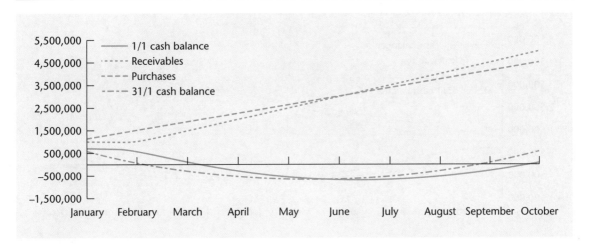

Figure 38.4

Managing profitability in these circumstances may be resolved in three ways:

1 Obtain a short-term bridging loan or a bank overdraft to finance the time-lag before increasing income translates into increasing liquidity.
2 Discount receivables for immediate cash.
3 Adjust the rate of growth to that which can be afforded without running out of cash.

Example 38.3 **Inflation under constant volume**

Assume that Bycel Limited is operating in a mature market, enjoying a constant sales volume yielding a steady level of net income. Government policy seeks to stimulate economic growth through fiscal and monetary policies that have resulted in an uncontrolled expansion of cheap credit, giving rise to massive monetary inflation without the real growth that it was intended to produce. The resulting impact on Bycel Limited was as follows:

	January	February	March	April	May
Sales (units)	10,000	10,000	10,000	10,000	10,000
Sales value (£)	1,000,000	1,500,000	2,000,000	2,500,000	3,000,000
Cost of sales (£)	750,000	1,125,000	1,500,000	1,875,000	2,250,000
Net income (£)	250,000	375,000	500,000	625,000	750,000
Purchases (units)	10,000	10,000	10,000	10,000	10,000
Purchases (£)	1,125,000	1,500,000	1,875,000	2,250,000	2,625,000
Receivables (£)	1,000,000	1,000,000	1,500,000	2,000,000	2,500,000
1/1 Cash balance	700,000	575,000	75,000	(300,000)	(550,000)
Receivables	1,000,000	1,000,000	1,500,000	2,000,000	2,500,000
Purchases	1,125,000	1,500,000	1,875,000	2,250,000	2,625,000
31/1 Cash balance	575,000	75,000	(300,000)	(550,000)	(675,000)

These figures are shown graphically in Figure 38.5.

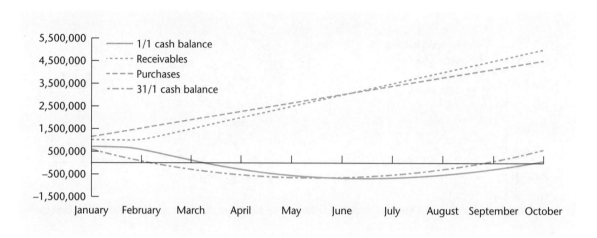

Figure 38.5

It is apparent that inflation and real growth are similar phenomena in their monetary and accounting expression and require financing in the same way. However, inflation has pernicious effects as higher corporate income attracts increased taxation and leads to claims for higher dividends out of higher reported corporate income.

Managing profitability in these circumstances may be resolved by obtaining short-term bridging loans or bank overdrafts to finance the time lag before increasing monetary income translates into increasing liquidity, or by resorting to discounting receivables. Government monetary policies aimed at controlling inflation through the restriction of bank credit lead to small and medium-sized businesses going into bankruptcy. Likewise, financial markets may freeze up and the willingness to discount trade bills for cash will lead to increased discounting rates. Large companies, being too large to fail, will receive the necessary financial assistance and will survive.

The option of reducing the level of inflationary growth to the level that a company can afford is not available. Unlike Example 38.2 above, the question is not 'how much growth can we afford?', but 'how much inflation can we handle?' Moreover, the combination of moderate growth levels expected in normal circumstances coupled with modest inflation has a cumulative impact on the financing requirement. Since the only option that exists is to reduce real growth, there will be a trade-off between real growth and inflation, leading to the phenomenon known as 'stagflation' (stagnation with inflation).

Example 38.4 Recession under constant prices

Assume that the economy entered into recession on 1 June 20X0, with the general level of demand falling without significant deflation. For the purposes of illustration, assume that Bycel Limited had been able to reach the higher income level of a volume of activity that resulted from unrestrained growth in the previous months by securing a bridging loan to cover accumulated cash deficit of £675,000 by 1 June 20X0. On 1 June 20X0, Bycel Limited reduced its volume of activity by 5,000 units per month until 1 October, when the market steadied. Import prices and selling prices for 'Gadget' remained unchanged during this period. The resulting impact on Bycel Limited was as follows:

	June	July	August	September	October
Sales (units)	25,000	20,000	15,000	10,000	10,000
Sales value (£)	2,500,000	2,000,000	1,500,000	1,000,000	1,000,000
Cost of sales (£)	1,875,000	1,500,000	1,125,000	750,000	750,000
Net income (£)	625,000	500,000	375,000	250,000	250,000
Purchases (units)	10,000*	15,000	10,000	10,000	10,000
Purchases (£)	750,000	1,125,000	750,000	750,000	750,000
Receivables (£)	3,000,000	2,500,000	2,000,000	1,500,000	1,000,000
1/1 Cash balance	(675,000)	1,575,000	2,950,000	4,200,000	4,950,000
Receivables	3,000,000	2,500,000	2,000,000	1,500,000	1,000,000
Purchases	750,000	1,125,000	750,000	750,000	750,000
31/1 Cash balance	1,575,000	2,950,000	4,200,000	4,950,000	5,200,000

*Purchases in May amounted to 35,000 units for June delivery, which was 10,000 in excess, actual deliveries of 25,000 units left 10,000 units in unsold inventory. August deliveries being revised downwards to 15,000 units, actual purchases in July were only 10,000 units to complement the 10,000 units in inventory for deliveries of 15,000 units in August. De-stocking resulted in cash savings of £750,000 in July.

These figures are shown graphically in Figure 38.6.

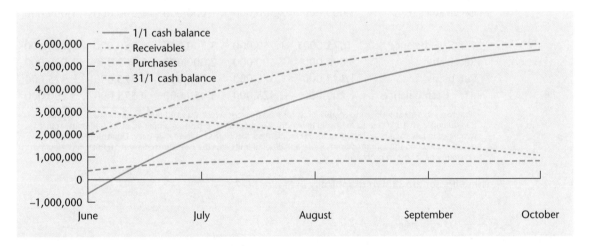

Figure 38.6

Under the simplifying assumption of constant prices used in this example, managing profitability under recession is a matter of dealing with reductions in activity volumes. It results in falling income and in disinvestment from inventories and receivables that progressively are converted into cash. These phenomena are consistent with periods of recession, when business confidence evaporates, investment ceases, assets are liquidated and debts reduced. The disappearance of investment opportunities takes investors to the sidelines, awaiting for a return of business confidence and renewed investment opportunities.

Example 38.5 Deflation under constant volume

Deflation is a phenomenon affecting the value of money against all other goods and is reflected in falling prices. Generally, it occurs during periods of recession, when price competition occurs between producers and suppliers seeking to protect activity levels. In this example, deflation is segregated from deflation in order to identify clearly its consequences for the management of profitability.

Given that Bycel Limited imports 'Gadget', payment being made in a foreign currency for sale in sterling in its home market. The demand for 'Gadget' in the home market remains constant, but by 1 June 20X0, the foreign currency is falling rapidly in relation to sterling. Bycel Limited decides to transfer the benefit of the reduction of the import cost to its clients and lowers selling prices in the same ratio. The activity volume remains constant, but prices are falling monthly, so that the same volume is being transacted at lower values, as follows:

	June	July	August	September	October
Sales (units)	25,000	25,000	25,000	25,000	25,000
Sales value (£)	2,500,000	2,000,000	1,500,000	1,000,000	1,000,000
Cost of sales (£)	1,875,000	1,500,000	1,125,000	750,000	750,000
Net income (£)	625,000	500,000	375,000	250,000	250,000
Purchases (units)	15,000*	25,000	25,000	25,000	25,000
Purchases (£)	1,125,000	1,375,000	875,000	375,000	375,000
Receivables (£)	3,000,000	2,500,000	2,000,000	1,500,000	1,000,000
1/1 Cash balance	(675,000)	1,950,000	3,700,000	4,950,000	5,700,000
Receivables	3,000,000	2,500,000	2,000,000	1,500,000	1,000,000
Purchases	1,125,000	1,375,000	875,000	375,000	375,000
31/1 Cash balance	1,200,000	2,325,000	3,450,000	4,575 000	5,200,000

*Purchases in May amounted to 35,000 units for June delivery, which was 10,000 in excess actual deliveries of 25,000 units, left 10,000 units in unsold inventory. August deliveries being maintained at 25,000 units, actual purchases in July were only 15,000 units to complement the 10,000 units in inventory. Due to the rate of deflation affecting the foreign currency, these additional units cost the same in sterling as 10,000 units would previously have cost to purchase.

These figures are shown graphically in Figure 38.7.

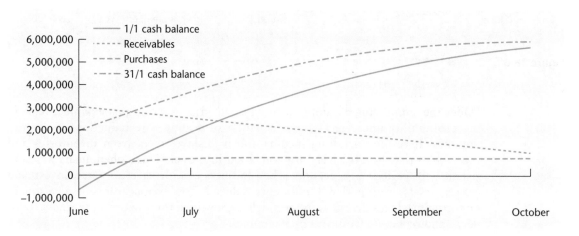

Figure 38.7

It is apparent that deflation has the same impact as recession on profitability and liquidity, with accompanying reduction in income and increases in liquidity as the activity level needs progressively less financing.

Summary

The traditional concern with costs for managing profitability has been criticized for being too narrow and inward-looking. The problems to which strategic management control is addressed broaden the range of information relevant to the management of profitability to include information on the market environment in which the enterprise operates, such as competitors, customers and product. This emerging discipline relates strategic planning to strategic management control. It adds a further dimension to conventional budgetary planning and control through its focus on activity analysis, customer profitability analysis, competitor analysis, market-led accounting and the development of non-financial measures of performance. The management of profitability also requires knowledge of the financial management implications of growth, inflation, recession and deflation.

Self-assessment questions

1 Contrast the objectives of strategic management control with conventional methods of budgetary planning and control.

2 State the four conditions necessary to the successful operation of a strategic management control system.

3 Define value-added and non-value-added. Give examples of each.

4 What kinds of questions does profitability analysis address?

5 Describe in general terms the steps taken in competitor analysis.

6 Explain what is meant by 'market-led accounting'.

7 Identify four non-financial measures of performance. Why are they important?

8 Discuss briefly the implications of managing profitability under growth, inflation and recession.

References

Bromwich, M. and Bhimani, A. (1989) *Management Accounting: Pathways to Progress,* Chartered Institute of Management Accountants.

Clarke, P.J. (1995) The old and the new in management accounting, *Management Accounting*, June.

Hiromoto, T. (1988) Another hidden edge: Japanese management accounting, *Harvard Business Review*, July–August.

Howell, R.A. and Soucy, S.R. (1990) Customer profitability – as critical as product profitability, *Management Accounting* (USA), October.

Kaplan, R.S. and Norton, D.P. (1996) *The Balanced Scorecard*, Harvard Business School Press.

Porter, M.E. (1985) *Competitive Advantage: Creating and Sustaining Superior Performance*, New York, The Free Press.

Richardson, R.R. (1988) *Cost Containment*, The Free Press.

Roslender, R., Hart, S. and Ghosh, J. (1998) Strategic management accounting: refocusing the agenda, *Management Accounting* (UK), December.

PART 4

Accounting for multinational corporations

Introduction to Part 4

The emergence and rapid expansion of a global market economy is a relatively recent phenomenon that has had a significant impact on traditional social, political and economic systems, and the values and beliefs with which peoples and nations had long established their identity. The success of Western industrial capitalism in raising living standards by applying the scientific method to develop knowledge, technologies and processes breached national barriers to economic growth, and projected its own culture throughout the rest of the world.

Commercial capitalism associated with early forms of international markets gave this evolution its earliest means with the development of structures such as international partnerships, early forms of banking to facilitate the management of funds, legal rules for defining business procedures and accounting methods for business control.

Industrial capitalism associated with the development of factory production gave this evolution its most significant legal structure in the form of the limited liability company, through the Companies Act 1844 followed by the Limited Liability Act 1855. It was adopted subsequently in the USA and on other Western countries. This legislation protected wealth from business risk and encouraged personal investment into corporate activity and endowed modern capitalism with most needed structure as it evolved through the Industrial to the Technological and Information Revolution. It opened the path to unrestricted access to funds for financing business expansion. It provided the universal model for structuring the global market economy using networks of legal structures that have their own identity, legal right, strategies and resources as supra-national entities operating under effectively de-regulated conditions.

By severing the link between ownership and control in corporate management and removing liability for business risk from corporate managers, the way opened for the development of banking and credit institutions and financial markets. Risk is an essential ingredient of business success and the management of risk an essential feature of corporate management. It was the eventual recognition of this truism that saw the evolution of financial capitalism in recent decades, giving ultimate authority and power to financial institutions.

The recent development of a global market economy may be argued to have had its genesis in financial capitalism, driven by wealth creation through profit-seeking. Today, hedge funds, equity funds, financial derivatives and a host of other structures and products have brought to an end that period of Western economic development that saw its essential problem as the manufacture of goods and the provision of services, and profitability as the measure of business efficiency.

Accounting for multinational corporations has its logic in the history, traditions and culture of Western European nations. The institutional framework that provides the rules, structures and the means that define the environment in which multinational corporations operate has its roots in the same context in which accounting philosophy, methods and practices have evolved. Accordingly, accounting for multinational corporations covers a wide range of issues of particular significance in dealing with the problems of the global market economy – social problems that involve accountability, political problems concerning regulations and accounting problems with respect to developing standards.

As noted earlier, financial capitalism has created a different accounting environment than that associated with industrial and commercial capitalism – the former is focused on creating and transacting values, the latter is concerned with business efficiency through the management of profitability. The result is seen in the presence of two business models. Financial institutions have a business model for managing credit; industrial and commercial enterprises employ a business model for managing resources. Financial institutions have enormous leverage on business enterprises, as may be seen in the importance attached to shareholder value and value-based accounting and away from traditional accounting based on profitability and historic cost accounting.

Our objective in this Part is two-fold. First, we aim to provide readers with an insight into the elegant simplicity of the mechanics for reducing the complexities of accounting consolidation in multinational corporations. Second, we refer this discussion to an examination of the management control systems used within industrial and commercial enterprises for effectively managing resources in attaining corporate business objectives.

SECTION 1

Financial accounting for groups of companies

CHAPTER 39

Financial reporting for groups of companies

Setting the scene

In simple terms, a group of companies is an economic reality existing whenever two or more separate companies operate under unified control. The dominant company is known as the parent company and the other companies are known as subsidiary companies. The parent company controls the subsidiary companies through a majority shareholding interest that enables it to control the board of directors of subsidiary companies. All companies within a group of companies retain their own legal personality, activities, assets and liabilities. They maintain their own separate accounting systems and prepare annual financial statements. In law, a group of companies is not recognized as a legal entity. It is an accounting fiction resulting from the need to give shareholders and investors a view of the group performance as a whole by unifying (consolidating) the year-end financial statement of its separate member companies. The mechanics of consolidation is a simple additive process based on accumulating the accounting numbers on all the separate balance sheets, income statements and cash-flow statements of individual companies into single statements for the group as a whole. All subsidiary companies, including foreign ones, are consolidated onto the parent company's own statements and, in the case of foreign subsidiaries, translated into the parent company's operating currency and brought into conformity with its accounting rules. It is a bottom-up process, requiring the elimination of all transactions between group companies to present a unified view of the financial performance of the group to external parties. It is a process through which complexity is reduced progressively through simplification, enabling the most complex structures and activities to be condensed into a single set of accounting numbers.

Learning objectives

After studying this chapter you should be able to:

1 define a group of companies;

2 understand the complexities of consolidating the financial statements of international groups of companies;

3 give examples of internal transactions requiring elimination on consolidation;

4 explain the procedures involved in the consolidating the financial statements of international groups of companies;

5 prepare a consolidated financial statement;

6 discuss the relevant international accounting standards issued by the International Accounting Standards Board.

Corporate growth has manifested itself in several ways. By the process of horizontal integration, firms engaged in the production or sale of comparable goods have combined to create monopoly or semi-monopoly situations. Similarly, the process of vertical integration has been important in the historical process by which the giant corporation has emerged. Vertical integration is the combination of firms having a supplier–customer relationship. Finally, the conglomerate is a group of companies having diversified activities, which has been brought under centralized control. The process of corporate growth has continued unabated for several decades. The multinational corporation has emerged, with activities straddling many nations, creating thereby special managerial and accounting problems. Through these processes groups of companies have emerged as a major feature of modern industrial and commercial organization.

There are many reasons why this external expansion by the process of 'acquiring' or 'merging with' another company is preferred to investing in internal expansion. External expansion provides a growing company with immediate access to productive capacity, distribution networks and suppliers, thereby avoiding startup delays which could be lengthy and costly. Also, by acquiring an existing company, the growing company obtains an existing experience of its problems, profitability and other factors relevant to the new management, indicating the success factors and the pitfalls associated with a new business venture. Similarly, the easiest way of entering a competitive market may be by acquiring an existing company, thereby avoiding the risks and problems which a new entrant to that market would face.

This chapter is concerned with setting out the framework within which the accounting problems of 'groups' of companies may be discussed. These revolve around two principal issues:

1 How should a group be defined?
2 How should consolidated accounts be prepared?

The regulatory framework

United Kingdom law and practice is defined in the Companies Act 2006 that consolidated the previous legislation contained in the Companies Acts 1985 and 1989 that contained detailed requirements governing consolidation, and FRS 2 'Accounting for Subsidiary Undertakings' (1992 amended 2009). Although the standard operates within and in accordance with these requirements, it made significant improvements to these provisions by reducing alternatives and by making definitions and requirements more precise. In addition, FRS9 'Associates and Joint Ventures' 1997 deals with companies which are closely related to a group, but do not fall within it for the purpose of consolidation.

FRS 2 Paragraph 57 provides that compliance with the FRS ensures compliance, and hence convergence, with IAS 27 'Consolidated Financial and Separate Financial Statements' 1989 (and as issued on 1 January 2009). Where directors of a company prepare International Accounting Standard group accounts, they must state in the notes to those accounts that they have been prepared in accordance with international accounting standards.

Definition of a group

If two separate companies operate independently of each other, they will maintain separate accounting records and prepare separate financial statements. However, if one company controls the other, a group is said to exist which consists of the controlling or parent company and the controlled or subsidiary company. Both companies will retain their separate legal identity and operations and separate accounting records. Equally, they will remain responsible in law for all their actions and liable to tax on their own profits. However, the objective of preparing financial statements in the form of balance sheets, income statements and cash flow statements assumes an additional dimension. If the shareholders of the parent company are to be fully informed of its activities, they will need to be informed about the substance of the controlling interest it has in the subsidiary company. This information need is met by the preparation of consolidated accounts for the group, in the form of a consolidated balance sheet and a consolidated income statement, created by aggregating the separate balance sheets and income statements of the parent and subsidiary companies.

The initial problem to be resolved is how to determine when an obligation to produce consolidated accounts exists. United Kingdom law and practice, as reflected in the Companies Acts and FRS 2, is based on the legal control concept. An undertaking is a parent undertaking in relation to another undertaking, a subsidiary, if:

1 it holds a majority of the voting rights in the undertaking; or
2 it is a member of the undertaking and has the right to appoint or remove a majority of its board of directors; or
3 it has the right to exercise dominant influence over the undertaking
   (a) by virtue of provisions contained in the undertaking's memorandum or articles; or
   (b) by virtue of a control contract; or
4 it is a member of the undertaking and controls alone, pursuant to an agreement with other shareholders or members, a majority of the voting rights in the undertaking.

This definition of a subsidiary is based on a company's ability to exercise control over another, rather than on the ownership of a majority of a particular class of shares. Accordingly, a group is said to exist whenever legal entities which are independent of each other are brought under central management, regardless of the situation of the equity ownership. In addition to implementing the EC Seventh Directive, this change to the definition of a subsidiary should curb the use of off-balance-sheet finance vehicles used, for example, to reduce the apparent level of group borrowing through special purpose vehicles controlled by the parent company but structured to fall outside the pre-1989 Companies Act definition. Some companies which were not subsidiaries under the previous definition have been consolidated by the requirements of the Act. Vehicles other than companies, including certain partnerships and joint ventures, can also come within the consolidation requirement.

Finally, as far as definitions are concerned, it is appropriate at this stage to note the existence of the concept of an associated company. FRS 9 'Associates and Joint Ventures' 1997 defines an associate as an investor who holds a participating interest and exercises a significant influence in the direction of its investee through participation in policy decisions. An associated company is not part of the group and its accounts are, therefore, not consolidated with those of other group companies. Instead, the concept of equity accounting is applied, the principles of which are dealt with in Chapter 40.

Preparation of consolidated accounts

The purpose of preparing consolidated accounts is to present the financial results and position of the companies in the group as though they were a single enterprise. Generally, all companies within a group adopt the same accounting year. When the final accounts of all the separate companies in the group have been prepared, the process of preparing group accounts is begun. To put it very simply, consolidated accounts are prepared by aggregating all the individual balance sheets and income statements. The balance sheet and income statement of the parent company are used as the basis for compiling the group balance sheet and income statement. Thus, the shareholders of the parent company receive a group balance sheet, a group income statement and a group cash-flow statement, which are expansions of those of the parent company, resulting from adding to the parent company's accounts those of its subsidiaries.

The objective of consolidation is to present the accounts of the group as if it were a single business. This objective requires that all internal group transactions are eliminated and that only the transactions external to the group are recorded in the consolidated accounts. Examples of internal transactions requiring elimination on consolidation include:

1 inter-company income and expenditure, such as sales, purchases, rents, royalties, interest or dividends;
2 inter-company profits and losses included in the assets of the group. Typically, this will affect closing inventory resulting from inter-company purchases and comprising the selling company's profit margin on sales. Accordingly, this profit margin must be excluded from the valuation of closing inventory and a corresponding adjustment made to net income (this is discussed further below);
3 inter-company debts and claims, whether short-term trading accounts or long-term advances;
4 the investment in the subsidiary recorded in the books of the parent company is cancelled with the issued share capital of the subsidiary.

In a simple situation, the above elimination followed by aggregation of the remaining balances is all that is required to produce a consolidated balance sheet and income statement. However, two further adjustment areas should be recognized and will frequently be encountered.

First, if the parent company owns less than 100 per cent of the total issued capital of the subsidiary, a minority interest is said to exist in that subsidiary. These non-group shareholders have an interest in the income and net assets of the subsidiary which must be reflected in the consolidation process. United Kingdom practice effects the consolidation on a control rather than an ownership basis and then separately recognizes any minority interest. Thus, even if less than 100 per cent of the issued capital of the subsidiary is owned by the parent company, the whole of the assets, liabilities and income statement items of the subsidiary are aggregated with those of the holding company, and the minority interest is then shown separately in the consolidated financial statements. As far as the balance sheet is concerned, it is necessary to compute the non-group shareholders' interest in the net assets (share capital and reserves) of the subsidiary at the balance sheet date. For income statement purposes, the minority shareholders' interest in the post-tax income for the year of the subsidiary is calculated and deducted in the consolidated income statement.

Reference was made above to the fact that inter-company income reflected in the assets of the group must be eliminated on consolidation, with an effect on the net income of the group. The question arises as to how the adjustment to income should be effected. While a number of possible methods may be encountered (some of which are discussed in Chapter 40), the general approach adopted in this book for illustration purposes is to treat all inter-company income adjustments as being adjustments to the reserves of the group as a whole, without any effect on the reserves of income of any individual group company. Through this approach, minority interests in subsidiaries are unaffected by the inter-company income eliminated.

The second additional adjustment area will arise where the parent company purchased shares in an existing, operating subsidiary and paid a price for the shares which differed from their par (or nominal) value. This difference would arise because the parent company perceived that the accumulated income (or losses) of the subsidiary at acquisition rendered the shares worth more than (or less than) their par value. Such income or losses existing at the date the parent company purchased its interest in the subsidiary are known as pre-acquisition income (or losses) and are capitalized as part of the consolidation process, i.e. they are removed from the group's reserves figures and, together with the par value of the shares purchased, are compared with the cost of the investment to the parent company.

If the cost of the investment exceeds the total of share capital plus pre-acquisition reserves purchased, then goodwill arises on consolidation. Should the cost of the investment be less than the total of share capital plus pre-acquisition reserves purchased, then negative goodwill arises. The current UK accounting practice applicable to goodwill and negative goodwill is discussed in Chapter 40.

Example 39.1 below is a comprehensive example, together with worked solution, of the preparation of consolidated financial statements. The problems relating to consolidated financial statements essentially relate to consolidated balance sheets and income statements. IAS 7 requires group companies also to prepare consolidated cash-flow statements, but as such statements are not significant to understanding the issues underlying the process of consolidation, we do not propose to discuss them further in this Part. As regards international groups trading in different currencies, they are required to consolidate on a standard currency, usually their national currency. In these cases, gains and losses on currency translation are shown in the consolidated income statement. Further practice questions are included at the end of the chapter.

Example 39.1 P plc is the parent company of S plc, the only subsidiary in the P Group. The following are their respective balance sheets and income statements as at 31 December 20X0.

Balance sheets at 31 December 20X0

	P plc			S plc		
	£	£	£	£	£	£
Non-current assets						
Tangible assets		210,000			180,000	
Investments						
Shares in S plc at cost		210,000			–	
Other shares		100,000			–	
Loan to S plc		50,000				
		570,000			180,000	
Current assets						
Inventory	220,000			80,000		
Debtors						
Trade debtors	420,000			260,000		
Owed by S plc	60,000			–		
Cash	130,000			80,000		
	830,000			420,000		
Creditors: amounts falling due within one year:						
Trade creditors	(480,000)			(79,000)		
Owed to P plc	–			(60,000)		
Net current assets		350,000			281,000	
Total assets *less* current liabilities			920,000			461,000
Creditors: amounts falling due after one year:						
Debenture loan		(100,000)			–	
Owed to P plc		–			(50,000)	
			820,000			411,000
Capital and reserves						
Called-up share capital		500,000			300,000	
Retained income brought forward for 20X0		270,000			90,000	
Income statement		50,000			21,000	
		820,000			411,000	

The following additional information is available:

1 P plc holds two-thirds of the issued share capital of S plc.
2 P plc has an issued capital of £50,000 shares of £10 each.
3 P plc also holds 10,000 shares in N plc acquired at £10 each. This holding represents 2 per cent of the equity of N plc.
4 P plc has made an interest-free loan of £50,000 to S plc, which is repayable in five years.
5 P plc is owed £60,000 by S plc in respect of sales made to the latter by the former. P plc has no outstanding debts towards S plc at the year end.
6 P plc's closing inventory comprised £30,000 purchased from S plc. S plc's profit margin on sales is 10 per cent. The opening inventory did not include any inventory acquired from S plc.
7 S plc's closing inventory comprised £20,000 purchased from P plc. P plc's profit margin on sales is 20 per cent. The opening inventory also included £20,000 purchased from P plc before it became the parent company of S plc.
8 Inter-company trading transactions were as follows:
   (a) P plc purchases from S plc amounted to £200,000 during the year.
   (b) S plc purchases from P plc amounted to £100,000 during the year.
   (c) P plc leased a building to S plc at an annual rent of £80,000.
9 S plc has paid a dividend of £30,000, being the dividend declared out of the previous year's income.
10 P plc purchased its interest in S plc on 1 January 20X0.

Income statement for the year ended 31 December 20X0

	P plc	S plc
	£	£
Turnover	2,320,000	1,000,000
Cost of sales	1,070,000	500,000
Gross income	1,250,000	500,000
Expenses	1,250,000	450,000
	0	50,000
Other operating income:		
Rent from S plc	80,000	–
	80,000	50,000
Income from shares in group companies: dividend S plc	20,000	–
Income from ordinary activities	100,000	50,000
Tax on ordinary activities	50,000	29,000
Income for the year after tax	50,000	21,000

Consolidated balance sheet as at 31 December 20X0 – worksheet

	P plc	S plc	P+S plc	Cancellation of inter-company debts and claims	Cancellation of parent company's investments in subsidiary and subsidiary's capital and reserves	Cancellation of inter-company profit/losses	Consolidated balance sheet
Non-current assets	£000	£000	£000	£000	£000	£000	£000
Tangible assets	210	180	390				390
Investments							
Shares in S plc	210	–	210		–210(c)		–
Other shares	100	–	100				100
Loan to S plc	50		50	–50(a)			
	570	180	750	–50	–210	–	490
Current assets							
Inventory	220	80	300			–7(e)	293
Debtors							
Trade debtors	420	260	680				680
Owed by S plc	60	–	60	–60			–
Cash	130	80	210				210
	830	420	1,250	–60(b)		–7(e)	1,183
Creditors: amounts falling due within one year:							
Trade creditors	(480)	(79)	(559)				(559)
Owed to P plc		(60)	(60)	–(60)			–
	(480)	(139)	(619)	–(60)(b)			(559)
Net current assets	350	281	631	–(b)	–	–7(e)	(624)
Total assets *less* current liabilities	920	461	1,381	50(a)	–210(c)	–7(e)	1,114
Creditors: amounts falling due after one year:							
Debenture loan	(100)	–	(100)				(100)
Owed to P plc		(50)	(50)	(–50)			–
	820	411	1,231	–a)	–210(c)	–7(e)	1,014
Capital and reserves							
Called-up share capital	500	300	800		-300(c)		500
Retained income brought forward	270	90	360		-90(c)		270
Difference on consolidation (non-distributable reserve)					50(c)	+20(f)	70
Consolidated income statement (20X0)	50	21	71			–34(g)	37
Minority interests					130(d)	+7(e)	137(h)
	820	411	1,231		–210	–7	1,014

(a), (b), (c), etc. refer to the accompanying explanatory notes.

Consolidated income statement for year ended 31 December 20X0 – worksheet

	P plc	S plc	P+S plc	Cancellation of inter-company income and expenses	Consolidation of profit on inter-company closing inventory	Cancellation of inter-company distributions	Consolidated income statement
	£000	£000	£000	£000	£000	£000	£000
Turnover	2,320	1,000	3,320	−300(i)			3,020
Cost of sales	(1,070)	(500)	(1,570)	+300(i)	(−7)(k)		(1,277)
Gross income	1,250	500	1,750	–	(−7)(k)		1,743
Expenses	(1,250)	(450)	(1,700)	+80(j)			(1,620)
Operating income	0	50	50	+80	(−7)		123
Other operating income:							
Rent from S plc	80	–	80	-80(j)			–
Total operating income	80	50	130	–	(−7)		123
Income from shares in group companies							
Dividend S plc	20	–	20			(20)(l)	–
Income from ordinary activities	100	50	150	—	(−7)	(20)	123
Tax on ordinary activities	(50)	(29)	(79)				(79)
Income for year after tax	50	21	71	–	(−7)(k)	(20)(l)	44
Minority interest in S plc's profit after tax for the year ($\frac{1}{3}\times$ 21)							(7)(m)
Consolidated income for the year							37

Explanatory notes: consolidated balance sheet as at 31 December 20X0

1 Cancellation of inter-company debts and claims

The rule requiring the cancellation of inter-company debts and claims is applied as follows:

(a) The cancellation of the loan of £50,000 by P plc to S plc. Therefore, it is eliminated from total group assets and total group liabilities, the net effect on the consolidated balance sheet being zero.

(b) The cancellation of the balance of £60,000 owed by S plc to P plc arising from inter-company sales. Therefore, it is eliminated from total group trade debtors and total group trade creditors, the net effect on the consolidated balance sheet being zero.

2 Cancellation of the parent company's investment in the subsidiary company and the cancellation of the subsidiary company's capital and reserves

The rule requiring the cancellation of the parent company's investment in the subsidiary company and the subsidiary company's capital and pre-acquisition reserves is applied as follows:

(c) The cancellation from total group assets of the shares acquired by P plc in S plc at their cost of £210,000.

The cancellation from total group capital and reserves of the called-up share capital and pre-acquisition reserves of S plc amounting to £390,000.

The substitution in the consolidated capital and reserves of a sum representing the difference between the value of the group's interest in the net worth of the subsidiary as against the cost at which this interest was acquired by the parent company. (It is calculated as shown on p. 290 of the 7th edition of this book.)

The negative goodwill is added to reserves on the consolidated balance sheet. (For the effect of the dividend paid by S plc on this figure, see (f) below.)

	£
S plc: Called-up share capital	300,000
Reserves	90,000
	390,000

	£
P plc: Two-thirds interest therein	260,000
Less: Cost of acquisition	210,000
Difference on consolidation ('negative goodwill')	50,000

(d) Where the subsidiary company is not wholly owned, the interest of minority shareholders has to be recognized on consolidation. It is shown as an external liability of the group, and is calculated as follows:

	£
S plc: Called-up share capital	300,000
Pre-acquisition reserves	90,000
	390,000

	£
Share of minority interests one-third thereof	130,000

This is subject to further adjustment for 20X0 profits – see (h) below.

3 Cancellation of inter-company profit/losses

The rule requiring the cancellation of inter-company income/losses is applied as follows:

(e) The closing inventory held by P plc and S plc resulting from inter-company transactions contain an inter-company income element which has to be eliminated from the valuation of closing inventory calculated as follows:

	£	£
P plc closing inventory purchased from S plc	30,000	
Inter-company income thereon being S plc's gross margin of 10 per cent		3,000
	£	
S plc closing inventory purchased from P plc	20,000	
Inter-company income thereon, being P plc's gross margin of 20 per cent		4,000
Inter-company income included in closing inventory		7,000

(f) The dividend of £30,000 paid by S plc was in respect of the previous year's income, i.e. a year before S plc became a subsidiary of P plc. The £20,000 of the dividend received by P plc is a dividend received out of pre-acquisition income and as such must be capitalized on consolidation.

In the books of P plc this £20,000 should have been credited to the investment account not to income, since it represents a return to P plc of part of the cost of its investment in S plc. Since this has not been done in the books of P plc, the adjustment must be effected on consolidation.

In the light of this, the negative goodwill arising on consolidation per note (c) above requires adjustment as follows:

	£	£
Two-thirds interest in the capital and pre-acquisition reserves of S plc ($\frac{1}{3} \times$ £390,000)		260,000
Cost of investment	210,000	
Less: Pre-acquisition dividend	(20,000)	190,000
Difference on consolidation (negative goodwill)		£70,000

(g) The group's consolidated income for 20X0 has to be calculated, and since no dividends were paid, the sum calculated will be shown on the balance sheet as at 31 December 20X0 as the income statement balance for the year. It is calculated as shown below.

	£	£
Total income of P plc and S plc as shown		71,000
Less: Cancellation of inter-company income on consolidation:		
Cancellation effected in respect of P plc:		
Dividends received from S plc	20,000	
Cancellation of profit element on closing inventory held by S plc and sold by P plc (note (e))	4,000	
Cancellation effected in respect of S plc:		
Cancellation of proft element on closing inventory held by P plc and sold by S plc (note (e))	3,000	27,000
		44,000
Less: Share of minority interests in S plc's income $-\frac{1}{3}$ of £21,000		7,000
		37,000

In accordance with the approach outlined earlier in this chapter, the minority interest in the 20X0 income of S plc is unaffected by the inter-company income elimination.

(h) It remains to show total amounts relating to minority interest, i.e.

	£
Share of S plc's income, calculated as above	7,000
Share of capital and pre-acquisition reserves (note (d))	130,000
	137,000

Explanatory notes: consolidated income statement for the year to 31 December 20X0

1 Cancellation of inter-company income and expenses

The rule requiring the cancellation of inter-company income and expenses is applied as follows:

(i) Inter-company sales and purchases are cancelled, as follows:

	£
P plc sales to S plc	100,000
S plc sales to P plc	200,000
–	300,000
P plc purchases from S plc	200,000
S plc purchases from P plc	100,000
–	300,000

It will be noted that these are, at this stage, self-cancelling adjustments as regards the consolidated gross income.

(j) Other inter-company income and expenses are cancelled, as follows:

	£
S plc rent paid to P plc	80,000

	£
P plc rent income received from P plc	80,000

It will be noted that these are likewise self-cancelling adjustments as regards consolidated operating income.

2 Cancellation of inter-company profits on closing inventory resulting from inter-company transactions

The rule requiring the cancellation of inter-company income on closing inventory resulting from inter-company transactions is applied as follows:

(k) The inter-company income on closing inventory amounting to £7,000, as calculated above (see (g)), have to be eliminated from the consolidated income. This is most conveniently effected by increasing cost of sales by £7,000, the amount of the income to be eliminated.

3 Cancellation of inter-company distributions

The rule requiring cancellation of inter-company distributions is applied as follows:

(l) The cancellation of inter-company distributions from group income on consolidation means that the dividends received by P plc from S plc must be eliminated from the consolidated income. Accordingly, the dividends amounting to £20,000 are eliminated from group revenues. Note (f) above pointed out that this is a pre-acquisition dividend, capitalized on consolidation.

4 Minority interest

The outside shareholders' interest in the subsidiary's net profit after tax for the year is calculated and deducted in the consolidated income statement: $\frac{1}{3} \times £21,000 = £7,000$.

Summary

Multinational groups of companies are associations of individual companies that act under unified control in the pursuit of their business objectives. They result from the process of mergers and acquisitions by companies, rather than through organic growth. Most large companies are international and constituted as groups, in which individual companies retain their legal and economic identity. The main objective of company legislation with regards to groups as such is to provide shareholders and investors with an annual global view of financial performance through the publication of annual consolidated financial statements in the form of balance sheets, income and cash-flow statements. They are founded on a legal fiction, for groups of companies have no legal personality, although effectively controlling their subsidiary and often controlling their associated companies. The procedure for consolidating the financial statements of group companies is a simple additive process that results in summarized numbers in which inter-company transactions have been eliminated.

1 Set out below are the balance sheets for Macro plc and Micro plc as at 31 December 20X0.

Balance sheets as at 31 December 20X0

	Macro plc			Micro plc		
	£000	£000	£000	£000	£000	£000
Non-current assets						
Tangible assets		5,121			1,230	
Investments						
Shares in Micro plc		962			–	
		6,083			1,230	
Current assets						
Inventory	1,244			514		
Debtors						
Trade debtors	2,048			390		
Owed by Micro plc	57			–		
Cash at bank	960			46		
	4,309			950		
Creditors: amounts falling due within one year						
Trade creditors	(2,825)			(634)		
Owed to P plc	–			(40)		
Taxation	(315)			(60)		
Net current assets		1,169			216	
Total assets less: current liabilities			7,252			1,446
Creditors: amounts falling due after one year						
Debenture loan			(750)			–
			6,502			1,446
			£000			£000
Capital and reserves						
Called-up share capital			1,800			600
Reserves brought forward			4,050			702
Income statement – 20X0			652			144
			6,502			1,446

Macro plc bought its holding of 400,000 ordinary shares in Micro plc when the latter's reserves stood at £312,000.

During the year ended 31 December 20X0, Macro plc regularly sold products to Micro plc at a selling price of cost plus $33\frac{1}{3}$ per cent. At 31 December 20X0, Micro plc's closing stock included £208,000 purchased from Macro plc.

The difference between the Micro plc's current account of £57,000 shown under debtors on Macro plc's balance sheet and Macro plc's current account of £40,000 shown under creditors on Micro plc's balance sheet is due to the fact that a cheque of £17,000 mailed by Micro plc on 31 December 20X0 was not received by Macro plc until 5 January 20X1.

Required:

Prepare a consolidated balance sheet for the Macro Group as at 31 December 20X0.

2 P plc is the parent company of S plc, the only subsidiary in the P Group. The following are their respective balance sheets and income statements as at 31 December 20X0:

Balance sheets at 31 December 20X0

	P plc			S plc		
	£000	£000	£000	£000	£000	£000
Non-current assets						
Tangible assets		40,000			20,000	
Investments						
Shares in S plc		12,000			–	
Other shares		3,000			–	
		55,000			20,000	
Current assets						
Inventory	7,100			6,600		
Debtors						
Trade debtors	8,000			4,000		
Owed by S plc	3,500			–		
Cash	3,400			2,400		
	22,000			13,000		
Creditors: amounts falling due within one year						
Trade creditors	(12,000)			(10,250)		
Owed to P plc	–			(3,500)		
Net current assets		10,000			(750)	
Total assets less current liabilities			65,000			19,250
Creditors: amounts falling due after one year						
Debenture loan			(23,000)			
			42,000			19,250
			£000			£000
Capital and reserves						
Called-up share capital			30,000			15,000
Reserves brought forward			10,000			4,000
Income statement for 20X0			2,000			250
			42,000			19,250

Income statements for the year ended 31 December 20X0

	P plc	S plc
	£000	£000
Turnover	300,800	150,500
Cost of sales	116,900	59,400
Gross income	183,900	91,100
Expenses	180,400	88,600
Operating income	3,500	2,500
Income from shares in group companies:		
Dividend S plc	500	–
Income on ordinary activities	4,000	2,500
Tax on ordinary activities	2,000	1,500
Income for the year after tax	2,000	1,000
Dividend	–	750
	2,000	250

The following additional information is also available:

1 P plc holds two-thirds of the issued share capital of S plc, comprising 1,000,000 shares of £10 acquired at £12 each.

2 P plc also holds 200,000 shares of £10 in N plc acquired for £3,000,000 representing 10per cent of the called-up capital of N plc.

3 P plc is owed £3,500,000 by S plc in respect of sales made to the latter by the former. P plc has no outstanding debts towards S plc at the year end, and does not purchase stock from S plc.

4 S plc's closing inventory included £5,000,000 purchased from P plc. P plc's profit margin on sales is 20 per cent. S plc's opening inventory did not include any inventory purchased from P plc. Total sales from P to S during the year were £15,000,000.

5 P plc purchased its shares in S plc on 1 January 20X0.

6 The dividend received by P plc from S plc is a distribution in respect of the year 20X0 income of S plc.

Required:

Prepare consolidated accounts for the group.

3 The balance sheets of Expanding plc and its two subsidiaries Growing plc and Declining plc as at 31 December 20X0 were as follows:

Balance sheets at 31 December 20X0

	Expanding plc	Growing plc	Declining plc
	£000	£000	£000
Non-current assets			
Tangible assets	525	210	60
Investments			
100,000 shares Growing plc	140	–	–
40,000 shares Declining plc	32	–	–
	697	210	60
Current assets			
Inventory	63	83	28
Debtors			
Trade debtors	60	36	15
Growing plc	24	–	–
Declining plc	16	9	–
Cash at bank	10	7	2
Creditors: amounts falling due within one year			
Trade creditors	(120)	(68)	(46)
Expanding plc	–	(22)	(16)
Growing plc	–	–	(8)
Net current assets	53	45	(25)
Total assets *less* current liabilities	750	255	35
Capital and reserves			
Called-up share capital (£1 shares)	400	150	50
Reserves brought forward	200	45	–
Income statement for 20X0	150	60	(15)
	750	255	35

The following additional information is available:

1 At 31 December 20X0, goods transferred at cost £2,000 were in transit between Expanding plc and Growing plc. A cheque for £1,000 was in transit between Declining plc and Growing plc.

2 The closing inventory of Expanding plc included goods supplied by Growing plc at an invoiced value of £3,600. Growing plc had priced these goods at cost plus 20 per cent, the standard group markup.

3 Expanding plc purchased all its investments in its subsidiaries on 1 January 20X0.

Required:

Prepare a consolidated balance sheet for the Expanding Group as at 31 December 20X0.

4* The balance sheets of Pip plc and its two subsidiaries Squeak plc and Wilfred plc as at 31 March 20X1 were as follows:

Balance sheets at 31 March 20X1

	Pip plc	Squeak plc	Wilfred plc
	£000	£000	£000
Non-current assets			
Tangible assets	315	120	77
Investments			
80,000 shares in Squeak plc	110	–	–
50,000 shares in Wilfred plc	45	–	–
Debentures in Squeak plc	5	–	–
	475	120	77
Current assets	250	70	41
Creditors: amounts falling due within one year			
Trade creditors	(100)	(20)	(30)
Proposed dividends			
Ordinary	(50)	(10)	–
Preference	–	(1)	–
Net current assets	100	39	11
Total assets less current liabilities	575	159	88
Creditors: amounts falling due after more than one year Debenture loan	–	(20)	–
	575	139	88
Capital and reserves			
Called-up share capital Ordinary shares of £1	500	100	80
10% Preference shares	–	10	–
General reserves	–	10	–
Income statement	75	19	8
	575	139	88

Income statements for the year ended 31 March 20X1

	Pip plc	Squeak plc	Wilfred plc
	£000	£000	£000
Balance at 31.3.X0	50	10	(2.4)
Dividend received from Squeak plc	2	–	–
Net income for year	73	32.5	10.4
	125	42.5	8
Transfer to general reserves	–	(10)	–
Dividends paid, ordinary shares		(2.5)	
Proposed dividends			
Ordinary shares	(50)	(10)	–
Preferrence shares	–	(1)	–
Balance at 31.3.X1	75	19	8

The following additional information is given:

1 The parent company purchased all its shares in its subsidiaries on 1 April 20X0.

2 There is no intra-group trading.

3 The parent company has recorded only dividend income received from its subsidiaries.

Required:

Prepare a consolidated balance sheet for the year ended 31 March 20X1.

CHAPTER 40

Understanding consolidated financial statements

Setting the scene

The process of consolidating the financial statements of many companies on the basis of the control exercised by the parent company, involves reducing the complexity that is mainly one of treating large numbers and eliminating the duplication arising through also accumulating inter-company transactions. Groups of companies are mostly brought into existence through market transactions in the shares of target companies leading to acquiring a controlling shareholding that allows restructuring through a legal and accounting merger. A shareholding in excess of 50 per cent of the relevant shares, is sufficient to give effective control. A parent company may control other companies with less than 100 per cent shareholding, so long as it has more than 50 per cent of the shares. The remaining shareholders are minority shareholders, whose financial interest must be shown and valued separately on consolidation. Likewise, depending on the level of diffusion in shareholdings, a shareholding of less than 50 per cent may give a company a significant interest in another company that will influence its management. Known as associated companies, their position in a group requires special treatment. The process of consolidation brings together local accounting rules and monetary measurements on to a common basis that these distinctions bring with them their own difficulties.

Learning objectives

After studying this chapter you should be able to:

1 appreciate the problems of accounting for minority interests in consolidated accounts;

2 explain the accountancy treatment of associated companies;

3 distinguish between merger and acquisition accounting;

4 discuss the problems of accounting for multinational groups.

Accounting for groups of companies is an important area of financial accounting by reason of the tendency of companies to grow by forming or acquiring subsidiary companies. Financial reporting for groups of companies by means of consolidated year-end accounting reports is complicated by a number of problems, which fall into two classes. First, there are technical problems of dealing with the complexity of data to be treated when preparing consolidated accounts. These problems have been explained in outline form in the previous chapter. Second, there are problems of understanding the nature of the consolidation process as it affects the meaning of the information which the accounts contain. This chapter deals with the following topics which are central to understanding consolidated financial statements:

1 minority interests present in subsidiaries that are less than 100 per cent owned;
2 the accounting treatment of associated companies;
3 mergers and acquisitions;
4 multinational groups.

The purpose of this chapter is to provide an introductory overview of the theory and practice of accounting for these complexities.

Accounting for minority interests

In this section, we discuss the problems of accounting for minority interests in consolidated accounts, where a parent–subsidiary relationship exists requiring the full consolidation of the balance sheets and income statements of companies so defined.

The assets, liabilities, revenues and expenses of the subsidiary must be consolidated in full with those of the parent company. The procedure for consolidation requires the elimination of inter-company transactions. The minority interests are represented as a separate item on the consolidated balance sheet and the consolidated income statement.

The problems relating to the recognition of minority interests in consolidated financial statements will be considered under the following headings:

1 the nature of the minority interest;
2 calculations required to quantify the minority interest;
3 the treatment of the elimination of extra group profits as far as the minority interest is concerned.

The nature of the minority interest

The question to be addressed here is: what is the nature of the minority interest, as reflected on a consolidated balance sheet? Two principal views exist. One view (the parent company concept) recognizes the parent company as being dominant in its relationship with the minority interest. The minority interest as depicted on the consolidated balance sheet is viewed as a liability of the group rather than a co-owner of the group. One result of this is that no attempt is made under this concept to attribute any goodwill relating to the holding company's acquisition of the subsidiary to the minority interest.

Example 40.1 H plc purchased 90 per cent of the issued capital of S plc for £90,000 when the net assets of S plc (at fair value) amounted to £80,000.

On consolidation, goodwill of £18,000 arises (i.e. £90,000 – 90 per cent of £80,000). Under the parent company concept, no attempt is made to attribute goodwill to the other 10 per cent of the capital held by the minority interest. (Any goodwill which was so attributed could be quantified as:

$$\frac{£18,000}{9} = £2,000$$

This could be added to goodwill and to minority interest on consolidation.)

FRS 2 'Accounting for Subsidiary Undertakings' states that the minority interest on a consolidated balance sheet should not be classified as part of shareholders' funds, thus indicating that UK standard practice adopts a parent company approach to the minority interest.

The alternative view is expressed in the entity concept which treats the parent company and the minority as partners or co-owners in the subsidiary. Under this concept, the minority interest is classified as part of shareholders' funds, and in quantifying the amount of that interest, parent company and minority would both be treated alike. Thus, referring back to Example 40.1, goodwill would be treated as being £20,000 (not £18,000) with £2,000 of that goodwill being added to the minority interest as shown on the consolidated balance sheet.

The calculation of minority interests

The objective of calculating minority interests on consolidation can be summarized as follows:

- for balance sheet purposes: to show the interest of the non-group shareholders in the net assets of the group as at the relevant balance sheet date;
- for income statement purposes: to show the non-group shareholders' interest in the profit after tax for the year of the subsidiary.

As far as the calculations are concerned, care is needed whenever there is more than one class of capital in the subsidiary, especially if the minority interest differs between the classes.

Example 40.2 Extracts from the financial statements of S plc for the year to 31 March 20X0 show the following:

Balance sheet		Income statement	
Called-up capital:			
£1 ordinary shares	£500,000	**Income after tax**	£65,000
£1 8% preference shares	50,000	**Preference dividend:**	
	550,000	Paid	(20,000)
		Proposed	(20,000)
Reserves:			
Retained income	160,000	**Ordinary dividend:**	
	£710,000	Proposed	(15,000)
Net assets	£710,000	Retained for the year	£10,000

It is known that H plc owns 80 per cent of the issued ordinary capital of S plc and 50 per cent of the issued 8 per cent preference shares. The calculation of the relevant minority interest figures is as follows:

Income statement

		Minority interest
Income after tax	£65,000	
Less: Preference dividends	(40,000) × 50%	£20,000
Equity income	£25,000 × 20%	£5,000
Total minority interest for the consolidated income statement		£25,000

Balance sheet

	Minority interest
Called-up share capital:	
Ordinary: £500,000 × 20%	£100,000
Preference: £50,000 × 50%	25,000
Reserves (all preference dividends have been paid or proposed	32,000
– so consider equity interest only) £160,000 × 20%	
Minority interest for the consolidated balance sheet	£157,000

Intra-group profit elimination

As mentioned in Chapter 39, a number of differing views exist as to how adjustments to eliminate unrealized intra-group income should be effected on consolidation. In some circumstances, the minority interest in the subsidiary may be affected by the choice of elimination method.

One view (as adopted for illustrative purposes in this book) is that the elimination of unrealized intra-group income is purely a 'consolidation' adjustment and is therefore dealt with in total group income or reserves, without allocating the adjustment to any specific company. On this view, where a subsidiary sells to a parent company and the goods remain in inventory, the calculation of any minority interest in that subsidiary is unaffected by income elimination.

A second approach is to allocate the income adjustment to the accounts of the group company which sold the inventory in question. Here, if S plc sells to P plc and the inventory remains in the parent company's balance sheet, any profit recorded by S plc on the transaction could be removed from its income figure. Consequently, the calculation of any minority interest in S plc will be based on the adjusted (reduced) income figure.

A third approach would, as in the first, treat any adjustment as a group adjustment but limit the adjustment to an amount equal to the parent company's percentage interest in the income of the selling subsidiary.

Example 40.3 H plc has owned 80 per cent of the issued capital of S plc since the incorporation of that company. During the year to 31 December 20X0, S plc sold goods to H plc at a profit of £10,000, these goods were unsold by H plc at 31 December. The retained income per the accounts of the two companies at 31 December 20X0 were H plc £100,000, S plc £50,000. The issued capital of S plc was £60,000 in £1 ordinary shares. The inventory in the balance sheets of the separate companies were H plc £250,000; S plc £170,000.

The three methods outlined above give the following results:

	Method one	Method two	Method three
Income adjustment	£	£	£
Group reserves	10,000		
S plc reserves		10,000	
Group reserves (80% of 10,000)			8,000
Consolidated reserves	£	£	£
H plc	100,000	100,000	100,000
S plc (80% of £50,000)	40,000		40,000
Income adjustment	(10,000)	(80% × 10,000)	(8,000)
S plc (80% of 50,000 – 10,000)	130,000	32,000	132,000
		132,000	
Minority interest for balance sheet	£	£	£
Subsidiary's capital	60,000	60,000	60,000
Subsidiary's reserves	50,000		50,000
(50,000 – 10,000)		40,000	
	110,000	100,000	110,000
Minority interest (20%)	22,000	20,000	22,000
Consolidated inventory	£	£	£
H plc	250,000	250,000	250,000
S plc	170,000	170,000	170,000
	420,000	420,000	420,000
Less: adjustment	(10,000)	(10,000)	(8,000)
	410,000	410,000	412,000

All these methods will be found in practice (together with others not covered here). It should be appreciated that no one method is viewed as being correct and often the amounts involved are immaterial in relation to the group's results and net assets.

Accounting for associated companies

The definition of an associated company was dealt with in Chapter 39. Here it is necessary to consider in detail the accounting treatment required by FRS 9 'Associates and Joint Ventures' 1997 in group accounts.

It will be recalled that an associated company holds a participating interest and exercises a significant influence on policy decisions. The associate is not consolidated in the group accounts, but instead is dealt with under the equity method of accounting for investments.

This method sets out to state the investment in the associate on the consolidated balance sheet, not at cost but at a figure approximating to the value of the equity interest in the associate. Also, because of the existence of participating interest, the income statement includes the investing company's share of profits of the associate, not just dividend income.

Table 40.1 summarizes and compares the equity accounting method with the consolidation method, and Example 40.4 then shows the FRS 9 balance sheet presentation of an investment in an associated company.

Table 40.1 Summary and comparison of equity, accounting and consolidation

	Consolidation	Equity accounting
Income statement	The dividend from the subsidiary is eliminated.	The dividend from the associate is eliminated.
	The income statement captions of the subsidiary are aggregated with those of the parent company.	The consolidated income statement includes as a separate item the group's share of the operating profit associate.
	A separate minority interest is calculated and disclosed.	No separate minority interest adjustment is necessary.
Balance sheet	The separate assets and liabilities of the subsidiary are aggregated with those of the parent company.	The investment account is retained, but stated at its equity value (per SSAP 1) i.e:
	The investment account and other internal items are cancelled.	Share of net assets of the associate (less goodwill) x
		Share of the associate's goodwill x
		Premium/discount on acquisition x x
		x
		=

Example 40.4 Octopus plc acquired a block of shares in Guppy plc for £100,000 on 1 January 20X0, giving it 25 per cent of the called-up capital. At that date the called-up capital and reserves of Guppy plc amounted to £360,000. In the balance sheet of Octopus plc, these shares would be shown at their historic cost of £100,000. On consolidation, Guppy plc would be defined as an associated company. Guppy plc's capital and reserves amount to £600,000 at 31 December 20X0, the net profit for the year being £240,000. Applying the equity method, the interest of the Octopus Group in Guppy plc will be shown as follows:

Consolidated balance sheet 31 December 20X0

	£
Non-current assets	
Investments:	
Shares in related company:	
25% of net assets (25% × £600,000)	150,000
Premium on acquisition (£100,000 – 25% × £360,000)	10,000
	160,000

The premium on acquisition above is, of course, purchased goodwill, the treatment of which is described below.

Mergers and acquisitions

Groups of companies may be formed in two ways. First, a parent company may form a subsidiary company. This is often the case with 100-per-cent-owned subsidiary companies. Second, a company may purchase shares in another company, that company becoming a subsidiary through a business combination.

Business combinations are a frequent topic of discussion in the financial press. They may result from discussions between two companies on the benefits which would flow from a merger of their business. On the other hand, negotiations between two companies may involve the acquisition of one company by the other. This is frequently a case of a big company acquiring a small successful company. Acquisitions may also result from aggressive expansionist policies of a company seeking to take over another company. In this case, the takeover will take the form of an acquisition of its shares by bidding up a price which will induce shareholders to sell them to the bidding company.

Current practice recognizes these differing situations by employing two different methods of recording business combinations in consolidated accounts:

1 acquisition accounting (also called the purchase method);
2 merger accounting (also called the pooling of interests).

Acquisition accounting

Under this, the consolidated balance sheet includes the assets and liabilities of the subsidiary at their cost to the group rather than at the values at which they are shown in the subsidiary's balance sheet.

The purchase method requires first the acquisition cost of the subsidiary to be established as a total by reference to the amount of cash paid and the value of shares exchanged for its shares. The second stage is to allocate the acquisition cost to the particular assets and liabilities of the subsidiary. The EC Seventh Directive gives little by way of guidelines on how this difficult task is to be performed, except to say that the acquisition cost should be allocated as much as possible to all identifiable assets and liabilities. FRS 2 'Accounting for Subsidiary Undertakings' includes a similar requirement, stating that allocation should be on the basis of the 'fair value' of the assets to the buying company. Any difference between the value of the subsidiary's net assets and the purchase consideration represents goodwill – positive or negative.

Merger accounting

Here, the business combination is treated as a merger which forms a new business as the result of the pooling of the assets and liabilities of two previously separate and independent businesses. The merger of two companies does not necessarily imply that one company disappears by liquidation. Frequently, mergers are implemented by the formation of a holding company to which the shares of the merging companies are transferred in exchange for shares in the holding company.

If the merging companies remain in business, but operate in the context of a group, then year-end consolidated accounts will have to be prepared. Accounting for mergers recognizes the on-going nature of the business by the pooling of the interests of the two companies. The assets and liabilities of both companies are therefore simply added together at the value at which they appear in the separate balance sheets, without 'fair value' adjustments arising.

The key income statement differences between merger and acquisition accounting is that the former consolidates for an entire year in the year of the merger and requires the prior year figures to be shown on a merged basis, while acquisition accounting does not. Acquisition accounting leads to the creation of goodwill, while merger accounting avoids it completely. Merger accounting was formally recognized in the Companies Act 1981, and the Accounting Standards Board issued FRS 6 'Acquisitions and Mergers' in 1995.

When is a combination a merger?

A business combination *may* be treated as a merger rather than as an acquisition in the following circumstances only:

1 if it results from an offer to all equity holders (and all holders of other voting shares), and
2 if the offer is accepted by at least 90 per cent of the equity shareholders (by value and by votes), and
3 if the new parent company did not hold more than 20 per cent of the equity or votes immediately before the merger, and
4 if at least 90 per cent of the fair value of the purchase consideration is in the form of equity shares.

Note that if the above four conditions are satisfied, the business combination *may* be accounted for on a merger basis, but it is not compulsory to do so. However, if the above four conditions are not satisfied, the combination *must* be accounted for as an acquisition. FRS 6 'Acquisitions and Mergers' seeks to introduce a new set of criteria for defining a merger, based on the guiding principle that the combining companies should be substantially equal partners with neither of them being identifiable as the acquirer or acquiree. The detailed conditions to be satisfied are all of the following:

1 neither party sees itself as acquirer or acquiree;
2 neither party dominates the management of the combined entity;
3 the equity shareholders of neither party have, or could have, disposed of a material part of their shareholdings, directly or indirectly, for shares carrying reduced rights in the combined enterprise or any non-equity consideration. (This would prevent transactions involving vendor placings from qualifying, as well as deals involving straight cash consideration);
4 no minority interests of more than 10 per cent of the equity remain in any of the enterprises to whom an offer is made;
5 neither of the combining parties is more than 50 per cent larger than the other, unless special circumstances (which could include voting and share agreements) prevent the larger from dominating the other; and

6 the share of the equity in the combination allocated to any party to it does not depend on the post-combination performance of the business previously controlled by that party. (This rules out deals involving earn-out clauses.)

The proposed rules are extremely restrictive and very few transactions would qualify for merger accounting.

Merger accounting: main principles

The principles of consolidated accounts outlined in Chapter 39 followed acquisition principles. It is now necessary to summarize the main points of merger accounting.

FRS 6 recommends the following accounting method for mergers. The shares transferred to the holding company as part of a merger should be recorded in the books of the holding company at the nominal value of the shares issued in exchange. No share premium is recognized or necessary on the new shares issued by the holding company. As a consequence of using the nominal value, the only difference to be dealt with on consolidation will be the difference between the nominal value of the shares issued as consideration by the holding company and the nominal value of the shares transferred by the shareholders of the new subsidiary company to the holding company.

Where the nominal value of the shares issued is less than that of the shares transferred, the differences should be treated as a reserve (non-distributable) arising on consolidation.

If the nominal value of the shares issued is greater than that of the shares received in exchange, the difference is the extent to which the reserves of the subsidiary have in effect been capitalized consequent on the merger. This difference should therefore be treated on consolidation primarily as a reduction of the existing reserves. It should be applied first against any unrealized surplus and second against revenue income or realized surpluses. Essentially, this indicates that to the extent that reserves are regarded as capitalized, non-distributable reserves are capitalized before distributable reserves.

Where there is some additional consideration in some form other than equity shares, for example cash or loan stock, the value of such additional consideration should be included by adding it to the nominal value of the shares issued by the holding company, so as to arrive at the total consideration paid for the shares in the merged subsidiary. This total of the consideration would be debited to the investment in the subsidiary account. By following these procedures, the reserves in the consolidated accounts will be either:

1 the total of the reserves of the constituent companies increased by any reserve arising on consolidation; or
2 the total of the reserves of the constituent companies reduced by any part of the reserves of subsidiaries which have been in effect capitalized as a result of the merger.

Example 40.5 In this example the reserves of the constituent companies are increased by a reserve arising on consolidation.

P Ltd has just increased its share capital by issuing 70,000 ordinary shares of £1 each plus a cash payment of £10,000 to gain 90 per cent control of the issued share capital of S Ltd. The separate balance sheets of the two companies immediately after the merger are as follows.

	P Ltd	S Ltd
	£	£
Ordinary shares of £1 each	270,000	100,000
Revaluation reserve		20,000
Revenue reserves	50,000	30,000
	320,000	150,000
	£	£
Non-current and current assets *less* liabilities	240,000	150,000
Investment – shares in S Ltd	80,000	
	320,000	150,000

Note that the cost of the shares in S Ltd is recorded in the books of P Ltd at the nominal value of the shares issued in exchange (£70,000) plus the value of any additional consideration (£10,000 in cash). The 70,000 ordinary shares of £1 each will have been issued at a premium (they must have been to comply with condition (4) above that 90 per cent in *value* of the offer is in equity voting capital) but such premium is not recognized when using the merger or pooling-of-interest method. In preparing the consolidated balance sheet the investment account in P's books is set against the nominal value of the shares purchased in S Ltd, thus:

	£	£
Nominal value of shares in S Ltd pooled by P Ltd		90,000
Cost of investment in S Ltd:		
Shares at nominal value	70,000	
Cash	10,000	
		80,000
Capital reserve arising on consolidation		10,000

and the full consolidated balance sheet appears as follows:

Consolidated balance sheet after merger

	£
Ordinary shares of £1 each	270,000
Capital reserve arising on consolidation	10,000
Revaluation reserve (90% × 20,000)	18,000
Revenue reserves (50,000 + 90% × 30,000)	77,000
Minority interest (10% × 150,000)	15,000
	390,000
Non-current and current assets *less* liabilities	390,000

The minority interest is calculated in the same manner in a merger as in an acquisition.

Example 40.6 In this example the nominal value of the shares issued by P Ltd exceeds the nominal value of the shares purchased in S Ltd, and the excess is treated as a capitalization of reserves of the subsidiary. The facts are as in the previous example, but P Ltd issues 110,000 £1 ordinary shares plus cash of £10,000 to gain control of a 90 per cent shareholding in S Ltd. In this case the separate balance sheets of the two companies immediately after the merger are as follows:

	P Ltd	S Ltd
	£	£
Ordinary shares of £1 each	310,000	100,000
Revaluation reserve		20,000
Revenue reserves	50,000	30,000
	360,000	150,000
	£	£
Non-current and current assets *less* liabilities	240,000	150,000
Investment – shares in S Ltd	120,000	
	360,000	150,000

The book value of the shares held by P Ltd in S Ltd is compared with the par value of the shares acquired, thus:

	£
Cost of investment	120,000
Nominal value acquired (90%)	90,000
Excess	£30,000

This excess is to be offset against group reserves, unrealized first, then realized. Thus:

	£
Offset against revaluation reserve (90% of £20,000)	£18,000
Offset against revenue reserves (balance)	12,000
	£30,000

The consolidated balance sheet will be as follows:

Consolidated balance sheet after merger

	£
Ordinary shares of £1 each	310,000
(Capital reserves – nil)	
Revenue reserves (50,000 + 27,000 – 12,000)	65,000
Minority interest	15,000
	390,000
Non-current and current assets *less* liabilities	£390,000

The above examples illustrate that one of the major differences between acquisition and merger accounting lies in the treatment of the reserves of the subsidiary at the date of acquisition. The acquisition (purchase) approach regards these as capitalized at the date of the takeover against the purchase price. The purchase price is based on a realistic assessment of the current values of the shares issued by the parent company. So where the purchase price exceeds the value placed on the proportion of the net assets acquired in the subsidiary, a difference, or figure for goodwill, will arise. The merger or pooling method regards the situation as being one where previously independent companies have merged as voluntary partners and that consolidation should be the mere amalgamation of balance sheets. Taking the valuation of the shares exchanged at face or par value is a mere bookkeeping device to cancel out the shares issued by P Ltd against those of S Ltd on consolidation, with any resulting difference being treated as an increase in reserves (as in Example 40.5) or as a capitalization of existing reserves (as in Example 40.6).

Multinational groups

Multinational groups face a number of complex accounting problems, which result from the economic, legal, organizational, managerial and fiscal environment in which they operate. Given that nation states see problems at a national level and set up rules for the conduct of business that reflect national interests, and that multinationals see problems at a global level, it follows that the resolution of conflict is a major preoccupation of multinational groups.

Conflict of accounting principles and procedures

A number of countries have codified accounting systems for business in the form of uniform charts of accounts, to which companies must adhere. In France, for example, the *Plan Comptable Révisé* is a nationalized accounting system setting out classes of accounts, detailing for each class the names of accounts and ascribing to them a number. In accordance with French commercial law, accounts are properly kept only if they accord with the *Plan Comptable Révisé*. A French subsidiary of a US multinational is required to keep its accounts in accordance with the *Plan Comptable Révisé*. At the same time, it must report year-end results for consolidation purposes to the US in the form which fits US practice, which is based upon US GAAP (generally accepted accounting principles). This means that the same accounting data must be rehashed again before it is suitable for consolidation. Moreover, French tax law regulates such items as depreciation charges and provisions, and in this way they regulate the extent to which amounts may be charged as expenses. In effect, the accounting income and the taxable income correspond closely as a result. When consolidating the accounts of the French subsidiary with the US parent, they must be redrafted to conform with US tax laws. The resolution of these conflicts of accounting and tax rules imposes a heavy burden of work on the French subsidiary.

The International Accounting Standards Board has produced a number of standards to help reduce these problems. It is also the objective of the EC Fourth and Seventh Directives to increase uniformity of accounting principles and methods, but the extent to which harmonization is possible is limited by fundamental differences in the institutions of nations.

The currency problem

The currency problem has two aspects. The financial aspect is the most important and complex one, for it involves the management of corporate resources across different currencies which fluctuate daily on world currency markets. Financial management decisions, the evaluation of investment and of corporate performance, the management of international cash balances and the avoidance of exchange risks are all part of this management problem. Generally, multinationals adopt a base currency as the functional currency for worldwide operations. For US multinationals, this currency is evidently the US dollar. Some non-US multinationals have found it useful also to adopt the US dollar as the functional currency. Some Dutch multinationals have adopted this option and prepare consolidated accounts in US dollars. This means that budgets are set in one base currency, but local activities involve the use of the local currency. It is possible, therefore, for a subsidiary of a US multinational to have a flexible budget as a result simply of currency movements rather than activity variances.

The currency translation problem

Multinational groups experience the currency translation problem in three different ways:

1 Inter-company transactions across currency borders are realized transactions which are translated at the rate of exchange ruling at the transaction date. It was noted in the previous chapter that these transactions are eliminated on consolidation. Therefore, they would be eliminated at the rate of exchange ruling on the transaction date. In practice, this requirement means that inter-company transactions have to be recorded separately from external transactions to facilitate consolidation at year end.

2 Inter-group dividends are also realized transactions involving the movement of funds through remittances. They crystallize on the due date of payment and are translated at the rate of exchange ruling on that date. Again, inter-group dividends are eliminated on consolidation at the rate of exchange ruling on the due date of payment.

The transactions falling under 1 and 2 above do not involve a problem of choice as to which exchange rate to apply. Moreover, they are eliminated on consolidation, and do not influence the overall presentation of group consolidated accounts.

3 The preparation of consolidated accounts involves the consolidation of all remaining assets, liabilities, revenues and expenses in order to show to shareholders the financial status and the net profit of the group as a single unit. It requires the translation of the income statements and balance sheets of all companies within a group into one currency, which is the base currency for the group.

The rate of exchange which should be applied for that purpose has been the subject of much controversy for two reasons:

(a) The assets, liabilities, expenses and revenues to be translated are not the subject of remittances to the parent company. In the case of assets and liabilities, they remain legal rights and obligations expressed in the local currency of the foreign subsidiary. Moreover, non-current items on the foreign subsidiary's balance sheet such as non-current assets, issued capital and reserves are not considered as involving any currency movements in the short term. In the case of current assets and liabilities, they form the substance of the foreign subsidiary's working capital. Given that inter-company items fall to be eliminated on consolidation, the items consolidated also are unlikely to involve currency movements. The expenses and revenue items on the subsidiary's income statement have been transacted across the accounting period, and to translate them with precise accuracy would mean tracking each transaction at a daily exchange rate, thereby imposing an impossible burden of accounting work. Also, they do not involve currency movements.

(b) The purpose of translating the accounts of foreign subsidiaries into the base currency of the group is to place all companies on to a uniform unit of measurement without infringing the historical cost rule of valuation. The problem lies in defining how the historical cost rule should be applied to the assets, liabilities, expenses and revenues of foreign subsidiaries at the close of each accounting period.

The currency translation debate is centred, therefore, on the issue of applying the historical cost principle in the process of consolidating the accounts of foreign subsidiaries, when the items to be translated do not imply any currency movements at balance sheet date.

Although a large number of translation methods have been put forward and used across the years, much of the debate has been resolved by the issue of SSAP 20 'Foreign Currency Translation' which sets out two permitted translation methods together with their uses and the accounting treatment of any resulting translation gain or loss. The two methods of translation permitted by the SSAP are known as the temporal method and the closing rate/net investment method. Table 40.2 provides a summary of the main points of each method as outlined in SSAP 20.

Table 40.2 SSAP 20 translation methods

	Temporal	Closing rate/net investment

1 Uses of method	Where the foreign currency transaction has a direct effect on the cash flows of the UK company, i.e.
	
	(a) 'individual company stage' (e.g. the UK parent company buying/selling overseas or receiving dividends from the overseas subsidiary);
	
	(b) 'consolidation stage' of the overseas entity is seen as being merely an extension of the UK company (e.g. overseas subsidiaries which are:
	  – selling agencies
	  – group finance
	  – companies
	  – group suppliers
		Used at the consolidation stage only, where the overseas entity is seen to be 'semi-independent' of the UK company.
		It is envisaged that this method would apply to the translation of the accounts of most subsidiaries for consolidation purposes.

2 Mechanics of method	Items are translated at the rate ruling when the amount was established in the accounts, *but* items on the balance sheet at 'current value' are translated at closing rate. Thus:
	(a) B/S items are:
	  Non-current assets
	    at cost – acquisition rate
	    at valuation – valuation rate
	  Inventory
	    at cost – acquisition rate
	    at NRV – closing rate
	    all monetary items – closing rate;
	(b) Income statement items are:
	  All except inventory and depreciation – at average rate for the period
	  Inventory – as for balance sheet
	  Depreciation – as for the related non-current asset
		All balance sheet assets and liabilities are translated at closing rate.
		All income statement items may be translated at *either* closing rates or average for the period.

3 Accounting for the translation gain/loss	Viewed as a normal risk/benefit of trading overseas and therefore included in the 'income on ordinary activities' before taxation.	Viewed as a revaluation in sterling of the net investment in an overseas entity and therefore presented as part of the movement for the period period of group reserves, profits being unaffected.

The inflation problem

Meaningful comparisons of balance sheets and income statements from year to year are rendered impossible under inflationary conditions, when the money unit of measurement becomes unstable. This problem had been recognized in the United Kingdom and in many other countries. Some countries, such as the United Kingdom and the United States, have required companies to disclose the effects of inflation in accounts. There is, however, no international standard for dealing with this problem, nor indeed is there a consensus as to how it should be treated. Multinationals are particularly affected because of the variety of inflation rates to which their business is exposed worldwide.

Moreover, although there is no connection in the short term between speculative changes in exchange rates and levels of domestic inflation, some assert that such a connection may be established in the long term. From an accounting viewpoint, financial statements deal with short-term periods of one year, and consequently fluctuations in exchange rates and changes in rates of domestic inflation may both affect the meaning of consolidated accounts involving foreign subsidiaries.

Summary

Understanding the consolidated financial statements of multinational corporations goes beyond the arithmetical simplicity of accumulating the accounting numbers of individual companies within a group and then eliminating the duplication created by inter-group transactions. Operating across international boundaries in the form of legal provisions, economic and social circumstances and accounting rules, an otherwise mundane appreciation of the arithmetic of consolidation is inadequate for a meaningful understanding of the consolidated financal statements. Accounting for minority interests, associated companies and the distinctive treatment that is accorded to acquisitions and mergers, as well as the problems of currency translation, adds complexity to the analysis of the financial performance of multinational groups.

Problems

1 Consider the following draft data relating to the year ended 31 December 20X0 of Royal plc and Butler plc.

Balance sheets	Royal plc	Butler plc
	£000	£000
Non-current assets (net) – tangible	6,500	4,000
Investment in Butler plc – cost	2,000	
Current assets	3,500	3,000
Current liabilities	(4,550)	(2,500)
Debentures (20X9)	(2,000)	(1,500)
	5,450	3,000
Issued ordinary share capital	2,000	1,000
Reserves	3,450	2,000
	5,450	3,000
Income statements		
Operating income before tax	1,100	500
Dividend from Butler plc including tax credit	143	–
Taxation	(433)	(200)
Income after tax	810	300
Dividends paid	(300)	(200)
	510	100

Royal plc acquired 50 per cent of the ordinary share capital of Butler plc on 1 January 20X0 for £2,000,000 when its reserves were £1,900,000 and sold this holding on 3 January 20X1 for £2,050,000.

Required:

1 Prepare the 'group' income statement and balance sheet on three bases: when Butler is treated as (i) a subsidiary; (ii) an associated company; and (iii) an investment.

2 Comment on the validity of these three alternatives.

2 On 3 July 20X0 Expo plc acquired 95 per cent of the issued share capital of Sition Ltd.

The terms of the merger were as follows:

For every 10 shares held in Sition, the shareholder received 8 shares in Expo at an agreed value of £1.90 per share plus £1.50 unsecured 15 per cent loan stock dated 20X0.

The draft accounts for the two companies at 31 December 20X0 were as follows:

	Expo plc	Sition Ltd
	(£000)	**(£000)**
Balance sheet		
Non-current assets	18,650	10,200
Goodwill at cost		1,000
Investments	9,025	
Current assets	3,550	6,650
Current liabilities	(2,850)	(3,200)
	28,375	14,650
Share capital		
£1 ordinary shares	21,600	10,000
Income statement	5,350	4,650
15% loan stock	1,425	
	28,375	14,650
Income statement		
Turnover	12,850	8,500
Income before tax	3,250	1,300
Taxation	590	30
	2,660	1,270
Dividends	1,200	
Retained income	1,460	1,270

Notes:

(i)   It is Expo's policy to write off goodwill over five years. Sition has not, to date, written off any goodwill and the balance in their accounts relates to a business bought in 19X9.

(ii) At the date of the takeover, Sition's estimated income for the year to date was £600,000.

Required:

1 Prepare a consolidated balance sheet and income statement in summary form for Expo group, adopting the merger accounting method in line with SSAP 23.

2 Explain the major differences between your statement and the way in which the same information would have been presented using traditional group accounting practices.

3 Assess the relative strengths and weaknesses of merger and group accounting. Explain why merger accounting has only been applied in the UK since 1981.

SECTION 2

Management control systems for multinational corporations

Introduction to Section 2

The consolidated financial statements of multinational groups portray their financial performance in an extremely summarized form. Groups of companies operate in complex economic, political and social environments that considerably aggravate the difficulties inherent in the management of business risk, which is the central problem in managing corporate financial performance. Earlier, we have seen that corporate financial management may be decomposed into three major areas of responsibility, namely, the management of operating profitability, asset management and debt management. We have also noted that focusing on shareholder value for the evaluation of financial performance reflects an approach to corporate management that places emphasis on improving the market value of shareholders' interest that reflect all the three foregoing management areas. Asset and debt management are specialist areas of financial knowledge, whereas online managers are emphatically concerned with the management of business activities in an operating context, with financial performance defined as operating profitability being the most evident and practical management objective.

A simplistic view of the role of management control systems would restrict their relevance and justification to the management of financial performance, lending support to narrow views of corporate objectives and ignoring the vast problem that links business success to the management of all factors that influence business risk and that are subsumed in financial results.

We noted in Chapter 1 that the foundation of accounting theory rested on the twin concepts of responsibility and accountability and that the methods and procedures of accounting are derived from these notions. Accounting theory has its roots also in the control paradigm, but its evolution has remained restricted to financial control. As we noted in Part 2, the transaction, money measurement and historic cost concepts have prevented accounting theory from expanding its role beyond traditional financial and costs accounting for responding to modern needs, as seen in modern management theory. As Drucker noted (in 1954 in *The Practice of Management*), management control systems are associated with the recent evolution of large corporations and the complex problems which they represent as regards management and control. The conceptual framework within which management control systems have evolved are remarkably free of *a priori* constraints imposed by accounting traditions. This conceptual framework has been able to absorb financial concepts in its methodology and methods and integrate them with concepts that have their roots in other management disciplines. In so doing, it has been able to overcome the measurement problem that restrict financial information to monetary values, extending the relevance and usefulness of the information base relevant to attaining more broadly based economic and social corporate objectives and refer to financial and non-financial numbers.

It is fitting, therefore, that the concluding discussion in this text should take the form of a broad and comprehensive view of the problems of managing multinational business corporations. The vehicle through which this objective may be attained requires an understanding of corporate management theory as expressed in the design of management control systems. This perspective has the added advantage of enabling the reader to gain an enhanced appreciation of accounting theory through such management concepts as responsibility and accountability, as well as an enlarged perception of the relevance and usefulness of the accounting methods and procedures that have constituted the subject matter of this text.

CHAPTER 41

Management control systems design: a conceptual framework

Setting the scene

The annual financial reports of multinational groups present an extremely condensed and therefore restricted view of their global activities and performance. It is left to the Chairman's statement and the Board of Directors' Report to provide additional information on corporate performance in general. Besides the traditional content of annual reports, investors and society at large are concerned with knowing whether the leadership of the group has chosen the right strategy and management executed this effectively. Drucker (1954) referred to these respectively as 'doing the right things' and 'doing things right'. Management control systems are the means by which large, complex organizations make these important choices, and ensure that resources are allocated accordingly and spent wisely.

Learning objectives

After studying this chapter you should be able to:

1 appreciate the nature of corporate leadership;

2 discuss the role of management in terms of its different functions;

3 understand the conceptual framework underlying management control systems;

4 comment on the McKinsey 7-S model and the John Lewis Sharing model;

5 understand the role of management control systems and strategy maps for maintaining coherence and cohesion in management action.

A conceptual framework

Peter Drucker, generally considered to be the founder of modern management and a pioneer in the development of management methods for the control of complex organizations, took the view that the Salvation Army was 'the most effective organization in America'. It merited this accolade because of the way it delivered what it had set out to do since its inception in 1865. This longevity is no small achievement considering that less than half of the 500 largest firms in the US in 1980 were still in business in 2000 (*Financial Times*, Monday, 18 January 2010, page 11). Drucker maintained that while management was about doing things right, leadership was about doing the right things. The Salvation Army was spectacularly good at both.

Whereas doing the right things normally has a moral and ethical connotation, in the business context the meaning expands to include other objectives. For instance investors in business corporations would consider that improving shareholder value to be a legitimate objective.

A philosophy of management that includes moral obligations as part of corporate responsibility, expects management to give account accordingly. In Chapter 1, we referred to accounting as the primary means by which management explains how it has discharged its responsibilities. In this vision, accounting and management enjoy a common heritage in those moral values proclaimed by Plato, and which are individually shared through the social conscience (Glautier, 2007). These values are made explicit in the insistence on truth, the importance of trust, the duty of care and the need for transparency. Viewed from this perspective, doing the right things is making manifest these moral obligations.

The apparent lack of morality and ethics in business has received considerable attention recently. The list includes: Siemens paying bribes to win lucrative contracts; the conviction of senior managers for various offences – Kenneth Lay and Jeffrey Skilling of Enron, Bernard Ebbers of WorldCom, Calisto Tanzi of Parmalat – other cases are still pending, such as the class action suit by investors against senior executives and their employer Vivendi alleging fraud which could result in the 'largest class action that has been tried to verdict, at least in the securities area'. The maximum damages could be $8bn (*Financial Times*, 18 January 2010, page 19). Moreover, in the wake of the financial crisis, business schools have defended themselves against charges of failing to devote enough time to ethics in their core curricula (*Financial Times*, 18 January 2010, page 13). More worryingly, when the chair of the Financial Crisis Inquiry Commission, appointed 'To examine the causes, domestic and global, of the current financial economic crisis in the United States', accused Wall Street of 'selling cars with faulty brakes and then taking out insurance on the buyers', Lloyd Blankfein of Goldman Sachs retorted, 'I do not think the behaviour improper' (*Financial Times*, 19 January 2010, page 19).

A philosophy of management that includes moral values as part of 'doing the right things' must consider society as a whole and all its members as partners in action and beneficiaries in success. Whereas such a preoccupation might be thought laudable but altruistic, recent research suggests that the benefits go beyond improving a company's image to also improving business performance (Kanter, 2009). Including society at large as one of the constituencies has a major influence on the design of management control system and implies a management style that promotes collaborative endeavour through appropriate structures. It sublimates in the common good the dysfunctional conflict induced by the excessive competition generally present in business behaviour. It requires effective and appropriate participation of employees in decision making at all levels and recognizes democracy as the relevant principle for a just and equitable society. The path to this ideal state has been a difficult and painful one in the evolution of the modern industrial state and is not by any means fully evident in current management practices.

Anyone entertaining doubts about the importance of these ideas and the potentially dire consequences of ignoring them need only consider the morality tales of Richard Fuld at Lehman's and Sir Fred Goodwin at The Royal Bank of Scotland. Few of the newspaper articles devoted to their respective rises and spectacular falls are complimentary. Neither was a shining example of a management style that promoted collaborative endeavour. The collateral damage caused by their tenures to others is immense.

The conventional philosophy of business management frequently defines 'doing the right thing' according to the dogma of classical capitalism. According to Milton Friedman, the sole objective of a business corporation is to make profits for its shareholders. This results in management control systems that reflect this objective. It is seen in the importance attached to financial results and the persistence of social conflicts at work.

Leadership and management

The vast literature on leadership is testimony to its importance and paradoxically to how little we actually know about it. We cannot even be sure that we can recognize good leaders and leadership when we see them. All too often heroes turn out to have feet of clay and companies celebrated as shining examples of success by some management guru have crashed in flames a decade later. The remarkable achievement of William Booth, the founder of the Salvation Army, is that the organization survived, outlived him and continues to 'prosper' in 2010. We could say that he designed and implemented management control systems that enabled the organization both to do the right things and do things right. Without him the organization would never have existed. Without his and his wife's (Catherine Mumford) extraordinary talent for leadership, it would not have flourished for 145 years.

In his book on companies that make the leap from being merely good to becoming great, Jim Collins devotes the first explanatory chapter to the topic of leadership (Collins, 2001). Every company that achieved and sustained great performance had what he called a Level 5 leader, without whom the leap would not have happened. Surprisingly these people did not conform to the popular conception of the role, namely leader as hero, but rather these leaders saw themselves as servants – of the corporation, its constituencies and society at large.

Plato's teachings on leadership and management have retained all their importance and relevance to this day (Plato, *trans.* Jowett 20th edn, 1937). Plato spoke of the relationship between Wisdom and Democracy that defined the Ideal State. Today the main social problems concern functional relationships within organizations and also ideals about the relationship between business and society. Similarly, Drucker saw corporate management as a partnership in collaborative endeavour between leadership and management – leadership doing the right things and management doing things right.

Management control systems: a functional analysis

Our discussion suggests that the design of management control systems should reflect the goals of the organization and the leadership style of top management – what they want to achieve and how they want to achieve it. Management control systems determine the flow of information and who is authorized to do what with it. It should be obvious that if information is used primarily to reward and punish subordinates, then the flow of bad news will be severely restricted. If on the other hand, it is used to learn, to devise new action programmes and generally to improve future performance, there will be much more willingness to share and seek help. If information is seen as power, it will circulate poorly: if it is seen as a collective good, it will circulate freely. Thus, management control systems are the vehicle by which organizations achieve goals, irrespective of the sector in which they operate. In Chapter 33, we examined how the planning and control cycle governed the choice of organizational objectives and the allocation of resources and monitored what was achieved with them. A good management control system is one that achieves coherence in decision making and cohesion in behaviour throughout an organization.

As mentioned previously, the classical view of business organizations structured on capitalist lines assumes the sole objective to be increasing shareholder wealth. Since employment costs are significant, there is constant pressure to reduce them through outsourcing, productivity improvements and headcount reductions. The persistence of these management philosophies and styles, despite demands for social justice and progress, generates organizational conflict, frequently resulting in industrial action – the only winners being competitors. An alternative path adopts a team approach to finding solutions to business problems and a conciliatory approach in resolving organizational conflicts through participation of employees in problem solving, decision making, profit sharing and power sharing, as discussed in Part 3.

The challenge of devising an appropriate management control system for a national company is demanding; doing it for multinational companies is an order of magnitude more complex. The idea that the parent management control system can be exported to foreign subsidiaries totally misunderstands the challenges presented by the complexities and diversity of the global market economy, such as different cultures, institutional and legal regulations, currencies, inflation levels, and comparative advantages, that now have to be integrated in a coherent manner to attain overall corporate objectives.

As we shall see presently, the complexities and diversity facing multinational companies frequently requires a divisional structure, either by product or geography, allowing decentralization of decision making within an overall set of corporate objectives and goals. While multinational companies share with national ones the need to achieve coherence in decision making and cohesion in behaviour, the task facing the former is much more difficult, and the penalty for failure greater.

Seven elements of strategic fit

Drucker's seminal work created considerable interest in organizational planning and control that focused on objectives, goals, strategies, structures, systems, performance evaluation and rewards. Rationalization in terms of coherence and cohesion between management functions in these regards were accepted as a basic condition for organizational efficiency. In the early 1980s McKinsey & Co., a leading management consulting company, developed the 7-S Framework for strategic fit, as shown in Figure 44.1.

This model consists of three 'hard elements', defined as those that are easier to define and to influence, namely Strategy, Structure and Systems and four 'soft' elements, that are less tangible and more cultural, namely, Shared values, Skills, Style and Staff. Figure 41.1 illustrates their interdependence.

Figure 41.1 The McKinsey 7-S Model

Hard elements

- *Strategy.* The purpose of strategy is to explain how the company is going to gain competitive advantage. It used to be visionary in nature, describing a future state, what it would be doing in five or ten years' time. This was a world in which according to Alfred Chandler, structure followed strategy. The pace of change and the volatility of the business environment have made this approach obsolete. Today firms must be adaptive, constantly evolving, to survive. Strategy and structure are different sides of the same coin – they are mutually interdependent.
- *Structure.* The division of tasks and responsibilities of managers is shown schematically on the organization chart. Apart from delineating the scope of the responsibilities of each manager, structure also defines the authority relationships: who does what, and who reports to whom. Along with responsibilities over certain domains of expertise (marketing, production, etc.), structure also spells out the nature of each manager's financial responsibility (cost, revenue, profit, investment).
- *Systems.* Every organization uses systems to implement strategy and run operations. Besides the usual formal systems such as planning, budgeting, reporting, capital budgeting, costing, performance evaluation and so forth, there are also the processes embedded in individual departments (HR, compliance, etc.) as well as work routines that get things done. Work flows horizontally through organizations, not vertically through different levels of functional hierarchies. These processes that govern how work is done are crucial to the effectiveness and efficiency of organizations, and have a decisive impact on the business model and competitive advantage (e.g. Dell's supply chain).

Soft elements

- *Shared values.* These represent the core ethical values and behaviours to which the organization aspires. They are placed at the centre because they are superordinate goals. One of these has to be whether or not the firm seeks to make profits (NGOs do not). They help create alignment within the organization, thus limiting the tendency for different parts of the organization and different executives to pursue their own agendas.

- *Style*. All organizations have a dominant culture and management style. Sometimes this is well articulated and widely shared, providing coherence but not necessarily conformity, which acts as an invisible glue binding the organization together. It takes a long time to develop and instil in an organization; recruits join the company because they 'feel at home'; existing employees leave because they do not. A CEO once declared that he would never take over another company, because of the near impossibility of abandoning an old culture and assimilating a new one – a testimony to the importance this executive attached to style and culture.

- *Staff*. The human side of organizations is specifically captured in this heading. The emphasis is on their intrinsic talent, rather than their skills, on their potential to grow and develop when given the opportunity. Building diversity into the organization is of critical importance: not just female and male, but culture, nationality, education, age, experience, etc. Doing this well creates the foundation for building competitive advantage: talented, committed, loyal, energetic employees.

- *Skills*. This comprises the things that the company knows how to do well and the skills of particular individuals. The former is epitomized by the Toyota System – much has been written about it; Toyota shows competitors round its factories, but replicating the System is extraordinarily difficult. Imbedding these skills in an organization requires a conscious effort and a lot of time. At the level of the individual employee, increased specialization is making their skills more and more important.

The model seeks coherence in the sense of '*fit*' between the elements and the attainment of strategic objectives. It is interesting to note how shared values are at the centre of the framework around which everything else revolves. The model recognizes that shared values transcend and infuse all other elements. The values represent a higher authority which must always be respected, even when the rules are silent. Adherence to the values enhances alignment and reduces internal conflicts.

The 7-S Framework, elaborated by Peters and Waterman (1982), identifies a constellation of interrelated factors that determine an organization's ability to create and sustain competitive advantage – they were after all distilled from the common characteristics of excellent companies. The absence of any hierarchical relationships suggests that change in any one element must be accompanied by complementary changes in others. Some 30 years after its inception the Framework remains a useful tool to help understand how complex organizations work and propose ways in which they can be made to work better. The nature and scope of the 7-S Framework help us understand why Jack Welch said that, 'On the face of it, shareholder value is the dumbest idea in the world' (*Financial Times*, 12 March 2009). He subsequently added that he was referring to the obsession with short-term profits and share price gains that have dominated the corporate world for many years. The fact that shareholders have residual claims on profits after all other claims have been satisfied is true but not germane to the debate. Shareholders' interests are best served by paying attention to the needs of the other stakeholders – returns to shareholders are a result of getting other things right, they are not an objective to be aimed at through financial engineering or short-term cost cutting.

An example of how looking after the interests of all the stakeholders is entirely consistent with doing the best for shareholders, is provided in the following section.

The John Lewis Sharing model

How to reconcile the political and social demand for greater democracy at the workplace, without constraining the leadership function of management, is one of the most important problems of this age.

One solution to this problem is seen in the management model developed by John Spedan Lewis, who experimented with putting the happiness and well being of his employees at the centre of policy making at the department store Peter Jones. Later this was extended to the family's main John Lewis department store in Oxford Street. Today the John Lewis Partnership has 69,000 Partners and owns three leading retail businesses – Waitrose, John Lewis and Greenbee. In 2009 sales were £7.0bn, profits £234m and bonuses amounted to £125m. The vision of John Lewis was a business owned by its Partners, powered by its people and its principles with profits and benefits shared by all Partners. Its founding principles were based on the notion of 'fair shares' in three domains:

1 sharing gains;
2 sharing knowledge; and
3 sharing power.

Authority is vested in the leadership which is required to obtain the consent of employees as partners. To this end, the objective of the management control system is to integrate leadership and management in collaborative endeavour, achieved through sharing gains, knowledge and power. Sharing gains is the driver for collaborative endeavour, sharing knowledge is the key to creating an effective management structure and sharing control provides the necessary cohesion between leadership and management in the action of the different management functions and systems.

John Spedan Lewis disliked socialism and was committed to capitalism as a social and economic model. However, he considered justice to be a fundamental moral value, which he identified with the principle of 'fair shares'. In this sense, he was faithful to the ideals that are seen in the teachings of Plato, Aristotle and St Thomas Aquinas, expressed in notions of the 'just price' and the 'fair wage'. He adapted the virtues of free trade reflected in competitive endeavour and capitalism to democratic ideals that are realized in collaborative endeavour and in a just society. He achieved this end by granting partnership status to all members of the business – directors, managers and ordinary employees, thereby making ownership and collaborative endeavour shared and core values.

The concept of sharing gains in the John Lewis Partnerships results in the distribution of the entirety of the year-end accounting income as a bonus for each employee, after reserving funds for future investment. This helps motivate employees to do their best, encourages collaborative behaviour (the bonus is based on group profits), and builds loyalty to the company. The effect is to forestall conflict between leadership and employees, secure cohesion between the different actors through management control systems and enhance overall business performance.

Corporate leadership through strategic planning and control

Multinational groups are formed in two different ways – organic growth through the extension of existing activities on a global basis and expansion by the acquisition of other firms through mergers and acquisitions (M&As). Both forms of growth are present in most large multinational corporations. As a result, multinationals are large and diversified, with multitudinous products and activities; they operate in very differing markets subject to their own economic conditions, including profitability; they invest under very different conditions of economic (inflation and currency instability) and political risk. Dealing with these challenges involves finding a way to reduce all this complexity into some form of manageable order, enabling the group to function under unified central control directed at attaining group objectives and goals. This is impossible without a high degree of '*fit*' between the 7-S Framework and the aspirations of the company. Among the 7-S elements, the 'hard' elements together with the shared values, govern the delegation of decision making, the alignment of these decisions with corporate objectives and the feedback information on the performance of responsibility centres.

One of the most recent, and acclaimed, suggestions about how the strategic planning and reporting process should be organized is by Kaplan and Norton (2004) in their book *Strategy Maps*. They emphasize that this should not be thought of as a tool, but as a management system. The purpose of the system is to sharpen execution of strategy, as this accounted for 70 per cent of failed strategies (Charan and Colvin, 1999). The unique contribution of Strategy Maps is that they provide a visual representation of the cause-and-effect relationships among the four perspectives of the Balanced Scorecard. A standard template is shown below in Figure 41.2. Strategy maps are based on the following five principles:

1 Strategy balances short and long term

Organizations have to invest for the long term and achieve performance targets in the short. Investing in product development, building brand awareness and increasing the skills of employees all require incurring costs in the short term in the expectation of generating returns in the long term. However, improving financial performance in the short term may require cost reduction programmes: the favourite targets are R&D, advertising and training budgets precisely because the benefits are felt immediately and the costs, if any, only appear later, perhaps during the tenure of a successor. Strategy maps help make visible, and therefore explicit, the balance to be struck between short-run objectives for cost reduction and productivity improvements and the long-run need for more revenues.

2 Strategy requires a differentiated customer value proposition

Without a clear statement of who the customers are and the value proposition that is being made, there is no strategy. Strategy maps again provide a vehicle for making these explicit together with the causal relationships linking them back to the internal perspective and forward to the financial.

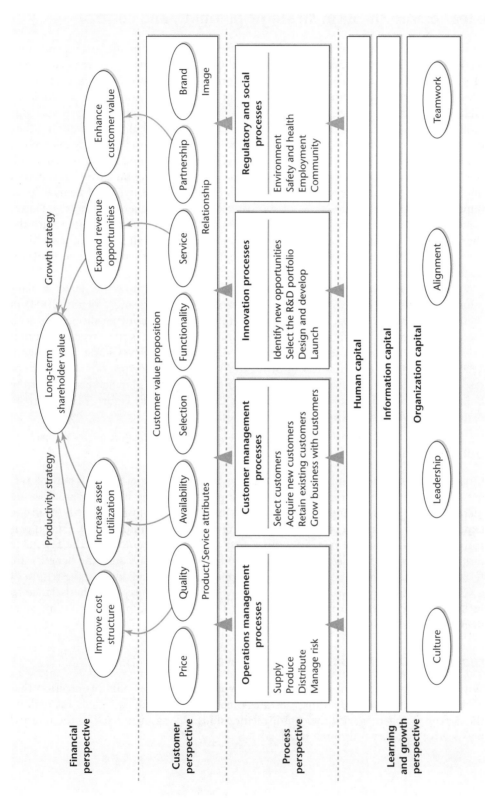

Figure 41.2 Strategy maps
(Adapted from Robert S. Kaplan and David P. Norton, Mastering the Management System, *Harvard Business Review*, January 2008 and *Strategy Maps*, Harvard Business School Press, 2004)

3 Internal business processes are the source of all value

While the customer and financial perspectives describe outcomes, these are generated by activities in the internal and the learning and growth perspectives. The internal perspective is concerned with developing, producing, selling and after-sales servicing of products (and services) together with regulatory and social processes: the learning and growth perspective is concerned with the capabilities and skills of employees in three critical dimensions – human capital, information capital and organization capital.

4 Strategy execution requires coordinated action on several fronts

The internal perspective has four generic processes which typically yield benefits over different time horizons: operational being the shortest and regulatory the longest. Sustainable growth in shareholder value can only be achieved by judicious balancing of initiatives in each of the four generic processes. Without balance the strategy and implementation efforts will be lopsided; either favouring the short term at the expense of the long or vice versa.

5 Strategic alignment is the key to execution

The last perspective, learning and growth, is at the bottom, not because it is the least important, but because it is the foundation stone on which the entire edifice reposes. The intangible skills and capabilities painstakingly built by programmes in three generic categories – human, information and organization – provide the alignment necessary for the execution of strategy. They have much in common with the 'soft' elements in the 7-S Framework and capture the organization's intangible assets.

Strategy maps are designed from the top down and executed from the bottom up. The financial and customer perspectives articulate what the company wants to achieve: the internal and the learning and growth perspectives explain how. Apart from being a visual representation of strategy, they also identify the processes and systems through which they will be implemented. The explicit identification of cause-and-effect links by which initiatives drive outcomes leaves as little as possible to chance.

However, sitting on top of the strategy map there has to be a statement of the mission and core values – why the organization exists, what it believes in and how it behaves towards its key constituencies – then comes the vision – a description of what the organization is aiming to be in the future. Strategy then explains the logic about how all this will be achieved.

Financial perspective

There are two levers of financial strategy: revenue growth and productivity improvements. Revenue growth can come from new customers or deepening relationships with the existing customer base. Productivity improvements are generated by reducing the cost base or using assets more efficiently. Productivity improvements tend to pay off quickly, growing revenues takes longer.

Customer perspective

The customer value proposition is the core of any business strategy: it explains how the company intends to differentiate its offerings from those of competitors and it provides the crucial link between these offerings and internal processes – what do they have to deliver and how well do they have to perform.

Internal process perspective

This perspective spells out how the company is going to deliver the customer value proposition in the customer perspective, and the productivity improvements and the financial perspective. Once again Kaplan and Norton helpfully identify four generic processes, based on their consulting and research interventions with over 300 organizations.

Learning and growth perspective

While the customer perspective is the core of any strategy, learning and growth is the foundation of its execution. Without the skills and capabilities, the motivation and commitment, the teamwork and collaboration, it simply will not happen. The learning and growth foundation rests on three foundation stones: human, informational and organizational. Individually and collectively these must be aligned to deliver the strategy.

The power of a well constructed strategy map lies in its ability to capture and articulate cause-and-effect relationships between action and effect across the four perspectives. These hypotheses are then used to allocate resources so that organizational units are aligned to deliver strategic outcomes. These hypotheses are continually tested by data gathered through the Balanced Scorecard: significant differences between actual and expected outcomes signal the need to revisit operational plans for the short term and strategic plans for the long.

Summary

Drucker, one of the founders of modern management, distinguished doing the right things and doing things right. The former is a characteristic of leadership, the latter of management. Doing the right things is capable of many interpretations, depending on the nature and purpose of the organization (public or private, profit making or not, etc.). Although organizations have a separate legal existence independently of the owners and managers, it does not mean that business is amoral or that anything goes. On the contrary, the moral values embraced by individuals and societies should be present in collections of individuals whatever form this may take. Among these values are the insistence of truth, the importance of trust, the duty of care and the need for transparency.

There is much evidence that these moral values are indeed present in business – concerns about fair trade and the movement for social responsibility are examples. There are also glaring failures – some due directly to the actions of top management, others to the actions of subordinates. However, in the latter case the question is asked what sort of company could allow these things, such as bribery, to happen. Why did the systems and procedures, the values of the company, not prevent it? Where were the whistle-blowers?

Neither the 'invisible hand' of Adam Smith, nor the free markets of capitalism are inconsistent with managing organizations in the interests of society as a whole. It depends on enlightened leaders such as John Spedan Lewis, who before Jim Collins coined the phrase, represented Level 5 leadership at its best.

The role of top management is not only to espouse doing the right things, but through management control systems to ensure that the organization carries these through by doing things right. The McKinsey 7-S Framework with its hard and soft elements is one approach to making sure that none of the levers for guiding and directing organizations has been neglected.

Once all the elements are in place (the structures, the systems, the financial responsibilities, etc.), the next task is to put the organization to work: set objectives and goals, agree targets, allocate resources, approve projects, etc. All organizations devise ways of doing this, some better than others. The strategy map of Kaplan and Norton provides a template and a process for thinking about the economics of the business and for allocating resources accordingly. The core of strategy is the customer value proposition and the key to execution depends on the intangible assets – human, informational and organizational capital. The loop is closed when the hypotheses, made explicit in the strategy, are tested by gathering data in the balanced scorecard which is then used to revisit operational plans and strategies.

Self-assessment questions

1 Explain what Drucker meant by saying that leadership was about doing the right things and management was about doing things right.

2 Should business corporations be concerned with moral values or simply with shareholder value?

3 Discuss the McKinsey 7-S Framework for the design of management control systems.

4 Discuss the John Spedan Lewis's management model based on sharing gains, sharing knowledge and sharing power. What do you consider to be its relevance to management control systems design?

5 What are the main problems in management control systems design for multinational corporations?

6 In what ways do strategic maps and balanced score cards help in dealing with complexity and coherence in management control systems design?

References

Chandler, A. (1977) *The Visible Hand: The Managerial Revolution in American Business*, The Belknap Press.

Charan, R. and Colvin, G. (1999) Why CEOs Fail, *Fortune*, 21 June.

Collins, J. (2001) *Good to Great*, Harper Business.

Drucker, P. (1954) *The Practice of Management*, Harper Collins Publishers Inc.

Glautier, M.W.E. (2007) *The Social Conscience*, Shepherd-Walwyn Publishing Ltd.

Glautier, M.W.E. (forthcoming) *The Caring Society*.

Kanter, R.M. (2009) *SuperCorp: How Vanguard Companies Create Innovation, Profits, Growth and Social Good*, Crown Business.

Kaplan, R.S. and Norton, D.P. (2004) *Strategy Maps*, Harvard Business School Press.

Peters, T.J. and Waterman, R.H. (1982) *In Search of Excellence*, Harper & Row.

Plato, *The Dialogues of Plato*, Jowett, B. (*trans.*) 20th edn (1937) Random House.

Solutions to self-assessment questions and problems

Solutions to self-assessment questions and problems

Chapter 1 Accountability and accounting

Answers to self-assessment questions

1 Responsibility and accountability have their roots in social relationships and in the duty that they impose to account for one's actions. Responsibility and accountability cement social relationships and ensure the permanence through rules of conduct accepted and recognized in law.

2 The social conscience is a shared conscience. It is the collective of all individuals seeking to do 'what is right'. It is the consensus that individual and group behaviour should conform to rules of conduct that are universally applicable and accepted. The social conscience considers 'what is right' by reference to moral values that are conducive to the common good.

3 The moral values that are implied in social relationships and necessary for social cohesion are truth, trust, care and transparency, which is needed for truth to be seen. Trust depends upon truth and both truth and trust are necessary for relationships to endure. The duty of care is the implicit intention that parties will seek to do 'what is right'.

4 Social theories are normative in nature and concerned with 'what should be'. They reflect beliefs that have much to do with social progress within civil society and the market economy. They are founded in moral value judgements and are addressed to the common good. They differ from theory construction in the natural sciences that are concerned with 'what is' and have the quality of being predictive.

5 Truth is the sole criterion by which knowledge is defined in the natural sciences. In the social sciences and in accounting, truth is defined by belief in the honesty and sincerity with which statements are made. Truth is essential to creating trust. Without truth, there is no trust. Therefore, truth is necessary for creating and maintaining trust in accounting and in accounting information contained in financial reports.

6 The moral values that are fundamental to accountability and accounting are truth, trust, transparency and care. They reflect the responsibilities that are implicit in social relationships that create a duty or obligations of accountability, that is, being accountable to others for one's behaviour in relation to such responsibilities. Accounting is the process that defines the form, content and procedures used for accountability.

Chapter 2 The scope of business accounting

Answers to self-assessment questions

1 Early definitions of accounting described the activities of accountants and focused on the importance of individual concepts (e.g. matching). More recent definitions have concerned the needs of users of financial reports and their role in making economic decisions. These

definitions have been extended into the social welfare arena and described accounting information in terms of the costs and benefits to society as a whole.

2 Stewardship accounting is concerned with accountability, i.e. reports by stewards to owners of wealth on how they have managed that wealth. Financial accounting addresses the role of financial reports in the economic decisions of shareholders and potential shareholders. Management accounting assists management in the planning and control of organizations. Unlike financial accounting, which reports on past events, management accounting is forward-looking. Social accounting widens the scope of accounting by considering the social effects of business decisions as well as their economic effects from the viewpoint of a caring society. It has arisen partly from the increasing attention which is being given to ethical and environmental problems over recent years.

3 The usefulness of the concepts upon which financial reporting is based has been questioned. Traditional management accounting techniques, it has been argued, are not suitable in fully technology-driven situations. Accounting concepts of growth and income are too narrow because they fail to address important social issues.

4 A standard-setting board aimed at developing a conceptual framework for external financial reporting has been established. New management accounting systems have emerged and social accounting issues are being increasingly debated.

Chapter 3 Accounting as an information system

Answers to self-assessment questions

1 Shareholders and investors are concerned with the value of their investment (or proposed investment) and the income they expect to derive from their holding. Management requires information for planning, control and decision-making purposes. Employees require information about the performance of their unit and how this contributes to the performance of the firm as a whole. Also, they require information for collective bargaining purposes. Governments use accounting information in making decisions about the economy. Creditors are concerned with whether or not an organization is creditworthy, i.e. will it be able to meet its financial obligations? The local community is concerned with job prospects and environmental issues.

2 Accounting information affects the allocation of resources. It is important that such information is relevant and reliable so that users' decisions do not result in a misallocation of resources. Also, the financial statements of different companies must be comparable.

Chapter 4 The universality of business accounting method

Answers to self-assessment questions

1 Historically, accounting responsibility was rooted in the idea of stewardship accounting. Estate owners appointed stewards (managers) to manage their properties and required them to keep proper records of all transactions and to present these accounts for approval. The concept of stewardship accounting is enshrined in accounting theory, which defines accounting responsibility in the keeping of proper records and preparing financial reports from these records for approval to the owners of businesses or company shareholders.

2 The transaction principle is key to understanding accounting method. The only business activity that is recognised and recorded in accounting systems are transactions that occur when contractual relationships of whatever nature are entered into with external parties to a

business. Transactions are evidenced in invoices that state the date, the nature of the transaction, the price and the amount involved. No transaction may be recorded without an invoice.

3 According to the double-entry principle of bookkeeping, a transaction is recorded in its legal meaning as involving an exchange in which something is given in exchange for something which is received. For example, a cash sale of £10 is recorded as a sale valued at £10 that has resulted in a receipt of £10. The double-entry principle requires both these aspects to be shown in the accounting records through two separate accounts, that are interlocking, namely the sales account and the cash account (often referred to as the cash book).

4 The terms 'debit' and 'credit' are used in double-entry bookkeeping for explaining transactions between inter-locking accounts as flows of constant money values from one account to another account. In the case of a cash sale of £10, the starting point is the sales that gives rise to a cash receipt of £10. Accounting language dates from the Italian Renaissance, when latin was in use. The term 'credit' is derived from the shortened Latin expression 'creditum', which means 'I give'. The sales accounting being starting point of the flow of £10 to the cash account, the sales account is shown as credited with £10, that is, giving £10 to the cash account. Similarly, the term 'debit' is derived from the shortened Latin expression 'I receive' and the cash account is shown as debited with £10, which is where the money flow terminates. The terms debit and credit have passed into universal accounting language and for all accounting and financial purposes are further shortened to 'Dr' and 'Cr'.

5 Accounting purports to record the truth with respect to transactions entered in the accounting records. Truth that is founded on facts is known as objective truth and it is validated by facts. The test of objectivity is applied in accounting by recording only facts obtained from invoices and verifiable from invoices. This ensures the purity of accounting data by preventing mere opinion from corrupting the objective truth that exists in invoices. Doctrinal purity in double- entry bookkeeping refers to the requirement that only data obtained from invoices should be recorded, when entering transactions.

6 The double-entry bookkeeping principle is used universally in all forms of accounting activity, whether in public or in private sector business firms, in manufacturing companies and in financial companies such as banks and insurance companies, or government and local authority accounting purposes and in non-profit organizations and global institutions such as the World Bank and the IMF.

Chapter 5 International rules for business accounting

Answers to self-assessment questions

1 Capitalism provides the theory, logic and structure of business organization in Western society. Classical economic theory, based on the concept of capitalism, defines the sole aim of business as concerned with producing goods and services and realizing profit through selling in free markets, which is the context of business accounting.

2 As a political philosophy, free trade is associated with classical economic theory. In arguing for free trade, Jeremy Bentham pleaded that every man was the best judge of his own advantage and should be allowed to pursue it without hindrance. The concept of free trade insists on freedom and is opposed to the regulation of trade. In this sense, free trade is opposed to international accounting rules that would limit choice open to individual companies to select accounting rules and would require conformity and uniformity as to financial reporting practices.

3 Profit is the reward for financing business risk. It is also expressed as the annual return on invested capital. Accounting profit is based on a simple arithmetic formula based on matching periodic revenues with the expenses of earning those revenues. The difference is the net periodic profit or net loss, as the case may be.

4 Accounting responsibility covers two major areas of accountability. First, maintaining proper records of business transactions on an on-going basis and ensuring that they are correctly recorded in accordance with generally accepted accounting principles, as stipulated in accounting law. Second, preparing periodic financial reports for shareholders showing the periodic financial result and the financial situation as the end of the period, in accordance with accounting law and certified as to truth and fairness by professional auditors.

5 The three areas of management responsibility and accountability concern profitability, asset values and financial risk. These concerns are addressed in the financial reports published to shareholders.

6 The evolution of international accounting rules may be seen as an organic process of adaptation to the needs of a market economy under constant progress and a market society under social change. Three distinct stages may be identified:

   (a) the early development of markets and of nascent capitalism prior to the Industrial Revolution of the seventeenth and eighteenth centuries;
   (b) the Industrial Revolution in Western Europe and rapid economic progress driven by commercial and industrial capitalism, flowing from manufacturing activities;
   (c) the recent global expansion of Western capitalism fuelled by financial capitalism, in the form of international financial capital flows, provoking revolutionary changes in world social order.

7 The International Accounting Standards Board was created in 1973, as the International Accounting Standards Committee (IASC) and changed its name to the International Accounting Standards Board (IASB) in 2001. Its role is to promote worldwide acceptance of accounting standards, known as International Accounting Standards (IAS) that would improve the comparability of financial information. It took its inspiration from the work of the accounting bodies in the USA and the UK, which was emphatically concerned with the substance of accounting information.

8 Three defining concepts underlie international accounting rules. They are the entity concept, the transaction concept and the money measurement concept.

9 The emergence of the global market economy under the auspices, direction and motivated in the interest of financial capitalism is creating a new world order in which there is an incompatibility between the insistence on free trade and the need for regulatory intervention to prevent the excesses that appeared in the recent banking and credit crisis. Regulatory intervention requires a framework of rules, and in particular international accounting rules adapted to the global economy.

Chapter 6 The scope and role of accounting theory

Answers to self-assessment questions

1 Theories are generalizations which serve to organize otherwise meaningless masses of data, and which establish significant relationships in respect of such data. They are concerned with explanation. Empirical theories assist in making predictions.

2 Accounting theories assist accounting policy makers in their deliberations on recommendations on accounting practice. Accounting policy makers have the responsibility of responding to the needs of users of accounting information.

3 Principles are directly related to the measurement of performance and financial status of an entity and include assets, liabilities, capital, revenue, expenses, income and transactions. Concepts determine the rules which are applied to accounting procedures. Procedures are the various activities concerned with processing transactions.

4 Descriptive theories are concerned with what accountants do and, therefore, describe current practice. Normative approaches prescribe what should be.

5 The welfare approach is an extension of the decision-making approach and considers the effects of decision making on social welfare. For example, the supply of information to one group of users may have implications for the welfare of other groups. According to the welfare approach these effects should be taken into account.

Chapter 7 Financial accounting statements

Answers to self-assessment questions

1 To report the income of a business for a specific period of time.

2 It lists the assets owed by a business, the liabilities owed to others and the accumulated investment of its owners at a specified date.

3 The income for a period is added to the owners' opening capital.

4 Non-current assets are used in the business and not intended for resale. Current assets are expected to be transformed into cash in the near future. Current liabilities are the amounts owing by the business which will fall due for payment within one year. Working capital is the difference between current assets and current liabilities.

5 Cost refers to original cost, i.e. the cost at which the asset was purchased. Depreciation is the apportionment to expense of the original cost of the asset over its productive life. Net book value is derived by deducting accumulated depreciation from the cost of an asset.

6 Income is derived by matching a period's sales revenue with the expenses incurred in earning those revenues. A statement of cash flows shows what cash has been generated by a business's operations and where the cash has gone.

7 In the United Kingdom, FRS 1 'Cash Flow Statements' classifies cash flows into six separate components, namely, net cash flow from operating activities, returns on investment and servicing of finance, taxation, capital expenditure, financing activities and increase/decrease in cash. International Accounting Standard IAS 7 'Statement of Cash Flows' adopts a presentation based on four separate components, namely, cash flow from operations, cash flow from investing, cash flow from financing and net change in cash flow over the period.

Chapter 8 Financial accounting concepts

Answer to self-assessment question

1 The role of so-called accounting concepts is to provide the ground rules for preparing financial reports. These concepts are discussed in the text.

Solutions to problems

1 (a) Assuming the company will not incur any significant costs relating to this contract, it seems reasonable in the light of the matching concept to take the advances into account when calculating income. However, if there is a possibility that the payments represent a figure which is in excess of the total fee due, then prudence suggests that the firm makes an appropriate allowance (presumably in the form of a provision). Any

payments received in advance of work carried out should certainly not be taken as income immediately. The aim is, so far as possible, to ensure that revenue is shown in the period in which it is earned and matched by the expenses relating to it.

(b) (i) If advances are discretionary, little difference should be made to their treatment. Such a system may be a better indicator that payments match work actually done.

(ii) Consultat Inc. should certainly make allowance for possible guarantee work. Again, the matching convention is particularly relevant since work we have to do later may be directly related to the income we are currently receiving. Instead of taking all the payments as income, the prudent course is to set up a provision to cover the potential cost. However, if in our experience these claims are unusual or immaterial, it would be more usual to take the income but note in the accounts the possibility of having to carry out guarantee work (a contingent claim).

2 (a) It might be argued that prudence would suggest that we should write down the machine to £30,000. However, it will often be the case that the resale value of an asset is less than its book value and it is not usual to write the asset down. The justification for this lies with the matching convention. The aim of depreciation is to match the cost of the asset to its use and not a temporary market value which is only of relevance if the asset is actually sold. In this case, it seems this is not so. Therefore, it is consistent with the conventions to maintain the asset at its existing written-down value.

(b) This is a different case because there is no intention to continue using the asset and its only value to the company is the value it can realize. Since the asset is to be sold forthwith and we know the price, prudence dictates that we should write the asset down to £15,000. It might even be argued that since there is £10,000 interest to be paid in the next year the true value of the asset is actually £5,000. This would, however, seem to be taking prudence too far and, in any case, the interest will be payable whatever happens to the asset.

Chapter 9 Financial accounting standards

Answers to self-assessment questions

1 See text. Standards are concerned either with how information might be presented, what information ought to be presented or how assets might be valued (e.g. inventory, depreciation). The general aim is to achieve a greater level of consistency along with more reliable accounting data. But it should be remembered that the need to produce a 'true and fair view' overrides any specific standard.

2 FRS 18 identified four particular accounting concepts (relevance, reliability, comparability and understandability) stating that 'their use is presumed unless otherwise stated'.

FRS 18 defines these concepts in a way similar to the conventions discussed in Chapter 8. It might be noted that the accruals concept is, in fact, consistent with both the accruals and matching conventions described in Chapter 8.

3 An accounting base is a way of expressing or applying concepts in practice. FRS 18 lists examples of cases where different bases might be applied such as depreciation, inventory valuation, hire-purchase arrangements, translation of foreign currency and others. Since there are many ways of applying concepts in practice there must be more bases than concepts.

Chapter 10 The generation of financial accounting data

Answer to self-assessment question

1 See text for examples of source documents. Source documents effectively start the accounting process. They also act as evidence when accounting records are verified by auditors.

Solutions to problems

1 (a) *Purchase day book*. Debit non-current assets (plant and equipment), credit trade creditors control.

(b) *Cash book*. Debit trade creditors control, credit bank (or, rather unlikely, cash).

(c) *Cash book*. Debit sundry expenses (bank charges account), credit bank.

(d) *Cash book*. Debit bank, credit trade debtors control.

(e) *Sales day book*. Debit trade debtors control, credit sales.

(f) *Sales day book* (or sales returns book). Debit sales, credit debtors control.

2   1 April   *Purchase day book*
            Debit plant and equipment   £400
            Credit creditors control   £400
    2 April   *Purchase day book*
            Debit purchases   £700
            Credit creditors control   £700
    4 April   *Cash book*
            Debit Bank   £50
            Credit debtors control   £50
            Debit creditors control   £250
            Credit bank   £250
    5 April   *Purchase day book*
            Debit purchases   £800
            Credit creditors control   £800
    6 April   *Sales day book*
            Debit debtors control   £98
            Credit sales   £98
    7 April   *Cash book*
            Debit bank   £70
            Credit debtors control   £70
    8 April   *Purchase day book*
            Debit rates expense account £500
            Credit creditors control   £500
    9 April   *Cash book*
            Debit bank   £700
            Credit cash   £700

Chapter 11 Data processing and double-entry bookkeeping

Solutions to problems

1

	Capital £	+	Liabilities £	=	Assets £
(a)	20,000				20,000
(b)			5,000		5,000
(c)	(1,000)				(1,000)
(d)			10,000		10,000
(e)					15,000
					(15,000)
(f)	2,000				2,000
(g)	(1,000)				(1,000)
	20,000		15,000		35,000

2

Transaction	Accounting effects	
	Balance sheet £	Income statement £
Cash sales £400	400	400
Cash purchases £75	75(75)	
Received from trade debtor £35	35(35)	
Equipment purchased on credit terms £345	345(345)	
Invoice received for repairs to machinery £67	(67)	(67)
Wages paid £78	(78)	(78)
Payment of rent due last month £90	90(90)	
Equipment sold as scrap £20 (book value £10)	20(10)	10
Loan received £600	600(600)	
Bank interest charged £49	(49)	49

3

Cash book			Bank account		
Ref		£	Ref		£
(A)	Capital	10,000	(1)	Rent	200
(14)	Debtors	50	(7)	Motor expenses	10
			(8)	Entertaining	20
			(10)	Entertaining	30
			(11)	Wages	70
			(12)	Creditors	1,000
			(13)	Creditors	150
				Bal c/d	8,570
		10,050			10,050
	Bal b/d	8,570			

Sales account

		£	Ref		£
			(5)	Debtors	50
	Bal c/d	110	(9)	Debtors	60
		110			110
				Bal b/d	110

Rent and rates account

Ref		£			£
(1)	Cash book	200		Bal c/d	200
	Bal b/d	200			

Non-current asset (equipment) account

Ref		£			£
(2)	Trade creditors	1,000		Bal c/d	1,000
	Bal b/d	1,000			

Sundry office supplies account

Ref		£			£
(3)	Creditors	150		Bal c/d	150
	Bal b/d	150			

Capital account

		£	Ref		£
	Bal c/d	12,000	(A)	Cash book	10,000
			(6)	Non-current asset (motor)	2,000
		12,000			12,000
				Bal b/d	12,000

Debtors account

Ref		£	Ref		£
(5)	Sales	50	(14)	Cash book	50
(9)	Sales	60		Bal c/d	60
		110			110
	Bal b/d	60			

Wages account

Ref		£			£
(11)	Cash book	70		Bal c/d	70
	Bal b/d	70			

Non-current asset (motors) account

Ref		£			£
(6)	Capital	2,000	Bal c/d		2,000
	Bal b/d	2,000			

Entertaining account

Ref		£			£
(8)	Cash book	20	Bal c/d		50
(10)	Cash book	30			
		50			50
	Bal b/d	50			

Motor expenses account

Ref		£			£
(7)	Cash book	10	Bal c/d		10
	Bal b/d	10			

Trade creditors account

Ref		£	Ref		£
(12)	Cash book	1,000	(2)	Non-current equipment	1,000
(13)	Cash book	150	(3)	Office supplies	150
		1,150			1,150

Bill Cashing Trial balance

	Dr	Cr
	£	£
Cash book	8,570	
Rent and rates	200	
Non-current assets (equipment)	1,000	
Office supplies	150	
Non-current asset (motors)	2,000	
Capital account		12,000
Entertaining	50	
Motor expenses	10	
Debtors	60	
Sales		110
Wages	70	
	12,110	12,110

4

AB Ltd Journal		Dr	Cr
		£	£
(a)	Stationery	100	
	Suspense		100
(b)	Sales account	36	
	Suspense		36
(c)	Sales account	60	
	Suspense		60
(d)	Sales ledger control	175	
	Suspense		250
	Purchase ledger control	75	
(e)	Inventory		2,250
	Suspense	2,250	
(f)	Discounts allowed	650	
	Suspense		650
(g)	Discounts received		521
	Suspense	521	
(h)	Cash at bank		20
	Suspense	20	

AB Ltd Suspense account

	£		£
Inventory account	2,250	Balance from trial balance	1,695
Discounts received	521	Stationery account	100
Bank account	20	Sales account	36
		Cash account	60
		Sales ledger control	175
		Purchase ledger control	75
		Discounts allowed	650
	2,791		2,791

6

Cash account

		£			£
(1)	Capital	4,000	(2)	Purchases	1,130
(10)	Victor	190	(3)	Wages	13
			(3)	Sundry expenses	2
			(7)	Fixtures and fittings	350
			(8)	Wages	38
			(9)	Drawings	80
			(11)	Rent	500
		4,190			2,113
				Balance c/d	2,077
		4,190			4,190
	Balance b/d	2,077			

Capital account

		£			£
	Balance c/d	5,750	(1)	Cash	4,000
			(1)	Motor car	1,750
		5,750			5,750
				Balance b/d	5,750

Motor account

		£			£
(1)	Capital	1,750		Balance c/d	1,750
	Balance b/d	1,750			

Purchases account

		£			£
(2)	Cash account	1,130		Balance c/d	1,215
(6)	William	85			
		1,215			1,215
	Balance b/d	1,215			

Wages account

		£			£
(3)	Cash	13		Balance	51
(8)	Cash	38			
		51			51
	Balance b/d	51			

Sundry expenses account

		£			£
(3)	Cash	2		Balance c/d	2
		2			2
	Balance b/d	2			

Sales account

		£			£
	Balance c/d	430	(4)	Victor	190
			(5)	Susan	240
		430			430
				Balance b/d	430

Victor's account

		£			£
(4)	Sales	190	(10)	Cash	190

Susan's account

(5)	Sales	£ 240	Balance c/d	£ 240
	Balance b/d	240		

Rent account

(11)	Cash	£ 500	Balance c/d	£ 500
	Balance b/d	500		

William's account

	Balance c/d	£ 85	(6)	Purchases	£ 85
				Balance b/d	85

Fixtures and fittings account

(7)	Cash	£ 350	Balance c/d	£ 350
	Balance b/d	350		

Drawings account

(9)	Cash	£ 80	Balance c/d	£ 80
	Balance b/d	80		

Trial balance as at 31 June 20X0

	Dr	Cr
	£	£
Cash	2,077	
Capital		5,750
Motor car	1,750	
Purchases	1,215	
Wages	51	
Sundry expenses	2	
Sales		430
Susan	240	
Rent	500	
William		85
Fixtures and fittings	350	
Drawings	80	
	6,265	6,265

7

Cash account

		£			£
(1)	Loan	10,000	(2)	Purchases	6,000
(3)	Sales	8,000	(4)	Bicycle	140
(7)	Cash	4,200	(5)	Rent	240
(8)	Capital	2,000	(6)	Creditors	3,000
			(9)	Electricity	180
			(10)	Drawings	240
				Balance c/d	14,400
		24,200			24,200
	Balance b/d	14,400			

Loan account

	£			£
Balance c/d	10,000	(1)	Cash	10,000
			Balance b/d	10,000

Sales account

	£			£
Balance c/d	15,600	(3)	Cash	8,000
		(7)	Debtors	7,600
	15,600			15,600
			Balance b/d	15,600

Purchases account

		£		£
(2)	Cash	6,000	Balance c/d	10,000
(6)	Creditors	4,000		
		10,000		10,000
	Balance b/d	10,000		

Bicycle account

		£		£
(4)	Cash	140	Balance c/d	140
	Balance b/d	140		

Rent account

		£		£
(5)	Cash	240	Balance c/d	240
	Balance b/d	240		

Creditors account

		£			£
(6)	Cash	3,000	(6)	Purchases	4,000
	Balance b/d	1,000			
		4,000			4,000
				Balance b/d	1,000

Debtors account

		£			£
(7)	Sales	7,600	(7)	Cash	4,200
				Balance b/d	3,400
		7,600			7,600
	Balance b/d	3,400			

Capital account

		£			£
	Balance c/d	2,000	(8)	Cash	2,000
				Balance b/d	2,000

Electricity account

		£			£
(9)	Cash	180		Balance c/d	180
	Balance b/d	180			

Drawings account

		£			£
(10)	Cash	240		Balance c/d	240
	Balance b/d	240			

Trial balance as at 31 March 20X0

	Dr	Cr
	£	£
Cash	14,400	
Loan – father		10,000
Sales		15,600
Purchases	10,000	
Bicycle	140	
Rent	240	
Creditors		1,000
Debtors	3,400	
Capital		2,000
Electricity	180	
Drawings	240	
	28,600	28,600

Chapter 12 Double-entry bookkeeping and periodic measurement

Answer to self-assessment question

1 The most significant conventions are:

(i) Accruals. Clearly it is most important that a proper matching of revenue and expense is achieved. This can be illustrated by accruals, prepayments, depreciation, the carrying forward of inventory values, deferred expenditure such as research and development and many other examples.

(ii) Going concern. If the company is on the verge of liquidation, many values may need modification.

(iii) Prudence. This implies that incomes are not recognized until they are realized by external sale. Similarly, expected losses, such as the situation where realizable value is less than cost, will be recognized immediately.

(iv) Related to prudence, assets will be valued at original cost. Clearly this has a 'knock-on' effect for revenue and expenses.

(v) Consistency. The same methods will generally be used each year in valuation and recognition of incomes/expenses. Thus changes in depreciation policy or inventory valuation would not normally take place and if they did, the effect of the change on income would need to be noted in the accounts.

Solutions to problems

1

Cost of goods sold

	£
Opening inventory	10,000
Plus: Purchases	40,000
	50,000
Less: Closing inventory	15,000
Cost of sales	35,000

2

Rent and rates account

		£			£
2.7.X0	Rent to 24.6.X0	400	1.7.X0	Rent owing b/d	400
2.7.X0	Rates to 30.9.X0	300	1.7.X0	Rates owing b/d	150
10.10.X0	Rates to 31.3.X1	300			
10.10.X0	Rent to 29.9.X0	400			
4.1.X1	Rent to 25.12.X0	400			
6.4.X1	Rates to 30.9.X1	300			
6.4.X1	Rent to 25.3.X1	400	30.6.X1	Rent owing c/d	150
30.6.X1	Rates prepaid c/d	400		Income statement	2,200
		2,900			2,900

Note that brought forward and carried forward figures have been estimated on the basis of whole months outstanding rather than accurately to the nearest day. The latter could, of course, be done but the charge to the income statement should still stand at £2,000, i.e. rent of £1,600 and rates of £600.

4

Rent payable account

		£			£
31 Dec	Balance b/d	300	31 Dec	Income statement	400
31	Balance c/d	100			
		400			400
			1 Jan	Balance b/d	100

Telephone account

		£			£
31 Dec	Balance b/d	60	31 Dec	Income statement	80
31	Balance c/d	20			
		80			80
			1 Jan	Balance b/d	20

Rates account

		£			£
31 Dec	Balance b/d	400	31 Dec	Income statement	300
				Balance c/d	100
		400			400
1 Jan	Balance b/d	100			

Insurance account

		£			£
31 Dec	Balance b/d	100	31 Dec	Income statement	75
			31	Balance c/d	25
		100			100
1 Jan	Balance b/d	25			

Electricity account

		£			£
31 Dec	Balance b/d	80	31 Dec	Income statement	96
31	Balance c/d	16			
		96			96
			1 Jan	Balance b/d	16

Rents receivable account

		£			£
31 Dec	Income statement	400	31 Dec	Balance b/d	500
31	Balance c/d	100			
		500			500
			1 Jan	Balance b/d	100

Commission receivable account

		£			£
31 Dec	Income statement	500	31 Dec	Balance b/d	300
			31	Balance c/d	200
		500			500
1 Jan	Balance b/d	200			

Chapter 13 Losses in asset values and periodic measurement

Answers to self-assessment questions

1 Clearly the overriding issue when deciding on a depreciation policy is the provision of a true and fair view within the constraints of accounting standards and company law. It should be noted that the usefulness of any depreciation charge will be limited by the more general accounting system in use, and even then it is based on a number of assumptions of varying reliability.

2 Having defined non-current assets, the standard describes depreciation as 'the measure of the wearing out, consumption or other reduction in the useful economic life of a non-current asset, whether arising from use, effluxion of time or obsolescence ...'.

FRS 15 requires that non-current assets be depreciated and that the income statement and balance sheet must be consistent. It prohibits the setting of depreciation directly to reserves. Its main thrust is to achieve realism (given the constraints that might be imposed by the more general accounting systems adopted). It requires a consistent approach, year by year, unless it can be shown that a change is desirable for the purpose of realism.

Land should not be depreciated unless it is depleted by, for example, extraction of minerals, but buildings are no different from other non-current assets.

Disclosure:

1 depreciation methods used;
2 useful economic lives or depreciation rates used;
3 total depreciation charged for the period;
4 gross amount of depreciable assets and related accumulated depreciation.

Any material changes in the method of depreciation should also be disclosed along with the reason for the change. Revaluations should be disclosed.

Solutions to problems

1 (a) Straight-line depreciation

$$r = \frac{c - rv}{n} \left(\frac{\text{cost} - \text{residual value}}{\text{life in years}} \right)$$

i.e. $\dfrac{\pounds 48,000 + \pounds 2,000 - \pounds 4,000}{8} = \pounds 5,750$ p.a.

provision for 20X0 = £5,750
accumulated depreciation end 20X1 = £11,500 (at end of 8 years = £46,000)

(b) Reducing balance

$$r - 1 - n \sqrt{\frac{rv}{c}}$$

i.e. $1 - 8 \sqrt{\dfrac{4,000}{50,000}} = 1\,0.73 = 27\%$

	Opening NBV	Provision (@ 27%)	Accumulated depreciation
19X9	£50,000	£13,500	£13,500
20X0	£36,500	£9,855	£23,355

2

Relevant cost

	£	
Invoice price	142,600	(*Note*: the cost related to the old
Transportation	2,000	machine has been written off)
Installation	3,400	
	148,000	

Estimated life 8 years, salvage value zero.

    (a) Straight-line depreciation produces an annual charge of:

        £148,000/8 = £18,500.

        There is a problem in calculating a rate for reducing balance depreciation here, because applying the normal formula to a salvage value of zero would produce a rate of 1 (i.e. 100% depreciation). One way around this would be to use a salvage value and accept that this would eventually need to be written off. If we arbitrarily use 1,000 we end up with:

$$1 - 8\sqrt{\frac{1,000}{148,000}} = 0.46, \text{ i.e. } 46\%$$

        This raises some interesting issues concerning the general realism of reducing balance depreciation.

    (b) FRS 15 states that where it is considered necessary to revise the estimated life of an asset 'usually . . . there will be no material distortion of future results or financial position if the net book amount is written off over the revised remaining useful economic life.' It goes on to recommend that any material distortions should be recognized in accordance with SSAP 6 'Extraordinary Items and Prior Year Adjustments'.

        In this case we are faced with a choice between:

      (i) Adjustment which is not really material.
          NBV end of year 20X0 = £148,000 – (£18,500 × 2) = £111,000.
      (ii) New estimate of life means 10 years remain;
          thus new charge = £11,100 p.a.
          Adjustment which is regarded as material.
          New charge from acquisition

$$\frac{£148,000}{12} = £12,333.$$

        New accumulated depreciation end of 20X0 = £24,666. Thus a prior year adjustment of £12,334 (i.e. reducing accumulated depreciation) with a charge of £12,333 for year 20X1 would be made.

3

Plant and machinery at cost

B/d	7,500	(4)	£500	Asset realization
(3)	1,000			disposal

Depreciation of plant and machinery

(4)	Asset realization disposal	£200	B/d	£3,000 (1)

Motor vehicles at cost

B/d	£3,500	(5)	£750	Asset realization disposal	

Asset realization account

		£			£	
(4)	Plant at cost	500	(4)	325	Proceeds	
	Income Statement (surplus on disposal)	25	(4)	200	Depreciation	
		525		525		
(5)	Motors at cost	750	(5)	400	Proceeds	
			(5)	300	Depreciation	
				50	Income Statement (loss on disposal)	
		750		750		

Depreciation of motor vehicles

(5)	Disposal	£300	B/d	£1,400 (2)

5

(a)

Bad and doubtful debts account

	£		£
19X9		19X9	
31.3		31.3	
Balance c/d	500	Income Statement bad debts	500
20X0		20X0	
(Bad debt w/o)		b/d	500
Debtors control	250		
Balance c/d	625	Income Statement bad debts	375
	875		875
20X1		20X1	
(Bad debt w/o)		b/d	625
Debtors control	270		
Balance c/d	400	Income Statement bad debts	45
	670		670

(b)

	£
Income Statement 19X9 Bad and doubtful debts	500
Income Statement 20X0 Bad and doubtful debts	375
Income Statement 20X1 Bad and doubtful debts	45

6

(a) (i) **Straight-line method**

	£
Cost	7,000,000
Less: Expected residual value	1,500,000
	5,500,000
Depreciation per annum	1,375,000

Annual charge	£
Year to 31 January 19X8	1,375,000
Year to 31 January 19X9	1,375,000
Year to 31 January 20X0	1,375,000
Year to 31 January 20X1 (balance)	1,675,000
Actual depreciation (£7,000,000 – £1,200,000)	5,800,000

(ii) **Flying hours logged method**

	£
Cost	7,000,000
Less: Expected residual value	1,500,000
Expected depreciation	5,500,000
Expected flying hours	10,000
Depreciation per flying hour	550

Annual charge	£
Year to 31 January 19X8 (3,000 × £550)	1,650,000
Year to 31 January 19X9 (2,800 × £550)	1,540,000
Year to 31 January 20X0 (2,300 × £550)	1,265,000
Year to 31 January 20X1 (balance)	1,345,000
Actual depreciation (£7,000,000 – £1,200,000)	5,800,000

(b)

Flying hours logged method Aircraft account

20X0		£	20X0		£
Feb 1	Balance b/f	7,000,000	June	Assets disposals	7,000,000

Provision for depreciation – aircraft

20X0		£	20X0		£
June	Assets disposals	4,455,000	Feb 1	Balance b/f	4,455,000

Assets disposals account

20X0		£	20X0		£
June	Aircraft	7,000,000	June	Provision for depreciation	4,455,000
				Bank	1,200,000
			20X1		
			Jan 31	Income and loss	1,345,000
		7,000,000			7,000,000

Straight-line method Aircraft account

20X0		£	20X0		£
Feb 1	Balance b/f	7,000,000	June	Assets disposals	7,000,000

Provision for depreciation – aircraft

20X0		£	20X0		£
June	Assets disposals	4,125,000	Feb 1	Balance b/f	4,125,000

Assets disposals account

20X0		£	20X0		£
June	Aircraft	7,000,000	June	Provision for depreciation	4,125,000
			Bank		1,200,000
			20X1		
			Jan 31	Income and loss	1,675,000
		7,000,000			7,000,000

7

Asset account

	£		£
Balance at 1 Jan 20X0	8,000	Balance at 31 Dec 20X0	8,800
Modification	800		
	8,800		8,800

Provision for depreciation account

	£		£
Balance at 31 Dec 20X0	4,320	Balance at 1 Jan 20X0	3,200
		Depreciation for 20X0 (W1)	1,120
	4,320		4,320

Income statement

	£
Depreciation	1,120
Maintenance and replacements (W2)	750

Workings:

1 The net book value of the asset is to be written off over the remaining useful life which is a further five years.

	£
Asset (cost)	8,800
Depreciation to date	3,200
	5,600

	£
Depreciation $\frac{1}{5}$	1,120

2 The £500 for renewal has been charged to income statement as it would appear to have no connection with the improvements which extend the useful life.

Chapter 14 Preparing an income statement and a balance sheet

Solutions to problems

1 (a) Adjustments to income:

		£
(i)	Cr income	100
	Dr bank	100
(ii)	Dr income	210
	Cr debtors	100
	Cr provision	110
(iii)	Non-current assets	500
	Cr Income Statement	500
	Dr Income Statement	50
	Cr Prov. Depreciation.	50
(iv)	Inventory	250
	Dr Income Statement	250
(v)	Cr cash	40
	Dr Income Statement	40

Net effect is income increased by £50 and now stands at £2,100.

(b)

	£		£	
Capital account	10,000	Plant cost	8,500	
Income for the year	2,100	Depreciation	2,050	6,450
	12,100	Vehicle cost	3,000	
		Depreciation	1,000	2,000
Creditors and provisions	5,000	Inventory		6,750
Bank overdraft	900	Debtors	3,100	
		Provision	310	2,790
		Cash		10
	18,000			18,000

727

2

	£	£
Sales		50,000
Purchases	30,000	
Inventory 1 Apr 20X0	35,000	
Admin expenses	5,000	
Selling expenses	5,000	
Trade creditors		27,000
Bank overdraft		32,000
Trade debtors	55,000	
Debentures		50,000
Plant and machinery at cost	80,000	
Depreciation of plant and machinery		30,000
Fixtures at cost	40,000	
Depreciation of fixtures		10,000
Capital account 1 Apr 20X0		51,000
	250,000	250,000

John Reeve Income statement

	£	£
Sales		50,000
Opening inventory	35,000	
Purchases	30,000	
	65,000	
Closing inventory	40,000	25,000
Gross Income		25,000
Less:		
Administration expenses	5,000	
Selling expenses	5,000	
Depreciation of plant	16,000	
Depreciation of fixtures	8,000	34,000
Loss for year		(9,000)

John Reeve Balance sheet

			£
Capital account b/f			51,000
Loss for year			9,000
			42,000
Debentures			50,000
			92,000

Represented by:	Cost	Depr	NBV
	£	£	£
Plant and machinery	80,000	46,000	34,000
Fixtures	40,000	18,000	22,000
	120,000	64,000	56,000

Current assets		
Inventory	40,000	
Debtors	55,000	
	95,000	
Current liabilities		
Creditors	27,000	
Bank overdraft	32,000	
	59,000	
Net current assets		36,000
		92,000

4

Matt Spode Income statement for year ended 31 December 20X0

	£	£
Sales		157,240
Opening inventory	19,250	
Purchases	92,400	
	111,650	
Closing inventory	22,400	
Cost of sales		89,250
Gross income		67,990
Motor expenses	7,300	
Rates	2,300	
Wages and salaries (42,000 + 1,200)	43,200	
Insurance (2,000 – 900)	1,100	
Sundry expenses	16,200	
Bad debts written off	800	
Increased provision for doubtful debts (1,200 – 560)	640	
Depreciation motors (30,000 – 8,200) × 0.25	5,450	
Depreciation fixtures and fittings (6,500 × 0.1)	650	
Loan interest	2,000	79,640
Net loss		(11,650)

Matt Spode Balance sheet as at 31 December 20X0

				£
Capital b/f				112,000
Loss for year				11,650
				100,350
Drawings				9,600
Capital carried forward				90,750
Long-term loan				20,000
				110,750

Represented by:

Non-current assets	Cost	Depr	NBV
Premises	64,000	–	64,000
Motors	30,000	13,650	16,350
Fixtures and fittings	6,500	1,750	4,750
	100,500	15,400	85,100

	£	£	£	
Current assets				
Inventory		22,400		
Debtors	17,200			
Less: Provision	1,200	16,000		
Prepayments		900		
Cash at bank and in hand		4,550		
		43,850		

			£	£
Current liabilities				
Trade creditors			15,000	
Accrued wages			1,200	
Accrued interest			2,000	
			18,200	
Net current assets				25,650
				110,750

5

A Merchant Income statement year ended 31 December 20X0

	£	£	Notes
Gross income		27,000	
Less: Expenses			
Selling and distribution	4,500		
Depreciation motors	4,000		
Rates and insurance	5,000		(1)
Office salaries	3,000		
Office expenses	1,250		
Bad debts written off	500		
Increased provision for doubtful debts	100		(2)
Discounts received and allowed (net)	(1,500)	16,850	
		10,150	

1 Prepayment of £1,000 re 3 months' rates to March.
2 Required provision 5% of £52,000 = £2,600. Provision brought forward £2,500.

A Merchant Balance sheet as at 31 December 20X0

	£
Capital account. A Merchant	
Balance brought forward	90,000
Introduced	1,500
Income for year	10,150
	101,650
Drawings	8,000
	93,650

Represented by:

Non-current assets	Cost	Depr	NBV
	£	£	£
Freehold premises	30,000	30,000	
Motor vehicles	20,000	8,000	12,000
	50,000	8,000	42,000
	£	£	£
Current assets			
Inventory		23,600	
Debtors	53,000		(3)
Less: Provision	2,600	50,400	
Bank balance		8,750	
		82,750	
Current liabilities			
Creditors		31,100	
			51,650
			93,650

(3) Includes prepayment of £1,000 re rates.

6

Movement in cash and bank

Closing	£(50)	Opening	£(450)
Increase	£400		

Other assets/liabilities

Closing	£	Opening	£
	3,300		2,600
	5,100		4,500
	(1,900)		(1,450)
	(2,500)		(4,000)
	4,000		1,650

		£	
Drawings 200 × 52 =		10,400	cash
Insurance for private house		100	
Furniture for private house		600	
		11,100	
Less: Payment of business expenses			
from private account		3,100	
Net		8,000	

Income for year =	2,750	Increase in assets
	8,000	Drawings
	(2,000)	Depreciation of shop
	(600)	Depreciation of fittings, etc.
	8,150	

Financial position at 31 December 20X0

Non-current assets	Cost	Depr	NBV	Notes
	£	£	£	
Shop	40,000	10,000	30,000	(1)
Fittings and fixtures	6,000	3,000	3,000	(2)
	46,000	13,000	33,000	
Current assets				
Inventory	3,300			
Debtors	5,100			
Cash	250			
	8,650			
Current liabilities				
Creditors	1,900			
Overdraft	300			
	2,200			

Net current assets		6,450
		39,450
Capital account		36,950	(3)
Loan from Mrs Jackson		2,500
		39,450

1 Depreciation 5 years @ 5% × 40,000
2 Depreciation 5 years @ 10% × 3,000
3 Balancing figure

8

	£	£	Notes
Sales		105,190	(1)
Opening inventory	24,000		
Purchases	67,940		(2)
	91,940		
Closing inventory	29,000		
		62,940	
		42,250	
Expenses			
General	7,630		(3)
Depreciation f, f & f	300		
Depreciation motor van	1,700		
Loss on disposal of motor vehicle	900	10,530	
		31,720	

Realization of motor vehicles

	£		£
Cost	5,625	Depreciation	1,125
		Proceeds	3,600
		Loss on disposal	900
	5,625		5,625

1 Bankings £98,740 plus increase in debtors £450 plus takings not banked £6,000.
2 Bank payments £57,180 plus increase in creditors £10,760.
3 Bank payments £6,720 plus £1,500 cash payments, less reduction in amount owing.

Balance sheet

Non-current assets (net)	£	£	Notes
Motor van		6,800	
Furniture, etc.		5,700	
		12,500	
Current assets			
Inventory	29,000		
Debtors	1,250		
Bank	27,140		
Cash	350		
	57,740		
Current liabilities			
Creditors	18,400		
Accrued expenses	730		
	19,130		
		38,610	
		51,110	
Snailsby capital account			
Balance brought forward		30,470	(4)
Income for year		30,540	
		61,010	
Drawings		9,900	(5)
		51,110	

4 Balancing figure derived from working backwards from balance sheet total.
5 Bank drawings £5,400 plus cash drawings £4,500.

9

Cash book

	£		£
Balance	12,600	Discharged cheque	70
Dividend received	340	Bank charges, etc.	60
		Trade subscription	15
		Balance c/d	12,795
	12,940		12,940

Bank reconciliation

	£
Balance per statement	13,500
Add: Uncleared lodgement	230
	13,730
Less: Unpresented cheques	935
	12,795

11

Tim Russell Income statement for the year ended 31 December 20X0

	£	£
Sales		105,560
Cost of sales		
Inventory at 1 Jan 20X0	7,154	
Purchases	71,812	
	78,966	
Closing inventory	8,221	70,745
Gross income		34,815
Expenses		
Salaries and wages	7,576	
Rent, rates and insurance	5,760	
Discounts allowed	1,206	
Carriage	2,000	
Postage and stationery	1,213	
Advertising	2,029	
Bad debts	1,234	
Depreciation	4,870	
Discounts received	(684)	25,204
Net income		9,611

Balance sheet as at 31 December 20X0

	Cost £	Depreciation £	Net book value £
Non-current assets			
Equipment	48,700	26,520	22,180
Current assets			
Inventory		8,221	
Debtors		13,170	
Prepaid expenses		213	
Cash at bank		3,054	
Cash in hand		312	
		24,970	
Current liabilities			
Creditors		11,640	
Accruals		177	
		11,817	13,153
Net current assets			35,333
Capital account			
Balance c/d			31,653
Income for year			9,611
			41,264
Drawings			5,931
			35,333

Chapter 15 Reporting recorded assets and liabilities

Answer to self-assessment question

1 The difficulty in accounting for research and development expenditure arises from the question as to how much of the expenditure might be interpreted as being of a capital nature and how much is really of a revenue nature. This is often so unclear that it is not possible to make an objective judgement. Pure research is viewed as being of a revenue nature because there is often little certainty as to its relationship with future revenue. (It should, however, be noted that this may be more of a measurement problem than one of principle.) Similarly, it is felt that applied research will be difficult to assess and this is to be treated as revenue.

IAS 38 'Intangible Assets' provides rules for the recognition and measurement of intangible assets, including research and development costs and requires that, initially, such intangible assets shall be measured at cost. A distinction is made between those intangible assets that have been acquired through purchase or a business combination. In the case of a purchase, the cost value applies and in the case of a business combination it is the fair value that applies. IAS 38 provides that expenditure in internally generated intangible assets, such as research and development, that expenditure shall be recognized as an expense as it is incurred. IAS 38 specifically prohibits the recognition of internally generated brands and views accounting for brands is inseparable from accounting for goodwill.

Solutions to problems

2 (a) The price paid for McMaltby was £120,000.

	£	£
Price paid		
Non-current assets		120,000
Premises	60,000	
Plant	25,000	
Current assets		
32,000 + 5,000 – 3,000	34,000	
	119,000	
Less: Current liabilities	15,000	
		104,000
Goodwill		16,000

(b) FRS 10 states that goodwill should be capitalized and written off over a period of time.

(c)

	£	£
Share capital		250,000
Reserves		95,000
		345,000
Debentures and loan		186,000
		531,000
Goodwill		16,000
Tangible non-current assets		
295,000 + 85,000		380,000
Current assets		
221,000 + 34,000 – 20,000	235,000	
Current liabilities		
85,000 + 15,000	(100,000)	
		135,000
		531,000

3

	19X8	19X9
Gross income margin	5,655/18,850 = 30%	7,722/25,740 = 30%

Debtors account

	£		£
Balance b/f	5,130	Balance c/f	6,050
Sales	31,000	Cash received	30,080
	36,130		36,130

Creditors account

	£		£
Balance c/f	1,870	Balance b/f	1,790
Payments	22,220	Purchases	22,300
	24,090		24,090

Gross income is a constant 30% of sales, therefore gross income for 20X0 = 30% × £31,000 = £9,300.

4

	£	£
Sales		31,000
Opening inventory	1,400	
Purchases	22,300	
	23,700	
Closing inventory	2,000	
Cost of sales		21,700
Gross income		9,300

Closing inventory is calculated by working back from the gross income figure and forward from opening inventory/purchases.

5 (a)

Inventory account (units)

19X8		19X8	
B/f	0	Sales	12,000
Purchases	15,000	C/f	3,000
	15,000		15,000
19X9		**19X9**	
B/f	3,000	Sales	15,000
Purchases	15,500	C/f	3,500
	18,500		18,500
20X0		**20X0**	
B/f	3,500	Sales	18,000
Purchases	16,500	C/f	2,000
	20,000		20,000

(b) Value of year-end inventory using FIFO:

19X8	3,000 units @ £30 =	£90,000
19X9	3,500 units @ £37 =	£129,500
20X0	2,000 units @ £45 =	£90,000

Value of year-end inventory using LIFO:

19X8	3,000 units @ £22 =	£66,000
19X9	3,000 units @ £22 =	£66,000
	500 units @ £32 =	£16,000
		£82,000
20X0	2,000 units @ £22 =	£44,000

Value of inventory using weighted average:

19X8	Units			Value
				£
B/f	0			0
Purchased	15,000	$\left(\dfrac{3,000}{15,000} \times (A)\right)$	(A)	388,000
	15,000			388,000
Closing inventory 19X8	3,000			77,600
19X9 Purchases	15,500	$\left(\dfrac{3,500}{10,500} \times (B)\right)$	(B)	528,000
	18,500			605,600
Closing inventory 19X9	3,500			114,573
20X0 Purchases	16,500	$\left(\dfrac{2,000}{20,000} \times (C)\right)$	(C)	698,500
	20,000			813,073
Closing inventory 20X0	2,000			81,307

(c)

Income statement

	FIFO		LIFO		AVCO	
	£		£		£	
19X8 Sales		600,000		600,000		600,000
Purchases	388,000		388,000		388,000	
Cl. Inventory	90,000		66,000		77,600	
		298,000		322,000		310,400
Gross income		302,000		278,000		289,600
19X9 Sales		900,000		900,000		900,000
Op. inventory	90,000		66,000		77,600	
Purchases	528,000		528,000		528,000	
Cl. Inventory	(129,500)		(82,000)		(114,573)	
		488,500		512,000		491,027
Gross income		411,500		388,000		408,973
20X0 Sales		1,170,000		1,170,000		1,170,000
Op. inventory	129,500		82,000		114,573	
Purchases	698,500		698,500		698,500	
Cl. Inventory	(90,000)		(44,000)		(81,307)	
		738,000		736,500		731,766
Gross income		432,000		433,500		438,234

(d) It is difficult to say which method of inventory valuation is 'most appropriate'. SSAP 9 implies that the use of base inventory or LIFO will generally be inappropriate. It may well be that the use of LIFO produces a more realistic cost of sales figure since inventory consumed approximates more closely to replacement cost. However, this is really part of a much bigger issue covered in later chapters. Generally speaking, both LIFO and AVCO will tend to undervalue inventory in the balance sheet.

6

SSAP 9 covers the treatment of long-term contracts and the taking of income during the period of the contract. It states that 'there can be no attributable income until the outcome of a contract can reasonably be foreseen'.

Accrued income is normally taken as:

$$[\text{Total contract price} - (\text{lists to date} + \text{estimate costs to completion})] \times \frac{\text{work certified}}{\text{total contract price}}$$

In this case, cost to date =

	£	£
Materials from store	42,000	
Less: Inventory	970	
		41,030
Wages		39,820
Expenses		12,130
Direct materials		4,910
Depreciation of plant		342
		98,232

The treatment of overheads depends on whether they are directly attributable to the project or merely an arbitrary allocation of general expenses.

In the case in question we have no indication of the estimated costs to completion, but it would seem that half the project has been completed (£100,000 grossed up to reflect 20% retention).

Assuming future costs to be consistent with past costs would produce a income to date of:

	£	£
		125,000
Less:	98,232	
Direct o/h	790	
		99,022
		25,978

How much of this income would be taken depends on assessments of guarantee costs, etc., as well as the likelihood of future costs remaining at the same levels as past costs. The figure calculated above would, effectively, represent the maximum income that might be taken at this stage.

7

	£	£
Costs to date		
Wages		60,000
Materials	42,500	
Inventory	1,250	41,250
Sundries		4,000
Head Office charges (deemed directly attributable to contract)		5,500
Plant: Cost	17,500	
Disposal	(1,500)	
	16,000	
Estimated residual value	4,500	11,500
		122,250

	£	£
Future costs		
Wages		52,800
Materials	1,250	
	35,000	36,250
Sundries		1,800
Plant b/f	4,500	
Additions	6,500	
	11,000	
Residual	3,750	7,250
Contingencies		3,500
		101,600

Attributable income =

[Total contract price – (Costs to date +

$$\text{Estimated costs to completion})] \times \frac{\text{Work certified to date}}{\text{Total contract price}}$$

Work certified to date = £125,000
(i.e. 100,000 grossed up for 20% retention)
Thus accrued income =

$$[250,000 - (122,250 + 101,660)] \times \frac{125,000}{250,000}$$

$$= 26,150 \times 0.5 = £13,075$$

Summarized contract account

	£		£	£
Costs to date	122,250	Payments rec'd		100,000
		Contract debtor c/d		
Income statement	13,075	certified	25,000	
		uncertified	10,325	
				35,325
	135,325			135,325

Chapter 16 The processes of management

Answers to self-assessment questions

1 Organizing involves setting up the administrative structure for implementing strategic decisions. It involves defining the tasks necessary to achieve strategic goals, determining who is to perform these tasks and assigning responsibility for their performance. The function of organizing is to coordinate these tasks in such a way that the organization is able to work efficiently in fulfilling its objectives.

2 The significance of the organizational structure lies in the manner in which tasks are structured in terms of different specialisms and areas of responsibility. A major purpose of any organizational structure is to facilitate the flow of information to and from decision makers. Management may be considered as a process of converting information into action. Hence, the organizational structure should be designed around information flows.

3 The term 'control' may be defined in a broad or in a narrow way. In a broad way, no distinction is made between planning and control. More narrowly, control may be defined as closely linked to planning in that its purpose is to ensure that the firm's activities conform to plans. It is effected by means of an information feedback system which enables performance to be compared with planned targets.

4 Communication involves linking all the management functions by transmitting information and instructions within the organization. Additionally, communication relates the organization to its environment by linking it to the suppliers of resources and to the consumers for whom its products are intended. A high degree of communication throughout the organization binds its various members together, uniting them in the pursuit of organizational

objectives. Hence, an organization may be viewed not only as a decision-making system, but also as a communication system.

5 Motivation involves getting all members of an organization to work together and to put their maximum efforts into the realization of organizational objectives by improving their personal performance. The purpose of motivation is to increase the level of congruence between the personal objectives of individual members of the organization and the objectives that the organization as a whole seeks to attain.

6 Information is the integrating force that combines organizational resources into a cohesive whole directed towards the realization of organizational objectives. Since the quality of information available is crucial to the quality of decision making, an efficient and adequate information system is a prerequisite of managerial success. A management information system provides individual managers with the information they require for making decisions within their own areas of responsibility. It consists of a network of information flows to which each decision is related.

7 Different levels of management activity may be related to the three major areas of decision making, namely, strategic planning, management control and operational control. Strategic planning involves the determination of corporate objectives and goals, and developing broad policies by which they may be achieved. Management control is concerned with the implementation of the strategic plan, ensuring that the necessary resources have been obtained and that they are being used efficiently and effectively. Operational control is the process of ensuring that specific tasks are being carried out efficiently and effectively. It focuses on individual tasks.

Chapter 17 Traditional cost accounting

Answers to self-assessment questions

1 Costs are collected for the following three purposes:

(a) To assist in planning decisions, such as the determination of which products to manufacture, the quantities that should be produced and the prices at which they should be sold.
(b) To assist in the control of operations by maintaining and improving the efficiency with which resources are employed.
(c) To assist in the measurement of reported income.

2 The three elements of product costs comprise:

(a) Direct material costs, that is, the material costs that can be directly associated with the finished product.
(b) Direct labour costs, that is, the wages of workers directly associated with a particular finished product.
(c) Factory overhead costs that include all the remaining manufacturing costs, after the direct costs have been determined. They include indirect materials, such as supplies of materials, indirect labour, such as the salary of inspectors, and cleaners, heat, light, power and depreciation of factory buildings, plant and equipment.

3 Manufacturing costs consist of the costs of transforming raw materials into finished products, namely direct materials, direct labour and factory overhead costs. Non-manufacturing costs comprise selling, administrative and financial costs that are not incurred in the manufacturing process. Consequently, the cost of sales is computed by reference to manufacturing costs only. Non-manufacturing costs are treated as 'period' costs and not 'product costs', and are expensed out against periodic income.

4 The term 'full product cost' refers to the method of determining product cost per unit by calculating the total unit factory costs. The direct material costs are calculated by reference to the quantities of materials used per unit of the product and the materials' purchase price. The direct labour costs per unit are calculated by the labour time taken to complete the operations involved in making the product and the appropriate wage rates of the operative involved. Full product costing requires that factory overhead costs be apportioned to each unit of the product. This is effected by means of a factory overhead rate that is an allocation key.

5 The problems involved in accounting for overhead costs are found where factories produce more than one product. In this case, the ascertainment of full product costs per unit means that factory unit costs have to be apportioned to the units of the different products. Since factory overhead costs are collected by departments, problems are involved in apportioning such costs to unit of a particular product, as follows:

(a) the allocation of factory overhead costs to production cost centres;
(b) the allocation of production cost centre costs to individual products.

The presence of fixed overhead costs means also that the choice of an appropriate level of activity is critical to correctly apportioning overhead costs at the unit level.

6 Once factory overhead costs have been allocated to production cost centres, the recovery of such costs is effected by charging out (apportioning) them to units of the product through an overhead rate (sometimes known as an overhead allocation key). Three overhead rates commonly used are:

(a) overhead rate based on direct labour costs per unit of the product;
(b) overhead rate based on direct labour hours per unit of the product;
(c) overhead rate based on machine hours per unit of the product.

7 The adoption of a plant-wide overhead rate means that all factory departments use the same overhead rate for allocating overhead costs. In effect, regardless of the specific nature of the operations needed for their manufacture, unit costs of the different products will include factory overhead costs charged out on the same basis. Thus, if one product is machine-intensive and another product is labour-intensive in the use of factory resources, the use of a plant-wide rate based on machine hours will load up factory overhead costs disproportionately on the product that is machine-intensive.

More accurate and reliable measurements of full product costs per unit will be obtained where departments select an overhead rate that more correctly reflects the predominant nature of the resource used in each department. This will be very important as regards establishing reliable product pricing policies.

8 Four major types of product costing systems are:

(a) job order costing;
(b) contract costing;
(c) process costing;
(d) service costing.

Job order costing and contract costing are similar in that production is undertaken on the receipt of the client's order and to that client's specifications. The difference between these two systems lies essentially in that contract costing is used in the case of contracts that take more than one accounting period to complete. Costs are accumulated per job order or per contract.

Process costing is a method of product costing used by manufacturing companies engaged in the mass production of standardized products. Production is undertaken in anticipation of market demand, and finished products are stocked until they are sold. Product costs are accumulated by reference to a standard quantity of the product, expressed in terms of quantity, volume or weight, as the case may be.

Service costing is a special application of process costing used where services rather than products are supplied. Particular problems involve the selection of cost units in relation to which costs can be accumulated, and the selection of charging rates for services.

Solutions to problems

1 (a) Estimated cost of job enquiry number 876.

	£	£
Direct material		1,000
Direct labour		
Plating	324	
Welding	42	
Assembly	20	386
Indirect departmental costs*		
Plating	197.6	
Welding	12.6	
Assembly	12.5	222.7
Total cost		1,608.7

*based on this year's budgeted rates per hour
Plating £22,000/9,000 = £2.44
Welding £9,000/10,000 = £0.90
Assembly £5,000/4,000 = £1.25

(b) If the customer accepts the estimated price, that is what should be charged for the completed job. The £1,608.70 calculated above is the cost of the job, which will be a starting point in the determination of the ultimate price, which will be set after considering factors such as the amount of spare capacity which the firm has, market conditions, alternative work which may be available and the attractiveness of doing work for this particular customer. From the information given, there is no way in which a price for the work can be estimated, but three considerations may be:

1 as an absolute minimum, assuming that there is spare capacity and that the indirect costs are all fixed, a price of £1,386 would recover all the incremental costs which are expected and would maximize the probability of getting the work, but it would result in no contribution being made;

2 the overhead cost in the Plating Department might be recalculated, since budgeted hours are less than last year's actual hours, this resulting in an increased overhead absorption rate which causes job costs to rise. If last year's actual hours are used, the rate per hour reduces to £2.20 (£22,000/10,000) in the Plating Department, which will reduce the charge to the job by 81 × (£2.44 − £2.20) = £19.44 and prevent a drop in activity from generating cost increases which cause further drops in activity;

3 in the long run, for all costs to be recovered and a profit to be made, the total costs of all the jobs undertaken have to be covered. For this job, therefore, long-run profitability would require a price in excess of £1,608.70.

3 Departmental overheads with capacity production

	Machining	Assembly	Canteen
	£	£	£
Allocated overheads	50,000	40,000	10,000
Apportioned overheads			
Rates (area)	300	600	100
Depreciation (equipment cost)	3,000	6,000	300
Light and power (Kw hours)	180	330	90
	53,480	46,930	10,490
			(10,490)
Re-apportionment of canteen costs			
(No of employees)	6,993	3,497	
	60,473	50,427	
Rate per hour			
Machine (8,000)	£7.56		
Labour (12,000)		£4.20	

Using normal capacity as an absorption base yields the following charge-out rates:

Total cost	£60,473	£50,427
Normal hours, rate per hour		
Machine (6,400)	£9.45	–
Labour (9,600)	–	£5.25

With expected activity as a base:

Total cost	£60,473	£50,427
Expected hours, rate per hour		
Machine (5,600)	£10.80	–
Labour (8,400)	–	£6.00

The above adjustments could have been calculated thus:
Machining rate per hour (capacity base) £7.56/0.8
= Normal capacity rate per hour, £9.45 × 0.8/0.7
= Budgeted rate per hour, £10.80.

Report
The above analysis demonstrates the difficulties involved in the use of overhead absorption rates:

    (i)   They are based on a subjective apportionment of cost over production centres (the 'benefit' principle).

   (ii)   No analysis of the cost by behaviour takes place.

  (iii)   The choice of activity level influences the charge-out rate quite substantially.

  (iv)   The determination of unit costs for 'general purposes' is not an adequate justification. It is not clear for example why overhead costs should be charged to products in parallel with production taking place.

   (v)   By setting an inappropriate overhead rate product cost can be distorted and poor decisions may result. If using expected hours as an absorption base a high overhead rate is the result, and this, if incorporated into a pricing decision may lead to overpricing and loss of orders.

4 (a)

Expense (basis)	Total	Cutting	Cooking	Canteen	Maintenance
Indirect labour (given)	340,000	120,000	140,000	30,000	50,000
Consumables (given)	82,000	24,000	32,000	20,000	6,000
Heating and lighting (area)	24,000	8,000	9,600	2,400	4,000
Rent and rates (area)	36,000	12,000	14,400	3,600	6,000
Depreciation (capital values)	60,000	30,000	24,000	2,000	4,000
Supervision (number of employees)	48,000	24,000	18,000	3,000	3,000
Power (kWh)	40,000	18,000	16,000	2,000	4,000
	630,000	236,000	254,000	63,000	77,000
Canteen (number of employees)		33,600	25,200	(63,000)	4,200
Maintenance (maintenance hours)					81,200
		46,400	34,800	–	(81,200)
	630,000	316,000	314,000	–	–

(b)

Labour hours	12,640
=	£25/direct labour hour
Machine hours	15,700
=	£20/machine hour

(c)

Direct materials cost percentage
This method is best used when the price of materials is constant and there is a direct relationship between the materials and labour costs incurred to manufacture the product. Consider the following example:

	Job A	Job B	Budget
	£	£	£
Materials	250	100	150,000
Labour	100	100	92,000

The overheads charged to a job will be distorted. Job A is charged with a greater proportion of overheads than Job B even though the labour costs were the same.

Direct wages cost percentage
This method is best used when the wages rates are the same throughout the company and the same for each job.

Prime cost percentage rate
This method combines the faults of the direct materials cost percentage and the direct labour cost percentage rates.

Labour hours method could have been used in the cooking department. But on the basis of the labour hours and machine hours for this department it is obviously machine-intensive and, therefore, machine hours should be used.

(d)

The under/over-absorption figures are:

	Cutting	Cooking
Actual overheads	£310,000	£312,000
Absorbed overheads	12,000	15,810
	× £25	× £20
	= £300,000	= £316,200
	= £10,000 under-absorbed	£4,200 over-absorbed

Chapter 18 ABC and JIT

Answers to self-assessment questions

1 ABC assumes that it is activities which cause costs, not products. Cost drivers are used to assign overheads. Traditional product costing assigns production overheads to products using volume-based recovery bases.

2 Activities are analysed and defined. The cost driver for each activity is determined. Activity centres are identified. Costs are assigned to products.

3 A cost driver is the action or transaction that results in costs being incurred. It is related to an activity, e.g. the number of purchase orders drives material procurement costs.

4 Where the company (i) has overhead costs that are not proportional to the unit volume of individual products; (ii) has a highly automated production system; (iii) produces a wide variety of tailor-made products or services.

5 JIT aims to reduce costs by eliminating inventories and production delays.

6 These costs are 'accepted' by traditional manufacturing.

7 JIT results in 'leaner' accounting systems.

Solution to problem

1 (a) Overhead rate = £220,000/4,000 = £55 per DLH

	Job 600	Job 700
	£	£
Direct materials	750	850
Direct labour	600	600
Overhead*	2,750	2,750
Total cost	4,100	4,200
Units	100	50
Unit cost	£41	£84

*Overhead assigned = £55 × 50 hrs = £2,750

(b) Pool rates
     Set-up: £60,000/300 = £200 per set-up
     Ordering: £45,000/4,500 = £10 per order
     Machine costs: £90,000/18,000 = £5 per machine
     Receiving: £25,000/50,000 = £0.50 per part

	Job 600	Job 700	
	£	£	
Direct materials	750	850	
Direct labour	600	600	
Overhead			
Set-ups	200	200	(£200 × 1; £200 × 1)
Ordering	40	20	(£10 × 4; £10 × 2)
Machine costs	100	150	(£5 × 20; £5 × 30)
Receiving	10	20	(£0.50 × 20; £0.50 × 40)
Total costs	1,700	1,840	
Units	100	50	
Unit cost	£17	£36.80	

(c) In a firm with product diversity and significant non-unit overhead costs, multiple rates using unit and non-unit drivers produce better cost assignments because the demands of the products for overhead activities are more fully considered. Specifically, there are three non-unit activities, causing £130,000 out of the £220,000 of overhead costs. These non-unit costs should be assigned using non-unit cost drivers.

Chapter 19 Cost–volume–income analysis

Answers to self-assessment questions

1 Cost–volume–income (CVP) analysis lies at the centre of short-term income planning because of its wider application to a series of decision problems. In examining the relationship between costs and volume of output, CVP analysis is helpful in establishing an optimal volume of output in relation to costs that will maximize short-term income. Likewise, it is helpful in determining a pricing strategy. CVP analysis is also relevant to the selection of the best sales mix, by selecting the most profitable combination of different products having regard to their cost and prices.

2 CVP analysis is widely used in income planning because it focuses on the distinction between fixed and variable costs in analysing the consequence of changes in activity levels. Fixed costs are costs that are fixed or constant regardless of the volume of output. Consequently, there is implied a minimum level of output to cover fixed costs. Failure to reach this level will result in an accounting loss. Variable costs are costs that vary directly with the volume of output. The firm's cost structure analysed as between fixed and variable costs will determine its profitability at given levels of output, and reveal the consequence of changes in levels of output on incomes.

3 Given the firm's cost structure, analysed as between fixed and variable costs, and the revenue associated with a given pricing policy, the break-even point signifies that level of activity at which the total revenues generated just cover total costs, producing a zero income zero loss result.

4 Three methods are commonly used to calculate the break-even point. These are:

(a) the equation method in which the break-even point is found either in terms of the volume of output or volume of revenue through the following equation:

sales = variable costs + fixed cost + zero profit

(b) the contribution margin method that makes use of the contribution margin per unit of output to determine the number of units of output or the sales revenues required to reach the break-even level. For example, to calculate the break-even volume of output, the formula is:

$$x = \frac{\text{fixed costs} - \text{zero profit}}{\text{unit contribution margin}}$$

(c) the graph method, using a break-even chart, in which the revenue and the cost structure, analysed in terms of total costs made up of fixed and variable costs, is plotted to indicate the break-even point.

5 The income–volume chart is a special type of break-even chart that is concerned with analysing income and loss at different levels of activity. As in the case of the conventional break-even chart, the horizontal axis is used to measure the volume of output or sales in units, but the vertical axis is employed to measure the income or loss at any given level. It represents an income line at different levels with the break-even point indicated on the income line.

6 Given that short-term profitability is dependent on four factors – fixed costs, variable costs, selling prices and sales volume – improvements in profitability may result from changes in any one of these factors. These changes may be analysed through the break-even chart. Thus, changes in fixed costs and variable costs will affect the break-even point differently, as will changes in selling prices and sales volumes.

7 The main limitations in using CVP lie in the assumptions upon which the analysis is based. These include the assumption that fixed costs are constant, and that both the variable cost and the revenue curves are linear over the relevant volume of output. It is also assumed that volume is the only factor affecting costs, and that the price both of the cost factors and of the product itself remain unaffected by changes in the volume of output. To overcome these limitations, it is necessary to limit the volume range to be examined, so that the behaviour of costs and revenue over the relevant range may be more reliably determined.

Despite its limitations, the real usefulness of CVP analysis is that it enriches the understanding of the relationship between costs, volume and incomes, enabling management to make assumptions that will assist in the management of short-term profitability.

Solutions to problems

1

	Per unit (£)	%
Selling price	0.25	100
Variable cost	0.15	60
Contribution	0.10	40

(a) £100,000/0.4   = £250,000 sales value
                                     = 1m units

(b) FC now £150,000
     break-even £150,000/0.1   = 1.5m bottles

(c) Required income £110,000

$$\frac{£100,000 + £110,000}{0.4}$$ = £525,000

(d) 2,000,000 × 1.6   = 3,200,000 bottles
     3.2m × 0.10p – £150,000   = £170,000 income

(e) (i)   Assumption of cost linearity.
     (ii) Difficulty in defining relevant range.
     (iii) Difficulty in separating cost into component parts.
     (iv) Assumption that all other variables remain constant – production methods, price levels, production efficiency.
     (v)   With multiple products, assumption of constant product mix.

3 (a)

Workings		£		£
Sales	8,736 × £30 =	262,080	6,552 × £30 =	196,560
Variable costs	8,736 × £8 =	69,888	6,552 × £8 =	52,416
Contribution		192,192		144,144
Fixed costs				
$\left(\begin{array}{l}65,000 + 39,000 + 75,000 \\ + 23,600\end{array}\right) \div 2$		101,300		101,300
Net income		90,892		42,844

(b) $\dfrac{\text{Fixed costs}}{\text{Contribution/rooms}}$

$= \dfrac{£101,300}{£17}$ = 4,605 rentals
= 177 per week
= 25/day
= 42% of capacity

(c) $= \dfrac{£101,300}{£17}$ = 5,959 rentals
= 299 per week
= 33/day
= 55% of capacity

(d) The financial factors which would need to be taken into account should the hotel be closed for two months are:

- No saving on depreciation.
- There may be a saving on reception staff if they are employed on monthly contract.
- There would be some savings on repairs and maintenance and miscellanies.

The non-financial factors would be customer goodwill, loss of staff goodwill and, possibly, motivation.

An alternative strategy would entail reducing fixed and variable costs whilst attempting to increase the number of rooms booked.

(e) The limitations of break-even analysis are:

- The problem of classifying costs into fixed and variable.
- The assumption that costs and revenues behave in a linear fashion.
- The assumption that fixed costs will remain fixed.

These three limitations are all applicable here.

Chapter 20 Marginal costing

Answers to self-assessment questions

1 Marginal costing is a method of costing that records only variable costs for product costing. The analysis of costs as between fixed costs and variable costs identifies such costs in terms of their behaviour in relation to changes in activity levels. Fixed costs are those that are constant, irrespective of the level of activity, whereas variable costs are those that vary directly in terms of the activity level. Accordingly, marginal costing ignores fixed costs in determining product costs, and uses only variable cost information for that purpose.

2 Overhead costs are defined as indirect product costs that require to be allocated to product costs by an appropriate allocation key. The distinction between direct and indirect costs is used for product costing purposes under both absorption and marginal costing. The distinction between fixed costs and variable costs is used only for the purpose of analysing cost behaviour through different levels of activity. Absorption costing ignores this consideration in addressing the problem of product costing. Marginal costing considers that fixed costs should not be included as product costs. Therefore, absorption costing will include, under full product costs, direct and overhead costs, both fixed and variable, whereas marginal costing will include under product costs only variable direct and overhead costs.

3 Different income results will be obtained using absorption costing and marginal costing whenever inventory levels vary as a result of differences between sales levels and production

levels. Given that the major difference between absorption costing and marginal costing is the valuation of inventory, either appearing as cost of sales in the year of sales, or carried forward to the following year as inventory, it follows that:

(a) where sales fluctuate but production remains constant, reported incomes will be higher under marginal costing whenever inventory are reduced to support a volume of sales greater than the volume of production;

(b) where sales are constant but production fluctuates, reported incomes will be higher under marginal costing whenever inventory are reduced because the volume of production is insufficient to meet the sales volume requirement.

Solutions to problems

1 (a)

	20X0	20X1	20X2
	£	£	£
Sales revenue	64,000	64,000	80,000
cost of sales*	(40,000)	(40,000)	(50,000)
	24,000	24,000	30,000
(Under-) over-absorption	(4,000)	4,000	(8,000)
	20,000	28,000	22,000
Fixed selling and admin	20,000	20,000	20,000
Income	–	8,000	2,000

*Unit production cost £10 VAR + £40 Fixed = £50.

(b) Contribution/unit = £70.

	20X0	20X1	20X2
Sales revenue	64,000	64,000	80,000
VAR costs	8,000	8,000	10,000
Contribution	56,000	56,000	70,000
Fixed units	60,000	60,000	60,000
Income/(loss)	(4,000)	(4,000)	10,000

(c)

	20X0	20X1	20X2
(i) Absorption income per (a)	£–	£8,000	£2,000
(ii) Difference in inventory levels (units) CS–OS	+ 100	+ 300	– 200
(iii) Fixed production overload cost/unit	£40	£40	£40
(iv) Additional MC charge (Credit) to income	£4,000	£12,000	£(8,000)
(v) Marginal costing income (i)–(ii)	£(4,000)	£(4,000)	£10,000

(d) In part (a) an absorption costing approach is used. Fixed production overhead costs are unitized and charged to products on the 'cost attach' principle, any eventual over- or under-recovery of these overhead costs being written off at the end of the year in the income statement. This method, when production exceeds sales, results in the carrying forward in inventory valuation of a proportion of the fixed production overhead costs, which in a marginal costing system would be written off. A marginal costing system would treat all fixed costs as period costs, writing them off in the period of incurrence. Thus, when inventory are rising absorption costing will report higher incomes, while when sales are in excess of production marginal costing incomes will be higher. Over the life of a business, or over a period in which opening and closing inventory levels are identical, both methods will yield the same income figure.

2

(a)

		20X0		20X1
Selling price		£80		£90
Variable production cost		48		55
Variable selling/admin cost		2		3
Contribution		30		32
Fixed overhead absorption rate/unit				
	$\dfrac{170,000}{28,000}$	£6.07	$\dfrac{180,000}{28,000}$	£6.43
Absorption unit cost		£54.07		£61.43

Marginal costing

	20X0
	£
Sales 20,000 × £80	1,600,000
Variable cost 20,000 × £50	1,000,000
Contribution	600,000
Fixed factory overheads	170,000
	430,000

	20X1
	£
Sales 25,000 × £90	2,250,000
Variable cost (2,000 × £51) + (23,000 × £58)	1,436,000
	814,000
Fixed factory overheads	180,000
Income	634,000

*OS brought forward in 20X1 will be sold in 20X1 at 20X1 level of variable selling costs (£3).

Closing inventory valuation 1,500 × £55 = £82,500

Note
In the following calculations, computations are based on unrounded unit costs.

Absorption costing

	20X0	
	£	£
Sales revenue		1,600,00
Opening inventory 1,500 × £54.07	81,105	
Production cost 20,500 × £54.07	1,108,435	
		1,189,540
Closing inventory 2,000 × £54.07	108,140	
Costs of sales		1,081,428
		518,573
Under-absorption 7,500 × £6.07		45,536
Selling and admin costs		473,036
		40,000
Income		433,036

*Assumption that OS in 20X0 is valued as per 19 × 5 standard costs.

	20X1	
	£	£
Sales revenue		2,250,000
Opening inventory (b/f)	108,143	
Production cost 24,500 × £61.43	1,505,000	
		1,613,143
Closing inventory 1,500 × £61.43	92,143	
Cost of sales		1,521,000
		729,000
Under-absorption 3,500 × £6.43		22,500
		706,500
Selling and admin costs		75,000
Income		631,500

	20X1	
	£	£
(b) **Reconciliation**		
20X0 Marginal income		430,000
Add: Fixed overhead		
C/F in inventory increase		3,036
500 × £6.07		433,036
Absorption income		634,000
20X0 Marginal income		
Fixed overhead B/F in		
absorption OS	12,143	
2,000 × £6.07		
Fixed overhead C/F in		
Absorption CS		
1,500 × £6.43	9,643	
Reduction in absorption income		2,500
Absorption income		631,500

The differences in income figures are caused by the different treatments of fixed production overheads, which are all written off as period costs in marginal costing systems, while a proportion is carried forward in inventory valuation in absorption costing systems. The above reconciliation shows why the income figures differ.

(c) **Advantages and disadvantages of marginal costing**

Advantages	Disadvantages
Useful information for decision making being based on cost behaviour.	Not in accordance with SSAP 9.
Removes the effect of inventory level changes on income.	May be less useful for long-term pricing or contract pricing on a cost-plus basis.
Avoids inclusion of Fixed overheads in unmarketable inventory valuations.	May lead to less attention being accorded to Fixed cost – possibly the most significant area of cost.
More prudent.	
Gives less ambiguous contribution figure rather than product incomes with multi-product production.	

Chapter 21 Costs for pricing

Answers to self-assessment questions

1 Income is a function of two elements, namely revenues and costs. Income may be improved, all things being equal, if sales revenues can be increased through price changes. It follows that a firm's relationship with the market for its products and services is intimately linked in one important respect to its pricing policy. Therefore, management needs to formulate a pricing strategy that takes into account the likely effect of price changes on the market's demand for its products. As a result, it will be able to plan a level of activity that, given the firm's cost structure, will produce the required income. Pricing may be viewed as having both short-term and long-range implications. Any alteration in the level of demand for the firm's products resulting from its pricing policy will also affect its capital budgeting programme. Thus, both short-term and long-range objectives are involved in the making of pricing policies.

2 Classical economic theory holds that the objective of pricing policy is to establish the optimal price, which is that price that will maximize the firm's incomes. The optimal price is found where the addition to total revenue resulting from the sale of the last unit is equal to the contribution to total costs resulting from the production of that unit. The objective of income maximization through the search for the optimal price is a strict condition that ensures the most efficient use of economic resources by the firm. Consequently, in a market economy, optimal pricing by all firms will lead to the most efficient allocation of resources between competing firms.

3 Cost-based pricing policies rely on product cost information for determining the selling price. They are concerned with two elements of price: first, that relevant costs should be recovered in setting the price; second, that a reasonable income margin should be added to relevant costs in arriving at the price. Cost-based pricing policies do not aim at determining the optimal price. Rather, they reflect a practical and prudent approach to price,

in which the first objective of price is to ensure that product costs are covered, thereby avoiding losses and allowing for the survival of the firm. Cost-based pricing policies also contain a moral view of what is a 'normal' profit. They are not concerned in a practical way with finding out that price that will maximize income, but rather that price that will reflect what the market is able and willing to bear, taking into account a reasonable profit for the firm and its shareholders.

4 'Full-cost' pricing reflects a cost-based approach to pricing that requires that all product costs be covered in setting the selling price. Once full costs have been determined, the required income margin is added to establish the selling price.

5 Accounting information relevant to making full-cost pricing decisions consists of all costs involved in bringing the product to the market. They comprise total manufacturing costs, consisting of direct and overhead production costs, to which are added marketing and administrative costs. Full product costs appear on first sight as relatively easy to determine. This is true in so far as direct costs are concerned. However, indirect costs, in the form of factory, administrative and marketing costs, have to be allocated to products. For this purpose, allocation keys have to be devised that produce satisfactory indirect cost allocation. In particular, such allocations should not produce biasing in the selling price of different products. A further problem stems from the nature of fixed costs in relation to levels of output. Fixed costs are fixed in aggregate terms, but are variable in relation to unit of the product. This means that as volume rises, fixed costs allocated to products decrease. Variable costs per unit remain constant. Hence, the variability of fixed costs at the unit level is a significant factor for pricing.

6 The statement that 'since prices are determined by supply and demand factors, accounting data is irrelevant in determining a firm's pricing policy' has some substance of truth in market situations where all firms are price-takers. This implies that there is a perfect market and that, as a result of perfect competition, individual firms compete as to costs. In this analysis, accounting data with respect to costs will be a key factor in providing the firm with knowledge of its own costs, and implicitly, where it is operating under efficiency conditions, with knowledge of the costs of competitors.

Where markets are imperfect, it is evident that firms may not necessarily be price-takers, but may be price-makers. In this case, accounting data will be significant in determining a firm's pricing policy.

7 Conversion-cost pricing takes into account only the costs incurred by the firm in converting raw materials and semi-finished goods into finished goods. It has to do with one of the limitations of full-cost pricing that makes no difference between two products that require different degrees of effort to convert them into a marketable condition. In effect, conversion pricing excludes direct material costs, providing a pricing policy that refers pricing to the internal efforts made in converting raw materials into finished goods.

Return-on-investment pricing attempts to link the markup on costs with a desired return on invested capital in establishing pricing policies. The formula used is as follows:

$$\text{selling price} = \frac{\text{total costs} + (\text{desired percentage return on capital} \times \text{capital employed})}{\text{volume of output}}$$

The attraction of this method is that it relates the problem of pricing to financial objectives, and integrates pricing decisions with the firm's overall planning objectives.

8 'Marginal-cost' pricing is a method of cost-based pricing that defines product costs only in terms of variable costs. Unlike full or absorption costing, this method of costing excludes fixed costs from product costs. This results in product costs that are comparatively lower than under full costing. Consequently, cost of sales and inventory values are understated

by reference to full-product costing. Fixed costs are treated as period costs, and are charged against incomes. This method of pricing is useful for developing aggressive sales policies, and in special marketing situations, for example, in expanding into export markets, and in introducing new products.

9 Target pricing is a recent innovation in the development of pricing theory. It is associated with the concept of target costing. This method of costing seeks to constrain product costs by imposing costs targets as desired cost objectives prior to introducing and producing products. Consequently, target pricing involves setting predetermined prices as targets for pricing policies that will meet targeted cost of production objectives as well as an income requirement.

10 Assuming that the exporting firm is a price-taker and not a price-setter, the initial attraction to exporting is expanding overall sales volume and revenue, with the possibility that export prices may be higher than domestic prices. There are substantial additional costs involved in exporting, notably packaging, transport, the margins of intermediaries such as agents, taxes and duties. The terms that normally apply to export contracts determine which costs are borne by the exporter and importer respectively. They are referred to as International Commercial Terms. These additional costs have to be brought into account in determining the viability of exporting in terms of the net profitability of exporting sales. The upper limit to the export price will be that price that the best customer is willing to pay, which in the case of a price-taker is the going-rate price. The lower limit is either the full-cost or the marginal cost, depending on the circumstances facing the export firm when determining the acceptability of an export order.

11 Pricing policies very significantly determine the firm's relationship with the market for its products and services. In the short term, pricing will affect the demand for those products, and thus directly impact on the firm's sales revenues. Since pricing affects the volume of demand, it is evident that the firm's long-term position in the market will be affected by its pricing policies. As a consequence of regulating the volume of demand, decisions relating to total production capacity will be affected by demand considerations. However, Western industrialized countries have hitherto tended to regard pricing as having emphatically short-term considerations. Setting pricing policies with long-term considerations predominantly in view has been contrary to this viewpoint. None the less, Japanese firms have developed alternative approaches that consider that long-term factors are more significant than short-term ones in determining pricing policies.

Solutions to problems

1

If the McTosh offer is accepted the financial effect will be:

	Per unit
	£
Price to McTosh	32.5
Manufacturing costs (variable)	(25.0)
Incremental overheads	(1.5)
Incremental benefit	6.0
Income increase	6,000

The effect of selling to Scotland at the price anticipated by McTosh would be:

	£	Per unit £
Price		42.5
Variable costs		
Manufacturing	25.0	
Transport	3.5	
		28.50
		14.0
Incremental fixed costs		1.5
Incremental benefit		12.5
Income increase		£12,500

If the price and terms set in Scotland were identical to those in England, the effect would be:

	£	Per unit £
Price		44.0
Variable costs		
Manufacturing	25.0	
Transport	3.5	
Commission	2.2	
Incremental PC	1.5	
		32.2
		11.8
Income increase		£11,800

Thus the offer should not be accepted, preferable options being:

(i) Schultz sells its production in Scotland on its own account, but on the McTosh terms re price and commission, resulting in a £12,500 incremental income.

(ii) Sell to Scotland on its existing price/commission terms. The income thus generated is £700 less than that at (i) above, being (a) an extra £1.50 per unit revenue + (b) an additional cost of £2.20 in commission = 70p per unit incremental cost × 1,000 sales units.

2

This is an awkward question, since the sales price, which is what the question asks for, is required in order to calculate the capital employed figure, yet one of the requirements which must be satisfied by the sales price is that it must 'yield a 16 per cent return on capital employed', and 'capital employed is considered to consist of 50 per cent of net sales for current assets'.

The problem can be solved by the use of simple algebra, where:

p = income
a = required net selling price
and (1) income is a function of sales revenue less total costs
(2) 16 per cent return on capital employed is calculated by dividing income by capital employed.

From (1) above:

p = sales revenue – variable costs – fixed costs
$p = 400,000a - (400,000 \times 8) - 460,000$ (Note 1)
$p = 400,000a - 3,660,000$

From (2) above:

$$0.16 = \frac{400,000a - 3,660,000}{0.5 \,(400,000a + 450,000)}$$

$400,000a - 3,660,000 = 32,000a + 72,000$
$368,000a = 3,732,000$
$a = £10.14$

The net selling price is £10.14 per unit, giving a gross selling price, before discount, of £10.14/0.98 = £10.35.

Note 1:

	£	
DM	6.00	
DL	1.60	($£1.50 \times 1.06$)
VFO	0.40	
	8.00	

Proof:

Calculation of income		£
Contribution	$400,000 \times £2.14$	856,000
Fixed costs		460,000
Income		396,000

Calculation of return on capital employed:

$$ROCE = \frac{396,000}{450,000 + (400,000 \times 10.14)} = 0.16$$

The above calculations assume sales to be constant at 400,000 units.

Chapter 22 Costs for short-run tactical decisions

Answers to self-assessment questions

1 Relevant costs are costs useful for making short-term tactical decisions involving alternative courses of action. Relevant costs have two important characteristics:

(a) they are future costs, that is, they are costs that have not yet been incurred;
(b) they are differential costs, that is, they are different according to the decision alternatives being considered.

2 Future costs are costs that have not yet been incurred. They will be incurred as the direct result of a decision now being taken. Sunk costs are costs that have been incurred in the past. They cannot be affected by a decision now being taken. Differential costs are future costs that will differ according to the alternatives being considered for decision making.

3 An example of future costs would be costs that will be incurred as the result of continuing a project, rather than abandoning the project. Costs that have been incurred in the acquisition of non-current assets would be regarded as sunk costs, once those assets have been purchased. Differential costs are future costs that will differ according to the alternative selected. For example, where a decision is being considered either to continue or to abandon a project, the costs associated with the decision to complete the project, rather than abandon the project, are differential costs.

4 In the analysis of special decisions, the contribution margin is the excess of the revenue of any activity over its relevant costs, which is available to make a contribution to fixed costs and incomes. Commonly, the contribution margin is the excess of revenue over variable costs.

5 Opportunity costs are not recorded in accounting. This is a cost concept found in economic analysis that is relevant to decision making. Opportunity costs only exist at a time when a decision has to be taken. They are defined as the value of the next best opportunity forgone, or the net cash-inflow lost as a result of preferring one alternative rather than the next best one. Opportunity costs are particularly useful for making special decisions, where choice is involved.

6 Four major classes of special decisions are the following:

(a) dropping a product line;
(b) selling or further processing a semi-manufactured product;
(c) operating or leasing an asset;
(d) making or buying a product.

A decision to drop a product line involves considerations that may be extended to a series of decisions of a similar nature, such as closing a branch, a division, or any area of organizational activity where revenues and costs are involved. These decisions have both short- and long-range consequences, affecting the contribution margin that such activities are considered to be making towards overall incomes.

A decision to sell or further process is also a decision that has short- and long-range consequences, affecting the contribution margin that is involved by a decision to extend an activity, thereby choosing to further process rather than to sell at a given cut-off point.

Similarly, decisions to operate or to use an asset in a different context are decisions of a tactical nature having both short-term and long-range consequences with respect to the structure of business activity.

Finally, decisions to make or not to make a product and rather obtain it by purchasing is a tactical decision having also short-term and long-range consequences with respect to the structure of business activity.

7 The significance of opportunity costs analysis to the four main categories of special decisions lies in clarifying the impact on overall incomes of selecting one alternative rather than the other. The best alternative is that which is the most advantageous by comparison to the next best one. The comparative advantage of selecting the best decision is calculated by taking into account as an opportunity cost the benefits forgone by not choosing the next best alternative.

8 Business enterprises are limited in the pursuit of income by the fact that they have limited resources and also limited opportunities and face constraints in maximizing incomes. Limiting factors may arise from shortages of labour, materials, equipment, productive capacity and a variety of other constraints.

9 The significance of a contribution margin analysis in the face of limiting factors lies in the clarification of the impact of choice on the contribution to overall incomes that results from the selection of one alternative as against another alternative, where limiting factors play a determining role.

The contribution margin analysis focuses on the contribution to organizational incomes that results from a particular activity, rather than a limited view of sector incomes involved in the activity itself. The contribution margin indicates that, even though a particular activity may not be profitable in a full cost accounting analysis, its contribution margin to organizational incomes is a more meaningful measure of its profitability. In effect, closing a loss-making activity that makes none the less a positive contribution margin will result in an overall loss of incomes.

By integrating the impact of limiting factors on the contribution margin, and expressing the contribution margin in relation to the limited factor, the contribution margin analysis allows optimal choice decisions to be made as between mutually exclusive alternatives.

10 Linear programming is a mathematical technique that seeks to make the best use of a firm's limited resources to meet chosen objectives. In accounting terms, this means maximizing incomes or minimizing costs. In the face of limited plant capacity, the level and cost of output will be determined by such capacity. Linear programming allows the analysis of the choice that has to be made with respect to the possibility of applying the available capacity to one or other of the products, or a combination of both. The problem of income maximization under such conditions under linear programming involves stating the problem in simple algebraic terms that have two aspects: first, an objective function to maximize income; second, the recognition of the production constraint. This formulation of the choice problem pinpoints the relative output volume of each product that will maximize overall incomes.

Solutions to problems

1

(a) (i) The differential cost of the order.

	Radwarm costs	Specials cost	Differential cost
	£	£	£
Materials	(8,000)	20,000	12,000
Labour	(9,000)	36,000	27,000
Special press write-off	–	4,000	4,000
Power	(400)	1,400 (1)	1,000
	(17,400)	61,400	44,000

Note 1 To determine the power bill for Specials it is necessary to know how many units of production are represented by the existing power budget. It has been assumed that the existing budget is based on the production of 1,000 Specials, a doubling of production therefore causing the power bill to double. It is clearly not logical to assume that by halving the output of Radwarms the power saving on that product will exactly match the power required to produce 1,000 Specials.

(ii) The full cost of the order

	£
Materials	20,000
Labour	36,000
Special press write-off	4,000
Depreciation	3,600
Power	1,400
Rent	1,000
Heat and light	100
Miscellaneous	900
	67,000

Note Because we are not aware of the quantities involved, some of the figures produced above look unusual. For example, the apportioned heat and light charge for the new order of 1,000 units is £100, while the cost for the existing (assumed) budgeted quantity of 1,000 is £1,200.

(iii) The opportunity cost of the order

	£	£
Radwarm		
Sales revenue		50,000
Variable costs:		
Materials	16,000	
Labour	18,000	
Power	800	34,800
Lost contribution		15,200

The opportunity cost of the order is therefore the loss of contribution of (£15,200/2) = £7,600 which would result from the transfer of half of the Radwarm production capacity to Specials.

(b)

To: Divisional manager   Ref: Special order
From: Management accountant
From the above figures it can be seen that the differential cost associated with the production of the Specials is £44,000. For the order to be accepted, additional working capital and plant financing would be required of up to this amount. If the differential costs are matched with the differential revenue from the order of £70,000 – £25,000 = £45,000, it can be seen that the new order is marginally worthwhile, generating a contribution gain of £1,000 (Note 2). This may not be a sufficiently attractive financial proposition. There may, however, be additional sound reasons for undertaking the work, such as that the customer is valued, and should not be turned away, or that the order represents an introduction to some new technology, and can be used as a springboard from which to obtain further work with other customers at higher prices, or that although £70 is a poor price now, in time, with productivity improvements, costs will fall so that £70 may be acceptable.

	£
Note 2 This can also be calculated as:	
Contribution gain from new order	8,600
Contribution loss from reduction	
in Radwarm sales	7,600
Net gain	1,000

In the above analysis the arguments depend upon the assumption that the current price is £100 per unit.

2

Using a marginal costing approach, eliminate common fixed costs from the analysis of product profitability.

	A	B	C	Total
	£K	£K	£K	£K
Sales revenue	60	15	25	100
Variable costs				
Materials	10	2	3	15
Labour	11	4	5	20
Overheads	8	3	4	15
Selling and admin.	5	2	3	10
Total variable cost	34	11	15	60
Contribution	26	4	10	40
Fixed costs				
Overheads				5
Selling and admin.				25
Income				10

Thus, all products make a contribution towards the common fixed cost pool, and in the absence of any reason for discontinuance which does not show up on this short-term financial analysis, all the products should be produced.

4 (a) Focus on the future costs and revenues and ignore the past (sunk) costs and revenues. Following this approach the following relevant costs can be identified:

(i) Materials:
- Value of materials in inventory (£10,000) is a sunk cost which should be ignored.
- Disposal costs of inventory will be incurred in the future and therefore are relevant to the decision.
- The agreed contract for £5,000 is a future cost and therefore should be included. The balance of the inventory is £65,000 – £5,000 – £10,000 = £50,000.

(ii) • Allocated supervision costs of £20,000 should be ignored as it is a fixed cost which will be incurred regardless of whether the contract is entered into or not.
- The cost of redundancy is a future cost, or in this case a saving if the contract goes ahead.

(iii) Depreciation should be ignored as it will be charged regardless of whether any work is carried out.

(iv) Variable overheads will be incurred as the costs vary with the contract.

(v) Fixed overhead allocation of £20,000 is another cost which will be incurred regardless of whether any sales are made or work carried out.

(vi) The modification of the machinery is a relevant cost and therefore it should be included. The opportunity cost of £5,000, resulting from the machinery being used on the contract instead of being sold, is also a relevant cost.

The full figures are:

	£	
Materials	50,000	Cost (balance)
	5,000	Cost
	(1,000)	Saving
Labour	(10,000)	Saving
Variable overheads	6,000	Cost
Machinery	3,000	Cost
	5,000	Opportunity costs
Net cost	58,000	

The contract should proceed as it will generate a contribution of £42,000 towards fixed costs and income.

Several other factors need to be borne in mind, such as whether there are other contracts which might be more profitable. What will be the effect on existing customers? Will discounts on materials be lost when the company purchases smaller quantities? Will the employees be demotivated by potential short-time working?

(b) The special contract will take up 3,600 direct labour hours and will displace the large new order. It is important to calculate the opportunity cost if the special order is pursued.

The limiting factor in this situation is direct labour hours. Therefore, the contribution for both the special order and the new order need to be calculated per labour hour:

$$\text{Special order } \frac{£42,000}{3,600} = £11.67/\text{labour hour}$$

$$\text{New order } \frac{£20}{5} = £4/\text{labour hour}$$

From a financial perspective, the special order should be accepted and the large new order should be rejected. However, if the large new order is from an existing customer, what will be the consequences of rejecting their order? Will the special order lead to further business? Why is the contribution on the large new order so low? This and other information will need to be evaluated before a decision is made.

(c) Non-financial factors which may be taken into account under various decision-making alternatives are as follows:
(i) *Make or buy.* Will the quality of the product be the same? Is the supplier reliable? Will the price fluctuate? Can the supplier keep the delivery schedules? What will happen to the existing labour? Is the order significant to the supplier?
(ii) *Dropping a product or department.* Are the products interdependent? Is there a suitable replacement? Will the costs be truly variable, particularly wages? What will be the customers' reaction? Will goodwill be lost?
(iii) *Limiting factors.* If products are lost because of a reduction in labour hours, will customers complain? Will the limiting factor change?

Chapter 23 Companies: their nature and regulation

Answers to self-assessment questions

1 Share capital represents a stake in the ownership of a company. The holders of ordinary shares are not guaranteed a dividend. When incomes are low they may get no return at all. Loan capital carries a fixed rate of interest. This is an annual commitment which has to be met each year regardless of whether the company has made any incomes and before any of the shareholders become entitled to any dividends.

2 Leverage is the relationship between 'risk' capital (i.e. ordinary shares) and fixed return funding. Ordinary shareholders will do well in a profitable year, but a poor year may result in no dividend being paid after the fixed charges have been met.

3 When a company sells its shares, it may ask a price in excess of the nominal value of those shares. This excess is known as the share premium and must be transferred to a special account.

4 According to the 'true and fair view' criterion, financial statements should contain sufficient information in quality and quantity to satisfy the reasonable expectations of the readers to whom they are addressed. Readers will expect such statements to comply with accounting standards.

5 (a) The Financial Reporting Council gives guidance to the ASB on priorities, work programme and issues of public concern, and acts as an instrument for promoting good accounting practice.
   (b) The ASB issues accounting standards.
   (c) The FRRP examines accounts in cases where departures from standard accounting practice have occured.
   (d) The UITF assists the ASB in areas where conflicts are likely to develop between Companies Act provisions and an accounting standard.

6 Accounting regulations in the UK are influenced by the EU and IASC.

7 The aim of a conceptual framework is to allow standards to develop in a coherent manner. Also it acts as a vehicle for evaluating current standards. Financial position information – concerning economic resources, financial structure, solvency and liquidity – is provided by the balance sheet. Performance comprises return on resources and embraces income statement information. Financial adaptability consists of the ability of an enterprise to alter its cash flows so that it can respond to unexpected events and opportunities.

8 Qualitative characteristics make the information provided in financial statements useful to users.

9 'Relevance' means relevance to decision making. 'Reliability' means that information is free from material errors or bias. Relevant information has the ability to influence the decisions of users. Reliable information can be depended upon by the users.

Chapter 24 Published financial statements

Solutions to problems

2 (a) By issuing ordinary shares, the company becomes less highly leveraged, i.e. less risky so far as those dealing with the company are concerned. There will also be a lower level of variation in returns to shareholders. However, the cost of issuing shares is high (especially for a PLC) and, unless this issue takes the form of a rights issue, the current

shareholders' stake in the company (and their control) will be diluted. However, because the company is already highly leveraged, this may be a preferred alternative.

(b) 50,000 preference shares would lead to a greater variation (and risk) to the holders of ordinary shares. Also 8 per cent may not be a particularly attractive return for this degree of risk. Advantages are that it would (a) reduce the company's leverage and provide greater financial flexibility, (b) not dilute the ordinary shareholders' control, (c) be less risky in terms of cash outflows than a loan.

It should be remembered that dividends on preference shares are not tax-deductible.

(c) The additional loan would increase leverage and thereby the existing shareholders' risk. However, debenture interest is tax-deductible and this may turn out to be the company's cheapest source of funds. Finance theory would suggest that there is a trade-off between tax benefit and the costs of leverage arising out of increased risk for shareholders. There will be an optimal capital structure for every company, but identifying it may be very difficult.

3

Huby Haulage Ltd Income statement

	£	£
Sales		365,000
Repairs to property	22,000	
Wages (60 + 15)	75,000	
Salaries (20 + 25)	45,000	
Drivers' subsistence	6,150	
Depreciation of vehicles	62,500	
Parts and consumables (70 – 18)	52,000	
Licences and insurance (20 – 4)	16,000	
Administrative expenses	12,000	
Debenture interest	5,000	295,650
Net income		69,350

Huby Haulage Ltd Appropriation account

	£
Trading income	69,350
Corporation tax	22,400
	46,950
Proposed dividend	20,000
Retained income	26,950
Income brought forward	70,000
Retained income carried forward	96,950

Huby Haulage Ltd Balance sheet as at 31 December 20X0

	£
£1 ordinary shares fully paid	200,000
Income statement	96,950
Shareholders' equity	296,950
10% Debenture	50,000
	346,950

Represented by:

Non-current assets	Cost	Depr	NBV
	£	£	£
Freehold property	165,000		165,000
Motor vehicles	360,000	172,500	187,500
	525,000	172,500	352,500

Current assets	£
Inventory of parts, etc.	18,000
Prepaid insurance and licences	4,000
Bank and cash	20,000
	42,000

Current liabilities	£	£
Drivers' subsistence owing	150	
Taxation	22,400	
Proposed dividend	20,000	
Accrued interest	5,000	
	47,550	
Net current liabilities		(5,550)
		346,950

4

Nether Edge plc Income statement for the year ending 31 December 20X0

	£000	Notes
Turnover	2,400	(1)
Cost of sales (Workings 1)	(800)	
Gross income	1,600	
Distribution costs (200 + 680)	(880)	
Administrative expenses (300 + 80 + 40)	(420)	
Operating income	300	(2)
Other income	30	(3)
Interest payable and similar charges	(10)	(4)
Income on ordinary activities before taxation	320	
Tax on income on ordinary activities	(100)	(5)
Income for the financial year	220	
Dividends paid and proposed	(70)	(6)
	150	
Earnings per share	39p	(7)

Nether Edge plc Balance sheet as at 31 December 20X0

	£000	Notes
Non-current assets		
Tangible assets	120	(8)
Investments	140	(9)
	260	
Current assets		
Inventory	600	
Debtors	558	(10)
Cash	118	
	1,276	
Creditors		
Amounts falling due within one year	(326)	(11)
Net current assets	950	
Total assets less current liabilities	1,210	
Creditors		
Amounts falling due after more than one year	(180)	(12)
	1,030	
Capital and reserves		
Called-up share capital	560	
Share premium account	140	
Income statement (180 + 150)	330	
	1,030	

Notes	£000
(1) Turnover	
Turnover represents the amount received, net of VAT, for goods sold during the year.	
(2) Operating income	
Operating income is stated after charging:	
Depreciation	80
Directors' emoluments	110
Hire charges for distribution activities	680
Auditors' remuneration	40
(3) Other income	
Other income arising from trade investments	30
(4) Interest	
Interest payable on debenture inventory	10
(5) Taxation	
Taxation on the income for the year:	
UK corporation tax at 30%	100
(6) Dividends	
Ordinary – interim 2.5p per share	14
– proposed final 10p per share	56
	70

(7) Earnings per share

The calculation is based on 560,000 ordinary shares of £1 each in issue during the year.

(8) Tangible non-current assets

Furniture and fittings at cost		400
Less: Accumulated depreciation to 31 Jan 19X9	£200	
Depreciation for the year	80	280
		120

(9) Investments

Shares at cost in respect of investments listed on a recognized inventory exchange (market value £170,000)

(10) Debtors

Trade	360	
Prepaid expenses	140	500
Amount falling due within one year		58
		558

(11) Creditors: Amounts falling due within one year

Trade creditors	120
Taxation	100
Accruals	50
Proposed dividend	56
	326

(12) Creditors: Amounts falling due after more than one year

Debenture loans	100
Deferred taxation	80
	180

Workings

1   Cost of sales

Opening inventory	400
Purchases	1,000
	1,400
Less: Closing inventory	600
Cost of sales	800

Chapter 25 Statements of cash flows

Solutions to problems

1

South Ltd
Statement of cash flows for the year ended 31 December 20X0

	£000	£000
Net cash inflow from operating activities		5,035
Returns on investments and servicing of finance		
Interest received		2,290
Corporation tax paid		(2,460)
Capital expenditure		
Payments to acquire intangible non-current assets	(150)	
Payments to acquire tangible non-current assets	(2,540)	
Receipts from sales of tangible non-current assets	96	
Net cash outflow from capital expenditure		(2,594)
		2,271
Dividends paid		(1,570)
		701
Financing		
Issue of ordinary share capital	400	
Expenses paid in connection with share issues	(10)	
Net cash inflow from financing		390
Increase in cash and cash equivalents		1,091

Notes to the statement of cash flows	£000
1 Reconciliation of operating income to net cash inflow from operating activities	
Operating income	4,100
Depreciation charges	1,080
Loss on sale of tangible non-current assets	20
Increase in working capital	(165)
	5,035

2

Walkley Ltd
Statement of cash flows for the year ended 31 December 20X1

	£000	£000
Net cash inflow from operating activities		912
Corporation tax paid		(470)
Payments to acquire non-current assets	(1,200)	
Receipts from sales of non-current assets	41	
Net cash outflow from capital expenditure		(1,159)
		(717)
Dividends paid		(230)
		(947)
Financing		
Issue of share capital	300	
Issue of loan capital	65	
Repayment of loans	(235)	
Net cash inflow from financing		130
Decrease in cash		(817)

Notes to the statement of cash flows

	£000
1 Reconciliation of operating income to net cash inflow from operating activities	
Operating income	1,195
Depreciation charges	401
Loss on sale of non-current assets	4
Increase in inventory	(640)
Increase in debtors	(37)
Decrease in creditors	(11)
Net cash inflow from operating activities	912

4

Zepf and Co Ltd
Statement for the year ended 31 December 20X1

	£000	£000
Net cash inflow from operating activities		204
Corporation tax paid		(60)
Capital expenditure		
Payments to acquire non-current assets	(460)	
Receipts from sale of non-current assets	6	
Net cash outflow from capital expenditure		(454)
		(310)
Dividends paid		(16)
		(326)
Financing		
Issue of debenture loan		60
Decrease in cash		(266)

Notes to the cash flow statement

	£000
1 Reconciliation of operating income to net cash inflow from operating activities	
Operating income	180
Depreciation charges	68
Loss on sale of non-current assets	10
Increase in inventory	(30)
Increase in debtors	(72)
Increase in creditors	48
Net cash inflow from operating activities	204

Chapter 26 Interpreting and comparing financial reports

Solutions to problems

1 (a)

$$\text{Current ratio} = \frac{\text{Current assets}}{\text{Current liabilities}}$$

We need first to define what we mean by 'current assets' and 'current liabilities'. For this exercise current assets are relatively straightforward being shown at book values. However, should current liabilities include taxation and dividends? We shall make the (reasonable) assumption that taxation will be payable in a short time, and the more heroic assumption that the same applies to dividends. However, this highlights a difficulty in this type of analysis because every approach we adopt will produce a potentially misleading position. If we exclude tax and dividends, we produce a misleading ratio in that we are hiding the fact that these amounts are payable, thereby producing a higher ratio than might otherwise be the case. If we include tax and dividends, we might also produce a misleading picture, since these liabilities will not appear throughout the year. On balance, it is probably better to include tax and dividends in current liabilities, but this is an interesting point for discussion and may help in educating students about the difficulties that are inherent in ratio analysis.

$$\begin{array}{cc} \textbf{20X2} & \textbf{20X1} \\ \dfrac{635 + 425 + 40}{496 + 15 + 52 + 30} & \dfrac{600 + 410 + 55}{492 + 17 + 43 + 25} \\ = 1.85{:}1 & = 1.84{:}1 \end{array}$$

(b) The acid test ratio is one where definitions (and interpretation) can be extremely difficult. The traditional definition has been that of the current ratio but with inventory being deducted from the numerator. However, it should be recognized that, for many types of business, the ratio will be rather meaningless. This is most obvious in the case of the cash retailer with a rapid inventory turnover, e.g. a good retailer such as a supermarket. In companies like this, the up-to-date quality of inventory will match that of trade creditors and it is thus difficult in the extreme to justify the use of the traditionally defined acid test ratio. Clearly, supermarkets represent a special case, but the general principle raised should be remembered when attempting to interpret such a ratio.

If we assume in this case that it is reasonable to exclude inventory and still derive a meaningful ratio, we would arrive at the following:

$$\begin{array}{cc} \textbf{20X2} & \textbf{20X1} \\ \dfrac{425 + 40}{496 + 15 + 52 + 30} & \dfrac{410 + 55}{492 + 17 + 43 + 25} \\ = 0.78{:}1 & = 0.80{:}1 \end{array}$$

(c) The major difficulty in calculating average inventory turnover is that we do not know what 'average inventory' is. We are forced into an assumption that (opening inventory + closing inventory) ÷ 2 is a reasonable approximation, but it should be remembered that seasonal patterns of sales and/or upturns/downturns in sales during the period around the year end would seriously affect the reliability of this approximation. Allowing for this we find inventory turnover of:

$$\text{Cost of sales} \quad \begin{array}{cc} \textbf{20X2} & \textbf{20X1} \\ \dfrac{600,000}{(635,000 + 600,000) \div 2} & \dfrac{550,000}{(600,000 + 520,000) \div 2} \\ = 0.97 \text{ times} & = 0.98 \text{ times} \end{array}$$

i.e. less than once a year.

(d) As with inventory turnover, we lack information concerning the average level of debtors and are thus forced to adopt an approximation. Often the simplest solution (i.e. using the closing debtors) is adopted, although in this case we will use an average based on opening and closing debtors. However, it should be remembered that year-end debtors are most closely related to sales in the period immediately preceding the year end. The correct way to assess days' sales in debtors would be to work back through the sales day book, but it is recognized that this course will, generally, be unavailable.

Our approximation will thus be:

$$\dfrac{(\text{opening} + \text{closing debtors}) \div 2 \times 360}{\text{sales}}$$

$$\begin{array}{cc} \textbf{20X2} & \textbf{20X1} \\ \dfrac{(425 + 410) \times 180}{1,000} & \dfrac{(410 + 440) \times 180}{2,015} \\ = 150 \text{ days} & = 170 \text{ days} \end{array}$$

(e) As a measure of leverage, the shareholders' equity ratio is much less problematical than the ratios that have gone before. It simply expresses shareholders' equity as a percentage of assets. One minor difficulty is whether we should use gross assets or net assets. Both are useful measures which convey slightly different information. We will use gross assets as our measure here.

$$\begin{array}{cc} \textbf{20X2} & \textbf{20X1} \\ \dfrac{(600 + 125 + 532) \times 100}{2,050} & \dfrac{(600 + 125 + 512) \times 100}{2,015} \\ = 61.3\% & = 61.4\% \end{array}$$

(f) The return on capital employed ratio also requires some definition as there are a number of alternatives. However, it is generally accepted that the most useful definition is that of net income before interest and tax divided by net capital, i.e. shareholders' equity plus any other long-term sources of finance (debentures, long-term loans, etc.).

$$\begin{array}{cc} \textbf{20X2} & \textbf{20X1} \\ \dfrac{100}{600 + 125 + 532 + 200} & \dfrac{75}{2,600 + 125 + 512 + 200} \\ = 6.86\% & = 5.2\% \end{array}$$

It should, however, be noted that we have included the closing income statement balances in our denominator and it might be argued that either the opening figure or some estimate of an average for the year might be more meaningful.

(g) Earnings per share is a more straightforward ratio to define since this is described in FRS 14 which states that 'earnings per share . . . should be calculated and disclosed on a comparable basis . . . so far as this is possible'. It is defined as:

The income in pence attributable to each equity share base on the consolidated income of the period after tax and after deducting minority interests, preference dividends and extraordinary items, divided by the number of equity shares in issue and ranking for dividend in respect of the period.

$$\begin{array}{cc} \textbf{20X2} & \textbf{20X1} \\ \dfrac{50}{600} \times 100 & \dfrac{37.5}{600} \times 100 \\ = 8.33p & = 6.25p \end{array}$$

3   Since Jack and Jill appear to be very similar, we are in a position to attempt a comparison through the use of accounting ratios. It is very difficult to assess the liquidity position of the company in any useful sort of way apart from saying that its position as regards current asset type ratios is much the same in 20X2 as it was in 20X1, as is its gearing position. Whether it is in a strong or weak position is impossible to say without access to much more information.

Profitability
Return on capital:

$$\begin{array}{cc} \textbf{Jack} & \textbf{Jill} \\ \dfrac{8,640}{108,000} & \dfrac{7,700}{30,800} \\ = 8\% & = 25\% \end{array}$$

Although the companies are supposed to be similar, Jill is operating on 28.5% of the capital of Jack. This may imply either that Jack is much less efficient in the use of assets than Jill or that Jack's and Jill's assets were acquired at different times and that interpretation is hampered through the use of historic cost accounting data. This can be further emphasized by calculating the turnover of capital, i.e. sales ÷ net capital employed:

$$\begin{array}{cc} \text{Jack} & \text{Jill} \\ 144,000 & 140,000 \\ \hline 108,000 & 30,800 \\ = 1.33 \text{ times} & = 4.55 \text{ times} \end{array}$$

It is difficult to imagine that one business could make so much better use of its assets if they are indeed similar. It is, of course, possible for a business to be more capital-intensive than another similar business but we would expect this to show up in an improved net income margin.

$$\begin{array}{cc} \text{Jack} & \text{Jill} \\ 8,640 & 7,700 \\ \hline 144,000 & 140,000 \\ = 6\% & = 5.5\% \end{array}$$

This would not appear to be significant enough to explain the difference in capital usage.

Liquidity ratios
If we now turn to the liquidity position of each company we find:
Current ratio:

$$\begin{array}{cc} \text{Jack} & \text{Jill} \\ 32 + 28.8 + 8.95 & 4.8 + 11.2 + 11.36 \\ \hline 15.5 & 30.4 \\ = 4.5\text{:}1 & = 0.9\text{:}1 \end{array}$$

Jack is clearly far more liquid than Jill and it is probably safe to suggest that Jack may not be controlling current assets sufficiently well. Jill may be slightly under-capitalized. However, if we consider the position with inventory excluded, we find:

$$\begin{array}{cc} \text{Jack} & \text{Jill} \\ 28.8 + 8.95 & 11.2 + 11.36 \\ \hline 15.5 & 30.4 \\ = 2.4\text{:}1 & = 0.74\text{:}1 \end{array}$$

If we assume that, in this case, inventories are not readily convertible into cash, we see that Jack still has very high coverage of creditors whilst Jill cannot cover creditors with short-term assets. There are potential problems here for Jill, but this might simply reflect an extremely effective use of resources and, since this is a sole trader, the proprietor may be in a position to solve the problems should they arise. Jack, on the other hand, carries far more inventory than Jill and is also carrying far more non-productive short-term assets.

Inventory turnover
Assuming opening and closing inventory ÷ 2 as a reasonable approximation for average inventory, we find:

	Jack	Jill
Cost of sales × 2	120×2	120×2
Opening + closing inventory	$28 + 32$	$3.2 + 4.8$
	= 4 times	= 30 times

Clearly, this is an enormous difference. It seems that Jill operates in an entirely different way from Jack. However, is it possible to operate one business effectively with so little inventory? Might it not be possible to reduce inventory holdings for the other company as well? A similar result is found for days' sales in debtors:

$$
\begin{array}{cc}
\text{Jack} & \text{Jill} \\
\dfrac{28.8 \times 365}{144} & \dfrac{11.2 \times 365}{140} \\
= 73 \text{ days} & = 29.2 \text{ days}
\end{array}
$$

Again, Jill seems to be using assets much more efficiently.

It is possible to calculate many more ratios but the picture remains the same. Jack uses assets far less effectively than Jill (assuming their valuation to be on the same basis). But, at the same time, Jack would seem to be a more stable, safer, business than Jill.

However, it is not really possible to draw more significant conclusions than this without more information about the proprietors' circumstances. It would certainly make a difference if these were limited companies, as Jill's capital does not even cover long-term assets, an indication of overtrading.

4 (a)

	Us	Them
Return on net assets	11.2%	11.5%
Sales/net assets	0.67 times	1.14 times
Sales/non-current assets	0.73 times	1.33 times
Net income/sales	16.8%	10.04%
Gross income/sales	33.9%	24.0%
Current ratio	1.35:1	1.57:1
'Acid test' ratio	0.87:1	0.81:1
Debtor period	106 days	60 days
Creditor period	126 days	60 days
Inventory turnover	4.0 times	5.1 times

(b) Improve utilization of non-current assets; dispose of surplus assets. Reduce prices to improve sales volume, asset utilization, inventory turnover. Examine purchasing policy. Improve liquidity through actions to reduce and control inventory, debtors, creditors.

(c) Different asset ages. Different accounting bases. Comparison with entire sector needed. Different stages in business cycle. Policy differences. Seasonal distortions.

Chapter 27 Capital, value and income

Answers to self-assessment questions

1 Accountants define capital by reference to the financial investment made in the enterprise by the owner(s). This financial investment consists of the personal capital that the owner(s) invested in the firm at the time of its creation, and the subsequent investments made, either in the form of further injections of personal capital or in the form of retained incomes. The accounting value of the enterprise capital is shown in the capital account, and represents an eventual liability by the firm to repay the owner(s) on winding up the firm.

2 Economists define capital by reference to assets. In this sense, economic capital is the source of future income or incomes when actively committed to business operations. Accordingly, economists define the capital of the business in terms of the assets found on the balance sheet, whereas accountants define capital in terms of the financial investment made by its owners and shown on the balance sheet as ownership equity in the assets of the business. In accounting, the capital of the business is measure as its net worth to the owners.

3 The concept of capital maintenance finds its significance in the measurement of income. Essentially, it is a criterion which evaluates income as a periodic surplus available for distribution. The strict condition imposed by the capital maintenance concept is that periodic income should be measured by reference to the value of the capital at the beginning and at the end of the year. If the value of the capital at the end of the year is larger than at the beginning (no further injections of capital having been made), the difference is income and it is available for distribution. This concept is linked to Hicks's definition of personal income as being that amount which a person may consume during a period, and as a result not be worse off at the end of the period than at the beginning.

4 Five concepts of capital maintenance are discussed in the literature:

(a) The money amount concept, which refers capital maintenance to the need to maintain the monetary value of the shareholders' equity constant.
(b) The investment purchasing power concept, which is based on the notion of economic income defined as being the present value of future cash flows generated by the firm's assets. Accordingly, the maintenance of capital is assured when the opening and closing value of the shareholders' equity based on this value remains constant.
(c) The financial capital concept, which requires that capital maintenance be assured by maintaining the financial value of shareholders' equity constant through adjustments to the historical cost of assets for changes in the value of money.
(d) The operating capability concept, which requires that the productive (operating) capacity of the firm should be maintained by making adequate provision for replacing asset values exhausted in the course of operations. This concept of capital maintenance is the main pillar supporting the case for replacement cost accounting.
(e) The disposable wealth concept, which suggests that the maintenance of capital should be viewed from the perspective of the realizable value of assets. It is based on the proprietorship theory of the firm, and views capital from the strict viewpoint of the owners of the business.

5 The general consensus is that the operating capability concept of capital maintenance is the most appropriate both for corporate shareholders and managers. It has been the major theoretical support for the use of replacement costs in measuring business income. From a management viewpoint, it ensures that the operating capability is maintained by providing for the replacement of assets as they are used in operating, and avoids the problem of excessive distributions to shareholders. From the viewpoint of corporate shareholders, some may argue that either the disposable wealth or the financial capital concept may be more relevant in making sell-or-buy decisions. However, the majority opinion has supported the relevance of the operating capability concept for shareholders' decision making.

6 Accountants measure business income on a periodic basis by identifying the revenues of the period and the expenses of the period. Hence, the measurement of business income results from a process of accruing revenues and expenses to an accounting period, and matching expenses with the revenues that they have produced. It should be noted that the principle of prudence requires losses to be recognized as soon as they are considered to have occurred. Consequently, some of the expenses charged against the revenues of a period are considered as expenses of the period rather than expenses of earning the revenues of that period.

7 Income measurement is relevant to the following decisions:

(a) for evaluating business efficiency in terms of profitability;
(b) for making investment decisions on the basis of the expected future cash flows resulting from different alternatives;
(c) for evaluating managerial performance both by reference to the effectiveness of managerial decisions and as stewards of business capital;

(d) as a basis on which annual income tax declarations may be made to the Inland Revenue. The tax authorities generally accept accounting conventions used in measuring business incomes when preparing tax assessments;

(e) as a guide to creditworthiness, on the principle that if a business is profitable it is able to pay its debts;

(f) as a guide to socio-economic decisions, for example, in wage-bargaining situations where the ability of the firm to afford bonuses and pay increases may depend upon current incomes;

(g) as a guide to dividend policy, for, generally, the ability to pay dividends depends upon the existence of incomes, either current or past incomes that may justify such dividends.

8 The meaning of 'value' has been the subject of considerable debate in the literature of economics. It finds its significance in the context in which it is used. Value has been associated with the notion of usefulness or utility. In that context, major problems have been encountered in measuring value in terms of utility. Another aspect is the notion of 'worth', which may be linked with the notion of capital. Capital is an economic and accounting concept of considerable significance. The notion of 'value' is also used as a measurement base. In this sense, one may refer to cost value, market value, etc. The terms value, capital and income form part of a complex of theoretical concepts concerning economic and accounting income.

9 The term 'valuation' refers to the measurement base by which value is determined. Commonly, value is established by reference to money as an exchange standard. In this sense, both economics and accounting utilize money value as a measurement base. Acquisition or input values, defined as historic cost, and realization or output values, defined as market values, also illustrate other approaches to valuation. These valuation bases are found in the measurement of accounting income. The 'present value' concept is an attempt to value on the basis of the current value of future expected cash flows. This notion of value is used in the measurement of economic income.

10 From the foregoing, it is evident that the use of different valuation bases in the measurement of capital and income will produce different conclusions or results. This may be seen from alternative valuations implied in different notions of capital maintenance, that result in different measurements of capital and income. The significance of these different values lies, therefore, in the problem of selecting the most relevant values for decision making.

Chapter 28 Accounting and economic concepts of income and value

Answers to self-assessment questions

1 The basis of valuation in accounting is historical cost. Underlying this convention is the assumption that the money measurement standard is stable through time. Given that this assumption is in practice false, its use leads to serious distortions in the measurement of income when the value of money changes through time. These distortions result from the fact that the historical cost of items charged as expenses is less than their current replacement cost. Consequently, historic cost income is overstated, leading to excessive taxation on income and the possibility of excessive distributions. Accordingly, the firm may be unable to finance the replacement cost of assets, and to maintain its operating capability.

2 The historic cost convention likewise leads to balance sheet valuation of assets being understated by reference to their current replacement cost. Asset values being understated, it follows that the value of the firm is itself understated. Conversely, liabilities that have been expressed at their historical cost will be exaggerated in real terms at a rate

corresponding to the rate of monetary inflation. These distortions are aggravated in direct proportion as the time gap lengthens between the entry date and the current year.

3 The modifications to historic cost accounting that need to be made to improve the quality of information for financial reporting are to be found in the selection of appropriate methods for correcting the instability of the money value measurement standard. Under conditions of zero price changes, historic cost accounting does not, of itself, distort the measurement of income or balance sheet values. It is only when price levels change that distortions appear. The translation of historic cost values into their current values is a problem that has been much discussed. Several different concepts and methods have been proposed, including indexing to assure constant purchasing power, and using current replacement costs.

4 The significance of the realization convention lies in the timing of the recognition of changes in values for the purpose of income measurement and balance sheet presentations. In effect, in accordance with the realization convention changes in value are not recorded until they have crystallized through a transaction. Accountants justify their attachment to the realization convention because a realized transaction assures an objective and verifiable measure of a change in value, and also because a sale is the most decisive and significant event in the chain of transactions that make up business activity. Nonetheless, the use of the realization convention may occasionally lead to absurd results.

5 The essential differences between the accounting and the economic approaches to income measurement stem from the transaction-based approach used in accounting to measure a historic result, and the economic approach that attempts to provide guidelines for consumption decisions. The transaction approach identifies revenues and expense transactions as relevant to the measurement of periodic income in an operational context. This implies that transactions that have an income-earning objective are segregated from those that are in the nature of investment. The latter are shown as balance sheet values. Accordingly, the measurement of accounting income is a matter of preparing a periodic income statement of operating transactions. The economic approach looks to changes in balance sheet values as affording a method of measuring periodic income. It does not require, as does the accounting approach, that changes in values be realized.

6 Hicks defined individual income as the amount that a man can consume during a period and still remain as well off at the end of the period as he was at the beginning. This definition links the measurement of income to the valuation of capital or wealth. It expresses income as limiting consumption to the maximum that may be consumed without eating into capital. Hicks's definition of income poses a measurement problem, since it requires an individual to estimate what can be consumed between two different points in time. The 'ex-ante' approach to economic income is really the only one that is relevant to the stream of consumption decisions that are made between two points in time. This requires the individual to have information about the year-end situation from the perspective of the beginning of the year.

7 Alexander extended Hicks's definition of individual income to the statement of business income. According to Alexander, the definition of the income of a company is the amount that it may distribute to shareholders during a period and still be as well off at the end of the year as it was at the beginning. Alexander's definition suffers from the same measurement problems as those that affect Hicks's concept of individual income, namely, the inability to estimate with certainty the situation at year end from the perspective of the situation at the beginning of the year.

8 In economics, income and value are closely related in the measurement of economic income, since income is a result of changes in value between two points in time. The economic concept of income treats asset values of all kinds as representing expected future

receipts. They are discounted to their present value to give in aggregate terms a valuation of present well-offness, or capital. It is the change in the perception of the value of future expected net receipts between two points in time that affords a measure of disposable income.

9 The 'ex-ante' approach to the measurement of economic income implies that income is measured from the standpoint of the beginning of the period by comparing the present situation with the situation at the end of the period. Since income is used as a guide to consumption in economics, the 'ex-ante' approach is fraught with uncertainty, since it relies extensively on forecasting. The 'ex-post' approach is historic in nature since the measurement of income is effected at the end of the period, rather than at the beginning of the period.

10 The major problems that are to be found in applying economic concepts of income and value to accounting measurements lie in the measurement problems implied in making the necessary forecasts of future expected receipts. These forecasts are information requirements both for asset valuations and for the measurement of periodic income. Many would agree that economic concepts provide valuations that are more relevant for decision making, but they also recognize the difficulties of providing the degree of objectivity that accountants seek. As noted, accountants seek objectivity in the notion of verifiability. This is obtained through transaction-based information.

Chapter 29 Accounting under monetary instability and market volatility

Answers to self-assessment questions

1 One of the major criteria of the quality of any form of data is that it should not have a fluctuating meaning, that is, a value that is unstable. Accounting data are transaction-based, and measured in terms of the money value established at the date of transaction. The application of historic cost accounting under conditions of monetary instability means, in effect, that goods and services recorded as acquisition costs will be valued in terms of their exchange rate against money at the date of the transaction. Under conditions of inflation, for example, the purchasing power of money over goods and services decreases through time. The result is that exactly similar goods and services acquired at different dates are represented as items of different accounting value. Thus, being unable to portray in a reliable manner the goods and services that are being recorded, the recording process registers misleading data. Under conditions of market volatility, market values themselves are changing constantly and this is seen particularly in financial assets and property values. Speculative factors play an important role in the market volatility. The application of historic cost accounting under conditions of market volatility means that assets values shown on balance sheets at their historical cost have no relationship with their latest market value.

2 Under both monetary instability and market volatility, accounting information based on historic cost accounting will be used for the purpose of financial reporting to shareholders that valuations which do not reflect current market values. The valuation rules applying to non-current assets require such assets to be maintained at their historic costs. As regards current assets, however, current market values may be substituted for historical costs at the lower of cost and market values in the case of inventory and provision for losses in the value of debtors are also allowed. Hence, it is really the application of the historic cost rule to non-current assets that is the basic problem as regards both monetary instability and market volatility.

3 The contradiction between the control paradigm and the valuation paradigm with respect to the use of historic cost has been a central issue in accounting theory for decades and remains unresolved. It goes to the very heart of the concept of accounting responsibility.

In terms of the control paradigm, the role of accounting is to keep a proper and orderly record of transactions that may be used for controlling purposes through verification. The control paradigm is concerned with truth, trust, objectivity and transparency values and considers that historic costs recorded from invoices is objective and verifiable truth. The valuation paradigm is founded on the view that accounting information should be relevant to the decision making needs of users of financial reports and, in particular, to investors and financial markets. As a basis for financial reporting, historic cost information is not relevant to users' needs in this regard. Financial markets have long criticized accounting information on these grounds and called for market related asset values to be used instead of historic cost for financial reporting purposes. However, as a basis for accounting measurements, valuations are subjective and rely upon opinions that are volatile in nature. Truth in accounting disappears when it is substituted for opinion and likewise trust in accounting information is impaired when speculation promotes corruption.

4 There are two aspects to the possible effects of monetary instability on accounting data. First, the legal basis of accounting data is founded on the legal rights and obligations established in binding contracts. They are stated at the contract value and are not indexed for changes in the value of money. Second, for income measurement purposes, under conditions of inflation, business income will be overstated by charging expenses at historic cost rather than at their current value. Used as a basis for the taxation of business income and dividend distribution, the failure to take inflation into account will result in inflated income measurement that will have serious consequences for the financial viability of businesses.

5 Current purchasing power accounting involves correcting for changes in the purchasing power of money over goods and services by reference to general price level changes. For accounting purposes, it does not involve altering the money value of recorded transactions, but, for the purposes of financial reporting only, restating the historical money values at the date of transaction to their current money values at the end of the accounting period. In effect, current purchasing power accounting means dealing with the instability of the money measurement standard by adjusting data to a common transaction date, assumed as the accounting year end.

Current purchasing power accounting, known as constant dollar accounting in the USA, was introduced in the United Kingdom by SSAP 7, later withdrawn. It recommended the use of the Retail Price Index for converting historical costs into current purchasing power equivalent at year end.

6 The method used to convert historic cost income into current purchasing power income relies on adjusting the figures shown on the income statement to the current purchasing power at the year end. This is realised by using the general index of price level changes across the year. Thus, if the index is 100 at the beginning of the year, and the index is 130 at the end of the year, the adjustment requires all values to be stated at the year-end index value.

Essentially, the problem lies in selecting the appropriate conversion factor to convert individual items to the year-end index value. This means that such items as sales, purchases and expenses running across the year have to be converted upwards by reference to the index at transaction date and the index at year-end date. Some items, such as depreciation, may relate to depreciable assets existing at the beginning of the year. In this case, the adjustment will correspond to the change in the index across the full year.

7 The method used to restate a historic cost balance sheet into current purchasing power involves restating all balance sheet items to their year-end index value. Non-monetary items are not treated as suffering purchasing power gains or losses, and hold their value in real terms. Hence, under current purchasing power accounting, these items are restated up to the year-end index value. The problem essentially lies in identifying the index value at the entry date of these items. For example, non-current assets existing at the beginning of the year and the accumulated depreciation thereon has to be converted up to the year-end index

value from the year-beginning index value. Other assets, such as inventory acquired across the year, have to be up-valued from the index at acquisition date to year-end index value.

Monetary item balances established as closing balances are treated as having appeared at year-end index values and, therefore, do not require an upward adjustment.

8 The instability of exchange rates between currencies is a form of monetary instability that affects businesses engaged in international trade. Foreign transactions stated in foreign currencies have to be translated into the local currency for accounting purposes as at the date on invoicing. At settlement date of foreign invoices stated in foreign currency, the rate of exchange between the currencies may have changed. As a consequence, more or less of the local currency may be needed to settle the foreign invoice in the foreign currency. This results in a difference between the recorded amounts and the amounts paid. Exchange gains or losses appear either as revenue or expense in the income statement. In this way, the commercial transaction is isolated from any instability in foreign exchange rates. The instability of exchange rate affects international corporations when translating the financial reports of foreign subsidiaries during the process of consolidating them into group financial reports.

9 Advocates of fair value reporting argue that financial statements should be relevant to the decision-needs of investors and financial markets and that financial statements based on historic costs are neither relevant nor useful in that context. Historic costs are argued not to be fair values, whereas end-year market values more correctly reflect the fair value of assets. Where there is a market value available to assets or liabilities, mark-to-market accounting consists of reporting them on financial statements at their market values, which may be assumed to be fair values. Where there is no market value, the fair value is the best price at which an asset could be bought or a liability settled between knowledgeable willing parties, other than in a liquidation.

10 According to IASB Exposure Draft on Fair Value Measurements, fair values should be measured in all international accounting standards that require such values in terms of a single unified definition. Consequently, the rules relating to balance sheet values remain much the same as in the past: non-current non-financial assets are valued at historic cost, current non-financial assets are to be valued at the lower of cost or market value, and financial instruments are to be classified according to their fundamental characteristics. Where cash flows are stable and predictable, such as in the case of loans and government bonds, financial instruments are to be valued at cost and impaired, if necessary. Where they are volatile or being traded, they must be marked to market.

11 FAS 157 Fair Value Measurement takes a different position from the IASB with respect to the application of fair value measurements. Both agree that historic cost should remain the rule for recording accounting data and preparing year-end financial statements that are subject to auditing requirements. They also agree that where legislation or accounting standards require the use of fair values and market values do not exist, fair values should be estimated in the best possible manner. The difference is found on the requirement under FAS 157 that fair value should be applied to financial and non-financial assets that are recognised or disclosed at fair value on a recurring basis. This rule is extended to other non-financial assets as from 2009, where fair values are required under other authoritative accounting pronouncements.

12 In terms of both the control paradigm and the valuation paradigm, accounting information disclosed in financial reports must be truthful. Truth is the fundamental ethical value. Falsehood, deceit and corruption destroy trust that is necessary in all relationships. It is for this reason that transparency is so necessary in securing truth and maintaining trust in financial reporting and protecting the interests of users of financial statements. The highest standard of truth is objectivity, that is, truth that is based on facts that are verifiable.

Objectivity is the standard of truth on which scientific knowledge is based. By contrast, subjective knowledge is a matter of opinion. Opinion is the essence of valuation, where different opinions support different valuations. Increasingly valuation enters into financial reports on matters of judgement, such as the valuation of current assets and fair values are required. In these cases, the criterion of truth is met by honesty and sincerity in formulating opinions on which valuations are based. It explains the requirement that financial reports should express a 'true and fair view'. Transparency is a fundamental ethical value, protects truth and maintains trust in accounting information disclosed in financial reports.

13 The objective of fair value measurement is to provide a concept of income for financial reporting purposes that satisfies criteria of relevance and usefulness, as against conventional financial reports based on historic cost measurements. Where market values exist, these may be taken as fair values. Where trading has collapsed or ceased, fair value measurements reflect the best price at which an asset could be bought or a liability settled between knowledgeable willing parties, other than in a liquidation. However, the difficulty in all cases with market values is that they are influenced by market sentiments in which speculation is a significant element that influences valuation.

Solutions to problems

1 **Vitex plc**
Calculation of the purchasing power gain or loss on monetary items

	HC		Factor	CPP	
	£	£		£	£
Opening capital contributed		150,000	120/100		180,000
Add: Sales		200,000	120/120		200,000
		350,000			380,000
Less:					
Purchases of equipment	40,000		120/100	48,000	
Purchase of goods					
(i) index at 100	88,000		120/100	105,600	
(ii) index at 110	90,000		120/110	98,182	
Expenses	32,000		120/110*	34,909	
		250,000			286,691
		100,000			93,309

*Based on the average index value for the year

	£
Net current monetary items at 31 December 20X0	100,000
Adjusted monetary items at 31 December 20X0	93,309
Purchasing power gain	6,691

In addition, the purchasing power gain on the long-term balance due on equipment is:

£50,000 × 120/100 = 60,000
less sum due   50,000
                                    10,000

Income statement for the year ended 31 December 20X0

	HC	Factor	CPP
	£000		£000
Sales	200	120/120	200
Less: Cost of sales	120	see below	140.5
Gross income	80		59.5
Less: Expenses	32	120/110	(34.9)
Depreciation	9	120/100	(10.8)
	41		
	39		13.8

	£
Cost of sales comprises £88,000 bought at index 100, CPP equivalent =	105,600
Cost of sales comprises £32,000 bought at index 110, CPP equivalent =	34,909
	140,509

Balance sheet as at 31 December 20X0

	HC	Factor	CPP	
	£000		£000	
Non-current assets				
Equipment (cost)	90	120/100		108.0
Less: Acc dep	9	120/100		10.8
	81			97.2
Current assets				
Inventory	58	120/110	63.3	
Trade debtors	36	120/120	36	
Bank	81	120/120	81	
	175		180.3	
Less: Creditors				
Amounts due within one year				
Trade creditors	17	120/120	17	
	158		163.3	
Total assets *less* current liabilities	239		260.5	
Less: Creditors				
Amounts due after one year	50	120/120	50	
	189		210.5	
Capital and reserves				
Issued share capital	150	120/100	180.0	
Income statement	39	–	13.8	
	189			
Accumulated purchasing power gain		Note 1	16.7	
			210.5	

Note 1	The accumulated purchasing power gain is made up of:	£000
	Purchasing power gain on monetary items	6.7
	Purchasing power gain on long-term liability	10.0
		16.7

Chapter 30 Reporting to investors

Answers to self-assessment questions

1   The text suggests the main reasons: the present system is backward-looking, much emphasis is placed on a single measure of earnings and historical cost is used.

2   The efficiency of the market will be helped, the control of investors over managers will be improved, investors will have more useful information and the reputations of forward-looking entities will be improved.

3   It will assist investors in forming their own forecasts, management's view of the future outlook will be disclosed, it will help prevent abnormal returns and it will provide investors with a better basis for evaluating managerial performance.

4   *MCRV* argues that NRV is market-based, is readily understandable, removes the need for depreciation, produces additive numbers, improves comparability and improves liquidity information.

5   Quarterly reporting helps users with a longer-term focus, provides reliable information and reduces inside information problems.

6   The findings of efficient market research show (i) financial accounting information does have economic significance in that share prices react to new information, (ii) the market does not respond to earnings increases that result from cosmetic changes in accounting policies.

Chapter 31 Social accounting and the caring society

Answers to self-assessment questions

1   Three approaches to corporate social responsibilities are distinguished in the text: (i) the classic economic theory objective of income maximization, (ii) the significance of social objectives in relation to income maximization and (iii) the view that the firm should seek a satisfactory level of income which is compatible with the attainment of a range of social goals.

2   In both cases, it is necessary to focus on their needs as users rather than on their wants. The information needs of employees are more complex than those of investors. In both cases, the disclosure of information is regulated by law. In both cases, traditional financial reports have limited usefulness. The impact of management decisions falls more obviously and directly on employees. The role of the auditor traditionally has been to protect investors and not employees, the important difference in financial reporting which is directed toward the interests of investors. There was little interest in reporting to employees before 1970.

3   The main aim of employee reports is to promote goal congruence by explaining how their interests and efforts relate to those of the firm and to improve communication with employees and their understanding of the manner in which the firm is being managed in the interests of all participants. Reporting in the context of collective bargaining is aimed at

providing information without which trade unions would be impeded in conducting negotiations. This information is primarily addressed to determining the minimum acceptable settlement and the firm's ability to pay.

4 Partnerships for the common good represent a significant move forward in the relationship between business and society and away from the strict view that the sole purpose of business is to increase shareholders' wealth by attributing the entire profit to shareholders as dividends. The crux of the problem is resolving the conflict between capital and labour that is a major source of conflict at the workplace. Partnerships for the common good address the manner in which business income should be shared equitably between all those who have participated and contributed to the firm's success.

5 The concept of employee ownership and control is a modification of modern capitalism that maintains the principle of free trade that is the hallmark of a market economy as its essential premise and opposes doctrinaire socialist theories favouring state ownership of business and bureaucratic public control. In effect, employee ownership and control extends the principle of democracy to the workplace through which the ownership basis is broadened to all employees, with management controlling the business in the interest of employees. The John Lewis Partnership Limited corporate management model is based on three operating principles – sharing gains, sharing knowledge and sharing power.

6 Six areas are discussed in the text: environmental protection, energy saving, fair business practices, human resources, community involvement and product.

7 The text examines three surveys undertaken to establish the nature and extent of social responsibility disclosures in the annual accounts of companies. The surveys show that the trend of mandated disclosure is upward, reflecting an increased response to legislation. No such conclusion could be drawn from voluntary disclosures, although two areas, community involvement and product, indicate an upward trend of disclosure.

8 The implications of the increasing concern for green issues are considered in the text. They are the depletion of natural resources, unacceptably high levels of pollution, global warming, acid rain and deforestation, among other issues affecting health and environmental conditions. The central focus is on the notion of sustainable development that meets the needs of the present without compromising the ability of the future to meets its own needs.

9 A caring society can exist in a market economy. The main achievements of the market economy include significantly raising living standards, encouraging the development of scientific and technological progress, providing employment and financing a vast range of social welfare activities. All these achievements are consistent with the aims of a caring society. The market economy is driven by self-interest, expressed in competitive endeavour. It is motivated by the profit-making motive and money is its sole value system. A caring society is based on two fundamental principles – the instinct to care that is the humane side of our existence and the necessity to share, which reflects the awareness of others in all we do. In that sense, a caring society is one that accepts caring and sharing with others in collaborative endeavour as its vision of society. It contrasts with the selfishness that drives the market economy and which is seen in the policies and behaviour of big business.

Chapter 32 Budgeting for planning and control

Answers to self-assessment questions

1 The first stage in budgeting is the determination of the key factors or constraints that impose overall limits to the budget plan. These include market conditions, productive

capacity and the financing available. Once the sales budget is determined, it is possible to determine the production budget, taking into account the level of inventory required to be maintained and the volume of production needed. The various production department budgets may then be prepared from the basis of the estimated costs involved in the output required. The overall financial needs are calculated in terms of a cash budget. This will represent the total finance needed to support all budgeted expenditure, including selling and distribution expenses, the production expenses, the capital expenditure budgeted for the period as well as the research and development budget. The overall budget will be expressed in terms of a budgeted income statement and a budgeted balance sheet at the end of the budget period.

2 A major problem in budgeting is forecasting sales, for many factors affecting sales are outside the firm's control. The importance of an accurate sales forecast cannot be overemphasized. If the sales forecast is too optimistic, the firm will commit itself to excessive expenditure, both on current production and on capital expenditure, which will result in excessive production and excessive production capacity. If the sales forecast is too pessimistic, the firm will underproduce and miss the opportunity of realizing sales, and the incomes involved in the lost sales.

3 There are four commonly used methods for forecasting sales:

(a) The salesforce composite method, which places the responsibility on individual sales representatives for developing their own sales forecasts. These are aggregated into an overall sales forecast.

(b) The analysis of market and industry factors, which recognizes the importance of factors that are not within the knowledge of sales representatives. They include statistical information relating to gross national product, personal income, employment figures, etc. This information is used to modify the internal forecasts developed by sales representatives.

(c) Statistical analysis of business trends and fluctuations, such as growth trends, business cycle fluctuations, seasonal fluctuations and irregular variations in demand. This analysis is applied to validating the sales forecast.

(d) Sales forecasting using mathematical models that have been developed in recent years to establish relationships between economic trends and a firm's sales forecast.

4 The sales forecast is the determining factor for planning the level of activity that the firm will wish to adopt as a target for developing the sales budget. The sales budget will dictate the volume of production required to meet the budgeted sales volume. The essential feature of the relationship between the sales budget and the production budget is the command position occupied by the sales budget. In a market economy, firms are generally sales-led in terms of budget planning. The importance of the production budget lies in the analysis of production costs. The production budget may be regarded as implementing the sales budget, and stating its implications in terms of the budgeted cost of sales, where goods are costed on the basis of factory cost of production.

5 The cash budget projects the cash flows arising from the planned activities for the budget period. It provides a forecasted profile of these cash flows across the budget period. It is a vital management planning tool, for it addresses the critical problem of cash flow management, both in terms of planned expenditure and the financing of such expenditure.

6 (a) Managers start from zero in estimating future budgets.
(b) Comparisons are made between forecasts.
(c) Flexible budgets take account of changes in the volume of activity.

7 ABB focuses on activities rather than on the functional organization structure.

Solutions to problems

1

(a) Debtors' budget

Quarter	July–Sept £	Oct–Dec £	Jan–March £	April–June £	Year £
Sales per month	5,000	6,000	7,000	4,000	
Month end debtors	5,000	6,000	7,000	4,000	4,000

(b) Cash budget

	July–Sept £	Oct–Dec £	Jan–March £	April–June £	Year £
balance b/f	2,000	1,500	2,700	10,600	2,000
Receipts					
From sales*	13,000	17,000	20,000	15,000	65,000
	15,000	18,500	22,700	25,600	67,000
Payments					
Purchases	12,000	14,000	10,000	8,000	44,000
Expenses	1,500	1,800	2,100	1,200	6,600
Balance c/f	1,500	2,700	10,600	16,400	16,400
	15,000	18,500	22,700	25,600	67,000

*Note Cash receipts in any quarter will equal sales for months 1 and 2 of that quarter plus receipts from the debtors at the end of the previous quarter, as follows:

	£	£	£	£
From debtors	3,000	5,000	6,000	7,000
From sales in qtr	10,000	12,000	14,000	8,000
	13,000	17,000	20,000	15,000

(c) Inventory budget

	units	units	units	units	units
Opening inventory	1,000	2,000	3,000	1,000	1,000
Purchases	6,000	7,000	5,000	4,000	22,000
	7,000	9,000	8,000	5,000	23,000
Units sold	5,000	6,000	7,000	4,000	22,000
Closing inventory	2,000	3,000	1,000	1,000	1,000

2

Income statement

Quarter	1	2	3	4
	£	£	£	£
Sales	42,000	45,000	48,000	51,000
Less:				
Direct materials (50%)	21,000	22,500	24,000	25,500
Direct wages (20%)	8,400	9,000	9,600	10,200
Variable overheads (10%)	4,200	4,500	4,800	5,100
	8,400	9,000	9,600	10,200

Balance sheet

Quarter	1	2	3	4
	£	£	£	£
Non-current assets	23,400	22,800	22,200	21,600
Current assets				
Inventory	28,000	30,000	32,000	34,000
Debtors	28,000	30,000	32,000	34,000
Total assets	79,400	82,800	86,200	89,600
Current liabilities				
Bank overdraft	27,500	27,900	27,700	26,900
Creditors	21,000	22,500	24,000	25,500
Total assets *less* current liabilities	30,900	32,400	34,500	37,200
Capital and reserves				
Share capital	40,000	40,000	40,000	40,000
Income statement	9,100	7,600	5,500	2,800
	30,900	32,400	34,500	37,200

Cash flow budget

Quarter	1	2	3	4
	£	£	£	£
Opening cash balance	(26,500)	(27,500)	(27,900)	(27,700)
Inflows from customers	40,000	43,000	46,000	49,000
Outflows				
Paid suppliers	21,500	23,000	24,500	26,000
Wages	8,400	9,000	9,600	10,200
Variable overheads	4,200	4,500	4,800	5,100
Fixed overheads				
Depreciation	6,900	6,900	6,900	6,900
	41,000	43,400	45,800	48,200
Net cash flow	(1,000)	(400)	200	800
Closing cash balance	(27,500)	(27,900)	(27,700)	(26,900)

	£	£	£	£
Opening debtors	26,000	28,000	30,000	32,000
Add: Sales	42,000	45,000	48,000	51,000
Less: Closing debtors	28,000	30,000	32,000	34,000
From customers	40,000	43,000	46,000	49,000
	£	£	£	£
Cost of sales	21,000	22,500	24,000	25,500
Add: Closing inventory	28,000	30,000	32,000	34,000
Less: Opening inventory	26,000	28,000	30,000	32,000
Purchases	23,000	24,500	26,000	27,500
	£	£	£	£
Opening creditors	19,500	21,000	22,500	24,000
Add: Purchases	23,000	24,500	26,000	27,500
Less: Closing creditors	21,000	22,500	24,000	25,500
Paid to suppliers	21,500	23,000	24,500	26,000

4

(a) (i) To assist the planning of the organization through the setting of objectives and goals.

(ii) To control the organization via setting plans and comparing the actual figures against them.

(iii) To coordinate the various departments and functions within the organization.

(iv) To motivate managers to achieve the budget, and thereby the organization's objectives.

To communicate the plans of the organization to the various parts of the organization.

(b) The organization can be classified by income centre as well as by functional area. The income centres are likely to follow the current organization structure, that is, swimming pool manager, diving pool manager, conference hall manager and so on. The functional budgets for this type of organization are: sales, purchases, labour and overheads. Each manager would be expected to prepare the figures for their particular area of responsibility.

The chart below is a proposed organization chart for the leisure complex, with each manager responsible for the staff, expenses and income in their area of responsibility.

(c) There are many software programs available for the preparation of budgets. These programs can be developed on spreadsheet software or can be run on a spreadsheet such as Excel, etc.

Chapter 33 Organizing for control

Answers to self-assessment questions

1 The purpose of 'control' lies in ensuring that the organization's activities conform with its plans. Control, therefore, is an activity affecting every aspect of the organization. The terms planning and control are frequently joined together in expressing the nature of their relationship.

2 The control process may be seen as a cycle that shows the origin of control in the objectives of the organization from which plans are developed. These plans include long-range and annual plans. The control cycle integrates both the long-range and the annual plan. Information feedback enables actual performance to be compared with planned performance, thus enabling management to control operations and the resources allocated to those operations. The control process allows achievements to be compared with the organization's desired objectives, thereby enabling new goals and new objectives to be formulated.

3 'Responsibility accounting' defines managerial responsibility in terms of an organizational framework in which responsibility centres are established, and individual managers appointed to manage such centres are made responsible for the centre's performance. There are different kinds of responsibility centres, that depend partly on the size of the organization and partly on the style of management adopted.

4 A support cost centre is a department that provides a service to the departments that are making a product or providing a service. A maintenance department is an example of a support cost centre as it incurs costs in maintaining machinery to produce a product. By contrast, a production cost centre is a production department in which costs are accumulated. The term 'production' is used loosely in this context to mean any department through which a product or service passes.

5 The distinction between 'controllable' and 'non-controllable' costs is significant for the purposes of responsibility accounting. Managers should only be held responsible for the costs that fall under their control. These are defined as 'controllable costs'. Costs over which they have no control are defined as 'uncontrollable costs'. Where systems of responsibility accounting have been installed, managers are not held responsible for 'uncontrollable costs', that is, costs over which they have no control. For example, a departmental manager would be held responsible for costs incurred in his/her department. S/he would not be held responsible for costs transferred into that department from another department as work-in-process.

6 A profit centre is a responsibility centre that involves a responsibility for profit. It represents a much higher level of management responsibility than expense centres and cost centres. In particular, it involves responsibility for factors affecting profit, namely revenues and expenses. It follows that a profit centre is a responsibility centre presenting specific features. First, it is generally a large responsibility centre, that includes subordinate responsibility centres, such as expense centres and cost centres. Second, given that management responsibility includes revenues, it follows that a profit centre must include revenue-producing activities. Third, given the broad nature of management responsibility involved, profit centres imply the existence of an organizational structure that allows the degree of centralized decision making that gives profit centre managers the necessary freedom of activity implied in the notion of running a segment of the organization as a business. Typical examples of profit centres are factories operating as profit centres, product and service divisions, and in large organizations, subsidiary companies that are managed as profit centres.

7 Large enterprises that have organizational structures that are decentralized and division-alized face particular problems in planning, controlling and evaluating income centres where intra-company trading occurs. This will occur in the following circumstances:

(a) where profit centres trade with the external markets as well as with each other with respect to finished products and services;
(b) where profit centres trade with each other in respect of intermediary products. This occurs where the activities of profit centres are interrelated, so that the output of one profit centre provides a substantial part of the input to another profit centre.

The purpose of transfer prices is to provide a price mechanism that allows trading between profit centres to take place, thereby permitting them to function as profit centres. Accordingly, transfer prices provide the profit centre that sells an output in the form of measurable revenue. Equally, it provides the buying profit centre with an input cost that would reflect efficient buying prices.

The availability of an efficient transfer pricing mechanism is of critical importance to the evaluation of profit centre performance in decentralized and divisionalized corporations.

Transfer prices should satisfy the following three criteria:

(a) they should promote goal congruence within the organization by harmonizing the interests of individual divisions with the interests of the organization as a whole;
(b) they should make possible reliable assessments of divisional performance for the following purposes:
   (i) making predictions for decision making;
   (ii) appraising managerial performance;
   (iii) evaluating divisional contributions to corporate incomes.
(c) they should ensure the autonomy of individual divisions is respected and profits are not dependent on the actions of other divisions.

8 Three main methods are used for establishing transfer prices, namely:

(a) market-based transfer pricing,
(b) cost-based transfer pricing,
(c) negotiated transfer pricing.

Market-based transfer pricing applies where external markets exist for the goods that are traded between profit centres. If the external markets are competitive, and divisional inter-dependence is minimal, market-based transfer pricing satisfies the required conditions for an effective transfer pricing mechanism.

Cost-based transfer pricing overcomes difficulties associated with the absence of market prices, for example, when intermediary goods are transferred between profit centres. Two commonly used cost-related prices are full-cost and variable cost prices.

Cost-based transfer prices can be simply at cost, in which case, the transferring profit centre simply recovers its costs and makes no income, or at cost-plus, in which case, the required profit markup is added to costs. Cost-based transfer prices pose a number of problems in actual practice.

Negotiated transfer pricing results from negotiations between profit centre managers. Given that their performance as managers is at stake, it is evident that this method will lead to disputes requiring arbitration.

9 Investment centres represent the ultimate stage in the decentralization of organizational decision making. Usually found in autonomous divisions and subsidiary companies, investment centres have managerial responsibility not only for cost goals (expense centres) and for income contribution (profit centres), but also for invested capital. They extend the principle underlying profit centres by evaluating investment centre profits with the capital

invested in the centre. The evaluation of investment centre performance implies selecting performance criteria that would apply to wholly autonomous enterprises.

10 The criterion most commonly applied for assessing the financial performance of investment centres is the return on capital employed (ROCE). It is a comprehensive measure of performance that enables comparisons to be made between companies and divisions for the purpose of evaluating the efficiency with which assets are utilized. It is calculated as follows:

$$\text{ROCE} = \frac{\text{earnings before interest and tax}}{\text{average capital; invested}} \times 100$$

Some limitations are inherent in using ROCE for the assessing of investment centre performance. They stem from the measurement of income and capital employed, the appropriation of costs and assets as between divisions, and some conceptual weaknesses affect ROCE. In particular, it is normal for different investment centres to have ROCEs that are different and that reflect the particular conditions affecting their particular sectors of business. Managers of investment centres having naturally lower ROCE than other investment centres will feel disadvantaged when evaluated on the basis of ROCE. This may well affect their behaviour.

Solutions to problems

1

To: Mr Jackson
From: Management Consultant
Dear Mr Jackson
EVALUATION OF DIVISIONAL PERFORMANCE
I have studied your proposals for the evaluation of the effectiveness of your divisional managers and the linking of their rewards with this evaluation. My comments are as follows:

(1) Any system of targets will influence the behaviour of those for whom the targets are set, indeed this is the purpose of the target setting exercise. Your composite index will avoid the problems associated with a single target, which is that desirable behaviour which does not have an immediate effect upon the target set will be much reduced. Your weighted targets do have problems, though. The weightings are subjective – are equal weights for the three objectives really in accord with the priorities of your business? Furthermore, change to the various criteria may not be equally easy to achieve, so that managers concentrate on improving the performance criteria which are easy to improve, and neglect those which are more difficult. Thus organizational 'improvement' effort becomes distorted. Finally, there may be conflict between achieving the different objectives, for example, by reducing volume a higher price in the market may be achieved, but the improved income margin may be countered by a reduction in the rate of capital turnover.

(2) There has to be a recognition that there may be a difference between managerial performance and divisional performance, and it may be inappropriate to reward managers for divisional performance improvements for which they are not responsible. To take the opposite as an example, it would clearly be inequitable to withhold a bonus from the manager of a division where growth, profitability and capital turnover are decreasing when the manager may be operating in a fiercely competitive market which is experiencing import penetration and a trade depression. In the particular situation, while in absolute terms the performance may be poor, in reality the management may be doing a superb job with the resources which they have available to them.

(3) It is necessary to ensure that the managers have control over the areas on which they are being assessed. To assess on capital turnover implies that capital acquisition decisions are taken by the managers, and not at Head Office. If the latter case holds, the

managers may justifiably complain that it is unfair to be assessed on the use of a capital base over which they have little influence, and which is not the one which they would have chosen.

(4) It might be better to assess each of your divisions separately, looking at their environments and their strengths and weaknesses, and then to produce, working with divisional managements, a statement of objectives for each of the divisions. This 'customized' statement of objectives may be more effective in promoting the kind of performance and decision making which is in the best interests of the division and of the company, at that particular time.

(5) In your assessment of effectiveness you might use a 'pyramid of ratios' approach, so that instead of simply looking at capital turnover, you look at particular components of this figure which may cause concern, such as the relationship between sales and, say, inventory. Greater emphasis may well be placed on non-financial factors when assessing performance, and you might consider looking at areas such as quality of production/service, which can be assessed by indicators such as number of customer complaints, length of order to delivery time and amount of repeat business generated.

(6) Your bonus of £200 for each 1 per cent improvement in the composite index seems a little arbitrary. It might be better to tie the bonus in more closely with the amount of savings made – say, as a percentage. This principle would require modification in the situation in which the management of a particular division is performing a holding operation in a hostile market, however, for in that case reduced losses rather than savings may be the mark of sound management.

I hope that you find these comments helpful, and shall be pleased to discuss them with you at any time prior to your October board meeting.
Signed
Management Accountant

Chapter 34 Standard costs and variance analysis

Answers to self-assessment questions

1 The principal difference between budgeted and standard costs lies in their scope. Budgeted costs impose total cost limits for the firm as a whole, for departments or for functions for the budget period. Standard costs impose total cost limits in respect of units of products. The relationship between budgeted costs and standard costs lies in the fact that the setting of standard costs as performance standards for control purposes at the product level implies that they must be used as a basis for calculating budgeted costs at the firm or departmental level, as the case may be.

2 There are several important applications of standard costing. First, it allows the evaluation of performance through the process of management by exception by highlighting only the variances between the standard cost set and the actual cost performance achieved. Second, a standard costing system may lead to cost reductions, since it involves a reappraisal of current production methods in the search for increased cost efficiency. Third, standard costs may be used for price setting, since they represent what products should cost. Hence, they are a better guide to selling prices than historic costs. Fourth, standard costing systems create an atmosphere of cost consciousness among managers.

3 The setting of standard costs involves problems in the following respects:

(a) establishing procedures for setting standards with respect to the price at which resources are acquired and in the manner in which they are utilized;

(b) establishing procedures for allowing participation by cost centre managers in setting attainable cost standards.

Particular problems exist in relation to setting cost standards for overheads, since there is no direct measurement of output against which they can be set. Hence, it is necessary to establish surrogate measures of output to which overhead costs can be related. As regards fixed overhead costs, it is necessary that there should be established a standard level of activity for the budget period.

4 A budget variance is defined as a difference between the budget allowance for the output achieved and the actual spending on the output achieved. Total expenditure budgeted for that output will have been calculated by reference to the standard costs per unit of the product multiplied by the number of units budgeted as the total output for the period. The actual expenditure recorded may reveal that budget allowances have been exceeded by actual expenditure, and will appear as an *unfavourable budget variance*. On the other hand, the actual expenditure may turn out to be less than the budget allowance, giving rise to a *favourable budget variance*.

The appearance of a budget variance allows for the process of management by exception by indicating the necessity to take corrective action to bring performance back to the standard performance set. Where the budget variance is considered to be significant, it must be investigated whether it be a favourable or an unfavourable budget variance. A favourable budget variance may be an indication that the standards need to be revised: an unfavourable budget variance may indicate that the desired performance is not being achieved.

The analysis of budget variances involves establishing which cost elements are involved, and then determining by reference to the analysis of standard costs whether the variance is due to price or to usage factors.

5 The formula for calculating the direct material price variance is:

actual quantity purchased × (standard unit price – actual unit price)

The formula for calculating the direct material usage variance is:

standard unit price × (standard quantity for the output achieved – actual quantity used)

The formula for calculating the wage rate variance is:

actual hours × (standard wage rate – actual wage rate)

The formula for calculating the labour efficiency variance is:

standard wage rate × (standard hours for the output achieved – actual hours).

6 Problems exist in setting overhead cost standards in the three important areas, namely setting cost standards, selecting a standard overhead rate and determining the standard volume for fixed overhead cost recovery.

The setting of cost standards implies that resources have been acquired at the best price, and that they have been used in the most efficient manner. The problem of setting efficient usage levels supposes that these costs will support a standard level of activity. Since overhead costs are not directly related to products, the problem is selecting a measurement of activity that can be used as a surrogate for the output expressed as product volume.

The selection of a standard overhead rate by which to allocate (recover) overhead costs to units of products depends on determining what measurement of activity should be used. In effect, this problem is resolved by using the concept of the standard hour, defined as *a unit of measurement representing the quantity of any product or service which can be produced or performed in one hour by any process, machine or operative*. It is not a measure of time, but a measure of performance in a period of one hour.

Fixed overhead costs, unlike variable overhead costs, do not vary with output. For this reason, the allocation (recovery) of fixed overheads to units of products requires that a normal (standard) output be budgeted as a reference base by which to calculate a fixed overhead rate. Should there be a volume variance, that is, a difference between actual and budgeted output level, there will necessarily be either an over-recovery or under-recovery of fixed overhead costs, according to whether actual output is greater or less than the standard output.

7 Fixed budgeting refers to the setting of budgets on the basis of a standard output for the purpose of establishing budget allowances throughout the firm. With fixed budgeting, standard fixed overhead costs will be over-applied (over-recovery) or under-applied (under-recovery) whenever actual output is greater or less than the standard output. These conditions manifest themselves as favourable or unfavourable volume variances.

Fixed budgets are useful for determining the financing requirement for the budget period, since they indicate that there is a target output volume that the firm aims to achieve, and for which finance is needed. The disadvantage of using fixed budgets for control purposes as well lies in the fact that where actual volume does not match exactly with the planned (standard) volume, there will always be a fixed overhead cost volume variance.

The objective of developing flexible budgets is precisely to overcome the problem caused by fixed budgets, when actual and standard volume differ. Flexible budgeting is used only for controlling performance. It involves recalculating the budget allowance for the actual volume of output achieved. Hence, fixed overhead volume variances are eliminated as regards the analysis of performance. This means, in effect, that managers are not made responsible for variances in activity levels for which they are not responsible.

8 The formula for calculating the variable overhead expenditure variance is:

actual overheads – (actual hours × standard variable overhead rate)

The formula for calculating the variable overhead efficiency variance is:

standard variable overhead rate × (actual hours – standard hours)

The formula for calculating the fixed overhead expenditure variance is:

actual fixed overheads – budgeted fixed overheads

The formula for calculating the fixed overhead volume variance is:

budgeted fixed overheads – (standard fixed overhead rate × standard hours in the output achieved)

9 The three variances that can be applied to the analysis of sales are:

(a) Sales price variance that indicates the effect on incomes of the difference between set prices and prices at which goods were actually sold. It is calculated as follows:

number of units sold × (actual contribution per unit – standard contribution per unit)

(b) Sales volume variance that indicates the effect on incomes of the difference between the planned and the actual sales volume. It is calculated as follows:

standard contribution per unit × (actual units sold – budgeted units of sales)

Sales mix variance indicates the change in total profitability that is due to changes in the mix of products sold, where these products have differing contribution margins. It is calculated as follows:

standard contribution per unit of each product × (actual quantities of units sold – actual total sales in budgeted mix proportions).

10 Standard costing allows the application of the concept of management by exception, which focuses managerial attention on variances between planned and actual performance as they appear. Therefore, the investigation of variances is concerned only with exceptional variances, that is, those regarded as being sufficiently significant to require investigation. Accordingly, the investigation of variances is a three-stage process consisting of:

(a) determining whether the variance is significant;
(b) if significant, determining its causes;
(c) if it can be corrected, taking action to prevent its recurrence.

Solutions to problems

1

(a) The master budget totals and actuals do not permit a breakdown of costs into those relating to A or to B, therefore total variances by cost element will be calculated.

	Fixed budget		Flexed budget		Actual		Variance
	A	B	A	B	. A	B	
Units	600	400	500	500	500	500	
Materials	13,200		13,500		13,300		200(F)
Labour	7,000		7,500		8,400		900(U)
Machining							
Var	1,600		1,500 ⎫				
Fixed	8,000		8,000 ⎭		9,450		50(F)
Overheads							
Var	1,400		1,500 ⎫				
Fixed	3,000		3,000 ⎭		4,400		100(F)
	34,200		35,000		35,550		550(U)

Note: The std variable cost/unit of input is:

Material	£13,200/4,400	= £3/kg
Labour	£7,000/1,400	= £5/direct labour hour
Machining		= £4/m/c hour
Overheads		= £1/direct labour hour

(b) 1,400 hours worked.

Actual labour cost	8,400	Rate variance	£1,400 (U)
Actual hours at std			
1,400 × £5	7,000	Efficiency variance	£500 (F)
Std cost of output	7,500		£900 (U)

3 (a) **Materials variances**

Actual materials purchased at actual price:		£
9,000 kg × 98p/kg	=	8,820
12,000 kg × 86p/kg	=	10,320
		£19,140
Less: actual materials at standard price:		
21,000 kg × £1	=	£21,000
Price variance		£1,860 (F)
Actual usage at standard price:		
19,500 kg × £1	=	£19,500
Less: actual production at standard price cost/unit:		
8,200 × £2	=	£16,400
Usage variance		£3,100 (U)

Direct labour variances

Actual hours at actual rate	=	£36,340
Less: actual hours × standard rate:		
15,800 × £2.20	=	£34,760
Rate variance		£1,580 (U)
Less: actual production at standard labour cost/unit		
8,200 × 2 × £2.20	=	£36,080
Efficiency variance		£1,320 (F)

Variable overhead variances

Actual expenditure	=	£14,250
Less: actual hours × standard rate		
15,800 × £1	=	£15,800
Expenditure variance		£1,550 (F)
Less: actual production × standard cost/unit		
8,200 × £2	=	£16,400
Efficiency variance		£600 (F)

(b) The purpose of variances is to provide feedback to management very quickly. The price variance on materials needs to be reported to the buyer; hence the calculation of the price variance is based on materials purchased, not used. The production manager would receive feedback on materials usage and labour efficiency. The rate variance is the responsibility of the personnel manager. It should be noted that some variances may be interrelated: for example, the materials price variance may have resulted from the purchase of cheaper and poorer quality materials. This would lead to more waste and an unfavourable materials usage variance. The unfavourable labour rate variance may have been caused by employing a higher grade of labour. This was reflected in the favourable labour efficiency variance.

(c) (i) The labour efficiency variance was favourable indicating that labour usage was efficient; therefore, the explanation is unacceptable.

(ii) The materials usage variance was unfavourable, indicating there was a higher level of waste than expected; therefore, the explanation is acceptable.

(iii) The labour rate was unfavourable which shows that the explanation is unacceptable. Labour was paid a higher rate than standard.

(iv) A discount on materials price would be reflected in a favourable variance, supporting the explanation.

(v) The variable overhead expenditure variance was favourable, indicating a saving on overheads and not on additional expense as suggested by the explanation.

Chapter 35 The control of managed costs

Answers to self-assessment questions

1. Essentially, managed costs are non-manufacturing costs. Their level is determined at the discretion of managers, rather than by strict requirements defined by manufacturing operations. They are often referred to as 'discretionary costs'. There are four categories of managed costs: administrative costs, research and development costs, marketing costs and training costs.

2. The problems involved in the control of managed costs arise from the fact that unlike engineered costs, they cannot be strictly defined in terms of short-term output. Administrative costs, for example, are considered as relatively Fixed. Research and development costs are related to long-term planning, and may be difficult to control by reason of the speculative nature of research. In effect, managed costs involve expenditure (inputs) without necessarily giving rise to results (outputs) that may be difficult to evaluate objectively. Methods of controlling managed costs are work study measurements, budgetary controls, activity-based costing, overhead value analysis, outsourcing and benchmarking.

3. Budgetary control is a method of controlling managed costs in terms of departmental spending budgets, relying on the principle of responsibility accounting. Two different methods are the marginal-costing approach and the fixed-cost approach. Under the marginal-costing approach, the development of department budgets assumes a cost–volume relationship, in which costs vary directly with activity volume and the relationship is quantifiable. The fixed-cost approach treats managed costs as fixed during the budget period, and not susceptible to variation in the short term. In this approach, control is focused on the spending variance.

4. Administrative costs refer to the costs associated with management activities and the various tasks involved in those activities. Management activities concerned with decision making are generally viewed as discretionary, and the tasks involved are of a non-routine and non-repetitive nature. Moreover, although cost inputs are often quite substantial in terms of salaries and other expenses, there is no measurable output that can be evaluated objectively. None the less, there are whole categories of lower-level activities that are found in the administrative function that may be exposed to some measure of control. These are routine tasks that are repetitive and routine, and can be controlled in terms of work study measurements.

   Generally, administrative costs are controlled in terms of spending budgets, and actual spending is reviewed in terms of budget allowances.

5. There are two main reasons why research and development costs are difficult to control. First, there is little connection between the costs committed and the benefits obtained. Second, there is usually a long lead-time between costs incurred and any ultimate result obtained.

   Research and development expenditure is an activity related to long-range planning, and the effectiveness of a research and development programme can only be assessed in terms of specified long-range goals. The control of research and development costs committed to a particular programme may be controlled in terms of progress made towards completion.

6. Marketing costs have become a significant cost element, owing to the costly nature of advertising and marketing. The development of the most efficient cost control methods in this is a most important consideration. This requires the analysis of all the activities involved in marketing, ranging from obtaining orders, warehousing and distribution, to handling returns and after-sales service. These activities may be analysed on three different bases: the nature of the costs involved, the functions performed, and the appropriate sector of the firm's activity.

7 The three bases on which marketing costs may be analysed, namely, cost classification, functional classification and sectorial classification, involve the following:

   (a) Cost classification, which is concerned with analysing costs as to their nature, for example, salespeople's salaries and commission, travelling expenses, and advertising.

   (b) Functional classification, which involves analysing costs classified as to nature in the context of particular functions, for example, selling, advertising, transportation, credit collection, warehousing and invoicing. In this way, it is possible to assess the burden of particular cost categories in different functions.

   (c) Sectorial classification, which involves analysing different sectors in which costs are committed in terms of particular functions, for example, sectors such as different territories, different products, different divisions, different customers, etc.

The end-purpose of such analyses is to provide the firm with analysed information permitting some form of evaluation of cost performance in relation to such goals as profitability and other indices of marketing performance.

Chapter 36 Capital investment decisions

Answers to self-assessment questions

1 Capital investment decisions fall in the category of long-range planning. They are concerned with maintaining and enlarging the firm's assets, and therefore affect directly the firm's future profitability. The reasons which render such decisions of major importance are the following:

   (a) usually, they involve substantial money outlays;

   (b) the funds are committed for a long period of time, and are exposed to the higher level of risk that is involved in long-range decisions;

   (c) once made, investment decisions are generally irreversible, if they should appear to have been ill-founded;

   (d) occasionally, the firm's entire future may depend on a single major capital investment decision;

   (e) such decisions are not only major ones for the firm, but they may be of great significance to an industry and to the economy.

2 Four common examples of capital investment decisions are:

   (a) the acquisition or replacement of long-lived assets, such as buildings or plant;

   (b) the investment of funds into another form of revenue-creating activity, such as a financial stake in another company;

   (c) a special project, which will affect the firm's future earnings, such as a research project;

   (d) the extension of the firm's range of activities, for example, a new production line or a new product line.

3 Capital investment decisions mostly focus on two aspects of long-range profitability, namely:

   (a) estimating the future net increases in cash inflows or net savings in cash outlays that will result from the investment;

   (b) calculating the total cash outlay required to undertake the investment.

Although such decisions are analysed in cash flow terms, it is evident that the range of information required for making the cash flow forecasts implied will cover all factors, both external and internal to the firm that will bear on such forecasts.

4   The three major factors affecting capital investment decisions are:

   (a) the net amount of the investment required, expressed as the total cash outlay needed to support the project during its entire life;
   (b) the net returns on the investment, expressed as the future expected net cash inflows. These may be actual cash flows or cash savings;
   (c) the rate of return on investment, expressed as a percentage. The determination of the lowest acceptable rate of return will be affected by a number of factors, among which are the firm's rate of return on other investment opportunities and the firm's cost of capital.

5   The payback method is an attempt to forecast the time it will take for the expected net cash inflows to pay back the investment outlay. The payback method has the advantage of simplicity, and by selecting the alternative that most quickly repays the investment outlay, it recommends the selection of the safest projects.

   However, the payback ignores the cash flows beyond the payback period. Hence, it ignores the overall profitability of the project, and emphasizes its liquidity. Moreover, the time pattern of cash inflows and outflows is also ignored, thereby treating cash flow through time as having a constant value.

6   The accounting rate of return method seeks to express the average estimated yearly net inflows as a percentage of the net investment outlays. This method overcomes the disadvantage of the payback method in that it attempts to calculate the profitability of projects. Its main disadvantage is that it also ignores the time pattern of cash inflows and outflows, and in this sense, suffers from the same defect as the payback method.

7   The discounted cash flow (DCF) method attempts to evaluate an investment by comparing the net cash flows accruing over the life of the investment at their present value, against the net cash outlay, also calculated at its present value. Thus, by comparing like with like, this method makes possible the calculation of the rate of return on an investment in a realistic manner.

   As compared to the payback and the accounting rate of return methods, the DCF method is much more demanding with respect to information. For example, the time profile of cash inflows and outlays is an important information requirement, as are other factors such as the impact of taxation and the cost of capital, in the analysis of investment decisions. The sensitivity of the DCF method to forecasting errors is a significant factor in using this method.

8   The present value method and the internal rate of return method both use discounted cash flows in the analysis of investment decisions. The net present value method assumes a minimum rate of return in discounting forecasted cash inflows and cash outflows to their present value. This minimum rate of return is the firm's cost of capital. Using this rate of return in the present value calculation of cash inflows and outflows results in either a positive or negative difference between these cash inflows that determines their relative acceptability. Alternatives having negative net present values are rejected.

   By contrast, the internal rate of return method does not assume a rate of return, but requires the expected rate of return on an investment to be calculated. This is the rate of return that will reduce the net present value of cash inflows to zero, after taking into account the net cash outlays. Accordingly, the selection of investment projects is effected by comparing the resulting rate of return with the firm's required rate of return.

   In effect, both methods produce the same 'yes' or 'no' decisions. The advantage of the present value method is its simplicity and its insistence on investment alternatives satisfying the minimum expected rate of return, which is the cost of capital.

9   The cost of capital has been extensively discussed in the financial literature. Its basic assumption is that there is a cost involved in financing investment projects. One interpretation of this cost is in the nature of the opportunity cost of applying funds to an

investment project. In this sense, the cost of capital is the cost of financing a project in terms of the return that could be obtained by investing in a similar project having similar risks. Another interpretation, which is more usually discussed in the literature, is that the firm has to meet the expectations of shareholders and lenders by providing them with a return on the funds invested in the firm. This involves estimating the cost of capital of a particular firm in terms of its capital structure. The cost of capital will be very much affected by the gearing (leverage), representing the proportion of interest-bearing capital to the total long-term capital.

In the latter sense, the cost of capital imposes a strict requirement on firms to finance only those investment projects that meet the firm's own bottom line with respect to the return that it has to ensure to its own investors, be they shareholders or lenders. In effect, this criterion resides in a more refined notion of profitability.

10 The impact of inflation is an important consideration in assessing investment decisions due to the manner in which inflation erodes the purchasing power of cash, on which investment decisions are based. Hence, inflation critically affects forecasts of investment profitability.

Several methods are available for dealing with inflation. For example, it is possible to incorporate cost-escalation estimates into cash flow forecasts. A commonly used method of correcting DCF calculation is to adjust cash flow forecasts for specific price increases. Such adjusted cash flows are then discounted by the monetary cost of capital.

Solutions to problems

1

	Machine A	Machine B
(a) Payback period	2 years	2.5 years
(b) Accounting rate of return depreciation	£50,000/3	£60,000/4
	£16,667	£15,000

$$\text{ARR} = \frac{\text{average cash flow} - \text{depreciation}}{\text{average investment}}$$

	$\dfrac{£25,000 - 16,667}{£50,000/2}$	$\dfrac{£24,000 - 15,000}{£60,000/2}$
	33.3%	30%

(c) Discounted cash flow

	Machine A		Machine B	
Year	Cash flow	Discounted	Cash flow	Discounted
	£	£	£	£
0	(50,000)	(50,000)	(60,000)	(60,000)
1	25,000	22,728	24,000	21,818
2	25,000	20,660	24,000	19,834
3	25,000	18,782	24,000	18,031
4	–	–	24,000	16,392
		12,170		16,075

From the above calculations it can be seen that machine A has the shorter payback period, but the method of calculating the payback period ignores the time value of money and ignores any cash flows occurring after the payback period.

Machine A also has a marginally higher accounting rate of return, but this measure of profitability is also compromised by considering all cash flows to be of equal significance no matter where in the life cycle of the machine they occur. Thus, machine A would have an identical ARR to that calculated above should all of its £75,000 lifetime cash inflow be concentrated into year 3.

The DCF figures, which incorporate adjustments to take account of the time value of money, show that machine B is the more attractive, yielding, in present-day money, a cash fund of £16,075, which is £3,905 more than that generated by machine A. The figures are not strictly comparable, however, since machine A yields its cash surplus one year before machine B, and to produce a true comparison it would be necessary to know what return would be made on the available funds yielded by machine A in year 4.

2 (a)

			Existing machine	
Year		Scrap	Fault correction	Operating costs	Total
		£	£	£	£
0		–	5,000	–	5,000
1		–	–	192,825	192,825
2		–	–	192,825	192,825
3		–	–	192,825	192,825
4		–	–	192,825	192,825
5		–	–	192,825	192,825
6		–	–	192,825	192,825
7		–	–	192,825	192,825
8		–	–	192,825	192,825
9		–	–	192,825	192,825
10		(1,800)	–	192,825	191,025

			New machine			
Year	Net	Operating	Total	Existing	Difference	DCF
	£	£	£	£	£	£
0	97,000	–	97,000	5,000	(92,000)	(92,000)
1	–	172,675	172,675	192,825	20,150	18,318
2	–	172,675	172,675	192,825	20,150	16,652
3	–	172,675	172,675	192,825	20,150	15,138
4	–	172,675	172,675	192,825	20,150	13,762
5	–	172,675	172,675	192,825	20,150	12,511
6	–	172,675	172,675	192,825	20,150	11,374
7	–	172,675	172,675	192,825	20,150	10,334
8	–	172,675	172,675	192,825	20,150	9,400
9	–	172,675	172,675	192,825	20,150	8,545
10	–	172,675	172,675	191,025	18,353	7,075
						31,109

The most profitable course of action to take would be to purchase the new machine, raising the net present value to the organization by £31,109.

(b) In coming to the above conclusion the discounted cash flow method has been used in order to calculate the discounted values of the cash flow differences between the two proposals over the ten-year period. An assessment of the profitability of the proposals cannot be made since there are no revenue figures.

In addition to considering the relative cash flows, the following should be considered in relation to the decision:

(i) reliability of the forecasts regarding future costs, lifespans and cost of capital;
(ii) desirability of any change upon labour requirements;
(iii) effect of any change upon labour requirements;
(iv) improvements in quality caused by the new machine.

3 (a) (i) NPV = £110,000

(ii)

Year	Discount factor	NPV
0	–	£10,000
1	0.833	
2	0.694	
3	0.579	
4	0.482	
5	0.402	
	2.99 × 35,000	104,650
		£114,650

(iii)

Year		Cash flow	Discount factor	NPV
0	£30,000 + £10,000 =	£(40,000)	1.00	(40,000)
1	Note (1)	–	0.833	
2		40,000	0.694	27,760
3		160,000	0.579	92,640
4		80,000	0.482	38,560
5		40,000 ⎱	0.402	22,110
	£10,000 + £5,000	15,000 ⎰		
				£141,070

Note (1)

			Fixed	
Units	SP	VC	costs	Depreciation

$20,000 \times (10 - 8) = 40,000 - (45,000 - 5,000)$

Based on NPV the optimum plan is (iii), as it results in the highest NPV. However, the choice would depend on Barry's attitude to risk; proposal (i) is low-risk while proposal (iii) is very high-risk.

(b) The choice of a required rate of return is sometimes based on the weighted average cost of capital. This comprises the return on shares, both ordinary and preference, from inventory, reserves and so on. The calculation is quite sophisticated and complicated. Therefore, companies tend to use surrogate measures such as the overdraft rate charged to the company of the average risk-free rate of return, plus a reward for the risk of running the business. Some companies appear to choose a figure almost at random (e.g. 20%).

(c) Using cash payback as the basis of assessment, the figures would be as follows: (i) and (ii) Immediate as cash payback is not a practical measure.

(iii) YR	0	(£40,000)	
	1	–	
	2	27,760	2 yrs 1.6 months
		12,240	
	3	92,640	

Chapter 37 Behavioural aspects of performance evaluation

Answers to self-assessment questions

1 Managerial style is said to be the 'set of behaviours exhibited by key managers in an organization' (Horngren and Foster, 1987). This means, in effect, that it is representative of the manner in which key managers relate to their subordinates and personnel throughout the organization. In this sense, two distinct and contrasting managerial styles are those that tend towards authoritative as against participative management styles.

2 Organization culture is said to be the 'set of beliefs and values that are shared by members of an organization'. It describes the prevalent interpersonal relationships that exist in an organization, and the constraints that exist as regards social behaviour. Much has been discussed about the importance of organizational culture of recent years, in particular in referring to the success of Japanese businesses. In this debate, organizational culture is deemed to determine the manner in which management and workers interact, and also the manner in which management decisions are made. Hence, managerial style may be viewed as subsumed in the concept of organizational culture.

3 The objectives of performance evaluation may be listed as follows:

(a) to assess how effectively managers have performed the tasks to which they were assigned;
(b) to identify where corrective actions should be taken;
(c) to ensure that managers are motivated towards organizational goals;
(d) to enable comparisons to be made between different sectors of an organization, and to discover where improvements may be made.

4 Theory X was defined by McGregor (1960) as a leadership style adopted by management. In effect, Theory X is a 'managerial style' that indicates an authoritarian style of management. It is based on a view of people in organizations that reflects the following sentiments:

(a) Management is responsible for organizing the elements of production.
(b) Management is responsible for directing the efforts of people, for motivating and controlling their actions, and modifying their behaviour to fit the needs of the organization.
(c) Management consists of getting things done through people. Without active intervention by management, people would be passive and even resistant to change. Their activities must be directed by management, by the means of persuasion, reward, punishment and on-going control.

5   By contrast to Theory X, Theory Y is a more modern view of management, the view that business firms should reflect the ideals of social democracy found in society evidenced in a willingness of managers to allow subordinates to participate in decision making.

Although both Theory X and Theory Y agree that the role of management is to manage, they differ markedly as regards their view of people in organizations. According to Theory Y, for example, people are not passive nor indeed resistant to change. It is the attitude of management that produces these reactions. The qualities that good management seeks, namely motivation, development potential, capacity for assuming responsibility, and the readiness to work for the realization of corporate goals already exist in people: they need only be brought out. According to Theory Y, the essential task of management is to arrange organizational conditions and methods of operation that will allow people to realize their own goals in the attainment of organizational objectives.

6   Managers may react negatively to budgets prepared in a traditional manner, that is, where the style of management reflects Theory X. The reaction to excessive budget pressure may lead to mistrust, hostility and eventually to poorer performance. There may be an over-emphasis on short-term performance at the expense of the long term. Excessive emphasis on income performance may tend to limit the ability of top management to correctly evaluate the all-round managerial qualities of their subordinates.

(a)   Among other negative reactions may be an unwillingness to communicate information, a stifling of initiative and biasing in preparing departmental budget information, where the style of management is authoritarian.

(b)   Proponents of participative budgeting argue that these negative reactions can be prevented, by altering management styles and creating conditions that allow managers to participate in setting attainable budgets.

7   Proponents of participative budgeting argue that the active participation of management in the budgeting process makes it possible to envisage three levels of cost performance. First, there is the budgeted level, which is decided as the planned level of cost performance. Second, managers will have their own aspiration level, defined as that level of future performance in a familiar task which individual managers explicitly undertake knowing their own past performance level. Hence, the aspiration level as regards costs is the spending level that managers regard as realistic. Third, the actual cost performance is that performance that is currently being achieved.

8   Management by objectives is a management concept that seeks to translate organizational objectives and goals in such a way that they become the personal objectives and goals of all management personnel. The aim is to create a high degree of goal congruence between organizational objectives and personal objectives throughout the organization and so encourage managers to take actions that are in the best interests of the organization.

9   Contingency theory is an approach to organization theory that starts with the premise that no single organizational design is the best in all situations. Contingency theory defines four factors as being of particular significance in the design of an organizational structure, as follows:

(a)   Forces in the manager. These are factors relating to the personalities of managers. Contingency theory states that organizations do not have objectives, only people have objectives. Hence, these objectives will vary from manager to manager.

(b)   Forces in the environment. Contingency theory argues that the most effective organizational structures are those that enable the organization to adjust to environmental requirements.

(c) Forces in the task. Contingency theory argues also that technology has an important impact on the design of organizational structures.

(d) Forces in subordinates. Organizations employing relatively more skilled than unskilled personnel will be faced with a greater desire for democratic structure.

Chapter 38 Managing profitability

Answers to self-assessment questions

1 The strategist is outward-looking and concerned with competitive market forces. The traditional management accountant is inward-looking and concerned with internal costs.

2 To remain sensitive to the needs and demands of clients and customers. To identify the forces which shape competitive rivalry. To understand environmental forces. To adopt a strategic perspective to internal data.

3 Value-added activities contribute something that is worthwhile to the enterprise and its customers, e.g. distinctive product features, superior customer service. Non-value-added activities can be reduced or eliminated without decreasing the enterprise's ability to compete and meet customers' demands, e.g. inspection of incoming materials.

4 All questions concerning the profitability of customers and customer groups, e.g. 'Which customer or group generates our greatest income contribution?'

5 Identify competitors and potential competitors. Identify substitute products. Place competitors into strategic groups. Analyse competitors and their strategy.

6 A competitive market price is estimated in the first instance from which is derived a target cost.

7 Lead time, set-up time, number of line stops and number of units scrapped. Non-financial measures provide fast feedback.

8 Growth, inflation, recession and deflation are four distinct phenomena that have their own characteristics that require clear understanding for profitability management. Income flows and cash flows are brought together in the management of profitability. Growth and recession reflect changes in demand, whereas inflation and deflation are monetary phenomena that are caused by changes in the value of money against all other things. Briefly, growth and inflation are seen in increases in monetary values that are reflected in accounting numbers. Both results in an increase in the need for cash to finance the expansion shown. However, growth is expansion of activity in real terms, whereas inflation is fictitious expansion in that it is not reflected in real growth with real activity remaining unchanged. The converse is true with regards to recession and deflation. The implications for the management of profitability is that the firm is able to control its own level of growth in activity and can likewise reduce it and is in a position to manage its level of activity with respect to its financing needs. By contrast, inflation and deflation are phenomena that are beyond the firm's control and, as a result, make it impossible for the firm to manage its finances by controlling its activity level.

Chapter 39 Financial reporting for groups of companies

Solutions to problems

1 First we assume that the consolidation falls under the acquisition provisions rather than merger accounting provisions as set out in FRS 6.

Workings
Goodwill

	Paid	Acquired
	£000	£000
Purchase price	962	
$\frac{2}{3}$ shares (600)		400
$\frac{2}{3}$ reserves (312)		208
	962	608
	608	
Goodwill	354	

Income and loss

	£000
Macro	4,050
Post ac	652
Micro $\frac{2}{3}$ res (702 − 312)	260
$\frac{2}{3}$ income (144)	96
Unrealized income on inter-company sales	
$208 \times 33\frac{1}{3}/133\frac{1}{3}$	(52)
	5,006
Minority interest $\frac{1}{3} \times$ (1,446)	482
Inventory 1,244 + 514 − 52	1,706
Debtors 2,048 + 390	2,438
Bank 960 + 46 + 17	1,023
Creditors 2,825 + 634	3,459
Tax 315 + 60	375
Non-current assets 5,121 + 1,230	6,351

Macro group consolidated balance sheet 20X0

	£000	£000
Non-current assets		6,351
Goodwill		354
Current assets		
Inventory	1,706	
Trade debtors	2,438	
Cash at bank	1,023	
		5,167
Trade creditors	(3,459)	
Taxation	(375)	
Net current assets c/f		1,333

	£000	£000
Net current assets b/f		1,333
		8,038
Less: Debenture loan		750
		7,288
Share capital		1,800
Reserves		5,006
Minority interest		482
		7,288

2

Workings (in 000s)
Goodwill

	Paid £	Acquired £
Shares in S	12,000	
$\frac{2}{3}$ Shares		10,000
$\frac{2}{3}$ Income statement at acquisition		2,666.667
	12,000	12,666.667
		12,000
		666.667
Minority interest		
$\frac{1}{3}$ of 19,250		6,416.667
Income statement		
Balance b/f		10,000
Income for year (from income statement)		1,166.667
		11,166.667
Inventory 7,100 + 6,600 − 1,000*		12,700
Trade debtors 8,000 + 4,000		12,000
Cash 3,400 + 2,400		5,800
Trade creditors 12,000 + 10,250		22,250
Non-current assets 40,000 + 20,000		60,000

*unrealized income

Consolidated income statement

	£	Notes
Turnover (300.8 + 150.5 − 15)	436,300.000	
Cost of sales (116.9 + 59.4 − 15 + 1)	162,300.000	(1)
Gross income	274,000.000	
Expenses	269,000.000	
	5,000.000	
Taxation	3,500.000	
	1,500.000	
Dividend paid to minority	250.000	
Retained income	1,250.000	
Minority interest in income	83.333	(2)
Group income for year	1,166.667	

Notes
(1) Holding company cost of sales + subsidiary company's cost of sales *less* inter-company sales plus unrealized income in inventory.
(2) $\frac{1}{3}$ of £250,000.

Consolidated balance sheet

	£000	£000
Tangible non-current assets		60,000
Shares in non-group companies		3,000
		63,000
Inventory	12,700	
Debtors	12,000	
Cash	5,800	
	30,500	
Trade creditors	(22,250)	
Net current assets		8,250
		71,250
Less: Debenture loan		(23,000)
		48,250
Share capital		30,000
Capital reserve arising on consolidation		667
Income statement		11,167
Minority interest		6,416
		48,250

3

Workings	Growing $\frac{2}{3}$	Declining 80%
Goodwill	Paid	Acquired
	£000	£000
Growing	140	
$\frac{2}{3}$ shares		100
$\frac{2}{3}$ reserves		30
Declining	32	
80% shares		40
80% reserves		–
	172	170
	170	
Goodwill on consolidation	2	

Income statement

	£000	
Expanding	350	
Growing $\frac{2}{3} \times 60$	40	
Declining 80% × (15)	(12)	
Unrealized income in inventory	(0.6)	
	377.40	
Inventory 63 + 83 + 28 − 0.6 + 2	175.4	(Inventory in transit 2)
Debtors 60 + 36 + 15	111	
Cash 10 + 7 + 2 + 1	20	(Cash in transit 1)
Non-current assets 525 + 210 + 60	795	
Creditors 120 + 68 + 46	234	
Minority interest		
Growing $\frac{1}{3} \times 255$	85	
Declining 20% × 35	7	
	92	

Reconciliation of group balances

	£000
Expanding shows growing debtor	24
Growing shows expanding creditor	22
Add: Inventory in transit	2
	24
Expanding shows declining debtor	16
Declining shows expanding creditor	16
Growing shows declining debtor	9
Less: Cash in transit	1
	8
Declining shows growing creditor	8

Expanding group consolidated balance sheet

	£000	£000
Tangible non-current assets		795
Goodwill on consolidation		2
		797
Inventory	175.4	
Debtors	111	
Cash	20	
	306.4	
Trade creditors	(234)	
Net current assets		72.4
		869.4
Called-up share capital		400
Income and loss		377.4
Minority interests		92
		869.4

Chapter 40 Understanding consolidated financial statements

Solutions to problems

1

(i) Subsidiary treatment

	Paid	Acquired
	£000	£000
Goodwill	2,000	
50% shares		500
50% reserves (1.9m)		950
	2,000	1,450
	1,450	
Goodwill	550	
Minority interest		
50% × 3,000	1,500	
Tangible non-current assets	6,500 + 4,000 = 10,500	
Current assets	3,500 + 3,000 = 6,500	
Current liabilities	4,550 + 2,500 = 7,050	
Debentures	2,000 + 1,500 = 3,500	

Royal Group Income statement

	£000	R	B	Adj
Operating income	1,600	1,100	500	
Taxation	(590)	(433)	(200)	43 Tax credit
Income after tax	1,010			
Minority share of income	150	50% × 300		
	860			
Dividends paid	300			
	560			
Balance b/f	2,940	3,450 – 510		
Carried forward	3,500			

Royal Group Balance sheet

	£000	£000
Tangible non-current assets		10,500
Goodwill		550
Current assets	6,500	
Current liabilities	(7,050)	
Net current assets		(550)
		10,500
Debentures		(3,500)
		7,000

	£000	£000
Share capital		2,000
Reserves		3,500
Minority interest		1,500
		7,000

(ii) Associate company treatment (equity)

Royal Plc
Income statement

		£000	
Operating income before tax		1,100	
Share of income of associate		250	
		1,350	
Taxation Royal	390		
Share of associate's tax	100	490	
Income after tax		860	
Dividends paid		300	
		560	
Write-off of goodwill		550	(see working above)
Retained income		10	
Retained income b/f		2,940	(see above)
Carried forward		2,950	

Balance sheet

		£000	
Tangible non-current assets		6,500	
Investment in associate		1,500	(50% net assets)
		8,000	
Current assets	3,500		
Current liabilities	(4,550)		
Net current assets		(1,050)	
		6,950	
Debenture		2,000	
		4,950	
Share capital		2,000	
Reserves		2,950	
		4,950	

(iii) Investment approach

In this case the accounting statements as shown for Royal in the question would be unchanged. There would, however, be a note to the accounts showing the valuation of Butler at the accounting date as £2,050,000. The income on the disposal would be taken in 20X1. In this case, it is clear that Royal did not invest in Butler with the intention of achieving long-term control since Butler was disposed of shortly after the accounting date. SSAP 14, para 2, states that 'the objective of group accounts . . . is to give a true and fair view of the income and loss and of the state of affairs of the group'. Similarly in paragraph 22 the statement says 'a subsidiary should be excluded from consolidation if . . . control is intended to be temporary'.

The statement then specifies valuation of the investment as the lower of cost or net realizable value and its inclusion in the balance sheet as a current asset.

There is little doubt that the investment approach provides the most reliable information in this case.

2

Workings

Value of shares acquired in Sition

		book		agreed prop	
95% of 10,000			9,500		
Consideration		book		agreed prop	
Shares 9,500 × 8/10		7,600		14,440	91%
Loan inventory 9,500 × 1.5/10		1,425		1,425	9%
		9,025			
Reserve arising on consolidation			475		
Goodwill in books of Sition			1,000		
Write-off at 20% p.a.			200		
Income before tax reduced by	200				
Income statement reduced by	200				
Goodwill reduced by	200				
Minority interest					
5% of 14,450	722.5				

(1) **Expo plc**
Consolidated income statement

	£000	
Turnover	21,350	
Income before tax	4,350	(3,250 + 1,100)
Taxation	620	
	3,730	
Dividends	1,200	
	2,530	
Due to minority	53.5	
Retained income	2,476.5	

Statement of retained earnings

	Group	Minority
Balance brought forward	7,101	169
Retained income for year	2,476.5	53.5
	9,577.5	222.5

Expo plc
Consolidated balance sheet

	£000
Non-current assets	28,850
Goodwill	800
Current assets	10,200
Current liabilities	(6,050)
	33,800
£1 ordinary shares	21,600
Capital reserve on consolidation	475
Income and loss	9,577.5
Minority interest	722.5
15% loan inventory	1,425
	33,800

(2) This requires coverage of the capitalization of pre-acquisition incomes and the calculation of goodwill. Students should be aware of the fundamental differences in approach that allow for the alternative treatment of reserves. This also requires appreciation of 'fair' or agreed values compared with book.

(3) The third part of the question should produce an analysis of the information content of the two alternatives. It should include reference to the inconsistency produced by valuing the acquired companies at agreed value while the holding company is at historic cost.

Chapter 41 Management control systems design: a conceptual framework

Answers to self-assessment questions

1 Besides the traditional contents of annual financial statements, investors and society at large are concerned to know whether the leadership of a multinational group has chosen the right strategy and whether management has executed it effectively. Drucker referred to these two notions as leadership doing the right things and management doing things right. Doing the right thing normally has a moral and ethical connotation. This is becoming an increasing concern in the light of expectations concerning the role of business in society and, in particular, in view of several high profile corporate scandals that have made the headlines in recent years. Doing the right thing is meaning that can be expanded to include other objectives than purely moral ones, for example, that it has fulfilled expectations of investors in improving shareholder value.

2 Whether business corporations should be concerned with moral values or simply share-holder value is very controversial. There is a strong and traditional view that business should be concerned solely with making profits for shareholders and that social welfare and social justice is a matter for government. Business corporations maintain the view that providing employment, paying taxing, improving living standards are in themselves valuable social contributions. Investors and other social groups do expect business corporations to uphold high moral standards. They expect business leaders to be truthful, to be worthy of trust, to accept the duty to care as one of the responsibility of leadership. In a broader social and political context, there is a public concern with the common good as the objective in which business and society should find their ultimate purpose.

3 The McKinsey 7-S model, developed in the 1980s was a significant step forward in seeking coherence and cohesion between management functions as basic conditions for organizational efficiency. It is concerned with the concept of strategic fit between 3 'hard' elements, namely strategy, structure and systems and 4 'soft elements', namely, shared values, skills, style and staff. Their interdependence is illustrated in the manner in which these elements interact in the 7-S Model, which seeks coherence in the sense of 'fit' between the elements in attaining strategic objectives. The model recognizes that shared values are at the centre of the model and represent a higher authority that must always be respected. These values enhance alignment and reduce internal conflicts.

4 The John Spedan Lewis 3-S Model was developed by the founder of the John Lewis Partnership Limited in the UK in the 1930s. Concerned with the notion of 'fair shares' as a basic condition for happiness and fulfilment at the workplace, Lewis thought that the conflict between capital and labour could be resolved within the context of a free market economy. He believed in free trade and the virtues of enterprise. By transferring owner-ship and control of his employees, he developed a management control systems around three basic principles, namely, sharing gains, sharing knowledge and sharing power. Transforming employees into owners and creating a management control system in which leadership provide wisdom is doing the right things and management doing things right with the consent of employees acting through layers of management committees and coun-cils, the John Lewis Partnership Limited has become one of the largest and most successful trading businesses in the UK. It highlights the importance of the three shared values that are enshrined in its constitution for all forms of businesses. In a practical sense, it provides a useful model for small and medium-sized businesses having succession problems and wish-ing to continue in activity.

5 Multinational business corporations are very large and diversified groups with multitudinous products and activities, operating in very different markets, subject to very different economic conditions and political risk. The main problem in management control systems design for multinational corporations involves reducing such great complexity into manageable order to enable the group to function under unified central control directed at attaining group objectives and goals.

6 Strategy maps provide a visual representation of the cause-and-effect relationships in five critical management areas, namely, strategy balances short and long-term, differentiated customer value propositions, internal business processes as the source of all values, strategy execution requiring coordinated action on several fronts and strategic alignment as the key to execution. They are designed from top down and executed from bottom up through the four perspectives of the balanced scorecard, namely, the financial perspective, the customer perspective, the internal processes perspective and the learning and growth perspective. The balanced scorecard itself is a performance management tool that focuses on these overall performance indicators and monitors progress toward organizations' strategic goals. Essentially, strategy maps state the mission and core values of the organization and its vision for the future. Strategy maps and balanced scorecards are particularly helpful in dealing with the problems of complex organizations and ensuring strategy fit in management control system design.

Index